A History of
Civilization
Prehistory to 1715

A History of
Civilization
Prehistory to 1715
Fifth Edition

Crane Brinton

John B. Christopher
University of Rochester

Robert Lee Wolff
Archibald Cary Coolidge Professor of History
Harvard University

Prentice-Hall, Inc., Englewood Cliffs, New Jersey

Library of Congress Cataloging in Publication Data

Brinton, Clarence Crane, 1898–1968.
   A history of civilization.

   Contents: v.1. Prehistory to 1715. v.2. 1715 to
the present.
   Includes bibliographies and index.
   1. Civilization—History. I. Christopher, John B.,
joint author. II. Wolff, Robert Lee, joint author.
III. Title.
CB69.B74 1976   909   75-20152
ISBN 0-13-389007-4 (vol. 1) pbk.
0-13-389809-1 (vol. 2)

© 1976, 1971, 1967, 1960, 1955 by Prentice-Hall, Inc., Englewood Cliffs, New Jersey

Printed in the United States of America

10 9 8 7 6 5 4 3 2 1

Design by A Good Thing, Inc.

Art research by Roberta Guerrette and Olivia Beuhl

Maps by Vincent Kotschar

Prentice-Hall International, Inc., London
Prentice-Hall of Australia, Pty. Ltd., Sydney
Prentice-Hall of Canada, Ltd., Toronto
Prentice-Hall of India Private Limited, New Delhi
Prentice-Hall of Japan, Inc., Tokyo
Prentice-Hall of Southeast Asia (Pte.) Ltd., Singapore

Contents

Preface

With this fifth edition *A History of Civilization* is available for the first time in a choice of paperback formats—two volumes, with the break at 1715, and three volumes, breaking at about 1300 and 1815. Readers familiar with earlier hard-cover editions will find that their generous allotment of maps, the end-of-chapter reading suggestions, and most of their other features have weathered the paperback revolution; the illustrations have been selected with particular care to tie in closely with the text. Throughout the book we have endeavored to take account of new historical evidence and interpretations that have appeared since the fourth edition as well as of increasing student interest in social and cultural history. We have reorganized some chapters to attain greater clarity and coherence, and sharpened the introductory sections of many chapters to provide a simplified chart of a particular historical terrain before elaborating on its detailed typography.

To summarize the most significant changes: We have revised Chapter 1 in the light of recent archaeological finds and of advances in deciphering languages. Chapter 4 includes a new section on the immediate background of Christianity as well as added material on Augustine, the most celebrated of the early Church fathers. We have completely revamped the chapters on the medieval West to aid the reader's understanding of a complex and often bewildering period. Chapter 7 discusses the Church and ecclesiastical culture

together with the great confrontation between the papacy and the Holy Roman Empire, and Chapter 8 the English and French monarchies plus secular literature. To enlarge the treatment of the forces that made possible the birth of modern western civilization, discussion of the burgeoning money economy has been shifted to chapter 11 (The Renaissance) from Chapter 10 (War and Politics in the Late Middle Ages). The much-debated crises of the fourteenth and seventeenth centuries receive augmented treatment in Chapters 10 and 15, respectively, and many sections on the arts are enriched, in Chapter 6 (Islam), 11 (Renaissance), 15 (Baroque) and 23 (19th century). We have added an entirely new chapter (32) on the major political developments since 1970 and have incorporated substantial new material in the final chapter (33) recapitulating the intellectual and cultural history of the twentieth century.

The successful completion of a complicated project requires help from many people. We wish to acknowledge our debt to our senior co-author, the late Crane Brinton, whose gift for catching the essential style of a civilization still informs this history; to readers who have taken the trouble to write down their specific suggestions for improving the text; and to the men and women of Prentice-Hall, Inc., for their patience and expertise in the lengthy process of converting manuscript into book form.

John B. Christopher
Robert Lee Wolff

A Note on the Reading Suggestions

A list of suggestions for additional reading is appended to each chapter of these volumes (except that the bibliographies for Chapters 30, 31, and 32 are consolidated into a single list). Since such brief bibliographies must be highly selective, we therefore stress four different categories of works: (1) standard authorities, both older and recent, and both concise and detailed; (2) diverse interpretations representing a spectrum of views, enabling the reader to realize that the past often provokes as much controversy as the present; (3) collections of source materials—texts of laws and decrees, memoirs, letters, chronicles and other items to help a student formulate his own interpretation of events; (4) historical novels and dramas that reflect with reasonable faithfulness the externals of the past and, what is even more difficult, its internal features as well, the motivations, values, and lifestyles of bygone generations.

Our lists star with an asterisk all titles available in paperbacks. New titles are constantly appearing in paperback, and old ones vanishing, so that an indispensable tool is the latest volume of *Paperbound Books in Print* (R. R. Bowker Co.), which lists tens of thousands of items by title, author and subject and is usually to be found in most libraries and bookstores. For a fuller list of works on a given topic, particularly scholarly books published only in hard covers, the handiest tool is the subject cards in a library catalog. In addition, useful up-to-date bibliographies may be found in the two volumes of P. Gay and R. Webb, *Modern Europe* (*Harper & Row), and in the revised *Harvard Guide to American History* (Harvard University Press, 1974).

New scholarly books are often reviewed in the Sunday book section of *The New York Times, The New York Review of Books,* and the London weekly, *The Times Literary Supplement.* Almost all scholarly titles are eventually reviewed in at least one of the major professional journals, such as *The American Historical Review* and *The Journal of Modern History,* or one of the more specialized ones, such as *The Middle East Journal* or *Speculum* (for medieval studies). Three periodicals consist entirely of critiques—*History: Reviews of New Books, Reviews in American History,* and *Reviews in European History.* Journals occasionally publish review articles evaluating at length a book of especial significance or assessing all the major recent publications in a given field, the French Revolution, for instance. Finally, the latest discoveries of historical evidence and innovations in interpretation appear frequently in journal articles months or even years before they do in books. A complete list of the journals concerned with history would itself require an article; a few useful titles, in addition to those already cited, include *History and Theory, The Journal of Interdisciplinary History, The Journal of the History of Childhood* (for psychohistory), *The Journal of the History of Ideas, The Journal of Medieval and Renaissance Studies, The Renaissance Quarterly, The Journal of British Studies, French Historical Studies,* and two British publications, *Past and Present* and *History Today.*

Maps

A History of
Civilization
Prehistory to 1715

What Good is History?

Roughly two centuries ago, just about the time of the American Revolution, a learned Englishman, Edward Gibbon, had completed a new volume of his famous work, *The Decline and Fall of the Roman Empire*, and called upon a royal duke, a brother of King George III, to give him a copy. The duke accepted the present with the remark "Another damned thick book. Always scribble, scribble, scribble. Eh, Mr. Gibbon?"

If you stop to think about it, there was really very little that Gibbon could say in reply. He might have pointed out that the earlier volume had been a best seller and was on the dressing tables of most of the fashionable ladies of the duke's acquaintance. But that would probably not have changed the duke's opinion very much. The duke was bored by history, and that was that. There have always been people like the duke and there always will be. Nor have they always been merely stupid, as one must admit that the duke was. The first Henry Ford, inventive genius whose cheap cars changed the whole way of life of twentieth-century America, once remarked feelingly "History is bunk," and there is no reason to think that he did not mean it or that he ever changed his views. And Henry Ford in his own way was brilliant. An even more brilliant man, a deep original thinker in the field of psychology, an active scholar and colleague of one of the authors of this history book you are reading, once said with deep feeling "I hate history." It is true that he said it at a cocktail party, but he surely meant it. Once his listener had overcome the shock of hearing so extravagant a statement from such a source, the remark even became understandable.

Like the duke and Henry Ford, the psychologist was made uncomfortable by history. How many complications we could avoid if we did not know anything about the past: what our forefathers in America and our ancestors in other countries and men and women in civilizations other than our own had done in their lives. If we could ignore everything that had happened yesterday or the day before or last year or ten or a hundred or a thousand years ago, we could face our own problems cleanly, without trying to hark back and solve them by remembering and acting upon some precedent. Or could we? We could avoid the clutter of past thinkers' unreliable, fumbling, inappropriate efforts to work things out, and so avoid a war, clean up a mess, end injustice (if any) by the sheer fresh simple use of our own brilliant intuition. Or could we? If indeed we could, why should we bother about the past? Yet if it were merely boring (as the duke said) or bunk (as Henry Ford said), we really could ignore it, and it would not only not be necessary to study it, or a good idea to reflect upon it, but it would be forgotten and better forgotten. Yet it is not forgotten, it is remembered; it somehow will not go away, and people do keep on trying to guide themselves by its lessons.

By introducing a necessary complication into human calculations, the past, or our memory of it, prevents the solution of human problems by simple, straightforward, direct means: it gets in the way of neatness, and somehow fogs things up, irritating our friend the psychologist. Remembrance of the past, of what happened to us the last time we crossed the street against the traffic light, of what happened to our father in the Korean War, or what happened to *his* father in the stock market crash of 1929 cannot help but affect us every day, as we go for a walk, think about the Middle East and the oil crisis, or contemplate investing in a speculative stock. Whether we get useful or non-useful signals from our memories of the past, good or bad advice, is another question. One traffic crossing is not the same as another; two wars are not the same; maybe the fact that grandpa was burned by speculating in 1929 should not stop us from trying the same kind of thing today, because times have changed, haven't they? Or haven't they? That is the thing that continues to puzzle us. And if times have changed, how ought the change to affect our decisions?

No sensible person will deny that these newer interpretations have greatly enriched and deepened the study of history. On the other hand, this new history is much more complex, difficult, and unwieldy than was the old. When you add China, India, the Aztecs, and a lot more in space, and add the centuries back to ancestral subhumans in time, and add all the innumerable activities of all men to the dramatic activities of a few in politics and war, you create an unmanageable mass of detail, and the result is sometimes a longer and more arid catalog of details than the lists of kings, queens, presidents, consuls, generals, popes, and cardinals that used to fill the older histories. After all, a list of poets, or even of inventors, is not in itself very illuminating; and even a hasty epithet or two—"ethereal" Shelley, "sweet-voiced" Keats, "ingenious and laborious" Edison—adds very little.

The present book is in part—though only in part—a reaction against the attempt to cover all the past everywhere on earth. We hope to retain the best of the old and add the best of the new. As for space, we shall concentrate on the history of one part of the world, the Europe sometimes scornfully called a "small peninsula of Asia." We shall trace the expansion of that Europe as Europeans explored, settled, colonized, and traded in all parts of the globe. But we shall be concerned with non-European peoples only as they and their histories impinged on the development of European cultures. We are not motivated by any self-worship, certainly not by any contempt for Asians or Africans, but rather by a desire to get our own record straight. We are not against the study of "world history," but we do hold that it is unwise to begin with world history; we think it wiser to know one's own civilization well before one tries to understand all others. As for time, after a very brief look at the ages-long prehistoric past of Western man and the beginnings of his history in the Near East, we shall be mostly concerned with the last two thousand years or so.

Obviously, this is not all a good American citizen of the second half of the twentieth century needs to know about the past of *Homo sapiens*. But it is an essential part of what he needs to know, probably the part he *most* needs to know if he is to face the problems of human relations on this planet.

In discussing the past of our own civilization, we shall try manfully to see our forebears in their religious and cultural lives and engaging in all their manifold social and economic activities. But "what really happened" still primarily means to us, as we think it must to all who are writing an introductory work, politics: politics in the sense of past government, past domestic policy, past foreign policy, and therefore—as always—past wars and past peace. So it will be around the political lives, political expediencies, political inventions, and political behavior of people from the first civilizations to the present that we hope to organize this work.

Prehistory to 1300

Man's First Civilizations

Before Writing
History and Prehistory

Within the lifetime of men now in their forties and fifties, archaeology, with the new tools supplied by other sciences, has revolutionized what human beings know about the remoter past of our earth and the people who live on it. Discoveries continue at a rapid pace. In the 1950s and 1960s no writer could have put on paper many of the major statements in this chapter. In the 1980s and 1990s, perhaps even sooner, our successors will know enough to dispute or modify or at least greatly add to what we say here.

It may at first seem strange that our concepts of the distant past are changing much faster than our concepts of the periods much closer to us in time and much better known. But when we consider the *ways* in which we know about the past we can quickly see that—far from strange—this is entirely natural. If we want to know about something—almost anything—that happened, let us say, during the American Revolution, we have the letters of George Washington and his contemporaries, the written records of the British government that tried to suppress the American colonists' rebellion, the proceedings of the Continental Congress, the Declaration of Independence, and literally thousands of other *written sources*—diaries, memoirs, documents, newspapers, propaganda leaflets—that take us instantly into the minds of the men of that time and enable us to work out for ourselves what probably happened. And if we cannot go directly to these written sources for history, we have hundreds of books written since the events of the Revolution by historians who have been interested in it and who have set down their views of what happened, for us to accept or challenge, but at least to consider. New sources may be discovered and fresh light thrown on some event we thought we understood: we may find out that Paul Revere's teacher at school had been reading radical pamphlets (something that previous students had not known) and that this helped prepare Paul as a youth for his famous ride.

But the new sources probably would not force us to reject or even to reconsider everything we had learned before they were discovered.

Most of the sources we would read about the American Revolution would be written in English. But if we wanted to find out about the part played by Lafayette and Rochambeau we would soon find ourselves compelled to read documents in French; if we asked ourselves why a Pole, Tadeusz Kościuszko, joined the American side, we might have to learn Polish—and Russian and German—in order to find out. If we were interested in the ideas of Thomas Jefferson, we would have to study several of his favorite classical authors—who wrote in Greek or Latin—and, though we would find translations available, we might feel it important to read them as Jefferson did, in the original. But whatever the problems of learning languages, or of trying to decide which of two contradictory accounts of the same event to follow, or of interpreting what we might find (this is what George III *said;* but what did he *really* think?), we would always be dealing with abundant written sources in languages that modern men know how to read.

For events two thousand years or more before the American Revolution, or less well known, or taking place in Europe or Asia, we would still usually have written sources in Persian or Sanskrit, Greek or Latin or Chinese, sometimes fragmentary instead of full, sometimes so biased as to be unreliable, but written. Where possible we would supplement these with all kinds of other evidence: the coins that rulers struck with pictures of inscriptions on them that might tell us things we could not find out any other way; the statues or paintings or poems or songs of the age that might reflect the attitudes of the artists and their society more surely than a document; indeed, anything that we could find from the period and the place to supplement our written sources.

But suppose our written sources were written in a language we could not read? Or suppose we had no written sources at all? As we move backward in time through human history these problems confront us more and more urgently. The discovery of texts written in both a known and a previously unknown language has over the last couple of centuries enabled scholars to read the language of the Egyptians, and those of the peoples of the ancient Mesopotamian river valleys in the Near East, although uncertainties often remain. Brilliant use of the techniques of cryptography in the 1950s cracked one of the two scripts commonly used in ancient Crete and on the Greek mainland. But the earlier Cretan script remains to be convincingly deciphered. Much work remains to be done before scholars can confidently read Etruscan, the language—written in Greek letters—of the people that ruled in Italy before the Romans.

And of course man lived on earth for many long thousands of years before he ever learned to write at all. Only his bones and the bones of his animals and some of the things he made remain to tell us about him: they are our only sources. The recent development of the carbon-14 technique, whereby radioactive carbon is used to enable us to date ancient objects within a couple of centuries, has proved to be a great help in straightening out chronology. Nothing seems surer, however, than that scholars will find many more new objects and new ways of dating them and so will enable our successors to write with more certainty than we can about our earliest ancestors.

The Old Stone Age

In the seventeenth century, an archbishop of the Church of England, named Ussher, carefully worked out from data given in the Bible the date of the creation of the world by God. It proved to be precisely 4004 B.C.; so if you added the sixteen hundred or so years since the birth of Christ, you came up with a figure of under six thousand years for the age of our earth. We smile now at the generations that accepted Ussher's views—though everybody did so until the nineteenth century—because all of us know that the earth is billions of years old and that organic life may go back several billion years.

Beginning in 1959, a series of digs in equatorial east central Africa in and around Olduvai Gorge turned up fragments of a small creature that lived between nineteen and fourteen million years ago, christened *Kenyapithecus* ("Kenya ape"), who seems to have made crude tools. He may not be a direct ancestor of man, but like man may have branched off from a primate ten million years older still, and still more primitive. By about two million years ago a creature more like true man had made his appearance, *Homo habilis,* "the skillful man." A mere quarter of a million years later came *Zinjanthropus,* who was perhaps related to a manlike animal about the size of a chimpanzee, but with a larger brain, called *Australopithecus* ("southern ape").

Australopithecus was a vegetarian (to judge by his teeth) and seems to have ceased evolving and come to a dead end, while *Homo habilis,* who ate meat, continued to evolve in the direction of true man, *Homo sapiens,* "the man who knows." All these manlike animals had larger skulls, with more brains, than apes. In another three-quarters of a million years (about a million years ago or a little less) *Homo habilis* began to look like a being long known as Java man, who lived about 700,000 B.C. First found in Java in the late 1880s and christened *Pithecanthropus erectus* ("ape-man that stands erect"), he is now recognized as a true man and has been renamed *Homo erectus.* A somewhat later stage is represented by Peking man of about 500,000 B.C., who advanced well beyond *Homo habilis.*

Much more is being learned and will continue to be learned as the origins of manlike beings and of true men continue to be studied. Especially we should like to know about the stages by which *Homo erectus* evolved into *Homo sapiens,* who appeared in Europe first only about thirty-seven thousand years ago. When he arrived there in a fashion still unknown, he entered into a land of forests and plains that had already been occupied for perhaps a hundred thousand years by Neanderthal man, named for the Rhineland valley where his remains were first discovered but spread far more widely, leaving remains, for example, also in the mountains of what is today eastern Iraq. Probably far less apelike than the traditional reconstructions of his skull have shown him to be, Neanderthal man was not yet *Homo sapiens.* We cannot yet locate him accurately on a hypothetical family tree, but he probably represents another offshoot from the main trunk. An excavation of a Neanderthal burial has shown that the corpse was placed on a heaping mound of flowers, an attention more delicate than one would have expected.

Even though we can identify our remote ancestors so many hundreds of thousands of years before 4004 B.C., when Archbishop Ussher thought the world was made, we know so little about what was happening during all those hundreds of millennia that for the historian—as distinguished from the anthropologist—almost all of that time belongs to "prehistory." During those long, long centuries the advance of the human animal was enormously slow. The first real tools were stones that he used to chip other stones into useful instruments. And it was by stone weapons and tools that early man lived for hundreds of thousands of years.

Archaeologists have named the early periods of human culture from the materials used by man for weapons and tools. During the Old Stone (Paleolithic) Age, the long, long period before roughly 8000 B.C.—give or take a few thousand years according to the region one is describing—man used chipped stone tools. About 8000 B.C.—in some places, much later in others—the development of farming and the use of more sophisticated stone implements marked the beginning of the New Stone (Neolithic) Age. Then, about

3000 B.C., the invention of bronze led to the Bronze Age and even greater transitions to new forms of human life and society. Still later, further experiments with metals ushered in the Iron Age.

Paleolithic man left remains scattered widely in Europe and Asia, and took refuge in Africa from the glaciers that periodically moved south over the northern continents and made life impossible there. Wherever he went, he hunted to eat, and fought and killed his enemies. He learned how to cook his food, how to take shelter from the cold in caves, and eventually how to specialize his tools: he made bone needles with which to sew animal hides into clothes with animal sinews; he made hatchets, spears, arrowheads, awls.

One day in 1940, when two boys in southwest France went hunting rabbits, their pet dog suddenly disappeared down a hole and did not come back. Following the dog, they literally fell into an underground grotto, hidden for thousands of years. The light of their torches revealed a magnificent series of paintings on its limestone walls and roofs, of animals portrayed in brilliant colors with astonishing realism and artistry: deer, bison, horses, and others. They were painted toward the end of the Paleolithic period by Cro-Magnon man, true *Homo sapiens*, often standing as tall as six feet four inches and with a large brain. Lascaux, where the paintings were found, became one of the great tourist centers of Europe. By 1960, despite all the precautions of the authorities, the breath of so many thousands of visitors gazing in awe and wonder began to damage the pictures; so the cave has had to be closed to the public. At Altamira, in northern Spain, similar contemporary cave pictures, not quite so splendid, had long been known, but had suffered somewhat from early souvenir hunters. Long exposed to air and changing temperatures, they are happily immune to moisture, and now remain the most easily visible monument of the great skills of Paleolithic man. There are many other caves with late Paleolithic paintings, but perhaps none so spectacular as Lascaux and Altamira.

We can only guess why the Paleolithic artist painted the pictures. Did he think that by putting animals on his walls he could improve his chances in the hunting field? Would their pictures give him power over them, and so ensure his supply of food? Were the different animals also totems of different families or clans? Sometimes on the walls of the caves we find paintings of human hands, often with a finger or fingers missing. Were these hands simple testimony of appreciation for one of man's most extraordinary physical gifts: the hand with its opposable thumb (not found in apes), which alone made tool-making possible? Or were they efforts to ward off evil spirits by upholding the palm or making a ritual gesture? Or were they prayers by hunters and warriors that they should not suffer mutilation of their fingers or that they might retain their strength despite some mutilation they had already suffered? Paleolithic man occasionally pro-duced small female statuettes, sometimes overemphasizing the breasts, buttocks, and sexual organs (and sardonically called Venuses by modern archaeologists). Were these fertility symbols? or love charms?

Until the late 1960s, such questions were the only ones that scholars had asked about the achievements of Paleolithic man, and hypothetical answers the only possible ones. But in addition to the cave paintings, and the Venuses, and the tools—known in such variety and with such increasing skill of manufacture from about 35,000 B.C. to about 8000 B.C.—archaeology had yielded up a rich variety of other finds. Prompted by some regular scratched markings on a bone from equatorial Africa carbon-dated at 8500 B.C., an inquiring scholar named Alexander Marshack has since 1965 reexamined the vast amount of material in European collections, and has made some amazing discoveries that he has judiciously explained by reaching new hypotheses about Old Stone Age man.

Marshack found numerous objects—a mammoth tusk, bones of various animals, a pebble, several short staffs of ivory, a pair of eagle bones—dating from perhaps 32,000 B.C. to 12,000 B.C., on which markings appeared in sequences like those on his initial bone tool from Africa, markings whose sequence and intervals he could interpret as notations recording lunar periods. Sometimes only one or two lunar months had been observed, sometimes six, sometimes an entire year. With the passing of the millennia, the Paleolithic craftsman

Bull from the cave at Lascaux, ca. 12,000 B.C.

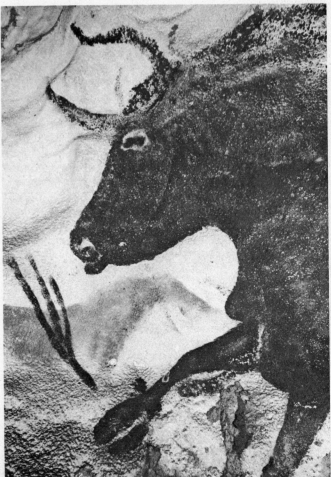

learned to make the notations more complex, sometimes engraving them in a crosshatched pattern that looks like mere decoration until one learns to read it, sometimes adding extra angled marks at important dates.

Once one realizes that late Old Stone Age man may well have been keeping a kind of calendar to enable him to predict the regular seasonal changes from year to year, and that therefore he was presumably regulating his hunting life and his other activities, such as the preparations of skins for clothing, one gets such a vivid new perspective on the quality of his mind and his perception of the importance of time in his life that the "mystery" of his extraordinary skills becomes far less mysterious. In the later Paleolithic art objects, the marks that Marshack has interpreted as time notations sometimes *accompany* artistic representations of animals. Where we find on the same piece of ivory from southwest France a budding flower, sprouting plants, grass snakes, a salmon, and a seal—which appeared in spring in the local rivers—Marshack proposes that we regard the object as a kind of symbolic representation of the earth's reawakening after winter; and when such symbols of springtime appear with the lunar calendric notation, we are looking at something very like an illustrated calendar. Other spring events celebrated in the art include the rutting of stags and bison.

In the same way, perhaps the "goddess" images should not be dismissed as "sexual" in any simple sense. In a hunting culture, a female image, with its suggestion of the female processes, serves to recapitulate the procession of the seasons. Certain animals—reindeer, bison, horses—appear on the artifacts associated with females; others—bears and lions—with males. Some representations can be interpreted as sacrifices. The men of the late Old Stone Age apparently had a mythology that involved tales of the hunt, successful and unsuccessful, a ritual that involved killing and sacrifice, and a deep awareness and knowledge of the passing of time in the world around them and in the bodies of animals and of mankind. A nude figure of a woman holding a bison horn that looks exactly like a crescent moon and is marked with thirteen lines, the number of lunar months in a year, we may now perhaps salute as mankind's first recognizable true goddess, the forerunner of the bare-breasted Neolithic moon goddess long known as the Mistress of the Animals, who appears with crescent, fish, flower, plant, bird, tree, and snake, and with a consort who plays sun to her moon and hunts the animals of nature and of myth. Though Old Stone Age man remains a dim and remote figure to us, these researches for the first time make him recognizable as fully man.

The New Stone Age

The advance from the Old Stone Age (Paleolithic) to the New (Neolithic) was marked by certain major changes in man's way of life, all first found in the Near East. One of these was the domestication of animals for food. Man had tamed dogs and used them in the hunt long before. But when he kept goats, pigs, sheep, and the ancestors of our cows in pens, he could eat them when their meat was young and tender without having to hunt them down when they were hardest to overtake. Parallel with this went the first domestication of plants for food—a kind of wheat and barley. Finally—and this always seems to have been the last step—man turned his shelter into a house, and settled down to live in it. Once he had done all these things, he had made the transition to the New Stone Age.

Accompanying these fundamental steps went the practice of a new art, the baking of clay vessels—pots and bowls and storage jars—much easier to make, of course, than stone ones. It is chiefly by studying the surviving varieties of such clay vessels and their fragments, and the types of glazes and decoration the potters used, that modern scholars have been able to learn how to date the sites where men lived in the times before writing, and often even later. Recent excavations in the Near East have pushed back our previous earliest Neolithic dates; and with the boundaries between periods thus in flux and the terms intended only to be useful and not to confuse, it is probably better here not to try to fix any firm boundaries between late Paleolithic and early Neolithic.

At Jericho in Palestine during the 1950s, archaeologists excavated a town radiocarbon-dated at about 7800 B.C. that extended over about eight acres and included perhaps three thousand inhabitants. These people lived in round houses with conical roofs—the oldest permanent houses known—and they had a large, columned building in which were found many mud-modeled figurines of animals and modeled statues of a man, a woman, and a male child; it was almost surely a temple of some kind. All this dates from a time when people did not yet know how to make pots, which appear only at a later stage. In Çatal Hüyük in southern Turkey, discovered in 1961 and dating to 6500 B.C., the people had a wide variety of pottery, grew their own grain, kept sheep, and wove their wool into textiles. A female sculptured in relief in the posture of giving birth to a child, a bull's head, boars' heads with women's breasts running in rows along the lower jaws, and many small statuettes were all found together in what we can be sure was their shrine. The bull and a double ax painted on a wall seem to look forward to the main features of the better-known religion of ancient Crete, as we shall see.

Far to the east, in modern Iraq (ancient Mesopotamia, "between the rivers" Tigris and Euphrates) lay Jarmo, to be dated about 4500 B.C., a third Neolithic settlement. A thousand years later than Jarmo, about 3550 B.C., and far to the south, at Uruk on the banks of the Euphrates River, men were using the plow to scratch the soil before sowing their seeds, and were already keeping the accounts of their temple in simple picture-writing. This was the great leap forward that took man out of prehistory and into history. Similar advances are found in Egypt too, at roughly the same time. But archaeology seems to show that Mesopotamia took the lead, and indeed that it was from Mesopotamia that major cultural contributions—especially the all-important art of writing—penetrated into Egypt and gave the Egyptians a great push into history.

Still further to the east, in various parts of modern Iran, archaeologists during the 1960s found several of these early Neolithic sites, some of which seem to go back in time as far as Jericho or even before—although no city so large or complex or advanced has been found from the eighth millennium B.C. The sites are scattered, and many of them are located in the highlands, indicating that the Neolithic revolution was not necessarily confined, as had usually been thought, to river valleys. Many of these Iranian discoveries are still unpublished, and much work remains to be done. But from 6000 B.C. there are several sites in northwest Iran rather like Jarmo, giving plenty of evidence of domesticated animals and grains. And even earlier, probably, perhaps around 7000, in the region of southwest Iran very near the Mesopotamian eastern border there are mud-brick houses and the same clear evidence of goat- and sheep- and cereal-raising. In a totally different region, in south central Iran, a brand-new site was discovered in the summer of 1967 at Tepe Yahya, where the earliest settlement in a large mound proved to be a Neolithic village of about 4500 B.C. Here along with the animal bones and cereal remains archaeologists found in a mud-brick storage area not only pottery and small sharpened flints set in a bone handle to make a sickle but an extraordinary sculptured figurine of dark green stone, which is simultaneously a female figure and a phallus.

The Neolithic people of the Near East were not necessarily any more intelligent than those elsewhere. Indeed, Neolithic remains have been found also in many places in the Mediterranean region, and even far to the north. But in those places climate was far less favorable, and even when Neolithic man managed to triumph over his environment—as in the lake settlements of Switzerland, where he built frame houses on piles over the water—the triumph came later (in this case about 2500 B.C.). In Australia and New Guinea and in South America there are people today who still live in the Neolithic Age. It was the inhabitants of the more favored regions who got to the great discoveries first. It was they who learned copper-smelting and the other arts of metallurgy, and who thus led the human race altogether out of the Stone Age—and into the Bronze Age. And it was they who first lived in cities. Writing, metallurgy, and urban life: these are the marks of civilization. Soon after these phenomena appeared in the Tigris-Euphrates valleys, along the Nile, and in Iran they appeared also in the valley of the Indus, and along certain Chinese rivers. But since it is not to India or China but to Mesopotamia and Egypt that we can trace our own civilization, it is to these that we must now turn, with some words on Iran as well.

The Venus of Willendorf, a Neolithic statuette found in Austria.

II The Valley Peoples and Iran
Mesopotamia and Elam

SUMERIANS The most recent discoveries have led some scholars to believe that the first Mesopotamian inventors of writing may have been a people whom the later Babylonians called Subarians. Traditionally they came from the north. In any case, by about 3100 B.C. they were apparently overpowered and were certainly superseded in southern Mesopotamia by the Sumerians, whose name became synonymous for the region immediately north of the Persian Gulf, in the fertile lower valleys of the Tigris and Euphrates and in the land between them. Here the Sumerians were already well established by the year 3000. They had invented bronze, an alloy of copper and tin that could be cast in molds, and they now made tools and weapons of it. Thus they had moved mankind into the Bronze Age, a momentous development. They lived in cities; they had begun to accumulate and use capital; and they wrote.

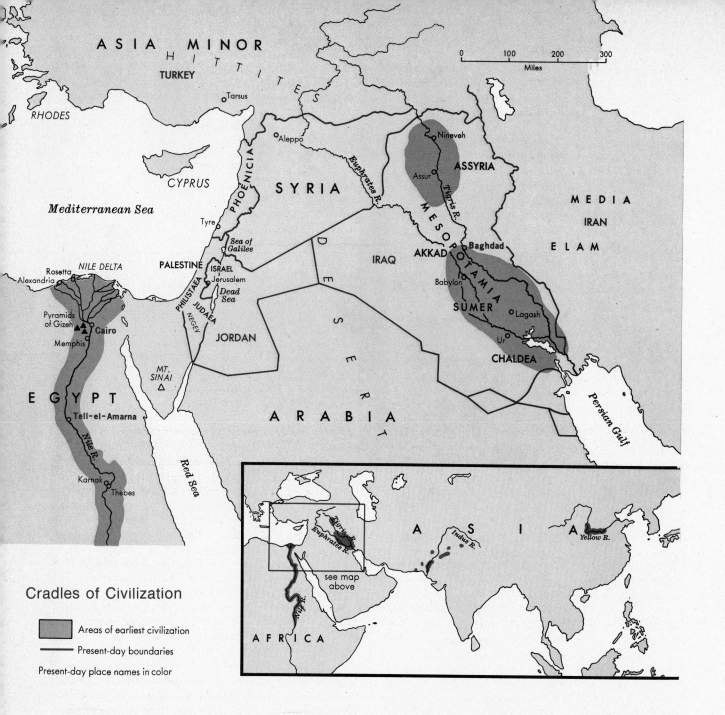

Cradles of Civilization

Areas of earliest civilization

Present-day boundaries

Present-day place names in color

We have known about the Sumerians for only a hundred years. Archaeologists working at Nineveh in northern Mesopotamia in the mid-nineteenth century found many inscribed clay tablets. Some they could decipher because the language was a Semitic one (Akkadian), on which scholars had already been working for a generation. But other tablets were inscribed in another language that was not Semitic, previously unknown. Because these inscriptions made reference to the king of Sumer and Akkad, a scholar suggested that the new language be called Sumerian.

But it was not until the 1890s that archaeologists digging far to the south of Nineveh found many thousands of tablets inscribed in Sumerian only. Because the Akkadians thought of Sumerian as a classical language (as we think of Greek or Latin), they taught it to their educated men, and they put onto tablets vocabularies, translation exercises, and other aids to study in both Akkadian and Sumerian. Working from known Akkadian to previously unknown Sumerian, modern scholars since the 1890s have pretty well learned how to read the Sumerian language. Vast quantities of tablets in Sumerian have been unearthed during the intervening years from numerous excavations.

Over the thousand years between 3000 and 2000 B.C. the Sumerians developed a phonetic alphabet.

With a reed pen they impressed into the wet clay tablet little wedge-shaped marks, producing a script that we call cuneiform, from the Latin *cuneus,* meaning a wedge. The first thousand years of Sumerian history we know from tens of thousands of these tablets, which are mostly economic or administrative in content. From the second thousand years (after 2000 B.C.) we have five thousand tablets that provide us with purely literary texts, some short, some very long, some of them not yet transcribed or translated.

In the earliest days, the Sumerians governed themselves through a council of elders, who derived their authority in turn from a general assembly of all the adult free men. This assembly, which decided on such questions as making war and peace, sometimes would grant supreme authority to an individual leader for a limited time. This arrangement—which seems astonishingly "modern" and "democratic" to us—apparently did not last long, and was replaced by one-man rule in each city. But the human ruler acted only as the representative on earth of the god of the city. In this capacity the ruler built temples to the god to keep him appeased, and especially to obtain his divine protection against the floods that often swept torrentially down the river valleys in the springtime with disastrous results for the people in their way.

The lives and religion and literature of the people of Mesopotamia were pervaded by terror of floods: the story of Noah and the ark in Genesis echoes the ancient tradition of the Sumerians that told of a single disastrous flood from which only a remnant of the people was saved, and from which (about 2900 B.C.) everything later was dated. The Sumerians devised an elaborate system of canals not only for irrigation but to control the force of the floods. Toward the south, near the Persian Gulf, the problem became one of drainage, to halt the flow of salt water that would have ruined the fields.

It took the toil of many centuries for the Sumerians to transform the bleak marshes of the river valleys into fertile and productive farmland, dotted with prosperous cities, each with its own political bureaucracy and its religious institutions; and, as with all human societies, each passing through occasional oppressions, upheavals, and political overturns, many of which are recorded by surviving inscriptions. The earliest known inscription recording the ambition of one city ruler to rule the entire region, to be the first universal monarch in history, dates from about 2350 B.C. The Sumerians also had to fight against infiltrating Semites from the Arabian deserts to the west and the hills to the north. And they campaigned eastward too, against "Elam," the peoples living in what today is western Iran. About 2300, Sargon, king of Akkad, a Semite from the north, conquered the Sumerian ruler of Uruk. Sargon and his successors called themselves kings of Sumer and Akkad, perhaps indicating that a fusion of the non-Semitic Sumerians and the Semitic Akkadians

had already begun. By about 2100, when scholars date the end of the early Bronze Age, Sargon's descendants had lost their power, and for a time there was no force to unify the petty states.

In taking the lead against invaders, Gudea, ruler of the city of Lagash, united the Sumerians about 2050 B.C. Soon after he died, Ur replaced Lagash as the capital city, and for a century its rulers played the role of universal monarch. They again called themselves kings of Sumer and Akkad. Much of what we know about the Sumerians comes from the recent systematic excavation of Ur. Very recently a portion of a series of statutes promulgated by the ruler Ur-Nammu (about 2000 B.C.) has been discovered, providing fixed punishment for certain crimes, such as a fine of five shekels of silver for the rape of a virgin slave girl without her owner's consent. Ur-Nammu is thus the first known true lawgiver for an entire people. And Ur enjoyed a brief period of great prosperity based on a farflung trade, a systematic tax system carefully recorded, and a revival of learning. But a decline set in, and Ur's subject cities fell away; invading Elamites from the east destroyed it. With Ur's destruction and the end of Sumerian power, the center of political might shifted to the north.

In addition to their city gods, the Sumerians worshiped a god of the heavens, a god of the region between heaven and earth (the air, hence storms and winds), and a god of earth. Another trinity included gods of the sun and moon, and a goddess of the morning star, who was also associated with fertility. With this female deity was associated a young male god who died and was reborn as a symbol of the seasons.

Here, in the first religion recorded in sources that we can read and therefore interpret surely, we find elements common to all subsequent efforts of men to deal with the supernatural. It was Enki, god of earth and of wisdom, for instance, who poured the water into the two great fertilizing rivers, Tigris and Euphrates, and stocked them with fish; who created grain, filled the land with cattle, built houses and canals, and set subgods over each enterprise.

The Sumerian gods were portrayed in human form, and lived recognizably human lives, with rivalries among themselves. Sumerians also believed in a multitude of demons, mostly bad. From the beginning, they used various arts in an effort to foretell the future. The entrails of slaughtered sheep or goats were carefully observed, and their shapes were given meaning. Interpreting dreams was also an important method, and the stars were observed, ever more scientifically but always with the purpose of obtaining omens. Because the temples of the city god and other gods actually owned most of the land, most of the population worked as serfs of the temple. But the produce of the land was distributed as pay to them.

Life was highly diversified: blacksmiths, carpenters, and merchants now appear alongside the hunters, farmers, and shepherds of the older days. Fathers exercised many rights over their children. The society was monogamous, and women held a high position. Punishments seem mild relative to those later found in the Babylonian society that grew out of the Sumerian; in Sumer, they consisted mostly of fines.

In their epic poems, the Sumerians celebrated the brave exploits of Gilgamesh, a mighty hero. He undertook perilous journeys, fought and overcame dreadful monsters, and performed great feats of strength. But even Gilgamesh, strong though he was, had to die; and a mournful tone, typical of the society, pervades Sumerian literature: hymns, lamentations, prayers, fables, and even schoolboy compositions.

Yet a Sumerian proverb sagely says,

> *Praise a young man,*
> *and he will do whatever you want;*
> *Throw a crust to a dog,*
> *and he will wag his tail before you.*

Obviously these were people who observed each other keenly. In their literature they often dealt with the seeming injustice of this life, where even righteous men who lead good lives must suffer. We can recognize the type of the future Old Testament Job, and the moral is the same: glorify God, await the end of life, which will set you free from earthly suffering.

Sumerian art was entirely religious, official in intent and impersonal in style. It changed very little for a millennium and more. The Sumerians built their temples of baked brick. In the shrine was an altar against a wall; other rooms and an outer courtyard were later added. The most striking feature of the temple was that the whole structure was set upon a terrace, the first stage toward a multiplication of terraces, each above and smaller than the last, with the sanctuary at the top, reached by stairs from terrace to terrace. This was the ziggurat, the typical Mesopotamian temple, whose construction itself suggests the rigidly hierarchical Sumerian social order. It was a great ziggurat that suggested the tower of Babel to the author of Genesis. Sumerian tombs were simple chambers, but were often filled with objects intended for use in the afterlife, which Sumerians envisioned as mournful and dreary. Their statuary consisted of clothed human figures, solemn and stiff, with large, staring eyes: gods were shown as larger than kings, and ordinary human beings as smaller. On monumental slabs (steles), on plaques, and especially on seals the Sumerians showed themselves skillful at carving in relief.

NEW DISCOVERIES IN IRAN Since 1967, the mound at Tepe Yahya in south central Iran, which contained the Neolithic city we have already mentioned, has also yielded startling finds from a later period. Here, five hundred miles east of the Mesopotamian region traditionally accepted as the birthplace of writing, archaeologists have turned up clay tablets dating to about the year 3500 B.C.—at least as early as, and perhaps even slightly earlier than, the early Sumerian writings. And at Tepe Yahya, the language of the tablets is what scholars call proto-Elamite, not Sumerian or Semitic but the earliest form of the language spoken in Elam, later Iran. In 1975 the tablets had not been read, but they are probably commercial records, since they were found in what appeared to be a storehouse, along with pottery storage jars. They were surely written where they were found, since similar tablets still blank were found with them.

Tepe Yahya, its discoverers believe, was a center of the soapstone manufacturing industry, and served as a midpoint between the civilizations growing up in Mesopotamia and that much farther to the east in the valley of the Indus. Another such midpoint appears to have been the island of Bahrein in the Persian Gulf. It will undoubtedly be many years before the details of such ancient trade and other relationships have been thoroughly investigated, and all conclusions are for the moment still tentative. But it is at least likely that the men of the Tigris and Euphrates valleys had such hitherto undemonstrable relationships with the men of the Indus valley, and that various centers in Iran were the midpoints. And at any rate the discovery of the proto-Elamite writings of so early a date, and of the soapstone industry of Tepe Yahya, are in themselves sensational brand-new developments in the exploration of the ancient Near East.

AKKADIANS: BABYLONIANS AND ASSYRIANS The successors of the Sumerians as rulers of Mesopotamia were the Semitic Akkadian-speakers, to whom belonged first the Babylonians and then their successors the Assyrians, both originally descended from nomads of the Arabian desert. They owed an enormous debt to Sumer. Power first passed to them with Sargon the Great (2300 B.C.) and returned to them after an interlude, about 2000 B.C., with the invasions from the west of a people called Amorite.

Since 1935, excavations at Mari in the middle Euphrates valley have turned up a palace with more than 260 rooms containing many thousands of tablets, mostly from the period between 1750 and 1700 B.C. These were the royal archives, and they include the official letters to the king from his own local officials scattered through his territories and from other rulers of local city-states and principalities, many of which were previously unknown to scholars. Among the correspondents was an Amorite prince named Hammurabi, who just before 1700 B.C. made his own Babylonian kingdom supreme in Mesopotamia. His descendants were able to maintain their power in Babylon and the regions surrounding it down to about 1530 but had to give up Hammurabi's great conquests.

Hammurabi's famous code of law, though in part modeled on its Sumerian predecessors, exhibits a much harsher spirit in its punishments. Yet, as its author, the king boasted not of his warlike deeds but of the peace and prosperity he had brought. Inscribed on a pillar eight feet tall, beneath a sculptured relief showing the king standing reverently before the seated sun god, the code reveals a strongly stratified society: a patrician who put out the eye of a patrician would have his own eye put out; but a patrician who put out the eye of a plebeian had only to pay a fine. But even the plebeian had rights that, to a degree at least, protected him against violence from his betters. Polygamy and divorce now made their appearance. One clause says that "if a merchant lends silver to a trader without interest, and if the trader loses on his investment, he need return to the lender only the capital he has borrowed." The word used for *capital* means "head," just as our word *capital* itself is derived from the Latin *caput,* meaning "head." The concepts of a capitalist system, expressed in identical terms, can here be found in Hammurabi's code; and it is also significant that the scribe used not the Akkadian but the Sumerian word for *silver,* to make the clause sound learned and classical. In its vocabulary as in its concept of the social order, the code reflects the Sumerian impact on the Akkadian-speaking Babylonians.

New nomads, this time from the east (Iran), the Kassites, shattered Babylonian power about 1530; and, after four centuries of relatively peaceful Kassite rule, supremacy in Mesopotamia gradually passed to the far more warlike Semitic Assyrians, whose power had been rising, with occasional setbacks, for several centuries in their great northern city of Assur. About 1100 their ruler Tiglath-pileser reached both the Black Sea and the Mediterranean on a conquering expedition north and west, after which he boasted that he had become "lord of the world." Assyrian militarism was harsh, and the conquerors regularly transported into captivity entire populations of defeated cities. By the eighth century the Assyrian state was a kind of dual monarchy: Tiglath-pileser III (744–727), their ruler, also took the title of ruler of Babylonia, thus consciously accepting the Babylonian tradition. He added enormous territory to the Assyrian dominions. During the 670s B.C. the Assyrian king Esarhaddon invaded and conquered Egypt. Then in turn the mighty Assyrian Empire fell to a new power, the Medes (Iranians related to the Persians), who took Nineveh (612 B.C.) with Babylonian and Palestinian help.

For less than a century thereafter (612–538) Babylonia experienced a rapid, brilliant revival, during which King Nebuchadnezzar built temples and palaces, made Babylon a wonder of the world, with its famous hanging gardens, and overthrew Jerusalem and took the Hebrews into captivity. But in 539, the Hebrew prophet Daniel showed King Belshazzar the moving finger on the wall of the banquet chamber that told him his kingdom was to be given to the Medes and the Persians. Daniel was right, of course, and Cyrus the Great of Persia took Babylon, ending the history of the Mesopotamian empires after two and a half millennia at least.

In religion as in all other aspects of life, the Babylonians and Assyrians took much from the Sumerians. The cosmic gods remained the same, but the local gods of course were different, and under Hammurabi one of them, Marduk, was exalted over all other gods and kept that supremacy thereafter. In Babylonian-Assyrian belief, demons became more numerous and more powerful, and a special class of priests was needed to fight them. Magic practices multiplied. All external happenings—an encounter with an animal, a sprained wrist, the position and color of the stars at a vital moment—had implications for one's own future that needed to be discovered. Starting with observation of the stars for such magical purposes, the Babylonians developed substantial knowledge of their movements, and the mathematics to go with it. They even managed to predict eclipses. They could add, subtract, multiply, divide, and extract roots. They could solve equations, and measure both plane areas and solid volumes. But their astronomy and their mathematics remained in the service of astrology and divination.

Like the Sumerians, the Babylonians were a worried and a gloomy people, who feared death and regarded the afterlife as grim and dusty, in the bowels of the earth. Even this depressing fate could be attained only if the living took care to bury the dead and to hold them in memory. Otherwise one had only restlessness and perhaps a career as a demon to look forward to. In Babylonian literature Marduk became the center of an epic of the creation; we encounter Gilgamesh again, in a more coherent epic than that of the Sumerians, in which he declines a goddess's offer to make him a god because he knows he is sure to die.

Similarly in art the inspiration remains unchanging, but some variations appear: unlike the Sumerians, the Babylonians in some regions had access to stone, and so now incorporated columns in their buildings; and especially the Assyrians showed greater interest, as one would expect, in scenes of combat. In Assyria, too, one finds the orthostat, a statue inserted into a wall and so appearing in high relief; typical Assyrian versions appear as bulls, lions, and fantastic winged beasts. Jewelry-making, goldsmithing, and ivory-carving now reached new and extraordinarily beautiful heights, as shown especially in the finds at Nimrud.

Egypt

CHARACTER OF THE SOCIETY What the Tigris and the Euphrates rivers did for the land between them—Mesopotamia—the Nile River, rising in the hills of Ethiopia and flowing a thousand miles north through Egypt into the Mediterranean, did for the strip of land along its banks on both sides, beyond which, east and west, stretched the dry and inhospitable sands of desert. Many millennia had passed during which the people along the Nile had slowly learned to take advantage of the annual summer flood by tilling their fields to receive the silt-laden river waters, and by regulating its flow. About 3000 B.C., at approximately the time when the Sumerian civilization emerged in Mesopotamia, the Egyptians had reached a comparable stage of development. Much better known to us than Mesopotamia—most of us even as small children already knew about the pyramids, the Sphinx, and King Tut's tomb—Egypt was the other ancient valley civilization that made major contributions to our own.

No sweeping generalizations about peoples and societies are ever wholly acceptable; yet, speaking roughly, the Egyptians were generally more cheerful and confident than the gloomy and apprehensive Sumerians, Babylonians, and Assyrians; more tolerant and urbane and less harsh and obdurate; more speculative and imaginative and less practical and literal-minded; and—despite the long centuries of apparent sameness—more dynamic and less static in their attitudes and achievements. Life after death the Egyptians regarded as a happy continuation of life on earth with all its fleshly pleasures, not as a dismal eternal sojourn in the dust. When we think of Mesopotamian art we think of temples made of brick and of public monuments; when we think of Egyptian art we think of tombs made of stone and of private monuments. The Mesopotamians left few statues, the Egyptians many. The Mesopotamian rulers—both the early city lords and the later kings who aspired to universal monarchy—were agents of the gods on earth; the Egyptian rulers from the beginning were themselves regarded as gods. The Mesopotamians were historically minded, the Egyptians not. So, despite the many similarities between the two societies, and the mutual influences we know to have passed from one to the other—though chiefly in the direction of Egypt from Mesopotamia—each had its own distinct characteristics.

Because Egyptian territory consisted of the long strip along the banks of the Nile, it was always hard to unify. At the very beginning—3000 B.C.—we can distinguish two rival kingdoms—Lower and Upper Egypt. Lower Egypt was the Nile Delta (so called because it is shaped like the Greek letter of that name), the triangle of land nearest the Mediterranean where the river splits into several streams and flows into the sea. Upper Egypt was the land along the course of the river for eight hundred miles between the Delta and the First Cataract. Periodically the two regions were unified in one kingdom, but the ruler, who called himself king of Upper and Lower Egypt, by his very title recognized that his realms consisted of two somewhat disparate entities, one looking toward the Mediterranean and outward to the other civilizations growing up around its edges, and the other more isolated by its deserts and more self-regarding. The first unifier, perhaps mythical, was a certain Menes, whose reign (about 2850 B.C.) scholars take as the start of the first standard division of Egyptian history, the Old Kingdom (2850–2200).

OLD, MIDDLE, AND NEW KINGDOMS When the king is god, his subjects need only listen to his commands to feel sure they are doing the divine will. As each Egyptian king died, his great sepulchral monument in the form of a pyramid told his subjects that he had gone to join his predecessors in the community of gods. The largest of the pyramids took several generations to build, and involved the continual labor of thousands of men, a token that the society accepted and took pride in the divinity of its rulers. A highly centralized bureaucracy carried out the commands of the king. A stratified society worked for him. His forces advanced at times westward into the Libyan desert, and at other times—drawn by the pull that we find exerted on every ruler of Egypt from Menes to President Sadat—east and north into Palestine.

The Old Kingdom was first disturbed and eventually shattered by a growing tendency among district governors to pass their offices on to their sons, who in turn tended to strike out on their own or at least to regard their territories as hereditary fiefs and thus to weaken the central authority. At the same time we know the priests of the Sun had also made good their claims to special privileges that helped diminish royal power. After an interim period of disorder lasting perhaps two centuries (2200–2000), a new dynasty (eleventh of the thirty in Egyptian history) restored unity in what is known as the Middle Kingdom (2100–1800), distinguished for its rulers' land-reclamation policies and its victories abroad.

To the south, the hostile Nubians were defeated and their movements controlled by the building of frontier fortresses. Palestine and Syria came under Egyptian influence. The bureaucracy flourished. Thebes ceased to be the capital, as a new city was founded south of Memphis, from which government could be exercised more effectively; the provincial governorship became hereditary, but had to be confirmed by the king; and the king's son at the age of twenty-one became co-ruler with his father. The king himself was less remote and more eager to be regarded as the shepherd of his people.

But secessionist movements took control of Egypt and the growing internal weakness combined with a foreign invasion and conquest put an end to the Middle Kingdom about 1800 B.C. The conquerors were called Hyksos, Asian nomads of uncertain origin who imported the war chariot and perhaps the bow. The Egyptians hated their rule, which lasted something over a century, and eventually rallied behind a new dynasty (the seventeenth) to drive out the invaders. By about 1550 and the eighteenth dynasty the task was accomplished and the New Kingdom (1550–1085) well launched.

The five centuries of the New Kingdom saw extraordinary advances: in foreign affairs, the Egyptians engaged in a struggle for Syria and Palestine not only with the great powers of Mesopotamia but with the mountain and desert peoples who lived between the two great valley civilizations. The Egyptian ruler (now called pharaoh) Thutmose I reached the Euphrates on the east, and marched far south into Nubia (what we today call the Sudan). Thutmose III (1469–1436) fought seventeen campaigns in the East, and even crossed the Euphrates and beat his Mesopotamian enemies on their own soil. The walls of the great temple of Karnak preserve his own carved account of his military achievements and the enormous tribute paid him by his conquered enemies. It is his obelisk, popularly known as Cleopatra's Needle, that stands in Central Park in New York. The Egyptians established their own network of local governors throughout the conquered territories, but ruled mildly, and did not, as the Assyrians were soon to do, deport whole masses of the population into captivity. The building program of the eighteenth dynasty was a vast one.

It was the pharaoh Amenhotep IV (1379–1362) who caused a major internal upheaval in the successful New Kingdom by challenging the priests of the sun god Amen, who had become a powerful privileged class. Amenhotep urged the substitution for Amen of the sun disk, Aten, and, even more dramatic, commanded that Aten alone be worshiped and that all the multitude of other gods be abandoned. Amenhotep changed his name to Akhenaten, "Pleasing to Aten," in honor of his only god. Some have seen in this famous episode a real effort to impose monotheism on Egypt; others disagree. To mark the new policy, Akhenaten and his beautiful wife Nefertiti ruled from a new capital in Amarna. Amarna gives its name to the "Amarna age"

The pharaoh Akhenaten. This statue from Karnak is a remarkable example of seemingly modern distortion in ancient art.

(ca. 1417-ca. 1358). Nearby, beginning in the 1880s A.D., were found the famous Tell-el-Amarna letters, a collection of about four hundred tablets including the diplomatic correspondence of Akhenaten and his father

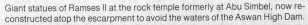

Giant statues of Ramses II at the rock temple formerly at Abu Simbel, now reconstructed atop the escarpment to avoid the waters of the Aswan High Dam.

with the rulers of western Asia, in many languages, an invaluable source for scholars.

Akhenaten's effort to overthrow the entrenched priesthood led to internal dissension and the loss of external strength. His son-in-law, Tutankhamen (1361–1351), was eventually sent to rule in Thebes, city of the priests of Amen, with whom he compromised: this was "King Tut," the discovery of whose tomb with all its magnificent contents was the sensation of the 1920s. With Akhenaten's death, the new religious experiment collapsed, and the pharaohs strove to make up for the interval of weakness by resuming their foreign conquests.

About 1300 B.C. Ramses II (nineteenth dynasty) reached a treaty with a people from Asia Minor, the Hittites. This treaty, of which we have texts in both Egyptian and Hittite, called for a truce in the struggle for Syria and provided for a dynastic marriage between the pharaoh and a Hittite princess. The interlude was short, however, and soon after 1200 B.C. the New Kingdom in its turn suffered severely as the result of an invasion of the eastern Mediterranean shores by mixed bands of raiders from the sea, sometimes called "Sea Peoples," possibly including ancestors of the later Greeks and Sicilians, and others.

Now Egypt entered into a period of decline, marked by renewed internal struggles for power between the secular authorities and the priests, and

Portrait head of Queen Nefertiti (fourteenth century B.C.), wife and sister of the pharaoh Akhenaten.

among local and central rulers. Then came the Assyrian conquest of the seventh century, the Persian conquest of 525 B.C., and the conquest by Alexander the Great of Macedonia in 331 B.C.

RELIGION Religion was the most powerful force animating Egyptian society. One of the greatest modern authorities writes that if one asked an ancient Egyptian "whether the sky was supported by posts or held up by a god, the Egyptian would answer: 'Yes, it is supported by posts or held up by a god—or it rests on walls, or it is a cow, or it is a goddess whose arms and feet touch the earth.'" * So the Egyptian was ready to accept overlapping divinities, and to add new ones whenever it seemed appropriate: if a new area was incorporated into the Egyptian state, its gods would be added to those already worshiped.

From the beginning, Egyptian cults included animals, totems perhaps: sheep, bulls, gazelles, and cats, still to be found carefully buried in their own cemeteries. As time passed, the figures of Egyptian gods became human, but often retained an animal's head, sometimes an animal's body. Osiris, the Egyptian god best known to most of us, began as a local Nile Delta deity. He taught mankind agriculture; Isis was his wife, and animal-headed Set his brother and rival. Set killed Osiris; Isis persuaded the gods to bring him back to life, but thereafter he ruled below (obviously a parallel to the fertility and vegetation-cycle beliefs we have already encountered in Mesopotamia and will encounter again in Greece). Naturally enough, Osiris was identified with the life-giving, fertilizing Nile, and Isis with the receptive earth of Egypt.

Horus the sun defeated the evil Set after a long struggle. But Horus was only one kind of sun god: there was also Re, later joined with Amen, and still later Aten, as we have seen. The moon god was the ibis-headed Thoth. In the great temple cities like Heliopolis, priests worked out and wrote down hierarchies of divinities. Out in the villages all the forces of nature were deified and worshiped: one local god was part crocodile, part hippopotamus, and part lion, a touching and economical revelation of what simple farmers along the river banks had to worry about. However numerous the deities, Egyptian religion itself was unified; unlike a Sumerian temple, however, which was the political center of its city, and for which the population toiled, the Egyptian temple had a limited religious function.

The Egyptians were preoccupied with life after death. They believed that after death each human being would appear before Osiris and recount all the bad things he had *not* done on earth: "I have not done evil to men. I have not ill-treated animals. I have not blasphemed the gods," and so on, a negative confession, to justify his admission into the kingdom of the blessed. Osiris would then have the man's heart weighed, to test

*J. A. Wilson, in *The Intellectual Adventure of Ancient Man* (Chicago, 1943), p. 44.

the truth of his self-defense; and he would be admitted or else delivered over to judges for punishment.

Egyptians believed not only in body and soul, but in *ka,* the indestructible vital principle of each human being, which left the body at death but could and did return at times. That is why the Egyptians preserved the body in their elaborate art of mummification: so that the ka on its return would find it not decomposed; and that is why they filled the tombs of the dead with all the objects that the ka might need or find delightful on its return to the body. Otherwise it might come back and haunt the living.

CIVILIZATION We know Egyptian civilization so intimately because of the great number of inscriptions, which give us the historical materials, and of papyri (fragments of the ancient material the Egyptians wrote on, made of the pith of a water plant), which give us the literary materials. Yet what we have represents a smaller percentage of what once existed and of what may yet be found than does our collection of Mesopotamian literature on its myriad, carefully copied clay tablets.

The Egyptians wrote in a form of picture-writing (hieroglyphics: sacred carvings), which yielded its secrets to modern scholars in the 1820s. They had possessed the key only since 1799, when a large inscribed stone was found near the town of Rosetta in the Nile Delta. This famous piece of black basalt has a long text chiseled into its surface in three languages: Greek, hieroglyphics, and another Egyptian script developed from hieroglyphics. Although the Greek version was imperfect, it could be read, and it proved to be a decree in honor of a pharaoh named Ptolemy V, from 196 B.C., in the period after Alexander the Great's conquest. Even so, it took three decades before a French scholar, Champollion, convinced himself that hieroglyphics were intended to be read phonetically, not symbolically, and so got beyond the mere decipherment of the name and title of Ptolemy V. Knowing the language of the Egyptian church of his own day, which was still close to ancient Egyptian although written differently, he gradually puzzled out the hieroglyphics of the Rosetta stone. In the century and a half since then, scholars have been able to read with certainty the vast number of surviving Egyptian texts. Visitors to the British Museum can still see the famous slab that made it possible for men of the nineteenth and twentieth centuries A.D. to understand ancient Egypt.

The equally famous Egyptian Book of the Dead brings together stories of the gods and hymns and prayers, and teaches us much of what we know of Egyptian religion. The Egyptian literature we have includes no epic story of a hero comparable to Gilgamesh, a mortal who cannot quite attain immortality, no doubt because the Egyptians confidently did expect to attain it. But it does include love songs, banquet songs, and what we would call fiction, both historical and fantastic. "If I kiss her," says an Egyptian lover,

The Rosetta Stone, discovered in 1799 at Rashid in the Delta and now at The British Museum.

"and her lips are open, I am happy even without beer," * a sentiment that seems irreproachably up to date. "Enjoy thyself as much as thou canst," says a banquet song, "for a man cannot take his property with him," † though actually nobody ever tried harder than the Egyptians to do so. The historical romance of Sinuhe tells the story of an Egyptian noble who was forced by intrigue into exile in Asia (early Middle Kingdom, ca. 1980 B.C.), was elected chief of a tribe there, won a magnificent single combat against a local champion, and, at the end, full of longing for Egypt, was happily recalled by the pharaoh and richly dressed, honored, and given a pyramid of his own for his future sepulcher. In another story we hear of the young man who resisted a lady's advances only to find that she was accusing him of having made advances to her: a predicament similar to that of Joseph in Egypt itself as reported by the Old Testament, and to many similar tales in the folklore of other peoples.

III Peoples Outside the Valleys

For well over a thousand years after their first flourishing, the peoples of the valley civilizations held the stage

*A. Erman, *Literature of the Ancient Egyptians,* trans. A. M. Blackman (London: Dutton, 1927), p. 244.
†J. H. Breasted, *The Dawn of Conscience* (New York, 1933), pp. 163–164.

virtually alone. But the Hyksos invasion of Egypt (ca. 1800 B.C.), the Kassite invasion of Mesopotamia, and the Hittite attacks on both have already warned us that the men of the mountains and deserts outside the valleys had begun to compete fiercely with the more settled valley societies. The outsiders too had centuries of history behind them, still not well known to scholars, but by 1500 B.C. the Kassites in southern Mesopotamia, the Hurrians with their state of Mitanni in northern Mesopotamia and smaller states in southeastern Anatolia (modern Turkey), and the Hittites in the remainder of Anatolia had all emerged as rivals both to Babylon and to Egypt.

All of them had strong Indo-European ethnic elements: that is, elements of a strain that would become predominant in Iran, and later in the Mediterranean and the West. All of them were ruled by kings, but their kings were neither the Mesopotamian agents of god on earth nor the Egyptian deified monarchs; rather they ruled as the most powerful among a noble class that controlled the instruments of conquest—horses and chariots—and shared the fruits of conquest, dividing new land among themselves. We begin now to find records, not only of war between these newly emerging peoples and the settled valley societies, but also of their diplomatic exchanges and their peace settlements.

For communication everybody used Akkadian, a Semitic tongue often foreign to both parties in a negotiation. The Egyptians, for example, corresponded in it with the peoples who ruled Syria, who did not speak it either. Even when they wrote in their own languages, some of them used Akkadian script. This enables scholars to pronounce the words even when they do not know what they mean, as is often still the case in Hurrian, written in Akkadian cuneiform but not related to well-known language groups and still by no means completely understood.

As with the language and the cuneiform letters in which it was written, so with the culture generally: the outside peoples were deeply influenced by Mesopotamian religion and literature and art. Though the outsiders dealt severe blows to the valley societies and sometimes seemed temporarily to have overthrown them, the valley societies—Mesopotamia and Egypt—did not in fact succumb during the centuries from 1500 to 1200 B.C., when the threat was greatest.

Hittites

Until the early twentieth century, scholars knew the Hittites chiefly from mentions in non-Hittite sources. Uriah, for example, whom King David so wickedly arranged to have killed in battle in order to keep his wife, Bathsheba, was a Hittite. And in Egypt a great inscription preserved the text in hieroglyphics of a treaty of 1280 B.C. between Ramses II and a Hittite king. Then, in A.D. 1906–1908, excavations at the ancient Hittite capital, Hattusas, now called Boğazköy,

on the plateau of Anatolia, brought to light several thousand tablets, largely in cuneiform script, and written in the Indo-European Hittite language and in many others as well. Painfully deciphered with the help of some texts that appeared in both Hittite and Akkadian and certain Akkadian and Sumerian signs in the Hittite scripts, these finds showed that a strong Hittite kingdom emerged about 1700 B.C.

Its Indo-European king and his aristocracy controlled a native Anatolian population. Between 1700 and ca. 1590, it made great conquests in Syria, and about 1530 resumed expansion toward Babylon. About 1530 there was an internal crisis, from which the state recovered about 1500, when the monarchy became hereditary. Under Suppiluliumas (1380–1346), a contemporary of Akhenaten, it reached its height, as the Hittites took advantage of Egyptian weakness to assert themselves.

Surely it was no coincidence that Suppiluliumas began after his intimate contact with the Egypt of Akhenaten to insist that he be addressed as "my Sun" and to use the solar disk as a symbol. Thenceforth Hittite sovereigns were deified, but only after death; it is from about this time that the written sources begin to speak of a king as "becoming a god" at death. The onslaught of the "Sea Peoples" that damaged the Egyptian New Kingdom about 1200 also put an end to the centralized Hittite state, although various smaller "neo-Hittite" petty principalities continued to exist in Asia Minor in the face of Assyrian expansion down to the late eighth century B.C. These wrote Hittite mostly not in cuneiform script but in hieroglyphics, whose decipherment made much progress during the 1930s, but the first major helpful bilingual text in hieroglyphic Hittite and Phoenician, a known Semitic language, was not found until after World War II, and still has not been fully published.

The native Anatolians, the Indo-European Hittite upper crust, the Mesopotamians, and the Egyptians all made contributions to Hittite religion: foreign gods were made welcome and domesticated. Once part of Hittite religion, no matter where they had originally come from, they received homage in forms derived from Mesopotamia. But there were differences here too: women played a more prominent role in Hittite religion and society than they did either in Mesopotamia or in Egypt. And alone among the peoples of the ancient Near East, the Hittites cremated their kings.

Hittite literature is full of Mesopotamian echoes. But the Hittites alone wrote sober official histories, which sought to determine and record the motives of rulers for their actions. The treaty, too, as a special literary and diplomatic instrument, was apparently a Hittite invention. Hittite architecture expressed itself in fortresses on peaks, which became the nuclei of cities. Otherwise, the buildings show Mesopotamian influence, as does the sculpture; but the Hittites produced no monumental human statues.

Hurrians, Canaanites, Philistines, Phoenicians

Far less well known than the Hittites and still posing many unsolved problems are the Hurrians, whose state, called Mitanni, was established about 1500 B.C. in northern Mesopotamia and lasted only about a century and a third. The language is still imperfectly read; no local archaeological finds comparable to Boğazköy for the Hittites have yet turned up. Like the Hittites, the Hurrians had an Indo-European ruling class, and worshiped some Indo-European deities. Their great importance was to act as intermediaries between the great civilization of Mesopotamia and the less advanced peoples to the north and west, especially the Hittites.

Like the mountains of Anatolia and northern Mesopotamia, the deserts of Syria (the Old Testament land of Canaan) gave rise to a number of Semitic peoples who from time to time invaded the valley societies. Indeed, the Akkadians themselves, both Babylonians and Assyrians, and the Amorites as well had first emerged into history along this path. But there remained behind, of course, other Semitic peoples who never penetrated into the valleys, and who created societies of their own along the Syrian coast of the Mediterranean and in its hinterland.

At Ugarit on the coast—in the northern portion called Phoenicia—archaeologists in 1929 found the royal palace of a Canaanite state that flourished between 1400 and 1200 B.C., complete with cuneiform tablets in a northwest Semitic tongue—Ugaritic—containing the archives of official correspondence, including a treaty with the Hittites written in Akkadian and showing that the Canaanites were under Hittite domination. There were also poems, including an epic about a hero named Kret, who is granted a son by divine favor, as was Abraham in the Book of Genesis in the Old Testament; and who also went to recapture his bride from the fortress of a king who had spirited her away, a leading theme in Homer's *Iliad.* At Ugarit, we are in an eastern Mediterranean world that seems to have cultural affinities with both the Hebrews and the Greeks. Ugarit was extremely important because of its farflung relationships with contemporary states and as a forerunner of the Phoenicians. But it was only one of many Canaanite city-states, and it went down in the general chaos of 1200 B.C. caused by the "Sea Peoples'" invasion. Among these invading "Sea Peoples," we know, were the Indo-European Philistines, who settled to the south of the Canaanites and gave their name to Palestine.

The Canaanites apparently matched their extreme political localism with extreme religious localism, and they seem often not to have taken much trouble to sort out their gods: several gods presided over any given department of life, and gods were sometimes masculine and sometimes feminine, as if nobody was quite sure or cared very much. If this seems primitive, the impression is reinforced by the Canaanite practices of human sacrifice and religious prostitution. The supreme Ca-

naanite god was El, whose name simply means "god" and who is little known. Baal, on the other hand, whose name means "lord," was a storm god—like the Sumerian god of the air, the region between heaven and earth. Baal and his wife Astarte, like Osiris and Isis in Egypt and parallel figures in Mesopotamia, symbolized the seasons and cyclical fertility.

In the period after 1300 the Phoenicians, still another Semitic people, flourished along the coast south of Ugarit, and carried on a brisk trade with the western Mediterranean, founding Carthage—Modern Tunis—as a colony about 800 B.C. The Phoenicians (whose very name comes from the word for the Tyrian purple dye made from shellfish found along the coast of their capital, Tyre) thus brought their Semitic tongue (Punic) more than halfway to the Straits of Gilbraltar, through which in fact their ships had often sailed. Many Phoenician names, as we shall see, appear among the names the Greeks gave to their gods; and the Phoenician alphabet, a genuine alphabet (not, like cuneiform, a collection of signs that stood for whole syllables), perhaps inspired by Ugaritic, became the immediate ancestor of the Greek alphabet.

Land of Canaan, Baal, Philistines: these names have been familiar to us all since childhood. For we have now come into the place and time of the Old Testament, and are prepared to understand some of the regional and cultural background of the Hebrews, who in turn were to pass on so much to the peoples of Europe and America.

Hebrews

HISTORY AND THE OLD TESTAMENT With the Hebrews we have reached our first people whose history is recorded in a series of books providing a consecutive story over many centuries. This is of course the Old Testament. The history is found in Genesis, Exodus, Joshua, Judges, Samuel, and Kings. But one also finds genealogy and ritual law (Numbers, Leviticus, and Deuteronomy), tales (Ruth and Job), proverbs (Proverbs, Ecclesiastes), prophetic utterances (Isaiah, Jeremiah, and the rest), and lyric poems (Psalms, the Song of Songs). For many centuries these books were held by Jew and Christian alike to express the literal and sacred truth; so it was not until relatively recently that scholars began to apply to them the same test of authenticity that they apply to ordinary works of history. Nineteenth-century scholars found much material in the Old Testament that they took to be legendary and mythical, and they often questioned its historical accuracy.

But most such doubts have tended to be dispelled in our own time, as hard archaeological evidence has piled up in support of the general narrative that the Old Testament gives us. It is true that the Old Testament was not written down as the events happened, that many of its earliest portions were compiled long after the event, that the writings were not arranged in their present form until the second century B.C., and that many folklore elements can be easily identified. But the weight of the evidence tends to confirm the biblical story.

Even the biblical account of the mist-shrouded beginnings of the Hebrews now seems authentic: they may well have migrated from Ur "of the Chaldees" sometime after 1950 B.C., when that Sumerian center in southern Mesopotamia was destroyed, northwest to the prosperous center of Harran. Abraham then may well have migrated westward into "Canaan," as Genesis says. The accounts in Genesis of the origins of the universe and the racial origins of the Hebrews, and the stories of Eden, the Flood, and the Tower of Babel all fit into the supposition of a northern Mesopotamian—and no other—place of residence for the Hebrews before about 1500 B.C., when the westward migration took place. Probably a racial mixture including some non-Semitic elements (Hurrian?) from the beginning, the Hebrews may well be the same as a people called Khapiru who appear beginning about 1900 B.C. in the cuneiform tablets and in both Hittite and Egyptian sources as raiders, wanderers, and captives. Historians also are convinced that some of the Hebrews at least did live for several centuries in the Nile Delta during the Hyksos period, before Moses (whose name is Egyptian) became their leader and led them about 1300 B.C. to within sight of the Promised Land. Even the miraculous crossing of the Red Sea in Exodus is not incompatible with the shallow waters, the reedy growth, and the winds of the region.

Outsiders battering their way back into Canaan against the entrenched resistance of those who already lived there, the Hebrew confederation of tribes was held together by the new religion that Moses gave them—the Ten Commandments, the ark of the covenant, the many observances that God prescribed. Gradually by ruthless conquest they added to their holdings (Joshua took Jericho about 1230 B.C.), and after the period of the Judges—when many minor leaders directed Hebrew affairs and battles were fought against Canaanites and Philistines—the loose confederation became a monarchy about 1020 B.C., when the prophet Samuel chose Saul to be the first king. Saul's son-in-law, rival, and successor, David, so well known to us by the virtually contemporary account (1000–960 B.C.) in the Book of Samuel, united the kingdom and strengthened it. His luxury-loving son Solomon brought the Palestinian kingdom of the Jews to new heights of prosperity, but even then it was small in size and resources compared to Sumer, Babylon, Assyria, or Egypt.

But under Solomon (960–922 B.C.) in 933 B.C. the kingdom split in two: the northern kingdom of Israel (933–722 B.C.), stronger but lacking the great center of Jerusalem, and the southern kingdom of Judah (933–585 B.C.), which held Jerusalem but had little real strength. The Assyrians destroyed Israel in 722 B.C., and the Babylonians—then, as we have seen, experiencing a brief revival—destroyed Judah in 586 and took the

Jews into captivity. When the Persians under Cyrus the Great in turn conquered Babylonia and freed the Jews to return to Palestine after 538, the Jews no longer had a state, but a religious community only. From then on they were held together by religion alone, and depended politically on three successive empires: the Persian, the Macedonian, the Roman.

RELIGION Indeed, had it not been for their extraordinary religion, the Hebrews would seem to us just another people of the ancient Near East, less numerous than most, less talented artistically than any. But of course we would probably not know much about them had it not been for their religion, which gave them and us the books of the Old Testament and an enduring tradition. Many of the most fundamental ideas of Hebrew religion go back to the days when the Hebrews were still nomads, before they had adopted a settled life. Thus God's commandments to Moses on Mount Sinai that "Thou shalt have no other gods before me," "Thou shalt not make unto thee any graven image," and "Thou shalt not take the name of the Lord thy God in vain"—which long preceded the settlement in Palestine—determined three fundamental and permanent aspects of Judaism that were new among Near Eastern religions.

First, the religion of the Hebrews was monotheistic, recognizing only a single god. Despite the experiment of Akhenaten in Egypt and a few Babylonian texts that try to associate all divine power with Marduk alone, the Jews were the first to insist that their god was the only god, and a universal god. Second, the Jews were forbidden to represent him in sculpture or painting—which was an enormous contrast with all other religions of the ancient world. More than that: they were forbidden to make *any* images of living beings, flesh, fish, or fowl, no doubt because their leaders feared that if they did make such images, they would end by worshiping them; and so from these earliest days their art was confined to nonrepresentational subjects. When they deviated from this law, as they often did, it was usually because of the influence upon them of neighbors whose traditions did not forbid animal or human representations in art. Third, the religion of the Hebrews from the beginning would regard the *name* of God—Yahweh or Jehovah, meaning "he causes to be," or "the creator"—as literally not to be spoken, a reverence quite different from any we have found in other ancient Near Eastern religions. From the nomadic period of Hebrew life also come the feast of the Passover, with its offering of a spring lamb and of unleavened bread, celebrating the escape from Egypt; the keeping of the sabbath on the seventh day; the annual day of expiation (Yom Kippur); and other holy days still honored by the Jews in our own times.

The Old Testament swarms with episodes in which the Hebrews proved unable to keep the first commandment, broke away from the worship of the single God, tried to propitiate other gods, and were punished. Yet however often they disobeyed, the first commandment remained the central feature of their religion. With monotheism from the first went morality, as shown in the remaining commandments forbidding murder, adultery, stealing, false witness, and covetousness of one's neighbor's property. Jehovah himself, both merciful and righteous, creator of all things, was human in form, but was not visible to the human eye. Unlike the gods of all the other peoples, he did not lead a human life; he had no family; he dwelt, not in a palace like a human palace only more splendid, but in heaven. When he wished to speak to the leader of his people, he descended onto a mountaintop (Mount Sinai) or into a burning bush or into the space left for him by his own direction between the golden cherubim to be set atop a sacred box in which the Ten Commandments on their two tablets of stone were to be kept.

This was the ark of the covenant, built by artisans to the special orders of God as relayed by Moses. The covenant was the special pact between God himself and his chosen people, all the tribes of the Hebrews, in tribal confederation, held together by their regard for this most sacred of objects. Kept at first in a very special tent, a portable tabernacle, the ark moved with the Hebrews, first to Shiloh, where the Philistines captured it about 1050 B.C., and then into the temple built for it by Solomon in Jerusalem, a royal chapel, whose decorations included many that violated the commandment about graven images. Solomon's temple was built by a Canaanite architect using Phoenician models, showing the increasing influence of non-Israelite peoples on the cult.

There were prophets (men called by God) among the Jews from the beginning; but they naturally multiplied during the division of the people into the two kingdoms of Israel and Judah. They summoned the people to return to the original purity of the faith and to avoid the paganism that seemed to be threatening if Canaanite influences continued. In ecstasy perhaps brought on by dances, they solemnly warned of fearful punishment to come if the people did not heed them. After the punishment, however, the prophets (notably Isaiah) promised that Israel would rise again, and that a descendant of David would appear as the Messiah to usher in a new golden age. The disaster came, of course, with the Babylonian captivity; and now that the prophecies of evil had been fulfilled, the prophet Ezekiel had a vision of new life being breathed into the dead bones of Israel, and urged the preparation for its restoration. (It was in exile, in the sixth century B.C., that the sacred writings were selected and arranged in a form not unlike the Old Testament we know.) The captivity once over, the priests became the dominant figures in the restored community, with its rebuilt temple but without a state of its own. They strove deliberately to return to what they believed to be the practices of their remote ancestors.

As one would expect, there was much about Hebrew society that recalls what we have already observed about the other peoples of the ancient Near East. The father exercised supreme authority within the family; polygamy and divorce were permitted; and, as among the Hittites, a widow married her dead husband's brother. The Hebrews had slaves, but a Hebrew slave could be made to serve no more than six years. A man who had injured his slave was required to set him free. Otherwise the law of an eye for an eye, a tooth for a tooth, held sway. Yet the general prescriptions, such as the Commandments, and even some of the specific regulations—not to wrong strangers, not to exact usurious interest for a loan, to help one's enemies as well as one's friends—strike an ethical note deeper than any found in the earlier Mesopotamian Near East, and presage the Christian principles that would—within another half-millennium—emerge from this Hebrew society, which by that time had been greatly influenced by Greek civilization.

IV Crete and Mycenae
Minoans before Mycenae

Among the notable finds in Ugarit was an ivory relief of a bare-breasted goddess, holding wheat ears in each hand and seated between two goats standing on their hind legs. She is like nothing from Mesopotamia or Egypt but she greatly resembles the goddesses frequently found on the large Mediterranean island of Crete, on the westernmost fringe of the Near East, where there developed beginning about 2600 B.C. the last of the Bronze Age civilizations we shall consider, preceded, like the others, by untold numbers of centuries of gradual Stone Age advance. Cretan civilization is often called Minoan, after Minos, the legendary founder of the local dynasty, whose monarchs were all called Minos after him.

Sir Arthur Evans, the British archaeologist whose brilliant work in Crete in the first half of our own century enabled modern scholars to appreciate Minoan society at its true worth, divided the culture into three main periods; Early Minoan (ca. 2600–ca. 2000), Middle Minoan (ca. 2000–1600), and Late Minoan (ca. 1600–1100). Each of these three is regularly further subdivided three times to enable easy discussion of the objects found. For all such dating, pottery is the key. Different styles found at different levels permit scholars to work out a chronological framework. In Crete such dating is of surpassing importance, partly because we have not yet learned how to read the earliest writing, some of it in hieroglyphics and some of it in a script known as Linear A.

Much is now conjectured about Linear A, and some words have been plausibly deciphered; but it cannot yet be read. There is no bilingual or trilingual Rosetta stone for Linear A, which, moreover, is surely not Greek. In the last twenty years Professor Cyrus Gordon of Brandeis University has argued strongly that it is a northwest Semitic dialect related to Phoenician

ever tribute is remembered in the Minotaur legend. Indeed, they now controlled the very center of the civilization that had already taught them so much. Certain military innovations now took place in Crete: chariots were introduced and arrows stored for large bodies of troops, but the invaders built no fortifications, presumably because they expected no new invasion. In the palace of Minos the Greeks installed a throne room of the type they were accustomed to build in their own mainland palaces. But, most important, the Minoans showed them how useful it was to keep records; and since Linear A, devised for a Semitic language, would not do, the scribes may have invented a new script—Linear B—in which to write the language of the conquerors: Greek. On the other hand, Linear B may have been developed gradually from Linear A.

The conclusive proof, worked out only in 1952 by Michael Ventris, that in fact the language of Linear B *is* early Greek has made possible the foregoing tentative reconstruction of events. Evans had found the Linear B tablets in great numbers at Knossos, but no such tablets were known *from mainland Greece* until 1939, when an American scholar, Carl Blegen, discovered the first of what proved to be a large collection of them in Pylos, where he was excavating a Mycenaean palace, and since then many more have turned up elsewhere in Greece, including some in Mycenae itself. Acting on the assumption that it was probably Greek (since he now knew that Greeks were keeping records in it on the mainland), Ventris used the techniques of cryptography to demonstrate that the script was a syllabary, not an alphabet (with each symbol representing not just a single letter but a syllable), and then cracked the code. The thousands of Linear B tablets have by no means all been read even now, and by no means all readings are certain; but Greek it is. The tablets are mostly prosaic inventories of materials stored in the palaces or lists of persons in the royal services.

But the disappearance in Crete of Linear A, and the substitution for it about 1460 B.C. of the new Linear B (Greek), points clearly to a Mycenaean occupation of the island that preceded the last great violent destruction of about 1400 and lasted almost a century. We cannot be sure to what degree the new Greek rulers of Knossos were independent of direct authority from the mainland; they may have been subordinate Mycenaean princes. The great palace of Knossos and a number of other major Cretan centers were burned down about 1400, apparently after looting. We do not know who did it. Perhaps the Cretans rose against their Greek masters and burned down their own cities; though it has been plausibly suggested that such an act would have invited fierce reprisals and continued occupation after reconstruction. There was no reconstruction. Instead there was permanent disruption. So perhaps it was the Mycenaeans themselves who—in revenge against Cretan rebelliousness that may have made the island ungovernable—decided to cut their losses and destroy the Cretan centers and sail away. Or

perhaps it was a volcanic upheaval of the seabed. The recent rediscovery (1967) and present active excavation of a Minoan city on the volcanic island of Santorin (Thera) to the north of Crete may provide new evidence and enable scholars to decide the question one way or another. After the disaster of 1400 B.C. Crete remained rich and populous but lost its Mediterranean predominance, which passed definitely to the aggressive mainland peoples.

Mycenae, 1400–1100 B.C.

We still know relatively little about Mycenaean politics and society. We can tell from excavated gold treasures that Mycenae itself was wealthy, which is not surprising considering that it had conquered Crete. But the Mycenaeans seem not to have been overseas empire builders even in the sense that the Cretans had been; their occupation of Crete may well have been undertaken by an invading captain who retained power for himself in Crete, however much of its revenue he sent back home. The Achaeans (Greeks) of whom the Hittite sources speak may well not have been the Greeks of Mycenae at all but Greeks of Rhodes, another island principality. And there were other settlements in the Peloponnesus itself—Pylos, Tiryns (the latter very close to Mycenae)—which seem to have been extensive too, and perhaps under local rulers equally powerful but bound in alliance to the Mycenaeans: a kind of loose confederacy among equals seems to fit best with the evidence. Each of the cities was walled. The walls of Mycenae survive, with their famous Lion Gate showing the two great sculptured beasts who lean forward to face each other, separated by a slender column, over the huge lintel above the gateway.

Tombs from the period before 1400 B.C. are of two sharply distinct types: those carefully built to take the bodies of kings and important noblemen, and simple burial places for the rest of the population. Tombs from the period between 1400 and 1200 show a rise in the general wealth: more chamber tombs with more gifts to the dead found in them. Similarly at Mycenae itself, Tiryns, Pylos, Athens, and Thebes, there arose now great palaces as community centers, with workshops, storage areas, guardrooms, and lesser dwelling houses attached. Others certainly existed, and more will be found. Good roads with bridges and culverts connected the main towns, and good water-supply systems characterized them. Artisans attached to the palace built and repaired chariots, made jars to hold the wine and oil, tanned leather, wrought bronze in the forge, made bricks, and sewed garments; workmen stored goods for preservation and for sale and exchange. A Mycenaean palace was a businesslike (and noisy) place.

The Linear B tablets preserve records of special royal furniture most elaborately inlaid in ivory, glass, and gold: like the Egyptian pharaohs, the Mycenaean rulers obviously valued things most when they took a lot of time and effort to make. Smaller than the great

was tamer in Greece, where songs were early written for the god.

Tragedy

From these songs there developed at Athens the art of tragedy: the word means "goat song" and shows the close connection with the god Dionysus. At first largely sung by a chorus and formally religious in tone, the tragedies later began to deal with more personal human problems, and individual actors' roles became more and more important. The first competition to choose the best tragedy was sponsored by Peisistratus in 534 B.C., and annual contests were held thereafter. Many hundreds of tragedies were written; comparatively few have survived in full—probably the best—and we have fragments of others. The later Greek philosopher Aristotle believed that it was the purpose of tragedy to arouse pity and terror in the spectators, to purge or purify them by causing them to reflect on the fearful punishments that highly placed men and women brought upon themselves by their own sins, the worst of which was hubris, arrogance.

The first, and some would still say the greatest, of the three chief tragedians whose works survive was Aeschylus (ca. 525–456), of whose seventy-odd tragedies we have seven. The earliest in time was *The Persians* (472 B.C.), in which Aeschylus explained the defeat of the Persians as the result of Xerxes' efforts to upset the international order established by the gods, and of the arrogance by which he offended Zeus. The audience could ponder recent history (it was only seven years since the Persians had been defeated) and consider the moral reasons for their own victories: such a play would

Dionysus sailing. Attic kylix (drinking cup) painted by Exakias ca. 540 B.C.

tend to sober up any fire-eater who thought one Greek could lick ten Persians.

In *Prometheus Bound,* Aeschylus dealt with the punishment inflicted by Zeus upon Prometheus the Titan, who had stolen fire as a gift to mankind and who now lay chained to a rock while a vulture pecked at his liver. Zeus behaved tyrannically—he was new to the job of being king of the gods when Prometheus committed his offense—and only gradually learned to temper his wrath with mercy. Just as Xerxes had offended against the proper order of things by trying to impose Persian rule on Greece, so Prometheus had, even out of good will, offended by trying to get mankind the great gift of fire too soon. In the trilogy *The Oresteia,* all three plays of which survive, Aeschylus dealt with the ghastly tragedies in the family of Agamemnon, who sacrificed his daughter Iphigenia to get a favorable wind to go to Troy, was murdered by his unfaithful wife Clytemnestra on his return, and was avenged by his son Orestes, who killed his mother on the order of Apollo. Orestes suffered torments by the Furies and was acquitted by a court presided over by Athena; but only Zeus succeeded in transforming the Furies into more kindly creatures. Crime and punishment, remorse and release, a benevolent god over all: these Aeschylus portrayed in lofty, moving verse.

Sophocles, the second of the three greatest tragedians (496–406), wrote many tragedies, of which only ten survive. He believed deeply in Athenian institutions and in the religion of his fellow Greeks, and he took an active part in the public life of Periclean Athens. In his *Antigone,* the niece of Creon, tyrant of Thebes, defied her uncle's harsh decision that the body of her brother, killed while leading a rebellion, must be exposed to be devoured by beasts of prey. Proclaiming that divine law required decent burial, she disobeyed Creon and caused the proper ceremonial earth to be sprinkled on the body. She knew she would die for her defiance, but she acted in obedience to her conscience and resisted the dictator. *Antigone* has carried its message of the sanctity of the individual conscience down the centuries, proclaiming the superiority of what is eternally right and decent to any mere dictator's brutal whim.

Living to be ninety, Sophocles saw the ruin brought by the Peloponnesian War, and his last tragedy, *Oedipus at Colonus,* produced after his death, dealt with the old age of the famous Theban king who in ignorance had killed his father and married his mother, and who had torn out his own eyes in horror when he discovered what he had done. A blind beggar, outcast, Oedipus now knew that he could not have avoided the pollution of his unwitting crimes, and that his self-mutilation too was justified. Tempered by years of suffering, he sought sanctuary to die, and received it from Theseus, king of Athens: Oedipus' tomb would forever protect the Athenians against Thebes. Reflecting upon the terrible story of Oedipus and on the trials of all human life, Sophocles' chorus sang that for mankind the best thing is never to be born, and the next best to die as soon as possible after birth: the passions of youth, the blows dealt one in middle life, and the anguish of old age are not worth it.

Nineteen plays remain of the many written by the third and last of the great Attic tragedians, Euripides (ca. 480–408), who focused more upon human psychology, with far less emphasis on divine majesty. More realistic in their introduction of children, slaves, and other characters upon the scene, his plays were also more romantic in their exploration of the far reaches of the human mind. The *Hippolytus* showed the uncontrollable sexual passion of a decent woman—Phaedra—for her ascetic stepson Hippolytus, who rejected it as he would all passion. She was ashamed of her lust

The theater at Epidaurus, ca. 330 B.C.

but, as in the case of Potiphar's wife and Joseph, accused Hippolytus of having attacked her; he was executed, she committed suicide. The *Medea* showed a woman so far gone in agony brought about by rejection of her love that she killed her children in a fit of madness. The *Alcestis* showed a husband so selfish that he gladly accepted the offer of his devoted wife to die for him so that she might prolong his life; and then suffered agonies of remorse at his folly, when he had lost her.

The Trojan Women presented the sufferings of the women of Troy at the hands of the Greeks. Staged in the same year as the Athenian atrocity at Melos, it must have caused the audience many uncomfortable moments of self-questioning. *The Bacchae* explored the excesses of religious ecstasy: in a frenzy a queen tore her own son to bits, thinking he was a lion. Was Euripides saying that men under the impulse of strong emotion were beasts, or that the old religion had too much that was savage in it, or only that the young king had defied the god and his hubris had brought him a fate that he well deserved?

Comedy

Comedy, like tragedy, also began at the festivals of Dionysus. Aristophanes (ca. 450–ca. 385) has left eleven complete plays and parts of a twelfth. Besides making his audience laugh, he hoped to teach them a lesson through laughter. A thoroughgoing conservative, Aristophanes was suspicious of all innovation. In *The Frogs,* for instance, he brought onto the stage actors playing the parts of the two tragedians Aeschylus (then dead) and Euripides (still alive). The god Dionysus himself solemnly weighed verses from their plays on a giant pair of scales. Every time, the solemn, didactic, and old-fashioned Aeschylus outweighed the innovating, skeptical, febrile, modern Euripides: a tragedian's duty, Aristophanes thought, was to teach.

In *The Clouds* Aristophanes ridiculed the philosopher Socrates, whom he showed in his "think shop" dangling from the ceiling in a basket so that he could "voyage in air and contemplate the sun." Aristophanes meant to call attention to the dangers offered to Athenian youth by the Sophists (see p. 55). Socrates himself, we know, thought the play very unfair; but, like the others, Socrates taught young men to question the existing order, and he was therefore fair game.

Aristophanes opposed the Peloponnesian War not because he was a pacifist but because he thought it unnecessary. In *Lysistrata* the women denied themselves to their husbands until the men made peace, and in other plays Aristophanes denounced the Athenian politicians, including Pericles himself, for going to war. In *The Birds* the leading characters set off to found a Birdville (Cloud-cuckoo-land) to get away from war. In one of his later plays, of which we have only two, the women took over the state and proposed to share all the men among them, putting prostitutes out of business; in the other, Poverty and Wealth appeared in person and argued their cases.

These later plays provided a transition to the New Comedy of the fourth century, gentler and more domestic. We have large portions of several New Comedies by Menander and one full text recently discovered and published for the first time only in 1958. The drama was of course only one form that Greek poetic genius took. From the earliest days, the Greeks were the masters of lyric poetry as well (we have quoted one or two of Solon's own poems above, p. 37): among the most celebrated are poems of love by the poetess Sappho, of war by Spartan poets in the very early days, and of triumph in the games by Pindar.

History

A large proportion of what we know about the Greeks before and during the Persian Wars we owe to the industry and intelligence of Herodotus (ca. 484–420), who began to write his history as an account of the origins and course of the struggle between Greeks and Persians, and expanded it into an inquiry into the peoples of the whole world known to the Greeks. Born in Halicarnassus on the Ionian coast of Asia Minor, Herodotus was a great traveler who visited Egypt, Italy, Mesopotamia, and the lands around the Black Sea, collecting information and listening to whatever stories people would tell him about their own past and about their present customs. He recorded what he learned, much of it of course tinged with myth, and he loved a good story; but he was both experienced and sensible, and he often put his reader on his guard against a story that he himself did not believe but set down in order to fill out the record.

Some have tended to scoff a little, especially at Herodotus' tales of a past that was remote even when he was doing his research; but these doubters have often been silenced by recent archaeological finds. Herodotus, for instance, said that the founder of Thebes, the semi-mythical Cadmus, was a Phoenician who had brought Phoenician letters with him from Phoenicia to Greece, where he founded Thebes about 1350 B.C., or about 900 years before Herodotus' own day. Herodotus added that Cadmus' dynasty was ousted about 1200 B.C. This was often disbelieved. But in A.D. 1964 archaeologists at Thebes found in the palace of Cadmus a large collection of fine cuneiform seals, one of which was datable to 1367–1346 B.C. These instantly demonstrated the high probability of Herodotus' account of Cadmus' origin, date of arrival, and bringing of letters. Even the date of the ouster was verified, since the seals were in a layer of material that had been burned about 1200 B.C. and had survived because they were already baked clay. Herodotus wrote so well and so beguilingly that we would read him with delight even if he were not so reliable. Nor was he a mere collector and organizer of material. Though he wandered far, he never lost sight of his main theme: the conflict between east and west, which he interpreted as a conflict between despotism and freedom.

Always coupled with Herodotus we find the equally intelligent but very different historian Thucydides (ca. 471–ca. 400), who wrote the account of the origins and course of the Peloponnesian War. The difference between the two arose partly from their subject matter: Herodotus was dealing largely with events that had happened before his own time, and he had to accept traditions and often hearsay accounts. Thucydides was dealing largely with events in which he himself had been a participant: he was an unsuccessful general on the Athenian side in the war, and had been punished for his defeat; but he remained impersonal, scientific, and serious, collecting and weighing his information with the greatest care. Though he followed Herodotus' custom of putting into the mouths of his leading characters words—sometimes long speeches— that represented what they might have said rather than what they actually said, he notified his readers that they must realize what he was doing: the actual words were not available, but the arguments on both sides of any issue could be revived and written up in the form of speeches. Pericles' funeral oration of 430 B.C. with its praise of Athenian democracy is perhaps the most famous; but Thucydides also wrote for the Melians, about to suffer terrible slaughter and enslavement at Athenian hands, all the moving arguments appropriate to those who were about to be massacred.

As deep a student of human psychology as any of the tragedians, Thucydides found in men and nations the cause of war; he knew as much about war and human behavior as anybody since has been able to learn. He wrote as a loser, but not as a mere loser in a sporting event, where time, and perhaps a return match, will assuage the hurt: Thucydides had seen his own Athens, so admirable in its best qualities, brought down by the Spartan militarists. He hoped that human intelligence would in the future realize how risky war was and what damage it did to the highest human values, but he knew that human nature would always respond to certain challenges by force, and that the lessons of the past were hard to learn. He wrote in pain and in iron detachment. His narrative of the great military events, such as the siege of Syracuse, Alcibiades' ill-conceived project, moves with great speed and well-concealed artistry. The much less talented and more pedestrian Xenophon, author of the *Anabasis* (see p. 43), wrote—in the *Hellenica*—a continuation of Thucydides' work down to the year 362 B.C. And the still less talented Arrian, writing very late but basing his work largely on the now lost account by Ptolemy I himself, has left us an account of Alexander's campaigns.

But for the century or so that followed the death of Alexander we have no historical work comparable with the histories of Herodotus, Thucydides, Xenophon, or Arrian. Therefore, we know the period less intimately than any since the Dark Age. It is only with the decade of the 220s that we once again encounter a narrative history, and then its author and his purpose themselves symbolize the change that has taken place. He was Polybius, a Greek who wrote in Greek but who had spent much time in Rome, where he had become an admirer and agent of the Romans, and the subject of his book was the rise to power of Rome. That he began his account with the year 221 B.C. clearly suggests that by that date the focus of world affairs had begun to shift from Greece to Rome.

Science and Philosophy

Possessed of inquiring, speculative minds, the Greeks showed a deep interest in science. Stimulated by their acquaintance with Egyptian science, the Ionians and later the European Greeks, though they lacked instruments to check and refine their results, correctly attributed to natural rather than supernatural causes a good many phenomena. They knew that the Nile flooded because annual spring freshets took place at its source in Ethiopia. They decided that the straits between Sicily and Italy and Africa and Spain had been caused by earthquakes. They understood what caused eclipses and knew that the moon shone by light reflected from the sun. Hippocrates of Cos (ca. 460–377) founded a school of medicine, from which there survive the Hippocratic oath, with its high concept of medical ethics, and detailed clinical accounts of the symptoms and progress of diseases so accurate that modern doctors have been able to identify cases of diphtheria, epilepsy, and typhoid fever.

The mathematician Pythagoras (ca. 580–500) seems to have begun as a musician interested in the mathematical differences among lyre strings needed to produce various notes. The theorem that in a right-angled triangle the square on the hypotenuse is equal to the sum of the squares on the other two sides we owe to the followers of Pythagoras. They made the concept of numbers into a guide to the problems of life, elevating mathematics almost to a religious cult, perhaps the earliest effort to explain the universe in abstract mathematical language. Pythagoras is said to have been the first to use the word *cosmos*—"harmonious and beautiful order"—for the universe. Earlier Greeks had found the key to the universe in some single primal substance: water, fire, or air; and Democritus (460–370) decided that all matter consisted of minute, invisible atoms.

When Alexandria became the center of scientific research, the astronomer Aristarchus, in the mid-third century, concluded that the earth revolves around the sun, a concept not generally accepted till almost two thousand years later, while his younger contemporary, Eratosthenes, believed that the earth was round, and estimated its circumference quite accurately. Euclid, the great geometrical systematizer, had his own school at Alexandria in the third century B.C., and his pupil Archimedes won a lasting reputation in both theoretical and applied physics, devising machines for removing water from mines and irrigation ditches ("Archimedes' screw," a hand-cranked device, is still in use in Egypt), and demonstrating the power of pulleys and levers by single-handedly drawing ashore a heavily laden ship. Hence his celebrated boast: "Give me a lever long enough and a place to stand on, and I will move the world." In the second century, Hipparchus calculated the length of the solar year to within a few minutes.

Greek scholars were usually not specialists like those in a modern university. The same man would study and write books on physics, mathematics, astronomy, music, logic, and rhetoric. Rhetoric became an increasingly important subject, as the Greeks reflected on their own language and developed high standards of self-expression and style. The subject really began with political oratory, as politicians wished to make more and more effective speeches—particularly essential in wartime, when the population was excited anyhow, and each leader strove to be more eloquent than the last. These multipurpose scholars who in the fifth and fourth centuries B.C. taught people how to talk and write and think on all subjects were called Sophists: wisdom-men. Sophists generally tended to be highly skeptical of accepted standards of behavior and morality, questioning the traditional ways of doing things.

How could anybody really be sure of anything?, they would ask, and some would answer that we cannot know anything we cannot experience through one or more of our five senses. How could you be sure that the gods existed if you could not see, hear, smell, taste, or touch them? Perhaps you could not know, perhaps they did not exist after all. If there were no gods and therefore no divine laws, how should we behave? Should we trust laws made by other men like us? And what sort of men were making laws and in whose interest? Maybe all existing laws were simply a trick invented by powerful people—members of the establishment—to protect their position. Maybe the general belief in the gods was simply a "put-on," invented by clever people to whose interest it was to have the general public docile. Not all Sophists went this far, but in Athens during the Peloponnesian War many young people, already troubled by the war or by the sufferings of the plague, were ready to listen to suggestions that the state should not make such severe demands upon them. Such young people would have burned their draft cards if they had had any, and their troubled parents, god-fearing and law-abiding, greatly feared the Sophists as the corrupters of youth.

It is only against this background that we can understand the career and the eventual fate of Socrates (469–399 B.C.), whose method was that of the Sophists —to question everything, all the current assumptions about religion, politics, and behavior—but who retained unwavering to the end his own deep inner loyalties to Athens and to God. Socrates wrote no books, and held no professorial chair; but we know him well from contemporary reports, chiefly those of his pupil Plato. Socrates was a stonemason who spent his life talking and arguing in the Assembly, in public places, and in the homes of his friends in Athens. He thought of himself as a "gadfly," challenging everything anybody said to him and urging people not to take their preconceptions and prejudices as truths. Only a never-ending debate, a process of question and answer—the celebrated "Socratic method"—could lead human beings to truth. Reasoning led Socrates to conclude that man was more than an animal, that he had a mind, and, above all, that he had a true self, a kind of soul or spirit. Man's proper business on earth was to fulfill this true soul and cultivate the virtues that were proper to it—temperance, justice, courage, nobility, truth. Socrates himself listened to the voice of God that spoke within him.

We have already seen Socrates in his basket in midair in Aristophanes' *Clouds*. Of course he irritated and alarmed those who were worried about the youth of the day, and who thought of him as just another Sophist and one of the most vocal and dangerous. So when he was about seventy years old he was brought to trial on charges of disrespect to the gods and corrupting the youth of Athens. He argued that he had followed the prescribed religious observances and that he wanted only to make men better citizens; and he defended his gadfly tactics as necessary to stir a sluggish state into life. But a court of 501 jurors voted the death penalty by a narrow margin. Socrates could have gotten off by suggesting that he be punished in some other way. Instead he ironically asked for a tiny fine and forced the court to choose between that and death. It condemned him again. Socrates drank the poison cup of hemlock, and waited for death serenely optimistic: he was "of good cheer about his soul." Many contemporaries and most men since have recognized that he was the victim of hysteria following a dreadful war.

Thereafter, it was Plato (ca. 427–347) who carried on his work. Plato founded a school in Athens, the Academy, and wrote a large number of notable dialogues: earnest intellectual conversations, in which Socrates and others discuss problems of man and the human spirit. Much influenced by the Pythagoreans, Plato retained a deep reverence for mathematics, but he found cosmic reality in Ideas rather than in numbers. As man has a "true self" (soul) within and superior to his body, so the world we experience with our bodily senses has within and superior to itself a "true world," an invisible universe or cosmos. In the celebrated dialogue *The Republic,* Plato has Socrates compare the relationship between the world of the senses and the world of Ideas with that between the shadows of persons and objects as they would be cast by firelight on the wall of a cave, and the same real persons and objects as they would appear when seen in the direct light of day. So man sees the objects—chairs, tables, trees—of the world as real, whereas they are only reflections of the true realities—the universals—the Idea of the perfect chair, table, or tree. So man's virtues are reflections of ideal virtues, of which the highest is the Idea of the Good. Man can and should strive to know the ultimate Ideas, especially the Idea of the Good.

This theory of Ideas has proved to be one of the great wellsprings of Western thought and has formed the starting point for much later philosophical discussion. Moreover, in teaching that the Idea of the Good was the supreme excellence and the final goal of life, Plato was advancing a kind of monotheism and laying a foundation on which pagan and Christian theologians both would build.

Politically, Athenian democracy did much to disillusion Plato: he had seen its courts condemn his master Socrates. On his travels he had formed a high opinion of the tyrants ruling the cities of Magna Graecia. So when Plato came to sketch the ideal state in *The Republic,* his system resembled that of the Spartans. He recommended that power be entrusted to the Guardians, a small intellectual elite, specially bred and trained to understand Ideas, governing under the wisest man of all, the Philosopher-King. The masses would simply do their jobs as workers or soldiers, and obey their superiors.

Plato's most celebrated pupil was Aristotle (ca. 384–322), called the "master of those who know." Son of a physician at the court of Philip of Macedon, and tutor to Alexander the Great, Aristotle was interested in everything. He wrote on biology, logic, literary criticism, political theory, ethics. His work survives largely

Greek vase, fifth century B.C., showing hunter and dog.

in the form of notes on his lectures taken by his students; despite their lack of polish, these writings have had a prodigious later influence. He wrote 158 studies of the constitutions of Greek cities. Only the study of Athens survives.

Aristotle concerned himself chiefly with things as they are. The first to use scientific methods, he classified living things into groups, much as modern biologists do, and extended the system to other fields—government, for example. He maintained that governments were of three forms: by one man, by a few men, or by many men; and that there were good and bad types of each, respectively monarchy and tyranny, aristocracy and oligarchy, polity and democracy (mob rule). Everywhere—in his *Logic, Poetics, Politics*—he laid the foundation for later inquiry. Though he believed that men should strive and aspire, he did not push them on to Socrates' goal of self-knowledge or to Plato's lofty ascent to the Idea of the Good. He urged instead the cultivation of the golden mean, the avoidance of excess on either side: courage, not foolhardiness or cowardice; temperance, not overindulgence or abstinence; liberality in giving, not prodigality or meanness.

Later, in the period after Alexander, two new schools of philosophy developed, the Epicurean and the Stoic. Epicurus (341–270) counseled temperance and common sense, carrying further the principle of the golden mean. Though he defined pleasure as the key to happiness, he ranked spiritual joys above those of the body, which he recommended should be satisfied in moderation. The Stoics, founded by Zeno, got their name from the columned porch (*Stoa*) in Athens where he first taught. They preferred to repress the physical desires altogether. Since only the inward man counted, the Stoics preached total disregard for social, physical, or economic differences among men. They became the champions of slaves and other social outcasts, anticipating to some degree one of the moral teachings of Christianity.

The Arts

The incalculably rich legacy left by the Greeks in literature was well matched by their achievements in the plastic arts. In architecture, their characteristic public building was a rectangle, with a roof supported by fluted columns. Over the centuries, the Greeks developed three principal types or orders of columns, still used today in "classical" buildings: the Doric column, terminating in a simple, unadorned square flat capital; the Ionic, slenderer and with simple curlicues (volutes) at the four corners of the capital; and the Corinthian, where acanthus leaves rise at the base of the volutes. Fluting gives an impression of greater height than the simple cylindrical Egyptian columns.

No matter what the order of the columns, a Greek temple strikes the beholder as dignified and simple. On the Acropolis of Athens, the Parthenon, greatest of all Doric temples, rose between 447 and 432 B.C. as the crowning achievement of Pericles' rebuilding program. By means of subtle devices—slightly inclining the columns inward so that they look more stable, giving each column a slight bulge in the center of the shaft so that it does not look concave—the building gives the illusion of perfection. In the triangular gable-ends that crowned its front and back colonnades (the pediments) and on the marble slabs between the beam ends above the columns (the metopes) stood a splendid series of sculptured battle-scenes, most of whose remains are now in the British Museum (the Elgin Marbles). Originally, the Parthenon and its statues were brightly painted. The building survived almost undamaged until 1697, when a Venetian shell exploded a Turkish powder magazine inside.

The achievement of Phidias and the other sculptors of the Periclean Age had gradually developed from the "archaic" statues created a century or more earlier, usually of young men rather rigidly posed, with their arms hanging at their sides and a curiously uniform serene smile on their lips. Probably influenced by Egyptian models, these statues have great charm for moderns, who sometimes find the realism of the finished classical work rather tiresome. Phidias' great gold and ivory statues of Athena and the Olympian Zeus long ago fell to looters. So did most of the Greeks' sculpture in bronze; but every so often a great bronze statue is fished out of the sea or (as happened in 1959) is found under the pavement of a street being excavated for a sewer.

Though Greek painting as such has almost disappeared, we know from written texts that public buildings were adorned with paintings of Greek victories and portraits of political and military leaders. Moreover, the thousands of pottery vases, plates, cups, and bowls that have been discovered preserve on their surfaces—in black on red or in red on black—paintings of extraordinary beauty and of great variety. They show mythological scenes, illustrations to the *Iliad* and *Odyssey,* and the daily round of human activity: an athlete, a fisherman, a shoemaker, a miner, even a drunk vomiting while a sympathetic girl holds his head.

In the Hellenistic age sculpture became more emotional and theatrical: compare the Laocoön group, with its writhing serpents crushing their victims, to a statue of the Periclean period. The Venus de Milo and the Winged Victory of Samothrace are two of the most successful Hellenistic works of art; but there are a good many imitative and exaggerated efforts which are regarded as comparative failures. In literature, too, beginning with Menander's New Comedy, vigor and originality ebbed, while sophistication and a certain self-consciousness took over.

Summary

Such a summary account runs the risk of creating the impression that the Greeks were supermen living in a paradise of physical and cultural triumphs. In fact, of course, few Greeks could understand or follow the ideas of a Plato or an Aristotle, or could afford to spend a great deal of time at the games, at the theater, or arguing with Socrates. Most Greeks worked hard, and their standard of living would seem extremely low today. In all of Athens at its height we know of only one establishment that employed over a hundred workmen. Even wealthy Athenians resided in small, plain houses of stucco or sun-dried brick: nobody until the Hellenistic period lived pretentiously. Athens was a huddle of mean little streets; there was little or no drainage; lighting was by inadequate, ill-smelling oil lamps. Inside a smithy or a pottery, it was so hot that the smith or potter often worked naked, as we know from vase paintings. But relaxation was at hand: a musician might play in the smithy; and the climate made outdoor living agreeable much of the year.

On the one hand, the Greeks discovered or invented democracy, drama, philosophy. But on the other, they clung to their old-fashioned religious rituals and could not make themselves give up civil war between their city-states. The freedom-loving Athenians executed Socrates. Though they formulated the wisdom of "Know Thyself" and the golden mean, created a beautifully balanced and proportioned architecture, and organized an education that trained the whole man, intellectual and physical, they too often exhibited hubris, the unbridled arrogance that they felt to be the most dangerous of mortal vices. And, as it did in the tragedies of the stage, so in their own lives, their hubris brought nemesis upon them. Their achievements, however, have lived after them, inspiring most of the values that Western man holds dearest.

Reading Suggestions on the Greeks
General Accounts
N. G. L. Hammond, *A History of Greece to 322 B. C.,* 2nd ed. (Oxford Univ. 1967). A good up-to-date survey.

M. I. Finley, *The Ancient Greeks* (*Compass). Compact, up-to-date, and perceptive introduction to Greek life and thought.

H. D. F. Kitto, *The Greeks* (*Penguin). Useful, though opinionated, introduction.

G. E. Robinson, *Hellas: A Short History of Greece* (*Beacon). Good survey by a scholar who has written extensively on Greek history.

M. I. Rostovtzeff, *Greece* (*Galaxy). A famous older account by a distinguished Russian scholar; now somewhat out of date.

J. B. Bury, *A History of Greece to the Death of Alexander the Great,* 3rd ed. rev. (Macmillan, 1951). Another celebrated older account, stressing war and politics.

A. Bonnard, *Greek Civilization,* 3 vols. (Macmillan, 1957–1961). Stimulating chapters on many aspects of Greece by a European scholar.

R. M. Cook, *The Greeks till Alexander* (Thames & Hudson, 1961). Well-illustrated survey stressing material accomplishments.

Special Studies: The Polis

G. Glotz, *The Greek City and Its Institutions* (Knopf, 1929). Celebrated study by a French scholar; now somewhat out of date.

A. Andrewes, *The Greek Tyrants* (*Torchbooks). Very informative comparative survey of emerging Greek constitutions.

V. Ehrenberg, *The Greek State* (*Norton). A solid scholarly introduction.

A. H. M. Jones, *Athenian Democracy* (Praeger, 1957). An up-to-date interpretation.

A. E. Zimmern, *The Greek Commonwealth* (*Oxford Univ.). A celebrated older account, highly sympathetic in tone.

A. R. Burn, *Pericles and Athens* (*Collier). Popular introduction to the Athenian Golden Age.

H. Michell, *Sparta* (Cambridge Univ., 1964). A comprehensive survey, rather more favorable in tone than most treatments of the subject.

K. Freeman, *Greek City-States* (*Norton). Excellent overview, focusing on interesting examples usually neglected in the concern for Athens and Sparta.

A. G. Woodhead, *The Greeks in the West* (Praeger, 1962), and J. M. Cook, *The Greeks in Ionia and the East* (Praeger, 1963). Volumes in the series ''Ancient Peoples and Places,'' highlighting the geographical outposts of the Greek world, likewise often neglected.

W. S. Ferguson, *Greek Imperialism* (Houghton, 1913). Brilliant lectures on the topic.

Special Studies: Greek Civilization

W. Jaeger, *Paideia,* 3 vols. (Oxford Univ. Press, 1939–1944; Vol. I also in paperback). An advanced study of Greek civilization and ideals.

C. M. Bowra, *The Greek Experience* (*Mentor). With stress on interpretation rather than fact; by a literary scholar.

Edith Hamilton, *The Greek Way to Western Civilization* (*Mentor). Enthusiastic popular treatment by a great admirer of the Greeks.

G. Lowes Dickinson, *The Greek View of Life* (*Collier). Greek culture appraised from an old-fashioned point of view.

M. Hadas, *A History of Greek Literature* (*Columbia Univ. Press). Helpful survey.

Edith Hamilton, *Mythology* (*Mentor). Brief introduction, centered on Greek myths.

W. K. C. Guthrie, *The Greeks and Their Gods* (*Beacon). Detailed but stimulating study of the origins and nature of Greek religion.

M. P. Nilsson, *Greek Folk Religion* (*Torchbooks). Informative lectures on popular beliefs and practices.

F. M. Cornford, *Before and After Socrates* (*Cambridge Univ. Press). First-rate short introduction to Greek science and philosophy.

E. Bréhier, *The Hellenic Age* (*Phoenix). The first volume of a detailed history of philosophy by a French scholar.

H. I. Marrou, *A History of Education in Antiquity* (*Mentor). A useful account, also treating the Romans and early Christians.

J. B. Bury, *The Greek Historians* (*Dover). Appraisal by a celebrated English historian.

Rhys Carpenter, *The Esthetic Basis of Greek Art* (*Midland). Analysis by an expert.

Special Studies: The Hellenistic World

W. W. Tarn, *Alexander the Great* (*Beacon). A sympathetic (and not always convincing) study by the foremost expert on the subject.

A. R. Burn, *Alexander the Great and the Hellenistic World* (*Collier). Brief popular account.

P. Bamm, *Alexander the Great* (Thames & Hudson, 1970). Beautiful pictures of the remains and scenery of Alexander's world; text disappointing.

W. W. Tarn, *Hellenistic Civilization* (*Meridian). Comprehensive survey of civilization under Alexander's successors.

M. Rostovtzeff, *The Social and Economic History of the Hellenistic World* (Clarendon, 1941). Detailed study by a great historian.

M. Hadas, *Hellenistic Culture* (Columbia Univ. Press, 1959). Good evaluation.

E. Bréhier, *The Hellenistic and Roman Age* (*Phoenix). Another volume of the French scholar's history of philosophy.

Sources

Note: The following list includes only the most famous works, many of which are available in many other translations and editions.

W. H. Auden, ed., *The Portable Greek Reader* (*Viking). Excellent short anthology.

A. J. Toynbee, ed, *Greek Civilization and Character* and *Greek Historical Thought* (*Mentor). Two volumes of excerpts from Greek writers affording a kaleidoscopic view of Greek attitudes.

Homer, *The Iliad.* Two of many translations: That of R. Lattimore (*Phoenix) is a good poetic translation; W. H. D. Rouse's (*Mentor) is in modern English prose.

W. J. Oats and E. O'Neill, Jr., eds., *The Complete Greek Drama* (Random House, 1938). A selection of dramas by the same editors may be found in *Seven Famous Greek Plays* (*Modern Library).

The Dialogues of Plato, trans. B. Jowett, (Clarendon, 1953). New edition of a famous (and controversial) old translation.

The Works of Aristotle, ed. W. D. Ross, (Clarendon, 1908–1931). Selections by the same editor are also available (*Scribner's).

Thucydides, *History of the Peloponnesian War,* trans. B. Jowett, (*Bantam).

Herodotus, *The Histories,* trans. A. de Selincourt (*Penguin).

Xenophon, *Anabasis: The March Up Country,* trans., W. H. D. Rouse (*Ann Arbor).

Historical Fiction

M. Renault, *The King Must Die* and *The Last of the Wine* (*Pocket Books). Two of the several novels with Hellenic backgrounds written by an accomplished practitioner of historical fiction. The first is set in Mycenaean Greece and Minoan Crete, the second in Athens during the Peloponnesian War.

The Romans

The Republic

The Romans cherished the legend that after the fall of Troy, Aeneas, a Trojan prince, half divine, led his fugitive followers to Italy and founded Rome on the banks of the Tiber. The poet Vergil (70–19 B.C.) immortalized the story in his *Aeneid*, written as Roman imperial glory approached its zenith. And as Vergil borrowed from Homer, so Rome borrowed extensively from the older Greek and Near Eastern civilizations. The tale of the mythical Aeneas symbolizes the flow into Italy of Greeks and Near Easterners as well as Rome's debt to the Greco-Oriental world. Yet Rome did not achieve greatness on borrowed capital alone. The Romans were builders, generals, administrators, lawgivers.

Compared geographically with Greece, Italy enjoys certain natural advantages: the plains are larger and more fertile, the mountains less of a barrier to communications. The plain of Latium, south of the site of Rome, could be farmed intensively after drainage and irrigation ditches had been dug; the nearby hills provided timber and good pasturage. The city of Rome lay only fifteen miles from the sea and could share in the trade of the Mediterranean; its seven hills overlooking the Tiber could be easily fortified and defended.

To the south, as we know, by the year 600 B.C. Greek colonies dotted the shores of Italy and Sicily: this was Magna Graecia. To the north, the dominant power was held by the Etruscans, a mysterious people, surely foreigners in Italy, perhaps from Asia Minor (and so the source of the Aeneas legend), who had invaded the peninsula and conquered the region north of Latium by 700 B.C. They extended their power southward, surrounding Rome, and then seized it soon after 600. Rich Etruscan remains have been discovered during the past century and a half, mostly in tombs. The Etruscans had an enormous admiration for Greek art, which they bought and imitated: in pottery, sculpture, and painting. They wrote their language in Greek letters, and

most of the ten thousand or so existing inscriptions are very short. Many can be read, since they give, for example, only a proper name and perhaps the age at which the person mentioned died. Until 1964 no key like the Rosetta stone had turned up. Then, on the seacoast thirty miles from Rome, archaeologists found three golden tablets with inscriptions in both Punic (Carthaginian, Phoenician) and Etruscan, which, although the total number of words is only about ninety, will throw more light on the language. Dated about 500 B.C., the tablets show the Etruscans sharing in the worship of a Carthaginian goddess.

Expert farmers and miners, the Etruscans built huge stone walls around their settlements. They practiced divination, foretelling the future from observing flocks of birds in flight or from examining the entrails of an animal slain as a sacrifice. Their tomb decoration seems to show that, like the Egyptians, they believed in an afterlife similar to this one, and that they accorded their women a more nearly equal status with men than was usual in ancient society. They also enjoyed gladiatorial combat as a spectacle, a taste that the Romans borrowed from them.

When the Etruscans moved into Latium and took over Rome, the people they conquered were apparently Latin tribesmen, descendants of the prehistoric inhabitants of the peninsula. Under its Etruscan kings, Rome prospered during the sixth century. The Etruscans built new stone structures and drained and paved what became the Forum. But the native population resented foreign rule, and joined with other Latin tribes in a large-scale rebellion. The traditional date for the expulsion from Rome of the last Etruscan king, Tarquin the Proud, is 509 B.C. What he left behind was an independent Latin city-state, still including some Etruscan notables, much smaller than Athens or Sparta, sharing Latium with other city-states. Yet in less than 250 years Rome would dominate the entire Italian peninsula.

We can understand this success only if we examine

Roman institutions. Once they had ousted Tarquin, the dominant aristocratic forces at Rome set up a republic. Only the well-established land-owning families, the *patricians* (Latin *pater,* "father")—perhaps not more than 10 percent of the population—held full citizenship. The remaining 90 percent were *plebeians* (Latin *plebs,* "the multitude"), who included those engaged in trade or labor, the smallest farmers, and all those who were debtors as the result of the economic upheaval after the expulsion of the Etruscans. The plebeians had no right to hold office; they could amass as much money as they pleased, however, and wealthy plebeians would eventually lead the campaign to gain political emancipation for their class. Fifth-century Rome, then, was not unlike sixth-century Athens before the reforms of Cleisthenes.

The patrician class supplied the two consuls, the executive chiefs of state who governed jointly for a term of a year, enjoying full *imperium,* supreme political power. Each had the right of veto over the other; so that both had to support a measure before it could be put through. Ordinarily they were commanders of the army, but in wartime this power was often wielded, for a period not longer than six months, by an elected *dictator.* In the Roman republic the word meant a commander who had obtained his authority constitutionally and had to give it up when his term was over.

The consuls usually followed the policies decided on by the Senate, a body consisting of about three hundred members, mostly patricians and all ex-officials like the members of the Athenian Council of the Areopagus. It wielded such prestige that it came first in the famous Roman political device: S.P.Q.R.—*Senatus Populusque Romanorum:* The Senate and the People of the Romans. The reigning consuls, who were themselves senators, appointed new senators. The Romans had another deliberative body, the Centuriate Assembly, based on the century, the smallest unit (a hundred men) of the army. Although some plebeians were surely present, the patricians dominated the deliberations of this body also. It enjoyed a higher legal prerogative but less actual power than the Senate, although it elected the consuls and other officials and approved or rejected laws submitted to it by both the consuls and the Senate.

Before a man could be chosen consul, he had to pass through an apprenticeship in other posts. The job that led directly to the consulate was that of praetor (*prae-itor,* "the one who goes in front"). Elected by the Centuriate Assembly for a term of a year, the praetor served as a judge; he often had an army command, and later a provincial governorship. At first there was only one praetor; but the number later rose to eight. Men seeking election as praetor or consul wore a special robe whitened with chalk, the *toga candida,* whence our word "candidate." From among the ex-consuls, the Assembly elected two censors, for an eighteen-month term, who took a census to determine which of the population was qualified for army service. They also secured the right to pass on the moral qualifications of men nominated for the Senate, barring those they thought corrupt or too luxury-loving, whence the connotation of our words "censor" and "censorship."

Early fifth-century bronze wolf ("the Capitoline wolf"). Figures of Romulus and Remus were added during the Renaissance.

Detail of an Etruscan mosaic from the Tomb of the Bulls, Cormeto, Italy.

This regime was well designed to carry on the chief business of the Roman state: war. The Roman army at first had as its basic unit the phalanx, about 8,000 foot soldiers, armed with helmet and shield, lance and sword. But experience led to the substitution of the far more maneuverable legion, consisting of 3,600 men, composed of 60- or 120-man bodies called maniples or handfuls, armed with the additional weapon of the iron-tipped javelin, which was hurled at the enemy from a distance. Almost all citizens of Rome had to serve. Iron discipline prevailed; punishment for offenses was summary and brutal, but the officers also understood the importance of generous recognition and reward of bravery as an incentive.

The plebeians naturally resented their exclusion from political authority. As early as the 490s, they threatened to withdraw from Rome and to found nearby a new city-state of their own, and when this tactic won them a concession, they continued to use it with great effect on and off during the next two hundred years. First (494) they got the right to have officials of their own, the tribunes of the people, to protect them from unduly harsh application of the laws. By 457 there were ten such tribunes. The plebeians also (471) gained their own assembly, the Tribal Assembly (so named because of the subdivision of the plebeian population into tribes), which chose the tribunes and had the right, like the Centuriate Assembly, to pass on new laws. Next they complained that the patrician judges could manipulate the law for their own purposes because it had never been written down.

So in 451 the consuls ordered the (extremely severe) laws engraved on wooden tablets—the Twelve Tables, beginning the epochal history of Roman law.

In the early days of the republic, debt meant that a plebeian farmer would lose his farm and be forced into slavery. Property therefore accumulated in the hands of the patrician landowners. The plebeians obtained legislation limiting the size of an estate that any one man might accumulate, abolishing the penalty of slavery for debt, and opening newly acquired lands to settlement by landless farmers. The farmer-debtor problem, though eased, remained to plague the Romans to the end. During the fifth and fourth centuries, the plebeians won the right to hold all the offices of the state, even that of consul (366 B.C.). They also forced the abrogation of the laws that forbade their intermarriage with patricians. The fusion of wealthy plebeians and patricians formed a new class, the *nobiles*, who were to dominate the later republic as the patricians had the earlier.

Roman Expansion

In a long series of wars the Romans made good their supremacy over the other Latin towns, the Etruscan cities, and the half-civilized tribes of the central Apennines (the mountain backbone of the peninsula). Early in the third century B.C. they conquered the Greek cities of southern Italy. Meanwhile, in the north, a Celtic people, the Gauls (see p. 66), had crossed the Alps and settled in the Lombard plain; their expansion was

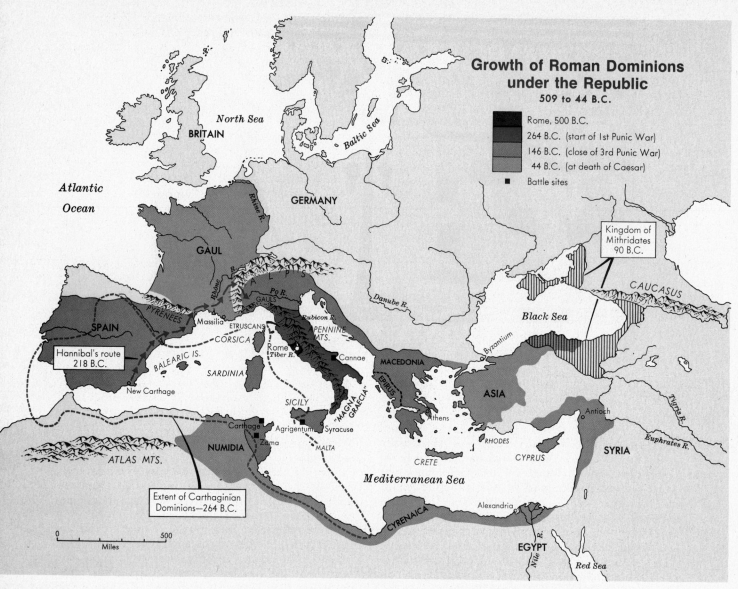

Growth of Roman Dominions under the Republic
509 to 44 B.C.

- Rome, 500 B.C.
- 264 B.C. (start of 1st Punic War)
- 146 B.C. (close of 3rd Punic War)
- 44 B.C. (at death of Caesar)
- ■ Battle sites

Kingdom of Mithridates 90 B.C.

Hannibal's route 218 B.C.

Extent of Carthaginian Dominions—264 B.C.

halted at the little river Rubicon, which formed the northern frontier of Roman dominion (Telamon, 225 B.C., a battle described by Polybius).

In conquered areas the Romans sometimes planted a colony of their own land-hungry plebeians. Usually they did not try to force the resident population into absolute subjection, but accepted them as allies and respected their institutions. The cities of Magna Graecia continued to enjoy home rule. Some of the nearest neighbors of Rome became full citizens of the republic, but more often they enjoyed the protection of Roman law as part citizens who could not participate in the Roman assemblies. So the expansion of Rome in Italy demonstrated imaginative statesmanship as well as military superiority.

The conquest of Magna Graecia made Rome a

near neighbor of the Carthaginian state. Carthage—modern Tunis—was originally a Phoenician colony, but had long since liberated itself from its motherland and expanded along the African and Spanish shores of the Mediterranean and into the western parts of Sicily. Ruled by a commercial oligarchy, Carthage held a virtual monopoly of western Mediterranean trade. When the Carthaginians began to seize the Greek cities in eastern Sicily also, the Sicilian Greeks appealed to Rome. So the Romans launched the First Punic (from the Latin word for Phoenician) War (264–241).

The Romans won by building their first major fleet and defeating the Carthaginians at sea. They forced Carthage to give up all claim to eastern Sicily and to cede western Sicily as well, thus obtaining their first province outside the Italian mainland. Sardinia and

Corsica followed (237). Seeking revenge, the Carthaginians used Spain as the base for an overland invasion of Italy in the Second Punic War (218–201). Their commander Hannibal led his forces across southern Gaul and then over the Alps into Italy, losing in the snow many of the elephants he used as pack animals. In northern Italy he recruited many Gauls and won a string of victories as he marched southward, notably at Cannae (216 B.C.).

Gradually the Romans rebuilt their armies, and in 202 B.C. Hannibal was summoned home to defend Carthage itself against a Roman invading force under Scipio. Scipio won the battle and the title "Africanus" as a reward. The Romans forced the Carthaginians to surrender Spain (where the native population resisted Roman rule for another two centuries), to pay a large sum of money, and to promise to follow Rome's lead in foreign policy. Hannibal fled to the court of the Seleucid king Antiochus III.

Carthaginian power had been broken, but the city quickly recovered its prosperity. This alarmed a war party at Rome. Cato the censor and senator would end each of his speeches with the words "Delenda est Carthago" ("Carthage must be destroyed"). In the Third Punic War (149–146) the Romans leveled the city, sprinkled salt on the earth, and took over all its remaining territory as the province of Africa (modern Tunisia).

While the Punic Wars were still going on, Rome had as early as 230 B.C. become embroiled in the Balkans and in Greece, sending ships and troops at first to put down the Illyrian pirates who were operating in the Adriatic from bases in what is now Albania, and then intervening again in 219 to punish an unruly local ally. The Greeks were grateful to Rome, and admitted Romans to the Eleusinian mysteries and the Isthmian Games. But Philip V (221–178), Antigonid king of Macedon, viewed with great suspicion Roman operations on his side of the Adriatic. He tried to help Hannibal during the Second Punic War, but a Roman fleet prevented him from crossing to Italy, and many of the Greek cities, opponents of Philip but not yet of Rome, came to Rome's aid in the fighting that ensued, helping to defeat him in the First Macedonian War (215–205).

Not eager as yet to expand on the eastern shores of the Adriatic, Rome contented itself with establishing a series of Illyrian buffer states. But Philip kept intervening in these, and the Romans feared for their loyalty. And in 202, several powers—Athens; Ptolemy V of Egypt; his ally Attalus, king of the powerful independent kingdom of Pergamum in Asia Minor; and Rhodes, head of a new naval league—appealed to Rome to intervene again against Philip V. In the Second Macedonian War (200–197) Rome defeated Philip's armies on their own soil (Cynoscephalae, 197) and forced him to withdraw from Greece altogether and become an ally of Rome. At the Isthmian Games

of 196, a solemn Roman proclamation declared that the Greeks were free. Two years later, after more fighting (chiefly against Sparta), the Roman armies left Greece and a largely disillusioned population.

Antiochus III (223–187), Seleucid king in Asia, profited by the defeat of Macedon to take over the Greek cities on the Aegean coast of Asia Minor and to cross into Europe and campaign there. Hoping to keep Greece as a buffer against him, and worried at his advance, the Romans, who had their hands full with wars in Spain, kept on negotiating with him. But Antiochus, who had with him the refugee Hannibal, challenged the Romans in Greece, hoping but failing to win wide native support. At Thermopylae in 191 B.C. the Romans defeated Antiochus, and then invaded Asia, forcing Antiochus in 188 to surrender all the Seleucid holdings in Asia Minor. Hannibal escaped, but poisoned himself in 183 as he was about to be surrendered to Rome. Rome had become the predominant power in the Greek world.

For the next forty years, the Romans found themselves obliged to arbitrate the constantly recurring quarrels among the Greek states. Rebellions forced repeated armed intervention. In the Third Macedonian War (171–168), Perseus, Philip V's son and successor, was captured and his forces routed at the decisive battle of Pydna (168). Rome imposed a ruthless settlement, breaking Macedon up into four republics and exiling from Greece many who had sympathized with Perseus. Twenty years later, the Romans annexed Macedon (148), their first province east of the Adriatic; and in 146 they defeated a desperate uprising of the Achaean League, and marked their victory by a particularly brutal sack of Corinth: all the men were killed, the women and children were sold as slaves, and the city was leveled. It was the same year as the total destruction of Carthage.

The Romans henceforth governed Greece from Macedon, but did not yet annex it as a province. Internal fighting in Greece came to an end; there was a religious and economic revival. Rome's prestige was now so great that in 133 the king of Pergamum, whose family had been helpful allies of the Romans—and much hated elsewhere for that reason—left his flourishing Asia Minor state to Rome in his will. It became the new province of Asia.

II Crisis of the Republic

As Roman territory increased, signs of trouble multiplied. The republic allowed a few overseas cities to retain some self-government, but usually organized its new territories as provinces under governors appointed by the Senate. Some of the governors proved oppressive and lined their own pockets, but as long as they raised recruits for the army and collected taxes, they had a free hand. In Italy, pressure mounted from Rome's allies, who demanded full citizenship and a share in the new wealth flowing into the capital. With the gradual exhaustion of Italian soil, grain had to be imported from Africa; former Italian grainfields were transformed into mixed farms or large cattle ranches run by slaves, whom only big landowners could afford. While veterans of overseas fighting and retired governors accumulated money and slaves as the spoils of conquest, more and more small farmers lost their land and became penniless and resentful refugees in the city of Rome.

The proprietors of *latifundia* (big estates), the successful generals and governors, and certain merchants and contractors who had built roads for the state or furnished supplies to the army combined to form a new class of very rich men, called *equites* (knights) because they could afford to equip themselves for service in the cavalry, the most expensive branch of the army. Sometimes they managed to join the Senate—increasingly influential because it had managed the Punic Wars successfully—but the small inner circle, where policy was made, continued to be dominated by the *Nobiles*. Among the senators themselves, those who were content with things as they were called themselves *optimates,* while those who found themselves unable to get things done their way sometimes tried to get support from the people at large in the Tribal Assembly, and so got from their opponents the name *populares*. Social tensions became acute: an old-fashioned, conservative nobilis like Cato, for instance, hated the rich men's taste for the luxurious new ways of life imported from Greece and the East. The political machinery of a small city-state could not cope with the problems of empire, of social tension, and of economic distress.

Two noble brothers named Gracchus, grandsons of Scipio, hero of the First Punic War, emerged during the late 130s and the 120s as the champions of the dispossessed. Tiberius Gracchus, who served as tribune of the people in 133 B.C., and Gaius, who held the post from 123 to 121, sought to increase the role of the tribunes and the Tribal Assembly at the expense of the Senate. The wild beasts, said Tiberius, have their dens, but the Roman soldiers have not a clod of earth to call their own. The brothers wanted to limit the size of estates that could be owned by one family; to resettle landless farmers either abroad or on state-owned lands in Italy that had been leased to capitalist farmers; and to give the city poor of Rome relief by allowing them to buy grain from the state at cost. Politically, they wanted to give certain judicial posts to the equites, to extend Roman citizenship to all Latins, and to raise other Italians to Latin status.

The efforts of the Gracchi failed. Of their economic program only the proposal to sell the Roman people cheap grain was adopted. In the succeeding centuries the state had to lower the price until the poor were getting their bread free. This in itself reveals the failure of the resettlement program: had the dispossessed farmers actually received new allotments, the number in the

city needing cheap bread would have fallen off sharply. The agrarian capitalists, after being forced by the Gracchi to give up some of the land they rented from the state, were soon expanding their holdings once more. The latifundia had come to stay. Moreover, on the political side, the Senate resented the extension of rights to the equites and balked at granting citizenship to other Italian cities. (Eventually, after an uprising in 91–88, this had to be done.)

Meantime, politics turned unconstitutional and violent. Tiberius Gracchus ousted a tribune of the people who was blocking his program; both brothers defied precedent and ran for reelection as tribunes. The senators themselves resorted to murder to stop the Gracchi and assassinated Tiberius in 133; in 121 Gaius killed himself to avoid a similar fate. Were the Gracchi high-minded "New Dealers" blocked by the vested interests of the senators, or unstable radicals whose high-handed methods only added to the discord? Probably both; at any rate the deadlock between Gracchan reformism and senatorial conservatism moved Rome toward autocracy.

After the Gracchan interlude, political leadership passed to generals who cared less for principle than for power. In the provinces the misrule of the governors provoked uprisings. Along the frontiers, at the end of the second century B.C., Germanic tribes were threatening. In 88 B.C. in Asia Minor, Mithridates, the king of Pontus, seized the Roman province of Asia, and provoked the massacre of eighty thousand Romans.

A general victorious in the chronic provincial warfare would celebrate in Rome with a great "triumph," a parade of his successful troops and of their prisoners and booty that would dazzle the public. And the troops, properly rewarded by their commanders, became loyal to them rather than to the state. The prescription for political success at Rome was to make a record as a successful general.

Political Generals: Marius, Sulla, Pompey, Caesar

The first of the generals to reach power was Marius, leader of the populares, who had won victories against the Numidians in North Africa—in what is now eastern Algeria (111–105)—and against a group of largely Celtic peoples called the Cimbri and Teutones, who had caused a great deal of trouble before he beat them at what is now Aix-en-Provence in southern France (102). Violating the custom that a consul had to wait ten years before serving a second term, Marius had himself elected five times between 108 and 103 B.C. He began a major reorganization of the army by abolishing the old requirement that a Roman citizen must pay for his own equipment, a rule that had automatically excluded the poor. Now that the state furnished the equipment, professional soldiers gradually replaced the former citizen soldiers, who in the past had gone back to their normal peacetime occupations once the fighting was over. When the Senate nullified a law extending

Roman citizenship to citizens of all other Italian cities, the cities rose in a rebellion that threatened Rome with the loss of her Italian power. After this savage war for independence (called the Social War, from *socius,* "ally"), the secessionists were mostly pacified by the year 89, but only by the gradual extension of Roman citizenship to all of Italy.

When Rome went to war against Mithridates in 88 B.C., Marius emerged from retirement and demanded the command. But the Senate chose Sulla, a younger general who was an optimate, and a bloody civil war broke out between the supporters of the two. Marius died in 86, and Sulla defeated Mithridates in 84, and then returned to assume the office of dictator. On the way to and from the east, his forces plundered Zeus's treasury at Olympia and Apollo's at Delphi, and sacked Athens for having sympathized with Mithridates. The Romans brought back Greek sculpture, painting, books, and other loot.

It took Sulla two years of bloody fighting to establish himself in power, and he took fierce reprisals against his opponents. He tried to move the Senate back into its ancient position as the chief force in political life. He put through laws designed to curb the rise of new younger politicians. He curtailed the powers of the tribunes and the Tribal Assembly. He broke all precedent by prolonging his tenure as dictator beyond the prescribed six months. He did retire in 80 B.C., but the Senate proved unable to govern.

Within ten years, Pompey, a ruthless and arrogant young veteran of Sulla's campaigns, rose to power. Having won victories first in Spain and then at home against a slave rebellion led by Spartacus (73–71), he became consul in 70 B.C. before he had reached the minimum legal age. With his colleague Crassus, a millionaire, Pompey forced the Senate to restore the tribunes and the Tribal Assembly to their old power. After defeating the troublesome pirates of the Mediterranean (67 B.C.), he took command of a new war against Mithridates for the kingdom of Bithynia in Asia Minor that had been left to Rome in the will of the king. By 65 B.C. Pompey had driven Mithridates into exile at the court of his son-in-law, Tigranes, king of Armenia. Mithridates committed suicide in 63 B.C., and Pompey reorganized Asia Minor into Roman provinces and subject kingdoms. Syria, where the last effective Seleucid had died in 129 B.C., had largely fallen to Tigranes by 83, and Pompey now made it too a Roman province (64 B.C.). He even took Jerusalem in that year. The western fringe of Asia was now virtually Roman, and much new revenue soon flowed to Rome.

On his campaigns Pompey enjoyed unprecedented special powers, forced through by the tribunes of the people against much senatorial opposition. He commanded huge resources in men and money. Foreseeing a showdown on his return, Crassus tried to build up his own power by vainly calling for the annexation of Egypt. And in 63 there came to light a celebrated conspiracy led by Catiline, leader of a group of discontented and dispossessed nobles who had been the victims of Sulla's purges and who now planned a revolution and a comeback. The consul and famous lawyer Cicero discovered the plot and arrested the plotters, some of whom he illegally had executed. His speeches in the Senate against the ringleader, Catiline, have given much instruction and some pain to generations of schoolboys. Cicero hoped to cooperate with Pompey in governing Rome and ending Roman domestic quarrels, but he lacked the family background and personal following necessary to get to the very top in Rome, and Pompey was not responsive.

Having returned to Rome as a private citizen (62 B.C.), Pompey reentered politics because the Senate would not ratify his Eastern settlement or give his veteran troops the usual land grants. He joined in a triumvirate, or team of three men, with Crassus and Gaius Julius Caesar, a man of enormous energy and talent, and impeccable ancestry. Caesar became consul in 59 B.C. Pompey married Caesar's daughter; Pompey's soldiers received large land grants to the south, near Naples, and the eastern Mediterranean settlement was confirmed.

The First Triumvirate in Action

Caesar became governor of the southern strip of Gaul (modern France), which Rome had annexed some sixty years earlier, and other adjacent lands rich in revenue. Between 58 and 50 B.C., he defeated the Celtic Gauls, conquering the huge area corresponding to modern France and Belgium. He even crossed the English Channel to punish the Celtic Britons for helping their fellow-Celts in Gaul, but he made no effort to conquer Britain permanently. The Gauls—distant relatives of the Celts we have already met—were predominantly a tall, fair-haired, blue-eyed people. The men were mostly beardless, but let their moustaches grow long, and wore trousers and ornamental neck rings. Recklessly brave in battle, hospitable, notably cleanly, loving bright-colored clothes, and enjoying feasts and quarrels, the Gallic tribes were governed either by kings (in the southwest and in the north) or by an aristocracy with appointed chief magistrates (in the central region). In order to give his achievements against these farming and cattle-raising Celts maximum publicity in Rome, Caesar wrote his *Commentaries on the Gallic Wars,* far easier Latin to read than Cicero and incidentally our chief written source of information about the Celts, greatly enlarged and supplemented by archaeological finds and surviving folklore.

Caesar found Gallic society divided into three chief classes: the magicians and seers, or druids; the nobles, for whom he used the Roman word *equites* (knights); and the common people, or *plebs.* As in Rome (and perhaps partly under Roman influence), a Gallic noble would have a group of adherents—clients—dependent on him and subject to his orders. A man who refused to comply with the order of a magistrate was excluded from the religious sacrifices and from the company of his fellows. Mostly rural elsewhere, the Celts in Gaul had some fortresses and urban trading centers.

They were excellent craftsmen in precious metals, bronze, iron, pottery, and textiles. For centuries they had traded with the Greeks and Etruscans, and were familiar with Greek painted vases and weapons; while they had also had contact with Iranian nomads skilled in metalwork. They expressed their own artistic ideas in mediums adapted from others; and they even struck their own coinage, inspired by Greek, Alexandrian, and Roman models. In Britain, they also used as money iron bars of a fixed weight, perhaps unfinished sword blades. They fought from fast, two-wheeled, two-horse war chariots. In earlier times, Celtic spear carriers had gone into battle naked, terrifying their opponents, as a means of invoking magical protection, and had beheaded their enemies and hung the heads on their saddles. They drank vast quantities of wine and beer, and gorged themselves on roast pork; and while they feasted bards played and sang to them. These were people living in a heroic age.

Like most peoples in that stage of development, the Celts were obsessed with magic, celebrating seasonal changes with festivals and sacrifice. They had a rich variety of gods and goddesses, some of them partly at least animal in form or closely associated with an animal, notably Epona, a goddess-mare and great queen. Some of the gods and goddesses were threefold, and the Celts often depicted them with three heads or three faces, rather to emphasize their triple power than to suggest a trinity. Caesar reported that the Gauls worshiped the chief Roman gods and goddesses, but they seem rather to have given the most suitable Roman name to their own divinities, using "Mars," for example, in inscriptions to their own god of war, who had many attributes of his own. Sacred trees, groves, and forest shrines also played a part in Celtic religion. The Celts sometimes piled their war trophies on the ground and left them exposed to view as a present to the god who had given them victory, but sometimes they threw the booty into a lake or a stream, and occasionally such a deposit has been found by modern archaeologists.

In Caesar's day the Gauls still performed human sacrifices, a practice the Romans had long since abandoned. Some victims were killed by a sword or spear, and their blood was then smeared on trees; others—chiefly criminals—were burned alive in groups in large wickerwork animal-images, or drowned or hanged. Recruited from the children of the fighting nobles, the Gaulish druids—whose name is connected with the Greek word for oak tree—foretold the future while in a frenzy or trance, preserved the secret knowledge of the magic rites, and arbitrated quarrels. Like the singers of the heroic tales of Greece, the druids also transmitted orally from generation to generation the sacred religious and legal wisdom of the tribe, including belief in the immortality of the soul. In fact, the Gauls were famous among the Romans for their eloquence; the Romans often hired Gallic orators as tutors to their sons, and the professors of rhetoric and oratory in the schools of Gaul after the Roman conquest were regarded as direct descendants of the druids.

While Caesar was fighting in Gaul, the German tribes from east of the Rhine often crossed the river and made trouble. Caesar massacred two entire tribes of them, building a bridge across the Rhine for a quick punitive raid into the territory on the east bank and destroying his bridge after his return. He temporarily taught the Germans the lesson that they should stay on their own side of the river. On the Gallic side, his victories meant the spread of Roman language and civilization. Like Italy and Spain, the future France would speak a largely Latin language, and share in the Roman heritage.

During Caesar's extraordinary campaigns in Gaul, Crassus had become governor of Syria, where he was drawn into war against the Parthians, a dynasty that had risen in Persia to replace the Seleucids. At Carrhae in Mesopotamia in 53 B.C. the Parthians defeated and killed Crassus. The triumvirate had begun to fall apart even before that, as Pompey's wife, Caesar's daughter Julia, died in 54 B.C. Pompey, who had been commander in Spain, stayed in Rome as the most powerful politician there, and became sole consul in 52 B.C. The former chief of Pompey's private gang now murdered the chief of Caesar's faction in Rome. This was Clodius, who had been acting to protect Caesar's interests in his absence, and had once succeeded in getting Cicero exiled for a period. A revolution in Gaul kept Caesar busy in 52 and 51 B.C.; when it was over, Caesar faced Pompey for supremacy.

In 49 B.C. Caesar defied an order from the Senate to stay in Gaul, and led his loyal troops south across the Rubicon river boundary. Within a few weeks, he was master of Italy. He then won another war in Spain, and in 48 B.C. defeated Pompey's troops at Pharsalus in Greece, to which most of the Senate had fled with Pompey. Pompey was later murdered in Egypt by troops of Ptolemy XII. Caesar now traveled to the East and to his famous love affair with Ptolemy's sister, Cleopatra. After new victories over former troops of Pompey in Asia Minor, North Africa, and Spain, he returned to Rome in triumph in 45 B.C. Less than a year later, on the Ides of March, 44 B.C., he lay stabbed to death on the floor of the Senate at the foot of Pompey's statue. Besides those who were merely jealous or disloyal, the assassins included patriots troubled at Caesar's assumption of supreme power and his destruction of the Roman constitution.

During his brief period of dominance, Caesar had carried further the subversion of the institutions of the republic that Marius and Sulla and Pompey had begun. Unlike Sulla, he was always merciful to conquered enemies. But he was consul five times; he took the title "liberator," and his dictatorship was twice renewed, the second time for life. As dictator he arrogated to himself many of the powers that usually belonged to the consuls, the tribunes, and the high priest. He packed the Senate with his own supporters.

Caesar showed a deep interest in the social and economic problems of Rome: he gave his veterans grants of land in outlying provinces; he tried to check the importation of slaves into Rome because they took work from free men; he made gifts to the citizens from his own private fortune, and then sharply curtailed the dole of grain that the Gracchi had instituted, forcing the creation of new jobs. He issued the first gold coins and reformed the calendar to bring it into line with the solar year. At the moment of his death he was projecting a great public works program: Tiber valley flood control, a trans-Apennine highway, and a canal through the Isthmus of Corinth in Greece.

The rank and file of the Romans seem to have regarded him as a benefactor, the restorer of order and prosperity. His opponents said he was planning to be crowned as king, and they may have been right. They also accused him of wishing to be worshiped as a god, and here—so far as Rome was concerned—they were probably wrong. But he was personally autocratic and had ridden roughshod over the Roman constitution.

After Caesar's death, the assassins found the public hostile; to escape punishment, they were forced to agree to accept the terms of Caesar's will. This document was in the hands of his former aide, the unscrupulous consul Mark Antony, who delivered a fiery funeral oration in Caesar's praise. He goaded the mob to fury against the conspirators, who had to flee from Rome. Antony's control proved only temporary, as Caesar in his will had adopted his grandnephew Octavian and had left him three-quarters of his huge fortune. Only nineteen years old, Octavian was ready to fight for his inheritance. He was supported by Cicero, who—like Demosthenes warning the Athenians against Philip—warned the Romans that Antony wanted to be a dictator. In order to freeze out the murderers of Caesar—Brutus and Cassius—Octavian reached an agreement with Antony and with Lepidus, another former aide of Caesar, and the three formally joined in the "second triumvirate" for a period of five years. Antony took most of Gaul, Lepidus Spain and the remainder of Gaul, Octavian Africa, Sicily, and Sardinia.

The assassins' armies threatened from Macedonia and Asia Minor, and Pompey's son, Sextus Pompeius, another aspirant for power, had a fleet. Reverting to Sulla's policy of executions and confiscations, the triumvirs raised money by terror. Among those murdered was Cicero. With their new forces, Octavian and Antony defeated Caesar's assassins in Macedonia (Philippi, 42 B.C.), whereupon Brutus and Cassius committed suicide. Lepidus began to be squeezed out, as Antony moved east, and Octavian took over most of the west. Rivalry between the latter two was postponed when Antony married Octavian's sister in 40, and in 37 the triumvirate was renewed for a second five-year term. Soon thereafter Sextus Pompeius was defeated

Bust of Julius Caesar.

and disposed of, and Lepidus was dropped by the other two triumvirs. Octavian, who now controlled the entire West, made his holdings more secure by mopping up the pirates of the Adriatic. Calling himself Imperator Caesar, he was highly regarded in Italy.

In the East, meanwhile, Antony had begun his famous affair with Cleopatra, who bore him three children. After a victory over the Parthians (34 B.C.), Antony made from Egypt his own bid for Empire. He put forward Cleopatra's young son by Julius Caesar as the legitimate heir to Rome, and assigned Roman provinces to her and to their own three children. Recognizing the threat, and capitalizing on Roman distaste for these oriental arrangements of Antony, Octavian dropped the triumvirate in 33, and war soon followed. At Actium, off the western coast of northern Greece (31), Octavian's ships won a critical naval battle. Antony and Cleopatra committed suicide. Rome thus acquired Egypt, the last of the great Hellenistic states to disappear. Egypt would not become a Roman province, but the personal property of Octavian and his successors, the Roman emperors, administered for them by their agents. And Octavian had become master of the entire Roman heritage. The republic had come to an end.

III The Roman Empire
Augustus and His Immediate Successors

Octavian was too shrewd, too conscious that he was heir to a long tradition, to startle and alienate the people of Rome by formally breaking with the past and proclaiming an empire. He sought to preserve republican forms, but at the same time to remake the government along the lines suggested by Caesar, so that Rome would have the machinery to manage the huge territories it had acquired. After sixty years of internal strife, the population welcomed a ruler who could guarantee order. Moving gradually, and freely using his own huge personal fortune, now augmented by the enormous revenues of Egypt, Octavian paid for the pensions of his own troops and settled them on their own lands in Italy and abroad. He was consul every year; imperator; governor in his own right of Spain, Gaul, and Syria; and princeps, first, among the senators. In 27 B.C. the Senate bestowed upon him the new title of Augustus ("revered one") by which he was thereafter known to history, although he always said his favorite title was the traditional one of princeps.

Of course he had far more power than anybody else, but since he called himself the restorer of the republic, Romans could feel that they were again living under republican rule. In 23 B.C. the Senate gave him tribunician power, "larger" powers than those held by any other provincial governor, and the right to introduce the first measure at any meeting of the Senate. It was he who summoned the Senate. He reduced its numbers in 29 B.C. from 1,000 to 800 members, and in 18 B.C. from 800 to 600. He gave it a small inner steering committee, on which he sat. To it he appointed men he thought able, regardless of their birth. He created a civil service where careers were open to talent. Having endowed a veterans' pension department out of his own pocket, he created two new taxes—a sales tax of one-hundredth and an estate tax of one-twentieth—to support it. His social laws made adultery a crime, and encouraged large families. He paid for the construction of splendid new buildings, boasting justly that he had found Rome a city of brick and had left it a city of marble. He also gave it its first police and fire departments, and he improved the roads throughout Italy.

The army, now numbering about 300,000 men, was stationed in permanent garrison camps on the frontiers, where the troops in peacetime worked on public projects such as aqueducts or canals. Roman citizens who volunteered to serve, and who retired after twenty-six years' service with a bonus equal to about fourteen years' salary, made up the legions. Noncitizens in equal number served as auxiliaries, becoming citizens after thirty years' service. Augustus also created the Praetorian Guard: 9,000 specially privileged and highly paid troops, of whom about one-third were regularly stationed in Rome.

In the East, Augustus reached a settlement with the Parthians and thus probably averted an expensive and perhaps a dangerous war. In 4 B.C., Herod, a client king of Jewish faith who governed Judea, died, and the Romans took over Judea and ruled through a Roman procurator, who remained outside Jerusalem as a concession to the Jews. Jews retained their freedom of worship, did not have to serve in the Roman armies, and were allowed not to use coins bearing "graven images," the portrait of Augustus. Under Augustus, most of Spain and Portugal were permanently pacified, and the Romans successfully administered Gaul. In what is now Switzerland and Austria and eastward along the Danube Augustus campaigned, extending Roman power into present-day Hungary, Yugoslavia, and Bulgaria, all the way to the Black Sea.

But in the year A.D. 9 the Roman armies suffered a disaster in Germany. A German chief named Hermann, who had served in the Roman army, become a Roman citizen, and had his name translated as Arminius, turned traitor and ambushed the Roman armies, wiping out three legions, perhaps sixteen or seventeen thousand men. Now an old man, Augustus made no effort to avenge the defeat, and so the Rhine frontier proved to be the final limit of Roman penetration into north-central Europe. Thus the Germans

Marble bust of Augustus as a youth.

never did become Romanized, a fact that had fateful consequences for all the subsequent history of Europe.

The Roman provinces were now probably better governed than under the republic. Regular census-taking permitted a fair assessment of taxes. In Gaul the tribes served as the underlying basis for government; in the urbanized East, the local cities performed that function. Except for occasional episodes, Augustus had done his work so well that the celebrated *Pax Romana*—the Roman Peace—lasted from his assumption of the title "Augustus" in 27 B.C. until A.D. 180, more than two hundred years. It was an enormous boon. As a second-century writer put it, "Through the Romans the world has peace, and we go wherever we like without fear, walking along the roads or sailing the sea." Whatever may have been Augustus' faults of character, one must cheerfully admit that he should be remembered as he wished to be remembered: he had maintained the Roman state firmly and had laid long-lasting constitutional foundations for its future.

When he died in A.D. 14, the only possible surviving heir was his stepson, Tiberius, son of his wife Livia by her first husband. Gloomy and bitter, Tiberius reigned until A.D. 37, emulating Augustus so far as possible during the first nine years but thereafter becoming involved in the efforts of a certain Sejanus, commander of the Praetorian Guard, to secure the succession to the throne. Absent from Rome for long periods, Tiberius became deeply unpopular, despite the fact that he reduced taxes and took steps to make interest-free loans available to debtors. His grand-nephew and successor Caligula (37–41), however, was perhaps insane and certainly brutish. The number of executions mounted, and the emperor enriched himself with the property of his victims. He made elaborate preparations for the invasions of Germany and of England, but in fact did nothing, while he convulsed Judea by insisting that his own statue be set up in the rebuilt temple. Caligula was assassinated in A.D. 41.

His uncle Claudius (41–54), youngest of Tiberius' nephews and the best of the first four emperors to succeed Augustus despite physical weakness and a miserable early life, was a learned student of history and languages—he even knew Etruscan—who strove to imitate Augustus by restoring cooperation with the Senate. He added to the number and importance of the bureaucracy by dividing his own personal staff of bureaucrats—mostly freedmen by origin—into regular departments or bureaus not unlike those in modern governments. So the private imperial civil service made strides in his reign. Claudius was generous in granting Roman citizenship to provincials. Abroad, he departed from Augustus' principles and added to Roman territory the region that is now Morocco, as well as certain smaller areas (Thrace and Lycia) in the Balkans and in Asia Minor. And in A.D. 43 he invaded Britain, ninety-eight years after Julius Caesar's first invasion. Southeast England became the province of Britain, whose frontiers were pushed outward toward Wales. The conspir-acies of Claudius' fourth wife, Agrippina, to obtain the succession for her son by an earlier marriage, Nero, culminated in her poisoning Claudius himself in 54. Nero (54–68) recompensed her by having her murdered in 59.

Dissolute and insanely proud of his own artistic talents, Nero sang, played the harp, acted, and drove a chariot at Roman public spectacles, which he wanted to transform into something like the Greek Olympic games. He had his mother put to death, murdered his wife, and married his mistress, whom he later kicked to death in a fit of temper. He did not start the great fire that burned down much of Rome in 64, nor did he fiddle while Rome burned; indeed he personally took part in the efforts to put the fire out and did what he could for those who had been left homeless. But the dispossessed did blame him, and to find a scapegoat he accused the new sect of the Christians, now for the first time attracting attention at Rome. Their secret meetings had led to charges of immorality against them, and Nero persecuted them to take attention away from himself.

There were serious revolts in Britain in 61, led by the famous queen Boudicca (Boadicea). She was "huge of frame, terrifying of aspect, with a harsh voice. A great mass of bright red hair fell to her knees; she wore a great twisted golden torc [neckring], and a tunic of many colors, over which was a thick mantle fastened by a brooch. She grasped a spear, and terrified all who saw her," a Roman historian reported. But the chief threat in the provinces arose in Judea, where Roman rule had alternated between extremes of tolerance (Augustus) and intolerance (Caligula). There were rival sects among the Jews, who detested each other and the Christians. Nobody except the small upper class supported Roman rule, and the Romans had too few troops to keep order. In 66, after the Jewish high priest refused to sacrifice to Jehovah for the special benefit of Nero, and a group of Jewish zealots massacred a Roman garrison, there was open warfare. The Roman general Vespasian had made much progress in the reconquest of Palestine when Nero found himself faced with a rising in Gaul and Spain of troops loyal to the governor, Galba. When the Senate proclaimed Galba emperor, Nero committed suicide (68).

From Nero to Marcus Aurelius (68–180)

Augustus' first four successors are called the Julio-Claudian emperors. Each had been a member, though sometimes a distant one—of the family of Julius Caesar and Augustus. But now the line had run out wretchedly in Nero, and the Senate and people of Rome learned that emperors could be found in other families and chosen in other ways. In 68–69 alone, four emperors, each a general supported by his own troops, ruled in rapid succession. The first three all died by violence, and the fourth was Vespasian, who had left his son Titus in command of the campaign in Palestine, where in 70 the Roman troops would sack Jerusalem and destroy the rebuilt temple.

Vespasian (69–79) founded the second Roman imperial dynasty, the Flavian; the throne passed successively to his two sons, Titus (79–81) and Domitian (81–96). Competent in every way, Vespasian added new blood to the Senate by appointing numerous non-Romans, especially Spaniards. He put through financial reforms, subdued a rebellion in Gaul, made gains in Britain, and managed to stave off the potential uprisings of other generals' troops against him by using some soldiers to build public works, stationing others in dangerous areas of the frontier, and keeping the numbers concentrated in any one place too few to encourage an ambitious commander to rebel.

It was in the brief reign of Titus that Vesuvius, the great volcano overlooking the Bay of Naples, erupted and wiped out the population of the provincial town of Pompeii, burying all the famous remains that testify so eloquently about daily life there. Domitian was a suspicious tyrant, seeing conspirators against him everywhere, and forcing the Senate to approve his own execution of suspects. In 96 a palace conspiracy brought him down.

When an emperor died, the Senate—so subservient during his lifetime—had the power of appointing his successor. In 96 they chose a mild sixty-five-year-old official named Nerva (96–98), who had no children and therefore could not found a dynasty. He promptly ended Domitian's persecutions of Jews and Christians, founded a new charity that gave loans to farmers in Italy to provide food for orphans, and most particularly discovered a method of providing for the succession: he adopted as his son, and so nominated as his successor, the great general Trajan (98–117), who succeeded him peacefully when he died. This was the first of a series of four successive fortunate adoptions that gave the empire its most prosperous and peaceful years at home, 98–177.

Abroad, in a series of successful but expensive campaigns, Trajan moved north of the Danube into Dacia—part of the Romania of today—which in 106 became a Roman province; but to the east, his campaigns across the Euphrates against the Parthians ended in failure in 115. A massive revolt of the Jews confronted Trajan's successor, his nephew Hadrian, when he succeeded his adoptive father in 117.

Hadrian (117–138), widely experienced as a soldier and administrator and a highly cultivated man, put down the Jewish uprising. He realized that Roman communication lines became too extended whenever Roman troops tried to cross the Syrian desert against the Parthians; so he wisely abandoned Trajan's war against them and eventually made peace with them. He made himself generally popular by canceling all private debts to the government, furthering charities, and putting on great spectacles in the circus. Among his advisers were some able lawyers who helped him

A street in the ruins of Herculaneum, buried with Pompeii by the eruption of Mt. Vesuvius in A.D. 79.

Relief of a Roman battle on the Column of Trajan, Rome.

adjust taxes and control prices in bad years and improve the legal position of slaves and soldiers. They codified all past decisions of the praetors, for the first time enabling a citizen to know when he ought to sue somebody and assuring him of uniform procedures.

Hadrian believed that all the provinces should be equal under Roman imperial benevolence, with himself as the "father of the fatherland" (*pater patriae*). So he caused each of the armies for provincial defense to be recruited within the province itself. And he himself lived much away from Rome. In Britain he built across the island the famous defensive system of walls and ditches still called Hadrian's Wall, to contain invasions from the Scots and Picts to the north. He thereafter resided successively in southern France, in Spain, in Morocco, in Asia Minor, in Greece, in Tunisia and Libya, in Greece again, in Syria and Palestine (where he replanned Jerusalem and changed its name, forbade circumcision, and had to put down another Jewish uprising), and in Egypt. Everywhere he inspected the troops and defenses, built buildings, and made himself known to the population, and everywhere except Palestine he was admired. After a decade abroad, he returned to Rome, where he began to build "Hadrian's Villa" at nearby Tivoli, something like a World's Fair exposition ground with whole areas built in his favorite Greek and Egyptian styles.

His successor, Antoninus (138–161), called Pius because he was so loyal an adoptive son to Hadrian, himself immediately adopted as his future successor his own nephew, Marcus Aurelius (161–180). The forty-two years of their combined reigns won glowing praise at the time and later as an era of peace and prosperity. The eighteenth-century English scholar Edward Gibbon remarked that there had never been another period "in which the happiness of a great people was the only object of government." He was echoing Antoninus Pius' contemporary, the Greek orator Aelius Aristides, who wrote that Persian rulers killed and exiled people and broke their oaths, while even the ancient Greek city-states, who had resisted the Persians, had failed in governing Greece. But within the Roman Empire, he said,

Neither sea nor land is any bar to citizenship, and Asia is treated exactly the same as Europe. In your empire, every avenue of advancement is open to everyone. No one who deserves office or responsibility remains an alien. A civil world-community has been set up as a free republic, under a single ruler, the best ruler and teacher . . . of order. From Rome, the center, there emanates throughout the world a security that rests on a power compared with which the walls of Babylon were mere child's play and women's work. All depends on the legions, who assure the perpetual peace, because Mars, whom you have never slighted, dances his ceaseless dance upon the banks of the outer rivers [Rhine, Danube, Euphrates] and thus averts the shedding of blood.*

*Adapted and abbreviated from the edition of J. H. Oliver, "The Ruling Power," *Transactions of the American Philosophical Society* 43 (1953), part 4.

Ruins of Hadrian's Wall in Northumberland.

Certainly, there was no civil strife; public buildings continued to rise; those who lived comfortable lives had never been more comfortable. For the less privileged, in Rome itself, and, more widely, in Italy, the Antonine monarchy showed great concern, and softened the worst pains of poverty. Egypt, as always, continued, however, to be ruthlessly exploited.

But unlike Hadrian, Antoninus Pius never left Italy, and the boasted dance of the war god Mars along the banks of the frontier rivers was less vigorous than Aelius Aristides claimed. So Marcus Aurelius, the cultivated Stoic philosopher, who got no pleasure at all from his powers as emperor, and whose melancholy *Meditations* (written in Greek) serve as a corrective to Aelius Aristides' official optimism, was forced to fight actively beyond the Danube in Dacia, and beyond the Euphrates against the Parthians. Although he was victorious, he allowed certain barbarians to settle within the imperial frontiers and to be enrolled in the Roman armies, thus jeopardizing the traditional defensive system.

During the pivotal reign of Marcus Aurelius began the steady and ever-increasing pressure from the Germanic tribes of central Europe. The more Germans who were allowed to settle inside the frontiers, the greater the pressure from those still outside who wanted to come in. The empire, with perhaps 60,000,000 people, an army of 300,000, and a small and very rich upper class, could in the long run not adjust to the demands made upon it. There was no modern technology to make possible a quick settlement of the frontier prob-

lem, which continued decade after decade for more than three hundred years. In the end, a population declining for reasons that cannot be satisfactorily explained could not be called upon to man the farms and the frontiers also. Although nobody in Marcus Aurelius' entourage could have predicted it, a long downward slide was now beginning. It was signalized for a century by a catastrophic falling-off in the quality of the emperors themselves.

The Downward Slide: Commodus to Diocletian, 180–284

Commodus (180–192), the true son of Marcus Aurelius, ended the line of fortunate adoptions, and proved to be a throwback to Caligula, Nero, or Domitian, a tyrant without talent. In the end, his closest advisers murdered him, and after two other emperors had been installed and murdered by the Praetorian Guard within a year, Septimius Severus (193–211), a native North African, commander of the Roman troops in what is now Hungary, marched his army into Rome and disbanded the guard, replacing it by a new elite body chosen from his own officers. He emerged successfully from the first civil strife Rome had known in more than a century, and rewarded his armies for their loyalty in a campaign against the Parthians (Mesopotamia was added as a province) by rewarding them with better food, better pay, and better conditions: his legionaries might marry native women and married legionaries might live off the base.

Killed campaigning in Britain, Septimius Severus

was succeeded by his two sons, one of whom (Caracalla, 211–217) killed the other and embarked on a series of other atrocious crimes until he was assassinated. He is also remembered for an edict of 212, which extended citizenship to all freeborn inhabitants of the empire, a natural climax to the earlier acts gradually expanding the circle of Roman citizens, but also a money-raising device, since all new citizens would be liable to inheritance taxes from which noncitizens were exempt.

Caracalla's sixteen immediate successors were all assassinated in their turn. It is an unedifying parade: the Moorish Macrinus (217–218) with his single earring and military incompetence, was followed by Elagabalus (218–222), a fourteen-year-old, immensely rich, homosexual Syrian priest of the sun god fobbed off on the Romans as a son of Caracalla. Alexander Severus (222–235), a cousin of Elagabalus, soberer and more virtuous, tried to revive cooperation with the Senate, and to restore the traditional virtues to Roman life, but he too was only fourteen on his accession and was dominated by his greedy and parsimonious mother. The Senate was now impotent, and the army resented Alexander's neglecting to appease it by the now traditional bribes. Though his campaign against the new Sassanian dynasty that had replaced the Parthians in Persia was a success (231–233), his military zeal was half-hearted, and in Germany on another campaign he fell victim to another military conspiracy.

During the next half-century (235–284), there were twenty-six emperors, of whom twenty-five were murdered: most of them were chosen by their troops, held power briefly, and were in turn supplanted by another ambitious military commander.

Attracted by Roman weakness, and pushed from behind by other people on the move, the barbarians crossed the Roman frontiers at many points. The emperor Decius was killed in battle by them (252). The emperor Valerian was captured (260) by the Persians and died or was killed in captivity. Plagues raged, whole provinces temporarily escaped from the central authority, population fell off, public order virtually vanished. The tide began to turn with the reign of Aurelian (270–275), the "restorer of the world," and definitely with the accession of Diocletian (284–305).

But to turn the tide demanded a thoroughgoing series of reforms, internal as well as external. Diocletian and his successors, especially Constantine (306–337), did put through such reforms, although we do not know exactly when some of the new measures were adopted. The result is usually called the new empire, but what looks new about it often proves to have been instead a return to earlier practice. It was the combination of all the experiments that was certainly new.

Under Diocletian there evolved gradually—each step resulting from local emergencies in one part or another of the empire—a system that when complete was called the tetrarchy, or rule by four men. Diocletian as Augustus first appointed a talented officer as Caesar, an action often taken previously, and then was forced by circumstances to promote him to Augustus, or co-emperor, though it was understood that Diocletian was the senior Augustus. Soon each Augustus had in turn appointed a Caesar of his own, whom he also adopted as his son. Such adoption too, we know, was an old practice. It was understood that the two emperors would eventually abdicate, each to be succeeded by his own Caesar, who upon becoming Augustus would appoint a new Caesar as his son and eventual successor. The scheme was obviously designed to assure a peaceful succession and to end the curse of military seizures of the throne. The empire, though in practice ruled by four men—a tetrarchy—still in theory remained a single unit.

This was particularly important, because accompanying the gradual establishment of the tetrarchy there was a territorial shift in administration, as each of the four new rulers took primary responsibility for his own large area. Diocletian made his headquarters at Nicomedia, on the eastern shore of the Sea of Marmara, in western Asia Minor, and from there governed Asia Minor, Syria, and Egypt, plus Thrace in Europe, the whole becoming the prefecture of the East. His Caesar had his headquarters at Sirmium in what is now Yugoslavia and governed from there the Balkans including Greece, which became the prefecture of Illyricum. Diocletian's co-Augustus, the junior emperor Maximian, had his headquarters at Milan and from there governed Italy and North Africa, together with parts of what is now Austria, which became the prefecture of Italy. And *his* Caesar had his headquarters at Trier (Treves) on the Moselle River and governed Gaul, Spain, and Britain, which became the prefecture of Gaul. Diocletian remained supreme over the others.

What is of course most obviously striking is that not even the prefecture of Italy was governed from the imperial capital of Rome. The new imperial territorial reorganization exposed as a hollow sham the ancient pretense that the emperor shared power with the Senate. Diocletian simply walked out on Rome, leaving the citizens with their free bread and circuses. It is of great importance too that he chose the East as the site of his own headquarters. Diocletian indeed now adopted the full trappings of oriental monarchy: he wore silk robes of blue and gold to symbolize the sky and the sun; he sprinkled his hair with gold dust to create a nimbus when light shone down upon him. His clothes glittered with jewels; he wore ruby and emerald bracelets, necklaces, and rings; his fingernails were gilded; and his boots—which were to become *the* new symbol of imperial power—were of purple leather. He entered his throne room carrying a golden scepter topped with a golden ball—the earth—on which was seated a Roman gold eagle with a sapphire in its beak—the heavens. Servants followed sprinkling the air with perfume, and fan bearers spread the scent abroad. Every person in the room sank to the floor until Diocletian was seated on his throne, after which the privileged might kiss the hem of his garment.

reliable historians. Still others have talked of climatic change, but with little evidence.

Economically, losses in population caused by plagues and civil war crippled agriculture, already hampered by backward methods. The growing concentration of land in large estates and the absorption of free farmers into the status of coloni diluted Roman prosperity, already suffering from feeble purchasing power and inflation. Psychologically, the masses became alienated from their rulers: the substitution of the mercenary for the old citizen-soldier testified to the decline of the old Roman patriotism. Yet even with all these factors, it would be hard to imagine Roman decline without the terrific pressure of outside forces: the third and fourth centuries were the time when the barbarian world began to move, and it was the barbarian threat that eventually brought about the collapse of the Roman structure in the West while permitting its survival in the East in a modified form.

IV Religion, Writing, and Thought
Greek Influences
In the years following the end of World War II, when American military power emerged as the decisive force in European affairs, many Europeans unkindly compared the Americans to the Romans and themselves to the Greeks. The Americans, they felt, were uncultivated boors without much of a civilization of their own, but with a great deal of impressive military hardware, trying to tell newly weakened peoples with old and proud military and political traditions how to run their affairs, and at the same time goggling admiringly at the surviving monuments of European culture.

It is of course true that American civilization is newer, and that if Americans wish to see ancient temples or medieval castles and cathedrals, they must go to Europe to do so. But the parallel breaks down in many places. America did not attack and conquer Europe or attempt to govern it. Rome did these things to Greece. America was founded by Europeans and inherited its civilization from them. Homer, Dante, and Shakespeare are as much a part of our tradition as of theirs. Rome was not founded by Greeks. And if many Americans regarded Europe as a museum for their entertainment and instruction, was it not because they recognized themselves as part of the same tradition rather than because they had found something new and different?

However faulty the modern part of the parallel may be, one ancient generalization still holds true: Greece, though conquered, took her conqueror captive. Indeed, Greek influence from Magna Graecia affected the Romans long before they conquered Greece itself. In the arts, the Romans found virtually their entire inspiration in Greek models. In literature the Greeks supplied the forms, and often much of the spirit, but the best Roman literary achievements could not be mistaken for Greek works: they have a Roman spirit and quality. In science and engineering the Romans had greater natural talent than the Greeks, as they did in law and the arts of government.

The Greece the Romans gradually conquered was not the Greece of Homer or Pericles; so that the Romans, for example, did not imitate the Greek tragedians of the fifth century B.C.: there was no Roman Aeschylus, Sophocles, or Euripides. This was the Greece of the decades after the death of Alexander, of the New Comedy of Menander, not the Old Comedy of Aristophanes, when literature—much of it produced in Alexandria—was more artificial, more purely charming and graceful, often trivial, less grand, less concerned with the central themes of human existence. The surviving Alexandrian epic, Apollonius Rhodius' *Argonautica*, which tells of the adventures of the mythical hero Jason on his way to find the golden fleece, was a scholar's careful (and not very successful) effort to be Homeric long after the heroic age was over. When the Romans first began to imitate the Greeks, the greatest Greek works, though deeply respected, were no longer being written: it was a lesser age.

Religion
Before the first contacts with the Greeks, of course, the Romans, in their central Italian provincial agricultural city-state, had already evolved their own religion, the worship of the household spirits, the lares and penates, that governed their everyday affairs, along with those spiritual beings that inhabited the local woods and springs and fields. Like the Greek Hestia, the Roman Vesta presided over the individual hearth and had in her service the specially trained Vestal Virgins. From the Etruscans the Romans took the belief, which they never abandoned, in divination: they too foretold the future through observing the flight of birds (the auspices) and examining the entrails of animals (the auguries). From Greece there came the entire Olympic collection of gods and goddesses, some of them merging their identities in existing divinities, and most of them changing their names. Zeus became Jupiter, Hera Juno, Poseidon Neptune, and so on, though Apollo remained Apollo. But the Romans had nothing like the Greek Olympic games or the festivals of Dionysus that had led to the writing of Athenian tragedy and comedy.

Julius Caesar, as we know—and after him most of the emperors beginning with Augustus—was deified after death, and Augustus consented to be worshiped jointly with Rome at the great altar in Gaul. But in the imperial cult as in other religious observances, except for certain notable festivals each year, the individual Roman took little part. The official priests performed most rites, headed by their chief priest, the pontifex maximus, a title and role taken over by the emperors themselves. The state religion early lost its appeal for the Romans, and, since there was no reason why they could not worship as many other gods as they chose in addition, after rendering due veneration to the ordinary deities, including the emperor, Rome early imported cults from other places, chiefly the East, which competed for popularity. Since Christianity eventually joined and won the competition, we postpone discussion of its competitors until the next chapter, where we can more easily examine the reason for its victory.

Literature

Quintus Ennius (239–169 B.C.), who was born and brought up in Magna Graecia, naturally turned to Homer for inspiration when he put into epic form his patriotic account (the *Annales*) of Roman successes down to his own time. Although only fragments (in all between six and seven hundred lines) are preserved, we have enough to appreciate Ennius' thoroughly Roman admiration for the military virtues, and to understand his lasting influence on later Roman writers.

Just as Ennius used Homeric verse to celebrate Roman toughness and resilience, Plautus (254–184 B.C.) and Terence (190–159 B.C.) found their inspiration in the Greek New Comedy of Menander. Plautus was the more raucous and knockabout: it was he who wrote the play about the two sets of twins, masters and servants who are always being taken for each other, that Shakespeare eventually imitated in *A Comedy of Errors*. And other characters from Plautus—the rich but stupid young gentleman with an immensely clever and resourceful valet, the money-grubbing miser—recur throughout the course of western European—and Russian—literary history. Gentler and milder in every sense, Terence stuck closer to the Greek originals, but he was not a success in his own day. After Plautus and Terence, various Roman authors tried to write comedies with a native Italian inspiration, but none of their work survives. In addition to these sophisticated works, the Romans enjoyed crude farces of the kind that had always been staged in the villages.

During the late republic appeared two of Rome's greatest poets, Lucretius (96–55 B.C.) and Catullus (84–54 B.C.), alike only in their mastery of their chosen verse forms and the genuineness of their emotions. Lucretius—a serious disciple of the Greek philosopher Epicurus—wrote a long poem, *On the Nature of Things* (*De rerum natura*), putting into moving poetry his master's beliefs that there is no human survival after death, and that the gods—far from governing the affairs of men—do not intervene at all. The universe is made of atoms, whose motions and behavior are governed by fixed laws, right out to the edges, the "flaming walls of the universe," except that men control their own actions.

Catullus, looking to certain Alexandrian poets of the emotions, wrote passionate love lyrics recording his feelings for his mistress Clodia (sister of the tribune Clodius), to whom he gave the name of Lesbia. Sometimes playful and charming, as in the poems addressed to Lesbia's pet sparrow or celebrating the first days of returning spring, sometimes bitter and obscene (Lesbia was unfaithful and made Catullus miserable), these brief poems, in a meter new to Rome, seem to some readers the highest achievement of Roman literature. Catullus also wrote a long, sustained, and extraordinarily moving poem about the exaltation and self-mutilation of the devotees of Cybele, the great mother-goddess of Asia Minor, and her consort Attis, whose cult was becoming popular at Rome.

In Cicero (106–43 B.C.), whom we have already so often encountered in his role as a lawyer and politician, the late republic produced its greatest writer of prose. His oratorical skill of course furthered his career as a successful lawyer and politician; his speeches in the courtroom or in the Senate were carefully prepared and effective pleas. He deliberately won his listeners with an occasional quick injection of a witty or ironical phrase into an otherwise somber and stately passage. He carefully studied not only what he wanted to say but how he could choose the most effective—sometimes the most unexpected—words in which to say it, and how he could combine them into a rhythmical and pleasing pattern, so that the sound and the sense would combine to make his point irresistibly. As the recognized supreme master of the art, he also wrote treatises on oratory. We also have almost a thousand letters that Cicero wrote to his friends and acquaintances, and some of their answers to him. The correspondence includes not only exchanges of letters with the most important Roman public figures of the period but also many intimate letters to Cicero's best friend, Atticus, that reveal his personal joys and sorrows.

Philosophically, Cicero in large measure agreed with the views of the Stoics as modified by Greek teachers who had adapted the originally abstract and remote concepts of Stoicism to Roman taste by allowing for the exercise in ordinary life of the Stoic virtues and admitting that one can have some virtues without possession of all knowledge. Cicero, himself not an original thinker, deliberately helped popularize these ideas in his philosophic essays—on Old Age, on Friendship, on the Nature of the Gods, and on other political and social subjects. Into the Latin language he introduced for the first time terms capable of conveying the meaning of the Greek concepts he was discussing. His fellow Romans first learned from him about the concept of a "natural law," for example, that existed independent of all human legislative actions, or a "law of nations" that should regulate the relationships of different peoples toward each other. The influence of these Ciceronian works radiated far into future human history: the early Christian church fathers went to school to Cicero, as did the humanists of the Italian Renaissance, and the men who made the eighteenth-century revolutions in America and in France and who wrote the Declaration of Independence and the Constitution of the United States.

It was the writers of the Age of Augustus who gave

Rome its literary Golden Age. And, as in the other enterprises of his era, Augustus himself took an active part in recruiting and subsidizing talent, even genius, to proclaim the glories of the new era, his new era. Vergil (70–19 B.C.) in his *Georgics* and *Eclogues,* following the models of Greek pastoral poetry, praised the pleasures and satisfactions of rural life. Written before Augustus reached political supremacy, these poems helped Augustus advance his later program of propaganda to get men back to the farm. He persuaded Vergil to write the *Aeneid,* the great epic of Rome's beginnings, in which the poet could "predict" the future glories that Augustus' rule would bring. Though designed in part to please Augustus, these passages nonetheless reveal Vergil's own sincere and intense patriotism. Vergil often reflects upon the sacrifices that necessarily accompany a rise to greatness, on sorrow, and on death.

His fellow poet Horace (65–8 B.C.) had more humor and expressed a greater variety of feelings in a greater number of meters. In short poems on more limited subjects he too praised the joys of rural life and the virtues of moderation, but also in more solemn terms celebrated the Roman qualities of quiet toughness, the simple life, the traditional religious attitudes. Ovid (43 B.C.–A.D. 17) gave worldly advice—often cynical—on the art of love; and elsewhere told the stories of the mythical transformations reported in Greek myths, as various divinities became birds or animals or plants. Ovid died in exile because of his involvement in a scandal affecting the granddaughter of Augustus.

To match in prose Vergil's epic of Rome's early days and to stress again the virtues that had made Rome great, the historian Livy (59 B.C.–A.D. 17) set out to write a prose history of the city from the moment of its founding. Only 35 of the 142 books into which he divided his work have come down to us complete, but we have summaries of the missing portions—most of the second and all of the first century B.C. Livy could use as his sources the compilations of many Roman writers now lost; but for the earliest periods he had to fall back on legend. He knew the difference between reliable and unreliable accounts, but often had only the latter available, and so used them. Vividly written, his work was indeed very long, and soon was put into *Reader's Digest* form for the unambitious. The future emperor Claudius had Livy as his tutor, and it would probably be safe to attribute Claudius' own success as emperor to the training he received from the historian.

The insistence on the great Roman virtues reflected an uneasy sense of their decline. In the period after Augustus, as the government became more arbitrary and autocratic, and writers began to fear the consequences of expressing themselves too freely, disillusionment set in. Moreover, the general admiration for the achievements of the Augustan writers, especially Vergil, became so intense that poets were often content to try to imitate the authors of the Golden Age and to suppress their own originality. The greatest of all the Roman historians, Tacitus (ca. 55–117 A.D.), himself

a master of prose style, was convinced that Romans had degenerated. In his *Germania* he wrote an essay ostensibly in praise of the rugged and still primitive way of life of the German barbarians, but in fact an acid commentary on the qualities the Romans had once had and had now lost. Similar disillusionment pervades his works of history, originally covering the period from Tiberius to Domitian, but not entirely preserved. Brilliant and prejudiced, allowing his personal opinions to color his accounts (sometimes in ways we cannot surely check), he was the greatest of the writers of the period between Tiberius and Hadrian, known as the Silver Age.

Silver Age poets included notably Seneca, Nero's tutor, by birth a Spaniard, a Stoic philosopher, and author of nine tragedies imitating Greek originals but far more bombastic and sensational. Seneca perhaps also wrote a satire on Claudius—a man easy to poke fun at, especially after he was dead, but morally worth several Senecas and any number of Neros. Seneca's nephew, Lucan, wrote an epic poem (*The Pharsalia*) about the struggle between Caesar and Pompey. In successive generations, Persius (34–62 A.D.) and Juvenal (50–130) satirized contemporary society, and, as satirists often do, overstated the case: Juvenal enjoyed painting the vulgarities and wretchedness, the cruelties and greed of Rome in the harshest colors. His crass characters the Romans would have met frequently not only on the streets but in the pages of a famous obscene novel, the *Satyricon,* attributed to one of Nero's court officials, Petronius, which has an unforgettable episode of a wild banquet given by a newly rich ex-slave.

Law and Science

The legal code published on the Twelve Tables in the fifth century B.C. reflected the needs of a small city-state, not those of a huge empire. As Rome became a world capital, thousands of foreigners flocked to live there to pursue their businesses, and of course they often got into disagreements with each other or with a Roman. But Roman law developed the flexibility to adjust to changing conditions: the enactments of the Senate and Assemblies, the decrees of each new emperor, and the decisions of the judges who were often called in as advisers—all of these contributed to a great body of legal materials.

It was the praetors, the chief legal officers, who heard both sides in every case and determined the facts before turning over the matter to the judex, a referee, for decision. The judices had to develop a body of rules for deciding cases that were not covered by existing law. As they dealt with many different breeds of foreigners, they worked out a body of legal custom common to all of them, the law of the peoples (*jus gentium*), that would be acceptable to all comers. As each new praetor took office for a year, he would announce the laws by which he intended to be bound, usually following his predecessors and adding to the body of law as necessary.

Romans too gradually acquired the benefits of the law of the peoples.

The expert advisors (jurisconsults) to both praetor and judex felt an almost religious concern for equity: it was the spirit rather than the letter of the law that counted. This humane view found support in the philosophical writings of the Stoics, who believed that above all man-made law stood a higher "natural" law, divinely inspired, and applying to all men everywhere. In practice, of course, judges were often ill trained, the emperors brutal or arbitrary; Roman law could be used to exalt the authority of the state over the individual. Yet the law recognized the rights of the citizen, afforded legal redress even to slaves, and gave wide scope to local legal practices. Its superiority gave it the victory over other legal systems; the law of much of western Europe today goes back to its provisions.

Roman surgeons made a variety of ingenious instruments for special operations, including the Caesarean operation—supposed (probably wrongly) to have been first performed at the birth of Julius Caesar—to deliver babies unable to be born normally. The Romans invented the first hospitals, military and civilian. Much superstition survived in Roman medicine, and it was the Greeks, notably Galen (A.D. 131–201), who continued to make the chief theoretical contributions, compiling medical encyclopedias and diffusing learning. What Galen did for medicine, a contemporary, Ptolemy of Alexandria, did for ancient geography; both remained the chief authorities on their subjects down to the sixteenth century. Some learned Romans followed the Alexandrian Eratosthenes in believing that the earth was round. Pliny the Elder in the first century A.D. made observations of ships approaching the shore to support this hypothesis: it was the tip of the mast that appeared first to an observer on shore and the hull last, a proof, Pliny felt, that the surface of the earth was curved.

Architecture, Sculpture, and Painting

Roman architecture borrowed the Greek column, usually Corinthian, but made much use also of the round arch, originated by the Etruscans, and from this developed the barrel vault, a continuous series of arches like the roof of a tunnel which could be used to roof over large areas. The Romans introduced the dome, and a splendid one surmounts the Pantheon at Rome, built to honor the divine ancestors of Augustus. Roman structures emphasized bigness: the Colosseum seated 45,000 spectators, the Baths of the emperor Caracalla accommodated thousands of bathers at a time (its ruins are still used for grand opera); Diocletian's palace at Split in modern Yugoslavia contains most of the modern city inside its walls. All over the Middle East and North Africa, as well as western Europe, one finds amphitheaters, temples, villas, and other monumental remains of the Roman domination.

Roman statues, though derived from Greek and Hellenistic models, often had a realism all their own, as in the cases of imperial portrait busts. In a sculptured frieze running spirally up a monumental column the victories of the emperor Trajan are vividly recorded. Of Roman painting we have chiefly the pretty—sometimes obscene—wall decorations of the villas at Pompeii (the resort town near Naples that was literally buried in A.D. 79 by the sudden eruption of Vesuvius that covered it in a rain of hot ash), and the mosaic floors of public and private buildings, where a favorite subject was a hunting scene in the landscape of the Nile, with crocodiles and hippopotamuses among the papyrus plants. The recently discovered imperial villa at Piazza Armerina in Sicily has a superb series of these floors, including a scene of bathing girls in bikinis tossing a beach ball from hand to hand.

A Final Appraisal

Tacitus was certainly right in thinking that Rome had lost some of its traditional virtues with its conquest of huge territories, its accumulation of wealth, and its assumption of imperial responsibilities. Nevertheless, the first two centuries of the empire mark the most stable and prosperous era that had yet occurred in human history. No doubt, the profits of flourishing commercial life were unevenly distributed, and there were glaring contrasts between riches and poverty. But many of the harshest aspects of ancient society elsewhere were softened at Rome: slaves could obtain their freedom more easily, and once free enjoyed all the privileges of citizenship, including that of owning slaves themselves; women had more rights and commanded more respect (we have much evidence of harmonious family life, though there were more divorces perhaps than at any time until our own day); physical comforts were abundant for those who could afford them.

In Rome itself, however, great areas were unsanitary, overcrowded slums: six- and seven-story wooden tenements that often burned down or collapsed and were rebuilt despite building codes and fire departments. Rents were exorbitantly high: streets were narrow and dark, noisy with cart traffic and full of crime at night, covered with hucksters' wares exposed for sale by day. Worst of all was the chronic urban unemployment: at the height of the Pax Romana, perhaps half the population of the capital was on the bread dole. The inhabitants also were given free circuses in the form of chariot races and gladiatorial combats, and the poor squandered their pennies on betting. Bloodshed exerted a morbid fascination: criminals were crucified and even burned alive on the stage as part of spectacles to entertain the populace, and in the last century of Roman life these shows had become so popular that they had superseded the circus, despite the protests of the occasional horrified citizen, pagan or Christian.

Though the structure of the Roman state had disappeared in the West by the end of the fifth century A.D., Roman influence has given a permanent shape to

Gladiators: detail of a mosaic pavement ca. A.D. 300 now in the Borghese Gallery, Rome.

western Europe. Italian, French, Spanish, and Portuguese were all languages derived from Latin, and our own English tongue is a hybrid with almost as many Latin as Germanic words. Roman legal concepts provided the foundations of respectability for many a squalid barbarian society. Rome itself, finally, became the capital of Christianity and its administrative organization a model for the structure of the Church.

Reading Suggestions on the Romans

General Accounts

M. Rostovtzev, *Rome* (*Galaxy). Excellent survey by a famous Russian scholar.

A. E. R. Boak, *A History of Rome to 565 A.D.,* 5th ed. (Macmillan, 1965). A standard textbook.

C. E. Robinson, *Apollo History of Rome* (*Apollo). A clear introductory account.

T. Mommsen, *The History of Rome* (*Meridian). A detailed study by a great German scholar of the nineteenth century; still worth reading, though its interpretations are sometimes out of date.

M. Grant, *The World of Rome* (World, 1960). General introduction to imperial Rome; handsomely illustrated.

R. H. Barrow, *The Romans* (*Penguin). Sound popular introduction.

T. Frank, *A History of Rome* (Holt, 1923). Useful, though opinionated, survey by an American scholar.

The Etruscan Background and the Roman Republic

O. W. von Vacano, *The Etruscans in the Ancient World* (Edward Arnold, 1960). Scholarly study carefully based on archaeological evidence.

M. Pallottino, *Etruscologia,* 3rd ed., trans. J. Cremona (*Penguin). The best introduction to the subject.

D. H. Lawrence, *Etruscan Places* (*Viking). Charming popular introduction by the famous novelist, somewhat outdated.

R. Bloch, *The Etruscans* (Praeger, 1958) and *The Origins of Rome* (Praeger, 1960). Two volumes in the series "Ancient Peoples and Places"; the first is a general introduction, generously illustrated; the second takes the story of Rome to the early fifth century B.C.

A. Alföldi, *Early Rome and the Latins* (Univ. of Michigan, 1963). Detailed and erudite study of relations of Rome with other Latin towns and with the Etruscans.

H. H. Scullard, *Roman Politics, 220–150* B.C. (Clarendon, 1951) and *From the Gracchi to Nero* (*Barnes & Noble). The first is a detailed study of the era when Rome began to dominate the Mediterranean world; the second an up-to-date, clear, and balanced history of the later republic and early empire.

R. E. Smith, *The Failure of the Roman Republic* (Cambridge Univ., 1955). A provocative essay critical of the Gracchi.

E. Badian, *Roman Imperialism in the Late Republic* (Blackwell, 1968). A brief and original series of lectures substantially revising previous scholarship.

L. R. Taylor, *Party Politics in the Age of Caesar* (*Univ. of California). Analytic as well as descriptive study of the way in which Roman politics worked; learned and stimulating.

T. G. E. Powell, *The Celts* (Thames & Hudson, 1963). Informative survey, often clumsily and pedantically written.

The Roman Empire

M. P. Charlesworth, *The Roman Empire* (Oxford Univ., 1951). Informative general sketch.

R. Syme, *The Roman Revolution* (*Oxford Univ.). Detailed study of the transformation of the Roman state and society under Caesar and Augustus.

H. T. Rowell, *Rome in the Augustan Age* (Univ. of Oklahoma, 1962). Sympathetic appraisal of Augustus and his work.

S. Dill, *Roman Society from Nero to Marcus Aurelius* (*Meridian). A classic of social history.

S. Perowne, *Hadrian* (Norton, 1960). Lively modern treatment.

G. C. Brauer, Jr., *The Young Emperors* (Crowell, 1967). The only recent monograph on the subject.

A. Birley, *Marcus Aurelius* (Little, Brown, 1966). Useful and well-written up-to-date study.

T. W. Africa, *Rome of the Caesars* (Wiley, 1965). The era of the Pax Romana interpreted through biographical sketches of some of its leading figures.

J. Carcopino, *Daily Life in Ancient Rome* (*Bantam). A lively introduction.

Roman Civilization

C. Bailey, ed., *The Legacy of Rome* (Oxford Univ., 1923). Informative essays on a variety of topics.

E. Hamilton, *The Roman Way* (*Norton). Sympathetic appraisal, based chiefly on Latin literature.

T. Frank, *Life and Literature in the Roman Republic* (*Univ. of California). Helpful survey.

H. Mattingly, *Roman Imperial Civilization* (*Anchor). Instructive study based largely on coins.

M. Clarke, *The Roman Mind* (Cohen & West, 1956). Studies in the history of thought from Cicero to Marcus Aurelius.

H. J. Rose, *Religion in Greece and Rome* (*Torchbooks). Detailed handbook.

E. Bréhier, *The Hellenistic and Roman Age* (*Phoenix). The second volume in a history of philosophy by an able French scholar.

M. Wheeler, *Roman Art and Architecture* (*Penguin). Clear, well-illustrated introduction.

Roman Decline

M. Rostovtzeff, *The Social and Economic History of the Roman Empire,* 2nd ed. (Clarendon, 1957). Detailed, scholarly study, magnificently illustrated, with interesting speculations on the reasons for Rome's decline.

R. M. Haywood, *The Myth of Rome's Fall* (*Apollo). Scholarly study of the centuries of decline, directed to the general reader.

E. Gibbon, *A History of the Decline and Fall of the Roman Empire* (*many editions, usually abridged). The earliest chapters of this famous old work relate to the third and fourth centuries.

G. Milner, *The Problem of Decadence* (Williams & Norgate, 1931). Comprehensive, if inconclusive, bird's-eye view of conflicting interpretations of the reasons behind Roman decline.

Sources

N. Lewis and M. Reinhold, *Roman Civilization,* 2 vols. (*Torchbooks). A highly useful compilation, with enlightening editorial comments.

B. Davenport, ed., *Portable Roman Reader* (*Viking). Helpful anthology.

Vergil, *The Aeneid,* trans. R. Humphries (*Scribner's). A good modern translation.

Tacitus, *On Britain and Germany,* trans. H. Mattingly (*Penguin) and *The Annals of Imperial Rome,* trans. M. Grant (*Penguin).

Plutarch, *Makers of Rome,* trans. I. Scott-Kilvert (*Penguin). Biographies by a cultivated Greco-Roman gentleman, who lived about A.D. 100.

Marcus Aurelius, *Meditations* (*several editions).

Historical Fiction and Drama

E. L. White, *Andivius Hedulio* (Dutton, 1933). A novel about the adventures of a Roman nobleman in the days of the empire.

W. E. Bryher, *The Coin of Carthage* (*Harvest) and *The Roman Wall* (*Vintage). By a first-rate historical novelist; the one is set against the Second Punic War, and the other against the Alpine frontier in the era of decline.

G. B. Shaw, *Caesar and Cleopatra* (*Penguin). Caesar characterized as a wise and talkative dictator.

Stimulating and imaginative, if not always historical, portraits of famous Romans are drawn by Shakespeare in *Julius Caesar, Antony and Cleopatra* (with a devastating characterization of the ambitious young Augustus), and *Coriolanus* (which takes a very disenchanted view of the Roman republic, especially the Tribunes of the People).

Christianity

I Religion in the Later Roman World

Greek scientific theory and Roman technical skills had brought the ancient world to the threshold of an industrial age. A century before Christ, Hero of Alexandria had even discovered the engineering usefulness of steam pressure in a boiler, and conceived a model of a fire engine, including the piston. It would have been only a short step to the building of steam devices. Why did more than 1700 years pass before man took that step?

The answer must lie in the attitudes of the ruling groups in Roman times. Science formed no part of their education, and scattered statements show that they scorned what we would call research. They feared new inventions that might put still more people out of work: the emperor Tiberius once executed a man who had invented a process for making unbreakable glass. Although the earlier advance of science in the Greek and Hellenistic world had given rise to small groups of rationalists who believed in improving their lives by using their reasoning powers, even these minorities seem virtually to have disappeared. Everywhere in Rome the student can observe a mounting pessimism and a lack of faith in man's ability to work out his own future.

The old gods seemed powerless to intervene; life appeared to be a matter of luck. And so, beginning as early as the third century B.C. and gathering increasing momentum later on, the cult of the goddess Fortune became immensely popular in the Mediterranean world: chance governed everything; today's prosperity might vanish tomorrow; the best thing to do was to enjoy luck while it lasted. Closely related was the belief in Fate: what happened was inevitable, because it had been fated from the beginning; when you were born, the moment of your death was already fixed. Some, like Cicero, protested that men could contribute to their own fate and so take advantage of fortune; Vergil attributed both fate and fortune to the will of the divine providence; but most Romans, like Tacitus, seem to have felt helpless to change their own fates or to influence events.

Astrology

To escape this feeling, most Romans came to believe that the movements of the heavenly bodies influenced the fortunes and the fate of men and governed the decisions they made. Thus the science of astronomy became lost in the false speculation of astrology. If you could do nothing to change your destiny, you could at least try to find out what it might be by consulting an expert astrologer. He would study the seven planets (Saturn, Jupiter, Mars, the Sun, Venus, Mercury, the Moon) each of which had its own will, character, sex, plants, numbers, and animals, and each of which was lord of a sphere. Seven transparent but impenetrable concentric spheres, with Earth at the center, cut man off from heaven. Each planet had its own day: hence the seven-day week. Seven itself became a mystic number: there were seven ages of man, seven wonders of the world. Then too there were the twelve Houses of the Sun, constellations of stars through which the sun passed on his way around the earth: these were the signs of the zodiac.*

From the position of the heavenly bodies and the signs of the zodiac at the moment of your conception or birth, astrologers would draw up a horoscope foretelling your fate. The Roman emperors, like most of their subjects, profoundly believed in astrology. And of course some people have continued to believe, even to our own day. Especially valuable for the art of prophecy were unnatural events: the appearance of a comet, the birth of a monster. Similarly, men believed in all sorts of magic, and tried by its power to force the heavenly bodies to grant their wishes.

*Not until the sixteenth century did man discover that the earth was not at the center of our universe, and that it revolved around the sun.

New Cults: Cybele, Isis, Mithra

The state religion of the Olympian gods and of the deified emperor still commanded the loyalty of many Romans, who regarded the proper observance of its rites as the equivalent of patriotism. But the old faith no longer allayed the fears of the millions of people believing in blind fate and inevitable fortune. More and more men sought for a religion that would hold out the hope for an afterlife better than the grim life here on earth. So, along with astrology and magic, a large number of mystery religions began to appear in Rome.

All the new faiths taught that a human being could save his soul by uniting it with the soul of a savior, who in many cases had himself experienced death and resurrection. Union with the savior was accomplished by a long initiation, marked by purifications, ritual banquets, and other ceremonies. As the candidate cast aside human unworthiness, the god would enter him, and so after death he would be saved. The initiate sought a mystical guarantee that he would not perish but would survive hereafter. It was perfectly possible to join as many of these cults as one liked and

yet at the same time continue to practice the state religion.

The Greeks had had such cults in the rites of Demeter at Eleusis and in the mysteries of Dionysus. The rites of Dionysus, now called Bacchus, became popular at Rome, celebrating as they did the animal side of human nature and the abandonment of all restraint. On hundreds of Roman sarcophagi can be seen the bacchic procession, celebrating the joys of drink and sex. But the cult of Bacchus was too materialistic to satisfy all Romans.

One of its major competitors was the cult of the great mother-goddess Cybele, transplanted from Asia Minor. Her young husband, Attis, died and was reborn annually (like Demeter's daughter, Persephone). Attis was thus a symbol of renewed fertility. The rites of Cybele included fasting, frenzied processions, and the self-flagellation and even self-mutilation of the priests. The first temple to Cybele at Rome dated from 204 B.C., but the zenith of the cult came in the second century A.D. and later. By that time the rites included the slaughter of a bull above a pit into which the

Wall of the nave of S. Apollinare Nuovo, a fifth-century church in Ravenna, Italy.

initiate had descended in order to be bathed by the blood. The cult, as we have seen, was the subject of a long dramatic poem by the poet Catullus.

Even more popular—especially among women—was the cult of the Egyptian Isis, whose consort, Osiris, also died and was reborn each year. All feminine elements, both lascivious and chaste, were concentrated in an elaborate ritual of worship for Isis, the loving mother-goddess, who promised her adherents personal immortality.

From Persia via Asia Minor came the cult of the god Mithra, allied to the supreme powers of good and light and so connected with the Sun. The male initiates passed in succession through seven grades of initiation (corresponding to the seven planets and named after animals), qualifying for each by severe tests. Baptism and communion were also part of the ritual. Unconquered, physically rough, and self-denying, Mithra be-

came a model for the Roman soldier, to whom he held out the hope of salvation. Mithraism had no priests and welcomed the gods of other cults; it tended to absorb the other sunworshiping cults, including that of Apollo, into one new cult, often heartily supported by the emperor. From London to Alexandria and from the Rhine to the Euphrates, temples of Mithra, with altars and statues, have been found.

Philosophy and Mysticism for the Intellectuals

In addition to these cults, most of which appealed to the masses rather than to the highly educated, there were certain notable new trends in philosophy and in mysticism that were popular among the intellectuals. Long before, after the death of Alexander the Great, the philosopher Epicurus had taught that unnecessary human fear lay at the root of the troubles of mankind.

Taurobolium (sacrifice of a bull in Mithraism): a Roman relief.

Adoration of the Magi: a panel from a fifth-century sarcophagus in Ravenna, Italy.

Anyhow, whatever gods might exist took no interest in what men might do; life after death was only untroubled sleep. A quiet life, and the cultivation of one's friendships would bring happiness; and if evil came, one could endure it. Both Horace and Lucretius were Epicureans. But as the ordinary man could hardly banish fear or pain or desire by following Epicurean formulas, the Epicureans were few in number.

So were the Stoics, who prescribed strict suppression of human emotions: man should accept the universe and simply defy evil to do its worst. These ideas fit well with certain aspects of the Roman temperament and won a large following among disillusioned Romans. But by compromising with astrology and with polytheism, by teaching that the universe was periodically destroyed and reconstituted, by harshly condemning human pity, Stoicism lost much of its validity and its appeal.

Halfway between religion and philosophy lay the writings of the so-called thrice-great Hermes (Hermes Trismegistus) and his school, who prescribed abstinence, concentration, and study as a preparation for a flash of ecstasy and a spiritual rebirth.

Stronger still was the current called Neoplatonic, since its adherents claimed to be disciples of Plato. They taught that each human soul makes a pilgrimage toward an eventual union with the divine incorporeal essence, the One, the True, the Good, the last great abstraction. By contemplation the mystic can gradually free himself from material ties and achieve ecstatic vision. Neoplatonism soon became contaminated with far less lofty and rarefied rites, like those of the cults. Incantations against demons helped the seeker on his way, and mumbo jumbo sometimes replaced philosophy. For the Neoplatonist the divine reason, the *logos* (literally, "the word"), joined with the divine soul and the ultimate divinity itself as a sort of Trinity.

Christianity

But no single one of the mystery religions or philosophic movements appealed to men and women of all classes at Rome. Mithraism, which perhaps had the most adherents, especially in the army, excluded women and lacked love and tenderness. Neoplatonism had no appeal for the masses. In the Roman world, we have already noted the presence of Christians, especially under Nero, who made them the scapegoat for the great fire of 64. Indeed, Christianity competed with the cults in the Roman world for more than three centuries after the death of its founder, with no assurance that it would triumph. Sharing some things in common with them, it also possessed qualities they lacked.

II   Jesus; The First Christians
The Setting for the Life of Jesus

Perhaps no problem—considered as a historical problem—has been more discussed and with more heat than the problem of the life and teachings and death of Jesus. He was born in Palestine sometime between the years we call 8 and 4 B.C. and was crucified probably A.D. 29 or 30 or 33. He was a Jew all his life, and stoutly declared that he had not come to lead a movement of secession from Judaism but one of reform and fulfillment within it: "Think not that I am come to destroy the law, or the prophets: I am not come to destroy, but to fulfill. For verily I say unto you, Till heaven and earth pass, one jot or one tittle shall in no wise pass from the law, till all be fulfilled" (Matt. 5:17–18). But one cannot understand this apparently straightforward and uncomplicated idea without appreciating the extraordinary complexity of the society in which Jesus was born, taught, suffered, died, and— his followers declared—was raised from the dead.

JUDEA TO THE ROMAN CONQUEST: HELLENISM AND THE HASMONEANS   When, after a century of struggle between Ptolemies and Seleucids for the rule of Palestine, the Seleucids won a permanent victory about 200 B.C., their monarch issued special tax privileges for the Jewish Temple and the Jews. The high priest of the Temple of Judea represented the Jews in their dealings with their Seleucid overlord, and was responsible for collecting the taxes for him. The upper classes among the Jews found themselves greatly attracted by Greek culture— Hellenism—as, to varying degrees, had all the other inhabitants of the Near East in the wake of Alexander's conquests and the establishment of the successor-kingdoms.

Some Jews engaged in athletics naked, in the Greek fashion; Jews discovered Greek music; Greek artistic motifs and symbols—acanthus leaves and grapevines—

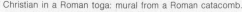

Christian in a Roman toga: mural from a Roman catacomb.

were carved on Jewish monuments. The heads of the ruler and even Apollo's tripod and Hermes' winged staff with a pair of entwined snakes (caduceus) appeared on Jewish coins. In some of the later books of the Old Testament—written in this period—notably Jonah, Jewish separateness, so notable elsewhere, seems to have disappeared in favor of a concern for all humanity, non-Jew and Jew alike. The Greek language spread widely; many Jews took Greek names. Certain Jewish writings echo Homer, such as Ecclesiasticus (*not* the same as Ecclesiastes—written about 185 B.C.) much honored among Jews in their day, although not finally accepted as canonical into the Old Testament, and regarded today as "apocryphal" or "pseudepigraphical."

This Hellenization of the upper class of Jews in Judea led to conflict and disapproval among the many Jews who sought to keep the traditions pure. And the poor population—tenant farmers on the lands of the rich, or humble artisans in the cities—hated their fellow Jews who oppressed them in association with the Seleucid monarchy. Party strife and civil war led to the intervention of Antiochus IV in 168, and to a concerted attempt to destroy Judaism by force: an altar on which pigs were sacrificed to Zeus was superimposed on the altar of the Temple. The Jews rebelled; the wars (called "Maccabean" after Judas Maccabeus the Jewish commander) were savage; Seleucid dynastic rivalries added to the political complexity.

In 153 Judas Maccabeus' brother Jonathan became high priest, and his descendants (called Hasmonean after a priestly ancestor, Hasmon) held the office for 117 years, until 37. In the last years of the Seleucids after 129, the Hasmonean state of Judea was virtually independent, and so remained until 63, when Pompey annexed it to the Roman Empire with the rest of Syria. The Hasmoneans made war on the territories neighboring Judea, forcibly circumcising non-Jewish men, and adding greatly to the anti-Jewish hatred already powerful among the Gentiles of the Mediterranean seacoast and the Transjordanian area.

To the Gentiles' agonized complaints the Hasmoneans replied that they were only reestablishing themselves in the lands of their ancestors. Another party of Jews, highly puritanical, participated in the war against the Seleucids until the Jewish faith was secure, but opposed the Hasmonean conquests. They would have been content to live under foreign rule so long as the Jewish religion was protected. They expected that the power of the Gentiles would in any case pass away, that the "Ancient of Days" would sit upon his eternal throne and grant to a Messiah—"one like the son of man"—an everlasting earthly dominion. To this party—the "pious people" (Hasidim or Assidaeans)—the Hasmoneans were arrogant usurpers.

FROM POMPEY'S ARRIVAL TO THE DEATH OF HEROD (63–4) As the Romans replaced the Seleucids in the role of foreign overlord of the Jewish lands, torn by dissent and by occasional civil war, Pompey liberated the areas the Hasmoneans had conquered and made the areas with Jewish majorities a client state (*civitas stipendiaria*) of Rome. In the mid-fifties, the Roman governor of Syria divided Judea into five sub-areas (*synhedria* or "councils") as a step toward later dismemberment.

Julius Caesar in 47 reversed this trend, reunited Judean territory, and gave the governorship to a certain Antipater, a convert to Judaism from one of the neighboring areas (Idumaea) that the Hasmoneans had conquered. Rivalry and a civil war between the last of the Hasmoneans and the family of Antipater, one of whose sons was Herod, was complicated by a Parthian invasion and culminated when the Roman Senate made Herod king of Judea. In 37, with the help of troops sent by Mark Antony, Herod was able to take Jerusalem. He was also able to survive the collapse of Mark Antony's hopes after Actium (31) by serving Augustus obediently.

The Jews hated Herod, not so much for being an outsider and a descendant of a forced convert as for his subservience to the foreign ruler and his ruthlessness in wiping out not only all those who engaged in acts of violence or sabotage but all suspects, including the last of the Hasmoneans, among them his own wife and his sons by her. Rome was far more powerful than the Seleucids had ever been and to the Jews was equally unacceptable as a source of the same Hellenistic influence. Tyrannical though Herod was, he was also a thorough realist: the Jews, he was sure, could survive only by reconciling themselves to living within the Roman Empire. The secret police, the prisons, and death were for resisters. For the others, survival lay through abandoning exclusiveness and adapting to the Greco-Roman world.

Herod built Greek cities with splendid public buildings; he patronized Greek artists and writers; and he sponsored musical and athletic contests, to which non-Jews were invited as guests. He even began to start a cult of himself in non-Jewish areas; and among Jews he represented himself as of the line of David, and as the restorer of the ancient glory of the kingdom. To that end he rebuilt the Temple on a grander scale than ever before. He managed to suppress opposition until he died in 4 B.C., by which time Jesus had probably been born.

PARTIES AMONG THE JEWS The Romans put down the rebellion that erupted on Herod's death; and ten years later they deposed Herod's son as king of Judea, at the petition of the Jews, and installed the first Roman prefect (not, we now know, called a procurator). By this time, there were at least three parties distinguishable among the Jews of Judea: the Sadducees, the Pharisees, and the Essenes.

The Sadducees were a small influential group of aristocrats who had long ancestral associations with the Temple priesthood, generally regarded as collaborationists with the Romans. What we know of their beliefs is derived from texts written by their enemies, but they apparently did not accept the idea of the resurrection of the dead or rewards and punishment after death. They repudiated the belief in good and evil spirits, rejected predestination, and believed in the full responsibility of men for their actions.

The Pharisees, who survived to become the prevailing force in later Judaism, we know much more about. Apparently originating in a wing of the Assidaeans, who about 160 abandoned the belief that at the last judgment only they would be saved and all other Jews forever damned, the Pharisees nonetheless held themselves strictly apart (the name itself means "the separated ones") from the common people who did not observe every letter of Jewish Law. Realists, they reconciled themselves to life under Herod and his Roman masters, and, after Herod, under the prefects. They strove to achieve the Kingdom of God here on earth, and they continued to oppose what they regarded as the unrealistic attitude that all expectations must be put off until the final day.

The Pharisees' reverence for the Jewish Law admitted of argument with respect to it, and of differing interpretations: they made divorce difficult, but they did not forbid it altogether; they believed in keeping the Sabbath, but they favored saving a man's life on that day. So the written Law, as laid down in the first five books of the Old Testament, was supplemented by an "oral" Law, the interpretations by rabbinical sages. Pharisees conceded that there were righteous men among non-Jews. They believed that fate determined some human actions, but not all, and that therefore some were in a man's own hands. Unlike the Sadducees, the Pharisees believed in the resurrection of the dead and in a last judgment separating the righteous from the sinners.

A third school of thought among the Jews was that of the Essenes, known before 1947 only by a few ancient texts. In that year began the famous series of discoveries, in the caves of Qumran near the Dead Sea, the so-called Dead Sea Scrolls. Dating from 200 to 70, the scrolls include fragments of the teachings of the Essenes, who lived in a monastic community nearby, dating back to before 100 B.C. Its buildings were destroyed by the Romans in A.D. 68, but we know that this was by no means the only Essene settlement and that some lived not in monastic communities but in cities.

In the Essenes' monastic community, men lived in celibacy, engaged in ritual baths and meals, and shared communal property. Some women and children buried nearby were probably relatives of members or wives and children of members not yet fully accepted. At the Essenes' communal meal, bread and wine were taken but were not thought of as transmuted, and the meal did not symbolize salvation. They took ritual baths, but repeated them often; so the baths were not parallel to the single ceremonial baptismal bath performed by John the Baptist for penitents, of whom Jesus was the most celebrated. When the present age of wickedness drew to an end, the Essenes believed that they, the "poor in spirit," in the end would prevail.

The scrolls refer to a Teacher of Righteousness, a Suffering Just One, who had been greater than all the prophets. He was not the same as the deliverer, the Messiah, whom they still awaited, and who would be a priest and a descendant of the House of David, the same "Son of Man" who appears in the Book of Daniel, and in whom the Essenes' forerunners, the Assidaeans, had also believed. In one passage in the scrolls, the Teacher of Righteousness referred to himself as the father of a man-child, who would have all his own powers. Thus, the texts that tell us about the Essenes reveal them as a reforming movement within Judaism that apparently had much in common with the Christianity that was still to appear.

In addition to the Sadducees, the Pharisees, and the Essenes, there were also groups of Jews who belonged to a "fourth philosophy," and who devoted themselves to resistance against the Romans, like modern guerrillas or partisans. They are sometimes called "Zealots" by modern scholars; but apparently they did not use this name for themselves, and they may have called themselves simply "Israel," to indicate that they were the only true Jews. As the Roman grip upon Judea loosened in the years immediately before the uprising that began in 66 and ended with Titus' suppression and the destruction of the Temple in 70, some of the resisters turned to terrorism, and committed many murders, after which they were called "the dagger men" (*sicarii*). Many Jews had indeed been moved by zeal against the Romans, but the true "Zealots," as a political party, did not come into existence before 67–68, as a grouping of rural peasant groups and urban militants, hostile to the Jewish upper classes as well as to the Romans. But all of this took place decades after the death and resurrection of Jesus. Anti-Roman Jews, however, though not yet organized formally in his day, formed part of the much divided population among whom he lived.

From the Roman point of view, the Jews were particularly privileged subjects. Their religion was protected by the Roman state. Unlike other Roman subjects, they could become citizens of any city without forfeiting the right to their beliefs. They were exempt from military service, which would have implied for them idolatry and required them to break their Sabbath; they were excused from participating in the imperial cult for the same reason, and said prayers for the emperor in the synagogues instead. Their local copper coinage was struck without the emperor's likeness. Their own judges (Sanhedrin) acted as local administrators and handled all purely Jewish court cases. Such privileges contributed to widespread anti-Jewish feeling among non-Jews in the empire, who resented the Jewish freedom from so many of the responsibilities of Roman citizenship. Non-Jews scoffed at the worship of a god who could not be portrayed and who required abstinence from pork; and they regarded Jewish abstention from emperor-worship as atheism and Jewish

separatism as incomprehensible. Despite what appeared to the Romans to be generous treatment, Jewish nationalism refused to die; and despite the apparent special lenience, most of the Roman prefects were inept and irritating.

The Teaching of Jesus

It was thus in a troubled and divided land that Jesus came to preach to his fellow Jews. He preached the love of God and of one's neighbor. He preached to the poor, the weak, and the simple. His "Blessed are the poor in spirit" has an Essene echo, but Jesus was not a revolutionary like the Essenes, not a revivalist or an ascetic. He preached the enjoyment of the good things of this world, an enjoyment freed from rivalry, ostentation, and vulgarity. He was kind but stern: good intentions are not enough; "he that heareth, and doeth not, is like a man that without a foundation built a house upon the earth. . . ." (Luke 6:49). Above all he preached gentleness and love: humility, charity, honesty, toleration ("Judge not, that ye be not judged"—Matt. 7:1); but he warned that "wide is the gate, and broad is the way, that leadeth to destruction" (Matt. 7:13). Though he preached that men should turn the other cheek, he also said at another time that he came not to bring peace, but a sword. Plain people understood him, and took comfort from his words.

From Jesus' preaching arose theological conclusions of enormous importance. He spoke of his Father in heaven, referred to himself as the Son of man, and taught that he was the Messiah whom God had sent to redeem mankind from sin. Those who hearkened and led decent lives on earth would gain eternal bliss in heaven; those who turned a deaf ear and continued in their wicked ways would be eternally damned in hell. Jesus was Christ, the anointed one. He was begotten by the Holy Spirit, and miraculously born of a virgin mother. He was baptized by John the Baptist in the waters of the Jordan, and his followers too were required to be baptized. He gave bread and wine to his followers at a feast of love and told them that it was his body and his blood, and that they should partake.

Such teaching—though not without its parallels in some earlier Jewish thought—aroused alarm and hostility among the Jewish authorities. Sadducees and Pharisees mistrusted all the reformist efforts, of which Jesus' seemed to them only one more. When the prefect, Pontius Pilate, asked Jesus, "Are you the king of the Jews?" and Jesus affirmed that he was, he was doomed; and on the cross itself the title was inscribed to show that a leader of the resistance had been executed. Pilate, as a modern scholar remarks, only "acted as any prudent Roman governor would have when all the local notables unanimously demanded the blood of a low-class agitator."

The crucifixion was the supreme act of redemption: Jesus died for mankind; his followers declared that he rose from the dead on the third day, and would soon

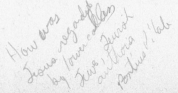

return—during their lifetime, they believed—to end this world in a final Day of Judgment, when he would sit at the right hand of the Father. Even in this bare summary one can single out elements of the Christian belief that are familiar from Judaism, and others that were present in the various mystery cults. But Christ's sacrifice of his life for mankind, and the intimacy with God promised in the future eternal life, gave Christianity an immediacy and an appeal that no mystery religion could duplicate. Christ's message of love for all mankind supplied the tenderness that was lacking in the world of every day.

The First Christians: Judaeo-Christianity

There are no historical sources contemporary with Jesus himself from which to draw an account of his life and teaching. Saint Paul's epistles to the Corinthians were written about A.D. 55, the Acts of the Apostles about 60–62, and the four Gospels that tell Jesus' story in the years that followed: Mark about 70, Matthew and Luke about 80–85, and John about 100. Late in the second century or early in the third, these texts were revised in Alexandria. We have no canonical Christian text written down before this revision.

Before the year 60 a collection of the sayings of Jesus himself existed, written in Aramaic, the Semitic language that he spoke. This collection is lost. In addition, many other texts existed that were not regarded as authentic. Among them was a so-called Gospel of Thomas, written in the native Egyptian language (Coptic) in the early second century, of which fragments including 114 sayings attributed to Jesus were found in Egypt in 1945 and later years.

All our New Testament sources, then, belong to a period at least several decades after Jesus' death. They were written in Greek for non-Jews and do not reflect the situation immediately after he died, which has only recently begun to be understood by scholars, who have studied inscriptions, monuments, and manuscripts that help tell the story. After the crucifixion of Jesus, a little group of his followers held together in Jerusalem. These first Christians were Jews who followed, as indeed Jesus himself had followed, the Jewish law. This was the Judaeo-Christian church, or "Church of the Circumcision," which had a succession of fifteen bishops. It regarded itself as the only true Israel, and was in conflict with Pharisees and Sadducees.

But Christian belief had drawing powers that were bound to exceed the limits of the Jewish communities. Christ had told his followers, "There be some standing here, which shall not taste of death, till they see the Son of man coming in his kingdom" (Matt. 16:28). Add to this doctrine of the Second Coming the immediacy of the emotional tie that Christianity created between the individual believer and Christ, and among individuals in the Christian brotherhood, and you have indeed an evangel, the "glad tidings" that appealed to Gentiles as well as to Jews.

Saul of Tarsus, who as a Jew had helped persecute Christians, and who had never known Christ himself, was miraculously converted to Christianity by a vision and changed his name to Paul. It was he and his followers who took the evangel to the Gentiles. Instantly problems arose: must a non-Jewish convert to Christianity be circumcised: a painful and even dangerous operation? Some Judaeo-Christians were willing to exempt pagan converts from circumcision and other Jewish observances; others were not; and even those who made the concession often were reluctant or unwilling to eat in company, or mingle socially, with such converts. Paul himself went further, however, than even the more liberal Judaeo-Christians; he would have freed even former Jews from Jewish ritual requirements.

Judaeo-Christians, led by Saint James, brother of the Lord, strongly opposed Paul's views. James's successor as bishop of Jerusalem was also a member of Jesus' own family, son of a cousin: the importance of the family as leaders is in line with Semitic customs. The last of the Judaeo-Christian bishops of Jerusalem governed the church in the time of Hadrian, when the last of the Jewish rebellions in Judea was crushed (132–135). Thereafter Judaeo-Christianity died out in its native habitat, but it was active in the Aramaic-speaking regions east of Palestine, where Paul did not work, and traces of it probably survive in the mighty Christian church of Roman North Africa and perhaps in that of Egypt, where we know that St. Paul did not labor as a missionary. But although the Judaeo-Christians held on in Jerusalem itself until the reign of Hadrian, it was Titus' capture of the city in 70 that put an end to their influence in the church. Thereafter—Paul himself was already dead—it was the church of the Gentiles that triumphed, and Christianity was truly separated from Judaism.

Saint Paul and Gentile Christianity

In the years between 48 and 62 Paul traveled twice to Syria and Asia Minor, twice to Greece, to Macedonia, back to Jerusalem, and eventually to Rome. Everywhere he took the position that "there is neither Jew nor Greek" (Galatians 3:28). The Jewish Law had been a forerunner, a tutor: "For by one Spirit are we all baptized into one body, whether we be Jews or Gentiles, whether we be bond or free" (1 Cor. 12:13), and most simply, "For the letter killeth, but the spirit giveth life" (2 Cor. 3:6). The Christian was to be saved, not by the letter of the Jewish law, but by the spirit of the Jewish faith in a righteous God. Christianity must be involved with the Hellenistic world as represented by the Roman Empire: Paul was from the first a hellenized Jew. He united in his own person the mystic who would transcend the world and the flesh, the gifted spiritual adviser of ordinary men and women troubled in their everyday lives, and the able administrator of a growing Church. In all Paul's writings there are passages that show him to have been ascetic in his morality and

good news

firmly convinced that Christian truth is not a matter of habit or reasoning, but of transcending faith:

> Howbeit we speak wisdom among them that are perfect: yet not the wisdom of this world, nor of the princes of this world, that come to nought: But we speak the wisdom of God in a mystery, even the hidden wisdom, which God ordained before the world unto our glory; Which none of the princes of this world knew: for had they known it, they would not have crucified the Lord of glory [1 Cor. 2:6–8].

Yet Paul was no oriental mystic who preached denial of this world in mystic ecstasy. Indeed he expressed clearly that characteristic Christian tension between this world and the next, between the real and the ideal, which has ever since firmly marked Western society. Paul's symbol for it was the mystic union of Christ and Christian: "Always bearing about in the body the dying of the Lord Jesus, that the life also of Jesus might be made manifest in our body" (2 Cor. 4:10). Christians are not merely animals, or merely men: They are children of God who are destined, if they are true Christians, to eternal bliss. But on this earth they must live in the constant imperfection of the flesh, not wholly transcending it, always aware that they are at once mortal and immortal.

A large part of the Pauline Epistles deals with matters of church discipline. Here we see Paul charged with the curing of souls, keeping a firm but not despotic hand over scattered and struggling Christian congregations in the lands to which he traveled. He tried to tame the excesses to which the emotionally liberating new doctrines so readily gave rise, urging the newly emancipated not to interpret Christian love as sexual promiscuity, not to take their new wisdom as an opportunity for wild ranting ("speaking with tongues"), but to accept the discipline of the Church, to lead quiet, faithful, but firmly Christian lives.

Paul, of course, was not one of the twelve apostles, actual companions of Christ, who, according to tradition, separated after the crucifixion to preach the faith in the four corners of the earth. But he has been accepted as their equal in his apostolate. Of the twelve, tradition holds that Peter (who disagreed with Paul about the purity of Gentile food) went to Rome, of which he was the first bishop, and so the first pope, and was there martyred under Nero on the very same day as Paul. Thus the Church of Rome had both Peter and Paul as its founders. In the imperial capital, the first Christians were a despised sect, suspected of all sorts of horrid crimes, such as incest and infanticide as well as ritual murder. But by the year 100, the new faith had penetrated into many of the eastern territories of the empire, and had even established a foothold in the West. It was still a small, obscure, persecuted sect, and only a visionary could have predicted its eventual triumph.

III Christianity in the Pagan World
The Reasons for Persecution

What to Christians is known as persecution was to the authorities of Rome simply their duty as defenders of public order against men and women who seemed to them traitors or irresponsible madmen. The Christians ran afoul of the Roman civil law not so much for their positive beliefs and practices, but rather for their refusal to make any concession to paganism. To cultivated Greeks and Romans of these first centuries Christians seemed wild and indecent enthusiasts, and to the masses they were disturbers, cranks, revolutionaries. "Who prevents you from worshiping this god of yours also, along with the natural gods?" a Roman official of Egypt in honest bewilderment asked a Christian as late as the year 257, when the Christian faith had spread widely throughout the empire.

But the empire was not very deeply concerned with the details of the morals and faiths of its hundreds of component city-states, tribes, and nations. Scores of gods and goddesses, innumerable spirits and demons, filled the minds of the millions under Roman rule, and the rulers, themselves usually Stoics with a philosophic, though scornful, toleration of mass superstitions, were willing to tolerate them all as part of the nature of things.

There was, however, a practical limit to this religious freedom, which after all was based on no ideal of religious liberty, and certainly not on any concept of separation of Church and State. To hold this motley collection of peoples in a common allegiance, to give them something like the equivalent of a modern national flag and pledge of allegiance, the emperor was deified. Simple rites of sacrifice to him were added to local religions and local rites. One more god did not offend the conscience of those who believed in the Greco-Roman pantheon or in Isis or Cybele or in any other conventional polytheism; one more pinch of incense on one more altar was simple enough. Those who did not believe in the customary local gods—and such disbelief was widespread in the Roman Empire—had no trouble in doing what was expected of them, for they did not take with undue seriousness any religion, new or old.

The Christians, however, could not sacrifice to the emperor any more than the Jews of old could sacrifice to Baal. Indeed, they felt that, insofar as the emperor pretended to be a god, he was in fact a devil. The more cautious administrators of the growing Christian Church were anxious to live down their reputation for disorderliness, and by no means sought to antagonize the civil authorities. These leaders may have been responsible for the familiar "Render therefore unto Caesar the things which are Caesar's; and unto God the things that are God's" (Matt. 22:21), which historians believe is clearly a later addition to the text of the New Testament. But sacrifice was a thing of God's. The true

ascetic - A person who renounces the comforts of society and leads a life of austere self-discipline especially as an act of religious devotion.

Christian, then, could not bring himself to make what to an outsider or a skeptic was merely a decent gesture, like raising one's hat today when the flag goes by in a parade. Moreover, if he was a very ardent Christian, he might feel that the very act of sacrifice to Caesar was a wicked thing, even when performed by non-Christians, and he might show these feelings in public.

The Persecutions

But the imperial authorities did not consistently seek to stamp out the Christian religion. Persecutions were sporadic. They came at intervals over the course of three centuries, and they varied in severity at different times and different places.

NERO AND TRAJAN Of the first, under Nero in 64, Tacitus said that the emperor was using the Christians as a scapegoat for the fire:

> To suppress the rumor [that he had started the fire himself] Nero substituted as culprits and punished with the most refined cruelty a class of men, hated for their vices, whom the population called Christians. Christus, the founder of the name, had undergone the death penalty in the reign of Tiberius . . . and the pernicious superstition was checked for a moment, only to break out again—not only in Judea where the plague began—but in Rome itself, where everything in the world that is horrible or shameful flows in and becomes a fad. First, the members of the sect who acknowledged that they were so were arrested; and on the basis of their disclosures, great numbers were convicted. . . . Although they were guilty and deserving of extreme penalties, a feeling of sympathy arose, because it seemed that they were being wiped out not for the public welfare but to gratify one man's brutality.*

While Tacitus had no doubt that the Christians deserved to die, he found Nero's methods distasteful. The emperor had had some of the Christians torn to pieces by wild beasts, or set alight as torches in the dark, and he had opened his gardens to the public for the entertainment; but even the bloodthirsty Roman mob obviously felt doubts and compassion.

A generation or so later, a conscientious imperial public servant, Pliny the Younger, wrote from his post in Asia Minor to his emperor, Trajan (98–117), that he was puzzled about how to treat the Christians, and asked for instructions. Should he make allowance for age, or punish children as severely as adults? Should he pardon a former Christian who now recanted? Should he punish people just for being Christians, or must he have evidence that they had committed the horrid crimes associated with their name? Up to now, Pliny had simply asked the accused if they were Christians, and if they three times said that they were, he

had them executed. Pliny had interrogated alleged Christians partly on the basis of an anonymous document listing their names. He had acquitted all who denied that they were Christians, who offered incense before the emperor's statue, and who cursed Christ, and all who admitted that they had once been Christians, but had recanted, and would perform pagan ceremonies. But these had said that, as Christians,

> the sum total of their offense or error was this: that they were in the habit of meeting on a certain fixed day before sunrise, to sing hymns antiphonally to Christ, as to a god, and to bind themselves by an oath—not for any criminal purpose—but that they would not commit theft, robbery, or adultery, or falsify their word, or deny that they had received a deposit at the moment when they should be called upon to give it back. Then they reassembled and partook of food, a meal taken in unison, but altogether innocent. This they had given up since . . . I forbade club-meetings. So I felt it necessary to make a further effort to discover the truth by torture from two slave-women, who were called "deaconesses," but I could discover nothing more than superstition, shameless and excessive.

Trajan was an emperor as unlike Nero as any that Rome ever produced, and he answered with moderation: Pliny had done right. Trajan left the question of sparing children to Pliny's own judgment. He said that Christians need not be sought out, though any who were denounced and found guilty must be punished, as Pliny had already done. But any who denied that they were Christians, even if they had been suspect in the past, should be pardoned if they offered prayer to the Roman gods. As for "any anonymous documents you may receive," they "must be ignored in any prosecution. This sort of thing creates the worst sort of precedent, and is out of keeping with the spirit of our times."* Even the relatively humane Trajan, however, who must have spared a good many Christians who escaped notice because of his policy that they were not to be hunted, was determined to execute those who were caught and who admitted that they were Christians.

LATER PERSECUTIONS Alone among the emperor's subjects Christians might be killed "for the name alone," presumably because their "atheism," as Trajan saw it, threatened to bring down the wrath of the gods on the community that tolerated it. Equally "atheist" in this sense, the Jews could be forgiven because they were continuing to practice their ancestral religion—a worthy thing in itself in Roman eyes—and because Rome had long since adopted an official policy of tolerating the Jewish faith, provided that the Jews did not rebel against the Roman state. A single act of religious conformity—a pinch of incense in the fire before the emperor's statue, for example—was enough to bring ac-

*Translation ours.

*Translation ours.

quittal. It took enormous spiritual and physical fortitude to risk torture and death when escape was ostensibly so easy.

As a Christian writer said, the Romans tended to blame the Christians for all public disasters. If the Tiber flooded, or if the Nile didn't flood, if there were a drought or an earthquake or a famine or a plague, the public instantly began to shout that the Christians should be fed to the lions in the arena. Except for such times of disaster or for an occasional lynching, there were long periods of toleration. When Christians were executed—usually by local governors, such as Pliny, concerned with keeping order in their provinces, rather than by imperial command—it was not specifically for refusing to worship the emperor, or as members of an illegal association, but for refusal to participate in the state religion as well as in their own, and for thus threatening the fabric of society.

Not until the third century, when the Roman world was apparently coming apart at the seams, did persecutions become more frequent and more severe. By then, too, Christians were far more numerous, as the faith had spread mightily. Decius (249–251), after an anti-Christian riot in Alexandria, commanded that on a given day everybody in the empire must sacrifice to the gods and obtain a certificate to prove that he had done so. Anybody who could not produce the certificate was liable to persecution. The dangers then threatening Rome were real enough; Decius himself would soon be killed by the Goths, and he wanted a single act of conformity from all his subjects to demonstrate that the empire was united in the face of peril.

The Pope, the Bishops of Antioch and Jerusalem, nineteen humble Christians of Alexandria, and six at Rome are known to have been executed. No bishop in North Africa died, but there were cases of torture. In Spain two bishops recanted. Many Christians who had not obeyed the edict were not arrested afterward for failing to have the certificate; some hid until the persecution had died down. In the Latin West, at least, others bribed officials to issue them false certificates saying that they had sacrificed, when they had not; and they were later with some protest received back into their churches. In the Greek East, the same bribery probably took place but was not regarded as sinful.

Under Valerian in 257–259, the government for the first time tried to interfere with the assembly of Christians for worship, and the clergy were ordered to sacrifice. After Valerian had been captured by the Persians, however, his successor granted toleration. The persecution begun in 303 by Diocletian (284–305) was the most severe of all, especially in the East, where it lasted a full decade as against only about two years in the West. Churches were to be destroyed, and all sacred books and church property handed over. In Palestine—for which alone we have the figures—nearly a hundred Christians were martyred. A good many actively sought martyrdom by violent anti-pagan acts of some sort, although church officials often discour-

aged such "voluntary martyrdom" out of fear that it would provoke mass anti-Christian retaliations. To court death in the Christian cause was a "baptism of blood," a passport direct to Paradise.

But persecution as a policy was a failure: it did not eliminate Christianity. Quite the contrary. Large numbers of influential persons in the empire had become Christians. Moreover, persecution did not avert disasters, which befell the Roman state whether it persecuted Christians or not. In 311 and 313, respectively, the persecuting emperors Galerius and Maximunus officially abandoned the policy. And Constantine (306–337), in agreement with his rival Licinius, in 313 confirmed the edict they had issued: "Christians may exist again, and may build their own churches, so long as they do nothing against public order."* Official persecution thus became a thing of the past.

While it raged, Christians had often called for universal toleration. "It is a privilege of nature," wrote the North African Christian Tertullian (150–225), "that everyone should worship as he pleases," and almost a century later Lactantius said that, while Christians believed that their God was the God of all men, whether they liked it or not, Christians did not force anybody to worship him and were not angry at anybody who did not. Once the Christians were free and clear from persecution, however, it was not very long before they forgot this view that religion was a matter of free choice; and in the later fourth century and in the fifth the pleas for toleration would come from pagans.

The Conversion of Constantine

In 312, the year before he associated himself with the edict of toleration, Constantine himself had a religious experience akin to that of Saint Paul. Just before going into battle against his rival Maxentius, north of Rome at the Milvian Bridge, it is said, the emperor saw in the heavens the sign of a cross against the sun and the words "conquer in this." He put the sign on the battle standards of his army, won the battle, and attributed the victory to the god of the Christians. Though the story has often been challenged, there is little evidence for the counterargument that Constantine acted because he simply foresaw the eventual triumph of Christianity. He continued to appease the sun god as well as the god of the Christians, but he regarded himself a Christian. At the time of his death in 337, the Church was on its way to becoming the official state religion of the Roman Empire.

One last major official attempt was made at a formal restoration—or, rather, reconstruction—of the old polytheism of the empire. The emperor Julian the Apostate (361–363), pagan and philosopher much influenced by the Neoplatonists, failed to restore paganism, and at his death only two years after he had assumed the imperial crown, Christianity quickly re-

*P. R. Coleman-Norton, ed., *Roman State and Christian Church*, vol. I, p. 20.

gained and extended its position. The emperor Theodosius I (379–395) made Christianity the official religion of the empire and began to persecute the pagans. Paganism continued in the countryside and among the upper classes and the intellectuals for another century or so, but in the cities it was no longer an organized force.

The Christian Triumph as a Historical Problem

[handwritten: Why did Christianity triumph]

Why did Christianity triumph? It was at the beginning a despised sect of simple enthusiasts in a rich, well-organized, sophisticated society. Yet it took over the society. In general, we may postulate the need for a religion of love in the savage world of Rome; and in particular we have noted some of the advantages that Jesus' teachings gave Christianity over the mystery cults. The cult of Isis lacked a missionary priesthood, that of Mithra any priesthood at all. Isis was chiefly for women, Mithra altogether for men. Apuleius, a second-century Latin novelist, in the eighth book of his *Golden Ass,* describes a troupe of emasculated priests of Isis carrying about an image of their "omnipotent and omniparent Syrian goddess" and behaving like a rowdy circus troupe. Apuleius himself was initiated into the cult of Isis, in a rite full of mumbo jumbo.

So the evangel was really "good news," with its promise of personal immortality, its admonition to behave with kindness and love to one's fellow human beings, its lofty moral code. The Church provided a consoling and beautiful and dramatic ritual, and the opportunity to become a part of the exciting, dangerous, and thoroughly masculine task of spreading the gospel. The would-be convert could find in it ideas and rites closely related to those of Egyptians, Greeks, and Jews. In the mysterious opening of the Gospel of John: "In the beginning was the Word, and the Word was with God, and the Word was God," the Word was the Greek *logos,* the divine reason, the intellect of the Neoplatonists. It was at Ephesus, the shrine of the peculiar virgin mother-goddess known as Diana of the Ephesians, that the quarrelsome Christian theologians of the fifth century would proclaim the Virgin Mary the mother of God.

From its cradle in Jerusalem, Christianity never penetrated far into the lands of Zoroastrian, Hindu, and other Eastern faiths, nor into Africa south of the Sahara. Instead it spread westward along the shores of the Mediterranean and north into Europe, essentially *within* the Roman Empire. It needed the political and cultural structure of the empire to work within. And, of course, only a few centuries later a fiery and militant new monotheism, Islam, arose and overwhelmed some of the outposts of Christianity.

Christianity succeeded not only because it set itself against the earthly compromises and indecencies of pagan cults, the dryness and sterility of later pagan philosophy, but also because it contained so much of Judaism and of paganism both religious and philosophical, Hellenistic and oriental. Even more important perhaps is the extent to which Christianity allowed the old uses, the old rites and habits, the unintellectual "practical" side of religion, to survive, and the extent to which it mastered and tamed pagan habits. So, when the crowds of Ephesus in the fifth century hailed the victory of the theologians who were defending the Virgin's motherhood, one might almost hear an echo, "Great is Diana of the Ephesians." Christmas is the birth of Jesus, but also the turning northward at last of the European winter sun, the promise of its returning warmth; and Easter is an echo of thousands of prehistoric years of celebrations of the actual coming of spring, the resurrection of life in nature.

So Christianity appealed to men and women because it offered a new and believable promise, yet preserved reassuringly familiar elements, because it concentrated upon mutual love, because it had a capacity for adaptation. All these things Jesus himself stood for and proclaimed. In addition, however, Christianity eventually triumphed within the Roman world because of the organization of the church, something that Jesus did not even foresee, much less plan.

IV The Organization of the Church

To maintain order, the Christian community clearly needed some authority to discipline, or even oust, those who misbehaved. It had to organize in order to survive in the midst of an empire committed in principle to its suppression. Prophets, or teachers, appeared in the very first churches, the informal groups of Christians organized by the missionaries; and soon elders, overseers and presidents followed.

More and more, the overseer (Greek *episkopos*) appeared in authority over a compact administrative area, his *see.* This was the bishop, who became the key figure in church administration. Each see claimed to have been founded by one of the original apostles; and its bishop thus held office through apostolic succession. Since it had been Christ himself who had chosen the apostles, every bishop, in effect, became a direct spiritual heir of Christ. Groups of bishoprics or episcopal sees often were gathered together into larger units, owing obedience to an archbishop, a head overseer (*archiepiskopos*). Just as the bishop often had his headquarters in a Roman *civitas,* or city-state unit, and exercised authority over the churches in the countryside roundabout, so the archbishop governed the *civitates* from a mother city, a *metropolis,* usually the capital of a Roman province, and his see was called a province.

At the top of the hierarchy stood the bishop of the imperial capital, Rome itself, the father of them all, *papa* or pope, who claimed supreme authority. The prestige of Rome contributed powerfully to his claim. So did the association of Peter and Paul with Rome. Christ had said to Peter, "Thou art Peter and upon

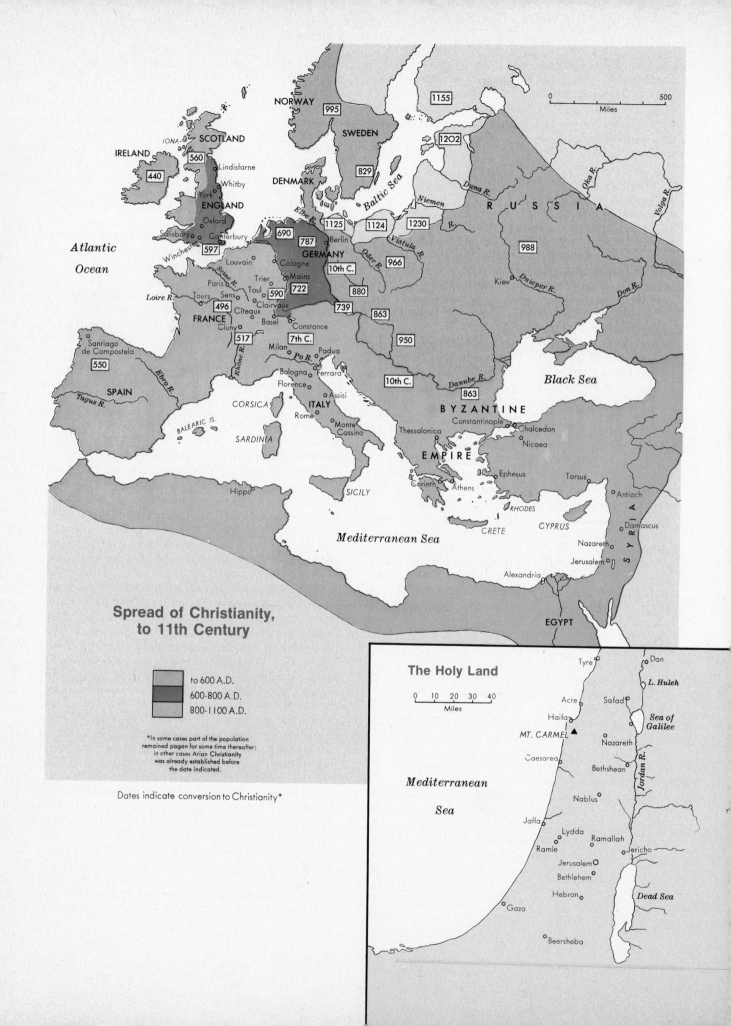

Spread of Christianity,
to 11th Century

to 600 A.D.
600-800 A.D.
800-1100 A.D.

*In some cases part of the population
remained pagan for some time thereafter;
in other cases Arian Christianity
was already established before
the date indicated.

Dates indicate conversion to Christianity*

The Holy Land

0 10 20 30 40
Miles

NORWAY 995
SWEDEN 1155
1202
829
DENMARK
Baltic Sea
1125 1124 1230
RUSSIA
IONA SCOTLAND
IRELAND 560
440 Lindisfarne
Whitby
York
ENGLAND 690
Oxford Berlin
Salisbury Canterbury GERMANY 966
Winchester 597 10th C. Oder R.
Atlantic Louvain Cologne 880 988
Ocean Seine R. Mainz 739 Kiev Dnieper R. Don R.
Trier 590 722 863
Paris Toul
Tours Sens Clairvaux 950
496 Citeaux Basel Constance 7th C.
FRANCE Cluny Milan 863
517 Po R. Padua 10th C. Danube R. Black Sea
Santiago Bologna Ferrara
de Compostela Florence BYZANTINE
550 Assisi Constantinople Chalcedon
SPAIN CORSICA ITALY Thessalonica Nicaea
Rome EMPIRE Ephesus Tarsus
Ebro R. Monte Corinth Athens
Tagus R. Cassino Antioch
BALEARIC IS. RHODES Damascus
SARDINIA CYPRUS SYRIA
Hippo SICILY CRETE Nazareth
Mediterranean Sea Jerusalem
Alexandria
EGYPT
Elbe R. Niemen R. Vistula R. Duna R. Oka R. Volga R.
Rhone R. Loire R.

Tyre Dan
L. Huleh
Acre Safad
Haifa Sea of
MT. CARMEL Galilee
Caesarea Nazareth
Bethshean Jordan R.
Mediterranean Nablus
Sea Jaffa
Lydda Ramallah
Ramle Jericho
Jerusalem
Bethlehem
Hebron Dead Sea
Gaza
Beersheba

0 500
Miles

this rock I will build my church," a celebrated pun, since the word for Peter is *Petros* and that for rock *petra*. Because Peter had been martyred in Rome, the bishops of that city could claim that Christ himself had picked Rome as the rock upon which to build: a claim that was embodied in their "Petrine theory." The bishops of the great cities of the eastern Mediterranean, Alexandria and Antioch, however, claimed to exercise a paternal rule equal in authority to that of the pope. They called themselves patriarch (fatherly governor). Still later, after Constantinople had been made the imperial capital (A.D. 330), its bishop, also a patriarch, would oppose papal claims to supremacy.

With the departure of imperial government from Rome, the popes gradually made themselves more and more responsible for the government of the great city. And as the barbarians began to pour in and Rome itself came under attack, the pope became the symbol of the old Roman regularities and certainties, a rock indeed. A succession of outstanding men became bishop of Rome, notably Leo the Great (reigned 440–461), a theologian, a splendid administrator, and a brave man, who saved the city from the Hun, Attila. By the time of the breakup of the Roman Empire, in the fifth century, nobody in the West would have disputed the claim of papal supremacy; the papacy had emerged as the firmest institution in a new and terrible world.

The government of the Church had taken shape gradually, in response to need. The Church strengthened its organization by utilizing the existing political machinery of the Roman Empire, placing its major officials in centers that were already administrative capitals. Bishops and archbishops, meeting in councils, determined which religious ideas or practices would be accepted and which rejected, which writings were truly Christian and which false. In this way the Church selected from other writings the twenty-seven canonical books of the New Testament, written in Greek, and the Old Testament writings as preserved in a Greek translation from the Hebrew. In the Greek church today, these versions are still in use; in the Roman church, the Latin version called the Vulgate, made by St. Jerome in the fourth century, is used. Many of the writings that the Church rejected have survived. Though not canonical, they have much interest for the modern historian and theologian.

Bishops and Their Duties: Church and State

Each bishop presided over several churches. Each church was under the care of a priest (Greek *presbyteros*, "elder"), who had been qualified by special training and by the ceremony of ordination. The area served by each church and its priest came to be known as the parish. In the early Church the office of deacon, often held by a man who had other occupations besides the service of the Church, had much importance. In some of the early churches, the congregation itself elected its officers, and the church was governed by boards of elders (presbyteries); but the system of appointment from above prevailed over that of election, although the congregation was often consulted. Before long, then, the distinction between those who were merely faithful worshipers (the laity) and those who conducted the worship and administered the affairs of the church (the clergy) became well defined. Despite frequent rumbles of protest during the two thousand years of Christianity, and despite differences of degree in the Christian churches, some distinction between laity and clergy is maintained in almost all.

By the seventh century the broad lines of church government in both the East and the West had been established. The organization was hierarchical—that is, there was a regular series of relations of subordinate to superior from priest to pope or patriarch, somewhat as military lines of command run from second lieutenant to general. But at almost every level—for bishoprics, for archbishoprics, and for the Church as a whole—there were councils made up of officials who met and debated problems and made decisions. Church government, then, was no simple relation of silent underling to commanding superior. Indeed, in these early centuries the critical decisions were made by assemblies rather than by individuals. Once the papacy had become firmly established, however, the popes maintained the position—when they could—that the pope was superior even to a general council, and was not bound by its decisions.

After the conversion of Constantine, the first Christian emperor, the election of bishops became a matter of particular concern to the state. In order to retain the initiative, the officials of the church worked to put the election of each new bishop into the hands of the clergy of the cathedral (episcopal church) of his see. Practice remained uneven, however. Sometimes the citizens simply gave assent to an accomplished fact by approving elections. At other times the people had real power, as when Roman mobs under the sway of rival political leaders controlled the choices to the papal throne. Since bishops often exercised actual governing power and had their own law courts, lay rulers often insisted on approving or even selecting them. The problem of the degree to which laymen could participate in the choice of the bishops remained acute in the West down into the eleventh century, as the popes strove to have the ultimate say, and this very struggle was one of the major sources of our present democratic institutions.

The point becomes clear when we look at the very different history of Church and State in the East. In the East, the emperor at Constantinople usually acted as the real head of both Church and State. No organized clerical body could tell him where to stop. Although religious disputes regularly broke out in the Eastern empire, no clear-cut moral or legal code emerged that set limits to the emperor's *rights*. The Russian church inherited this Eastern tradition. In

The abbey at Monte Cassino in southern Italy.

the West, however, pope and emperor struggled over the issue. And gradually it became accepted that no single person or institution could wield both political and religious power. Such an understanding helped pave the way for further acceptance of the rights of smaller groups and of individuals.

Monasticism

Deacons, priests, bishops, archbishops, all serve the laity of this world, and are called *secular* clergy (*sæcularis,* "temporal"). Early in the history of the Church, however, another kind of devotee to Christianity appeared in Syria and Egypt—the monk, a man who felt that he must deny the urges of his own flesh and become an ascetic. The New Testament itself, in Paul's own writings and elsewhere, extolled the merits of abstaining from sexual relationships if possible, and from all other fleshly indulgence. Therefore, monks would leave civilization behind and go into the desert to live in solitude, meditation, and prayer, subsisting on the minimum of food and drink. By the third century, there were many of these hermits, who enjoyed reputations for extreme holiness and often competed with each other in torturing themselves or in self-denial; some lived in trees or in holes in the ground, others on the tops of columns, to which they would haul up food supplied by pious devotees.

To keep the extremists from using the cloak of holiness to cover un-Christian self-assertion, certain leaders, such as St. Anthony, early collected groups of monks around themselves and formed communities,

living by a rule. The Greek St. Basil (329–379) wrote the most famous of these rules, which became standard in the Greek church and still regulates Greek monasticism today. Basil prescribed celibacy and poverty but combated the dangers of extreme asceticism by requiring that the monks work in the fields or elsewhere to make their communities as self-supporting as possible. Because, after Basil, monks lived by a rule, they are known as the regular clergy (Latin *regula,* "rule"), as contrasted with the secular clergy. In Greek monasticism, the monks not only worshiped but also ate and worked together. Although dedicated to a life outside this wicked world, they were also to do works of charity, such as setting up orphanages and hospitals.

Similarly, in the West the problem was met by the rule of St. Benedict, who founded the great abbey at Monte Cassino in southern Italy in the 520s. His Latin rule, like Basil's Greek rule, prescribed hard work for all and urged the monks to try to be tolerant of one another's interests and infirmities. In the West particularly, the monks broke new ground around their monasteries, acted as pioneers in opening up the wilderness, performed missionary service among the still unconverted heathen tribes, and did much charitable and medical work among the poor and the sick. In both East and West, scholarship early became one of the recognized occupations for monks, and the monastic scribe, who copied the works of the ancients and built up the library of his foundation, helped preserve the literature of the past.

Tensions often arose between secular and regular clergy, each feeling that its own work was more valuable to Christianity as a whole. Constant care and strict government were needed to maintain the high ideals of the monasteries and of the convents for women that soon appeared. This continuing need prompted the successive monastic reform movements that played a major role in Christian history. The abbots of the greater monasteries often participated, along with the bishops, in the councils of the Church that helped form Christian doctrine and frame the rules of Church observance and discipline.

V The Ideas of Christianity

The Christian clergy could hardly have attained their great power had they not been essential intermediaries between this visible world of actuality and an invisible other world that to the true Christian is as real as this one. In Christianity certain important ideas about the other world are embodied in ritual acts called *sacraments*. These sacraments, administered by the clergy, are central to Christianity.

Sacrament and Salvation

The central mystery of Christianity is the sacrament of the Eucharist. It is a mystery made available to simple men and women, as a part of ordinary living, by the services of the church. The sacrament stems from Jesus' last supper with his disciples, where he

> . . . took bread, and blessed it, and brake it, and gave it to the disciples, and said, Take, eat; this is my body. And he took the cup, and gave thanks, and gave it to them, saying, Drink ye all of it; For this is my blood of the new testament, which is shed for many for the remission of sins [Matt. 26:26–28].

By the third century, the Eucharist had become the miraculous ceremony that made the Christian believer feel emotionally his link with God, that made him feel the wonder of salvation. If the sacrament of *baptism* figuratively washed away the stain of original sin, and made the individual a Christian, then the sacrament of the *Eucharist* enabled him to remain in the Christian communion—subject always to good behavior—and sustained him in its faith and fellowship. There were to be many grave theological disputes over the doctrine of the Eucharist, notably at the time of the Protestant revolt. But it has remained central to the drama of the Christian faith even when, as for some Protestants, it is but a commemoration of the Lord's Supper.

For this symbolic act of the Mass, or Eucharist, theological explanations were given. Adam, who began with the chance for a perfect life on earth, disobeyed God, was driven from Eden, and was exposed to death and suffering here on earth. This was Adam's "original sin," and all his descendants shared his fate. But the Jews, in spite of individual and group backslidings, kept alive their faith in God; and after generations of suffering God took mercy and sent to earth his only begotten son, Jesus. By his sufferings on the cross, Jesus atoned for human sins, made redemption to God the Father, and made it possible in the future for good Christians to be saved, in spite of Adam's sin, to enjoy in the other world after death the immortal happiness they could only anticipate in this one, since this world is no longer the Garden of Eden.

Even so elementary an outline of the doctrine of salvation bristles with the kind of difficulties Christians have been arguing about for centuries. What *was* the relation between God the Father and his only begotten son? In this context, what does the term *begotten* actually mean? What was Adam's original sin? How did a man go about the task of attaining salvation; was it enough to belong to the Church, or must he have some inward sign? This latter question raises what has been for two thousand years perhaps the central point of debate in Christianity, the problem of faith or good works.

Those who believe that salvation is primarily an inward and emotional matter for the individual Christian, a matter of faith, tend to minimize the importance of individual outward acts, even the sacraments. Those who believe that the individual must behave externally in strict accordance with God's directions in order to be saved put more emphasis upon "good works." Either simple position, carried to its logical extreme, poses great dangers: on the one hand, the withering of the Church and the usurpation of the priestly role by the individual believer; on the other, the withering of the individual's role and the dictatorship over his daily behavior by the clergy. Neither extreme is acceptable to the Christian. In his life, both faith and good works are necessary; indeed, neither is possible without the other.

The Seven Sacraments

As time passed, the sacraments grew in number to seven. They were: (1) baptism, by which the infant was washed of the stain of original sin and brought into mystical union with Christ; (2) confirmation, by which, on attaining an age at which he could understand Christian doctrine, the child was formally brought into the discipline of the Church; (3) the Eucharist, the central act of the Christian drama; (4) penance, whereby the confessed and repentant sinner was forgiven (granted absolution) by the priest, had the guilt of his sin and *eternal* punishment remitted, subject to a *temporal* punishment assigned as penance; this temporal punishment might or might not be sufficient to satisfy God's justice, and hence a given penance itself could not guarantee the penitent's salvation; (5) extreme unction, "the last rites of the Church," a ceremony performed by the priest at the dying moments of the Christian to prepare him for the life to come; (6) ordination, the ceremony by which a candidate was made a priest; and (7) matrimony. Baptism and the

Virgin and saints, from the chapel of a Coptic monastery in Egypt.

Eucharist (the latter is often called the Lord's Supper or Communion) have remained as sacraments in almost all the Protestant groups. Of the other sacraments, the one that has been most heavily attacked and most vigorously rejected by Protestants generally is that of penance.

Heresy

The early centuries of Christianity saw a series of struggles to define the accepted doctrines of the religion—orthodoxy—and to protect them against the challenge of rival doctrinal ideas—heresy. The first heresies appeared almost as soon as the first clergy. In fact, the issue between those who wished to admit Gentiles who were outside the law and those who wished to confine the gospel to the Jews foreshadowed the kind of issue that was to confront Christianity in the first few centuries, when heresy followed on heresy. The points at issue sometimes seem unreal and unimportant, even ludicrous to us today. But we must not regard these religious debates as trivial or childish. Men believed that their future salvation depended upon the proper

definition and defense of religious belief and practice. In addition, bitter political, economic, and national issues often underlay disputes that took a theological form.

Gnostics and Manichaeans

Men have always had difficulty in understanding and explaining how evil can exist (as it obviously does) in a physical world created by a good God. The Gnostics (from the Greek word for "knowledge") affirmed that only the world of the spirit is real (and good); the physical world is evil, or an evil illusion. Thus they could not accept the Old Testament, whose God created this world; they regarded him as a fiend or decided that this world had been created by Satan. Nor could they accept Jesus' human life and work and martyrdom in this world, an essential part of Christian belief. They could not accept baptism, because to them water was matter, or venerate a crucifix, which to them was just two pieces of wood. Like the Zoroastrians with their god of good and their god of evil, the Gnostics were *dualists*. Clearly heretical, the Gnostics focused on

Christ's miracle-working and on other sorts of magic. Among them there arose a sharp distinction between an elite, whose members led especially pure lives, and the ordinary flock, less able to bear self-denial or the mysteries of the faith, who usually worked hard to support the elite.

Closely related to Gnosticism were the ideas of Mani, a third-century Mesopotamian prophet, who preached that the God of light and goodness and his emanations were in constant conflict with the god of darkness, evil, and matter, and his emanations. These Manichaean views became immensely popular, especially along the North African shores of the Mediterranean during the third and fourth centuries. The Christians combated them, and throughout the Middle Ages tended to label all doctrinal opposition as Manichaean. Yet the dualist ideas persisted, more or less underground, and cropped up every few decades for a thousand years.

Donatists and Arians; The Council of Nicaea

Within Christianity, heresy sometimes involved very practical problems. The emperor Constantine faced the so-called Donatist movement in North Africa. The movement arose because, during the Roman persecutions of the Christians after 303, a number of priests yielded to the demands of Roman authorities and had handed over to them the sacred books. After the edicts of toleration of 311 and 313, these "handers-over" (traditores) had resumed their role as priests. Donatus, bishop of Carthage, and his followers maintained that the sacraments administered by such a traditor were invalid. Donatus' wish to punish weakling or collaborationist priests is understandable but dangerous, because, once a believer suspected the validity of the sacraments as received from one priest, he might suspect it as received from any other. Amidst much bitterness and violence Constantine ruled that once a priest had been properly ordained, the sacraments administered at his hands had validity even if the priest had himself acted badly. But the Donatists persisted in their views, and North Africa was much troubled by the continued rivalry between them and their opponents.

Heresy also arose over essentially philosophical issues. Such was Arianism, named after Arius, a priest of Alexandria, who early in the fourth century put forth the view that if God the Father had begotten God the Son (through God the Holy Ghost), then God the Son, as begotten, could not be exactly of the same essence (homoousios in Greek) as God the Father, but must be somehow inferior to, or dependent upon, or at least later in time than his begetter, of a similar essence (homoiousios in Greek) but not the same. It is difficult to refute this position on the basis of logical argument alone. Far from a quarrel over one letter (homoousios or homoiousios), Arius' view threatened to belittle the divinity of Christ as God the Son and to separate Christ from the Trinity.

Arius' bitter opponent, Athanasius, bishop of Alexandria, fought him passionately, disdaining logic and emphasizing mystery. Athanasius and his followers maintained that Christians simply had to take it as a matter of faith that Father and Son are identical in essence and that the Son is equal to, independent of, and contemporaneous with the Father. Even though the Father begat the Son, it is heresy to say that there was ever a time when the Son did not exist. In the Greek East especially, this abstract philosophical argument was fought out not only among churchmen and thinkers but in the barbershops and among the longshoremen. A visitor to Constantinople complained: "I ask how much I have to pay; they talk of the born and the unborn. I want to know the price of bread; they answer 'the father is greater than the son.' I ask if my bath is ready; they say 'the son has been made out of nothing.'" The fact that most people did not understand what they were talking about did not prevent their rioting against their opponents.

After trying hard to stay out of the quarrel and urging the bishops to stop discussing it, Constantine realized that it would have to be settled. He himself summoned in 325 the first council of the whole Church, a council called ecumenical (from the Greek oikoumene, "the inhabited world"), at Nicaea, across the straits from Constantinople. A large majority of the bishops decided in favor of the Athanasian view, which was then embodied in the famous Nicene Creed, issued with all the force of an imperial decree by Constantine himself:

We believe in one God, the Father all-sovereign,
    maker of all things, both visible and invisible:
And in one Lord Jesus Christ,
    the Son of God,
begotten of the Father, and only-begotten,
that is from the essence [ousia] of the Father.
    God from God
    Light from light,
    True God from true God,
begotten not made,
being of one essence [homoousion] with the Father;
by whom all things were made,
    both things in heaven and things on earth;
who for us men and for our salvation came down
from heaven and
    was made flesh, was made man
    suffered and rose again on the third day,
    ascended into heaven,
    cometh to judge quick and dead:
And in the Holy Spirit.
But those who say
    that there was once when he was not
    and before he was begotten he was not
    and he was made of things that were not
Or maintain that the Son of God is of a different
    essence or substance
    or created or subject to moral change or alteration—
Them doth the Catholic and Apostolic Church
    anathematize [condemn to damnation].

The emperor had presided over the council, and against his will found himself assuming the role of head of the church, giving legal sanction to a purely doctrinal decision and so playing the role both of Caesar and of pope. This "Caesaro-papism," in fact, became the tradition of Empire and Church in the East.

But the decree of Nicaea did not dispose of Arianism. Arians disobeyed; Constantine himself wavered; and his immediate successors on the imperial throne were themselves Arians. Between 325 and 381, there were thirteen more councils that discussed the problem, deciding first one way, then another. One pagan historian sardonically commented that one could no longer travel on the roads because they were so cluttered up with throngs of bishops riding off to one council or another. Traces of Arianism remained in the empire for several centuries after Nicaea, and, because the missionary Ulfilas preached the Arian form of Christianity to the barbarian Goths beyond the frontiers of the empire, the heresy was spread among most of the Germanic peoples then being converted to Christianity.

The Two Natures of Christ

Long before Arianism disappeared, a new and related controversy had shaken the Eastern portion of the empire to its foundations. Exactly what was the relationship of Christ the God and Christ the man? He was both man and God, but just exactly how was this possible? And was the Virgin Mary—a human woman—perhaps the mother only of his human aspect, or, if not, how could a human being be the mother of God?

One extreme position was that of the dyophysites (two-nature-ites), who separated the human nature of Christ from the divine and so refused to regard the human virgin as the *mother of God*. The dyophysite view later became (unfairly) linked with the name of Nestorius, bishop of Constantinople in the early fifth century, and its followers were called Nestorians. They took refuge in Asia—Persia and beyond, all the way to China. The other extreme view was that of the monophysites (one-nature-ites), who argued that Christ's human and divine natures were totally merged; but they carried their thesis so far that they almost forgot Christ's human attributes and tended to make him a god only.

Again the dispute flared up in physical violence in the East; again the decision hung in the balance; again the emperor (Marcian, reigned 450–457) called an ecumenical council, this one at Chalcedon, near Constantinople, in 451. Supported by Pope Leo the Great, the council condemned monophysitism and, like the Council of Nicaea, took a mystical rather than a rational decision: the true believer must believe in the two natures of Christ, human and divine, coexisting yet not distinct from each other; the Virgin is properly called the mother of God.

But like the decision at Nicaea, the decision at Chalcedon did not completely or definitively dispose of the opposition. Monophysites were concentrated in the provinces of Egypt and Syria and apparently expressed in their religious beliefs the resentment of the ancient Mediterranean cities of Alexandria and Antioch against the new domination by the upstart Constantinople, and the dislike of Egyptians and Syrians for the Greeks who dominated at the capital. So, perhaps partly because it was identified with what we would call nationalism, monophysitism did not die out, and the emperors strove to deal with it by one compromise or another. But, since there were no monophysites in the West, the Roman Church regarded the issue as closed; every time an emperor at Constantinople tried to appease his Egyptian and Syrian monophysite subjects, he would be condemned by the pope for heresy. For two centuries the problem remained unsolved.

The disaffection of the monophysite provinces of Syria and Egypt was to facilitate their conquest in the seventh century by the new religion of Islam. To this day there are still monophysite Christians in Egypt and Syria, and Nestorian remnants in farther Asia. The continuing quarrel illustrates the lasting political impact that theological disagreement sometimes provided.

VI Thought and Letters in the First Christian Centuries

Though a good deal of dislike and misunderstanding had always characterized the attitudes of Greeks and Romans toward each other, Roman admiration for Greek literature and art had given its stamp to the works of Roman writers and artists. The triumph of Christianity tended to contribute, as we have seen, new sources of misunderstanding and tension to the relationships between Easterners and Westerners. The political division imposed by Diocletian and repeated by many of his successors expressed the geographic distinction between Eastern and Western provinces. As the barbarian inroads began increasingly in the fourth and fifth centuries to disrupt communications and threaten all the established institutions in the West, the opportunities for Westerners to know Greek and embrace the great classical tradition were fewer. In the Eastern provinces few except soldiers and professional administrators had ever spoken or read Latin, though it remained the official language of legislation at Constantinople down through the fifth century. Despite the growing division, however, the literature of the late Roman and early Christian world may be treated as a single whole.

The Turn from Pagan to Christian Literature: Julian, the Cappadocians, Jerome, Ambrose

In the West, pagan literature declined and virtually disappeared, while in the East a few passionate devotees of the old gods still made their voices heard. Constantine's nephew Julian was taught by a group of anti-Christian pagan scholars. As emperor (361–363) he revived the sacrifices in the temples, forbade Christians to teach, threatened to revive persecution, and even tried to construct a new pagan hierarchy like that of the Christian Church to make paganism more effective as an organized religion. He wrote satirical and moralistic essays and orations, but his program was doomed to failure.

Christian letters began to take the center of the stage. In the East, writers devoted much energy to polemical writings on the burning doctrinal questions and disputes of the day. In both East and West the best minds among Christians faced the problem of how to treat Greek and Roman literature. A few thinkers, mostly in the West and especially at first, advised against the reading of anything but Scripture, for fear of pagan error. They later came to acknowledge that one had to read the great pagans of the past in order to be able to refute pagan philosophical ideas. Still, there was always the danger that in the pleasure of reading a delightful classical author one might forget that the prime concern was to expose his errors and refute his arguments. The Greek Christians worried far less about this problem, and in the fourth century the three great Cappadocian fathers (so called from the province of Asia Minor where they were born)—Basil, author of the monastic rule; his brother, Gregory of Nyssa; and their friend, Gregory of Nazianzos—all had an excellent classical education and used the techniques of the pagan philosophers in discussing religious ideas.

One of the most important writers in Latin was Jerome (340–420), who studied with Gregory of Nazianzos, produced the Latin Bible, the Vulgate, as the climax of a life of devoted scholarship that had made him the master of Hebrew and Greek as well as Latin. Ambrose (ca. 340–397), a Roman civil servant who became bishop of Milan, wrote many theological works and commentaries, christianizing much that he found in the classics, particularly in Cicero; he transformed Cicero's Stoic concept of duty to the state into a Christian concept of duty to God. But he felt so guilty about his love for the classics and his indebtedness to Cicero that he once had a nightmare in which Christ himself called him a "Ciceronian, not a Christian." Ambrose put his own preaching into practice when he publicly humiliated the emperor Theodosius I (reigned 379–395) and forced him to do penance for savagely punishing some rioters. The act symbolizes the Western church's insistence that, in matters of morals and of faith, the Church would be supreme, an attitude that ran exactly counter to the practice already growing up in the East.

Augustine

HIS EARLY LIFE Augustine (354–430), the greatest of the Western church fathers, we know intimately through the famous autobiography—*The Confessions*—written when he was forty-three. His life and writings introduce us vividly to his world. He was born in a small market town in what is now Algeria, some distance inland from Carthage, the administrative and cultural center of the African provinces. Here the population still spoke Punic (Phoenician), but the upper classes were Latin-speaking, wholly Roman in their outlook, and deeply imbued with the classical traditions of Rome. Prosperous landowners lived on their great estates, while peasants toiled in the fields and olive groves. The Africans admired eloquence, lawsuits, and education. They loved their friends, hated their enemies, were often sarcastic in their speech, and yearned for fame with an unusual vehemence. They pursued religion ecstatically, indulging in trances, chanting, and drunkenness, even at Christian feasts, haunted still by memories of their pagan father-god Saturn and the even more terrifying mother-goddess who still influenced even the Christians.

Of modest means, and often at odds with one another, Augustine's father and his devoutly Christian and possessive mother were determined that he should be given a proper education. But all that his teachers did was force him to memorize a few classical Latin texts and to comment on them in detail. Augustine was so bored that he never did learn Greek, and so was cut off from the original philosophers, and forced to pick up their ideas at second hand, largely through Cicero. His parents' ambitions for him prevented him—and he resented it—from getting married at seventeen, like most of his contemporaries. At the university in Carthage, where fraternities of upperclassmen hazed the freshmen and heckled the professors, Augustine, barely out of his adolescence, took a concubine, as was the custom, with whom he lived happily for some years, and by whom he had a son.

Disappointed with his reading of the Bible, which he found insufficiently polished and too confining in the Old Testament requirements that were still followed in North Africa, Augustine at nineteen joined the Manichaeans. Rejecting the Old Testament and its stern paternal Jehovah and considering themselves true radical Christians, the Manichaeans were highly influential in fashionable Carthaginian society, where they had been preaching for about eighty years. Nonetheless, they were regarded by pagans and Christians alike as subversive, and they had been declared illegal. The "elect" among them fasted and abstained from sexual relations and from labor in the world, while the "hearers" learned Mani's wisdom from their secret books and supported the elite. Gone were Augustine's plans to become a lawyer as his parents had wished; he determined to learn and teach the Manichaean "wisdom," passively keeping the good side of his nature unsullied by the encroaching baseness of the fleshly side.

When he went back to his birthplace as a teacher, his mother was so angry with him for having become a Manichaean that she would not let him into the house. But the static quality of Manichaean belief, the naiveté of its rituals, and the disappointing intellectual level of its leaders began to disillusion Augustine, who returned to Carthage to teach rhetoric.

Highly placed friends invited him to move on to Italy, and, steeling himself against his mother's pleas, he sailed off. At twenty-eight he was appointed professor of rhetoric at Milan, the seat of the imperial court. The job required him to compose and deliver the official speeches of praise for the emperor and for the consuls: propaganda for the official programs. He owed his advancement partly to the wishes of influential pagans to balance Christian influence at court by that of a non-Catholic Manichaean.

CONVERSION; THE CONFESSIONS But at Milan, Augustine abandoned the Manichaean faith, and fell under the spell of Ambrose, who stood out staunchly against the pagan and pro-pagan elements in the city and against the Arian Goths, who formed the main force of the imperial garrison. Better educated than Augustine, a superb preacher, indifferent to the demands of the flesh, Ambrose stimulated Augustine to reexamine all his ideas. And Augustine's mother, who had followed him to Milan, eagerly drank in Ambrose's words "as a fountain of water."

Augustine toyed briefly with Stoicism. He also liked the Neoplatonist idea that material things of this world were reflections of ideas in the eternal other world, and that there were means—to be painfully achieved—by which a man could move in his inner life away from the external world of the senses and toward the One. Augustine's world widened, and evil, instead of looming at the center of it, took a less terrifyingly prominent place; his god became more distant, more powerful, more mysterious than Mani's god. But Augustine could not in the end accept the Neoplatonist view that individual man, unaided, could by reason alone attain to the vision of God. He was therefore ready for conversion to Christianity.

This was a major step, involving not only the abandonment of Augustine's promising worldly career (including his engagement to marry a girl of a rich and prominent family) but also the fateful rite of baptism, which was then felt to be so great a spiritual ordeal that many Christians preferred to put it off until their deathbeds, as the emperor Constantine himself had done. In temporary rural retirement near Lake Como, in a household presided over by his widowed mother and including congenial friends, Augustine devoted himself to philosophic contemplation and conversation. When they found and dissected a centipede, and watched the separate portions continuing to move, they debated the question whether the creature's soul had also been subdivided. Here Augustine elaborated his theories of Christian education and wrote a little book on the immortality of the soul, so complicated that he later found he could barely follow his own arguments. At Easter 387, aged thirty-three, he was baptized by

Ambrose, who three times held his shoulders under a stream of cold water as he stood naked in a deep pool, and who then conducted the impressive services in which the newly baptized Christians participated for the first time in the mysteries of Christ's resurrection, symbolizing their own entry into a wholly new life. Soon afterward—his mother having died—Augustine returned to his native North Africa.

In his home town he soon found himself in intellectual combat with his former co-religionists, the Manichees, debating them publicly, writing pamphlets against them, arguing that evil—the central problem that worried them—was in large part a matter simply of human bad habit: once a man had derived pleasure from an evil act, the memory of the pleasure prompted him to do it again. So he tried to break men of the bad habit of swearing oaths, like an Alcoholics Anonymous campaigner working against the evils of drink. The problem was to allow God to make one take pleasure in good actions, to make one long for perfection. Within three years Augustine had literally been forced into the priesthood by the demands of a local congregation, and in 395, he became bishop of the large town of Hippo, the modern Bône in Algeria.

Here in his early forties he wrote the *Confessions*, describing his spiritual journey and making an appeal to those who, like himself only a few years before, still clung to the doctrines of Mani or of the pagan philosophers and who remained skeptical about Christianity. Written in the Neoplatonic tradition as an effort to lead his reader to God, Augustine's great book, in its selection of individual experiences, in its vivid sketches of persons and places and scenes, in its communication of Augustine's familiar intimacy with God, and in its honesty in reporting his past behavior and feelings, was nonetheless wholly original. So was the message that mere conversion was not enough: temptations would persist; human nature was full of uncertainty and mystery.

BISHOP OF HIPPO Like other prosperous Roman provincial seaport towns, Hippo had its baths, temples, forum, theater, its luxurious suburban villas of the rich, with their lavish floors covered with pictures of hunting scenes or mythological episodes in multicolored mosaics. It depended for its livelihood upon the rich grain-producing fields that surrounded it; and its citizens lived a life far removed from that of the poor pagans or Donatists or of the villages not far off, where little Latin was spoken, only Punic. No revolutionary, Augustine was dependent on the secular authorities for support of the church. As bishop, he had heavy administrative tasks in settling lawsuits and arbitrating quarrels. With a small circle of friends surrounding him, he wrote book after book, always showing his training as a classical prose stylist, as a lawyer, and as a philosopher. He corresponded at length with many who consulted him, and with Jerome, with whom he often disagreed.

But his gravest problem was posed by the Donatists, who with Old Testament fervor regarded themselves as the only true church, and who outnumbered the Catholics in Hippo. He preached against them, wrote pamphlets against them, even turned out a popular set of verses satirizing them, which was intended to be sung. Certain extremists among them (called Circumcellions), wandering bands of violent men, aroused his particular eloquence. Convinced that there could be no salvation outside the Church, Augustine persecuted the Donatists when the Christian emperors about the year 400 took severe measures to suppress paganism (itself so recently the imperial persecuting faith).

When, in the year 410, the Goths sacked Rome, refugees poured into North Africa with accounts of the fear that had gripped the inhabitants and the ruthlessness of the barbarians. Though no longer the imperial capital, Rome was still the symbol of the imperial tradition and of all ancient culture. The North African governors, worried about the stability of the province, issued an edict of toleration for the Donatists. Augustine protested. It was a time of trial for the world, of punishment and testing; the sack had been a disaster without precedent; the world was nearing its old age, like Augustine himself. But he was certain, one must not fear: youth would be renewed.

THE CITY OF GOD   In his new book, *The City of God*, carefully planned in twenty-two books, written between 413 and 425, Augustine combated the pagan argument that it was Christianity—by undermining the traditional Roman virtues and offending the gods—that had been responsible for the catastrophic sack of Rome. It was easy to show that many pagan empires had fallen in the past, and Augustine quickly moved beyond his original subject. Virtually ignoring the recent mystery religions, he attacked the core of traditional pagan worship and of pagan interpretations of Roman history, systematically demolishing—even debunking—pagan philosophy, in particular the erudite Neoplatonists who had so attracted him in earlier years. All of them were limited to earthly values, to the mere "earthly city," the *civitas terrena*.

Honest in seeking and generous in spending their wealth, the Romans had been allowed by God to acquire their great empire; but they were too eager for praise, for glory. True glory, however, belonged only to the citizens of the City of God, *civitas Dei*. Though apparently mixed together on earth, the community of those who served the devil and the demons in the earthly city would be separated in the afterlife from those who served God, the Christians, who even in this world lived in a heavenly community. As the demons took over Rome because the Romans had not submitted to the authority of Christ, so only in that heavenly city of God—when death itself should have been defeated—could the true Christian achieve true peace.

In elaborating a complete Christian philosophy of history, *The City of God* exceeded its initial purpose—which became no more than an excuse for Augustine to leave the world one of its greatest achievements of the human intellect and human spirit. When it was completed, Augustine was seventy-two.

AUGUSTINE AND PELAGIUS: FREE WILL   In the later years of his life, Augustine found himself engaged in a final philosophical controversy: with Pelagius, a British-born Christian layman, who had lived for many years in Rome, and who believed that man not only could but *must* perfect himself. He denied original sin, and believed in man's free will. Yet such an exaltation of human possibilities, highly attractive at many times in history to many men, is in its essence non-Christian, since it exalts man and diminishes God's majesty by diminishing his role.

Moreover, Pelagius' ideas instantly affected questions of Christian behavior: for example, if there was no such thing as original sin, then newborn infants could not be guilty of it, and infant baptism was unnecessary. The Pelagian message, that one must simply will oneself to obey God's commandments wholly, meant virtually that every real Christian must lead a monk's life. In Rome many rich upper-class Christians, who served the imperial regime, used judicial torture on prisoners, and led luxurious lives, regarded Pelagius' views as a summons to reform and purify themselves. They and they alone were "perfect" Christians.

Augustine fought these ideas and claims. On the practical level, he preferred to see zealous, rich, puritanical radicals give their property to the church rather than directly to the poor. On the theological level, he argued that not all sins were committed willfully or could be willfully avoided: some came through ignorance, weakness, and even against the will of the sinner. It was for these sins that the Church existed. Baptism was the only way to salvation. Once one accepts this, one can become far more tolerant of human failings, far more realistic about probable, possible human behavior than the all-or-nothing Pelagians.

For Pelagius, man was no longer an infant, dependent on his heavenly Father; he was an emancipated individual being, who could and must choose to be perfect. The idea required true stoicism. For Augustine, man was still dependent for his behavior upon God, as a nursing infant upon the breast. Human beings were not stoics, not perfect. In a controversy, hotly fought not only by written argument but also by suborning officials, by unduly influencing successive popes, and with ruthless determination, Augustine eventually won the victory.

Yet in his last years, a young and brilliant disciple of Pelagius, Julian of Eclanum, continued the controversy from a refuge in Palestine. Cleverly attacking Augustine as an African who was interfering with the church in Italy, Julian denounced the ruthless suppression of free speech and the exiling of bishops that Augustine's followers had imported from their persecution of the Donatists in Africa and had used against Pelagians in Italy. The controversy was still going strong when Augustine died in 430.

To a modern, the psychological aspects of the argument come as a fascinating surprise. Augustine defended the concept of original sin by citing the passage in Genesis in which Adam and Eve instantly cover their genitals when they have eaten of the forbidden fruit: *there* was the place, Augustine said (reminding the males of his congregation of the shame they felt at seminal emissions in their sleep), whence sin had arisen. All man's sexual feelings create guilt; only baptism and the Christian life can wipe it out. Julian answered in disgust that this imagery was blasphemous, making the devil into the creator of mankind, destroying free will, and sullying the innocence of the newborn. Sexual power, he said, was a natural good, a sixth sense; but Augustine crudely and violently repudiated this: would Julian have people jumping into bed whenever they felt the itch, have married couples not even waiting until bedtime?

Both men were devout Christians. Yet, to Julian, Augustine's God seemed a persecutor of infants and not the loving God who sacrificed his only Son for our salvation, an unjust God; whereas justice—like the fabric of the Roman law—must underlie all society and all religion. For Augustine, God's justice was indisputable but not susceptible to definition by mere human reason, not to be questioned: God had said he would visit the sins of the fathers upon the children, and so Adam's unspeakable sin had been visited upon mankind. The world of the fifth century was large enough for both points of view to be heard; but the prevalence of evil and wretchedness made it certain that Augustine's would prevail.

PREDESTINATION In his old age, Augustine came to believe, and to write, that God had already chosen those men who would attain salvation, the elect, and that men's actions were foreordained, predestined. Early African views of the Church as a group of saints helped Augustine arrive at his ideas of predestination. The conflict with Pelagius and with Julian of Eclanum—in which Augustine had been concerned to minimize man's free will, which they were maximizing—also made an important contribution. In the face of new barbarian onslaughts—this time from the Vandals—on the hitherto safe shores of North Africa itself, and in the anticipation of terror and destruction, predestination was a message with some comfort for the man aware that he had persevered in God's work: the elect would survive all earthly disaster.

When Augustine died, a year before the Vandals devastated Hippo, a disciple listing his writings said that no one man could ever hope to read them all; and yet that any man who did would still have missed the greatest experience: knowing Augustine as a human

being, or seeing him in the pulpit and listening to him preach. While the Catholic Church turned away from the doctrine of predestination—always insisting that God's grace must be supplemented by a man's good works before he could be saved, it has rightly seen in Augustine the greatest of the Western fathers of the Church. And more than a thousand years later, other non-Catholic Christians would turn again even to his teaching of predestination.

The Christian Way of Life

Although the heavenly city is a Christian's goal, his conduct and attitudes while sojourning in the earthly city are of the utmost importance. He must curb his pride and ambition, control his natural appetites, and avoid yielding too exclusively to the pull of family ties. This does not mean the annihilation of self in extreme asceticism, but rather the combination of control of self with love and kindness for others: all others, high and low. The Christian must love even the sinner, though not the sin. Nor may he, out of softness, attribute sin to environment or temporary influences; sin is *there,* and will be permanent in the earthly city. Nor may a Christian trust too fully the experiences of his senses alone, and try to explain all phenomena by reason and by naturalistic arguments. He must have faith, "the substance of things hoped for, the evidence of things unseen." He must not try to put himself in the place of God, who alone can "understand" the universe. Instead he must believe in God, for then he can feel that the universe is not the puzzling or hostile place it seems to men who do nothing but reason. Yet he must also strive to improve the world around him and the other human beings who live in it, in order to make the earthly city as nearly as possible resemble the city of God.

The Christian at his highest moments is alone with God, responsible to God alone. State, vocation, family are all distractions of this world, yet in daily living Christianity accepts and emphasizes social and family responsibility. In the true Christian life all men are one, and subsidiary groups are a distraction—or, worse, a manifestation of selfishness. The important thing is for the individual to avoid all kinds of personal triumphs over others, all competitive successes, all the things that set off and sharpen his ego. Although Christianity as a great world religion, especially in its Catholic form, has never carried this annihilation of the individual ego to an extreme, the ideal of unselfishness is there.

Christian loving-kindness, for all its affinities with gentler emotions, is also based on resignation in the face of a universe that is not to be shaped wholly by man's will. For the Christian regards sin as a fact. He may not deny the existence of sin, nor hold that, left to himself, treated permissively, the sinner will somehow cease to sin. He must forgive the truly repentant sinner, he must pity the sinner, he must indeed love the sinner. But he may not love the sinner for his sin. Above all, he may not regard sin as an illusion, nor as the result of poor physical and social environment alone, nor as the result of temporary and wholly human or physical influences. For the orthodox Christian, loving-kindness can therefore never be optimistic about the perfectibility of man, nor can it ever be pure humanitarianism.

Like all men, Christians have their five senses, through which they perceive the external universe. But for a Christian the universe so perceived is incomplete. Not even when man's senses are aided by scientific instruments of great delicacy and power can they apprehend it more than partially. God alone "understands" the whole universe: common sense, logic, science will not bring a man close to that kind of understanding. Beyond the senses, beyond intellectual activity, beyond reason there lies for a Christian the acceptance of a universe made by God for man's salvation: an acceptance and understanding that can come only through *faith,* which may at times require the submergence, even the abandonment of reason.

This helps explain why, in their concern lest the human mind try to think away the miraculous, the supernatural, the transcendental, Christian churches have at times opposed full intellectual freedom or viewed modern science with skepticism or even hostility. At the same time, a Christian must strive, in the perceived world of the senses, the real world, to be good himself, to help others to be good, and to make this imperfect world approximate as nearly as he can the perfect world that only his faith teaches him about. The Christian hopes to make things better, despite his tough awareness that the world is full of pain and injustice.

Reading Suggestions on Christianity

General Accounts

L. M. O. Duchesne, *Early History of the Christian Church,* 3 vols. (Longmans, 1912–1924). A lengthy standard account; very readable.

H. Lietzmann, *The Beginnings of the Christian Church, The Founding of the Church Universal, From Constantine to Julian,* and *The Era of the Church Fathers,* trans. B. L. Woolf (Lutterworth, 1949–1951). A learned and well-written survey of the early church.

K. Latourette, *History of Christianity* (Harper, 1953). A short survey well balanced and sympathetic.

C. Dawson, *Religion and the Rise of Western Culture* (*Image). Excellent survey to the thirteenth century.

A. C. McGiffert, *A History of Christian Thought,* vol. 1 (Scribner's, 1932). A good, brief account from a Protestant position.

H. B. Parkes, *Gods and Men: The Origins of Western Culture* (Knopf, 1959). A clear and sympathetic account with a fine reading list.

R. M. Pope, *The Church and Its Culture* (Bethany, 1965). A brief, sympathetic account, with a full bibliography.

Special Studies

F. Cumont, *The Oriental Religions in Roman Paganism* (Open Court, 1911; *Dover). A classic introduction to the general religious climate in which Christianity took root.

J. Ferguson, *The Religions of the Roman Empire* (Cornell Univ., 1970). Up to date and comprehensive.

A. D. Nock, *Early Gentile Christianity and Its Hellenistic Background* (*Torchbooks). An important essay by a great scholar with two shorter studies, of which one, "Hellenistic Mysteries and Christian Sacraments," is also a landmark.

A. Toynbee, ed., *The Crucible of Christianity* (World, 1969). Learned essays by leading scholars, including the editor, on Judaism, Hellenism, and the historical background of Christianity. Splendidly illustrated.

M. Goguel, *Jesus and the Origins of Christianity, The Birth of Christianity,* and *The Primitive Church,* trans. H. C. Snape (Allen & Unwin, 1933, 1953, and 1964). Highly scholarly studies of Christianity down to the year A.D. 150.

M. Burrows, *The Dead Sea Scrolls* (Viking, 1955). Of the many books on the subject this is perhaps the most useful for the student of general history.

E. Wilson, *Scrolls from the Dead Sea* (Oxford Univ., 1955). Readable and thought-provoking.

S. Mowinkel, *He That Cometh* (Oxford Univ., 1956). A study of the Jewish concept of the Son of man.

A. Schweitzer, *The Quest of the Historical Jesus,* new ed. (Macmillan, 1948). An excellent introduction to the question.

B. H. Streeter, *The Four Gospels* (Macmillan, 1930). By a Protestant cleric.

E. R. Goodenough, *The Church in the Roman Empire* (Holt, 1931). A brief, balanced account directed to the beginning student.

R. Bultman, *Primitive Christianity in Its Contemporary Setting,* trans. R. H. Fuller (*Meridian). An up-to-date scholarly treatment.

J. Daniélou, *The Theology of Jewish Christianity,* trans. and ed. John A. Baker (Darton, Longman & Todd, London, 1964). The fullest treatment of the subject by a great modern authority.

A. D. Nock, *St. Paul* (Oxford Univ., 1955). A classic treatment, originally published in 1938.

W. H. C. Frend, *Martyrdom and Persecution in the Early Church* (Basil Blackwell, 1965). A scholarly yet readable account with a full bibliography.

P. Brown, *Augustine of Hippo: A Biography* (*Univ. of California). A truly brilliant and learned biography, well-written, taking all modern scholarship into account, yet enthusiastic and original.

Sources

The New Testament is, of course, the best source reading. The inquisitive reader may wish to compare several versions: the Authorized version (many editions) is substantially the King James version; the Revised Standard version (Nelson, 1952) has created some unfavorable comment both from literary reviewers and from fundamentalist Protestants; a recent American edition of the Douay (Roman Catholic) version was published in 1950 (Catholic Book Publishing Company); finally, there is an American Protestant version by Smith and Goodspeed (Univ. of Chicago, 1939).

Next to the New Testament may be ranked the writings of St. Augustine—his spiritual autobiography, *The Confessions*, trans. J. F. Sheed (Sheed and Ward, 1947), and *The City of God,* trans. G. E. McCracken, 6 vols. (Harvard Univ., Loeb Classical Library).

H. S. Bettenson, ed., *Documents of the Christian Church,* 2nd ed. (Oxford Univ., 1963). An excellent collection, accompanied by enlightening summaries and editorial comments; useful not only for the early period but also for the whole history of Christianity.

P. R. Coleman-Norton, ed., *Roman State and Christian Church,* 3 vols. (S.P.C.K., 1966). Translations of the key legal documents down to 535.

The West

Early Middle Ages

I The Breakdown of Roman Civilization

The period from the collapse of the Roman Empire in the West down to about A.D. 1000 provides an outstanding example of the breakdown of a whole civilization. Historians used to call the centuries from 500 to 1000 by the name still used for the centuries between 1100 and 800 B.C.: the Dark Ages. This properly suggests a gloomy barbarian interruption between a bright classical flowering and a later bright recovery or rebirth (renaissance). But today historians prefer the more neutral term "early Middle Ages"; for they have come to believe that "dark" is a misleading exaggeration. "Middle Ages" accurately enough suggests a time lying *between* the ancient and the modern world, and the adjective "medieval"—of the middle age—is in general use.

Much of Roman civilization was lost in these years, but much, notably Christianity, was retained and developed, and many new ways of life and even new techniques were adopted and discovered. New kinds of social relationships arose, combining Roman and barbarian practices. New inventions such as deeper plowing and better drainage, the horse collar (a great improvement on the old yoke), and the seaworthy Norse ships (which could face the hazards of Atlantic navigation in a way the old Mediterranean vessels never could) marked technological advance over the ancient ways of farming and sailing. Yet, by the standards of classical civilization, the early Middle Ages by and large represented a catastrophic decline into a dark and barbarous age.

Viewed in the long perspective of world history, the barbarian conquest of the Roman Empire is no more than another instance of a mature, somewhat decadent, civilization falling to simpler peoples of primitive background. Even the centuries of the *Pax Romana* had been filled with Roman combat against the barbarians on the far side of the Rhine-Danube line. Tacitus had lectured his fellow Romans on the contrast between their own soft degeneracy and the simple toughness of the Germans. His account of the Germans is the fullest report we have on their simple tribal life before their first major breakthrough to the Roman side of the frontier, which did not take place until the fourth century. In spite of Tacitus' fears, it was apparently not so much Roman decline that opened the way to the Germans as sheer pressure on the Germans from other tribes that drove them in panic to try to cross the Roman borders, by force if necessary.

Indo-European in language, like the Greeks, the Romans, and the Celts, the Germans originated along the shores of the Baltic, both on the Continent and in Scandinavia. Very early in ancient times some of them migrated southward. When the Romans first began to write about them, they were already divided into tribes, but had no overall political unity. One group of Germanic tribes, the Goths, had settled in what we now call Romania, on the north side of the Danube boundary, and in the adjacent plains of what is now southern Russia, the Ukraine. In the fourth century, conditions in central Asia about which we still know almost nothing precipitated a fierce Asian people known as the Huns into the territory of the Goths.

Living on horseback for days, traveling swiftly, and reveling in cruelty, the Huns started a panic among the Goths and other Germanic tribes. The shock waves, beginning in the last half of the fourth century, continued throughout the fifth and into the sixth. They shattered the Roman structure in the West and left its fragments in barbarian hands. The Eastern territories suffered much less, and the imperial tradition continued uninterrupted in Constantinople.

In addition to barbarian military raids, penetrations, and conquests, there were slower and more peaceful infiltrations lasting over long periods. German laborers settled and worked on the large Roman estates, especially in Gaul. Moreover, before, during, and after

The Oseberg ship, from the early Viking period, excavated in 1904 and now in the Viking Ship Museum in Oslo.

the invasions, individual barbarians joined the Roman side, often rising to high positions and defending the old empire against their fellow barbarians. The Romanized barbarian became as familiar a figure as the barbarized Roman.

Thanks to chronicles and histories, almost all written in Latin by monks, we know a great deal about the routes of the invading bands, about their chiefs, and about the politics of the separate states they set up. But these accounts are inferior to the best Greek and Roman historical writings not only in style and in wealth of detail but in psychological insight and accuracy. Moreover, because these narratives were written by clerics, whose ideals and property suffered so much from the invaders, they almost certainly exaggerate the cruelty and destructiveness of the invasions.

We do not know how numerous the invaders were in proportion to the invaded population; we do not know to what degree the barbarians replaced peoples who were there before them; we do not know whether the total population of western Europe was greater or less under the barbarians than under the late Roman Empire. Modern research has generally tended to diminish the numerical importance of the German invaders. Clearly there were more Germans in proportion to non-Germans in Britain and Belgium, and the proportion of Germans steadily diminished south of Belgium.

But may not this German addition to the West European racial mix have been qualitatively important? Proud patriots, especially in Germany and Britain during the nineteenth and early twentieth centuries, used to argue that this "new blood" brought a youthful energy that ultimately made possible medieval and modern civilization. But nowadays we are properly more than skeptical about all such unscientific racial claims.

How complete was the breakdown of Roman civilization in the West? The loss can be seen most clearly at the level of large-scale political and economic organization. These early medieval centuries, with the brief but important interlude of Charlemagne's revived empire, just before and after the year 800, were marked by a failure in human ability to organize and administer as an effective state and society any large territory. Only the Roman Catholic church consistently asserted its authority beyond the relatively narrow limits of the medieval duchy, county, or other small unit that was coming into existence, and maintained an effective organization to which millions of human beings adhered. And even the Church was subject to grave lapses of discipline and control. Its local clergy were caught up in the web of local lay rule, and weakness and disorder appeared in its very heart at Rome.

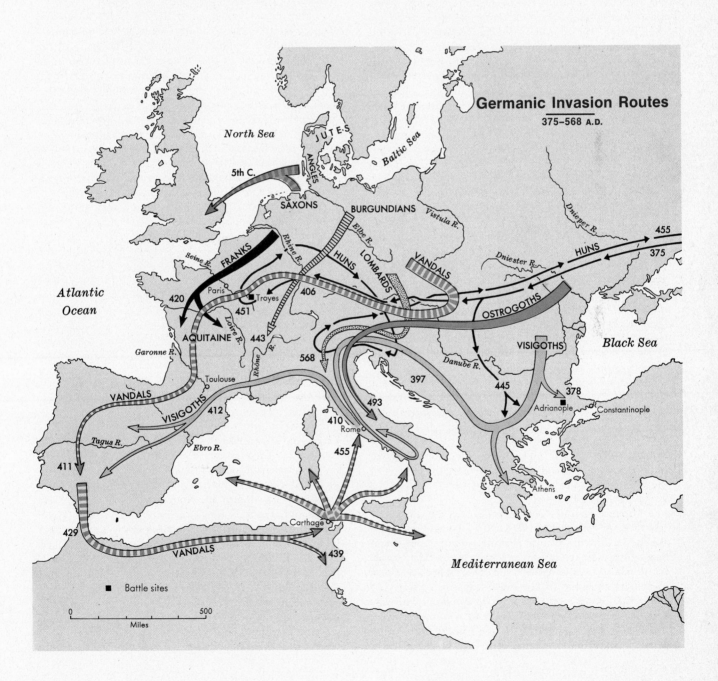

Germanic Invasion Routes
375–568 A.D.

Roads, postal systems, and communications declined from the Roman efficiency that had allowed both men and things freedom and ease of travel. Thousands of little districts came to depend on themselves for almost everything they used, and thus became relatively autarkic (self-sufficient). And these same little districts took to fighting among themselves. Some invading Germanic tribes did exercise a loose control over sizable areas, but these areas were much smaller than the old empire had been, and the control was uncertain and unsophisticated, when compared to that made possible by the complex Roman governmental machinery.

With this loss of ability to run anything big, there went a loss of discipline, a loss of morale, a loss of the older, orderly ways. Save for rare exceptions, mostly in the Church, the almost instinctive network of habits of command and obedience that keep a great, complex community together was rudely cut. Long centuries later, it had to be gradually and painfully restored.

The early Middle Ages lost command over the classical tools of scholarship and science. Spoken Latin gradually broke down into local languages—"vernaculars"—French, Italian, and Spanish in the making. Even where it survived as a learned tongue, written as well as spoken, Latin was debased and simplified. The general level of cultivated literature and philosophy was primitive. Most writers in Latin—and there were not many—were clumsy and inept imitators of the already enshrined "classics" like Cicero and Vergil. Similarly, as we shall see in detail, traditional skills in the arts underwent a profound change.

But much of ancient civilization did survive the early Middle Ages. Men could weave, farm, use horses, and make the necessary implements of peace and war quite as well in the year 1000 as in the year 100; in some ways and in some places, they could do these things better. Among churchmen there survived, in libraries, and to some degree in the education of the cleric, an admiration for and some varying familiarity with the classics. The barbarian chiefs so admired the Rome they were destroying that they retained an almost superstitious reverence for its laws and institutions even if they understood them only faintly and in part. As we shall see, the most striking political event of the early Middle Ages is the actual revival in the West, under Germanic kings, of the title and the claims of the Roman Empire.

Visigoths, Vandals, Anglo-Saxons

When the fourth-century Hunnic push against them began, one tribe of Goths, the Visigoths, or West Goths, petitioned to be allowed to cross the Danube and settle in Roman territory, on the south bank, in present-day Bulgaria. The Roman border guards took cruel advantage of their fear and hunger; and soon there were many desperate Goths milling about only a few miles from Constantinople. In the year 378, at Adrianople,

the mounted Goths defeated the Roman legions of the Eastern emperor Valens, who was killed in battle. More and more Goths now freely entered the empire. Unable to take Constantinople or other fortified towns, they proceeded south into the Balkans, under their chieftain, Alaric, ravaged Greece, including Athens, and then marched north again around the head of the Adriatic and south into Italy. In 410, Alaric and his Goths sacked Rome itself, an event that made a staggering impression on the inhabitants of the empire. Pagan and Christian blamed each other for the disaster, and, as we know, it inspired Augustine to write his *City of God.* Alaric died soon afterward, and his successors led the Visigoths north across the Alps into Gaul, and then south again across the Pyrenees into Spain.

Here, in the westernmost reaches of the continental Roman Empire, the Visigoths, after their long wanderings, founded a Spanish kingdom that lasted until the Muslim invasions of the seventh century. In southern Gaul they had a large area (Aquitaine) given them by the Western Roman emperor Honorius (ruled 395–423), into whose family their king married; but this area they would lose in less than a century to a rival German tribe, the Franks. Since the Visigoths were Arians, they had some difficulty in ruling the orthodox Christians among their subjects.

Almost simultaneously with the Visigothic migration, another Germanic people, the Vandals, still resident in Germany, crossed the Rhine westward into Gaul and moved southward into southern Spain, where they settled in 411. The Roman governor of North Africa made the mistake of inviting them across the straits to help him in a struggle against his Roman masters. The Vandals came in 429, but soon seized North Africa for themselves. They moved eastward across modern Morocco and Algeria—partly destroying Augustine's bishopric at Hippo—and established their capital at Carthage (Tunis). Here they built a fleet and raided the shores of Sicily and Italy, finally sacking Rome (455) in a raid that has made the word *vandalism* synonymous to this day with destruction of property. Like the Visigoths, the Vandals were Arian, and they, too, often persecuted the orthodox. They held on in North Africa until the 530s, when the Eastern emperor Justinian put an end to their state.

Under pressure on the Continent, the Romans early in the fifth century began to withdraw their legions from Britain. As they left, Germanic tribes from across the North Sea in what are now northern Germany and Denmark began to filter into Britain. These Angles, Saxons, and Jutes, coming from an area that had undergone little Roman influence, were still heathen. In England they gradually established their authority over the Celtic Britons, many of whom survived as a subject class. The barbarians soon founded seven Anglo-Saxon kingdoms, of which Northumbria, Mercia, and Wessex successively became the most important. Scotland and Wales remained Celtic, as of course did Ireland, which was in large measure converted to Christianity in the fifth century by Catholic missionaries from Gaul, led by Saint Patrick.

Ireland escaped the first great wave of barbarian invasions, and its Celtic church promoted learning, poetry, and the illustration of manuscripts by paintings. By the end of the sixth century Catholic Christianity was moving into England both from Celtic Ireland and from Rome. "Celtic Christianity" developed several practices that differed from those of the Roman church, notably in the method of determining the date of Easter. In Britain heated disputes over these questions were eventually settled by the Synod of Whitby (664). Irish monasticism became so strong that many Irish monks and scholars moved out of Ireland as missionaries to convert the heathen on the Continent too. Columban, for example, born in Leinster, headed missions from the Low Countries up the Rhine to Switzerland and even into Italy in the seventh century.

Huns, Ostrogoths

Not only the Germanic peoples but the Asian Huns themselves participated in the onslaught on Roman territories. Emerging into Europe from the East early in the fifth century, the Huns soon conquered what we call Romania, Hungary, and parts of Yugoslavia, Poland, and Czechoslovakia. Under their domination lived a large collection of German tribes. The Hunnic rulers extracted tribute-money from the Roman emperors of the East at Constantinople. Under their ruler Attila, the Huns pressed westward, crossed the Rhine, and met with defeat in Gaul in 451 (Châlons) at the hands of a Roman general. Pope Leo the Great persuaded Attila to withdraw from Italy without attacking Rome.

Like many nomad empires, that of the Huns in central Europe fell apart after the death of the conquering founder (452). A plague decimated their ranks, and many withdrew into Asia once more. But other related Asian peoples, nomads and pagans like the Huns, and like them Mongol in appearance, entered Europe before the age of the barbarian invasions was over: Avars in the sixth century, Bulgars in the sixth and seventh, and Magyars or Hungarians in the ninth. The Magyars eventually set up a lasting state in the Danubian plain, and their europeanized descendants still inhabit modern Hungary. As the first Asian invaders, the Huns had not only touched off the invasions of the terrified Germanic tribes but had directly helped to smash Roman influence in central Europe.

Among the German tribes liberated by the collapse of the Hunnic empire, the first to make a major impact were the Ostrogoths (East Goths). They moved into the general disorder left in Italy after the last of the Western emperors, Romulus Augustulus (the little Augustus), had been dethroned by his barbarian protector Odovacar in 476, a date often used by historians to mark the "end" of the Roman Empire in the West. Actually, like his immediate predecessors, Romulus Augustulus

had been an ineffectual tool of the nearest barbarian general who could command loyal troops. Roman imperial power, however, continued uninterrupted in the East. In fact, it had been the Eastern emperor Zeno in Constantinople who had hired the Ostrogoths to intervene in Italy on his behalf against Odovacar.

The leader of the Ostrogoths, Theodoric, who had been educated in Constantinople, admired both Greek civilization and the Roman Empire as an institution. For most of his long rule in Italy (489–526) he was content to serve as nominal subordinate to Emperor Zeno and his successors in the East, as a kind of governor of Italy. Theodoric was also king of his own Gothic people, and established his capital at Ravenna. Like many other christianized German tribes, the Ostrogoths were Arian. In the eyes of the popes and of the Italians, they were therefore heretics as well as German foreigners. Although Theodoric hoped to impose upon his Germanic subjects the civilization of the Roman Empire, he did not have enough time to bring about any real assimilation. Moreover, toward the end of his reign, Theodoric, who had made dynastic marriages with the Vandal and other Germanic ruling houses, became suspicious of the empire and planned to go to war against Constantinople, but died before he could do so.

Many other barbarian peoples participated in the breakup of Roman territory and power in the West during the fifth and sixth centuries, but failed to found any lasting state. They remain mere tribal names: Sciri, Suevi, Alamanni—the German forests seem to have had an inexhaustible supply of them. There were two other German tribes, however, whose achievements we still remember: the Burgundians, who moved into the valleys of the Rhone and Saône rivers in Gaul in the 440s and gave their name to a succession of "Burgundies," varying in territory and government, and the Franks—most important of all—from whom modern France itself derives its name.

II The Franks:
The Building of an Empire

Destined to found the most lasting political entity of any of the Germanic tribes, the Franks appeared first as dwellers along the lower Rhine. They engaged in no long migrations, but simply expanded gradually west and south from their native territory until eventually they were to create an empire that would include most of western Europe except for the Iberian peninsula and the British Isles. Clovis (reigned 481–511), descendant of the house of Merwig or Merovech, called Merovingian, was the founder of Frankish power. Moving into Gaul, he defeated successively a Roman army (486), the Alamanni (496), and the Visigoths of Aquitaine (at the battle of Vouillé, 507). Large areas of modern France, northwest Germany, and the Low Countries were now Frankish.

The most important factor in Clovis' success, aside

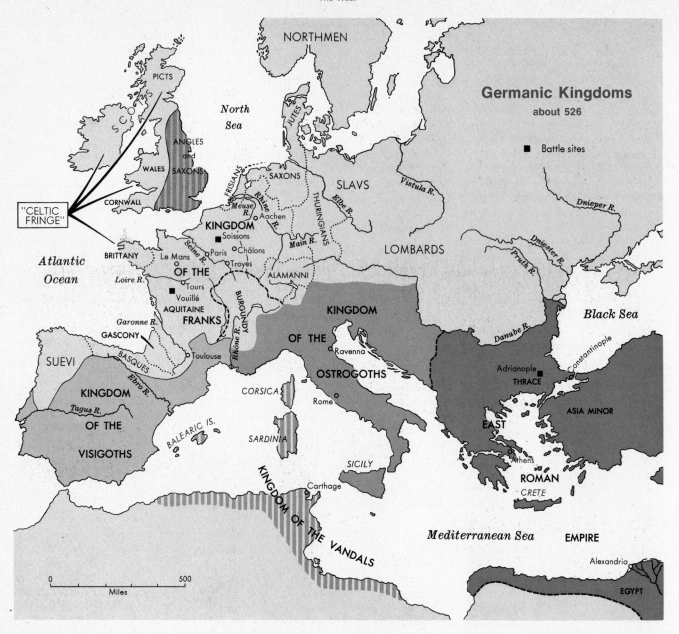

Germanic Kingdoms
about 526

■ Battle sites

from his skill as a general, was his conversion to Christianity, not as an Arian heretic but as an orthodox Catholic. This gave him the instant support of the clergy of Gaul, especially of the powerful bishops of Aquitaine, who welcomed the Franks as a relief from the Arian Visigoths. Probably the greatest liability of the Franks was their habit of dividing up the kingdom between the king's sons in every generation. This meant not only a constant parceling out of territory into petty kingdoms and lordships but constant secret intrigues and bloody rivalries among brothers and cousins and other relatives who strove to reunite the lands. Indeed, Merovingian history forms one of the most sordid and savage chapters in the whole record of Western society.

According to the sixth-century historian Gregory

of Tours, King Chilperic, Clovis' grandson, married the wicked Fredegund, who stopped at nothing to achieve her ambitions. She sent her husband's son by an earlier marriage into a plague-infested region in the hope of killing him off, and when that failed she stabbed him. Next, she sent an assassin to kill her sister-in-law, Brunnhild, and when the assassin returned unsuccessful, Fredegund had his hands and feet cut off. Finally, she turned against her own daughter, and lured her into reaching her arm into a chest full of "necklets and precious ornaments." Fredegund

seized the lid and forced it down upon her neck. She bore upon it with all her strength, until the edge of the chest beneath pressed the girl's throat so hard that her eyes

Egypt

We have all seen pictures of Egyptian pyramids and temples, gigantic sculptured pharaohs and divinities, and the rich and ostentatious gold and jewels of a splendid sepulcher like King Tut's. The use of stone in building, the skillful use of great spaces, the skillful portraiture of individuals rather than types, the obelisks and sphinxes, the absence of perspective: these are familiar characteristics of Egyptian art. Less well known are the many scenes of ordinary country or family life that show a characteristic enjoyment and even a sense of humor distinctly not found in other early civilizations. Within an Egyptian tomb were placed many objects from daily life: a boxwood chair, a gameboard. On the walls of the tombs men spear fish and snare birds; a young man and his wife sit happily playing checkers or listening to music or watching the dancing girls. The people who lived along the Nile all those millennia ago speak to us clearly, and we listen with fascination and recognition.

Boxwood and acacia chair from the tomb of Ramose, Thebes. The household god Bes is depicted between symbols of stability and protection.
The Metropolitan Museum of Art, Rogers Fund, 1936.

Limestone Statue of Queen Hat-shepsut. From the temple of Hat-shepsut, Thebes, Deir el Bahri.
The Metropolitan Museum of Art, Rogers Fund and contribution of Edward S. Harkness, 1929.

The Angel of the Four Winds: a ceiling panel in the Church of St. Martin,
Zillis, Switzerland, ca. 1350.

European Art Color, Peter Adelberg, N.Y.C.

seemed about to start from her head. . . . The attendants outside . . . broke into the small chamber, and brought out the girl, whom they thus delivered from imminent death.*

By the end of the seventh century, the Merovingian kings themselves became so degenerate that they are known as *rois fainéants* (do-nothing kings). They delegated real power to their chief officials, the "mayors of the palace," a title showing the close connection between the household service of the monarch and the actual government. By the eighth century one particular family had made this office hereditary from father to son—the Carolingians (from *Carolus*, Latin for *Charles*). One of the mayors, Charles (ruled 714–741), called Martel, "the hammer," organized the Frankish nobles into a dependable cavalry and in 732 near Tours defeated a roving band of Muslims that had been raiding northward from Spain. There was no real danger that the Muslims would conquer Frankish territory, yet since Tours was the farthest north in Europe that the Muslims ever came, the battle is a landmark in Western history. Charles Martel's son, Pepin the Short (ruled 741–768), assumed the title of King of the Franks and consolidated the kingdom once again. Pepin's adventurous policy with regard to Italy initiated a whole new chapter in Western history.

Italy from Theodoric to Pepin

Soon after the death of Theodoric, the great Eastern emperor Justinian (ruled 527–565—see Chapter 6) launched from Constantinople an ambitious effort to reconquer the major areas of the West that had been lost to the barbarians. The imperial forces first tackled the Vandals of North Africa, and then, before consolidating their successes, invaded Italy from Carthage, via Sicily. For almost twenty years (535–554) increasingly savage and destructive warfare ravaged the peninsula. The towns and countryside were left depopulated, and the survivors reduced to misery. So Justinian's proclamation of an imperial restoration (554) was hollow indeed. In the same year imperial forces took back a portion of southern Spain from the Visigoths.

But only three years after Justinian's death, a new Germanic tribe, the Arian Lombards, entered Italy (568) from the north. They easily conquered the north Italian plain that still bears their name (Lombardy) and established a kingdom with its capital at Pavia. Further to the south, they set up two duchies (Benevento and Spoleto). Italy lay once again in fragments.

Still under imperial domination were Ravenna and the territory surrounding it, the island settlement of Venice, Rome, Naples, and the toe and heel of the peninsula, as well as Sicily. The emperor at Constantinople appointed a governor called the exarch, who had his headquarters at Ravenna and was particularly charged with organizing the defense of Italy.

*Gregory of Tours, *History of the Franks*, ed. O. M. Dalton (Oxford, 1927), Book IX, 34.

But Constantinople was far away; dangers threatened the emperors from the East, and they often could not afford to pay much attention to Italy's needs or send money and troops to help the exarchs to fight the Lombards. In this situation the Church emerged more and more as the protector of the Catholic population; the bishops often received privileges from the Arian Lombard conquerors that conferred upon them virtual governing rights in the towns. Among the bishops, the pope of course took the lead, and, among the popes, the most remarkable in every way was Gregory I, the Great (reigned 590–604).

Child of a rich and aristocratic Roman family, Gregory abandoned worldly things and became a monk and founder of monasteries. His administrative talents were extraordinary: he served as papal ambassador to the Roman imperial court at Constantinople before becoming pope in 590. Besides his religious duties, he had to take virtually full responsibility for maintaining the fortifications of Rome, for feeding its population, for managing the great financial resources of the Church and its lands in Italy, for conducting diplomatic negotiations with exarchate and Lombards, and even for directing military operations. It was he who sent the mission to Britain (596) that began the papal contribution to the conversion of the Anglo-Saxons. Gregory had an exalted conception of papal power, and he stoutly defended its supremacy over the Church in his letters to the emperor and to the patriarch at Constantinople.

During the seventh and early eighth centuries, the alienation between the empire in the East and the papacy was greatly increased by religious disagreements and a related political and economic dispute (see Chapter 6). And simultaneously, the Lombards gradually consolidated and expanded their power, taking Ravenna in 751 and putting an end to the exarchate. Menaced by the Lombards and unable to count on help from Constantinople, Pope Stephen II in 753 paid a visit to King Pepin of the Franks.

Pepin was unsure of his position, being only a descendant of a line of Mayors of the Palace for the Merovingians. So, in exchange for papal approval of his new title of king, he attacked the Lombards and forced them to abandon Ravenna and other recent conquests. Then, although these lands did not truly belong to him, he gave a portion of them to the pope, as the celebrated Donation of Pepin. Together with Rome itself and the lands immediately around it, the Donation of Pepin formed the territory over which the pope ruled as temporal sovereign down to the nineteenth century. These were the Papal States, and Vatican city is their present-day remnant. Pepin's son, Charles the Great (Charlemagne), completed the destruction of the Lombard kingdom in 774.

The new alliance with the Franks marked the end of papal dependence upon the empire at Constantinople and the beginning of the papacy as a territorial power. The Franks, too busy to take over these Italian lands themselves and no doubt also aware of the pious responsibilities that they had acquired when they became the protectors of the Church, did not try to dictate to the popes. Soon after Pepin's donation, the clerks of the papal chancery forged "proof" that Pepin had only been confirming a gift of lands to the Church made long ago by the emperor Constantine. The forgery (the so-called Donation of Constantine) stated, in addition, that Constantine had directly declared that:

> inasmuch as our imperial power is earthly, we have decreed that it shall venerate and honor his most holy Roman Church and that the sacred see of blessed Peter shall be gloriously exalted above our empire and earthly throne. We attribute to him the power and glorious dignity and strength and honor of the Empire, and we ordain and decree that he shall have rule as well over the four principal sees, Antioch, Alexandria, Constantinople, and Jerusalem, as also over all the churches of God in all the world. And the

pontiff who for the time being presides over that most holy Roman Church shall be the highest and chief of all priests in the whole world, and according to his decision shall all matters be settled which shall be taken in hand for the service of God or the confirmation of the faith of Christians.*

For about seven hundred years, until the Italian Renaissance scholar Lorenzo Valla proved it a forgery, men believed this extraordinary document to be genuine.

Charlemagne and the Revival of Empire

Pepin's son Charlemagne (Charles the Great, reigned 771–814)—so Einhard, his contemporary biographer,

*Documents of the Christian Church, ed. Henry Bettenson (New York, 1947), p. 140.

A thirteenth-century fresco, depicting the Donation of Constantine.

tells us—was a vigorous, lusty, intelligent man who loved hunting, women, and war. All his life he wore Frankish costume and thought of himself as a Frankish chieftain. Although he could read, and kept pen and ink under his pillow, he could never teach himself how to write. He spoke Latin, however, and understood some Greek. A great conqueror, Charlemagne turned his armies east and crossed the Rhine. In campaigns lasting more than thirty years, he conquered the heathen Saxons, living south of Denmark, and converted them at sword's point to Christianity. Monks and priests followed his armies.

Charlemagne thus made the first successful invasion of Germany. Only then did this spawning ground of the barbarians who had shattered Roman society in the West begin the long, slow process of assimilation to Western civilization. In addition to the lands of the Saxons, Charlemagne added to his domain the western areas of modern Czechoslovakia (Bohemia), much of Austria, and portions of Hungary and Yugoslavia. The eastern boundaries of his realm reached the Elbe River in the north and the Danube, where it turns sharply south below Vienna. Along these wild eastern frontiers he established provinces (marks or marches). His advance into eastern Europe brought him victories also over the Asian Avars, successors to the Huns along the lower Danube. Far to the west, Charlemagne challenged Muslim power in Spain and set up a Spanish march in what is today Catalonia. A defeat of his rear guard at the pass of Roncesvalles in the Pyrenees Mountains in 778—though only a skirmish—formed the theme of the heroic epic *The Song of Roland* (*Le Chanson de Roland*), which in its surviving form was composed several centuries later.

By the end of the eighth century, Charlemagne had reunited under Frankish rule all of the western Roman provinces except for Britain, most of Spain, southern Italy, Sicily, and North Africa, and had added to his domains central and eastern European areas which the Romans had never possessed. On Christmas Day, 800, the pope himself, Leo III, crowned Charlemagne emperor in Rome. So mighty was the tradition of Roman Empire and so great its hold on the minds of men that, more than three centuries after the disappearance of Romulus Augustulus, last of the Western emperors, the chief bishop of the Christian church, seeking to honor and recognize his mighty Frankish patron, automatically crowned him "Roman" emperor. Even before the coronation, a poet in Charlemagne's own circle had hailed him as "Augustus." Indeed, Einhard modeled his biography of his imperial master so closely upon Suetonius' famous biography of Augustus that a modern reader has to be careful in its use.

It is quite possible that Charlemagne himself was surprised and not altogether pleased by the coronation; he probably relished his title, but he almost surely disliked the role played by the pope and the implication that the pope had the right to choose and crown emperors. The Roman emperors at Constantinople were horrified at the insolence of the barbarian Charlemagne in assuming the sacred title.

Within his territories, Charlemagne was, by virtue of his consecration, a sacred ruler, with spiritual rights and duties as well as temporal ones. His lofty concept of his office and his personal power enabled him to influence the Church—even in matters of doctrine—more like Constantine or other Eastern emperors than any other Western monarch. He himself named Louis the Pious, by then his only living son, his successor in 813; the pope had no part in the ceremonies.

Charlemagne's government was very simple. Had not all but one of his sons died before him he would have divided the kingdom in the standard Frankish way. His personal household staff were also the government officials: the chamberlain, the count of the stable (constable), and so on. On major decisions the emperor conferred with great nobles of state and church, but he told them what he (and they) were going to do

This restored eighth-century mosaic from St. John Lateran shows Saint Peter conferring symbols of spiritual authority and temporal power on Pope Leo III and Charlemagne.

rather than asking them for advice and permission. Since the Franks, like other Germans, believed that law *existed* and could not be made by men, even Charlemagne could not in theory legislate. But he did issue instructions to his subjects, divided into subheadings or chapters (and therefore called *capitularies*), which usually dealt with special administrative problems. It was a highly personal rule. Einhard says about it:

> When he had taken the imperial title he noticed many defects in the legal systems of his people; for the Franks have two legal systems, differing in many points very widely from one another, and he therefore determined to add what was lacking, to reconcile the differences, and to amend anything that was wrong or wrongly expressed. He completed nothing of all his designs beyond adding a few capitularies, and those unfinished. But he gave orders that the laws and rules of all nations comprised within his domains which were not already written out should be collected and committed to writing.
>
> He also wrote out the barbarous and ancient songs, in which the acts of the kings and their wars were sung, and committed them to memory. He also began a grammar of his native language.*

Early Lives of Charlemagne, ed. A. J. Grant (London, 1922), pp. 44–45.

Detail of a fourteenth-century reliquary bust of Charlemagne.

Since Einhard also tells us that Charlemagne himself could not write, we know that this passage must mean that Charlemagne did not do this writing himself but ordered it to be done.

Charlemagne's territories included about three hundred counties, each governed by a count. The counties that lay in former Roman territory each corresponded to the lands of a former Roman *civitas.* The count had to maintain order, render justice, and recruit and command soldiers. Alongside the count, the bishop of the diocese and the various local magnates might have considerable powers of their own on their own lands. Only a powerful king could keep the local authorities from arrogating too much power to themselves. Charlemagne required his counts to appoint teams of judges, called *scabini,* whose appointment he would then ratify, and who would actually take over much of the counts' role in rendering justice. He also sent out from his own central administrative staff pairs of royal emissaries (the *missi dominici,* literally "the lord's messengers"), usually a layman and a cleric, to investigate local conditions and correct abuses. As representatives of the emperor, they could overrule the count.

The Carolingian empire depended heavily upon Charlemagne personally. He had assembled more territory than could any longer be effectively governed, in view of the degeneration of administrative machinery and of communications since Roman days. Under his less talented successors, the old Frankish habit of dividing lands and authority among the heirs to the throne reasserted itself. Quarrels over the allotment of territory raged among brothers and cousins. The title of emperor descended to a single heir in each generation, but as early as the middle of the ninth century it had become an empty honor.

Thus Charlemagne's achievement was short-lived if brilliant. Historians have taken differing views of it; some have emphasized its brevity and denied its lasting influence. Others have stressed its brilliance and declared that the mere resurrection of the Roman imperial title in the West helped determine the future direction of European political action: the next time a new revival began, men instinctively launched it by resuscitating the Roman Empire once again. But these historians add that, as events turned out, this title lured later generations of German rulers over the Alps into Italy in search of an illusory honor, prevented them from forging Germany into a national unity, and so kept Italy and Germany tied together in an utterly unnatural relationship that helps explain why neither became a nation until the nineteenth century.

Some insist that Charlemagne's revival of the imperial title kept alive, even though in a tenuous and almost unreal form, at least the ideal of a unified Christian Western society, not merely a collection of parochial states devoted to cutthroat competition. Others maintain that, thanks to Charlemagne's act, a lay

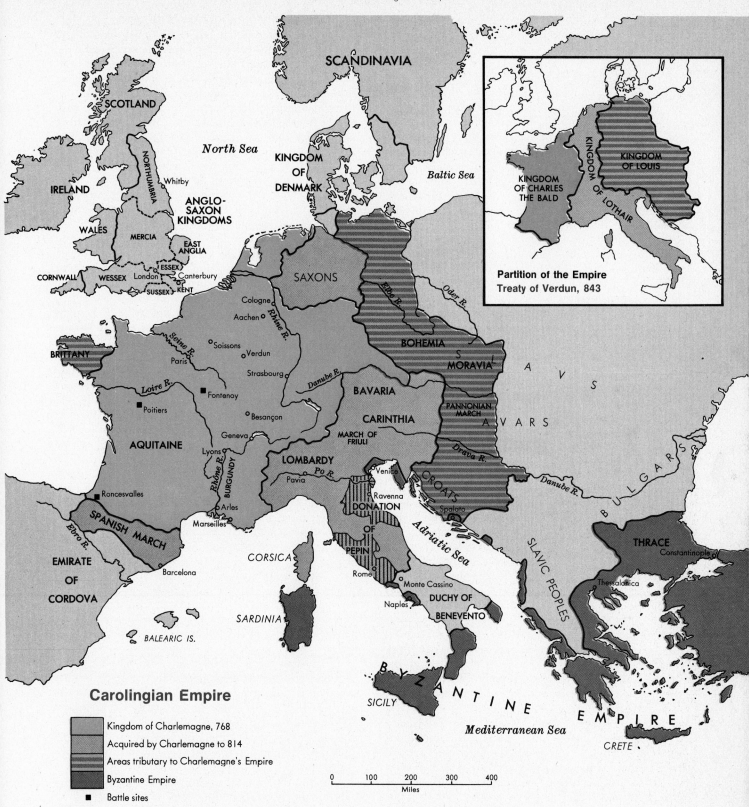

Partition of the Empire
Treaty of Verdun, 843

Carolingian Empire

- Kingdom of Charlemagne, 768
- Acquired by Charlemagne to 814
- Areas tributary to Charlemagne's Empire
- Byzantine Empire
- ■ Battle sites

power with universal or at least pan-Western temporal aspirations was able through the medieval centuries to oppose the temporal claims of a spiritual power, the papacy; and, of course, a spiritual power well anchored in Italy could oppose the temporal power. The existence of these two claimants to supreme power, the pope and the emperor, saved the West from the extremes of lay domination of religion on the one hand and religious domination of the state on the other. This rivalry and tension—they argue—helped promote such typically Western institutions and attitudes as individual rights, the rule of law, and the dignity of man.

All of this lies in the realm of political theory and speculation and of course none of it can be "proved." Nevertheless, it is clear that the revival of the old Roman imperial idea is one of the great threads that run through all subsequent European history. With Charlemagne the "Roman" empire became in fact largely a German one, but there always remained about the very name "empire" some suggestion of a common political order within which war was somehow "unnatural," not right. In this sense, the medieval empire, reinforced by the concept of Christendom, serves as a link between Roman unity and all later dreams of unity. And apart from political theorizing, all students of the intellectual and artistic revival in the time of Charlemagne and his successors would agree that the period provided a dazzling flash of light after centuries that had indeed been relatively dark.

In the struggle among Charlemagne's grandsons, one episode deserves special notice: the Strasbourg Oaths of 842. Two of the grandsons, Charles the Bald, who held the Western regions, and Louis the German, who held the Eastern regions, swore an alliance against their brother, the emperor Lothair, whose lands lay between theirs. Each swore in the language of the other's troops: Louis in a Latin-like language on its way to becoming French, which scholars call Romance, and Charles in Germanic. Of course this does not mean that there was a France or a Germany in 842: only that the western and eastern Frankish lands spoke divergent tongues. But the symbolism is a striking sign of things to come in European history. Charles and Louis could hardly have chosen a more appropriate place than Strasbourg—chief city of Alsace, in the heart of the middle zone, long a bone of contention between modern France and Germany—to swear their bilingual oath. In the ninth century, however, there were as yet no national states in Europe. Indeed, instead of coalescing into large national units, the Frankish dominions were even then in the process of breaking up into much smaller ones. As the power of the central Frankish state was frittered away in family squabbles, smaller entities, duchies or counties, emerged as virtually autonomous units of government, many with names we still recognize as belonging to provinces of modern France or Germany: Champagne, Brittany, Saxony, Bavaria.

III After Charlemagne: The Northmen

Charlemagne's conquests in Germany had for the first time brought into the area of Western civilization the breeding ground of many of the barbarians. Still outside lay Scandinavia, from whose shores there began in the ninth century a new wave of invasions that hit Britain and the western parts of the Frankish lands with savage force. The Northmen conducted their raids from small ships that could easily sail up the Thames, the Seine, or the Loire. Their appetite for booty grew with their successes, and soon they organized fleets of several hundred ships, ventured farther abroad, and often wintered along a conquered coast. They ranged as far south as Spain, penetrated into the Mediterranean through the Straits of Gibraltar, and raided Italy. To the west they proceeded far beyond Ireland, and reached Iceland and Greenland. Later on, some almost certainly landed in Newfoundland, Labrador, or even New England, although some scholars still question the validity of the evidence we have for this.

The longing for booty may not by itself account for the Norse expansions. Polygamy was common among the upper classes of the pagan Scandinavians (the lower ones could not afford it), and it is probable that the younger sons of these Viking chiefs either had to leave home or stop living in the style to which they had grown accustomed. This possible cause for the Norse expansion is suggested by the fact that even after the Vikings had conquered their first European base of settlement, the younger sons continued to go abroad to plunder and to settle.

The Norsemen's first captured base was the region along the lower Seine River, which is still called Normandy after them. In 911, the Frankish king was forced to grant the Norse leader Rolf (or Rollo) a permanent right of settlement. The Normans became an efficient and powerful ruling class—in fact, the best administrators of the new "feudal" age. From Normandy soon after the year 1000 younger sons would go off to found a flourishing state in the southern Italian and Sicilian territories that still belonged to the Eastern Roman Empire. And from Normandy in 1066, as we shall see, Duke William and his followers would conquer England.

Kinsmen of these Norsemen who had settled in Normandy also did great deeds. In the 860s the first wave of Viking invaders crossed the Baltic Sea to the territory that is now Russia and penetrated deep inland to the south along the river valleys. They conquered the indigenous Slavic tribes and, at Kiev on the middle Dnieper, consolidated the first Russian state (see Chapter 6).

While the Normans were raiding and developing Normandy, other Scandinavians were almost paralleling their achievements in the British Isles. In Ireland the Northmen were soon firmly established, especially in the ports of Dublin and Waterford, and in the Shannon River port of Limerick. But in the interior, the Celtic chieftains held on. In 1014, under the leadership of Brian of Munster, these chieftains won the battle of Clontarf against the Northmen and their native allies. Finally, the Northmen were absorbed into the texture of Irish society. But the two centuries of struggle had provided a fatal interruption in the brilliant development of Irish civilization, and thereafter tribal warfare was to reign unchecked until the English invasion of the twelfth century.

The Anglo-Saxon Kingdoms and the Danes

In England, savage Danish attacks on the northern and eastern shores soon led to settlement. The chief organizer of defense against the Danes was the Anglo-Saxon kingdom of Wessex under Alfred the Great (ruled 871–899). Although Alfred defeated the Danes, he was not strong enough to expel them, and he had to concede the whole northeast of England to them, a region thereafter called the Danelaw. By the mid-tenth century, Alfred's successors had reunited the Danelaw to Wessex, whose royal family ruled over all England.

Soon after the turn of the eleventh century, new waves of Danes scored important successes under the command of Canute (Knut), the king of Denmark. In 1017 Canute was chosen king of England by the Anglo-Saxon *witenagemot,* a council of wise men. Able ruler of a kind of northern empire (he was also king of Norway), Canute allied himself with the Roman church, and brought Scandinavia into the Christian community. His early death (1035) without competent heirs led to the breakup of his holdings, and England reverted to a king of the house of Alfred (Edward the Confessor).

Like the Carolingian monarch, the Anglo-Saxon king was crowned and anointed with holy oil, and ruled by the grace of God and as his deputy on earth, with corresponding responsibility for church as well as state. His revenue came in part from an ancient practice, the *feorm*—originally a tax on food levied for the support of the monarch and his household as they moved about England, but by the time of Edward the Confessor it was often paid in money. In addition, there was the Danegeld, a war tax on land first levied in 991 to bribe the Danes, which continued to be regularly collected long after its original purpose was unnecessary. The king also had income from his own estates and from fines levied in court cases. His subjects were required to work on the building and repair of bridges and defense works, and had to render military service in the *fyrd,* the ancient Germanic army.

The Anglo-Saxon king was the guarantor of law, and serious crimes were considered to be offenses against him as well as against the victims. And he was a lawgiver, like the Carolingian monarch. His great council of wise men (*witenagemot*) made up of important landholders, churchmen, and officials, advised him when asked on major questions of policy (war, taxes, new laws) and sometimes acted as a court to try important cases. It played a major role in the election and deposition of kings. In the king's personal household staff, which moved with him and did his business from day to day, lay the origin of future specialized governmental departments. The Anglo-Saxon monarchy resembled the Carolingian, but it flourished while that of the Carolingians declined.

Carolingian Decline: The Saxon Empire

By the end of the ninth century, the power of the Carolingians in their German territories had almost disappeared in the face of domestic challenge by ambitious local magnates and foreign threats from Norsemen, Slavs, and the Asian Magyars, who poured into the Hungarian plain in the mid-890s. Their predecessors, the Huns and Avars, had vanished, but the Magyars stayed, forming the nucleus of a Hungarian state. The Hungarian language thus remains today the only non-Indo-European tongue in Europe except Finnish and Basque.

When the last nominal Carolingian ruler, Louis the Child, died in 911, the German magnates elected the duke of Franconia as King Conrad I (reigned 911–918). The most important units in Germany were now the duchies—Franconia, Saxony, Swabia, and Bavaria—each under its autonomous ruler. Conrad I failed to control either the other dukes or the Magyars, and finally nominated his strongest enemy, Henry, duke of Saxony, to succeed him. Henry's son, Otto I (936–973), both checked the rival dukes and, at the Battle of Lechfeld, 955, defeated the Magyars.

Master of his German territories, the Saxon Otto next sought to revive Charlemagne's title of Roman emperor, which had passed from one shadowy Carolingian prince to another until it lapsed in 924. Deep in decline after the reign of the great pope Nicholas I (858–867), the papacy had fallen into the hands of rival Roman noble families, corrupt and ineffectual. Without strong central administration and under a two-pronged attack from Muslims and Magyars, Italy had become anarchic. Yet Rome, even at its lowest depths in the mid-tenth century, continued to act as an irresistible magnet for those seeking supreme power. Like Charlemagne almost two hundred years before him, Otto went to Italy. He had himself crowned emperor by the degenerate Pope John XII (962), and then had John deposed for murder and installed his own candidate on the papal throne. He forced the Roman aristocracy to promise that imperial consent would hereafter be necessary to papal elections, and he renewed the Donation of Pepin and the subsequent grants of the Carolingians to the papacy. Though the

A French manuscript illumination of the eleventh century, showing Otto I receiving the homage of the nations.

king who was feebler than his great supporters; Germany was divided into duchies, one of which—Saxony—had asserted its supremacy and claimed the old imperial title; and Italy still remained anarchic, although a revived papacy had begun to emerge. Out of the debris of the Roman Empire, buffeted by two successive waves of barbarian invasions and held together only by their common Christian faith, these major fragments had begun to take on, even as early as this, certain features that we can still recognize today. Elsewhere, the Scandinavian kingdoms had imposed order on the turbulent peoples who had made the Viking expansion, and the little Christian kingdoms in the north of Spain were only beginning their struggle with the Muslim tide that had engulfed the peninsula (see Chapter 6).

In the East, the empire, with its direct descent from Rome and its Greco-oriental character, still stood firm at Constantinople after many shocks. It had started its work of christianizing those Slavic peoples nearest to it—the Bulgarians, the Russians, the Serbs. The western Slavs—Czechs, Poles, Croats, and others—and the Magyars, lying between the Germans and the influences radiating from Constantinople, had received the attention of Roman missionaries. By the year 1000 there was already visible a fateful line of demarcation between the Western Catholic world and the Eastern Orthodox world, with its different alphabet and its different outlook.

papacy for the next hundred years was hardly more than an instrument manipulated by Otto's German successors, Otto's action eventually ensured the continuity of the papacy as an independent institution; it also tightly linked the political fortunes of Germany and Italy for centuries to come.

In the western Carolingian lands, which we may now call France, partitioning, strife, and feebleness led to the fragmentation of both territory and power among ambitious landowners. As early as 887 one faction of these magnates chose a non-Carolingian, Odo, count of Paris, as king, and civil war between him and the Carolingian claimant added to the chaos. For the next century the families of the two rivals alternated in power. Finally, in 987 the magnates elected as king a descendant of the early count of Paris, Hugh Capet. Though several of the nobles who chose Hugh were actually more powerful than he, he founded the dynasty that lasted almost to our own time. (When Louis XVI went to the guillotine in 1793, his executioners called him "Citizen Capet.")

Europe about 1000

About the year 1000, then, England was a centralized monarchy; France was nominally ruled by an elected

IV Feudal Europe

If the old Roman ways of governing largely collapsed, as they did, during the centuries that we have called the early Middle Ages, what replaced them? It is all very well to speak of relative "anarchy" before and after the interval provided by Charlemagne, but what was "anarchy" like, and how were human relations governed? Did everybody just slaughter everybody else indiscriminately? What were the rules that enabled life to go on, however harshly?

In fact, of course, there were mutual arrangements between men that allowed people to work and fight, and to survive if they could. In these arrangements, about which we still know much less than we might like to know, we can discern elements surviving from Roman times, innovations introduced by the barbarians, and changes linked with conversion to Christianity. The settled inhabitants of western Europe and the invaders underwent a long period of slow mutual adjustment, as new and old ways of regulating human affairs competed and often combined with each other.

Feudalism: The Rulers

To these widely varied social and political combinations scholars give the name *feudalism*. Feudal institutions were the arrangements—personal, territorial, and governmental—between persons that made survival possible under the conditions that obtained in western Europe during the early Middle Ages. The arrangements were made between important people who were concerned with maintaining order; feudal institutions involved the governors—the upper classes, both laymen and clerics—not the masses of the population. Because central authority was no longer able to maintain itself locally, local authority had to be improvised to replace it. But because the processes and their results were anything but systematic, we do not here use or recommend the outmoded term "feudal system."

One of the most influential arrangements between persons among the barbarians was the war-band (or *Gefolge*) of all the early Germans, the *comitatus,* as Tacitus called it in Latin. In the war-band, the leader commanded the loyalty of his followers, who had put themselves under his direction for fighting and winning of

booty. It was one of the most important institutions of the Scandinavian invaders of future Russia, where it acquired the Slavic name *druzhina.* Among the Anglo-Saxons, the word for its chieftain was *hlaford,* the direct origin of our word "lord." Chief and followers consulted before a raid or before making peace; those who disagreed might go and serve another chief; booty was divided.

In the Roman provinces, too, local landowners had often built their own private armies, while in Rome itself the magnates had long maintained their groups of *clients,* to whom they acted as *patron* and gave legal protection. When a humble man wanted to enter the client relationship, he asked for the *patrocinium* of the great man and secured it by performing the act of *commendation,* recommending or entrusting himself to the patron. He remained free, but obtained food and clothing in exchange for his services, whatever they might

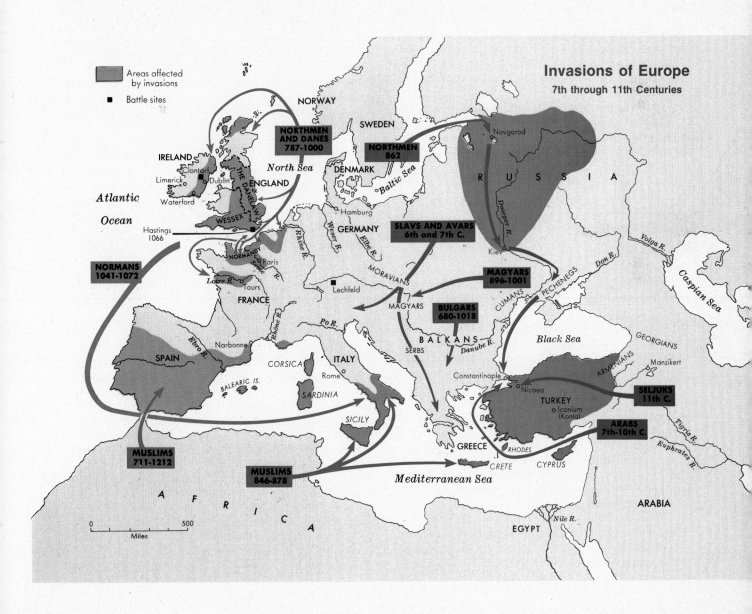

be. If the man was of the upper classes, he was called *fidelis,* a faithful man. By the Carolingian period, the term *vassus,* originally denoting a man of menial status, had come to mean a man who rendered military service to his patron, or lord. To be a vassus or vassal meant no disgrace; it was the new name for status gained by the act of commendation. So a combination of old Germanic and old Roman practices contributed to new relationships described in new terms.

A Roman patron sometimes had retained the title to a piece of property but granted a client the temporary use of it, together with the profits to be derived from it so long as he held it, often for life. The Romans used the term *precarium* for this kind of tenure, and the Carolingian rulers commonly adopted the old practice—sometimes using the old Roman term, sometimes the newer *beneficium,* benefice, to describe the land temporarily held by the vassal in exchange for service. By the year 1000 the act of becoming a vassal usually meant that a man got a benefice; indeed he might refuse faithful service or loyalty unless he was satisfied with the land he received. The feeble later Carolingians and their rivals outbid each other in giving benefices to their supporters in order to obtain armed support and service. This was one of the practices that depleted the royal estates.

In the later Carolingian period, the benefice came to be called *feudum,* a fief, the term that has given us the words "feudal" and "feudalism." When the benefice became a fief, it also became hereditary. Though title to the fief remained with the lord who granted it, the fief itself passed, on the death of a vassal, to the vassal's heir, who inherited with it the obligations to serve the lord and his heirs.

The man who received a fief often got with it certain rights to govern the farmers who lived and worked on the lands that made it up. This practice too had its precedents: in late Roman times, the emperors had often granted an *immunity* to their own estates, an understanding that imperial tax collectors or other law-enforcing officials would stay away from the inhabitants. Because the immunity exempted the farmers from onerous duties, it was hoped that they would enjoy their privileged status and therefore stay put and supply the emperor with needed produce. The Frankish kings adopted this practice, sometimes extending it to lands of the Church and even to those of private proprietors. By the tenth century an immunity meant that the king undertook to keep his officials off the privileged lands and that the holder of the lands would himself perform such governmental functions as collecting taxes, establishing police arrangements, and setting up a court of justice, of which he might keep the profits coming from fines or assessments.

From late Roman times, too, came the local offices of duke and count. Originally military commanders, they took over increasing civil authority as the power of the central government relaxed. In Frankish times they were sometimes very powerful rulers, kings in all

but name. In the disorders of the Carolingian decline, these offices gradually became hereditary; at the same time, the dukes and counts were the vassals of the Carolingians. So the title and office, the duties of the vassal, and the fief (or territory of the office) all became hereditary.

Vassals and Lords

Feudalism and feudal practice did not extend uniformly over all of Europe. Northern France and the Low Countries were the most thoroughly feudalized areas, Germany perhaps the least. Everywhere some pieces of land never became fiefs but remained the fully owned private property of the owners; these were called *allods.* Feudal practices varied from place to place, and they developed and altered with the passage of time. But certain general conceptions were held pretty much everywhere.

One of the most significant was that of a feudal contract: the lord—or *suzerain,* as he was often called—owed something to the vassal just as the vassal owed something to the lord. When they entered upon their relationship the vassal rendered formal homage to his lord; that is, he became the lord's "man." He also promised him aid and counsel. *Aid* meant that he would appear when summoned, fully armed, and fight as a knight in the lord's wars (subject perhaps to limits on the number of days' service owed in any one year). *Counsel* meant that he would join with his fellow vassals—his *peers,* or social equals—to form the lord's court of justice, which alone could pass judgment on any one of them. He might also be required at his own expense to entertain his lord for a visit of specific length, and to give him money payments on special occasions—the marriage of the lord's eldest daughter, the knighting of his eldest son, or—later on—his departure on a crusade. The vassal also swore *fealty* (fidelity) to his lord. The lord was understood to owe, in his turn, protection and justice to his vassal.

If the vassal broke this contract, the lord would have to get the approval of the court made up of the vassal's peers before he could proceed to a punishment such as depriving the vassal of his fief (*forfeiture*). If the lord broke the contract, the vassal was expected to withdraw his homage and fealty in a public act of defiance before proceeding to open rebellion. Sometimes the contract was written, sometimes it was oral. Sometimes the ceremony included a formal *investiture* by the lord: he would give his kneeling vassal a symbol of the fief that was being transferred to him, a twig or a bit of earth. When lord or vassal died, the contract had to be renewed with his successor. The son of a vassal, upon succeeding to his father's fief, often had to pay *relief,* a special, and often heavy, cash payment like a modern inheritance tax. If the vassal died without heirs, the fief would *escheat,* or revert to the lord, who could bestow it on another vassal or not as he saw fit. If the vassal's heir was still a minor, the lord exercised the right of *wardship* or guardianship until he came of age; this meant that the lord received the revenues from the fief, and if he was unscrupulous he could milk it dry.

Within a feudal kingdom, the king theoretically occupied the top position in an imaginary pyramid of society. Immediately below him would be his vassals, men who held fiefs directly from the king, called *tenants-in-chief.* But they in turn would be feudal lords: that is, they would have given out various parts of their own property as fiefs to their own vassals. These men, the king's vassals' vassals, would be the king's *rear vassals,* and so at the next lower level of the theoretical pyramid. But they too would often have vassals, and so on, for many more levels—a process called *subinfeudation.* But this was only theory.

Practice was more complicated still. A tenant-in-chief might hold only a very small fief from the king and not be a very important person at all, while a vassal's vassal's vassal might be rich and powerful. The dukes of Normandy, who were vassals to the king of France, were for some centuries much stronger than their overlord. An individual might receive fiefs from more than one lord, and so be a vassal, owing homage and fealty, to both. What was he to do if one of his lords quarreled with another and went to war? Which of his lords would have a prior right to count on his military help? This kind of thing happened very often: one Bavarian count had twenty different fiefs held of twenty different lords. Gradually, there arose a new concept, that of a *liege* lord, the one to whom a vassal owed service ahead of any other. But in practice the difficulties often persisted. Even though feudal law became more and more subtle and complex, this was an era when armed might counted for more than legality.

Manorialism

All the complicated arrangements we have been discussing directly involved only the governing persons who fought on horseback as mounted knights and whose fiefs consisted of landed property known as manors or estates. Even if we include their dependents, the total would hardly reach 10 percent of the population of Europe. Most of the other 90 percent of the people worked the land. In late Roman times, the large estate, owned by a magnate and worked by tenant farmers, had been called a *latifundium.* The tenant farmers, or *coloni,* were often descendants of small landowners who had turned over their holdings to the magnate in exchange for a guarantee of protection and a percentage of the crop. While the coloni were personally free, not slaves, they could not leave the ground they cultivated, nor could their children.

If the coloni lived in groups of houses close together, the latifundium could be described as a *villa.* Though conditions varied widely, we shall not be far wrong if we think of the late Roman latifundium becoming the medieval manor, the late Roman villa be-

becoming the medieval village, and the late Roman coloni becoming the medieval serfs. As we shall see, the early German village community also contributed to the new social structure. While the Roman landed estate had often produced its food for sale at a profit in the town and city, the long centuries of disorder beginning with the Germanic invasions led to a decline of commerce, of cities, and of agriculture for profit. The medieval manor usually produced only what was needed to feed its own population.

The oldest method of cultivation was the two-field system, alternating crops and fallow so that fertility could be recovered. Later, especially in grain-producing areas, a three-field system was devised—one field for spring planting, one for autumn planting, and the third lying fallow. Elsewhere—in the mountains, in winegrowing areas, in the "Celtic fringes" of Brittany and Wales, and in the new areas of pioneer settlement in Eastern lands—there were many variant agricultural techniques and social arrangements. Here, as so often, there was no simple "typical" medieval way.

On the manor, oxen had originally pulled the plow, but the invention of the horse collar (so that the horse would not strangle on the old-fashioned strap around his neck) and the use of horseshoes (which allowed horses to plow stony soil that hurt oxen's feet) helped make it possible to substitute horses for oxen. So did the increasing use of tandem harnessing, enabling the horses to work in single file instead of side by side. A heavy-wheeled plow made its appearance in advanced areas.

The pattern of agricultural settlement, then, varied from region to region. But so far as a "typical" manor existed, each of its peasant families had holdings, usually in the form of scattered long strips, in the big open fields. In theory this gave each family a bit of the good arable land, a bit of the less good land, a bit of woodland, and so on. The strips might be separated from each other by narrow, unplowed *balks,* but there were no fences, walls, or hedges. The lord of the manor had his own strips, his *demesne* (perhaps a quarter to a third of the land), reserved for the production of the food that he and his household needed. It was understood that the peasants had to work this demesne land for the lord, often three days a week throughout the year, except perhaps in harvest time, when the lord could command their services until his crops were safely in the barns. Of course, the size of the lord's household varied, depending on how important a person he was in his feudal relations with the king and other magnates. The more important he was, the more armed men he had to feed, and the more dependents and servants they all had, the more numerous and bigger would be his fiefs, and the more peasants he would need to work the manors that made up the fiefs.

When a serf died, his son made the lord a payment (*heriot*) in order to inherit his father's right to cultivate the family strips. In exchange for permission to pasture their beasts in the lord's meadows, the serfs might per-

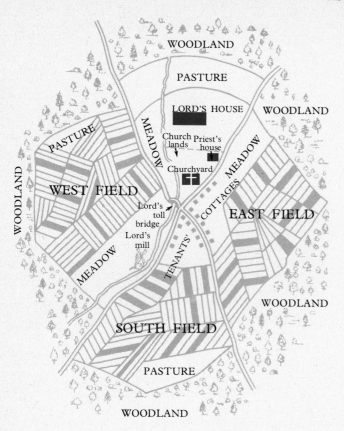

Plan of a medieval manor; the solid strips are the lord's demesne.

earliest developed in eastern France and in parts of Italy and Germany. Even at its height, it did not include some parts of these and other European countries. But in the large areas where manorialism did prevail, the old Roman landlord's economic power over his tenants had fused with the traditional Germanic village chief's political power, and, by the eleventh century, with the governing rights that the lord received with his fief. The deep respect for custom often, no doubt, tended to prevent the lord's extorting from his peasants more work or more food than they traditionally owed him. But they had no rights, and nowhere to appeal in cases where the lord was oppressive. Custom prevailed in the lord's court of justice, when he or his steward sat in judgment on the serf-tenants, enforcing the traditional rules of the village community. Custom regulated the bargaining agreements reached among the peasants for the use in common of plows and plowteams. Custom no doubt retarded inventiveness and stifled initiative, but it was the only thing that gave a serf the sense that he was protected against exactions and cruelties.

As for true slavery, the sale and purchase of human beings like chattels, it hardly existed in early medieval Western Europe. If the serf was tied to the land, the land, in effect, was also tied to the serf. The serf could not be dispossessed unless he failed to live up to his obligations. Thus he could claim certain rights, even if they were only customary rights—his share of the complex manorial farming operations, his use of the strips which he *felt* to be his own. Moreover, as a Christian, the serf had a soul and could not be treated as a mere animal. Christianity never fitted well with a slave society, and throughout the Middle Ages the Church sought to make the serf's customary rights into real rights.

By no means all the peasants on every manor were serfs, however. Some of them were freemen, called *franklins* in England, who virtually owned the land they worked. And between the freemen and the serfs there were probably always landless laborers who were not tied to the land as serfs, and peasants with dues so light that they were almost freemen.

The manor was nearly, but not wholly, self-sufficient. Only rarely can the manorial forge have produced all plowshares and other implements for farming and all the weapons needed for defense, the manorial quarry all the stone, its forests all the lumber needed for building, and its fields and its animals everything necessary to eat or to wear. At least the iron that went into implements had to be bought, and often such luxuries as furs or salt or occasional spices had to be bought also. The manor, then, was only *comparatively* self-sufficient and unspecialized. It had surpluses and deficiencies that gave it the motives and the means for trade with outsiders. It provided something above a bare minimum of livelihood for at least a minority of its residents.

form other duties. They often had to dig ditches or maintain the roads. They paid to have their grain ground at the lord's mill and their bread baked in his oven. They could not marry or allow their daughters to marry outside the manor without the lord's permission and usually the payment of a fine (*merchet*). They were bound to the soil, a hereditary caste of farm laborers, serfs. But they were not slaves; the lord could not sell them; they and their children descended with the land to the lord's heirs. On such a manor the peasants would live in a cluster of houses. A big manor might be several such villages, with perhaps isolated farmsteads in addition. On the other hand, a single village might lie partly in another belonging to a different lord.

Undoubtedly the bulk of the man-hours of labor on the manor went directly into farming, and the bulk of the farming was grain-farming. But everywhere some of the manor's inhabitants were craftsmen, such as blacksmiths or tanners. They too cultivated their own plots of land. Each manor had at least one church of its own, with its priest. If the lord was a great lord, he might have several priests, including his own chaplain for the household and a village priest for the local church.

The organization of the countryside by manors was

V   The Civilization of the Early Middle Ages in the West

A General View

In letters and in the arts, the early medieval centuries saw a severe, perhaps catastrophic, decline in the skills that had characterized the men of the Roman Empire, even in its latest periods. Judged by comparison with the achievements of Greek, Hellenistic, or Roman civilizations, or by those of the contemporary eastern Mediterranean world, Byzantine and Muslim, those of western Europe in these centuries may sometimes seem feeble or primitive, sometimes even pathetic. But this is only what one would expect in a world where the masters usually did not have the taste or the judgment to patronize writers or artists, and where life was often too turbulent to give men much leisure for the exercise of creative skills. The efficient Roman communication system now deteriorated. Cities, generally in human history the homes of culture and the commerce that makes the culture possible and available, often subsided into mere shells of their former splendor: mere forts in the countryside, where they had once been vibrant centers of communication, both physical and human. Technical skills were lost, and so was the command over what had become the whole western European language of intellectual and literary men: Latin. Nobody spoke good Latin any more, and few could write it. The slowly developing vernacular languages: the Romance-French, or the German, were used only infrequently, and usually hesitantly, for literary purposes.

Yet a large question remains. Can one fairly use classical standards to judge the writing and the art of a postclassical age, now evolving in many new directions? Most scholars would today be reluctant to do so, which is of course why we have not adopted the term *Dark Ages*. We now know enough about the original barbarian contributions to the culture of this period to dismiss old prejudices against it. Not only did many barbarians love and admire the Roman world that their fellow barbarians were engaged in destroying, and therefore painstakingly keep alive, however crudely, the Roman literary and artistic tradition, but the widely traveled invading tribesmen brought with them art forms of their own, poetry, sculpture, and painting that only recently have begun to receive from scholars the appreciation that is their due.

Everywhere in the West, then, the story in general is the same, although it varies greatly in detail: the men of these centuries were moving gradually away from their Roman past, though still cherishing, and often trying with varying degrees of success to imitate, Roman models; and at the same time they were also creating new and original writings and works of art that reflected their own barbarian past. While the Christian faith that the invaders took from the dwellers in the Roman Empire gave them a more permanent and firmer link with Rome itself and with its traditions than they would otherwise have had, they could neither absorb the Roman heritage entire nor wholly abandon their own traditions and practices.

In the cultural realm, then, as in the realm of institutions, what we shall find is an amalgam, a new combination of old elements. If we meet no Homer, no Vergil, no Phidias in the pages that follow, it may not necessarily mean that the men we shall encounter—many of them anonymous—are less worthy of our study or deserve our contempt. It means instead that they lived in different times, under different pressures, and expressed their artistic and intellectual drives in new and different ways. Far less well known than the civilizations of the ancient world, this early medieval western European civilization merits far more attention than it usually gets.

Latin Literature: Italy

It was naturally in Italy that the fight against the loss of the classical heritage was waged most vigorously and most successfully. Under the rule of the Ostrogothic king Theodoric (489–526), a great admirer of the Greek and Latin cultural tradition, two distinguished intellectuals combated the general decline: Boethius and Cassiodorus.

Boethius (ca. 480–524), unlike most of his contemporaries, knew both Greek and Latin. Learned and versatile, he advised Theodoric on many points. He gave detailed directions to the king's brother-in-law, ruler of the Burgundians, for the making of a water clock. A recognized authority on music, he selected the best available harpist to play at the court of Clovis, the king of the Franks. Boethius thwarted an effort of Theodoric's military paymaster to cheat the troops, by showing that the paymaster had "sweated" the silver from the coins. He held the posts of consul (now of course honorary, but still carrying enormous prestige) and of Master of the Offices, something very much like a prime minister and by no means honorary only.

Boethius planned a Latin translation of all the voluminous works of Plato and Aristotle, and in those small portions of the work that he completed he took care to make his translation as literal as possible. He also made the first efforts to use in Christian theological writings the logical methods of Aristotle, writing works of his own about the art of argument. These were to serve as the inspiration, not to men of his own time, most of whom had little interest or ability in philosophical discourse, but to scholars and thinkers who lived six hundred and more years after his death, when philosophical disputation on theological questions became the fashion and the chief sign of an intellectual revival (see Chapter 8). Had Boethius survived to complete or even carry very far his plans for rendering the greatest Greek philosophers into Latin, western Europe perhaps would not have been denied these materials for another half millennium, and intellectual development in the West might have been speeded up. But only two years after making him Master of the Offices, Theodoric imprisoned Boethius on a charge of treasonable plotting against him. After a year in jail, Boethius was executed at the age of forty-four, perhaps because he was sharply opposed to Arianism, the form of Christianity to which Theodoric and the Ostrogoths adhered.

In the later years of his life, Boethius wrote a treatise on music, and several influential works on theology, against the Arian and monophysite heretical views. In jail, he wrote his most famous work, *The Consolation of Philosophy*, a dialogue between himself in his cell and the female personification of Philosophy, who appears to him. Partly in verse, partly in prose, and wholly in excellent Latin, the *Consolation* is a moving and noble book, in which the prisoner seeks—and is helped by Philosophy to find—answers not only to the injustice he feels he is suffering, but also to the larger questions of human life and death on earth, and the relationships between man and God. Full of reminiscences of classical authors (Boethius was extremely well read in the classics and probably had few if any books to refer to in prison) and so sometimes criticized for its lack of originality, the book dwells on the commonness of suffering, on the fickleness of fortune, which often punishes unjustly an innocent man, and on the transitoriness and relative worthlessness of worldly triumphs. Everything we gain here on earth, even fame, will vanish away. Largely owing to this book, however, Boethius' own fame survived far more securely than that of any other mere successful Master of the Offices: *The Consolation of Philosophy* became one of the most popular books (and schoolbooks) of all later medieval centuries.

Cassiodorus (ca. 490-580) managed to stay in Theodoric's good graces, and long survived him. During the life of the Ostrogothic king, Cassiodorus, like Boethius, became consul and Master of the Offices. He collected his royal master's official correspondence. But his great ambition was to found a new Christian university in Rome, where the sadly neglected classical subjects could be taught and where a real revival of learning and scholarship might take place. Perhaps it was too late for this in any case, but the terrible disorders that accompanied Justinian's reconquest of Italy from the Goths between 535 and 554 made fulfillment of the idea altogether impossible. Thwarted, Cassiodorus founded instead a monastery near Squillace, his birthplace on the Adriatic shore of the heel of Italy. Here among the brethren of his community—who lived, of course, according to the Rule of St. Benedict (see Chapter 4)—Cassiodorus tried to keep learning alive in its Christian form. The monks copied by hand not only the Bible but the best pagan Latin authors—Cicero, Vergil, and the rest—and those who had no taste for this bookish work cultivated the gardens and wheatfields and took care of the fishponds, which became especially famous, in order to feed the community. Cassiodorus himself wrote books on spelling, to help the monastic scribes with their task, on the Psalms, to provide the biblical text with a classical commentary,

and on the Soul, following in the footsteps of Cicero and his Greek masters. Some of his monks translated Greek works into Latin.

Far more typical of the period, however, were the views of Pope Gregory the Great (ca. 540-604, pope 590-604), whom we have already encountered as the talented administrator who kept the Church alive and kept Italy from falling into total chaos in the strife between Lombards and exarchate. Practical in every way, Gregory was ready to abandon the classical past if he could bring more order into the barbarian and Christian present. "The same lips," he wrote one of his bishops, "cannot sound the praises of Jupiter and the praises of Christ," and he firmly enjoined him to stop holding conferences where ancient literature was read. In Gregory's own writings, the same practical tendency appears: his so-called *Dialogues* deal in four volumes with the lives and miracles of the Italian church fathers, providing edifying anecdotes in order to attract Christian readers away from pagan authors and toward the proper contemplation of their own future salvation. His commentary on the Book of Job interprets the Old Testament story in New Testament terms: Job becomes a type of Christ in his suffering, and the aim of the book is to make its readers behave better in this world.

But perhaps the most important of Gregory's writings is the great body of his surviving correspondence, more than a thousand letters dating from the fourteen-year period of his papacy. Sent to all corners of the Christian world, and dealing with every sort of problem in the management of the Church and its relations to the secular rulers, from the Byzantine emperor and the exarch down, these letters reflect Gregory's humanity, commanding habits, enormous sense of the importance of his office, and even, at times, unexpected humor. To a bishop in far-off Asia Minor, who had been trying unsuccessfully to convert a refugee Persian prince to Christianity, Gregory wrote that it was too bad the bishop had not yet succeeded in his pious aim, but that what really mattered was the effort, and the bishop would surely reap his heavenly reward just for trying. To lend point to this, he quoted a proverb apparently popular at the time: "Black the Ethiopian goes into the bath, and black he emerges, but the bathman gets his fee just the same." No other pope of the Early Middle Ages has left us so large a number of letters, nor is there anything remotely resembling these documents as a vivid historical source: they provide a sustained flash of light for the scholar in a period very little known to us both before and after they were written.

Latin Literature: Gaul and Spain

As one moves away from Italy, the center of the Roman world, the survival and cultivation of Latin letters naturally grows even feebler. In Gaul, a highly romanized province, there did remain even into the period of the invasions a cultivated group of upper-class landowners and churchmen who still found it natural to communicate with each other in Latin, in the old-fashioned way, and with much of the old-fashioned style. There were good poets among them, but perhaps the most distinguished writer of all was chiefly a prose stylist, Sidonius Apollinaris (ca. 431–ca. 475).

Born of a family long prominent in imperial affairs, and educated at the school of Lyon (still a major Roman provincial center), Sidonius eventually became bishop of Auvergne in south-central France during the invasions of Visigoths and Burgundians, while Huns and Franks were active nearby. Yet in 147 letters, written with a conscious eye to preservation and future publication, Sidonius—essentially an aristocrat in his habits and tastes—writes almost as if nothing very alarming were happening in the outside world and as if he and his fellow nobles, well born and well educated, still had the say about what would happen in the future. True, he refers to the Germanic invaders, but with gentlemanly distaste, as underbred and coarse, not with the apprehension that they were bringing with them the doom of Sidonius and all his friends. He sneers at one of his fellow nobles who had forgotten himself so far as to learn the language of the barbarians.

Decorous parties on beautifully situated country estates, with luxurious baths, tastefully decorated, sparkling drawing-room discussion full of epigram, careful cultivation of ornamental gardens as well as of vineyard and olive grove, lavish picnics spread by devoted servants, due attention to setting a new mosaic floor, reading in the estate's library, and discussion of Vergil or Terence, games of tennis and dice: these are the occupations that chiefly concerned Sidonius and his wide circle of friends, all as proud of their noble Roman origins as he was himself. But he was also a good Christian, made financial sacrifices for his flock, and showed vigor in combating the Arianism and barbarism of the Germans. His letters provide a corrective to the oversimple view of the barbarian inroads as producing a chaotic social upheaval.

By the time of the Frankish triumph in the next generation, the Gallo-Roman culture that Sidonius so proudly stood for had virtually died. There was now very little literary activity. We have some moving Latin hymns by a writer called Fortunatus, and of course we have the prose document already cited, the history of Gregory, bishop of Tours. As we know, it chronicles in a Latin that would have shocked Sidonius, much less Cicero, the unedifying behavior of the Merovingian rulers. But there is a vigorous if primitive quality about Gregory, a mixture of credulity, native goodness, and calm acceptance of atrocities that gives the reader deep insight into the Merovingian age. In Spain, too, farther from Rome than Gaul but still a romanized province, there was a good deal of writing in Latin, at least down into the seventh century, which saw the *Etymologies* of Isidore (ca. 570–636), archbishop of Seville, a sort of encyclopedia. It reflects Isidore's own learning, extraordinary for its time, and his superstition and ignorance,

which were far more typical. With all the defects that make a modern reader smile or shudder, Isidore's book became a standard reference work for several centuries after he wrote it.

Latin Literature: Britain, and the Continent Once More

The seventh century, then, saw the virtual end of literary activity in the classical vein on the Continent, and marks the low point of intellectual effort there as of political stability. For a different spirit, destined eventually to restore Roman culture to the Continent, we must turn to Britain, during Roman times a peripheral province, hardly participating in Roman civilization, and producing no Latin authors before the barbarian invasions. Christianity came to Britain, as we have seen, in two waves: one from Ireland, where it was of Gallic origin, and the other from Rome, at the very end of the sixth century and the beginning of the seventh, in the mission sent by Gregory the Great, headed by a Greek from Asia Minor. And it was Christianity that produced in England not a revival but the very first original writing in Latin. The combined influence of the Celtic and the Roman traditions brought such fruitful results that by the end of the eighth century it was men from Britain who stimulated a revival on the Continent—sponsored by Charlemagne himself, who provided the necessary interest and patronage.

Of a large number of cultivated men, the greatest was Bede (ca. 672–735). Abbot of his own monastery, he could read Greek, knew the Latin writings of the church fathers intimately, and himself wrote a famous *Ecclesiastical History of the English People,* covering the story of the spread of Christianity in England from the arrival in 597 of the missions sent by Gregory the Great down to 732, almost to the moment of Bede's own death. Written in a Latin of astonishing vigor and purity, it tells us almost everything we know of the progress of the new religion among the pagan Anglo-Saxons, about the Church's relationship with the Anglo-Saxon kings, and about the foundation of the many monastic houses, where book-loving monks found a shelter for themselves and the books they loved. Bede's own even-tempered personality shines through the work, which sometimes rises to true poetic greatness.

For example, Bede tells how, in 627, when the still pagan king Edwin of Northumbria had received a letter from the pope, and a Latin missionary was at his court urging him to accept Christianity, he naturally called his witenagemot to consult them on the matter. One of Edwin's counselors then said:

Man's life here on earth, O King, seems to me—so far as its uncertainties go—just the same as if, when you were sitting at dinner in the wintertime with your companions in arms and their servants, and a great fire had been kindled in the middle of the hall, and the hall was warm with its heat, but outside all about there raged the storms of winter rain and snow, a sparrow might come to the house, and fly through it swiftly, entering at one window and flying out at another. For the time while the bird is inside the house, it feels no chill from the winter blast, but after this tiny spell of fair weather has passed, that lasts only for a moment, the sparrow quickly passes again from winter to winter, and so is lost to your view. In the same way, this life of men comes into being for a brief moment, but what follows it and what went before it we certainly do not know. So if this new teaching [i.e., Christianity] has brought us anything surer to cling to, I think it should be followed.*

Soon after, Edwin was converted. And the metaphor about human life on earth remains a moving and effective one more than thirteen centuries later.

It was churchmen from this cultural world of Britain that thrived while the Continent stagnated who helped make possible the great flowering of Latin letters that took place under Charlemagne. Alcuin of York (ca. 735–ca. 804), who had studied under a pupil of Bede, came to Charlemagne's court in 782 and helped to transform the palace school there into a serious and practical educational institution, where men studied the seven liberal arts, as generally understood by the medieval layman and cleric alike: grammar, rhetoric, and dialectic (the art of argument), and arithmetic, geometry, astronomy, and music. Alcuin wrote much himself, prose and verse, and took the lead in reviving biblical scholarship and in teaching such practical subjects as legible handwriting to the scribes who now began to copy manuscripts in monasteries. The survival of much of Latin literature we owe to the efforts of these Carolingian scribes.

Other literary men in great numbers worked in Charlemagne's time. Einhard imitated Suetonius in his biography of Charlemagne, but he also turned his hand to various other arts, including bronze-foundry and metalwork in general, taking the nickname of Bezaleel (the artisan in Exodus to whom the making of the Ark of the Covenant was entrusted) to show his craftsmanship. The splendid bronze grill around the gallery in Charlemagne's palace church at Aachen, still to be seen there (though now a part of the much later city hall), is thought to be Einhard's own work, or at least executed under his direction.

Another prolific writer was Theodulf, bishop of Orléans, born in southern Gaul near the Spanish border, where classical civilization had never died out. He is now recognized as the author of the anonymous *Libri Carolini* (*Books of Charles*, i.e., Charlemagne), an imposing theological treatise dealing with the problem of whether it was idolatrous to venerate holy images—a problem then severely agitating the Byzantine Empire (see Chapter 6), with which Charlemagne had diplomatic relations. Theodulf, who traveled widely (he was one of Charlemagne's *missi dominici*), wrote verse accounts of his voyages and of the works of art he saw on his way. He had at least two of the most splendid surviving Bibles of the entire Middle Ages copied for him, written in gold letters on vellum entirely stained purple. On his estate of Germigny-des-Près along the Loire River, he also built for himself a private chapel that can still be seen, altered in many ways but containing the only surviving mosaic picture of the period in the West, a picture of the Hebrew Ark of the Covenant described in Exodus: it is no coincidence that Theodulf's chapel is the only church in Christendom dedicated to no saint, not even to Christ, but to God the Father himself.

The foundations laid by men such as these and others like them permitted their successors in the next two generations, after Charlemagne's empire had disintegrated, to write history, poetry, saints' lives, works on theology and ethics, and vast numbers of personal letters in Latin. In new monastic centers such as St. Gall in Switzerland, and across the Rhine in newly christianized Germany, the literary work made possible by the British immigrants who had been responsible for the "Carolingian Renaissance" went on, and the continuity of Western civilization had been assured.

Vernacular Literature: *Beowulf*

As we have seen, the distance of Britain from Rome and its failure to become completely latinized during antiquity paradoxically allowed it to profit greatly from the double wave of Latin Christian missionaries—Celtic and papal—and so provide the needed stimulus for the Carolingian Latin literary revival. But by the same token, the thinness of the Latin veneer probably encouraged the Angles and Saxons and Jutes to produce a literature in their own language (we call it Anglo-Saxon or Old English) while the continental former Roman provinces were too inhibited by the overpowering prestige of Latin, and perhaps also delayed by far less stable political conditions than prevailed in Britain. At any rate, there were a good many writers in England who did not hesitate to write in their own language. Sometimes they were translators: Boethius' *Consolation of Philosophy* was rendered into Old English, and King Alfred the Great himself translated Bede's *Ecclesiastical History*. Sometimes they were original writers, setting down a group of proverbs, or the life of a saint, or a chronicle, or—in verse—an account of one battle or another.

But by far the most remarkable Old English literary survival is *Beowulf,* a poem of almost 3,200 lines, preserved in only a single manuscript in the British Museum, written down about the year 1000. Hundreds of scholars have written thousands of pages about this poem: almost every statement about it might be questioned by some authority, and what we say here is no exception. A fire damaged the unique manuscript in 1731; it was rebound in the 1860s in such a way that more words disappeared; after the fire but before the

*Bede, *Historia Ecclesiastica Gentis Anglorum,* Book II, chap. xiii (London and New York: Loeb Classical Library, 1930), I, 283 ff. Translation ours. In the distant Soviet Union there survives a manuscript of Bede's history contemporary with the author, with some notes written in a handwriting that scholars believe is that of Bede himself.

rebinding, two copyists, one an Icelander, had made transcripts of it in the 1780s: all this has naturally tended to keep scholarly controversy alive.

It is clear that the poem was composed well before the date of the surviving manuscript, perhaps as early as about 680 (it includes historical characters from the 500s), perhaps as late as 800 or even later. Until 1939, some scholars thought it had been composed in Northumbria, some in Mercia; but in that year a spectacular archaeological discovery at Sutton Hoo in Essex (East Anglia) turned up the ship-tomb of an East Anglian king dating from the late seventh or early eighth century and containing a harp, jewels, and armor like those described in *Beowulf*, which also includes a description of a ship-funeral. So now some scholars think the poem may be of East Anglian origin. Some scholars argue fiercely that the poem was written by a single author, others that it is a composite; some that it is a pagan poem with Christian interpolations, others that it breathes a wholly Christian spirit. Some think it has two parts, some six, some three. These arguments and others are likely to go merrily on without resolution. The poem has been described as "a museum for the antiquarian, a sourcebook for the historian, a treatise for the student of Christian thought, and a gymnasium for the philologist." It is, however, also unmistakably a poem.

Beowulf begins in Denmark, where it tells of the founding of the Danish royal line, and the building of the great hall called Heorot by King Hrothgar. Heorot is repeatedly raided by a savage monster, Grendel, who seizes and eats the Danish warriors as they lie asleep after dinner, until from over the sea in southern Sweden comes a hero, Beowulf, a Geat in the service of the Geatish king, Hygelac. Beowulf has come to rescue the Danes from the curse of Grendel; he lies in wait for the monster and in single combat so severely grips his hand that Grendel has to flee, leaving his entire arm, ripped out at the socket, in the hands of Beowulf. The wound is fatal, of course. But Grendel's mother, in some ways more terrifying than her son, tries to avenge him, and Beowulf has to do combat with her at the bottom of a wild and lonely lake; he kills her too, and the Danes celebrate in delight. Then Beowulf returns home to the land of the Geats and reports to his master, Hygelac, who receives him warmly. Eventually Beowulf himself becomes king of the Geats, and at the very end of a long life has a last victorious combat with a dragon who has stolen a hoard of treasure and is ravaging the country. The treasure is recovered, but Beowulf dies in the fight, and his funeral ceremonies end the poem.

Such a narrative of fighting and treasure would have surely provided rich entertainment to warriors gathered in a hall, perhaps like that of Edwin in the excerpt from Bede we have quoted above. *Beowulf* exalts the ideal of heroic behavior, but, again like Edwin's counselor, is deeply concerned with the transitoriness of human life: the climax of all Beowulf's heroism, and the end of the poem, is the hero's death and funeral.

The monsters may be thought of as mere mythical creatures, but they have been assimilated by the poet into the framework of Christianity: he tells us that Grendel and his mother are descendants of Cain. But it is an almost incidental Christianity: the name of Christ is not mentioned nor is there reference to the Incarnation, the Crucifixion, or the Resurrection. The Christianity of the poem seems to have been superficially grafted on to a pagan stem. The fierceness of combat itself, the immense sensitivity of heroes to slights, real or imagined, and the heroic response to courteous treatment for a traveler or a man who saved one's life: these are familiar from other poems of heroic ages, like the *Iliad* and the *Odyssey*.

Here is a recent translation into modern English of several short passages from the poem.

Beowulf's trip to Denmark:

> Foaming at the prow and most like a sea-bird
> The boat sped over the waves, urged on by the wind;
> until next day, at the expected time
> so far had the carved prow come
> that the travellers sighted land,
> shining cliffs, steep hills,
> broad headland. So did they cross the sea;
> their journey was at an end [ll. 217–224].

Hrothgar's queen, Wealhtheow, thanks Beowulf for killing Grendel:

> To him she carried the cup, and asked in gracious
>   words
> if he would care to drink; and to him she presented
> twisted gold with courtly ceremonial—
> two armlets, a corselet and many rings,
> and the most handsome collar in the world.
> I have never heard that any hero had a jewel
> to equal that. . . [ll. 1190–1196].
>
> Applause echoed in the hall.
> Wealhtheow spoke these words before the company:
> "May you, Beowulf, beloved youth, enjoy
> with all good fortune this necklace and corselet,
> treasures of the people; may you always prosper;
> win renown through courage, and be kind in your
>   counsel
> to these boys [her sons]; for that, I will reward you
>   further.
> You have ensured that men will always sing
> your praises, even to the ends of the world,
> as far as oceans still surround cliffs,
> home of the winds. May you thrive, O prince,
> all your life. I hope you will amass
> a shining hoard of treasure. O happy Beowulf,
> be gracious in dealing with my sons.

Exterior of San Pedro de la Nave, from the southwest.

Here, each warrior is true to the others,
gentle of mind, loyal to his lord;
the thanes are as one, the people all alert,
the warriors have drunk well. They will do as I
ask.”
    Then Wealhtheow retired to her seat
beside her lord. That was the best of banquets. . .
[ll. 1215–1234].

Beowulf goes to Grendel's mother's lake:

Then the man of noble lineage left Heorot far
*   behind,*
followed narrow tracks, string-thin paths
over steep, rocky slopes—remote parts
with beetling crags and many lakes
where water-demons lived. He went ahead
with a handful of scouts to explore the place;
all at once he came upon a dismal wood,
mountains, trees standing on the edge
of a grey precipice, the lake lay beneath,
blood-stained and turbulent. . . [ll. 1407–1416]. *

Although we shall find a spirit somehow similar to

*Reprinted by permission of Farrar, Straus & Giroux, Inc., and Macmillan & Co. Ltd. from Kevin Crossley-Holland's translation of *Beowulf.* Translation © 1968 by Kevin Crossley-Holland; introductory matter © 1968 by Bruce Mitchell.

Beowulf in the later Old French *Song of Roland,* there is no contemporary vernacular poem truly comparable to it in any language.

The Arts

In the arts, as in literature, the story is one of a very gradual transition away from Roman forms, thoroughly standardized and understood in all the continental provinces, and adapted to Christian needs and uses for at least two centuries before the barbarians arrived, toward newer achievements introduced as the barbarians themselves became more cultivated. The early great churches of such important imperial cities as Milan (San Lorenzo) or Trier were still the large rectangular basilicas taken over from the secular architecture of the Romans, but for certain smaller Christian structures, especially baptisteries, then built detached from the main church, innovations were tried: some were square, with corner niches and a drum (Fréjus, in southern France), others were polygonal (Albenga, in northern Italy), and rich mosaic decoration was characteristic. As soon as a barbarian tribe was firmly established in its new territory, its kings as a matter of prestige built churches, often small, it is true, but generally imitative of the Roman models. Most of these have disappeared, but we know from contemporary written accounts and from archaeological research that they often had domes, and tin or gilded bronze roof tiles that shone in the sun. In Merovingian times, marble quarries were worked, especially in southwest France, and fine stone capitals and slabs were even exported.

From the Visigothic occupation in Spain there survive several churches, such as the seventh-century San Pedro de la Nave near the Portuguese frontier, whose architecture is late Roman but whose sculpture is clearly unclassical and in a new mood: in a capital showing the sacrifice of Isaac, the hand of God emerges from the heavens representing the voice of the Lord telling Abraham to hold his upraised hand and spare his son.

For a still-existing Merovingian building one must examine the seventh-century Baptistery of St. John at Poitiers, remodeled to some extent but still clearly showing its debt to later Roman buildings, even though the sculptural decoration and the ornamentation in terra-cotta are far cruder. At Poitiers too is the underground mausoleum of a seventh-century abbot, Mellebaude, modeled on the Gallo-Roman tomb-chambers in which such a noble as Sidonius, or indeed any of his ancestors for centuries before him, might have been buried. In very good Latin on the wall are painted inscriptions, well lettered, one of which says, "Everything goes from bad to worse, and the end of time is near," a quite un-Roman sentiment that reflects the pessimism of men who felt the degeneration of the times they lived in. Even more representative of a new era is a sculptured representation in the tomb-chamber itself: the two thieves crucified with Christ, each bound to a cross of his own that no Roman sculptor could have carved, so primitive are the figures, so staring the eyes, so crude the execution. Here, as for example in certain sculptured slabs of the same period found in

The sculptured figures in Mellebaude's tomb: the two thieves who were crucified with Christ, bound to their crosses.

The sacrifice of Isaac: capital at San Pedro de la Nave. The hand of God, representing the voice of the Lord, emerges from the heavens at the critical moment to stop Abraham from killing his son.

The carved wooden reading desk of the saintly Merovingian queen Radegund.

excavations at St. Denis, just outside Paris (a most ancient and celebrated church in which French kings were later buried), one sees unmistakably the barbarian hand working in a tradition that is all its own.

Also still almost miraculously preserved at Poitiers by the nuns at the Abbey of the Holy Cross is a small carved wooden bookstand owned by a Merovingian queen, Radegund, at the end of the sixth century. In the center of the carved reading surface is a lamb, representing Christ, and in each corner is the symbol of one of the four apostles, an eagle's head for John and a man's for Matthew, a bull's for Luke and a lion's for Mark. At the top, between two doves, is the Greek monogram for Christ, while at the bottom, between two doves, is a cross in a circle. Along the sides two crosses in still another form balance each other. The whole is simple and harmonious, and thoroughly Mediterranean in inspiration, but in execution perhaps more primitive, showing possibly the limitations of a barbarian wood-

carver, and suggesting—if one is impressionable—both the piety and the ingenuousness of a Christian barbarian queen.

Two sculptured tombs in the crypt (underground chapel) of Jouarre, east of Paris, further illustrate the complexity of the era. The tomb of Agilbert, of the late seventh century, with its extraordinarily vivid and poignant representation of men and women praying at the Last Judgment, their arms upraised, is so unlike all other sculpture of the period in its intensity that it has been conjectured that the artist was an Egyptian Christian, one of those known to have fled from the Arab Muslim conquest (see Chapter 6). By contrast, the tomb of Theodechilde, of the first half of the eighth century, with its splendid carved shells and beautifully lettered Latin inscription, is in the fullest Roman tradition. Jouarre had close connections with Britain, and its sculptures have been compared with those of the early sculptured crosses of Ireland and northern England, where it is possible also that Egyptian influences had penetrated.

Not only Egypt but the Byzantine Empire too made its contribution to the art of the West during these centuries. There were of course the great monuments built in Rome and Ravenna itself by Greeks or artists trained in the Greek school, dating back to the sixth century, all well known. But this was imperial territory down to 751. More striking are the frescoes in the tiny church in a remote village in northern Italy, Castelseprio, where the bishops of Milan had a summer residence. Totally unknown until 1944, these were revealed when some soldiers scraped the plaster off the wall. Although there is still much debate among scholars as to the date when they were painted, it seems probable that they belong to the eighth or early ninth century, and they reflect a classical revival that had been taking place at Byzantium itself since the seventh century. Compared with the figures of the tomb of Mellebaude, these frescoes reveal an extraordinary sophistication.

To find clear-cut examples of the kind of art the barbarians brought with them, it is easiest to turn to

Details from two sculptured tombs in the crypt of Jouarre: (left) the tomb of Agilbert; (right) the tomb of Theodechilde.

the "minor arts" of goldsmithing and jewelry. As the Huns drove before them into Europe the Germans who had settled along the shores of the Black Sea, the Germans brought with them objects made there by local craftsmen working in an Iranian or other Eastern tradition, and characterized by brilliant color and the use of gems (often from as far away as India) or colored glass for ornamentation. Once inside the borders of the Roman Empire, the tribesmen, notably the Ostrogoths, naturally retained their taste for this sort of thing, and presumably artists they had brought with them as well as their own craftsmen continued the tradition. Many of these marvelous (and altogether unclassical) objects have been found in barbarian graves in central Europe, and also in Gaul, Spain, and Italy. An eagle-shaped clasp from Spain is a fine example of a not uncommon type of ornament of this school.

To understand the influences exerted by the Byzantine outpost of the exarchate at Ravenna, we must make a point often overlooked: between 642 and 752 virtually all the popes were themselves Greek or Syrian by origin. These Eastern popes surely sponsored further imports from the East and fostered a continued popularity of Eastern objects. The magnificent jeweled gold bookcovers made probably in Rome for the Bible that Pope Gregory the Great himself gave to the Lombard queen Theodelinde provide a convincing example. Four large jewels in the corner of each cover are actually classical portrait-gems, often now taken out of some treasured collection to embellish this sort of artwork of a quite different tradition.

From later in the seventh century comes the jeweled gold crown of the Visigothic king Recceswinth, one of a large collection of Visigothic royal crowns, of which several can be seen in the Cluny Museum in Paris. Similar jeweled objects—a purse, a harp, and weapons—were found in the great Sutton Hoo ship-burial in Essex, England, in 1939, to which we have referred in connection with *Beowulf*. To those astonished archaeologists and students of Old English poetry who first looked at the Sutton Hoo find, it must have seemed as if they were seeing illustrated in real life the lines of the poem that tell how

> . . . then they laid their dear lord,
> the giver of rings, deep within the ship
> by the mast in majesty; many treasures
> and adornments from far and wide were gathered
>   there.
> I have never heard if a ship equipped
> more handsomely with weapons and war-gear,
> swords and corselets; on his breast
> lay countless treasures that were to travel far
> with him. . . .*

*Reprinted by permission of Farrar, Straus & Giroux, Inc., and Macmillan & Co., Ltd. from Kevin Crossley-Holland's translation of *Beowulf*. Translation © 1968 by Kevin Crossley-Holland; introductory matter © 1968 by Bruce Mitchell.

And the presence in the royal funeral-ship at Sutton Hoo of a massive round silver plate made at Byzantium in the period 491–518, and of two silver spoons with Greek inscriptions, helped to emphasize the continuous contacts between the barbarians and the East.

It was indeed the influences from the East greatly stimulated by the influx of barbarians that led to the gradual abandonment of the realistic representation of men and beasts in art. Imported Byzantine silver, ivories, and textiles, as well as the Byzantine monuments like those of Ravenna, on Italian soil, surely helped speed the change in styles. Though the story of Eastern influences and its expression by Western artists is a complicated one, it is strikingly exemplified by an extraordinary row of six stucco statues of saints that decorates the front of a small church (Santa Maria in Valle) at Cividale in northern Italy. These saints were carved by sculptors whose skills would have permitted them to do anything they chose. The stiff ceremonial garments obviously cover genuine human bodies; and though hieratic positions are preferred for the figures, the detail is deliberately realistic. Scholars now date these remarkable statues to about the year 800 and ascribe them to Byzantine artists working in Italy.

In strong contrast is the almost abstract effect of a relief of the Adoration of the Magi on the altar of Duke Ratchis, in the same small town of Cividale, ascribed to native Lombard craftsmen and to a period a little more than half a century earlier. Here we are almost back to the primitive quality of the two thieves in Abbot Mellebaude's tomb at Poitiers. But we have come the full distance and more when we consider a seventh-century German tomb-slab (stele) now at Bonn. On one side the warrior stands sword in hand, about to be bitten by the serpent of death; on the other, Christ stands over his tomb with a halo (but also with a spear!).

Although in a few cases, such as the paintings at Castelseprio and the stucco saints at Cividale, we have found monuments reflecting powerful classicizing influences, we must wait until the Carolingian period for a full revival. Surviving monuments in Italy gave the artists some of their inspiration, and Charlemagne's desire and ability to attract the best craftsmen from anywhere in Europe enabled them to put it into effect. Paintings and mosaics in Roman churches—Santa Maria Antiqua and Santa Maria Maggiore in particular, dating to the fifth and sixth centuries, illustrated for the men of the eighth and ninth centuries, as they do today, what could be made of Christian subjects treated in the classical style.

Wall paintings and mosaics are fixed monuments, and only a traveler can visit them if they are widely separated from each other; but books are transportable, and it was largely through book illustration—the famous illumination of manuscripts—that inspirations from one region and one school intermingled in other regions with influences from other schools. So north Italian books in which all these classical and Byzantine

Sculptures from Cividale: (above) three holy women; (below) the Adoration of the Magi.

influences had been brought to bear traveled across the Alps, into Gaul, and into Britain with Gregory the Great's missionaries: there actually survive two illustrations from a Bible that came along on the expedition, which together with other books and objects, now lost or unidentifiable, brought the Mediterranean traditions into England, already exposed to them indirectly by the Celtic missionaries from Ireland. And in due course the same influences penetrated into Germany by the same route, where artists under the Ottonian Emperors would pick them up.

Illustrative of this north Italian school of painting, so influential in transmitting its influences northward, is a drawing from a manuscript of a book of church law (early ninth century) at Vercelli. Constantine the Great is shown on his throne at the Council of Nicaea with the bishops who signed its decrees, while below the throne, books propounding the Arian heresy are being burned.

To the "Carolingian Renaissance," notably marked by manuscript illustration, the specifically barbarian contribution came not in the form of figure-drawing, either of persons or of animals, but in the decorative geometric patterning that often characterized barbarian craftsmanship in the metal objects we have discussed. It appears as well in the contemporary written descriptions of other objects (Beowulf was given by a Dane a sword whose "iron blade was engraved with deadly twig-like patterning"—ll. 1458–1459—which we are specifically told was an heirloom); and it reappears in book illustration with the breathtaking patterns to be seen in the great Celtic manuscripts: the Books of Durrow, Echternach (brought from Britain to Germany), Lindisfarne, and Kells, executed in the seventh and eighth centuries. A page with interlace border from the earliest of these, the Book of Durrow, shows St. Matthew in a cloak of complex checkerboard design; both border and cloak are of barbarian inspiration. The Celtic missionaries who went from Ireland to the Continent and founded the monastery at Bobbio in Italy took these talents with them, and there learned what the indigenous craftsmen had to teach them. By the time we reach the celebrated Book of Kells the earlier stiffness of the human figure is gone, and the geometric patterns have enriched themselves and proliferated; in some cases the birds and fish that were used by continental artists for ornamentation also appear. Coptic influences from Egypt, and even Iranian ones, can also be seen in some of the manuscript illuminations produced just before the time of Charlemagne, notably at the French monastery of Corbie.

Charlemagne himself made five trips to Italy, which have been called "the stages by which Frankish culture climbed to the level of Carolingian culture," deepening and carrying further the connection begun by Pepin. Lombards from northern Italy joined the Anglo-Saxons like Alcuin at a court that had no per-

A tomb stele now at Bonn: on one side a warrior, on the other, Christ.

manent residence during the long years of continual campaigning but that settled in 794 at Aachen, where the new royal (soon imperial) residence was built at forced-draft speed. From Rome and Ravenna there poured in exciting works of art, many of which have of course disappeared, like the equestrian statue of Theodoric, itself an imitation of that of Marcus Aurelius. We have preserved a model in bronze of a similar statue of Charlemagne himself. In the chapel at Aachen, Charlemagne's marble throne is still in place.

To Aachen came Romans, Lombards, Greeks from southern Italy and probably from Byzantium itself, Syrians, Anglo-Saxons, Irishmen, Spaniards from the Visigothic parts of Spain, Jews, Arabs, and every sort of inhabitant of Gaul and Germany. Architects and artisans—including, perhaps, some Greeks—were striving to create a kind of synthesis between the imperial palace in Constantinople and the papal residence in the Palace of St. John Lateran in Rome. Charlemagne especially enjoyed receiving foreign travelers, who came from everywhere, many of them, especially officials, bringing rich gifts—relics, books, textiles, jewels. In 796 arrived the treasure captured from the Avars, who had been pillaging for two centuries. It filled sixteen oxcarts. The most sensational present was sent in 802 by the caliph at Bagdad, Harun al Rashid (see Chapters 6 and 9): the famous white elephant, Abu'l Abbas, who became a general favorite at Aachen, and whose bones remained a wonder for many centuries after he died. Harun also sent Charlemagne a marvelous clock of gilded bronze, with twelve mounted mechanical knights who on the stroke of noon emerged from twelve little doors that shut behind them. Silken tents, perfumes, oriental robes abounded. The exotic atmosphere of the

Book illustration: Constantine at Nicaea, from a canon-law book at Vercelli.

court remained a vivid memory for many centuries after the glory had departed. Charlemagne had a good many beautiful daughters, whom the gentle aging Alcuin nicknamed "the crowned doves that flit about the chambers of the palace" and against whom he warned his students.

In a New Testament made expressly for Charlemagne in the early 780s and richly illustrated, the dedication verses read "Charles, the pious king of the Franks with Hildegard his glorious wife ordered me to write down this work," and the simple words conceal only momentarily the appearance of a new factor in early medieval art, the presence and determination of a powerful royal patron that provided a wholly new stimulus to artists. A portrait of Christ from this early manuscript reflects the influence of paintings recently done at Rome. It is only one of literally hundreds of miniature paintings from surviving Carolingian books, among which scholars distinguish between those painted at court and those produced in provincial centers. Similarly the art of the worker in precious metals and jewels flourished with new vigor, and that of the bronze-founder—having virtually perished—was revived at Aachen, where the still-existing grillwork around the gallery of Charlemagne's palace chapel illustrates the development of a variety of styles, and where great bronze doors, several with ornamental lion's-head handles, testify to classicizing influences at work. And these and all the other currents can be seen in ivory carvings of the period.

Reflecting upon the Carolingian artistic explosion as well as upon a galaxy of writers that ranges from Boethius to Pope Gregory the Great to Bede and the author of *Beowulf*, no student would now seriously maintain that the early Middle Ages in the West were dark. Troubled, yes; often agonizingly wretched, yes; but not dark.

Reading Suggestions on the West in the Early Middle Ages

General Accounts

T. Hodgkin, *Italy and Her Invaders*, 8 vols. (Clarendon, 1885–1899). A detailed treatment of these centuries in Italy, a monumental work of nineteenth-century scholarship, by no means superseded.

J. B. Bury, *The Invasion of Europe by the Barbarians* (Macmillan, 1928). A helpful shorter account.

E. A. Thompson, *The Early Germans* (Oxford Univ., 1965). A brief up-to-date general study.

F. Lot, *The End of the Ancient World and the Beginnings of the Middle Ages* (Knopf, 1931). A balanced survey by a French historian.

The Cambridge Medieval History, Vol. II (Macmillan, 1913). One of the few scholarly surveys of the whole period in a single volume.

C. Dawson, *The Making of Europe* (Macmillan, 1933; *Meridian). A scholarly Catholic account.

Special Studies

J. M. Wallace-Hadrill, *The Barbarian West: The Early Middle Ages, A.D. 400–1000* (*Torchbooks). Up-to-date, brief account.

J. H. Clapham and E. Power, eds., *The Cambridge Economic History*, Vol. I (Cambridge Univ., 1941). A scholarly study of agrarian life in the Middle Ages.

A. Dopsch, *The Economic and Social Foundations of European Civilization* (Harcourt, 1937). An important work revising earlier notions of the breakdown that occurred after the "fall" of Rome.

S. Dill, *Roman Society in Gaul in the Merovingian Age* (Macmillan, 1926) and *Roman Society in the Last Century of the Western Empire*, 2nd ed. (Macmillan, 1899; *Meridian). Useful social and cultural accounts.

C. Stephenson, *Medieval Feudalism* (*Great Seal Books). The best simple introductory manual.

M. Bloch, *Feudal Society,* English trans., 2 vols. (Univ. of Chicago, 1961–1964). The masterpiece of a great French scholar.

L. J. Daly, *Benedictine Monasticism: Its Formation and Development through the Twelfth Century* (Sheed & Ward, 1965). A valuable general account of a major monastic order.

H. Pirenne, *Mohammed and Charlemagne* (Norton, 1939). Propounds and defends the highly controversial thesis that the Arab conquest of the Mediterranean harmed western Europe more than the German invasions had done.

R. Winston, *Charlemagne: From the Hammer to the Cross* (Bobbs-Merrill, 1952). The best biography available in English.

H. Fichtenau, *The Carolingian Empire: The Age of Charlemagne* (*Torchbooks). A competent study.

C. H. Haskins, *The Normans in European History* (Houghton, 1915). A very readable and sympathetic introduction.

G. Duby and R. Mandrou, *A History of French Civilization,* trans. from the French (Random House, 1964). Though this admirable book is useful for all French history right up to the present, its first few pages provide a particularly good bird's-eye view of France at the end of the early Middle Ages.

F. M. Stenton, *Anglo-Saxon England,* 2nd ed. (Clarendon, 1950). A standard account.

P. H. Blair, *Roman Britain and Early England, 55 B.C.–871 A.D.* (Nelson, 1963). Supplements Stenton and is equally scholarly.

D. Whitelock, *The Beginnings of English Society* (*Penguin). A briefer introduction to Anglo-Saxon England.

D. Wilson, *The Anglo-Saxons* (*Penguin). An excellent summary account of Anglo-Saxon archaeology.

C. Brooke, *The Saxon and Norman Kings* (*Fontana Library). The first nine (of thirteen) chapters carry the story of the kingship to the reign of Canute in authoritative, up-to-date, crisp prose.

E. K. Rand, *Founders of the Middle Ages* (Harvard Univ., 1928). Excellent essays on early medieval men of letters.

M. L. W. Laistner, *Thought and Letters in Western Europe, A.D. 500 to 900* (Methuen, 1931). A good scholarly study.

R. W. Chambers, *Beowulf: An Introduction to the Study of the Poem,* suppl. C. L. Wrenn, 3rd ed. (Cambridge Univ., 1959). A full compendium of the scholarship on the poem.

G. Jones, *The Norse Atlantic Saga* (Oxford Univ., 1964) and *A History of the Vikings* (Oxford Univ., 1968). The two latest and best studies.

Sources

Gregory of Tours, *History of the Franks,* ed. O. M. Dalton (Clarendon, 1927). The account of a sixth-century historian.

A. J. Grant, ed., *Early Lives of Charlemagne* (Chatto & Windus, 1922).

Sidonius, *Poems and Letters,* trans. W. B. Anderson (Harvard Univ., 1936). The observations of a fifth-century Roman aristocrat.

Venerable Bede (Beda Venerabilis), *Ecclesiastical History of the English Nation* (Dutton, 1954). An adequate translation.

Beowulf, trans. K. Crossley-Holland (Farrar, 1968). A good recent translation.

Historical Fiction

H. Muntz, *The Golden Warrior* (Scribner's, 1949). A well-written, historically sound novel of the Norman Conquest of England.

W. Bryher, *The Fourteenth of October* (Pantheon, 1952) and *The Roman Wall* (Pantheon, 1954). Two good novels: the first about the Norman Conquest of England, the second about life on the frontier of the Roman Empire during the decline.

Eastern Christendom and Islam

To the Late Eleventh Century

Byzantium: The State

At the far southeastern corner of Europe, on a little tongue of land still defended by a long line of massive walls and towers, there stands a splendid city. Istanbul it is called now, a Turkish corruption of three Greek words meaning "to the city." After 330, when the first Christian Roman emperor Constantine the Great made it his capital, it was often called Constantinople, the city of Constantine, but it also retained its ancient name: Byzantium. For more than eleven hundred years thereafter it remained the capital of the Roman Empire, falling to the Ottoman Turks in 1453.

The waters that surround it on three sides are those of the Sea of Marmora, the Bosporus, and the city's own sheltered harbor, the Golden Horn. A few miles north, up the narrow swift-flowing Bosporus, lies the entrance into the Black Sea. To the southwest of the city, the Sea of Marmora narrows into the Dardanelles, the long passage into the Aegean, an island-studded inlet of the Mediterranean. The Dardanelles, the Sea of Marmora, and the Bosporus not only connect the Black Sea with the Mediterranean but separate Europe from Asia. Together, these are the "Straits," perhaps the most important strategic waterway in European diplomatic and military history. The city dominates the Straits. In the fifth century B.C., a shrewd Persian general was told that the earliest Greek settlers had built a town across the Straits in Asia, some seventeen years before anyone had colonized the European site of Istanbul. "Then," said he, "they must have been laboring under blindness. Otherwise, when so excellent a site was open to them, they would never have chosen one so greatly inferior." *

To the Slavs, both of Russia and of the Balkans, who owe to it their religion and their culture, Byzantium has always been Tsargrad, city of the emperor.

This was the center of a civilization in many ways similar to that of western medieval Europe, yet in others startlingly different.

The Emperor

After Constantine, Byzantium called itself New Rome. Its emperors ruled in direct succession from Augustus. Its population, predominantly Greek in race and language, called itself not Hellene (the name of the ancient Greeks for themselves) but Rhomaean, Roman. Yet many non-Roman elements—Christian, Greek, Armenian—became increasingly important in Byzantine society. A Roman of the time of Augustus would have found himself ill at ease and out of place in Byzantium. After Constantine himself had become a Christian, the emperor was of course no longer a god. But he was ordained of God, and his power remained divine. As there could be but one god in heaven, so there could be but one emperor on earth. The pagan tradition of the god-emperor was modified, not abandoned.

In theory, the will of God manifested itself in the unanimous consent of the people, the senate (established at Constantinople in the Roman pattern by Constantine himself), and the army to the choice of each new emperor. A reigning emperor usually followed the Roman practice and chose his heir, often his son, by co-opting him during his own lifetime. When an emperor selected somebody not his son, public opinion required that he should adopt him formally. Byzantine dynasties sometimes lasted several centuries. But politicians and the mob often intervened. They imprisoned and exiled emperors, murdered them, blinded or mutilated them (which made them ineligible to rule again), and enthroned their own candidates.

Each new emperor was raised aloft on a shield as a sign of army approval, so becoming *Imperator*, com-

formally crowned by the highest dignitary of the Church, the patriarch of Constantinople. He would swear to defend the Christian faith, and in addition to the crown received a purple robe and a pair of high purple boots. In the seventh century, the emperor began to call himself *basileus,* King of Kings, in token of his military victory over the Persians. Later still, he added the term *autocrat.* Empresses bore corresponding feminine titles and in general played an important role. Their images often appeared on the imperial coinage. Three times in Byzantine history women ruled alone, without a male emperor.

The emperor was an absolute ruler. Though now only the servant of the Christian God, he was still hedged about by the old imperial divinity. God bestowed his position upon him and lent victory to his arms. Although the individual autocrat might be overthrown by the conspiracy of a rival, autocracy as such was never challenged. And of course these divinely-awarded powers entailed immense earthly responsibilities: "Imperial power," says an eighth-century text, "is a legal authority established for the good of all subjects. When it strikes a blow, it is not through hatred; if it grants a reward, it is not through favoritism; but like the referee in a fight, it awards to each man the recompense he deserves." "And if," added a ninth-century patriarch more daring than most, "the Em-

peror, inspired by the devil, gives a command contrary to the divine law, no one should obey him. Every subject can rebel against any administrative act which runs counter to the law, and even against the Emperor if he allows himself to be governed by his passions." Thus the Byzantines believed that revolution was the only recourse against imperial tyranny.

An elaborate and rigid code of etiquette governed every movement the emperor made every day of the year. So complex were the rules of his life that entire treatises were written to describe them. His subjects remained silent in his presence. He spoke and gave his commands through simple, brief, and established formulas. When he gave gifts, his subjects hid their hands beneath their cloaks, a Persian ritual gesture implying that the touch of a mere human hand would soil his. Those admitted to audience approached him with their arms held fast by officials and ceremoniously fell on their faces in obeisance when they reached the throne. On public occasions the emperor was acclaimed in song, to the sound of silver trumpets.

The Law

As the direct agent of God, the emperor was responsible for the preservation of the tradition of the Roman law. He alone could modify the laws already in effect or

Sixth-century mosaic in the Church of San Vitale, Ravenna, showing the emperor Justinian and attendants.

proclaim new ones. From time to time the emperor ordered the periodic redrafting and recompiling of the statute books. Thus he had ready to his hand an immensely powerful instrument for preserving and enhancing his power.

Justinian (reigned 527–565) between 528 and 533 ordered his lawyers to dispose of obsolete, repetitious, and conflicting enactments, thus codifying existing law. His *Code* included all legislation since Hadrian (117–138). The authoritative opinions of legal experts were collected in the *Digests,* an even bulkier work. The *Institutes,* a handbook for students, served as an introduction to both compilations. All these were set down in the Latin in which they had been issued, but Justinian's own laws, the *Novels,* or newly passed enactments, appeared in Greek.

Not until the eighth century did a new collection appear—the *Ekloga* (wholly in Greek)—which modified Justinian's work in accordance with Christian attitudes toward family relationships and with the decreasingly Roman and increasingly Greek and oriental character of the empire. The *Ekloga* softened the death penalty provided for many offenses by earlier law, and substituted punishments less severe, though still often entailing cruel mutilations. Under Leo VI (886–912), a new collection, called the *Basilics,* made its appearance. Leo's own new laws show the emperor rejecting much that dated from an earlier period when the absolutism of the emperor had not been so fully developed.

In the Byzantine Empire, justice could be rendered only in the emperor's name. He was the supreme judge, and the rendering of justice was perhaps his most important function. Subordinate officials handed down decisions only by virtue of the power he had delegated to them, and could in theory always be overruled on appeal to him. The emperors themselves often rendered judgment in person in quite ordinary cases brought to them by their subjects. Heraclius (610–641) executed an officer who had stolen the land of a poor widow and had beaten her son to death. Theophilus (829–842) appeared every week on horseback at a given church and handed down judgments so fair and equitable and unbiased that they have passed into legend:

One day when the Emperor appeared, a poor woman threw herself at his feet in tears, complaining that all light and air had been shut off from her house by a huge and sumptuous new palace which a high official of the police was building next door. Moreover, this official was the brother of the Empress. But the Emperor paid no heed to this. He ordered an instant inquiry, and when he found that the woman had told the truth, he had the guilty man stripped and beaten in the open street, commanded the palace to be torn down, and gave the land on which it stood to the woman. Another time, a woman boldly seized the bridle of the horse which the Emperor was riding, and told him that the horse was hers. As soon as Theophilus got back to the palace, he had her brought in, and she testified that the general of the province where she lived had taken the horse away from her husband by force, and had given it to the

Emperor as a present to curry favor with him. Then he had sent the rightful owner of the horse into combat with the infantry, where he had been killed. When the general was haled before the Emperor and was confronted by the woman, he finally admitted his guilt. He was dismissed from his post, and part of his property confiscated and given to the plaintiff.*

The emperors of the later ninth century took greater care in the systematic appointment of judges and created a kind of legal-aid bureau to enable the poor of the provinces to make appeals to the capital. Judges were obliged to render written decisions and to sign them all. New courts were set up and new officials were created. Later, even in the provinces, side by side with the martial law administered by the local commanding general, we find instances when even soldiers were tried in civil courts for civil offenses.

The "sacred palace," the emperor's residence, was the center of the state, and the officials of the palace were the most important functionaries of the state: administrative, civil, and military. All officials had a title that gave them a post in the palace, as well as a rank among the nobility. At Byzantium, many of the greatest and most influential officials were eunuchs, an oriental feature of the state that astonished Westerners and made them uneasy. There was never a prime minister, but in practice an imperial favorite often controlled policy.

War

As defenders of the faith, the Byzantine emperors fought one enemy after another for eleven hundred years. Sometimes the invaders were moving north and west from Asia: Persians in the seventh century, Arabs—adherents of the new Islamic religion—from the seventh century on, and Turks beginning in the eleventh century.

The Byzantine Empire was often shaken by these blows: the provinces of Syria and Egypt—Roman for more than seven hundred years—were lost forever in the seventh century as a result of the impact of Persians and Arabs. And western Europe was not entirely spared the effects of these invasions. The Arab expansion swept westward over North Africa, into Sicily and southern Italy, and across the Straits of Gibraltar into Spain, whence a small force even challenged the Franks at Tours in 732. But Charles Martel's victory at Tours was a far less significant achievement in checking the Muslim tide at high-water mark than the victory of the Byzantine emperor Leo III, who had repelled a major Arab attack on Constantinople itself in 717, fifteen years before.

Byzantium thus served as a buffer that absorbed the heaviest shock of Eastern invasions and cushioned the West against them. The Byzantine state was also

---

*C. Diehl, "La Légende de Théophile," *Seminarium Kondakovianum,* IV (1931), 35. Our translation.

engaged on all its frontiers in almost constant warfare against a variety of other enemies. Sometimes they were Asians, who had drifted into Europe from what is now Russia. In this category belong the Huns of the fifth century, the Avars of the sixth and seventh, the Bulgars of the seventh and succeeding centuries, the Magyars of the ninth and later centuries, and the Pechenegs and Cumans of the eleventh, twelfth, and thirteenth centuries. All these peoples were initially Turkic or Finnish or Mongolic nomads, living in felt tents, drinking fermented mare's milk and eating cheese, and quite at home for days at a time on the backs of their swift horses.

Sometimes the enemies were native Europeans, like the Slavs, who first appeared in the sixth century and filtered gradually south into the empire thereafter in a steady human flow that covered the entire Balkan peninsula, even inland Greece, with Slavic settlement. In the northeastern part of the peninsula just south of the Danube, the Slavs were conquered by the Hunnic tribe of the Bulgars, but slowly absorbed their conquerors. By the tenth century the Bulgarians had no recognizable Asian traces left but were thoroughly Slavic. These Bulgars, and much later the Slavic Serbs to the west of them, fought long and exhausting wars against Byzantium.

So did the Russians, another Slavic people, whose Scandinavian upper crust was gradually absorbed by a Slavic lower class. They first assaulted Byzantium from the water in 860, having sailed across the Black Sea; and they several times repeated the attack. Beginning in the eleventh century, the enemies were western Europeans: Normans from the southern Italian state in Italy and Sicily, Crusaders from France and Germany and Italy, freebooting commercial adventurers from the new Italian cities seeking to extract economic concessions by force or to increase the value of the concessions they already held.

For more than seven hundred years after Constantine, until the late eleventh century, when Turks and Normans alike inflicted serious defeats, the Byzantines were able to hold their own. Though hostile forces sometimes swarmed to the very foot of the land walls or threatened to launch a maritime invasion from across the Straits, Constantinople itself remained inviolable until 1204. In that year it was taken for the first time by a mixed force of Venetian traders eager for profit, and French, Italian, and German Crusaders, who had set out to fight the Muslims in Palestine but had been detoured.

Only a state with phenomenally good armies and navies could have compiled so successful a military

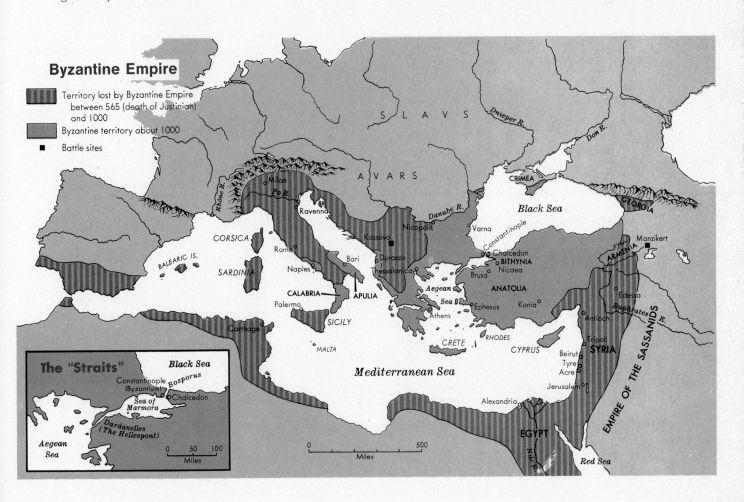

Thirteenth-century manuscript illumination illustrating the use of Greek fire.

record. From all periods of Byzantine history there survive treatises on the art of war, discussing new ways of fighting, new weapons. The Byzantines were adaptable, learning and applying lessons from their successive enemies. Often commanded by the emperor in person, carefully recruited and thoroughly trained, well armed and equipped, entertained by bands playing martial music, served by medical and ambulance corps, by a signal corps with flashing mirrors, and by intelligence agencies far more competent than those of their rivals, the Byzantine armies, though occasionally defeated, by and large maintained their superiority.

The same is almost as true of the Byzantine navies. The appearance of a Muslim fleet in the eastern Mediterranean in the seventh century forced a naval reorganization by the Byzantines, who by the tenth century had recaptured their former control of these waters. In the eleventh century, like all other Byzantine institutions, the navy suffered a decline from which it never recovered. Gradually, the developing Italian merchant cities replaced Byzantium as the great Mediterranean naval power. This was one of the main causes of the empire's downfall. At its height, however, the Byzantine fleet played a major role in imperial defense. It was equipped with one of the real secret weapons of the Middle Ages: Greek fire, a chemical compound squirted from tubes or siphons in the shape of lion's heads of gilded bronze mounted on the prows of the Byzantine ships, which would set enemy vessels aflame, and strike terror into the hearts of their sailors.

Diplomacy

The Byzantines fought only when they had to, preferring to negotiate whenever possible. Diplomacy too

they brought to a high level: we have the records and reports of a good many Byzantine embassies and can appreciate the subtlety of the instructions given the envoys. First Persia and then to some extent the Muslim caliphate were the only states whose rulers the Byzantine emperors regarded as equals. All others were barbarians, and when they claimed an imperial title, as in the case of the Franks or the later German emperors, the claim was usually passed over in scornful silence or openly disputed.

Yet, although the theory of empire proclaimed that the Byzantine Empire was universal, in their constant effort to protect their frontiers the Byzantine emperors dealt realistically with those "barbarian" peoples whom they could not conquer. They negotiated treaties, obtaining military assistance, and graciously allowing the vassal peoples to bask in the reflected light of imperial prestige and to enjoy the luxuries that Byzantine money could buy. A kind of "office of barbarian affairs" kept imperial officials supplied with intelligence reports on the internal conditions of each barbarian people so that a "pro-Byzantine" party might be created among them and any internal stresses and quarrels might be turned to the advantage of the Byzantines.

As in Roman times, when the emperor sent arms for the chieftain of a foreign tribe, the act was the equivalent of adoption. The Christian Byzantine emperor could make the paternal relationship even stronger by sponsoring a pagan barbarian ruler at his baptism. The son of such a chief might be invited to be educated at Byzantium and thus introduced to all the glories of Byzantine civilization. Titles in the hierarchy of the palace, with their rich and valuable insignia, were bestowed on barbarian rulers; and even a royal crown might be granted. Marriage was also a most useful instrument. Barbarian leaders were delighted to marry Byzantine girls of noble family; and when it was a question of a particularly desirable alliance, the emperor himself might marry a barbarian princess or arrange to give a princess of the imperial house to a foreigner.

A solemn formal reception at the imperial court usually dazzled a foreign ruler or envoy, even a sophisticated Western bishop like Liudprand, ambassador of the king of Italy, who has left us this account from the year 948:

> Before the emperor's seat stood a tree made of bronze gilded over, whose branches were filled with birds, also made of gilded bronze, which uttered different cries, each according to its varying species. The throne itself was so marvellously fashioned that at one moment it seemed a low structure and at another it rose high into the air. It was of immense size and was guarded by lions, made either of bronze or of wood covered over with gold, who beat the ground with their tails and gave a dreadful roar with open mouth and quivering tongue. Leaning upon the shoulders of two eunuchs I was brought into the emperor's presence. At my approach the lions began to roar and the birds to cry out, each according to its kind. . . . After I had three times made obeisance to the emperor with my face upon the ground, I lifted my head and behold! the man whom just before I had seen sitting on a moderately elevated seat had now changed his raiment and was sitting on the level of the ceiling. How it was done I cannot imagine, unless perhaps he was lifted up by some sort of device as we use for raising the timbers of a wine-press.*

The Economy

Good armies and navies and shrewd diplomacy always cost money. Byzantium was enormously rich. It was a great center of trade, to which came vessels from every quarter of the compass. From the countries around the shore of the Black Sea came furs and hides, grain, salt, wine, and slaves from the Caucasus. From India, Ceylon, Syria, and Arabia came spices, precious stones, and silk; from Africa, slaves and ivory; from the West, especially Italy, merchants eager to buy the products sold in Constantinople, often the products of the imperial industries.

The Byzantine emperors themselves were able for many centuries to maintain a monopoly of the manufacture and sale of silk textiles, purple dye, and gold embroidery, which were not then merely luxuries but absolute necessities for the dignitaries of church and state in the West as in the East. Long a closely guarded secret of the Persians, silk manufacture came to Byzantium in the middle of the sixth century, when—so the story goes—two monks explained to the emperor that the mysterious cloth was the product of silkworms. Later, bribed by the promise of a great reward, they actually brought back silkworms' eggs hidden in a hollow cane. They taught the emperor that the worms must be fed on mulberry leaves; great plantations of mulberries were established, especially in Syria; and a mighty enterprise was under way.

The power that was derived from the control over the manufacture and sale of silk has been compared with modern controls over such strategic materials as oil. But it was not only the imperial treasury that profited: the rich were able to embellish their persons and their homes; many middle-class merchants and craftsmen found a livelihood in the industry; and the flow of revenue into the imperial treasuries made it possible for the emperors to tax the lower classes less than would otherwise have been necessary for national defense and other official expenses. An elaborate system of control over manufacture (which was in the hands of carefully regulated guilds) and over sales (which were permitted only in official salesrooms) safely secured the monopoly down to the eleventh century.

Besides controlling silk, the emperor forbade the export of gold, in order to prevent the depletion of reserves. The *nomisma*, as the Byzantine gold coin was called, was standard all over the Mediterranean and even in the East. Until the late eleventh century it was almost never debased, and even then only under the impact of crisis brought about by civil strife and foreign invasion, and only gradually. But for eight hundred years this money was stable.

All visitors noticed and envied the wealth of Byzantium, especially those from the West, whose own largely rural society and meager way of life contrasted so strikingly with the urban glitter and sophistication of the imperial capital. Westerners admired the splendid silken garments embroidered with gold, the palaces and churches aglow with mosaics and richly carved columns of semiprecious stones imported at great expense from distant lands, the jewelry and gold and ivory worn by the wealthy citizens and displayed in their houses. Beneath the splendor and the show lay the hard economic realities that preserved the state for centuries: a thriving commerce and industry and a substantial revenue.

Throughout Byzantine history, the sources of state income remained pretty much the same. Money came in from state property in land—farms, cattle ranches, gold and silver mines, marble quarries—as distinct from the money that came in from the emperor's personal estates. Booty seized in war or fortunes confiscated from rich men in disgrace provided cash. And of course there was also revenue from taxation: on land and persons, sales and profits, imports and exports, and inheritances.

From Diocletian (284–305) the Byzantines inherited the concept that land and labor were taxable together. The territory of the empire was considered to be divided into units called yokes, each of which was defined as the amount of land that could feed a single laboring farmer. In order to be taxable as a unit of land, each yoke had to have its farmer to work it; in order to be taxable as a person, each farmer had to have a yoke to work. In a period of labor shortage, the

Antapodosis, VI, v, in *Works of Liudprand of Cremona*, trans. F. A. Wright (London, 1930), pp. 207–208.

government thus had to find a person to cultivate every yoke; otherwise there would have been no revenue.

It was this concept that led to the binding of many peasants to the soil and to their slow degeneration into serfs. Large private landowners naturally flourished under such a system, since it was easier for the state to lease them large tracts of land and leave it to them to find the supply of labor. Moreover, inferior land or abandoned or run-down farms were compulsorily assigned to nearby landowners, who were responsible for the taxes on this property as on their more productive acres. Only if a landowner had a substantial acreage of rich and productive farm land could he be expected to pay such taxes on the more marginal farms. So this aspect of the system also contributed to the growth of large private estates. Yet, though the large estate may have predominated in the early period, the small private freeholder seems never to have disappeared. In later centuries, the balance between the two types of holding would several times swing one way or the other.

The Capital and the Factions

As the capital, Constantinople had its own special administration, under a prefect of the city, or *eparch*. He was mayor, chief of police, and judge rolled into one, responsible for public order, inspecting the markets, fixing fair prices for food, and supervising the lawyers, notaries, money changers, and bankers, as well as merchants. The city artisans and tradesmen were organized into guilds or corporations, each with its own governor, under the authority of the eparch. He upheld standards of quality in food supplies and in manufactured goods, and he punished misrepresentations of quality by overenthusiastic or dishonest salesmen. By the eleventh century, the eparch was often left in charge in the emperor's absence.

Byzantium inherited from Rome rival parties of chariot racers, each with its own stables and equipment and colors, the Blues and the Greens. We can best understand these circus factions if we imagine that in, let us say, present-day Chicago, the White Sox and the Cubs were not only the city's passionately loved baseball teams who played each other exclusively, and about whose rivalry the entire community got wildly excited but also represented opposing factions on all the political, religious, economic, and social issues of the day, and in addition had certain military duties in defense of the city in time of war.

The Blues and Greens were influential during the early centuries of the empire; the emperor himself always joined one group or the other. He fixed the days on which races were to be held at the Hippodrome, a vast stadium attached to the sacred palace and close to the Cathedral Church of Saint Sophia (Hagia Sophia). On the appointed days, the turbulent populace would throng the stands and root frantically for the charioteers of their party.

Blues and Greens seem to have come from different quarters of the city, and from different social classes. The Blues were apparently the party of the aristocracy, the Greens of the lower classes; the Blues were the party of strict Christian orthodoxy, the Greens were frequently the party of questionable orthodoxy, since new heresies naturally took root among the poor. Those emperors who were strictly orthodox themselves enrolled as Blues; those who leaned toward heterodoxy and felt the need for mob support enrolled as Greens. This division existed in the great provincial cities, too, but at Constantinople it took on special virulence. The factional strife manifested itself sometimes in the Hippodrome, when the faction opposed to the emperor would riot against him, and sometimes in the streets of the city, when roving bands belonging to one faction would invade the quarter of the other and burn down houses.

The most celebrated riot in all Byzantine history was the Nika revolt of 532 (so called because of the cry of the rioters, meaning "victory"). On this occasion the Blues and Greens temporarily united to try to force Justinian to be merciful to two condemned criminals, one Green and one Blue, who had escaped execution by accident. When the emperor, who had been a Blue, but who now tried to assume an impartially severe attitude toward both parties, failed to assent to their joint request, they revolted simultaneously and burned most of the public buildings of the city. The seriousness of the riot was greatly increased by the presence in the city of a large number of poor peasants from the country, who had fled their farms as a result of heavy taxation, and who joined the factions in what became a revolution.

Justinian might well have lost his throne had it not been for the coolness and bravery of his celebrated empress, Theodora, who said,

> Now, above all other times, is a bad time to flee, even if we get away safely. Once a man has seen the light, he must surely die; but for a man who has been an emperor to become a refugee is intolerable. May I never be separated from the purple [the symbol of imperial rank] and may I no longer live on that day when those who meet me shall not call me mistress. Now if you wish to save yourself, O Emperor, that is easy. For we have much money; there is the sea, here are the boats. But think whether after you have been saved you may not come to feel that you would have preferred to die. As for me, I like a certain old proverb that says: royalty is a good shroud.*

The emperor took heart, and the revolt was put down. It was the destruction of the old cathedral during this riot that made necessary the construction of the new Hagia Sophia.

The Nika affair was exceptional in its severity and in the combination of the rival factions. But every reign from the end of the fourth century to the middle of the seventh was marked by outbursts of disorder be-

*Procopius, *History of the Wars*, I, xxiv, 35–38. Our translation.

tween the two parties. All this time, both the Blues and Greens also had military and municipal duties, helping with the construction of the walls and bearing a heavy share of the responsibility for defense. This made for instability, since it was never certain that mutual hatred would yield in the face of common danger. In the seventh and eighth centuries the emperors in some unknown fashion finally succeeded in clipping the wings of the factions. They took over the management of the public entertainments in the Hippodrome and left only an unimportant role to the leaders of the Blues and Greens, who were restricted to acclaiming the emperor on public occasions.

II Byzantine Christianity and Relations with the West

Religion at Byzantium

In the Byzantine world, religion governed men's lives from birth to death. In the life of every person, the Church governed marriage and family relations, filled leisure time, helped determine any critical decision. Religion pervaded intellectual life: the most serious intellectual problems of the age were theological, attacked by brains second to none in power and subtlety. Religion dominated the arts and literature, economic life and politics. What we would call domestic issues, about which the people got excited, were political issues centering on theological problems. What was the true relationship of the members of the Trinity to one another? What was the true relationship of the human to the divine nature of Christ? Was it proper to worship the holy images? It was not only in monasteries and universities that such problems were argued, but also in the streets. Either faction would riot in the Hippodrome if the emperor opposed its views on such questions. The right answer meant salvation and future immortality, whereas the wrong answer meant damnation and eternal punishment.

What we would call the issues of foreign policy too were pervaded by religion: when the emperor went forth to war, he went as the champion of the faith. Most often, the enemies were not Christians, or were heretics or schismatics. The emperor went into battle against them with a sacred picture borne before him, an icon (image) of the Virgin, perhaps one of those which legend said had been painted by Saint Luke, or not even made by human hands at all, but miraculously sent from heaven itself.

Contrast with the West

Yet much of this was true also in the medieval West. The real contrast we see most clearly when we compare the relationship between Church and State in the West with that in the East. In the West, the imperial departure from Rome permitted the local bishops to create a papal monarchy and challenge kings and em-

perors. In Constantinople, however, the emperor remained in residence. No papacy could develop. Constantine himself summoned the Council of Nicaea in 325; he paid the salaries of the bishops, presided over their deliberations, and as emperor gave to their decrees the force of imperial law. When he legislated as head of the Christian church in matters of Christian dogma, he was doing what no layman in the West could do; he still had some of the attributes of the Roman pontifex. In the East, the emperor regularly deposed patriarchs and punished clerics. He took the initiative in church reforms. The faith was a principle of civil law; the emperor often helped prepare canon law. Constantine's imperial successors were often theologians themselves and enjoyed argument and speculation on theological questions. Sometimes they even legislated on matters of faith without consulting churchmen. In short, the Church was a kind of department of state, and the emperor was the effective head of it as he was of the other departments. One of his titles was "Equal to the Apostles."

A system in which a single authority plays the role of both emperor and pope is known as *Caesaropapism*. Sometimes, it is true, a patriarch of Constantinople challenged an emperor successfully. Moreover, absolute though they were, none of the emperors could afford to impose new dogma without church support or could risk offending the religious susceptibilities of the people. Some scholars therefore prefer not to use the term *Caesaropapism*, but it seems to us in general an accurate one.

As we know, Constantine had not wanted to intervene in the theological quarrel over Arianism, but he did so because the very structure of the empire was threatened. The Council of Nicaea failed to impose a settlement, and the quarrel continued for another three-quarters of a century. Then, after a pause of only fifty years, there began the new and even more desperately fought battles over the relationship between the human and divine natures in Christ, concentrated in the eastern Mediterranean world. Egyptian, Syrian, Ethiopian, and Armenian Christians were monophysites, as they are to this day, and they successfully resisted the attempts to force them to compromise that were repeatedly made by the emperors, notably Zeno (474–491), Justinian (527–565), and Heraclius (610–641).

Monasticism and the Sacraments

The Byzantines assumed, to a far greater extent than the western Europeans, that the individual had very little chance of salvation. In the East, more than the West, monasticism became *the* Christian life, since to become a monk was to take a direct route to salvation. Worldly men, including many emperors, became monks on their deathbeds to increase their chances of going to heaven. At Byzantium, monks enjoyed enormous popular prestige and often influenced political decisions; monks provided the highest ranks of the Church hierarchy; rich and powerful laymen, from the emperor down, founded new monasteries as an act of piety. Often immune from taxation, monasteries acquired vast lands and much treasure. Some emperors tried to check monastic growth, but the monks continued to influence policies because of their hold over the popular imagination.

For the ordinary Christian, the sacraments of the Church provided the way to salvation. In the East every religious act took on a sacramental quality. Every image, every relic of a saint, was felt to preserve the essence of the holy person in itself. God was felt to be actually present in the sanctuary; he could be reached through—and only through—the proper performance of the ritual. In the East the emphasis fell on mystery, magic, ritual, a personal approach to the heavenly Saviour, more than on the ethical teachings of Christianity. Once a believer had accepted the proper performance of a magical action as the right way to reach God, he could not contemplate any change in it: if the old way is wrong, one's parents and grandparents are all damned.

Quarrels and Schism with the West

A slight difference in the wording of the liturgy, it is sometimes argued, caused the schism, or split, between the Eastern and Western churches in 1054. The Greek creed states that the Holy Ghost "proceeds" from the Father, the Latin adds the word *filioque,* meaning "and from the son." But this and other differences might never have received much notice, and would probably not have led to schism, had it not been for the political questions at issue and for the increasing divergences between the two civilizations.

More than three hundred years earlier, in the eighth century, a new religious controversy arose in the Byzantine Empire over the use of sculptured and painted sacred images and the nature and amount of reverence that a Christian might properly pay them. Something very like idolatry was widespread, and twice for long periods (726–787 and 813–842) the emperors adopted the strict Old Testament rule that all images must be banned (iconoclasm, image-breaking). The impulse apparently came from a puritanical revulsion against superstitious excesses in venerating the images. The popes, who believed that images were educational and might be venerated (but of course not worshiped), were shocked, and they condemned iconoclasm.

In the end, the emperors restored the images, but as early as the 730s an iconoclastic emperor had punished the pope by removing from papal jurisdiction southern Italy, with its rich church revenues, and Illyricum (the Balkan provinces), and placing them under the patriarch of Constantinople. The papacy was determined to recover its rights and incomes in these territories. But even more decisive than iconoclasm was the papal belief that Byzantium could not or would not defend Italy and the papacy against Lombards and Muslims, and the consequent decision of Pope Stephen II to turn to Pepin and Charlemagne.

Again, in the 860s, competition between papal and Byzantine missionaries to convert the Bulgarians led to a political quarrel. It was only then that the Byzantines "discovered" the Roman "error" in adding *filioque* to the creed. Though this quarrel too was eventually settled, underlying mistrust persisted. It was increased by the deep corruption into which the papacy fell during the tenth century. The Byzantines became accustomed to going their own way without reference to the bishops of Rome. When the papacy was eventually reformed in the eleventh century, the Byzantines did not at first understand that they were no longer dealing with the slack and immoral popes they had grown used to.

Under these circumstances, they were unprepared for a revival of the old papal efforts to recover jurisdiction over southern Italy from the patriarch of Constantinople. As Norman adventurers, newly arrived in southern Italy just after the year 1000, began to make conquests in this Byzantine territory, they restored to the pope churches and church revenues there. The pope naturally welcomed the action, while the Byzantine patriarch naturally was unhappy over his losses. A violent and powerful man, he dug up the old *filioque* controversy as a pretext for pushing his more solid grievances. In answer to his complaints, the pope in 1054 sent to Byzantium one of his most energetic and unbending cardinals. Patriarch and cardinal excommunicated each other. The papal envoy shook the dust of Constantinople from his feet and sailed for home. This was *schism,* a split between the Roman Catholic and Greek Orthodox churches. Despite numerous efforts at reconciliation since 1054, these mutual excommunications were lifted only in 1965.

Antagonism between East and West

In addition, Eastern and Western Christians disliked one another instinctively. To the visiting Westerner, no doubt in part jealous of the high Byzantine standard of living, the Greeks seemed soft, effeminate, and treacherous. To the Byzantine, the Westerner seemed savage, fickle, and dangerous, a barbarian like all other barbarians. Nowhere is the Western attitude shown any better than in the writings of Bishop Liudprand, who had been so impressed by the emperor's movable throne when he visited Constantinople in 948. On a second official visit in 969, as ambassador from Otto I, he describes his reception by the emperor Nicephorus Phocas:

On the fourth of June we arrived at Constantinople, and after a miserable reception . . . we were given the most miserable and disgusting quarters. The palace . . . was . . . large and open, but it neither kept out the cold nor afforded shelter from heat. Armed soldiers were set to guard us and prevent my people from going out and any others from coming in. . . . To add to our troubles the Greek wine we found undrinkable because of the mixture in it of pitch, resin, and plaster. The house itself had no water, and we could not even buy any to quench our thirst. . . . Nicephorus himself . . . is a monstrosity of a man, a dwarf, fatheaded and with tiny mole's eyes; disfigured by a short broad thick beard half going gray; disgraced by a neck scarcely an inch long; piglike by reason of the big close bristles on his head; in color an Ethiopian, and, as the poet, says, "you would not like to meet him in the dark."*

As might have been expected, Liudprand, the defender of the West, and Nicephorus, the Byzantine, whose unattractiveness his guest certainly exaggerated in order to curry favor with his German imperial master, had a violent disagreement on questions of prestige. When Liudprand left, he scrawled on the wall of his uncomfortable quarters a long anti-Greek poem, beginning

Trust not the Greeks; they live but to betray;
Nor heed their promises, whate'er they say.
If lies will serve them, any oath they swear,
And when it's time to break it feel no fear.†

On the other side, the Byzantine reaction to Westerners is illustrated by the famous *Alexiad*, written by the princess Anna Comnena more than a century later, a history of her father, Emperor Alexius I Comnenus (1081–1118). She says that two Normans, Robert Guiscard and his son Bohemond

might rightly be termed "the caterpillar and the locust"; for whatever escaped Robert . . . Bohemond took to him and devoured. . . .

For by nature the man was a rogue and ready for anything; in roguery and cunning he was far superior to all the Latins [Westerners]. . . . But in spite of his surpassing them all in superabundant activity in mischief, yet fickleness like some natural appendage attended him too. . . .

He was such a man . . . as no one in the Empire had seen before, . . . for he was a wonderful spectacle . . . so tall that he surpassed the tallest man by a cubit [about eighteen inches]; he was slender of waist and flank, broad of shoulder, and fullchested; his whole body was muscular. . . . very white; his face was mingled white and ruddycolor. His hair was a shade of yellow, and did not fall upon his shoulders like that of other barbarians; the man avoided this foolish practice, and his hair was cut even to his ears. I cannot say whether his beard was red or some other color; his face had been closely shaved and seemed as smooth as chalk. . . . A certain charm hung about the man but was partly marred by a sense of the terrible. There seemed to be something untamed and inexorable about his whole appearance, . . . and his laugh was like the roaring of other men. . . . His mind was manysided, versatile, and provident. His speech was carefully worded and his answers guarded.‡

* *Works of Liudprand of Cremona*, trans. F. A. Wright (London, 1930), pp. 235–236.
† Ibid., p. 270.
‡ Translation partly ours, partly from E. A. S. Dawes' translation of the *Alexiad* (London, 1928), pp. 37–38, 266, 347.

The mutual dislike between Byzantines and Westerners was to grow steadily more intense in the period after the late eleventh century, until it reached a climax in the tragedy of 1204.

III The Fortunes of Empire, 330–1081

When we are dealing with a period of more than eleven hundred years of history, as in the case of Byzantium from its dedication by Constantine in 330 to its capture by the Turks in 1453, it is useful to subdivide it. The late eleventh century provides the major break in Byzantine history: by then the decline in imperial strength can be plainly seen. So in this chapter we shall bring the story down only as far as 1081. In each of the shorter periods that can for convenience be distinguished between 330 and 1081, we single out for emphasis the major trends of foreign and domestic policies, and trace the more gradual course of changes to be found in government, society, and economic life.

The Main Periods of Byzantine History, 330–1081

The first period runs from Constantine's dedication of his capital in 330 to the accession of the emperor Leo III in 717. Despite their efforts, the Roman emperors at Constantinople could not reconquer the West and thus reconstitute the Roman Empire of Augustus. Indeed, theological controversy, reflecting internal political strain, and combined with Persian and Arab aggression, cost the empire Syria and Egypt. The internal structure was modified in accordance with the new situation.

From 717 to 867, the threat of Arab conquest was safely contained, the Bulgarians were converted, the major religious and political struggle over church images was fought and decided, and the big landowners began to emerge as a threat to the financial and military system.

From 867 to 1025, the Byzantine Empire was at its height; the emperors went over to the counterattack against the Arabs and regained much territory and prestige; the grim Bulgarian struggle was fought to a bloody conclusion; the Russians were converted; and the emperors made every effort to check the growth of the great landowning aristocracy.

The years 1025–1081 represented a period of decline, slow at first, but accelerated as the period drew to a close: external military disaster accompanied, and was related to, the triumph of the landowners.

From Constantine to Leo III (330–717)

As we know, the emperors immediately following Constantine were Arians until Theodosius I (379–395), who proclaimed Orthodox Nicene Athanasian Christianity (381) to be the sole permitted state religion. All those who did not accept the Nicene Creed were to be driven

Silver plate showing the emperor Theodosius, with his sons, Honorius and Arcadius, on either side, bestowing the insignia of office on a local official. Found in the mid-nineteenth century in western Spain by two peasants, who, before they could be stopped, split it in order to divide the profits.

from the cities of the empire. Theodosius' enactment is a landmark along the road to the creation of the Orthodox Eastern empire, illustrating the close relation of theology to politics and to imperial initiative. Although the empire east and west was united under Theodosius, his sons Arcadius (395–408) and Honorius divided it, with Arcadius ruling at Constantinople. It was never again fully united in fact, although in theory it had never been divided.

Until the accession of Justinian in 527, the eastern portion of the empire successfully used Goths and other barbarians as troops and usually managed to deflect the new blows of further invaders westward. Despite the challenge from Huns and Persians, the East continued to prosper. Only the monophysite controversy warned of internal weakness. The subtleties of theological argument only partly revealed the challenge of Alexandria to Constantinople and the dangers of Syrian and Egyptian defection.

Justinian (527–565) was so controversial an emperor that even his own historian, Procopius, wrote—in addition to several works praising him to the skies—a *Secret History,* never published in his own day, which denounces Justinian in the most unrestrained way and reports much dirty gossip about his famous empress, Theodora, who in her youth had been an entertainer

in the Hippodrome. We do not have to believe that Justinian was greater than Cyrus the Great or Themistocles, as Procopius says when praising him, but neither do we have to believe that he was a demon who walked around the palace at night without his head, as Procopius tells us in the *Secret History.*

In an epic series of wars, Justinian's armies reconquered North Africa from the Vandals, Italy from the Ostrogoths, and southern Spain from the Visigoths, a last desperate effort to reunite all of Rome's Mediterranean lands and recreate a territorial unity that was by now in fact unmanageable. Both the long drawn-out campaigns and a vast new system of fortifications proved extremely costly. By limiting his wars with the Persians on the eastern frontier to defensive efforts, Justinian permitted the Persian danger to grow. His immediate successors could not check it, while in Europe Slavs and Avars were able to dent the Danube line and filter into the Balkans.

Justinian began a process of administrative reorganization that his successors would finish. In the provinces of the Roman Empire, Constantine had seen to it that civil and military authority were never united in the hands of the same official. He had also subdivided large territorial units of government. These were obvious precautions against revolts by ambitious generals like those that had characterized the third century. But now, Justinian's conquests in the West imposed so severe a strain on the system, and unrest in Egypt and elsewhere was so alarming, that the emperor occasionally entrusted both civil and military power to a single officer, giving him a comparatively large area to administer. After Justinian's death the military emergency caused in Italy by the invasion of the Lombards and in North Africa by the savage native Berbers forced the authorities to create in both regions large military districts. In Italy and Africa, the military commanders, called exarchs, also served as civil governors, and their areas of command were called exarchates. With their headquarters respectively at Ravenna and Carthage, they became virtual vice-emperors.

The empire did not have to pay the full bill for Justinian's policies until the early years of the seventh century. During the reign of Phocas (602–610), internal bankruptcy and external attacks from the Persians seemed to threaten total destruction. But Heraclius (610–641), the son of the exarch of Africa, sailed in the nick of time from Carthage to Constantinople and seized the throne. He spent the first years of his reign in military preparations, absorbing heavy losses as the Persians took Antioch, Damascus, and Jerusalem, bearing off the True Cross in triumph. Soon afterward they entered Alexandria, and Egypt too was gone. After 622 Heraclius began his counteroffensive. At one moment in 626 the Persians threatened Constantinople from the Asian side of the Straits, while the Slavs and Avars were besieging it in Europe; but the Byzantines beat off the double threat. Heraclius defeated the Persians on their own territory, recaptured all the lost provinces, and returned the True Cross to Jerusalem in 629.

But only a few years later, the new movement of Islam exploded out of Arabia and took away once more the very provinces that Heraclius had recaptured from the Persians. In both the Persian and the Muslim victories over Byzantium, the disaffection of the monophysite Syrians and Egyptians played a major part. From Egypt the Muslims pushed on westward and took Carthage in 698, putting an end to the North African exarchate. Muslim ships began to operate from Cyprus and Rhodes. In northern Italy the Lombard kingdom had increased its power, while two separate Lombard duchies, one at Spoleto in central Italy, the other at Benevento farther south, threatened the imperial possessions. Heraclius' work and that of Justinian were seemingly undone.

The Reorganization of the Seventh and Eighth Centuries

Despite the desperate crisis, the emperors, beginning— tradition said—with Heraclius, completely overhauled the administrative machinery of the state. Gradually they extended to their remaining territories in Asia Minor and the Balkans the system of government previously introduced into the two exarchates. The loss of Syria and Egypt required the transformation of Asia Minor into a reservoir of military manpower and an orderly stronghold of defense. The perpetual raids of Slavs, Avars, and Bulgars into the Balkan provinces made the emergency more acute and increased still more the dependence on Asia Minor. So over a period of time the emperors divided Asia Minor and the Balkans into what we would call army corps areas, with the local military commanders also exercising civil authority.

These new military districts were called *themes,* from a word meaning a permanent garrison. In each theme the troops were recruited from the native population; in return for their services, the independent farmers were granted land, but they were not allowed to dispose of it or to evade their duties as soldiers. Their sons inherited the property along with the obligation to fight. Though in theory responsible to the emperor, the commanding generals of the themes often revolted, and in the late seventh and early eighth centuries such rebellious generals often seized the imperial throne. The imperial government strove to combat this danger, inevitable when military and civil powers were united in the same hands, by dividing the large original themes into smaller ones. From seven big themes at the end of the seventh century, the number mounted to about thirty smaller ones by the year 900. From the start, one of the themes was naval. In addition to the troops supplied by the commanders of the themes, the emperors had at their disposal other non-thematic forces, both land and sea, quartered in the capital itself.

The emperors also asserted more and more their direct supervisory authority over the civil service departments. As the reorganization proceeded, the old title of a formerly influential job was sometimes bestowed as a purely honorary reminder of past duties, much as the English title of duke, for example, today no longer means that the bearer is a true dux, or army commander. In this way a hierarchy of honorary titles came to exist side by side with the hierarchy of real jobs. Military and civil officials, eunuchs, clerics, and even foreign ambassadors to the Byzantine court all had their places both in the galaxy of honorary titles and in the hierarchy of real positions. Special treatises were needed to remind court officers of the proper precedence at banquets and other festivities.

The new system also embodied a change in concepts of taxation. New immigration and settlement had apparently put an end to the labor shortage of earlier centuries. It was now possible to separate the land tax from the tax on persons. The latter was transformed into a hearth tax, which fell on every peasant household without exception. For purposes of the land tax, each peasant village was considered a single unit. Imperial tax-assessors regularly visited each village, calculated its total tax, and assessed the individual inhabitants the portion of the tax that each would owe. The community as a whole was held responsible for the total tax, and often the neighbor of a poor peasant or of one who had abandoned his farm would have to pay the extra amount to make up the total. This obligation was onerous, and when the tax could not be collected the state itself sometimes had to take over the property and resell or re-lease it.

From Leo III to Basil I (717–867)

In 717, Leo III—who had come to the throne as a successful general of an important theme—won a victory over the Arabs who were besieging Constantinople. Thereafter the Byzantine struggle against the Muslims gradually became stabilized along a fixed frontier in Asia Minor. But the Muslim capture of Crete and Sicily opened the way for repeated pirate raids against the shores of imperial lands in Greece and southern Italy. In northern Italy, the Lombards extinguished the exarchate of Ravenna in 751, and Byzantine rule was interrupted by the alliance between the Franks and the papacy. The Byzantine *dux* of Venetia moved his headquarters to the famous island of the Rialto, and thus became the forerunner of the *doges* of Venice. And in the Balkans, the Bulgarian menace reached a new peak of severity.

During the periods when iconoclastic emperors held the throne (726–787 and 813–842) the movement took on in its later phases a violent antimonastic aspect, since the monks at Byzantium were the great defenders of the images. During this phase of the struggle some of the monks actually challenged the right of the emperors to legislate in matters of religion. But the images were twice restored by imperial decree (each time by an empress) as they had twice been banned by imperial decree. The position of the emperor in church affairs remained supreme despite these murmurs against his authority, and the restoration of the images was a concession to the weight of public opinion. As a result of the struggle, the Byzantines drew more careful distinctions between superstitious adoration paid to images and proper reverence. When the controversy closed, it was tacitly understood that no more religious statues would be sculptured in the round.

Although the new system of military small-holdings and the growth of a free peasantry retarded the development of large estates during the eighth and ninth centuries, we have clear evidence that once again large landlords were beginning to accumulate big properties. One cause may have been the ruin of the small farmers in Asia Minor as a result of the dreadful disorders that accompanied a great rebellion led by a certain Thomas the Slav. After threatening to subvert the throne, this rebellion was put down in 823.

From Basil I through the "Time of Troubles" (867–1081)

Although intrigue and the violent overthrow of sovereigns remained a feature of Byzantine politics, the people developed a deep loyalty to the new ruling house that was established in 867 by the Armenian Basil I (867–886) and called the Macedonian dynasty. Even usurpers now took pains to legitimize themselves by marrying into the imperial house. As political disintegration began to weaken the Muslim world, the Byzantines went over to the counteroffensive in the tenth century. Their fleets and armies recaptured Crete (961), and soon afterward Antioch and much of northern Syria, after three centuries of Arab domination.

A new Muslim dynasty in Egypt, which took over in Palestine also, stopped the Byzantine advance short of Jerusalem. But like the later Crusaders from the West, the Byzantine emperors hoped to liberate Christ's city from the infidel. While pushing back the Muslims, the Byzantines allied themselves with the Armenians, penetrated the state of Armenia, and at the end of the period annexed it. This was almost surely an error in judgment. Armenia, which had been a valuable buffer against the Turks of Central Asia, now beginning to raid into eastern Asia Minor, lay open to direct attack. Firmly reestablished in southern Italy in the face of the Muslim threat from Sicily, the Byzantines dominated the neighboring Lombard duchies until after the advent of the Normans in the early eleventh century. These adventurers displayed their usual ability in carving out estates for themselves and gaining a foothold in the peninsula. With the critically important fight against the Bulgarians we deal below.

Under the early emperors of the Macedonian dynasty the large landowners continued to flourish. Whole dynasties of nobles lived on their great estates. They were "the powerful," who were constantly acquiring more land at the expense of "the poor." The more they got, the more they wanted. They bought up the holdings of "the poor" and made the peasantry once more dependent upon them. The growing might of "the powerful" threatened the state in two important ways: not only was it losing its best taxpayers, the free peasants, but also its best soldiers, the military settlers.

During the tenth and eleventh centuries, there developed a great struggle between the emperors and "the powerful," parallel in some ways to the struggle between the monarchy and the feudal nobility in France, but destined to end differently. In France over the centuries the nobility was curbed and a strong centralized monarchy was established. But in the East, where absolutism as such was never questioned, "the powerful" thwarted all imperial attempts to check the growth of their economic and military power, and eventually seized the throne itself. Repeated laws striving to put an end to the acquisition of land by "the powerful" could not be enforced; in times of bad harvest especially, the small free proprietor was forced to sell out to his rich neighbor.

The great emperor Basil II (976–1025) made the most sustained efforts to reverse this process. A law of Basil has been preserved, with marginal notes and comments of his own, which vividly illustrates the problem and his attitude toward it. It tells how Basil, in the course of his travels in the empire, had received thousands of complaints about "the powerful." The emperor names names:

The patrician Constantine Maleinos and his son the magistros Eustathius have for a hundred years, or perhaps even a hundred and twenty, been in undisputed possession of lands unjustly acquired. It is the same way in the Phocas family, who, from father to son, for more than a century, have also succeeded in holding on to lands wrongly obtained. In more recent times certain newly rich men have done the same. For example Philokales, a simple peasant who lived for a long while in poverty by the work of his hands and paid the same taxes as the other peasants his brothers, now has obtained various offices of the palace, because he made a fortune . . . and acquired vast estates. He has not gone unpunished. When we arrived in the region where his property is located, and heard the complaints of those whom he had dispossessed we commanded that all the buildings he had built be razed and that the lands ravished from the poor be returned to them. Now this man is living again on the small piece of property which he owned at the start of his career and has once more become what he was by birth, a simple peasant. Our imperial will is that the same should happen to all those of our subjects, whether of noble birth or not, who have in this way seized the land of the poor. It is for this reason that we proclaim what follows: Every estate which was established before the time of our maternal grandfather Romanos I [919–944] shall remain in the hands of its proprietor, provided that he can prove by authentic documents that his title goes back before that time. All estates acquired since, and contrary to my grandfather's laws, shall be considered to be illegally owned. . . . The peasants, the original owners, who were long since expelled by the owners of the large estates, have the right to reclaim the immediate and complete restitution of their property without being required to repay the sales price, or to pay for any improvements which may have been installed by the proprietors who are about to be dispossessed.*

Shortly afterward, the emperor visited the enormous estates in Asia Minor belonging to that very Eustathius Maleinos whom he had denounced in his law. Maleinos not only entertained the emperor himself in sumptuous style but fed the entire army. On the pretext of wishing to repay his hospitality, Basil took this great potentate back to Constantinople with him, where he kept him, like a bird in a cage, until he died. Thereupon all his estates were seized by the crown. As a final blow to "the powerful," Basil II ordained that they would have to pay all the tax arrears of the delinquent peasants, thus relieving the village communities of the heavy burden that was so difficult for them to bear, and placing it on the shoulders of the rich.

But a few years after Basil died, this law was repealed under the influence of "the powerful," and thenceforth they did indeed prove "more merciless than famine or plague." As the landlords got more and more of the free military peasants as tenants on their estates, their own military role grew more and more important, and they became virtual commanders of private armies. After Basil, only the civil servants acted as a counterweight to the landowners. In an effort to reduce their power, the civil servants tried to cut down the expenses of the army, in which the landlords were now playing the leading role. Strife between these two parties weakened the imperial defenses.

The Macedonian dynasty died out in 1057, and a "time of troubles" began. The Normans drove the Byzantines from the Italian peninsula by taking the great southern port of Bari in 1071. In the same year, after three decades of raids across the eastern frontier of Asia Minor, the Seljuk Turks defeated the imperial armies at Manzikert in Armenia and captured the emperor Romanos IV. Asia Minor itself, mainstay of the empire, now lay open to the Turks, who pushed all the way to the Straits and established their capital in Nicaea. Meanwhile other Turkic tribes, Pechenegs and Magyars, raided southward into the Balkans almost at will. In 1081, there came to the throne one of the "powerful" magnates of Asia Minor, Alexius I Comnenus. The story of the ways in which he and his successors built a new military and social system and staved off collapse for more than a century properly belongs to a later chapter.

IV Byzantine Learning and Literature

Until less than a century ago, the study of Byzantine history was under a cloud. German classical scholars felt that it was somehow not decent to investigate the history of a people who could not write good classical Greek. The French usually referred to Byzantium as the *bas-empire*, literally "the low or degenerate empire," whose achievements they scornfully contrasted with the glorious literary and artistic performance of Greece and Rome. From Gibbon on, the English were equally indifferent or scornful. The Victorian scholar Lecky wrote:

> Of that Byzantine Empire the universal verdict of history is that it constitutes, without a single exception, the most thoroughly base and despicable form that civilization has yet assumed. . . . There has been no other enduring civilization so absolutely destitute of all the forms and elements of greatness. . . . The history of the empire is a monotonous story of the intrigues of priests, eunuchs, and women, of poisonings, of conspiracies, of uniform ingratitude, of perpetual fratricides.*

Lecky was writing a history of European morals; and one must cheerfully admit that a Victorian moralist would find much to shudder at in the private lives of the individual Byzantine emperors. Yet this is almost irrelevant to the historian's estimate of Byzantine civilization.

That achievement was varied, distinguished, and of major importance to the West. Byzantine literature does indeed suffer by comparison with the classics; but the appropriate society with which to compare medieval Byzantium is not classical antiquity but the contemporary Europe of the Middle Ages. Both were Christian and both the direct heirs of Rome and Greece. The Byzantines maintained learning on a level much more advanced than did the West; the West itself owes a substantial cultural debt to Byzantium.

Byzantium as Preserver of the Classics

In the West, long centuries passed during which the knowledge of Greek had disappeared and nobody had access to the great works of ancient Greek philosophy, science, and literature. During all this time the Byzantines preserved these masterpieces, copied and recopied them, by hand of course, and gave them constant study.

Again, in contrast to the West, study was not confined to monasteries, although the monks played a major role. It was also pursued in secular libraries and schools. The teacher occupied an important position in Byzantine society; books circulated widely among prominent men in public life; many of the emperors were scholars and lovers of literature. In the early days of the empire, the greatest university was still at Athens, but because of its strong pagan tradition the pious Christian emperor Justinian closed the university there in the sixth century. The imperial university at Constantinople, which probably dates from Constantine himself, supplied a steady stream of learned and culti-

*G. L. Schlumberger, *L'Epopée Byzantine* (Paris, 1896–1905), II, 122. Our translation.

*W. H. Lecky, *History of European Morals from Augustus to Charlemagne* (New York, 1869), II, 13–14.

vated men to the bureaucracy, the church, and the courts. The emphasis in its curriculum was on secular subjects: philosophy, astronomy, geometry, rhetoric, music, grammar, law, medicine, and arithmetic. The School of the Patriarch, the Archbishop of Constantinople, also in the capital, provided instruction in theology and other sacred subjects.

Had it not been for Byzantium, it seems certain that Plato and Aristotle, Homer and Sophocles would have been lost. We cannot even imagine what such a loss would have meant to Western civilization, how seriously it would have retarded us in science and speculation, in morals and ethics, how crippled we should have been in our efforts to deal with the fundamental problems of human relationships, what a poor and meager cultural inheritance we should have had. That these living works of the dead past have been preserved to us we owe to Byzantium.

Original Writing: Epic, History, Theology, Hymns

Too often, however, people have thought of the Byzantine cultural achievements as limited to preservation and transmission. The Byzantines were themselves creative. We have, for instance, an epic poem, from the tenth or eleventh century, describing the heroic activity of a frontier warrior who had lived some two to three centuries earlier, Basil Digenes Akritas (Basil, of the two races, the frontiersman). Half Greek, half Arab, he fights wild beasts and brigands, preserves order on the border between Byzantine and Muslim territory, seizes a fair bride and forces her family to consent to the marriage, defeats a magnificent Amazon (female warrior), and even tells the emperor how to behave. Though the creator of this hero was no Homer, he is fully comparable with the Western authors who sang of Roland, of the Cid, and of the Scottish borderers. Like Basil, all these heroes were men of the frontiers, Daniel Boones of the Middle Ages, pursuing adventure and righting wrongs among the medieval equivalents of the Red Indians.

In prose, we find an almost unbroken line of those who over the long centuries wrote the history of the empire. Writing in a popular style, the chroniclers took their story back to the Creation or continued the work of a predecessor who had done so. The true historians wrote for intellectuals and limited themselves to the story of their own times, perhaps with an introduction describing a period immediately before their own about which they had some firsthand information. We must be careful to weigh what they tell us, because they were often violently partisan in the quarrels of their day and may sometimes be found blackening the innocent or whitewashing the guilty for their own purposes. But if we proceed cautiously, the great series of Byzantine historians opens up for us a world as yet little known. There is no comparable body of literature to tell us about men and events in the medieval West, which all too often can be discovered only from the bare bones

of legal documents or from a tantalizingly dry and brief mention in some book of annals.

As we might expect, theological writing forms a substantial part of the prose literature. In the early period the Byzantine theologians hotly debated the great controversies that rent the empire about the true relationship between God the Father and God the Son, or between the divine and human natures of Christ. In a society like the Byzantine, such works had the importance that may be ascribed, for example, to those of Freud or Marx in our own day. Too difficult for most people to read or understand, they none the less had enormous influence over the lives of everybody: the leaders of the society were directly or indirectly affected by their answers to the problems of human social and economic life in general, or of the life of the human individual in particular and of his prospects of eternal salvation or damnation. The early theologians also drew up appropriate rules for monks, balancing the need for denying the desires of the flesh by providing reasonable opportunities for work, an arrangement that worked in the East to prevent many of the difficulties that arose in Western monasticism. Later, in the eleventh century, under the influence of the Neoplatonic philosophers, theologians developed a mystic strain, in which they urged contemplation and purification as stages toward illumination and the final mystic union with God. For the ordinary man, the mysteries of his faith were enhanced by the beauties of the church service, where magnificent hymns were sung, often composed by men whom we would consider to be major poets.

Original Writing: Saints' Lives

Saints' lives, usually written for a popular audience, took the place of the novel in our society. They told a personal story, often including adventure, anxiety, deprivation, violence, and agony of various sorts, and they set forth the final triumph of virtue and piety. The eyes of the reader were elevated to consider his heavenly reward, since the hero of the story was often martyred here on earth. Exciting and edifying, these tales not only were immensely popular in their day but they help the scholar of our own. They were not, of course, deliberately designed to do so, but they often supply valuable bits of information about daily life, especially among the humbler classes, and about the attitudes of the people, for which we sometimes have no other source.

Here is an episode from the life of Theodore of Sykeon, a seventh-century saint who wrought miracles in Asia Minor:

. . . The holy Theodore sent his archdeacon to the capital, Constantinople, to buy a chalice and a paten of silver. . . . The archdeacon went and bought from a silversmith a pure and well-finished vessel, so far as concerned the quality of the silver and the workmanship, and he brought it back to the monastery. . . . When the Saint looked at them, he . . . condemned them as being useless and defiled. But the archdeacon who looked at the appearance and not at what was hidden, pointed out the perfect and well-wrought workmanship and the quality proved by the five-fold stamp upon it, and thought by these facts to convince the Saint. But the Saint said "I know, yes, I know, son, that so far as eyes can see, it appears a beautiful specimen of craftsmanship and the worth of the silver is evident from the stamps on it, but it is another, an invisible cause which defiles it. I fancy the defilement comes from some impure use. But if you doubt it, pronounce the verse for our prayers and be convinced." Then whilst the archdeacon chanted the verse of Invocation, the Saint bent his head in prayer, and after he had filled the chalice, the chalice and the paten turned black. . . . Then the archdeacon returned to Constantinople and gave them back to the dealer in silver and told him the reason. The dealer made inquiries of . . . his manager and his silversmith who fashioned the vessels, and found out that they came from the chamberpot of a prostitute. . . . He gave him other and very beautiful vessels, and these the archdeacon carried to the Saint, and reported to him and to the monks the cause of defilement in the earlier vessels, and they all gave thanks unto God.*

From this passage we learn quite incidentally a good bit about the organization of the silver business in Byzantium: a merchant is shown employing a manager and an artisan, and we find that a fivefold hallmark was the Byzantine equivalent of our "sterling" stamped on an object. Also, we discover that then as now ladies of easy virtue sometimes became quite prosperous.

Unique among these saints' lives is one extraordinary document of the tenth century: a highly polished tale of an Indian king, who shuts away his only son Ioasaph in a remote palace to protect him from the knowledge of the world and especially to prevent his being converted to Christianity. But the prince cannot be protected; he sees a sick man, a blind man, and a dead man; and when he is in despair at life's cruelties a wise monk in disguise, named Barlaam, succeeds in reaching him by pretending to have a precious jewel that he wishes to show. The jewel is the jewel of the Christian faith, and the rest of the long story is an account of the wise monk Barlaam's conversion of Prince Ioasaph. In the course of the conversion, Barlaam tells Ioasaph ten moral tales illustrating the Christian life. One of these reappears in our own literature as the casket story of Shakespeare's *Merchant of Venice;* another is the tale of Everyman, which later became common in all Western literatures; others of Barlaam's stories were used by hundreds of other Western authors and preachers of all nationalities.

Yet what is most extraordinary about this piece of Byzantine literature is that it originally comes from India: the life of Ioasaph is a Christianized version of the life of Buddha, the great Indian religious leader of

*N. H. Baynes and E. A. S. Dawes, *Three Byzantine Saints* (Oxford Univ., 1948), pp. 117–118.

the sixth century B.C. His life story passed through Persia via the Arabs to the Caucasian kingdom of Georgia before it was turned into Greek legend and transmitted to the West. And the stories that Barlaam tells to convert Ioasaph are also Indian in origin and are either Buddhist birth-stories (recitals of the Buddha's experiences in earlier incarnations used as comment upon what was going on around him), or Hindu moral-comic tales. Indeed the very name "Ioasaph" was once "Bodasaph," and so is the same as the Indian word "Bodhisattva," which means a person destined to attain Buddhahood. Prince Ioasaph has been canonized a saint of both the Orthodox and the Roman Catholic churches, and it is thus an odd but true fact that through this legend Buddha himself became and has remained a Christian saint.

The Arts

When we turn to the field of the plastic arts, we can see the Byzantine achievement with our own eyes. In Constantinople the Church of Santa Sophia, built in the sixth century, was designed to be "a church the like of which has never been seen since Adam nor ever will be." The dome, "a work at once marvelous and terrifying," says a contemporary, "seems rather to hang by a golden chain from heaven than to be supported by solid masonry"; and Justinian (527–565), the emperor who built it, was able to exclaim "I have outdone thee, O Solomon!" "On entering the church to pray," says Justinian's historian, Procopius, "one feels at once that it is the work not of man's effort or industry, but in truth the work of the divine power; and the spirit, mounting to heaven, realizes that here God is very near, and that He delights in this dwelling that He has chosen for Himself." The Turks themselves, who seized the city in 1453, ever since have paid Santa Sophia the sincerest compliment of imitation; the great mosques that throng present-day Istanbul are all more or less directly copied after the great church of the Byzantines.

Before Santa Sophia could be built, the other cities of the empire, particularly Alexandria, Antioch, and Ephesus, had produced the necessary architectural synthesis: a fusion of the Hellenistic or Roman basilica with a dome taken from Persia. This is just one striking example of the way in which Greek and oriental elements were to be blended in the new society. In decoration, the use of brilliantly colored marbles, enamel, silken and other fabrics, gold, silver, and jewels, and the paintings and glowing mosaics on the walls and ceilings, reflect the sumptuousness of the Orient.

The tourist of today wishing to see a Byzantine church of Justinian's time need not go all the way to Istanbul. On the Adriatic coast of Italy, south of Venice at Ravenna, there are three wonderful smaller churches of the sixth century with superb mosaics still well preserved, including portraits of Justinian himself and of his Empress Theodora. And at Venice itself, first the client, then the equal, and finally the conqueror of

The creation of the world: mosaic scenes from Genesis in St. Mark's, Venice.

Byzantium, St. Mark's is a true Byzantine church of the later period, whose richness and magnificence epitomize perhaps better than any surviving church in Istanbul itself the splendor of later Byzantine architecture.

Along with the major arts of architecture, painting, and mosaics went the so-called minor arts, whose level the Byzantines raised so high that the term "minor" seems almost absurd. The silks, the ivories, the work of the goldsmiths and silversmiths, the enamel and jeweled bookcovers, the elaborate containers made especially to hold the sacred relics of a saint, the great Hungarian sacred Crown of Saint Stephen, the superb miniatures of the illuminated manuscripts in half a

hundred European libraries—all testify to the endless variety and fertility of Byzantine inspiration.

Even in those parts of western Europe where Byzantine political authority had disappeared, the influence of this Byzantine artistic flowering is often apparent. Sometimes we are dealing with actual creations by Byzantine artists produced in the West or ordered from Constantinople by a connoisseur. These are found in Sicily and southern Italy, in Venice, and in Rome itself. Sometimes the native artists work in the Byzantine manner, as in Spain, in Sicily, and in the great Romanesque domed churches of southern France. Often the new native product is not purely Byzantine, but rather a fusion of Byzantine with local elements, a new art diverse in its genius, but one of whose strands is clearly native to Constantinople.

V Byzantium and the Slavs

Perhaps the major Byzantine cultural achievement was the transmission of their civilization to the Slavs. Much as Rome christianized large groups of "barbarians" in western Europe, so Constantinople, the new Rome, christianized the Slavs. Many of the problems that beset the West today in its dealings with the Soviet Union arise from the fact that the Soviet Union is first and foremost Russia, a country in the Orthodox and not in the Western Christian tradition, a country that still shows the effects of having experienced its conversion from Byzantium rather than from Rome.

Conversion of the Bulgarians

The first of the Slavic peoples to fall under Byzantine influence were the Bulgarians, product of a fusion between a Slavic population and a smaller group of Asiatic Bulgar invaders. From the time these barbarians crossed the Danube in the late seventh century, they engaged in intermittent warfare against the Byzantine Empire. In 811, their ruler, Krum, defeated the imperial forces, killing the emperor Nicephorus I (802–811), the first emperor to fall in battle since the death of Valens at Adrianople in 378. Krum took the skull of Nicephorus, had it hollowed out and lined with silver, and used it as a drinking cup. Bulgarian religion was still primitive: the sun and moon and stars were worshiped and propitiated with sacrifices of horses and dogs.

Yet the Bulgars created a powerful state, which by the middle of the ninth century was prepared for conversion to Christianity, the religion that alone could accompany a position of prestige in the medieval world. Greek artisans were imported into Bulgaria to build the palaces of the native rulers. Since there was no Bulgarian alphabet, Greek letters had to be used in the royal inscriptions. But the Bulgarian rulers hesitated to accept missionaries from Byzantium, fearing the extension of Byzantine political power.

At the same time, a Slavic people called the Moravians, far to the west in what is now Czechoslovakia, had also established a state and had reached a similar stage. Their rulers were ready for Christianity, but associated it with their powerful neighbors the Germans, and feared both German and papal encroachment, as the Bulgarians feared Byzantium. In order to avoid German or papal influence, the king of the Moravians in 862 sent to Byzantium and asked for a Greek missionary to teach the Moravian people Christianity in their own Slavic language.

The Byzantine emperor Michael III sent to Moravia two missionaries, Cyril (or Constantine) and his brother Methodius, called the Apostles to the Slavs. They knew the Slavic tongue and had invented two alphabets in which it could be written. The simpler and more useful is the alphabet still employed by the Russians, the Bulgarians, and the Serbs, and still called *Cyrillic* after its inventor. Almost at once, as a countermove, Boris, ruler of the Bulgarians, asked for Christianity from the Germans. But these efforts on the part of the two Slavic rulers to avoid accepting conversion at the hands of their powerful neighbors and to obtain it instead from a less threatening distant court were doomed to failure. In spite of the efforts of Cyril and Methodius among the Moravians, German pressure and papal dislike for church services conducted in any language but Latin proved too strong. The German clergy and the Roman form of Christianity eventually triumphed in Moravia.

Similarly, despite Boris' long correspondence with the popes—during which he once got good advice about wearing trousers (permissible) and eating all his meals by himself (permissible but rude)—the nearby power of Byzantium was too strong. Although Boris tried a second flirtation with Rome when Byzantine patronizing behavior annoyed him, he found that he could not obtain an independent church from the papacy. Byzantium permitted the Bulgarians virtual ecclesiastical autonomy. Only in the fold of the Eastern church could Boris unify his country and consolidate his own autocratic power. The Byzantine patriarch, unlike the pope, made no temporal claims. In Bulgaria, then, from the late ninth century on, the language of the church was the native Slavonic tongue preached by followers of Cyril and Methodius.

But the ambitions of the Bulgarian rulers were too great to permit friendly relations with Byzantium. Under Simeon (893–927), second son of Boris, educated in Constantinople and called "half-Greek," there began a bitter hundred-years' war, during which the Bulgarians tried to make themselves emperors by conquering Constantinople itself. Toward the end of the tenth century, the rivalry became more intense than ever under a Bulgarian ruler named Samuel. In 1014, Basil II (976–1025), whom we have already seen curbing his own great landowners, captured fourteen thousand Bulgarian prisoners and savagely blinded ninety-nine out of every hundred. The hundredth man was allowed to keep the sight of one eye, so that he could lead his miserable fellows home. At the ghastly sight of his blinded warriors, Samuel fell dead of shock. Basil II took the appropriate name of "Bulgar slayer." Shortly afterward, Byzantine domination over Bulgaria became complete, and the country was ruled as a conquered province. But its inhabitants were never deprived of their own church, whose archbishop had just as much jurisdiction as he had had in the days of Bulgarian independence.

The great expenditures of money and manpower incidental to the long pursuit of the Bulgarian war

Fourteenth-century Slavonic manuscript depicting Basil II's defeat of the Bulgarians (top). Basil blinded the prisoners and sent them back to King Samuel, who died of shock at the sight (bottom).

into the Black or Caspian seas. Beginning in the eighth century, the Scandinavians, whom we have already encountered in the West, expanded into Russia also. First taking control of the Baltic shore, they then moved south along the rivers to the Sea of Azov and the northern Caucasus. Their name, in the period of expansion, was Rus, which has survived in the modern term *Russia.* Gradually they overcame many of the Slavic, Lithuanian, Finnish, and Magyar peoples who were then living on the steppe. The details of this process are very little known. The story told in the Old Russian *Primary Chronicle,* compiled during the eleventh century, is suggestive of what may have happened among the inhabitants of Russia sometime in the 850s:

> There was no law among them, but tribe rose against tribe. Discord then ensued among them, and they began to war one against another. They said to themselves "Let us seek a prince who may rule over us and judge according to the law." They accordingly went overseas to the Varangian [i.e., Scandinavian] Russes . . . and said to the people of Rus, "Our whole land is great and rich, but there is no order in it. Come to rule and reign over us."*

This is the story of the "calling of the princes." The *Chronicle* goes on to tell how Rurik (who has now been successfully identified with a Danish warrior known from other sources) accepted the invitation and settled in the town of Novgorod, already an important trading center. From Novgorod, within a few years, Scandinavian princes moved south along the Dnieper River. On the middle course of the Dnieper they seized the settlement called Kiev, still today the major city of the Ukraine, and made it the center of a state at first very loosely controlled and devoted especially to trade. And in 860, for the first time, a fleet of two hundred of their warships appeared off Constantinople, where they at first caused panic but were eventually repulsed. During the next two centuries there were three further attacks of varying seriousness, as well as other wars, which the Byzantines won.

But the normal state of affairs was not war between Byzantium and Russia. The texts of the trade treaties concluded between the two reflect close economic ties. We find the Byzantines promising to feed the visiting Russian traders and to furnish them baths and supplies for the homeward voyage. The Russians agreed to live in a special quarter outside the city during their stay in Constantinople and to be registered by imperial officials. One treaty reads, "They shall not enter the city save through one gate, unarmed and fifty at a time, escorted by soldiers of the emperor." The Byzantines were anxious to protect the lives and property of their citizens from the wild barbarians, but they were also eager to obtain the merchandise that the Russians brought them.

*Samuel H. Cross, *The Russian Primary Chronicle,* in *Harvard Studies and Notes in Philology and Literature,* XII (1930), 145.

played their part in weakening Byzantium for the military disasters that were to come at Manzikert and at Bari in 1071. But the events we have reviewed helped to determine where the line between East and West would be drawn for all future history. The Bulgarians are an Orthodox people to this day, and their civilization throughout the Middle Ages directly reflected the overpowering influence of Byzantium. In much the same way, more than three hundred years later, the western neighbors of the Bulgarians, the Serbs, also took their faith from the Greek East after a flirtation with the Latin West.

The Early Russian State

To the north and east of the Balkan Bulgarians between the Baltic and the Black Seas lie the great plains of European Russia. Here movement is easiest by water, along the rivers that flow north into the Baltic or south

Conversion of the Russians

Most important was the continuing religious influence that Byzantium exercised upon the Russians. No doubt numerous individual Russians were converted from their primitive polytheistic faith as a result of their impressions during a visit to Byzantium. In the trade treaty of 945, we find that some of the Russian envoys were already Christians, swearing by the Holy Cross to observe the provisions of the treaty. In the 950s, Olga, the ruling princess of Kiev, visited the emperor at Constantinople:

> Olga came before him, and when he saw that she was very fair of countenance and wise as well, the Emperor wondered at her intellect. He conversed with her, and remarked that she was worthy to reign with him in his city. When Olga heard these words, she replied that she was still a pagan, and that if he desired to baptize her, he should perform this function himself: otherwise she was unwilling to accept baptism. The Emperor, with the assistance of the Patriarch, accordingly baptized her. . . . After her baptism, the Emperor summoned Olga and made known to her that he wished her to become his wife. But she replied, "How can you marry me, after baptizing me yourself and calling me your daughter? For among Christians that is unlawful, as you must know." Then the Emperor said, "Olga, you have outwitted me."*

The Russians were converted as a people during the late 980s in the reign of Vladimir. He felt the inadequacy of the old faith, about which we do not know very much except that the Russians worshiped forest and water spirits and a god of thunder. According to the partly legendary story in the *Chronicle,* Vladimir was visited by representatives of the different faiths, who told him about their beliefs. He discarded the faith of Mohammed, because circumcision and abstinence from pork and wine were disagreeable to him. "Drinking," said he, "is the joy of the Russes. We cannot exist without that pleasure." Judaism he rejected because the God of the Jews had not been strong enough to enable them to stay in their native Jerusalem. Roman Christianity he rejected because it required a certain amount of fasting, as of course did the Christianity of the Greeks. But the cautious Vladimir did not accept this fourth possibility, Orthodox Christianity, until he had sent a commission to visit the countries where all the faiths were practiced and to report back to him.

> The envoys reported, "When we journeyed among the Moslems, we beheld how they worship in . . . a mosque, . . . and there is no happiness among them but only sorrow and a dreadful stench. Their religion is not good. Then we went among the Germans [Roman Catholics], and saw them performing many ceremonies in their temples; but beheld no glory there. Then we went on to Greece [Byzantium], and the Greeks led us to the edifices where they worship their God, and we knew not whether we were in

heaven or on earth. For on earth there is no such splendor or such beauty, and we are at a loss how to describe it. We only know that God dwells there among men, and their service is fairer than the ceremonies of other nations. For we cannot forget that beauty.*

Shortly afterward, Vladimir was baptized and married a Byzantine princess. Returning to Kiev, he threw down all the idols in the city, and in one day forcibly baptized the entire population in the waters of the Dnieper.

Despite its legendary features, the whole story reflects the various cultural influences to which the Kievan state was in truth exposed. It had Muslim, Jewish,† and Roman Catholic Christian neighbors; but the most powerful and influential neighbor was the Orthodox and Greek Byzantium, and doubtless the marriage alliance with the Byzantine princess and the resulting gain in prestige played a part in Vladimir's decision. To secure the conversion of the Russians to the Byzantine form of Christianity was also important for the Byzantines, who needed to protect their possessions along the Black Sea and their capital itself against Russian attack.

Effects of Conversion

Conversion meant great changes in the Russians' way of life. The church became an important social force in Kievan society, and the clergy formed a new and influential social class. In spite of the fact that the Byzantines always asserted theoretical sovereignty over the Russian church, and in spite of the fact that the archbishops of Kiev in the early period were mostly Greeks appointed from Byzantium, the Russian church early asserted its practical independence. The church in Russia from the first became an important landowner, and, as in the Byzantine Empire, monasteries multiplied. The clergy came to have legal jurisdiction over all Christians in cases involving morals, family affairs, and religious matters. The advanced concept that crimes should be punished by the state replaced the old primitive feeling that punishment was a matter of personal revenge. For the first time, formal education was established. The Cyrillic alphabet was adopted, and literature in Russian began to appear, almost all of it ecclesiastical. Byzantine art forms were imported and imitated; the great Church of Saint Sophia at Kiev is in its way as magnificent as its namesake in Constantinople. The old pagan faith persisted in the countryside; enormous rural areas remained backward, and culture was largely confined to the few cities and to the monasteries. In the main, however, the conversion of the Russians had a civilizing effect.

Yet, many have agreed that the short-run gain was outweighed by a long-run loss. The very use of the

*Ibid., pp. 168–169.

*Ibid., p. 199.
† The Turkic tribe of the Khazars, settled along the lower Don River, had been converted to Judaism.

Arctic Ocean

URAL MTS.

Novgorod
Pskov
Tver
Polotsk
Suzdol
LITHUANIA
Moscow
Vladimir
Smolensk

Kiev

Sarai

Danube R.

Black Sea

Sea of Azov
CAUCASUS MTS.

Caspian Sea

Ob R.
Irtysh R.
Tobol R.
Ural R.
Volga R.
Don R.
Donets R.
Dnieper R.
Dniester R.
Baltic Sea
Dvina R.

Early Russia

about 1100

native language in the liturgy (so great an advantage to the Byzantines when, as missionaries, they sought to spread their faith without insisting on the use of Greek) meant that the culture of Russia remained poor by contrast with that of the West. In the West, every priest and every monk had to learn Latin. As soon as he did so, he had the key to the treasures of Latin classical literature and the works of the Latin church fathers, themselves formed in the schools of pagan rhetoric, philosophy, and literature. The educated man in the West, usually a cleric, had access to Vergil, to Ovid, to Cicero, and to the other Roman authors, some quite unsuitable for clerical reading, but all giving the reader a sense of style, a familiarity with ancient taste and thought, and sometimes solid instruction. He had Jerome, who had gone to school to Cicero, and Augustine, whose *City of God* was the classic expression of Christian philosophy, written in magnificent Latin prose. He had a whole library of commentaries on the classical authors designed to reconcile them with Christian doctrine. For those in the West who had the leisure, the talent, the inclination, and the luck to find themselves in a monastery with a good library, the opportunity for learning and cultivation was open.

The fact that the Byzantines did not insist on the use of Greek in the liturgy meant that the Russian clergy did not automatically learn Greek, as French or English or German or Spanish priests had to learn Latin. And of course the Latin heritage was not avail-

able to the Russians either. A very few Russians did learn Greek, but by and large the great Greek classical heritage of philosophy and literature was closed to the Russians. Byzantine sermons, saints' lives, some chronicles and history, and certain other pieces of Byzantine literature were indeed translated and circulated in Slavonic. But these were no substitutes for Plato and Aristotle, Homer and the dramatists. The conversion to Christianity from Byzantium thus had the effect of stunting the intellectual and literary progress of Russia. The Kievan Russians of the tenth century were not ready for Plato and Aristotle, but when the time in their development came when the Russians were ready, they were cut off from access to the treasurehouse.

Indeed, in the nineteenth century an influential group of Russian thinkers argued that conversion from Byzantium had led Russia into stagnation and intellectual sterility, because it had cut Russia off from Rome, the fountainhead of the intellectual and spiritual life of the West, without providing a substitute. Their opponents argued just as vigorously that it was precisely the Orthodox faith accepted from Byzantium that gave modern Russia her high degree of spirituality, her willingness to bend to the will of God, and indeed all the virtues that they found in the Russian character and the Russian system. This difference of opinion persists, but most students argue that modern Russia has shown a considerable cultural lag in comparison with Western countries, that this cultural lag is partly attributable to the fact that Christianity was accepted from Byzantium, and that the very privilege of using Slavonic in the church services prevented the growth in Russia of a class of men educated in the wisdom of the ancient world.

It would be a grave mistake, however, to attribute the cultural lag solely to these factors. It was perhaps in even greater measure due to the effect on Russian development of the Tatar invasions and domination of the thirteenth and fourteenth centuries.

Kievan Russia

Kievan Russia itself, in spite of whatever drawbacks conversion from Byzantium may have had, developed a society not very unlike that in contemporary western medieval Europe. From being a mere Scandinavian war band sworn to assist the prince in battle and entitled to divide the booty with him, the prince's entourage had now become that upper ruling group of councillors appropriate to a settled state. The Kievan law codes reflect the social conditions of the time and place: arson and stealing horses were the worst crimes, more heavily punished than murder or mutilation. The penalty was the same for stealing a beaver out of another man's trap, for trespassing on his land, for knocking out his tooth, or for killing his slave. This was a society that put due emphasis on the value of property.

Scholars have disputed whether agriculture or commerce was more important in Kievan Russia, and the answer seems to be commerce. In this trade, with Byzantium in particular, the Russians sold mostly furs, honey, and wax, not products of agriculture at all, but of hunting and bee-keeping. Since the Byzantines paid in cash, Kiev had much more of a money economy than did western Europe. Viewed from the economic and social point of view, Kievan Russia in the eleventh century was in some ways more advanced than backward manorial western Europe, where markets, fairs, and industries were only beginning to spring up in Flanders, along the Baltic shore, and in northern Italy.

During the period before the Tatar invasions, which began in the early 1200s, this Kievan state began to have close diplomatic and political relations with the West. Dynastic marriages were arranged between the ruling house of Kiev and the royal families of Sweden and France, and alliances were reached with the Holy Roman Empire of Germany. Merchants from the West appeared in Russia, especially at Novgorod in the north, and at Kiev itself. It is then conceivable that whatever handicap was imposed by Byzantine Christianity might have been overcome had Kiev been allowed to maintain its free lines of communications and its vigorous and valuable exchange with the West. But as things turned out, Russia was denied this opportunity.

The Kievan state had internal political weaknesses. It failed to make any rules for the succession to the throne, and it followed the practice (similar to that of the Franks) of dividing land among a prince's sons as if it were the private property of the prince. The fragmentation of the Kievan state into mutually hostile provinces weakened it in the face of outside dangers. Beginning in the eleventh century the Turkish tribe of Polovtsy or Cumans appeared on the southern steppes of Russia just as the Huns had swept into Europe earlier. The Russian princes warring against one another made a tragic error by hiring bands of Polovtsy. Thus when the Mongol Tatars appeared in the early thirteenth century, Kievan Russia had been softened for the blow. The sole surviving heroic poem of the Kievan period, *The Song of the Expedition of Igor*, reproves the Russian princes:

> Voices have grown mute, revelry has waned. . . . Lower your banners, sheath your damaged swords, for ye have already strayed far from the glory of your grandsire. For with your own treasons ye began to bring the infidels upon the Russian land. . . . For through civil strife came violence from the land of the Polovtsians.*

Never entirely centralized politically, the Kievan

state nonetheless strove for unity. It bequeathed the ideal of unity, together with a literary language and a single Christian faith, to the future Russian state of Moscow that was to emerge after more than two centuries of Mongol domination. Moscow would take from the Byzantines not only their form of religion, already deeply entrenched in the Russia of Kiev, but also their political theory of autocracy, and much of their political practice.

VI Islam before the Crusades

Islam (the Arabic word means "submission") is the most recently founded of the world's great religions. Its adherents (Muslims, "those who submit") today inhabit the entire North African coast of the Mediterranean, part of Yugoslavia and Albania, Egypt, Turkey, the entire Near and Middle East, Pakistan, parts of India, the Malay Peninsula, Indonesia, and the Philippine Islands, to say nothing of Soviet Central Asia and portions of China. From the point of view of Western civilization, relationships with the Muslim world have been of crucial importance since Muhammad founded Islam in the early seventh century. In an incredibly short time Islamic society joined the Latin and Greek Christian societies as the third major civilization west of India.

Muhammad

What we know of Muhammad is derived from Muslim authors who lived some time after his death; it is not easy to decide what is true and what is fictional in their accounts. The Arabia into which he was born in 571 was inhabited largely by nomadic tribes, each under its own chief. These nomads lived on the meat and milk of their animals, and on dates from the palm trees. They raided each other's flocks of camels and sheep and often feuded among themselves. The religion of the Arabs was pagan, centering around sacred stones and trees. Their chief center was Mecca, fifty miles inland from the coast of the Red Sea, where there was a sacred building called the Kaaba (the Cube), in which the Arab worshipers did reverence to a large number of idols, especially to a small black stone fallen from heaven, perhaps a meteorite. This building seems to have been the object of religious pilgrimages by the pagan Arabs.

In the sixth century, Mecca was inhabited by a tribe called the Kuraish, a trading people who lived by caravan commerce with Syria. Muhammad was born into one of the poorer clans of the Kuraish. Early orphaned, he was brought up by relatives and as a young man entered the service of a wealthy widow much older than himself, whom he later married, after successfully performing several trading journeys for her. We do not know how he became convinced that he was the bearer of a new revelation.

La Geste du Prince Igor, ed. H. Grégoire, R. Jakobson, and M. Szeftel (New York, 1948), p. 171, trans. S. H. Cross. The *Igor Tale* was preserved in a single manuscript only, which perished in the burning of Moscow during Napoleon's invasion of Russia in 1812. Scholars have long debated its authenticity, and recently the theory that it may be a brilliant eighteenth-century forgery has once more gained some currency. But we believe these arguments are far from conclusive, and prefer to accept the poem as a genuine—and remarkably beautiful—Kievan work.

He was keenly aware of the intense struggle going on between the two superpowers, Byzantium and Persia. News of the shifting fortunes of war reached him, and he apparently sympathized with the Christians, and perhaps even thought of himself as destined to lead a reform movement within Christianity. He could read no language except Arabic, and there were no religious books written in Arabic. His ideas and information on other religions must therefore have been derived from observations on his caravan journeys and from conversations with members of Christian and Jewish communities.

He seems to have spent much time in fasting and

Sixteenth-century Persian miniature showing Muhammad, his face veiled, ascending to Paradise.

in vigils, perhaps suggested by Christian practice. He suffered from nervousness and hysteria, and seems to have had paroxysms during which he suffered high fevers. He became convinced that God was revealing the truth to him and had singled him out to be his messenger. The revelations came to him gradually over the rest of his life, often when some crisis arose. He probably wrote them down himself, in a rhythmic, sometimes rhyming Arabic prose, and included entertaining stories from the Old Testament of the Hebrews, and from popular and current Arabian folklore, such as the legends that had come to surround the memory of Alexander the Great.

The whole body of Muslim revelation was not assembled in a book until some little time after Muhammad's death. This is the Koran. The chapters were not arranged in order by subject matter, but mechanically by length, with the longest first. This makes the Koran difficult to follow. Moreover, it is written in a peculiar style, full of allusions to things and persons who are not called by their right names. Readers are often puzzled by the Koran, and a large body of Muslim writings explaining it has grown up over the centuries. Muhammad regarded his revelation as the confirmation of the Old and the New Testaments. Muslims call Jews and Christians, as they call themselves, "people of the Book." Islam is a religion designed for all men, the perfection of both Judaism and Christianity, the final revelation of God's truth.

Muhammad was a firm monotheist. His God—Allah—is the God of the Jews and Christians, yet Muhammad did not deny that his pagan fellow-Arabs had knowledge of God. He declared only that it was idolatry to worship more than one god, and he believed the trinity of the Christians to be three gods and therefore polytheism. If Judaism emphasizes God's legal covenant with the Jews and his justice, and Christianity God's mercy that tempers his wrath, Islam may be said to emphasize his omnipotence—his absolute ability to do anything he may wish to do. Acknowledgment of belief in God and in Muhammad as the mediator with God for men, and acceptance of a final day of judgment are the basic requirements. A major innovation for the Arabs was Muhammad's idea of an after-life, which was to be experienced in the flesh. The delights of paradise for a Muslim are fleshly indeed, and the punishments of hell are torture.

The demands of Islam are not severe. Five times a day in prayer, facing toward Mecca, the Muslim—having first washed face, hands and feet—must bear witness that there is no god but Allah and that Muhammad is his prophet. During the sacred month of Ramadan—perhaps suggested by Lent—he may not eat or drink or have sexual relations between sunrise and sunset. He must give alms to the poor. And, if he can, he should at least once in his lifetime make a pilgrimage to the sacred city of Mecca. This was, and is, all, except for regulation of certain aspects of daily life—for example, the prohibition against strong drink, and other rules about food and its preparation, mostly taken from Jewish practice. The rest is social legislation: polygamy is sanctioned, but four wives are the most a man, save the Prophet himself, may have. Divorce was easy for the husband, who need only repeat a prescribed formula. The condition of women and of slaves was markedly improved by the new laws.

At first, Muhammad preached this faith only to members of his family; then he preached to the people of Mecca, who repudiated him scornfully. In 622, some pilgrims from a city called Yathrib, two hundred miles north of Mecca, invited Muhammad to come to their city to settle a local feud. He accepted the invitation. This move from Mecca is the famous Hegira, from which the Islamic calendar has ever since been dated. The year 622 is the Muslim year 1. And Yathrib, to which he went, had its name changed to al-Medina, *the* city. Medina became the center of the new faith, which grew and prospered.

The Jews of Medina, however, on whom Muhammad had been counting to become converted, did not do so, and aroused his hostility. He came to be more dependent upon the Arabs of the desert, the nomads, and became less universal in his appeal. Allah told him to fight against those who had not been converted. The holy war, or *jihad,* is a concept very like the Christian crusade: those who die in battle against the infidel die in a holy cause. Soon after Heraclius defeated the Persians (whom Muhammad considered to be pagan), Muhammad returned in triumph to Mecca (630). Muslim historians believe that he appealed to Heraclius and other rulers to recognize him as a prophet, and was disappointed when they did not do so. He cleansed the Kaaba of all the idols except the black stone, and made it a shrine of his new religion. Two years later, in 632, he died. Much of Arabia had by then become Muslim, but it seems clear that many Arabs had not yet even heard of the new faith. Yet only one century later, Charles Martel was having to battle Muhammad's co-religionists in far-off France; the great Byzantine Empire was locked in a struggle with them for its very existence; and Islam had reached India.

Expansion of Islam

Scholars used to believe that this startling expansion was due to the religious zeal of the converts to the new faith. Now, students of early Islam often argue that overpopulation of the Arabian peninsula set off the explosion of the Arabs into so huge an area. In fact, Arabs had been quietly emigrating from Arabia for some time, to settle in Iraq, Palestine, and Syria. Now they had the new faith to serve as a symbol of their new unity, and the first stages of their advance took them into lands already infiltrated by fellow Arabs. So the movement quickly gathered momentum: Islam was its battle-cry, but its motives seem to have been the age-old ones of conquest for living-space and booty. Moreover, the organization of the Arab Muslims into

armies dispatched abroad to fight surely prevented the disruption of hard-won unity inside Arabia itself. Toward Christians and Jews the conquering Muslims generally were tolerant, regarding both as fellow monotheists and "peoples of the Book."

Syria and Persia were conquered almost simultaneously by two armies. The Syrian province, disaffected from Byzantium by monophysitism, fell easily. And the Persians, because of their weakness after recent defeats at the hands of Heraclius, failed to put up the resistance that might have been expected. By 639 Jerusalem had been captured; in 641 the native Persian dynasty was ended. During 639–640 the Arabs added Egypt, the major Byzantine naval base, which was also monophysite in religion and ripe for conquest. Launching ships, they seized the islands of Cyprus and Rhodes and began attacking southern Italy and Sicily. Moving west across North Africa, they took Carthage in 698 and conquered the native Berber tribes, who had resisted Romans, Vandals, and Byzantines. In 711 with a mixed force of Berbers and Arabs, under the command of a certain Tarik, they launched the invasion of Spain across the Straits of Gibraltar. The very name *Gibraltar* is a corruption of Arabic words meaning "Rock of Tarik." By 725, the first Arabs had crossed the Pyrenees, to meet Charles Martel at Tours seven years later. Meanwhile, they had been spreading east from Persia throughout what is today Soviet Turkestan, and in 724 they had reached the Indus and the western frontiers of China. Simultaneously, they moved south from Egypt and North Africa into the little-known and uncivilized desert regions of Central Africa. These conquests of the first century of Islam were virtually final. Only the Mediterranean islands and Spain were ever permanently reconquered by Christians.

Disunity in Islam

The unity of these enormous conquests was of course more apparent than real. The Arabs had overrun a vast collection of diverse peoples with diverse customs. Moreover, the Arabs themselves were experiencing internal dissensions that made impossible the establishment of a unified state to govern the whole of the conquered territory. After Muhammad's death, there was disagreement over the succession. Finally, Muhammad's eldest companion, Abu Bekr, was chosen *khalifa* (caliph, the representative of Muhammad). Abu Bekr died in 634, and the next two caliphs, Omar (ruled 634–644) and Othman (ruled 644–656), were also chosen from outside Muhammad's family, to the distress of many Muslims. Moreover, many Arabs resented the caliphs' assertion of authority over them and longed for their old freedom as nomads. In 656, Othman, the third caliph, was murdered. By then, those who favored choosing only a member of Muhammad's own family had grouped themselves around Ali, cousin of the Prophet. This party also opposed all reliance on commentaries, or supplemental works explaining the

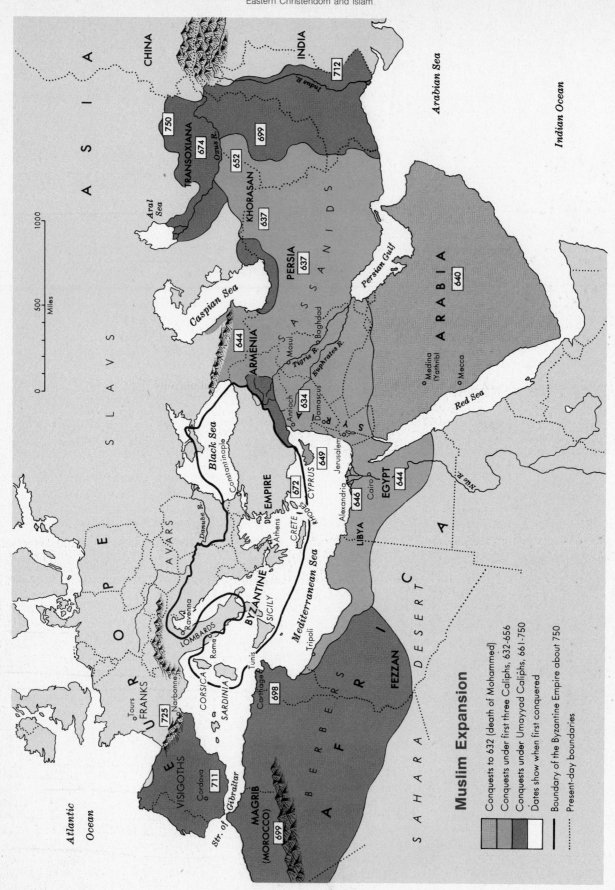

Muslim Expansion

Conquests to 632 (death of Mohammed)
Conquests under first three Caliphs, 632-656
Conquests under Umayyad Caliphs, 661-750
Dates show when first conquered
Boundary of the Byzantine Empire about 750
Present-day boundaries

Koran. Fundamentalists with regard to the Koran, they became known as Shiites (the sectarians). Opposed to them were the members of a prominent family, the Umayyads, who backed one of their members—Muawiyah—as caliph.

In 656 Ali was chosen caliph. Civil war broke out. Ali accepted arbitration of the quarrel, and a sect began (Kharidjites) who opposed Ali's decision. Ali was murdered in 661. His opponent, Muawiyah, had already proclaimed himself caliph in Damascus in 660. Thus began the dynastic Umayyad caliphate (660–750). On the whole, it saw ninety years of prosperity, good government, brisk trade, and cultural achievement along Byzantine lines, of which the famous "Dome of the Rock" mosque in Jerusalem is the outstanding example. The civil service was manned by Greeks, and Greek artists worked for the caliph; the Christian population, except for the payment of a poll tax, were on the whole unmolested and better off than they had been before.

Shiite opposition to the Umayyads, however, remained strong. The enemies of the Shiites called themselves Sunnites (traditionalists). There was almost no difference between the two groups with regard to religious observances and law. But the Shiites felt it their duty to curse the first three caliphs, who had ruled before their hero, Ali, while the Sunnites deeply revered these three caliphs. The Shiites were far more intolerant of the unbeliever, conspired in secret against the government, and were given to self-pity and to wild emotional outbursts of grief for Ali's son Hussein, who was killed in 680. Southern Iraq was then the center of Shiite strength, although in modern times Persia (Iran) has become the center.

From these Eastern regions came the leadership of the plot which in 750 was responsible for the overthrow and murder of the last of the Umayyad caliphs at Damascus, together with ninety members of his family. The leader of the conspirators was Abu'l Abbas, not a Shiite himself, but the great-grandson of a cousin of Muhammad. The caliphate was shortly afterward moved east to Baghdad, capital of present-day Iraq, and was thereafter known as the Abbasid caliphate. The days when Islam was primarily an Arab movement under Byzantine influence were over. At Baghdad, the caliphate took on more and more of the color of the Persian Empire, in whose former territory it was situated. But even now, its Christian subjects were on the whole well treated.

Other sects appeared in Islam with varying views of how one might interpret the Koran. Some were mystics seeking and sometimes finding ecstatic union with God—Sufis, like the Neoplatonists. And politically the rest of the Muslim world fell away from its dependence upon the Abbasids. One of the few Umayyads to escape death in 750 made his way to Spain, and built himself a state centered around the city of Cordova. Rich and strong, his descendants declared themselves caliphs in 929. Separate Muslim states appeared in Morocco, in Tunis, and in Egypt, where still another

dynasty, this time Shiite, built Cairo in the tenth century and began to call themselves caliphs. Rival dynasties also appeared in Persia itself, in Syria, and in the other Eastern provinces. At Baghdad, though the state took much of its character and culture from its Persian past, the power fell gradually into the hands of Turkish troops. And it was the Seljuk Turks who emerged supreme from the confused struggle for power when they took Baghdad in 1055. Although the caliphate at Baghdad lasted down to 1258, when the Mongols finally ended it, the caliphs of its last two centuries were mere puppets in Turkish hands.

Islamic Civilization

More interesting perhaps than the shifts in political and military fortunes of Islamic rulers is the extraordinary development of Islamic civilization. The Arab conquerors were moving into provinces that had an ancient tradition of culture, regions which, until the Arabs appeared, had been parts of the East Roman or Persian empires. The Arabs brought their new religion and their language to the peoples whom they conquered. The religion often stimulated new artistic and literary development, and, through its requirement of pilgrimage, brought about mobility among the Muslims and encouraged the exchange of ideas with fellow Muslims from the other end of the Muslim world. The language had to be learned by everybody who wished to read the Koran, since it was the rule that "the Book" might not be translated. Since Arabic is an extraordinarily flexible and powerful instrument, it became the stan-

The Dome of the Rock, Jerusalem.

Contributions

dard literary language of the whole Islamic world. Indeed, the Muslims were highly conscious of its merits. They felt that incessant study of it was necessary for comprehension, and they gave the highest position among the arts to the composing of poetry, rating it even above science.

Spreading their religion, though seldom by force, and clinging to their family and social traditions, the Arabs in the early stages of their expansion founded new cities in the conquered territories that were purely Arabic in population. But as conversions increased, the Arabs absorbed the non-Arab converts. And in their way of life—houses, clothes, gardens—the Arabs borrowed much from the older urban societies they were now absorbing. So, aside from religion and language, the chief contribution to Muslim culture came from the civilizations of Persia and of the Greco-Roman world. Islamic government learned much from the Persian tradition; Islamic philosophy learned much from the classical tradition; and Islamic literature learned much from both.

Like both Roman and Greek Christianity, Islam was convinced of its superiority to all other religions and ways of life. Like Byzantium, Islam aspired to dominate the civilized world, which it thought of as divided between those lands already part of Islam and those lands still to be conquered. Like the Byzantine emperor, the caliph was an absolute autocrat, a vicar of God, chosen by a mixture of election and hereditary principle, who could not be mutilated and still keep the throne. The caliph, of course, could not add to or change the religious law, although we have seen the emperor pronounce on dogma. Both courts went in for show and ceremony.

Christians and Muslims, however strong their mutual hatred, felt themselves to be worshipers in two religions that were on the same level of intellectual advancement and parallel in many respects: in their attitude toward creation, human history, the last judgment, and the instability of everything mortal. When at peace with the Muslims, the Byzantines thought of them as the successors of the Persians, and as such the only other civilized nation. As a concession to the Muslim attitude toward women, diplomatic protocol prescribed that ambassadors from the caliph were not to be asked the customary questions about the health of the ladies of the caliph's household. And the caliph's ambassadors had the highest places at the imperial table. Each court had the highest respect for the other's attainments in science.

Science

The reign of Mamun (813–833) is often said to mark the high point in the civilization of the caliphate. In Baghdad he built observatories, founded a university, and ordered the great works of Greek and Indian scientists and philosophers translated into Arabic. We hear of a young Byzantine geometry student who was taken prisoner by the Muslims and brought to Baghdad as a slave:

> One day his master's conversation turned on the Caliph, and he mentioned Mamun's interest in geometry. "I should like," said the Greek youth, "to hear him and his masters discourse on that subject." . . . Mamun . . . eagerly summoned him to the palace. He was confronted with the Moslem geometers. They described squares and triangles; they displayed a most accurate acquaintance with the nomenclature of Euclid; but they showed no comprehension of geometrical reasoning. At their request he gave them a demonstration, and they inquired in amazement how many savants of such a quality Constantinople possessed. "Many disciples like myself," was the reply, "but not masters." "Is your master still alive?" they asked. "Yes, but he lives in poverty and obscurity." Then Mamun wrote a letter to the master, Leo, inviting him to come to Baghdad, offering him rich rewards. . . . The youth was dispatched as ambassador to Leo. Leo discreetly showed the Caliph's letter to an imperial official, who brought the matter to the Emperor's attention. By this means Leo was discovered and his value appreciated. The Emperor gave him a salary and established him as a public teacher. . . . Mamun is said to have communicated with Leo again, submitting to him a number of geometrical and astronomical problems. The solutions he received made him more anxious than ever to welcome the mathematician at his court, and he wrote to the Emperor begging him to send Leo to Baghdad for a short time, as an act of friendship, and offering in return eternal peace and 2,000 pounds of gold [about a million dollars]. But the Emperor, treating science as if it were a secret to be guarded like the manufacture of Greek fire, and deeming it bad policy to enlighten barbarians, declined.*

Although the charge that the Muslim mathematicians did not understand geometrical reasoning is surely an absurd invention, the story nonetheless reflects a real situation—the immense eagerness of the Muslims to acquire Greek learning, which seems to have served as a stimulus to the Byzantines to appreciate their own neglected men of science. In any case, the last portion of the story, showing how jealously guarded were not only the secret weapons of the Byzantines but also what we would call today their basic research in mathematics, has a modern ring indeed. Aristotle and the other philosophers and scientists of the ancient world were in any case available to the Arabs, whether in the original Greek or in Syriac or Persian translations. Under Harun al-Rashid (785–809), the caliph of *Arabian Nights* fame, who walked about the streets of Baghdad in disguise looking for amusement and adventure, schools of translators were set up and manuscripts were ordered from Constantinople and elsewhere. Even more was done by Mamun.

One of the chief fields of interest was medicine, which the Muslims developed beyond the standard works of the Greek masters. They wrote textbooks, for instance, on diseases of the eye, on smallpox, and on

---

*Slightly adapted from J. B. Bury, *A History of the Eastern Roman Empire* (London, 1912), pp. 437–438.

measles, which remained the best authorities on those subjects until the eighteenth century. Al-Razi, a Persian of the tenth century, wrote a famous twenty-volume compendium of all medical knowledge, and Avicenna (980–1037) was perhaps even more famous for his systematization of all known medical science. In physics, Al-Kindi (died 870) wrote more than two hundred and fifty works, on such diverse fields as music, optics, and the tides.

Muslim scientists adopted the Indian numerals, the very ones that we use today and call "Arabic." The new numerals included the zero, a concept unknown to the Romans, without which it is hard to see how higher mathematical research could be carried on. The Muslims began on analytical geometry and founded plane and spherical trigonometry. They progressed much further than their predecessors in algebra; and "algebra" is itself an Arabic word like "alcohol," "cipher," "alchemy," "zenith," "nadir," and others that testify to early Muslim scientific achievement.

Philosophy, Literature, and the Arts

On the philosophical side, the Muslims eagerly studied Plato, Aristotle, and the Neoplatonists. Like the Byzantines and the western Europeans, the Muslims used what they learned to enable them to solve their own theological problems. These did not involve such questions as the relationships of the members of the Trinity to each other or the human and divine natures in Christ, but focused on the nature and the power of God and his relationship to the universe or on the distinctions to be drawn between the apparent (outer) meaning and the true inner meaning of the Koran. Al-Ghazali (died 1111), having written a *Refutation of Philosophy,* became a Sufi mystic for a decade before returning to his desk to write an autobiography and more theological works, all Sunni. In opposition to al-Ghazali's dismissal of philosophy and interpretation, the great Spanish Muslim Averroës (1126–1198) strove to reconcile philosophy and the Koran. Their debate deals with the problem always present in every faith. Averroës' commentaries on Aristotle translated from Arabic into Latin were available to the Christian West before the original Greek text of Aristotle himself. Thus it was that the Muslims came to share with the Byzantines the role of preserver and modifier of the classical works of philosophy and science. And eventually, in the twelfth century and later, when the West was ready and eager for the intellectual banquet of ancient learning, it was the Muslims in Sicily and in Spain, as well as the Greeks, who could set it before them.

Indeed, the process began even earlier in Spain, where the physical splendor and intellectual eminence of Cordova caused its fame to spread abroad. Cordova was only dimly known to non-Spaniards, but they were deeply aware of its superiority to their own cities. In Spain itself, a Spanish Christian in 854 complained that his fellow Christians were irresistibly attracted by Muslim culture:

> My fellow-Christians delight in the poems and romances of the Arabs; they study the works of Moslem theologians and philosophers, not in order to refute them, but to acquire a correct and elegant Arabic style. Where today can a layman be found, who reads the Latin Commentaries on the Holy Scripture? Who is there that studies the Gospels, the Prophets, the Apostles? Alas! the young Christians who are most conspicuous for their talents have no knowledge of any literature or language save the Arabic; they read and study Arabian books with avidity, they amass whole libraries of them at immense cost, and they everywhere sing the praises of Arabian lore.*

These Arabic poems of which the Spaniard spoke went back in part to the pre-Islamic classical Arab tradition, and portrayed life in the desert, with its camels and horses, its warfare and hunting, its feasts and drinking-bouts. Love is a favorite subject, but it was bad form to mention a lady's real name unless she was a slave girl. Composition was governed by a strict code of convention. It was customary, for example, for the poet to praise himself, but not possible for him freely to portray human character. Still, much understanding of fundamental human experience shines through. Here is a portion of a poetic treatise on the calamities of love, which describes the kinds of "avoidance" a lover encounters:

> The first kind is the avoidance required by circumstances because of a watcher being present, and this is sweeter than union itself. Then there is the avoidance that springs from coquetry, and this is more delicious than many kinds of union. Because of this it happens only when the lovers have complete confidence in each other. Then comes avoidance brought about by some guilty act of the lover. In this there is some severity, but the joy of forgiveness balances it. In the approval of the beloved after anger there is a delight of heart which no other delight can equal. Then comes the avoidance caused by boredom. To get tired of somebody is one of the inborn characteristics of man. He who is guilty of it does not deserve that his friends should be true to him. Then comes the avoidance brought about when a lover sees his beloved treat him harshly and show affection for somebody else, so that he sees death and swallows bitter draughts of grief, and breaks off while his heart is cut to pieces. Then comes the avoidance due to hatred; and here all writing becomes confused, and all cunning is exhausted, and trouble becomes great. This makes people lose their heads.†

Arabic love poetry, especially as developed in Spain, deeply influenced poets—called *troubadours*—across the Pyrenees in Provence, in the south of France. "Earthly love" became an important element of medieval literature. The troubadours' songs spread to Germany, where the *minnesinger* adopted the convention.

---

*G. E. von Grunebaum, *Medieval Islam* (Chicago, 1946), pp. 57–58.
†Ibid., pp. 269–270. Slightly adapted and abridged.

Some of the greatest masterpieces of Western poetry thus find their ancestry in the songs of the Muslims of Spain.

But of course love was not the only theme of Arabic verse. The famous blind Syrian poet, al-Ma'arri (979–1057), lamented the helplessness of men faced by the vicissitudes of life, sometimes in verses of a haunting beauty:

> *My friend, our own tombs fill so much space around us,*
> *imagine the space occupied by tombs of long ago.*
> *Walk slowly over the dust of this earth;*
> *its crust is nothing but the bones of men.* *

Besides poetry there is a great deal of interesting autobiography and excellent history in Arabic, but no drama. The fiction is of a limited sort only—sad misfortunes of a pair of lovers, exciting incidents of urban life in the capital, with the caliph and his chief minister the vizier participating, or the adventures of a rogue. These stories were collected in the celebrated *Arabian Nights* between 900 and 1500. Stories of Persian, Indian, and Jewish origin are included, as well as some that derive from the Greek classics and from works of the

*Wilson B. Bishai, *Humanities in the Arabic-Islamic World* (Dubuque, Iowa: Wm. C. Brown Company, 1973). Slightly modified.

Hellenistic period. Even when the plots are not so derived, much of the detail, especially geographical detail, is. Thus Sinbad the Sailor's famous roc with its enormous egg came from the Greek romance of Alexander, and the *Odyssey* supplied the adventure with the blinded giant.

Deeply appreciative of secular music and dancing, the Arabs in the early Islamic period seem to have preferred the role of audience and spectators to that of performers, most of whom were slaves or former slaves. Stringed instruments like lutes, whistles and flutes, and drums were and still are favorites in the Islamic world, whose music can be rendered only by instruments that can produce quarter tones. Many musical words we take for granted derive from Arabic. The Morris dance, for instance, is simply a "Moorish dance." "Lute," "tambourine," "guitar," and "fanfare" are all words of Arabic origin. From the Muslims of Spain across the Pyrenees into France and thence to the whole western European world came not only the poetry of courtly love but the instruments which the singer played while he sang of his beloved. Through Sicily and through Spain came Greco-Roman and Muslim science, philosophy, and art. When we consider the contributions of the Byzantines and the Muslims to the culture of our Western society, we are altogether justified in saying that much light came from the East.

Reading Suggestions on Eastern Christendom and Islam
General Accounts

G. Ostrogorsky, *History of the Byzantine State*, trans. J. Hussey (Rutgers Univ., 1957). A brilliant historical synthesis, with rich bibliography.

A. A. Vasiliev, *History of the Byzantine Empire, 324–1453*, 2 vols. (*Univ. of Wisconsin). A good comprehensive work.

J. Hussey, *The Byzantine World* (Hutchinson's University Library, 1957). Useful shorter sketch.

The Cambridge Medieval History. Vol. IV: *The Byzantine Empire.* Part I: *Byzantium and Its Neighbours,* ed. J. M. Hussey (Cambridge Univ., 1966). Collaborative work with contributions by many excellent scholars. Full bibliographies.

H. J. Magoulias, *Byzantine Christianity: Emperor, Church, and the West* (*Rand McNally). Good, brief account of the religious aspects of Byzantine history.

V. O. Kluchevsky, *A History of Russia*, 5 vols. (Dent, 1911–1931). The greatest single work on Russian history, its usefulness impaired by a poor translation.

M. Florinsky, *Russia: A History and an Interpretation,* Vol. I (Macmillan, 1953). A good textbook, solid and accurate.

H. A. R. Gibb, *Mohammedanism: An Historical Survey* (*Galaxy). An excellent essay by the greatest Western authority on the subject.

B. Lewis, *The Arabs in History*, 3rd ed. (*Torchbooks). A reliable short treatment.

P. K. Hitti, *History of the Arabs from the Earliest Times to the Present,* 8th ed. (*St. Martin's). A detailed treatment, useful for reference.

G. E. von Grunebaum, *Medieval Islam,* 2nd ed. (*Phoenix). A learned essay on Islamic culture, in part controversial.

F. Rahman, *Islam* (Weidenfeld & Nicolson, 1966). Sound comprehensive introduction by a Muslim scholar.

W. Montgomery Watt, *Muhammad: Prophet and Statesman* (*Oxford Univ.). Clear and informative study.

W. B. Bishai, *Humanities in the Arabic-Islamic World* (*Wm. C. Brown). Concise, learned, up-to-date.

Special Studies

A. H. M. Jones, *Constantine and the Conversion of Europe* (Macmillan, 1948). A sensible and helpful introduction.

C. Diehl, *Byzantine Portraits* (Knopf, 1927). A collection of excellent essays on important Byzantine personalities.

J. B. Bury, *A History of the Later Roman Empire, 395–802,* 1st ed., 2 vols. (Macmillan, 1889). The first edition of a work later revised only down to 565. The second edition (*Dover) is the best work on the period 395–565.

J. B. Bury, *A History of the Eastern Roman Empire, 802–867* (Macmillan, 1912). Distinguished scholarly treatment.

R. J. H. Jenkins, *Byzantium: The Imperial Centuries, A. D. 610–1071* (Random House, 1967). Reliable narrative.

G. Every, *The Byzantine Patriarchate, 451–1204* (S.P.C.K., 1947). A good summary.

J. M. Hussey, *Church and Learning in the Byzantine Empire, 867–1185* (Oxford Univ., 1937). Good introduction to the subject.

G. Ostrogorsky, "Agrarian Conditions in the Byzantine Empire in the Middle Ages," and R. S. Lopez, "The Trade of Mediaeval Europe: The South," in *The Cambridge Economic History,* Vols. I and II, respectively. Brief modern discussions of these topics.

S. Runciman, *History of the First Bulgarian Empire* (Bell, 1930). Lively and reliable.

A. Grabar, *Byzantine Painting* (Skira, 1953). Superb reproductions of mosaics and frescoes.

D. Talbot Rice, *The Art of Byzantium* (Thames & Hudson, 1959). A beautiful picture-book.

G. Vernadsky, *Kievan Russia* (Yale Univ., 1948). Vol. II of the Yale History of Russia, authoritative and complete.

G. P. Fedotov, *The Russian Religious Mind,* 2 vols. (Harvard Univ., 1946, 1966). A study of the Kievan period of Russian history from a most unusual point of view.

W. Muir, *The Caliphate,* rev. ed. (Grant, 1915); and G. Le Strange, *Baghdad during the Abbasid Caliphate* (Oxford Univ., 1924). Standard works on these subjects.

Sources

C. M. Brand, *Icon and Minaret* (*Spectrum). A well-chosen series of excerpts from Byzantine and medieval Islamic sources.

Procopius, trans. H. B. Dewing, 7 vols. (Harvard Univ., 1914–1940). The writings of a major historian who lived through the events he recounts. His work includes histories of Justinian's wars and of his activities as a builder, and also a scurrilous secret denunciation of Justinian.

Constantine Porphyrogenitus, *De administrando imperio,* ed. G. Moravcsik, trans. R. J. H. Jenkins (Budapest, 1949). A letter of advice written by an emperor to his son and heir, telling much about the various "barbarian" peoples on the imperial frontiers.

Michael Psellus, *Chronographia,* trans. E. R. A. Sewter (Yale Univ., 1953). A contemporary account of eleventh-century history.

Digenes Akrites, trans. J. Mavrogordato (Clarendon, 1956). The first English translation of the Byzantine frontier epic, with a good introduction.

Saint John Damascene, *Barlaam and Ioasaph,* trans. G. R. Woodward and H. Mattingly (Harvard Univ. 1967). The transformed life of Buddha discussed in the text above. The attribution to Saint John of Damascus is no longer regarded as correct. See D. M. Lang's introduction and bibliography.

The Russian Primary Chronicle, Laurentian Text. ed. S. H. Cross and O. P. Sherbowitz-Wetzor (Mediaeval Academy, 1953). Our oldest source for early Russian history.

A. J. Arberry, *The Koran Interpreted* (*Macmillan).

Historical Fiction

W. S. Davis, *The Beauty of the Purple* (Macmillan, 1924). The career of Leo the Isaurian in eighth-century Byzantium.

F. Harrison, *Theophano* (Harper, 1904). Byzantium toward the end of the tenth century.

Yet despite the growth of towns and of trade, society in the West did not become predominantly urban, but remained rural. And its rulers generally preserved the attitudes of large country landowners, interested in the productivity of their estates, on which their wealth depended; regarding the great lords and their fellow landowners as sharing their interests, even when they quarreled with them; and respecting the clergy as men of education who were often useful in administering their affairs and who were indispensable to their salvation. They spent their money ostentatiously, but felt committed to give to the poor and to build churches. They were countrymen, not townsmen.

II The Medieval Church as an Institution

The Church Universal

The twentieth-century student must stretch his imagination powerfully to realize that for about a thousand years, down to perhaps 1600, western European society was identical with the Church, as indeed it was in Byzantium also. The separation of church and state, the existence indeed of several, even many, different churches—things we take for granted—were simply unimaginable for any inhabitant of medieval Europe, powerful or humble. Everybody, save only the Jews, belonged to the Church. And the Church's own laws protected the Jews: from being killed or converted by force or having their worship impeded, although often they suffered disabilities and sometimes persecution or worse. The Jews were the only exception; any others who sought to leave the Church or departed from its teachings were outside the law, and it was the duty of society to exterminate them.

So the medieval Church had the attributes of the modern state. Once baptized, everybody was subject to its laws, paid its taxes, and led his life at its mercy. Yet, while the rulers of the Church—the popes—often strove mightily to create the machinery that would make this absolutism work, they never fully succeeded. The story of their efforts, the degree of their success, the measures of their failure, the nature of their opposition, is in some degree the history of the western Middle Ages.

Having no armies of their own, the popes depended upon laymen—the kings and princes of Europe—to raise armies for the purposes of the Church; and often got the troops but sometimes failed to get them. But even a mighty secular ruler often bowed to the commands of a pope who seemed in every respect far weaker than he. Princes were terrified of the spiritual weapons at the disposal of the pope: excommunication and interdict. Excommunication deprived the victim of the sacraments and threatened him with hell-fire if he died while excommunicated. Interdict stopped all church services in his lands except baptism and the rites

for the dying; none of the population could be married, take communion, confess and be absolved, or be buried with the assurance of salvation. A population under interdict sometimes became desperate, and its prince often succumbed and made his submission.

As a super-state, the medieval church gradually saw its secular authority diminished by the growth of secular states. Yet the rulers of those secular states, even those who challenged the popes and struggled with them the hardest, all took it for granted that they and all their subjects and the subjects of other kings and princes were automatically members of Christian humanity, which was synonymous with human society. Holy relics were inserted into hollows built in the throne of Charlemagne, who often disagreed with the pope; the proudest possession of Otto the Great—who deposed one pope and installed another—was the holy lance, which had been thrust into the side of Christ, and which, legend said, had once been in the possession of Constantine the Great. Such relics symbolized the total dependence of even the most powerful ruler in this world upon the will of God, and served as a sign that he had God's favor. Coronation ceremonies, in the West as in the East, emphasized the sacred character of the monarch being consecrated and were indispensable, not only for the public acceptance of the ruler, but for the ruler's belief in his own mission.

But the economic expansion—it was almost an explosion—and the new drives of the eleventh century tended to diminish the sacred character of secular monarchy, as society grew more complex and more sophisticated and elaborate methods of government needed to be devised. As the king was perceived to be merely a human being doing a political job in this world, and ceased to share with the churchmen his former aura of sanctity, the churchmen alone, for a time, seemed to have a monopoly of spirituality. And, since the secular rulers and their men were often unable to read, and were almost always poorly educated, the tasks of secular government often fell to clerics, who performed them for lay rulers as well as for ecclesiastical rulers. The western European church organization—the hierarchy—from the eleventh century to the fourteenth—has been well compared to a most efficient guild or labor union.

These centuries saw the sustained effort to build what has often been called a "papal monarchy" to develop a system of ecclesiastical—canon—law, and to think through an overarching theological system. They saw also the expansion and proliferation of the monasteries as new orders of monks came into being, often with reform as their aim.

Theories of the Papal Monarchy

Those who use the term "papal monarchy" believe that the papacy strove steadily to dominate the temporal as well as the spiritual government of medieval man.

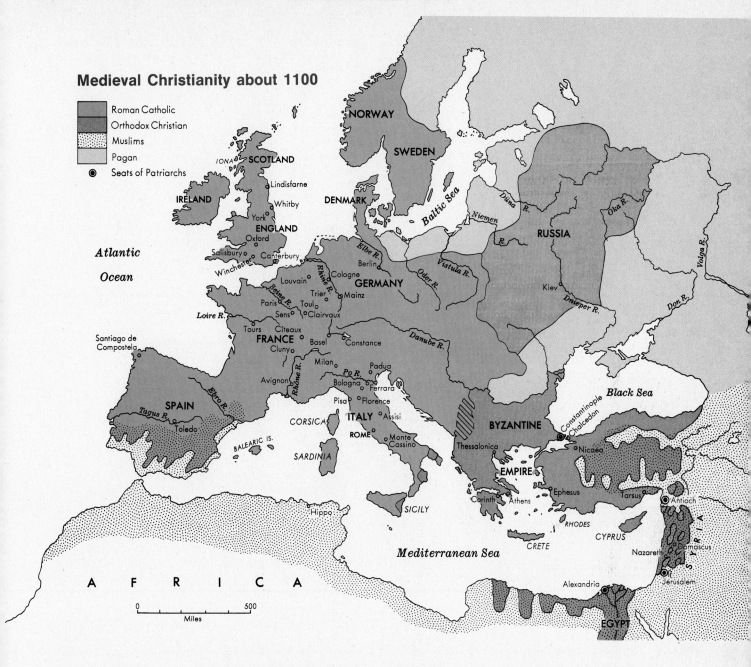

Medieval Christianity about 1100

- Roman Catholic
- Orthodox Christian
- Muslims
- Pagan
- ◉ Seats of Patriarchs

When secular states—France, England, the Holy Roman Empire that included so much of modern Germany and Italy—came into being, that in itself constituted a defeat of papal purposes. Others argue that Christian theorists had always understood that human affairs must be governed jointly by a secular and a religious authority and that, even when secular rulers came into severe conflict with the papacy, the popes, though voicing strong claims of supremacy, would never have wished to see secular rulers altogether powerless. A third group maintains that, at least in the heat of their battle with secular authorities, the popes in fact did voice extreme claims to complete supremacy. In the controversies that marked the period between

the eleventh and fourteenth centuries, both sides engaged in active propaganda warfare, in the course of which many extreme views were expressed. It is often difficult to judge how far such statements were put forward with complete sincerity, how far as arguments to win adherents, or how far as expressions of "way-out" claims that might be used as bargaining positions, and from which at least some retreat was always envisioned as safe.

Christ himself had cautioned the faithful to distinguish between the things that are Caesar's and the things that are God's (Luke 20:25), and to Peter he gave the keys of the kingdom of heaven, and the power to "bind" and to "loose" both on earth and in heaven

(Matthew 16:19); while Paul cautioned all Christians that "the powers that be are ordained of God" (Romans 13:1); so for Paul the secular powers were there to be obeyed. When Christ and Paul spoke, Christians were a tiny minority in the Roman world, and their precepts became difficult to interpret later when the Christian church was supreme among men. As early as Saint Ambrose we have seen a bishop excommunicate an emperor (Theodosius I) and force him to do penance; while Augustine conceded the necessity of a civil state with laws and police to enforce them, but cautioned the true Christian to lift his eyes above the affairs of the mere earthly city. It was Pope Gelasius (ruled 492–496), only two generations after Augustine, who wrote to the emperor at Constantinople that there were "two by which the world is ruled": the "sacred" *authority* of priests and the royal *power,* and that the priests had the higher responsibility, since at the last judgment they would have to answer for the behavior of kings. In Gelasius' Latin, the priests had *auctoritas,* the kings *potestas.*

To this day scholars argue whether *auctoritas* meant "moral authority" or "the natural right to rule," whether *potestas* meant "sovereign power" or only "a power delegated by a superior instructing church"; or even whether both words really meant essentially the same thing. Gelasius was surely thinking of the still more cryptic words of Luke 22:28, in which the apostles said to Christ, "Lord, behold, here are two swords," and Christ answered, "It is enough": a passage constantly used in the Middle Ages to refer to the roles of the church and the state in human society. It is clear enough from the rest of Gelasius' letter that he intended to admonish the emperor to obey the ecclesiastical authorities with regard to matters of religion.

Having broken with Byzantium, and having been strengthened by the Frankish alliance and the protective role of Pepin, of Charlemagne, and of their successors, the papacy in the tenth century sank into impotence, as the individual popes became instruments in the hands of rival Roman aristocratic families contesting for power in the city. Drunkenness, incest, arson, and murder were among the charges against the pope whom Otto I deposed in 962. In such an atmosphere, the buying and selling of church offices (the sin of simony) was not uncommon, and immorality of other kinds—including the marriage or irregular union of priests and monks—was not curbed.

As early as the year 910, at Cluny, in the east-central region of modern France, was founded a Benedictine monastery, whose successive powerful abbots refused to tolerate among their own flock or elsewhere concubinage, the sale of church offices, and other abuses; and who created a series of "daughter" monasteries all imbued with the same reforming principles. More than three hundred new monastic foundations took their inspiration from Cluny, which was probably the chief, though by no means the only, center of reforming currents in the Church during the tenth and early eleventh

centuries. Themselves living in strict accordance with the ascetic rule of Benedict, the Cluniac monks acted as an organized pressure-group to spread reform everywhere in the Church.

Sanctified by the presence of the body of Saint Peter himself in his church, the goal of pilgrims from all over western Europe, Rome, as the home of the papacy, remained the core of the church, and papal business continued to be conducted even when the popes were unworthy. But it was not until the mid-eleventh century that full-fledged reform came to the papacy itself. When it did so, the impulse was indeed partly Cluniac. But more important in papal reform, ironically enough, were the continued secular interests of the German monarchy. For this reason papal and German history now become inextricably entwined. In this chapter we deal with both and with their mutual involvement, as well as with the roles of the Church in medieval society.

III Germany and the Papacy, 911–1152: The Investiture Controversy

German Dukes and German Kings

As the Carolingian Empire gradually disintegrated in the late ninth and early tenth centuries, five duchies (Franconia, Saxony, Thuringia, Swabia, and Bavaria) arose in the eastern Frankish lands of Germany. These were military units organized by the local Carolingian administrators, who took the title of duke (army commander). After the Carolingian dynasty had become extinct, they chose one of their own number, Conrad, duke of Franconia, as their king in 911, to protect their lands against the threat of the Magyar invaders. But Conrad was a military failure and a newcomer; so the dukes for the first time asserted themselves as rivals to the Crown, built up their duchies into petty kingdoms, and made themselves hereditary rulers and took control over the Church in their own duchies, dominating the local administrators of the king, the counts.

Conrad's successor, the duke of Saxony, became King Henry I (919–936). He and his descendants—notably Otto I (936–973) and Otto III (983–1002)—successfully combated the ducal tendency to dominate the counts and to control the Church; they made the counts serve under the Crown, and regained the right to appoint bishops. In 939, moreover, the Crown obtained the duchy of Franconia; thenceforth the German kings, no matter what duchy they came from, would also have Franconia as the royal domain.

Saxon Administration and the German Church

The Saxon dynasty established by Henry I relied on the Church to perform much of the work of governing Germany, since bishops, unlike counts, could not pass on their offices to their sons, and bishops were better educated than laymen. The Church welcomed the alliance because a strong central government was its best guarantee of stability; the papacy itself recognized the rights of the German kings to appoint their own bishops. The Saxon monarchs received church and abbey lands into their special protection, exempting them from the authority of the counts, and bringing them directly under the Crown. Like the former counts, the bishops obtained the right to administer justice within their own domain. In 1007, for instance, the bishops of the great sees of Bamberg and Würzburg were given all the rights that had formerly belonged to counts.

In addition to efficient administration, the Church supplied the German king with much of his revenue, and tenants of church lands furnished three-quarters of his army. The Church also shared largely in the German expansion to the east—the celebrated *Drang nach Osten*—in the defeat of the Magyars (955), in the push into Slavic lands along the Elbe and Saale rivers, and in the advance into Silesia. New German bishoprics were set up, with Magdeburg as center, and subject sees were established east of the Elbe. The Church, in consequence, was now able to impose Christianity upon the vanquished Slavs.

The Empire

When King Otto I took the title of emperor in the year 962, he created for his successors a set of problems that far transcended the local problems of Germany and that profoundly affected Germany itself. The old concept of the Roman Empire as the only possible true secular power had continued unchanged in the Eastern empire of Byzantium.

In the Carolingian West, however, this idea had become much diluted, and *emperor* had come to mean a ruler who controlled two or more kingdoms, but who did not necessarily claim supremacy over the whole inhabited world. The kingdoms that the Western emperor was likely to control were Germany, Burgundy, and Italy. Burgundy had grown up under ambitious rulers in the region between the eastern and western Frankish lands. Italy, on the other hand, was weak, divided, and open to invasion.

Thus the king of Germany had something to gain if he could secure the title of emperor even in its diluted new meaning. And, if he did not make himself emperor, he faced a real danger that somebody else would. That somebody might easily be the duke of Swabia or of Bavaria, in which case the struggle of the Saxon kings to control the dukes would have proved unavailing. When viewed in this light, Otto I's fateful trip to Italy and his assumption of the imperial title appear not as a mere urge for conquest but as a move in self-defense. Moreover, it was the natural step for the heir to the Carolingians to take.

Otto I's grandson, the brilliant young Otto III

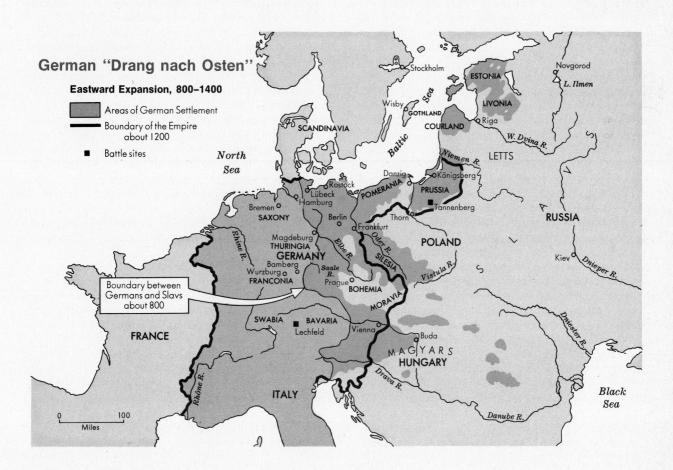

German "Drang nach Osten"

Eastward Expansion, 800–1400

- Areas of German Settlement
- Boundary of the Empire about 1200
- Battle sites

(983–1002), used a seal with the words *Renewal of the Roman Empire*. In Rome itself he strove to restore a Roman imperial palace, Roman titles, and Roman glory, possibly acting under the influence of his Byzantine mother, and surely hoping to win the support of the Roman aristocracy. He also tried to make imperial power real in Italy by putting German officials on Church lands to keep these lands out of the hands of the Italian nobility, and by appointing German bishops to Italian sees in an effort to build up the sort of government he had at home. Since Otto III did not ignore Germany but paid careful attention to relations between Germany and the Slavs, German contemporaries seem to have felt that his intervention in Italy was proper and legitimate. He was not trying to dominate the entire West, but rather to establish himself as emperor in the new sense, and to consolidate the rule of the Saxon dynasty in Italy, Burgundy, and Germany.

German culture and German trade benefited from the Italian connection. By the early eleventh century, the right of each new German king to be king of Italy and emperor was taken for granted; even if a new king had not yet been crowned emperor by the pope, he called himself "king of the Romans, still to be promoted to emperor." Italy benefited, as the long period of anarchy finally came to an end. The emperors raised the level of the papacy from the degradation it had reached in the tenth century. But, as the emperors sponsored reforming movements within the Church, they set in motion forces that would make the papacy a world power and bring about their own eventual ruin.

Salian Administration

The hereditary principle had by now been established in the German monarchy; regional barriers within Germany were gradually disappearing; and a sense of German national unity was asserting itself, evidenced by the general use of the term *teutonici* (Teutons or Germans). When the Saxon dynasty died out in 1024, the widow of the last Saxon designated Conrad II (1024–1039) of the Salian dynasty. The new dynasty, which came from Franconia, produced some first-rate administrators. Conrad II modified the Saxon policy of entrusting the duchies and the great episcopal sees to members of the imperial family. Instead, he experimented with a political alliance between the Crown and the lesser nobles (the counts) against the pretensions of the great dukes and allowed the office of count to become hereditary. But he found the counts more likely to ally themselves with the dukes against the Crown than the other way around, and his successors therefore abandoned the dangerous alliance with the counts.

They did accept and develop another of Conrad's administrative innovations: the training of members of the lower classes to serve as administrators: the *ministeriales*. The Church had long used such men to run its great estates, and now the kings used them to run the lands of the Crown. Though they often received lands as a reward, their lands were usually not hereditary, and so did not become fiefs. Thus the *ministeriales* depended directly on the Crown, had a status that could not be described as feudal, and remained a class peculiar to Germany. Often they had highly successful careers, though scorned as low-born by the great nobles.

Henry III (ruled 1039–1056) chose Goslar in the Harz mountains as the first permanent royal residence, and the German royal court gave up its previous practice of moving from place to place. Henry IV (ruled 1056–1106) ordered a survey of Crown lands in 1064–1065 to discover how much revenue he could count on. The survey did not extend to other people's land, and so was by no means as comprehensive as the one that William the Conqueror would soon be ordering on conquered England. But by the 1070s the German monarchy was as effectively administered as Norman England, and far more so than France would be for more than a century to come.

Moreover, Germany, unlike France, was not a fully feudalized country. In France, the Carolingian counts had become feudal lords, each in his own county, whereas in Germany the dukes had no such feudal position. Free men in Germany did not have to choose between becoming vassals of the dukes and ceasing to exist; both large and small estates continued to be owned outright by free men. Although the social distinction between the rich and poor was great, both were more often free of feudal ties than anywhere else in western Europe. Technically, as we have seen, land that was still free was called an *allod* (from *allodium*, the opposite of *feudum*, a fief) and allods were far more numerous in Germany than elsewhere.

Though the class of free landholders had no feudal ties, it had no royal ties either. So, when the attack came on the increasing centralization of the eleventh-century German monarchy, it came from these free landowners, a class that had no exact counterpart elsewhere in the West. They had strengthened their position by becoming the guardians or "advocates" (German: *Vogt*) of monasteries, a process that was aided for a time by the Crown itself. In 973 there were in Germany 108 abbeys, probably all attached to the Crown; in 1075, there were more than 700, and almost all the new ones were attached to members of the landowner class. A new monastic foundation in Germany was not only a sign of the founder's piety. Monks opened up and colonized new lands, and the resulting revenues went to the founder of the house, who as "advocate" also had jurisdiction over the tenants. (The English term for this practice is *advowson*; the German, *Vogtei*.)

To keep these valuable monasteries out of royal hands, the German nobles often made them the legal property of the pope, who was far away and could not interfere as readily as the king could. Thus, side by side with what may be termed the "royal" church and its bishops, there grew up in Germany a "noble" church based largely on monastic foundations.

Opposition to the royal church, to the low-born ministeriales, and to the trend toward monarchical centralization all led the German nobility to revolt. In 1073, the nobles rose in Saxony against the emperor Henry IV; in 1075, Henry crushed the uprising. But only a few weeks later there began the open struggle with the papacy that gave the nobles new occasion to rebel. This was the Investiture Controversy. It lasted half a century.

The Investiture Controversy

TO 1077 The origins of this struggle go back to the year 1046, when the emperor Henry III found three rival popes simultaneously in office while rival mobs of their supporters rioted in the streets of Rome. Henry deposed all three. After two successive German appointees had died—perhaps by poison—Henry in 1049 named a third German, his own uncle, Bishop Bruno of Toul, who became pope as Leo IX (ruled 1046–1051). Leo was committed to the Cluniac program of monastic reform. But he and his younger assistant, Hildebrand, also favored the extension of reform beyond the monasteries. The whole church hierarchy, they insisted, must be purged of secular influences, and over it all the pope must reign supreme. The emperor Henry III had thus put into power reformers whose chief target would be his own imperial system of government in Germany. And Leo began to appoint *cardinals* (from the Latin *cardo,* a hinge), who now served as key advisers and administrators instead of merely ornamental dignitaries, which they had been. By 1059 the papacy had given these cardinals the power to elect new popes, depriving the German emperors of their role. And the Normans of southern Italy promised to give the cardinals military backing, so that they could do their job without fear of German intervention.

In 1073 Hildebrand himself became pope as Gregory VII. He was determined to push ecclesiastical reform by ensuring the canonical (legal) election of all bishops and abbots. This would mean sweeping away the system of royal selection and appointment, and the subsequent ceremony of lay investiture—that is, the conferring of the prelate's insignia of office (for bishops a ring and a staff)—by a layman, the emperor. Yet the German royal administration largely depended on this royal appointment of prelates, which involved not only lay investiture but the sale of church offices and many other corrupt practices.

Gregory VII now girded himself for the attack. And, though personally humble and saintly, he was a statesman of such vigor, shrewdness, intellect, and passion that modern historians agree with his contemporaries in judging him as one of the Church's greatest

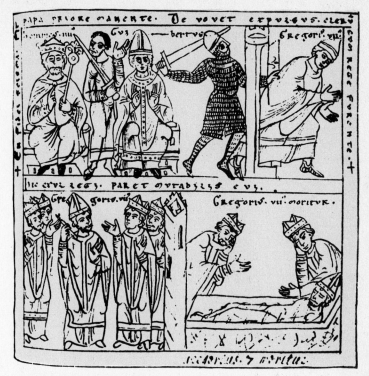

Illumination from a twelfth-century chronicle. Top: Henry IV and his antipope expelling Gregory VII from Rome. Bottom: Gregory's death.

and most effective popes. He believed that, as the wielder of supreme spiritual authority, the pope had jurisdiction over temporal things as well, and that temporal princes who defied his command were followers of Antichrist. To some, these ideas seemed and still seem revolutionary; to others, an appropriate extension of traditional theory.

Gregory himself denied that he was ambitious for temporal power for any purpose except the holiest. He was unquestionably committed to moral reform, yet he also declared that the pope was subject to no human judgment; that the Roman church had never erred, and never could err; that the pope alone could make new laws, create new bishoprics, depose bishops, and change his own mind; that all temporal princes should kiss his feet; that the imperial insignia were his alone to use; that he could absolve the subjects of a temporal prince from their allegiance, and could depose emperors. By the merits of Saint Peter, he declared, all popes were saints. Such a series of claims was indeed an unprecedented stretching of Pope Gelasius' words of six centuries earlier.

Gregory VII took the offensive in 1075 by forbidding lay investiture. After another exchange of charges, Henry IV and his bishops responded in 1076 by declaring Gregory's election as pope null and void. Gregory then excommunicated Henry as a usurper, declared him deposed, and deprived the bishops loyal to the emperor of their offices. In a letter to the pope, Henry began, "Henry, King not by usurpation but by the pious ordination of God, to Hildebrand, now no longer Pope but false monk." The German nobles, opponents of Henry, joined forces with the pope and made Henry promise to clear himself of the excommunication within four months, on pain of the loss of his crown, and meanwhile to accept the papal sentence and to withdraw from public life. They also invited the pope to Germany.

To prevent this unwelcome visit, Henry himself secretly went to Italy in 1077, and appeared before the castle of Canossa, where Gregory was temporarily staying on his way north. Henry declared himself a penitent, and Gregory kept him waiting outside the castle for three days, barefoot and in sackcloth. When he was finally admitted he did penance, and Gregory absolved him. The drama and symbolism of this famous episode have often led historians to marvel at the power of the pope. But it struck contemporaries the other way: by allowing himself to be publicly humiliated, Henry had actually forced Gregory's hand. The pope had had to absolve him, and once absolved, Henry could no longer be deposed.

1077 TO 1122 Before Henry returned home, his German opponents, in their resentment at his stealing a march on them, had elected a new ruler, an "anti-king," Rudolf of Swabia. This development resulted in a fearfully destructive civil war in Germany. By refraining for three years (until 1080) from making a decision between the rival kings, Gregory VII did what he could to prolong the civil war. When he did decide, it was in favor of Rudolf and against Henry, whom he solemnly deposed and excommunicated once more. But the pope's efforts failed. Rudolf was killed in battle, and a new anti-king commanded even less support. The German clergy again declared the pope deposed, and Henry marched to Italy in 1081, took Rome in 1084, after three years of bitter siege, and installed an antipope, who proceeded to crown him emperor. Gregory's Norman vassals and allies did not arrive until after Henry had returned to Germany. They looted Rome and took Gregory with them to southern Italy, where he died defeated (1085). By 1091, the last vestige of the revolt against Henry in Germany had been stamped out.

Political propagandists for both sides engaged in a pamphleteering war throughout: extremists on the royal side proclaimed the superiority of secular power, while conceding that mankind needed priestly power also; extremists on the papal side supported Gregory's claim to the right to depose a king, but only if the king were a tyrant. To many pious men this claim seemed a dreadful thing. The pope was destroying monarchy, they argued, something that had been established by God at the beginning of time. Thus the imperial theorists in the struggle were the conservatives, and the papal theorists were the revolutionaries.

Gregory VII's successors were reformers like him. They renewed his excommunication of Henry IV, supported civil war in Germany, and virtually put an end to imperial power in Italy. In 1106, Henry IV died and was succeeded by his son, Henry V (1106–1125). Just as Henry IV had tried to make his peace with the Church at Canossa in 1077 in the hope of defeating the princes, so now his son, Henry V, made his peace with the princes in the hope of defeating the Church. In doing so, he changed the character of the German monarchy. The nobles kept most of the gains they had won in the revolt of 1077. Consequently, feudal warfare continued in Germany, the ravaged royal lands could not be reassembled and put in order, and Henry V was unable to carry out the thorough survey of German lands that he had planned.

No final settlement could be reached before 1122. In his famous Concordat of Worms, Henry V renounced the practice of investing bishops with the clerical symbols of ring and staff. The pope permitted the emperor to go on investing bishops with the *regalia* (worldly goods pertaining to the bishop's office). The investiture was to take place before the bishop was consecrated, thus assuring the emperor of a previous oath of fealty from the bishop. Moreover, clerical elections in Germany were to be carried out in the presence of the emperor (or his representatives), thus giving him an opportunity to exercise a strong influence over the decisions. In Italy and Burgundy, the emperor retained less power; consecration was to take place *before* the regalia were conferred, and the emperor could not attend clerical elections. The Concordat of Worms was a compromise that in effect ended the Investiture Controversy, despite its failure to settle many other issues.

GERMANY, ITALY, AND THE PAPACY AFTER THE STRUGGLE By 1122, Germany had become feudalized. During the years between 1076 and 1106 the princes and other nobles acted on the pretext that there was no king, since the pope had deposed him. They extended their powers, and administered their lands without reference to the monarchy. Castles multiplied and became centers of administrative districts; free peasants fell into serfdom; the weakness of central authority drove lesser nobles to become dependent on greater nobles—in short, the familiar feudalizing process that had gone on in ninth- and tenth-century France now was operating in eleventh- and early twelfth-century Germany.

The princes had many assets in addition to their great allodial holdings. They employed ministeriales of their own, had a variety of vassals bound to them by feudal ties, and increased their power by combining and pyramiding their monastic "advocacies." The royal government did not extend outside the royal domains. The aristocracy were the "lords of the land" and their lands were their own. The foundations of the future German territorial principalities and of what is known as German *particularism* had been laid.

In Italy, the Investiture Controversy had seen the

further rise of the Norman kingdom of the south, controlling the island of Sicily, and the toe and heel of the Italian boot to a point well north of Naples. The struggle had also been responsible for the growth of communes in the cities of the north. The communes had begun as sworn associations of lesser nobles, who banded together to resist the power of the local bishops. In Lombardy, the communes were favored by Gregory VII.

They took advantage of his support to usurp the powers of municipal government. In Tuscany, where the ruling house was pro-papal, the communes allied themselves with the emperor, who granted them their liberties by charter. Thus, in Germany, the Crown faced a newly entrenched aristocracy; in Italy, it faced a new society of powerful urban communes.

The German nobles now controlled the election of the emperor. In 1138 they chose Conrad of Hohenstaufen, a Swabian prince, who became Emperor Conrad III (ruled 1138–1152). In so doing, they passed over another claimant, Henry the Proud, duke of Bavaria and Saxony and marquis of Tuscany in Italy, a member of the powerful Welf family. Because of their ancestral estate, the Hohenstaufens were often known as Waiblings; in Italian, *Waibling* became *Ghibelline* and *Welf* became *Guelf.* Thus in the first half of the twelfth century, the Guelf-Ghibelline, or Welf-Hohenstaufen, feud—one of the most famous, lasting, and portentous in history—got under way. Henry the Proud, the Welf leader, refused homage to Conrad III; Conrad, in turn, deprived Henry of Saxony and Bavaria. Once more feudal warfare raged in Germany.

As for the papacy, although its theorists had not been able to establish beyond question their more extreme claims, future popes could and would try again to depose emperors and kings. Moreover, occasional voices had been raised even on the papal throne itself to say that—while superior to all secular rulers—the pope could best achieve supremacy by renouncing altogether the things of this world and leaving them to secular princes. The pope possessed both swords, the ecclesiastical and the secular, but he should never attempt to wield the secular sword except in extreme necessity. True papal supremacy lay in the things of the spirit, in morality, in ethics, in otherworldliness. But this remained a minority view.

IV Papacy and Empire, 1152–1273

In the next phase of the contest between popes and emperors—which lasted a little more than a century—the greatest popes were themselves lawyers. And the lawyers for both sides got down to fine points. Though often still making the traditional claims to priestly or royal authority in general terms, they now argued about details of jurisdiction: what *kinds* of cases belonged in papal courts, and what *sorts* of appeals from royal judgments could the pope entertain. With the revival of the study of Roman law during the twelfth century went a corresponding interest among churchmen in the systematization of church (canon) law. As the texts of Justinian's great law books of the civil law became familiar to the students in the law schools—of which Bologna in Italy was the most important—the Bolognese monk Gratian about 1140 published the *Decretum,* a corresponding effort to codify for the first time past decrees of popes, the enactments of Church councils, and the decisions of Church fathers, dating back a full millennium. Gratian tried to reconcile apparently conflicting decisions and produced for the Church lawyers an indispensable tool, emphasizing the major importance of the papal role.

Investiture was replaced in the papal-imperial struggle by what we would call today "the Italian question." How could an emperor be sovereign over Italy—including Rome—without trespassing on papal sovereignty? But if an emperor did not have effective sovereignty over Italy, did not his title "Roman Emperor" become meaningless? Or was the pope in some sense the emperor's feudal overlord for his Italian possessions, and was the emperor therefore the pope's vassal? By the 1140s a mosaic picture in the papal palace of Saint John Lateran showed the emperor kneeling at the pope's feet, and, as the inscription said, becoming his liege man, and receiving the crown from him in return. This was not the sort of claim that a powerful or ambitious emperor would accept. And in 1152, when Frederick I Hohenstaufen (ruled 1152–1190)—nicknamed Barbarossa, "red-beard"—came to the throne of divided feudal Germany, the issue was joined again.

Frederick Barbarossa

Using the Roman law as the source for his arguments, Frederick maintained that he was the lawful heir to the lands and titles that Charlemagne had won by conquest, and not merely king by God's grace. Unable to rely upon the great churchmen as administrators, and not possessing enough lands in Germany itself to give him a basis for a full restoration of royal power, he focused his attention on Burgundy, near his native Swabia, and on Italy with all its riches.

In 1156, he married the heiress to Burgundy, which had slipped out of imperial control during the Investiture Controversy. He made Switzerland the strategic center of his policy; adjacent to Burgundy and Swabia, it controlled the Alpine passes into Italy. In Swabia he tried to build a compact, well-run royal domain, but he needed the loyalty of cooperative great vassals. And in northern Italy (Lombardy) he needed also an alliance with the communes in the towns.

Frederick Barbarossa made six trips to Italy. He intervened first at Rome, where, in 1143, a commune had risen up in protest against papal rule. The leader of the commune, Arnold of Brescia, strongly favored the Church's return to apostolic poverty and simplicity.

Frederick Barbarossa portrayed as a crusader, from a Bavarian manuscript of 1188.

that was designed to define his *regalia*—that is, the rights of the emperor in the Italian towns, which over three centuries had been passed from the Frankish counts to the bishops, and had then been seized from the bishops by the communes: the right to appoint dukes and counts, to coin money, and to collect taxes for the imperial army, customs dues, and other purposes. Although Frederick did not necessarily intend to resume exercising the regalia, he wanted it recognized that they really belonged to him. He was prepared to appoint imperial officials "with the consent of the people" in those towns he did not trust; elsewhere he left the choice of officials to the communes themselves.

But the pope—worried about imperial power so close to Rome—opposed this consolidation of imperial power, and so did the Lombard League of communes, headed by Milan. Frederick supported rival popes (anti-popes) of his own between 1159 and 1177. He had to fight the Lombard League and the anti-imperial Pope Alexander III. Although he defeated the pope and occupied Rome in 1168, a devastating plague forced him to retreat. Then he was defeated by the Lombard League at Legnano in 1176. In 1177, at Venice, Frederick reached an agreement with the pope. In 1183 he made the Peace of Constance with the Lombard towns, which kept the regalia within their own walls; but outside the walls retained only rights they had bought from the emperor. Communal officials were to take an oath of fealty to the emperor. Frederick continued to levy the special tax to support the imperial army and recognized the Lombard League as a legitimate organization. The league paid a large sum of money in return for this peace. Although Frederick had made concessions of self-government to the communes, he had succeeded in establishing his claims as feudal suzerain. The Peace of Constance enabled the emperor to assert himself strongly in central Italy, where he established a direct imperial government rather than a feudal government, as he had in the north.

Barbarossa won papal good will by offering the pope assistance not only against Arnold but also against the Normans and against a Byzantine threat to southern Italy. He was crowned emperor in Rome in 1155, after a famous argument over whether he would hold the pope's bridle and stirrup as well as kiss his foot. (Frederick lost.) At the pope's request, the emperor hanged and burned Arnold, whose death he is later said to have regretted. The pope, however, soon reached an accommodation with the Normans and quarreled with Frederick once more (1157); the Pope claimed—or seemed to be claiming—that Frederick held the empire for him as a *benefice*, not just "a good deed," but a fief.

Frederick, the Papacy, and the Italian Towns

Frederick returned to Italy in 1158 for the special purpose of subduing the leading north Italian commune, Milan. At Roncaglia (1158) he held a conference (diet)

Frederick's German Policies

To free himself for his Italian policies, Frederick Barbarossa made concessions to the German princes. His great Welf rival, Henry the Lion, obtained the right to invest the bishops of several important sees, and led a great wave of German eastward expansion into the Slavic lands across the Elbe, where he ruled independently of Frederick. Henry married the daughter of Henry II of England, received envoys from the Byzantine emperor, and conducted an almost independent foreign policy. But in the 1160s, when Henry tried to bargain with Frederick over troops needed for Italy, Frederick summoned him to his royal court. A refusal to come enabled the emperor to declare Henry a "contumacious" vassal and to seize his property (1180).

The great territorial possessions of the Welf family were now broken up and divided among other smaller princes. The very act of parceling them out instead of

Emperor Frederick II in the ship on the left, watching his soldiers assaulting
churchmen on their way to the council summoned by Gregory IX.

royal justice, mints, runaway serfs, and the rest. In
Germany, both the ecclesiastical and the secular princes
had become virtually independent potentates. The
German crown had surrendered its hard-won rights.
Frederick's reign condemned Germany to six hundred
years of disunity.

The Struggle between Frederick II
and the Papacy and Its Aftermath

Yet the keynote of Frederick II's reign was his tremendous conflict with the papacy, beginning in the 1220s.
His opponents were three successive popes—Honorius
III (1216–1227), Gregory IX (1227–1241), and Innocent
IV (1243–1254)—who were not only consistently determined to prevent him from achieving his aims but
entirely competent to fight him on even terms. Honorius, who was Frederick's former tutor, did crown him
emperor in 1220, but before Honorius died Frederick
was already asserting himself in sensitive Lombard territory. During the emperor's absence from Italy on a
crusade, Gregory IX's newly-hired mercenary armies
attacked his southern Italian lands. When Frederick
returned, he was able to make peace temporarily. But
he soon created further trouble. After he had defeated
the Lombard towns in 1237 for refusing to keep the

Peace of Constance, he announced a new plan to extend
imperial administration to all Italy, including Rome.
So in 1239 the pope excommunicated him, and war
was resumed. Violent propaganda pamphlets were
published and circulated by both sides. The pope called
Frederick a heretic who was trying to found a new
religion. Frederick called the pope a hypocrite, and
urged all monarchs in Europe to unite against the
pretensions of the Church. Hemmed in at Rome by the
encroaching imperial system, the pope summoned a
church council, presumably to depose Frederick. But
Frederick's fleet captured the entire council of more
than one hundred high churchmen. Just as Frederick
was about to enter Rome itself, Pope Gregory IX died
(1241); Frederick tried to install a new pope favorable
to himself, but failed. The new pope, Innocent IV, fled
from Italy, summoned a council to Lyons (1245), and
deposed Frederick. There followed five more years of
struggle. Frederick died in 1250, before the conflict had
been settled.

In its last phases, when he was locked in combat with
Innocent IV, Frederick—who had hitherto always protested that he was a good Christian and had proper
reverence for the papal office—wrote a letter to the
princes of Europe, furiously attacking the clergy for
their greed. He himself, he said, would reform the

North Sea

PRUSSIA

Danzig

POMERANIA

Lübeck
Hamburg
Bremen
Elbe R.
Weser

FRIESLAND

SAXONY

BRANDENBURG

Vistula R.

HARZ MTS.
Magdeburg
Goslar

POLAND

SILESIA

Cologne
Aachen

LOWER
LORRAINE

KINGDOM

THURINGIA

Saale R.

Elbe R.

Oder R.

Rhine R.

Trier
Mainz
Worms

Frankfurt
Würzburg
Bamberg

Main R.

OF

Prague

BOHEMIA

MORAVIA

PALATINATE

FRANCONIA

UPPER
LORRAINE

Strasbourg

SWABIA

Ratisbon
Augsburg
Danube R.

GERMANY
BAVARIA

AUSTRIA

Vienna

FRANCE

Constance

Saône R.

STYRIA

CARINTHIA

TYROL

CARNIOLA
Trieste

Danube R.

Drava R.

Danube R.

H U N G A R Y

R.

Legnano
LOMBARDY
Brescia
Milan
Pavia
Roncaglia

Adige R.

Po R.

Venice

S E R B I A

KINGDOM OF BURGUNDY
(KINGDOM OF ARLES)

Rhône R.

Alessandria
Genoa
Canossa

Ferrara

Bologna
Ravenna

ROMAGNA

Zara

Avignon
Arles

KINGDOM
OF ITALY

Pisa

Florence

Siena

Ancona

Adriatic Sea

Ragusa

TUSCANY

Assisi

CORSICA
(to Pisa)

PAPAL

Rome
Anagni

STATES

Tagliacozzo

Bari

Melfi

APULIA

Naples
Amalfi
Salerno
Taranto

SARDINIA
(to Pisa and Genoa)

KINGDOM
OF THE
TWO SICILIES
(Hohenstaufen, 1194)

CALABRIA

Palermo

SICILY

Syracuse

**Medieval
Germany and Italy**

at Death of Frederick II, 1250

0   100   200
Miles

■ Battle sites

Boundary of the Holy Roman
Empire

Kingdom of the Two Sicilies

Papal States

Claimed by Papacy

Venetian possessions

M e d i t e r r a n e a n   S e a

church by confiscating all its wealth. Maybe a return to the poverty of the early Christian days would bring into existence once again a breed of saints who would heal the sick and perform an occasional miracle rather than sticking their noses into political affairs that were none of their business. Although his letter was obviously a cynically intended piece of propaganda—which seems to have startled its recipients, and won over nobody at the time—the very enunciation of such a plan foreshadowed the days, not far off, when powerful laymen would move vigorously against the organized church. In response, Innocent IV's propagandists had to fall back on a new interpretation of the Donation of Constantine, claiming that the popes had always had the right to make and unmake emperors.

After Frederick's death, the papacy pursued his descendants with fury. His son, Conrad IV, died in 1254, leaving a young son who was called Conradino, "little Conrad." In 1255, Frederick's illegitimate son, the gifted and capable Manfred, gained control of Sicily, which the popes had been trying to give to an English prince. But in 1266 a long-maturing papal plan succeeded. Charles of Anjou, a ruthless and able French lord, brother of Louis IX, King of France, was brought into Italy as the papal candidate for the southern territories. He defeated and killed Manfred, and established himself as king in the south. When Conradino, aged fifteen, led an army south from Germany against Charles, he was defeated and captured at the Battle of Tagliacozzo in 1268, and soon afterward executed at Naples. Angevin rule continued in Naples until 1435, although the Aragonese took Sicily in 1282.

By 1268 the breed of the Hohenstaufen was extinct. The Holy Roman Empire, begun by Frederick Barbarossa, and given an Italian rather than a German base by Henry VI and Frederick II, had been destroyed by the papacy. Yet within forty years of Charles of Anjou's entry into Italy as the instrument of papal vengeance, Charles' grandnephew, King Philip IV of France, called Philip the Fair, would puncture the inflated temporal claims of the papacy and take it off to "captivity" in France.

In Germany the imperial throne remained vacant from 1254 to 1272. The princes consolidated their power during this interregnum by taking advantage of the large grants made by rival candidates to the throne, all foreigners, in the hope of receiving their support. But the princes were pleased for a time not to have an emperor; their usurpation of rights that had formerly belonged to the monarchy was now well on its way to completion. Meanwhile, the old links with Italy were virtually broken, and the earlier form of the imperial idea vanished. The allodial nobility, the Investiture Controversy, and the preoccupation with Italy had ensured that the princes would emerge as the real rulers of Germany. Ultimately, the monarchical papacy and the German kingdom destroyed each other.

V The Church in Society
Reform and Renewal

Frederick II's denunciation of the Church was obviously a partisan document issued for his own selfish purposes. Yet of course he was right in believing that the Church needed reform almost as much as ever. Innocent IV, in fighting Frederick, had, for instance, approved the appointment to a bishopric in German territory of an illiterate and dissolute young man of nineteen just because he was a member of a powerful anti-Hohenstaufen noble family. The bishop was forced to resign after twenty-five years, when the last Hohenstaufen was dead, but only because his public boasting about his fourteen bastards (some by abbesses and nuns), all of whom he had provided with ecclesiastical benefices, had become a matter of scandal. Because the Church had an efficient bureaucracy in each bishopric, it probably did not matter so much if the bishop were incompetent or even wicked; and in the end the papacy, which had installed him, removed him. The need for reform was constantly felt in the Church itself, and successive waves of reforming zeal manifested themselves especially in monastic movements.

We have already mentioned the reforming movement of Cluny within the Benedictine order. Its puritanical determination to rid the Church of abuses, and its centrally organized rule over the daughter-houses were both its strength and its weakness. Reforming enthusiasm is difficult to sustain over a long period, especially after the particular abuses that aroused it have begun to yield to its force; while the effectiveness of centralized control depends on the personality of the abbot of the ruling house. Weak or selfish or cynical abbots would endanger the whole enterprise. Those who began determined to leave the world and live in poverty and humility found themselves admired by the rich, and often took gifts that in turn transformed their order into worldly men of business all too concerned with the things of this life. Thus, by the late eleventh century, the Cluniac houses had become wealthy, and their rule had relaxed.

Augustinians and Cistercians

One newly founded order actually broke with the Benedictines and the rule of Benedict, finding its inspiration in a letter of Augustine that prescribed simply that they share all their property, pray together at regular intervals, dress alike, and obey a superior. Some of the "Augustinians," as they called themselves, interpreted these general rules severely, living in silence, performing manual labor, eating and drinking sparingly, and singing psalms; others ate meat, conversed among themselves, and did not insist on manual labor. Beginning often as small informal foundations without large endowments, the Augustinians helped the sick and did useful, if humble, actions in the world, rather than leaving it altogether. They attracted modest donations from relatively modest donors. Unlike Cluny, with its vast collections of buildings crowned by a great and splendid church, the Augustinian foundations were simple and humble. Nor were the Augustinians particularly learned or fanatically pious. They wore neither splendid vestments nor hairshirts and ropes; but they preached, baptized, heard confessions, and helped the poor unobtrusively. They multiplied rapidly—testimony to their attraction to many decent, unimportant people—and in the thirteenth century there were thousands of Augustinian houses in England and on the Continent.

Founded only a little later, the Cistercians abandoned the world instead of living in it. Their original house, Cîteaux (Cistercium), in Burgundy lay in a dismal waste-land far from the distractions of the world. They considered themselves the only true Benedictines, aggressively declaring that the rule of Benedict when lived purely was identical with the message of the gospels: life as Christ himself had lived it. Yet the self-denial, poverty, and wholly spiritual life in retirement that the Cistercians adopted was seen by their contemporaries as often in fact arrogant, militant, worldly, and even greedy.

This came about partly because the Cistercians multiplied so quickly and won so much success. Within half a century after their foundation, they had three hundred abbeys. Their very insistence upon opening up remote, uncultivated lands helped bring them an unpredicted financial return, and their organization—with each house autonomous, yet all governed by a supreme assembly (General Chapter) of the abbots meeting once every three years—made them efficient. Within each abbey, the same military effectiveness prevailed: rules provided for everything, including even the daily habits of the swineherds and their pigs. Much of the labor was performed by lay brethren (*conversi*), illiterate and compelled to remain so, subject to the rigor of monastic discipline but unable to aspire ever to become full-fledged monks, celibate of course, and taking a vow to the abbot of life-long obedience. They outnumbered the monks, did much of the work, got no pay, and served for their lifetimes. By the end of the twelfth century, occasional revolts took place among them, and a century later the practice of taking in *conversi* was abandoned. But in the years when pioneers were needed in the expanding society of the late eleventh and first half of the twelfth century the *conversi* of the Cistercians were among the most active, successful, and unsung heroes of monasticism. It was a rare chance for the unlettered to assure themselves of eternal salvation.

Moreover, the Cistercian rule forbade expenditure on architectural or sculptural decoration of their buildings, on illuminated manuscripts, or on rich vestments of the sort on which other Benedictines always spent money. So Cistercian profits from agriculture and stock-raising were spent on more lands for more agriculture and more stock. To less economical and rigorous men this looked like greed. But in their favorite frontier regions the Cistercians offered landowners the manpower necessary to cultivate, develop, and even to defend the waste and dangerous areas. Cistercian houses flourished in remote parts of Spain, Portugal, Scotland, and Hungary, as well as in the less developed areas of France, Germany, and England. It was tempting to become a benefactor of such developers, to see estates well managed, and thus to avoid hell-fire. One Cistercian house founded on a desolate sandy shore in Belgium eventually was able to profit by taking advantage of nearby industrial and commercial development, running its own fleet of vessels, and turning its *conversi* into a skilled band of craftsmen of all sorts.

The most celebrated Cistercian leader was Saint Bernard of Clairvaux (1091–1153), who in 1115 led a small band of Cistercians to Clairvaux, a nearby spot as unpromising as Cîteaux itself. From here the ostensibly unworldly Bernard influenced the affairs of the world to a degree almost beyond our modern understanding. He not only upbraided clergymen for their laxity in observing ecclesiastical rules but also helped to organize a crusade to the Holy Land, advised the kings of France, and chastened even the greatest feudal nobles. When the duke of Aquitaine expelled bishops from their sees, Bernard, after trying unsuccessfully to win the duke over in a conference, celebrated the Mass in his presence. Bearing aloft the sacred Host in the midst of the congregation, Bernard challenged the duke to pit his will against God's. The duke had armies, Bernard had none; but the duke collapsed—literally, for he could not stand—and the bishops were restored.

But in the end, the Cistercians too succumbed to worldly temptations. Display conquered austerity, and aristocratic traditions quenched humility. By the thirteenth century, great Cistercian monasteries—Fountains Abbey in Yorkshire, for instance, whose ruins are still magnificent—were great and wealthy centers of production. The expensive arts of architecture and sculpture—scorned initially by Bernard as devilish devices that took men's attention from worship—were lavished on their buildings. These Cistercian monasteries had become great corporations, thoroughly tied into the increasingly complex web of medieval economic life.

Friars: Dominicans and Franciscans

In the early thirteenth century, the reforming movement within the Church took on quite new aspects. As town population grew, the new urban masses, often neglected by the Church, hostile to the rich and worldly clergy, eager to "get religion" in a revivalist sense, and sometimes subject to waves of mass hysteria and guilt-feelings, cried out for attention. Late in the century, in Italy, there briefly appeared a small and not very important group of men and women calling themselves "Apostles," who had a leader, in whose presence they chanted and stripped off their clothes until he clad them and dispatched them on their errands to distant places. Even such mild manifestations—amounting to nothing more than indecent exposure—seemed to threaten public order, and eventually their leader was burnt at the stake. But mass outbreaks and the terror that led to them were the cry of the inarticulate for spiritual help, and long before the Apostles the two famous new orders of friars, Dominican and Franciscan, had arisen in response.

Dominic was an Augustinian canon of Spanish birth, who saw some richly dressed Cistercian abbots wholly failing in their mission to convert heretical townspeople in southern France in 1206. He revived the idea of apostolic simplicity that had given birth to the Augustinians, founded an order called the "Order of Preachers" within the Augustinian rule, and until his death in 1221 directed them in their work of preaching and living the life of simple, primitive Christians. Francis was the son of a wealthy Italian merchant, who gave all he had to the poor in 1206, and with a few followers, all of whom had also given up all possessions, and wished only to preach to the poor, obtained Pope Innocent III's approval of his new order of the "Friars Minor" ("little brothers") in 1210. Poverty was not new, but the heavy emphasis that Francis placed upon it—the brothers were to be dependent for their daily bread upon alms from the charitable—was new. The Franciscan movement grew much faster than the Dominican, and much against his will Francis soon was the head of a large, somewhat amorphous, organization. So Dominic raised the Augustinian duty of preaching to the highest level of obligation, subordinating all else, while Francis led a truly grass-roots urban movement of protest against wealth and show.

They were in a sense rivals, and the Franciscans soon adopted the more efficient organizing principles of the Dominicans, while the Dominicans took over the Franciscan emphasis on poverty. The Dominicans from the first had emphasized the need of study as a fundamental duty, while the Franciscans, who began by repudiating book-learning and books, soon emulated the Dominicans, moved into the universities, and became distinguished scholars. Both orders divided Europe into "provinces" and spread widely. By about 1300 there were perhaps twenty-eight thousand Franciscans and twelve thousand Dominicans.

Both orders owned monastic buildings (even before Francis died in 1226 the papacy against his will had revised his rule and permitted this), but were not supposed to derive income from them. Both were concentrated in towns, where almsgivers were thickest. As professional beggars, both were tempted to be over-kind to those who gave them money, and so as time passed both developed a reputation for greed. Sons of the well-to-do would horrify their parents by repudiating their parents' way of life and joining the friars, much as modern children of affluent parents have found equivalent modern forms of action. Dominicans and Franciscans both served on the staff of the permanent papal tribunal of the Inquisition, founded in 1233 to search out, try, judge, and punish heretics, and to deliver those who persisted in their heresy to the secular authorities to be burnt at the stake.

Education

The Church alone directed and conducted education in medieval Europe. Unless destined for the priesthood, young men of the upper classes had little formal schooling, though the family chaplain often taught them to read and write. Their training was in war and hunting, and sometimes in the problems of managing their property. But the monastic schools educated future monks and priests, and the Cluniac reform, with its increased demand for piety, stimulated study and the copying of manuscripts. Medieval men divided knowledge into seven liberal arts: the trivium (grammar, rhetoric, dialectic) and the quadrivium (arithmetic, geometry, astronomy, and music). The first three included much of what we might call humanities today, the last four corresponded to the sciences. In the eleventh century only a few monastic schools were prepared to offer instruction in all seven. In general, monks thought of their work as the preservation rather than as the advancement of knowledge.

The cathedral schools, on the other hand, whose teachers were often less timid about studying pagan writings from the great classical past, fostered a more inquiring spirit. In France during the eleventh century at the cathedral schools of Paris, Chartres, Reims, and other towns, distinguished teachers now were often succeeded by men whom they had trained themselves, and distinguished pupils went on to join or found other schools. Scholarship no longer depended on the occasional advent of a single first-class mind. In Italy, where the connection with cathedrals was not so close, the medical school at Salerno had a tradition stretching back into the early Middle Ages; at Bologna law became the specialty, beginning as a branch of rhetoric and so within the trivium. Students were attracted to Bologna from other regions of Italy and even from northern Europe, and in the early twelfth century, as education became fashionable for young men ambitious for advancement in the Church or in the royal service, the numbers of students grew rapidly.

Universities

The student body at Bologna organized itself into two associations: students from the near side of the Alps and students from the far side, and the two incorporated as the whole body, the *universitas*, or university. As a corporate body, they could protect themselves against being overcharged for food and lodging by threatening to leave town; they had no property, and could readily have moved. If the students did not like a professor, they simply stayed away from his lectures, and he

Scenes of student life in the Middle Ages, from "Statutenbuch des Collegium Sapientiae."

starved or moved on, for he was dependent on their tuition fees for his living. Soon the *universitas,* that is to say the students, fixed the price of room and board in town, and fined professors for absence or for lecturing too long. The professors organized too, and admitted to their number only those who had passed an examination, and so won a *license* to teach, remote ancestor of all our academic degrees.

In Paris and elsewhere in the north, the cathedral schools were the immediate forerunners of the universities, and it was the teachers, not the students, who organized first, as a guild of those who taught the seven liberal arts and who got their licenses from the cathedral authorities. By the thirteenth century pious citizens had founded in Paris the first residence halls for poor students, who might eat and sleep free in these "colleges." The practice crossed the Channel to Oxford and Cambridge. As in later times, the authorities of these medieval universities stoutly defended them against encroachment by the secular powers. Students were not very different then:

Well-beloved father, I have not a penny, nor can I get any save through you, for all things at the University are so dear: nor can I study in my Code or my Digest, for they are all tattered. Moreover, I owe ten crowns in dues to the Provost,

and can find no man to lend them to me; I send you word of greetings and money.*

The friction of "town and gown" also dates from medieval times. The students played, drank, sang, hazed freshmen, organized hoaxes and practical jokes, and staged riots. University authorities did not like this sort of thing and passed many ordinances, usually in vain, against student sports and brawls. Student life in the Middle Ages was hard; it was little softened by what we call "activities."

Much of the study meant mere memorizing by rote. But in the days before printing, ready reference works were scarce. Moreover, though the formal rules of scholarly debate were fixed, there was, nonetheless, lively discussion available for those who worked to sharpen their minds, not just to load their memories.

The Question of Universals
Much of the learning taught and studied in the Middle Ages seems strange to us today, and it requires imagination to understand how exciting intellectual exercise

*Quoted in G. G. Coulton, *Life in the Middle Ages* (Cambridge Univ., 1929), III, 113.

was to men discovering it for the first time. At the turn of the eleventh century, Gerbert of Aurillac, who spent the last four years of his life as Pope Sylvester II (999–1003), stood out as the most learned man of his day; the smattering of mathematics and science that he had been able to pick up caused his contemporaries to suspect him of witchcraft. Because he was interested in logic, he turned to the work of Boethius (see Chapter 5). For the first time, across the gulf of centuries, a probing mind moved into the portions of Aristotle that Boethius had translated, and discovered in logic a means to approach the writings of the ancients and of the church fathers in a systematic way. By the end of the century, churchmen could debate whether it was proper to use human reason in considering a particular theological question (for example, was Christ actually present in the sacramental wafer and wine?), and in all efforts to explain away inconsistencies in the Bible and the Fathers in general. Even those who attacked the use of reason used it themselves in making new definitions that enabled them to argue that bread and wine could indeed, in a certain way, become flesh and blood.

Once the new method became available, the men of the late eleventh and early twelfth centuries employed it largely in a celebrated controversy over the philosophical problem of "universals." A universal is a whole category of things; when we say "dog" or "table" or "man," we may mean not any specific dog or table or man, but the idea of all dogs, tables, or men: dogdom, tabledom, mankind. The question that exercised the medieval thinkers was whether universal categories have an existence: *is* there such a thing as dogdom, tabledom, or mankind?

If you said no, you were a *nominalist;* that is, you thought dogdom, tabledom, mankind were merely *nomina, names* that men give to a general category from their experience of individual members of it. We experience dogs, tables, men, and so we infer the existence of dogdom, tabledom, mankind because the individual members of the category have certain points of resemblance; but the category, the universal, has no existence in itself.

If you said yes, you were a *realist;* that is, you thought that the general categories did exist. Many realists took this view a large step further, and said that the individual dog, table, or man was far less real than the generalizing category or universal, or even that the individual dog, table, or man was a mere reflection of one aspect of the category, and existed by virtue of belonging to the category; a man exists only because he partakes of the nature of mankind, a dog because he partakes of the nature of dogdom.

If one transfers the problem to politics, and thinks of the state and the individual, one can see at once how great its practical importance may be. A pure nominalist would say that the state is just a name, and exists only by virtue of the fact that the individuals who make it up are real; he would argue that the state must then serve its subjects, since after all it is only the sum of their individualities. A pure realist would say that the state is the only real thing, that its individual subjects exist only in so far as they partake of its general character, and that the state by virtue of its existence properly dominates the individual. In religion, an extreme nominalist, arguing that what one can perceive through one's senses is alone real, might even have trouble believing in the existence of God. An extreme realist would tend to ignore or even to deny the existence of the physical world and its problems. Moderate realists have to start with faith, to believe so that they may know, as the English Saint Anselm put it.

Peter Abelard (1079–1142), a popular lecturer in the University of Paris, tried to compromise the question. He argued that universals were not merely names, as the nominalists held, nor did they have a real existence, as the realists held. They were, he said, *concepts* in men's minds, and as such had a real existence of a special kind in the mind, which had created them out of its experience of particulars: mankind from men, dogdom from dogs, and so on. Abelard's compromise between nominalism and realism is called conceptualism.

Abelard insisted on the importance of understanding for true faith; he put reason first, and thus understood in order that he might believe, instead of the other way around. His most famous work, *Sic et Non (Yes and No)*, lists over 150 theological statements and cites authorities both defending and attacking the truth of each. When Scripture and the Fathers were inconsistent, he seems to argue, how could a man make up his mind what to believe unless he used his head? A rationalist and lover of argument, Abelard was nonetheless a deeply pious believer. Saint Bernard the Cistercian, who was a mystic and suspicious of reason, believed him heretical, and had his views condemned and denounced repeatedly.

Thomas Aquinas

By the time of Abelard's death in the mid-twelfth century, the Greek scientific writings of antiquity—lost all these centuries to the West—were on their way to recovery, often through translations from Arabic into Latin. In the second half of the century came the recovery of Aristotle's lost treatises on logic, which dealt with such subjects as how to build a syllogism, how to prove a point, or how to refute false conclusions. Using these instruments, medieval thinkers were for the first time in a position to systematize and summarize their entire philosophical position.

Yet the recovery of Aristotle posed certain new problems. For example, the Muslim philosopher Averroës, whose comments accompanied the text of Aristotle's *Metaphysics,* stressed Aristotle's own view that the physical world was eternal; since the soul of man—a nonphysical thing—was essentially common to all humanity, no individual human soul could be saved by itself. Obviously this ran counter to fundamental Christian teaching. Some scholars tried to say that both views could be true, Aristotle's in philosophy and the Christian in theology; but this led directly into heresy. Others tried to forbid the study and reading of Aristotle, but without success. It was the Dominican Albertus Magnus (1193–1280), a German, and his pupil Thomas Aquinas (1225–1274), an Italian, who—in massive multivolume works produced over a lifetime— succeeded in reconciling the apparent differences between Aristotle's teachings and those of the Christian tradition. They were the greatest of the Schoolmen, exponents of the philosophy historians call Scholasticism.

Aquinas' best-known writings were the *Summa Theologica* and the *Summa contra Gentiles*. He discussed God, man, and the universe, arranging his material in systematic, topical order in the form of an inquiry into and discussion of each open question. First, he cited the evidence on each side, then he gave his own answer, and finally he demonstrated the falsity of the other position. Though Aquinas always cited authority, he also never failed to provide his own logical analysis. For him, reason was a most valuable instrument, but only when it recognized its own limitations. When reason unaided could not comprehend an apparent contradiction with faith, it must yield to faith, since reason by itself could not understand the entire universe. Certain fundamentals must be accepted as unprovable axioms of faith, although, once they had been accepted, reason could show that they were probable.

If a man put a series of arguments together and came out with a conclusion contrary to what orthodox Christians believed, he was simply guilty of faulty logic, and the use of correct logic could readily show where he erred. Indeed, Aquinas delighted in the game of inventing arguments against accepted beliefs, matching them with a set of even more ingenious arguments, and then reconciling the two with an intellectual skill suggesting the trained athlete's ability in timing and coordination.

Here is an example of the mind and method of Aquinas. It is a relatively unimportant part of the *Summa Theologica*, but it is fairly easy to follow, and it brings out clearly how close to common sense Aquinas can be. He is discussing the specific conditions of "man's first state," the state of innocence before the Fall. He comes to the question of what children were like in the state of innocence. Were they born with such perfect strength of body that they had full use of their limbs at birth, or were they like human children nowadays, helpless? In the Garden of Eden, one might think that any form of helplessness would detract from perfection, and that God might well have made the human infant strong and perfect, or might even have had men and women born adult. Aquinas did not think so; even his Eden was as "natural" as he could make it:

By faith alone do we hold truths which are above nature, and what we believe rests on authority. Wherefore, in making any assertion, we must be guided by the nature of things, except in those things which are above nature, and are made known to us by Divine authority. Now it is clear that it is as natural as it is befitting to the principles of human nature that children should not have sufficient strength for the use of their limbs immediately after birth. Because in proportion to other animals man has naturally a larger brain. Wherefore it is natural, on account of the considerable humidity of the brain in children, that the sinews which are instruments of movement, should not be apt for moving the limbs. On the other hand, no Catholic doubts it possible for a child to have, by Divine power, the use of its limbs immediately after birth.

Now we have it on the authority of Scripture that *God made man right* (Eccles. vii. 30), which rightness, as Augustine says, consists in the perfect subjection of the body to the soul. As, therefore, in the primitive state it was impossible to find in the human limbs anything repugnant to man's well-ordered will, so was it impossible for those limbs to fail in executing the will's commands. Now the human will is well ordered when it tends to acts which are befitting to man. But the same acts are not befitting to man at every season of life. We must, therefore, conclude that children would not have had sufficient strength for the use of their limbs for the purpose of performing every kind of act; but only for the acts befitting the state of infancy, such as suckling, and the like.*

This apparently trivial passage contains much that is typical of Thomism, as the philosophy of Aquinas is termed. It reveals the clear supremacy that is granted to "truths which are above nature," which we hold by faith and receive through divine authority; the belief that God usually prefers to let nature run its course according to its laws; the belief that there is a "fitness" in human action conforming to these laws of nature; and, finally, the appeal to authority, in this case the Old Testament and Augustine. Notice also that Aquinas never even brings up the kind of question anticlerical rationalists were later to ask, such as just how were children procreated before the Fall? Or were there any children, anybody but Adam and Eve, in Eden before the Fall?

Political Thought

In dealing with problems of human relations, medieval thinkers again used a vocabulary that is different from ours. Yet they come fairly close in many ways to modern democratic thinking. Except for extreme realism, medieval thought was emphatically not totalitarian. To the medieval thinker the perfection of the kingdom of heaven could not possibly exist on earth, where compromise and imperfection are inescapable.

Full equality could not exist on earth. Medieval

*The Summa Theologica of St. Thomas Aquinas, 2nd ed. (London, 1922), Vol. IV, pt. I, Quest. XCIX.

political thought accepts as its starting point an order of rank in human society. The twelfth-century *Policraticus (Statesman's Book)* of the English Scholastic philosopher John of Salisbury (ca. 1115–1180) provides a complete statement of this social theory. The prince (or king) is the head of the body of the commonwealth; the senate (legislature) is the heart; the judges and governors of provinces are the eyes, ears, and tongue; the officials and soldiers are the hands; the financial officers are the stomach and intestines; and the peasants "correspond to the feet, which always cleave to the soil." This "organic" theory of society is a great favorite with those who oppose change. For obviously the foot does not try to become the brain, nor is the hand jealous of the eye; the whole body is at its best when each part does what nature meant it to do. The peasant, the blacksmith, the merchant, the lawyer, the priest, and the king himself all have been assigned a part of God's work on earth.

Medieval thought thus distinguished among vocations, but it also insisted on the dignity and worth of all vocations, even the humblest. It accepted the Christian doctrine of the equality of all souls before God and held that no man can be a mere instrument of another man. Even the humblest person on this earth could in the next world hope to enjoy a bliss as full and eternal as any king's. Furthermore, medieval political theory was by no means opposed to all change on earth. One might assume that it would have opposed any and all resistance to existing authority. Certainly the medieval thinkers were not democratic in the sense of believing that the people have a right to, or can, "make" their own institutions. But they did not hold that, since God has arranged authority as it now is in this world, we should preserve existing conditions, come what may. If existing conditions were bad, it was likely to be a sign that originally good conditions had been perverted. The thing to do was to try to restore the original good conditions, God's own plan.

Living after Church and Empire had passed through the Investiture Controversy and the century of struggle that followed its close, and familiar with the extreme claims sometimes made for the papacy and for its opponents, Thomas Aquinas, nurtured on Aristotle, repudiated Augustine's views that the state was a necessary evil and the result of human sin. He concluded that kings were needed; good kings were best; limited monarchy had the least chance of becoming a tyranny. And, he said, though the pope was at the peak of both temporal and spiritual power, he had "an indirect rather than a direct authority in temporal matters"—another example of Aquinas' bent toward moderation.

Marsiglio of Padua (ca. 1290–1343), the author of *Defensor Pacis (Defender of the Peace)*, found the only true source of authority in a commonwealth to be the *universitas civium*, the whole body of the citizens. Marsiglio probably did not mean to be as modern as this may

seem. He still used medieval terms, and the constitutionalism, the notions of popular sovereignty, that have been attributed to him are a long way from our notion of counting votes with "one man, one vote" to determine political decisions. But Marsiglio did in all earnest mean what a great many other medieval thinkers meant: No man's place in the order of rank, even if he is at the top of it, is such that those of lower rank must always and unquestioningly accept what he commands. If worst came to worst, medieval political thinkers—even in autocratic Byzantium—were often willing to approve tyrannicide.

To the medieval mind, even to that of the lawyer, the law was not made but found. Law for common, everyday purposes was custom. But beyond custom lay the *law of nature* or natural law, something like God's word translated into terms that made it usable by ordinary men on earth. It was the ethical ideal, the "ought to be," that was discernible by men of good will who were thinking rightly. Only by using our full human facilities as God intended, can we answer questions of right and wrong. To do so, we need the whole resources of the human community. We need the word of God as revealed in the Christian church, the wisdom handed down to us by our ancestors, the skills and learning each of us has acquired in his calling, and the common sense of the community. Of course, due weight must always be given to those who are specially qualified by their position. Protection from sin is afforded only by being a full member of the Christian church. Such a member will know right from wrong, natural from unnatural, by the fact of his membership.

The medieval intellectual assumed that the universe was at bottom static; the modern intellectual assumes that it is at bottom dynamic. The one assumed that laws for right human action had been designed for all time by God in heaven, and that those laws were clear to the good Christian. The other assumes that laws for right human action are in fact worked out in the very process of living, that no one can be sure of them in advance, and that new ones are constantly being created. The medieval man, puzzled, tended to resolve his problem by an appeal to authority, the best or the natural authority in which he had been trained to put his faith. He turned to Aristotle and Aquinas if he was a Schoolman, to the customary law of the land if he was a lawyer, to his father's farming practices if he was a farmer. And—this is very important—he usually believed that no perfectly satisfactory solution of his problems would be available until he went to heaven. The modern man, puzzled, tends at least to consult several different authorities and to compare them before he makes up his own mind. He may also try some experiments on his own. He usually feels that if he goes about it in the right way, he can in fact solve his difficulty. The right way for the medieval man already existed, and had at most to be *found;* the right way for the modern man may have to be *invented, created.*

Mysticism

Although Scholasticism set faith above reason, nevertheless it held that the instrument of thought is a divine gift, and that it must be used and sharpened here on earth. Those who distrust reason and intellect, men of a mystic bent, could never accept this view. There were many mystics in the Middle Ages. Saint Bernard, mystic and activist, denounced Abelard, thinker and rationalist teacher. Saint Francis also distrusted formal intellectual activity; for him, Christ was no philosopher. Christ's way was the way of submission, of subduing the mind as well as the flesh. "My brothers who are led by the curiosity of knowledge," Francis said,

> will find their hands empty in the day of tribulation. I would wish them rather to be strengthened by virtues, that when the time of tribulation comes they may have the Lord with them in their straits—for such a time will come when they will throw their good-for-nothing books into holes and corners.*

The quality of Francis' piety comes out in this fragment of a work, which is almost certainly by his own hand, the *Canticle of the Brother Sun:*

> Most High, omnipotent, good Lord, thine is the praise, the glory, the honour and every benediction;
>
> Praised be thou, my Lord, with all thy creatures, especially milord Brother Sun that dawns and lightens us;
>
> Be praised, my Lord, for Sister Moon and the stars that thou hast made bright and precious and beautiful.
>
> Be praised, my Lord, for Brother Wind, and for the air and cloud and the clear sky and for all weathers through which thou givest sustenance to thy creatures.
>
> Be praised, my Lord, for Sister Water, that is very useful and humble and precious and chaste.
>
> Be praised, my Lord, for Brother Fire, through whom thou dost illumine the night, and comely is he and glad and bold and strong.
>
> Be praised, my Lord, for Sister, Our Mother Earth, that doth cherish and keep us, and produces various fruits with coloured flowers and the grass.†

Aquinas' Franciscan contemporary Bonaventura (John of Fidanza, 1221–1274) preached to his students in Paris that the human mind, as an organ of Adam's sinful and unredeemed descendants, could understand only things of the physical world. Only by divine illumination could men hope to gain cognition of the divine or supernatural. Prayer, not study; love and longing for God, not reason—this was the answer of Bonaventura, as it always is for mystics. Yet Bonaventura was an accomplished philosopher, quite able to deal on even terms with rationalist opponents. In his *Voyage of the Mind to God* he echoes Augustine and the earlier Platonists: the grace of God helps the mind achieve the degree of love it needs to undergo the ultimate mystical experience of union with the divine.

Science

The Middle Ages saw considerable achievement in natural science. Modern scholars have revised downward the reputation of the Oxford Franciscan Roger Bacon (ca. 1214–1294?) as a lone, heroic devotee of "true" experimental methods; but they have revised upward such reputations as those of Adelard of Bath (twelfth century), who was a pioneer in the study of Arab science, and Robert Grosseteste (ca. 1170–1253), who clearly did employ experimental methods. No doubt much theological and philosophical thinking of the Middle Ages was concerned with forms of human experience that natural science is not concerned with; but in many ways even modern Western science goes back at least to the thirteenth century.

First, especially in the late Middle Ages, real progress took place in the arts and crafts that underlie modern science—in agriculture, in mining and metallurgy, and in the industrial arts generally. Accurate clockwork, optical instruments, and the compass all emerged from the later Middle Ages. Even such sports as falconry, and such dubious subjects as astrology and alchemy, helped lay the foundations of modern science. The breeding and training of falcons taught close observation of the birds' behavior; astrology involved close observation of the heavens, and complicated calculations; alchemy, though it was far short of modern chemistry, nevertheless brought the beginnings of the identification and a rough classification of elements and compounds. Second, mathematics was pursued throughout the period. Thanks in part to Arab influences, it had been fashioned into a tool ready for the use of early modern scientists. Through the Arabs, medieval Europeans learned Arabic numerals and the symbol for zero, which originated apparently in India—a small thing, but one without which the modern world could hardly get along. If you doubt this, try doing long division with Roman numerals—dividing, say, MCXXVI by LXI. The process is difficult and time-consuming.

Finally, and of major importance, the intellectual discipline of Scholasticism, antagonistic as it often was to experimental science, formed a trained scholarly community that was accustomed to a rigorous intellectual discipline. Natural science uses deduction as well as induction, and early modern science inherited from the deductive Scholasticism of the Middle Ages the meticulous care, patience, and logical rigor without which all the inductive piling up of facts would be of little use to scientists. There was no direct "psychological" transfer of skills from the medieval philosophers to the early modern scientists; the transfer was the inheritance of an intellectual tradition of close, almost "unnatural" attentiveness and hard mental work that cannot grow up overnight in any society.

All the educators, all the philosophers, all the mystics, and all the scientists were churchmen. And in a less formal sense, every European (save only the Jews)—even Henry IV, even Frederick II—was in some sense a churchman too.

---

*Quoted in H. O. Taylor, *The Mediaeval Mind* (New York, 1930), I. 444–445.
†Ibid., 455-456.

Reading Suggestions on Medieval Western Society:
The Church and the Empire
Social and Economic Foundations

R. S. Lopez, *The Birth of Europe* (Lippincott, 1967). Basic work by a distinguished economic historian.

The Cambridge Economic History, Vols. I and II (Cambridge Univ., 1944, 1952). Detailed investigations of the medieval European economy with chapters by scholarly specialists.

L. White, Jr., *Medieval Technology and Social Change* (*Galaxy). Scholarly, readable, and full of original insights.

H. Pirenne, *Medieval Cities* (*Princeton Univ.). Classic essay by a notable scholar.

S. Painter, *Mediaeval Society* (*Cornell Univ.). Useful introduction.

The Church and the State: General Accounts

W. Ullmann, *Medieval Papalism: The Political Theories of the Medieval Canonists* (Methuen, 1949); *The Growth of Papal Government in the Middle Ages,* 2nd ed. (Methuen, 1968); *Principles of Government and Politics in the Middle Ages* (Barnes & Noble, 1961); *A History of Political Thought in the Middle Ages* (*Pelican, 1965). By one of the leading scholars in the field, whose views are highly controversial.

G. Tellenbach, *Church, State, and Christian Society at the Time of the Investiture Controversy,* trans. R. F. Bennett (Oxford Univ., 1948). Useful and convenient.

R. W. Southern, *Western Society and the Church in the Middle Ages* (*Penguin). Volume II of the Pelican History of the Church, 1970. Recent, authoritative, well written: a fine introduction to the subject.

B. Tierney, *The Crisis of Church and State (1050–1300)* (*Spectrum). A valuable collection of excerpts from original sources, with particularly authoritative commentary.

J. M. Powell, ed., *Innocent III, Vicar of Christ or Lord of the World?* (D. C. Heath, 1963). Another valuable collection of excerpts from original sources.

The Empire and Medieval Germany and Italy

G. Barraclough, *The Origins of Modern Germany* (*Capricorn). The best general treatment of medieval Germany in English.

J. Bryce, *The Holy Roman Empire* (*Schocken). A brilliant undergraduate essay, whose conclusions have been modified by recent investigation.

G. Barraclough, ed. *Mediaeval Germany, 911–1250,* 2 vols. (Blackwell, 1938). A series of scholarly essays by German historians, conveniently translated and commented upon.

J. W. Thompson, *Feudal Germany* (Univ. of Chicago, 1928). The only work in English on this subject.

E. Kantorowicz, *Frederick the Second, 1194–1250* (R. R. Smith, 1931). Scholarly and imaginative treatment; some scholars deplore the imagination, but not the scholarship.

Church and Civilization

H. O. Taylor, *The Mediaeval Mind,* new ed. (Harvard Univ., 1949). Sympathetic and objective in its treatment of the Middle Ages, but in some respects outdated.

F. B. Artz, *The Mind of the Middle Ages,* A.D. *200–1500,* 2nd ed. (Knopf, 1954). A very useful survey.

G. C. Coulton, *Medieval Panorama* (Macmillan, 1938; *Meridian). This and other writings of Coulton are full of interesting details, but are basically "anticlerical" and unsympathetic toward much of medieval culture.

M. De Wulf, *Philosophy and Civilization in the Middle Ages* (*Dover). Popular lectures by a great medieval scholar of an older generation.

D. Knowles, *The Evolution of Medieval Thought* (*Vintage). Stresses the continuity between classical and Scholastic thought.

C. Dawson, *Religion and the Rise of Western Culture* (Sheed & Ward, 1950; *Image). An admirably sympathetic but also realistic survey in terms of cultural history.

E. Gilson, *The Spirit of Medieval Philosophy* (Scribner's, 1936) and *Reason and Revelation in the Middle Ages* (*Scribner's). By a distinguished French Catholic scholar, author of many other important works sympathetic to the Middle Ages.

H. D. Rops, *Bernard of Clairvaux* (Hawthorne, 1964). An excellent account translated from the French.

M. D. Chenu, *Toward Understanding St. Thomas* (Regnery, 1964). Standard work translated from the French.

P. Sabatier, *Life of St. Francis of Assisi* (Scribner's, 1912). A well-balanced biography of a personality hard to evaluate objectively.

H. Rashdall, *The Universities of Europe in the Middle Ages,* new ed., 3 vols. (Clarendon, 1936). The classic account; full and readable.

C. H. Haskins, *The Renaissance of the Twelfth Century* (*Meridian) and *The Rise of Universities* (Peter Smith, 1940; *Cornell Univ.). The first is an important work, stressing "modern" elements in medieval civilization; the second is a delightful series of short essays.

A. C. Crombie, *Medieval and Early Modern Science,* 2 vols. (*Anchor). Good introductory account.

Historical Fiction

There are many historical novels about the Middle Ages, a few of them good (see the reading suggestions for Chapters 5 and 8). But the best literary introduction to the many-sided human beings of the Middle Ages is provided by Chaucer's *Canterbury Tales.* E. Power's *Medieval People* (*Anchor) is an admirable set of brief biographical sketches of a half-dozen people from various walks of medieval life. Z. Oldenbourg's *The Cornerstone* (Pantheon, 1955) is a remarkably frank realistic novel about an early thirteenth-century French noble family. H. Waddell's *Peter Abelard* (*Compass) is a novel about the famous love affair with Heloise. An interesting narrative poem is C. Whitman's *Peter Abelard* (Harvard Univ., 1965).

8

Medieval Western Society

National Monarchy, Secular Literature, and the Arts

I The Peoples of Western Europe

We have seen that the overarching institution of the Middle Ages was the Roman Catholic Church, to which all Christians in medieval western Europe owed their allegiance—the single institution that bridged the gap between the earthly city and the City of God. In the last chapter we saw how the popes were drawn into the politics of Italy and Germany, and how the German emperors intermittently from the mid-eleventh to the late thirteenth century struggled with the papacy in a war of political theory and of action. Italy was left disunited—as indeed it had been since the collapse of Roman rule—and men's political loyalties went in the north to one or another of the city communes, in the center to the pope as temporal ruler of the papal territories, and in the south successively to the Norman, Hohenstaufen, and Angevin masters of Sicily and of the toe and heel of the mainland. Germany, under a strong central monarchy in the mid-eleventh century, had in the course of two hundred years shattered into many small political units ruled by its princes, both ecclesiastical and secular.

The impact of this disunity in Germany and Italy has been lasting, and many of the modern generalizations about Germans or Italians that we tend to make, perhaps too carelessly, derive whatever truth they may have from this medieval experience. We tend to think of Germans as talented and hardworking, eager both to exercise authority over others and to have it exercised over them, convinced of their own superiority to men of other nations, disciplined but sometimes gulled by demagogues with glittering promises, and given to aggression against others. And Italians, we would say, are volatile, artistically brilliant and sensitive, but indifferent to or cynical about politics, and willing to accept great social and economic contrasts: the poor and illiterate forever poor and illiterate and the rich and powerful forever rich and powerful.

If asked to explain historically how Germans or Italians got the way we think they are, we would probably say of the Germans that they were not unified as a nation until the late nineteenth century, and that when unity came it brought with it a general acceptance of Prussian discipline, military and political, and a willingness to accept the dictation of government. This in turn led to defeat in World War I and to the punitive Treaty of Versailles, and so made it possible for Hitler to triumph. Only since World War II, we might add, can one see a real change. And of the Italians we might say that here too political unity was delayed until recent times, and indeed has in fact actually never been fully achieved, so that Italian loyalties still go to whichever of their great cities gave them birth; while the Roman heritage and the Mediterranean tradition that social differences reflect God's will have contributed to the remainder of our stereotype.

Such stereotypes are wholly unscientific, and such explanations only partly satisfactory. Why were German and Italian unity retarded so long? At least our return to the eleventh century took us back to a time when there were no Germans and Italians in the modern sense, and the later national differentiation between the peoples of Europe was still in its earliest stages. Similarly, in this chapter, we return to the tenth and eleventh centuries and examine the national experience of the people who would later be French and English. In France, our stereotype of a modern Frenchman would be an intelligent and volatile person, individualistic, disliking authority and regimentation, cynical about sweeping statements of principle, passionately patriotic but hating his French political opponents because they refused to share his assumptions about the framework within which France's destinies were to be worked out. As for the Englishman, we would probably think of him as sensible and calm, feeling the need to act on principle, devoted to political freedom, law-abiding, accepting more readily than other men a measure of social inequality, and willing to work with even his bitterest political enemy, since all agreed in principle about their basic assumptions, and took political stability for granted.

Once again, we might try to explain our Frenchman's behavior by saying, "France has been attacked by Germany three times since 1870, and has been left weakened and disillusioned. In any case, since the Revolution of 1789, the French have never been able to agree on whether they should have a democratic republic." Or we might say of our Englishman, "In the eighteenth century the English got such a head start on the Industrial Revolution that in the nineteenth London became the economic capital of the world. Economic power and the far-flung British Empire created a stability that survived even the troubles of the mid-twentieth century." But in giving these answers we would only have begun to chip away at the answer to our basic questions. Next we would need to ask, *Why* have so many Frenchmen never reconciled themselves to democracy? *Why* did the English get their head start on industrialization and imperial expansion? The trouble with our answers is that they come out of the recent past, the period since the eighteenth century. They are good as far as they go, but they do not go far enough. We could answer our second question accurately but inadequately with answers out of the sixteenth and seventeenth centuries, but a new set of unanswered questions would instantly present itself that could be answered only from a still earlier period. Until we get back to the tenth century and apply our questions to the French and English, as we have done with the Germans and Italians, we shall not have come to grips with the mystery of national development.

II The Development of France: From Hugh Capet to Philip the Fair

The central thread of French history during the period between 987 and 1314 is royal success. The French monarchy grew in power and prestige from small and not altogether promising beginnings until it found itself dominating the machinery of government, which it had largely created, in a large and unified state that it had largely built.

The Capetians

When Hugh Capet came to the throne of France in 987, there was little to distinguish him from the last feeble Carolingians. Yet he was different, if only because he was the first of a male line that was to continue uninterrupted for almost 350 years. Like the Byzantine emperors, but with better luck, the Capetians procured the election and coronation of the king's eldest son during his father's lifetime, and then took him into the government. When the father died, the son would al-

ready be king. After two centuries, when Philip II Augustus (ruled 1180–1223) decided for reasons of his own not to follow this practice, the hereditary principle had become so well established that the succession was no longer questioned.

For a hundred years before the accession of Hugh Capet, his ancestors had been rivals of the Carolingians for the throne. As king of France, Hugh was recognized by all the feudal lords as their suzerain, but they were actually more powerful than he and could if necessary defy him with impunity. Thus he might not be able to collect the aid (military service), the counsel, and the feudal dues which his vassals in theory owed him. He was also, of course, lord of his own domain, the Île de France. This was a piece of land including Paris and the area immediately adjacent, and extending south to Orléans on the Loire. It was far smaller than the domain of any of the great feudal lords: the dukes of Normandy or Burgundy or Aquitaine, the counts of Flanders, Anjou, Champagne, Brittany, or Toulouse. It may indeed have been for this very reason that Hugh was chosen to be king: he seemed less likely to be a threat than any of the better-endowed lords. Yet the Capetian domain was compact and central, easy to govern and advantageously located. Hugh and his immediate successors concentrated on it.

In addition to their position as the suzerain of suzerains and as feudal lords of their own domain, the Capetians enjoyed the sanctity of kingship that came with coronation and unction (anointing) with the holy oil, which tradition said a dove had brought down from heaven for Clovis at his baptism. In the eyes of his people, this ecclesiastical ceremony brought the king very close to God. He could work miracles, some believed. In this way the king was raised above all other feudal lords, however powerful: he had no suzerain.

Furthermore the Church was his partner: he defended it, according to his coronation oath, and it assisted him. In the great sees near Paris, the king could nominate successors to vacant bishoprics and archbishoprics, and he could collect the income of bishoprics during vacancies. As in Germany, these royal powers aroused the opposition of the papacy, but the French kings abandoned lay investiture—the actual presentation of ring and staff to a new bishop—without a prolonged struggle. The king retained his right of intervention in episcopal elections, and the bishops still took oaths of fealty to the king and accepted their worldly goods at his hands. This unbroken partnership with the Church greatly strengthened the early Capetian kings.

The history of the Capetians, during their first two centuries of rule in France, is on the surface far less eventful than the contemporary history of several of their great vassals, such as the dukes of Normandy, who were conquering England, and whose vassals were establishing a great state in Sicily, or the dukes of Burgundy, whose relatives were taking over the throne in Portugal. The Capetian kings stayed at home, made

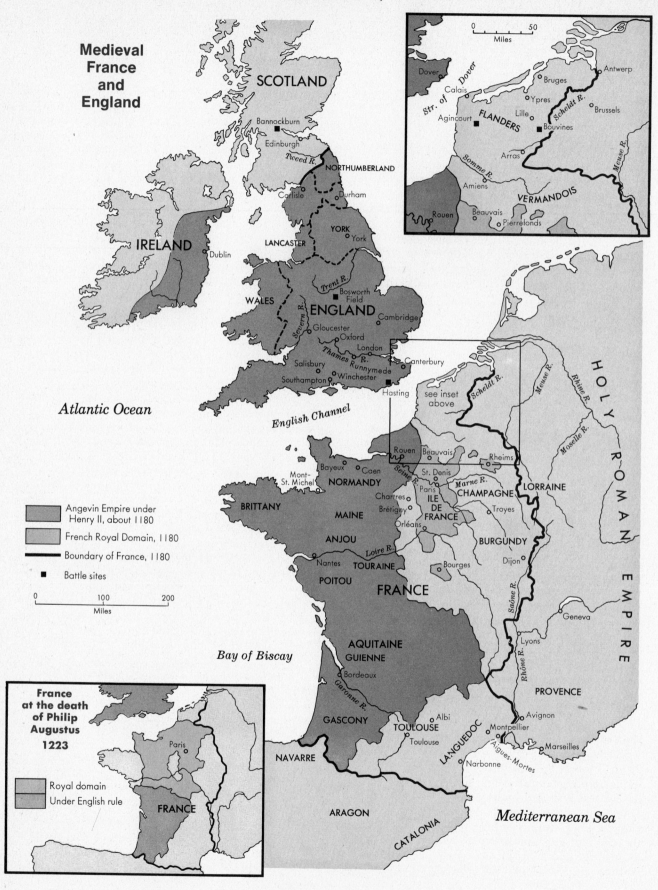

Medieval France and England

Scotland

Bannockburn
Edinburgh
Tweed R.

NORTHUMBERLAND

Carlisle   Durham

IRELAND

Dublin

York
YORK

Trent R.

WALES   Bosworth
            Field
            ENGLAND   Cambridge

Severn R.

Gloucester
Oxford
London
Thames R.   Canterbury
Salisbury   Runnymede
Southampton Winchester
            Hasting

LANCASTER

Atlantic Ocean

English Channel

see inset
above

Inset (upper right)

0   50
Miles

Dover
Str. of
Dover
Calais
Bruges   Antwerp
Ypres   Scheldt R.
Lille   Brussels
Agincourt FLANDERS
            Bouvines
Arras
Somme R.
Amiens   Meuse R.
Beauvais
Rouen   Pierrefonds
VERMANDOIS

Main map (France)

HOLY ROMAN EMPIRE

Scheldt R.   Meuse R.
Rheims   Rhine R.
Moselle R.
Rouen   Beauvais
Bayeux   Caen   Seine R.   LORRAINE
Mont-   St. Denis
St. Michel   Paris
NORMANDY   Marne R.
            Chartres   ILE   CHAMPAGNE
BRITTANY   MAINE   DE   Troyes
            Brétigny   FRANCE
        Orléans   BURGUNDY
ANJOU   Dijon
            Loire R.
Nantes   TOURAINE   Saône R.
POITOU   Bourges
            FRANCE   Geneva
                    Lyons
AQUITAINE   Rhône R.
GUIENNE
Bay of Biscay   Bordeaux   PROVENCE
            Garonne R.   Avignon
GASCONY   TOULOUSE   Montpellier   Marseilles
            Albi   LANGUEDOC   Aigues-Mortes
NAVARRE   Toulouse   Narbonne

            ARAGON   **Mediterranean Sea**

            CATALONIA

Legend

Angevin Empire under
Henry II, about 1180

French Royal Domain, 1180

Boundary of France, 1180

■   Battle sites

0   100   200
Miles

Inset (lower left)

France at the death of Philip Augustus 1223

Paris

Royal domain

Under English rule

FRANCE

good their authority within their own domain, and, piece by piece, added a little neighboring territory to it. They put down the brigands who made a mockery of their authority on the roads. By the time of Louis VII (ruled 1137–1180), faraway vassals in the south of France and elsewhere, recognizing royal prestige and authority, were appealing to the king more and more often to settle local disputes. The king's duty to maintain peace throughout the realm had become more than a theoretical right.

Within the royal domain itself, the Capetians increased their control over the *curia regis*, the king's court, which consisted of an enlargement of the royal household. The great offices had at first tended to become hereditary, thus concentrating power in the hands of a few families. Under Louis VI (ruled 1108–1137) one man held the key household offices of chancellor and seneschal (steward) as well as five important posts in the Church. Louis VI, however, ousted this man and his relatives from their posts, and made appointments of his own choosing. These new men were lesser nobles, lower churchmen, and members of the middle classes that were now emerging in the towns. Since they owed their careers to the Crown alone, they were loyal and trustworthy royal servants, not unlike the *ministeriales* in Germany. Most important among them was Suger, the abbot of Saint Denis, a man of humble origin who efficiently served both Louis VI and Louis VII for decades.

Besides ensuring the loyalty and efficiency of the central administration, the Capetians replaced hereditary local officials. They introduced royal appointees known as *prévôts* (provosts) to administer justice and taxation in the lands of the royal domain. Furthermore, Louis VI granted royal charters to rural colonists and to new towns, because he recognized that the colonization of waste lands and the growth of new towns would be advantageous to the monarchy. In these ways, the French kings began their long and significant alliance with the middle classes.

The Contest with Normans and Angevins

The most important single factor in the development of Capetian France, however, was the relationship of the kings with their most powerful vassals, the dukes of Normandy. By the mid-eleventh century, the dukes had centralized the administration of their own duchy, compelling their vassals to render military service, forbidding them to coin their own money, and curbing their rights of justice. The viscounts, agents of the ducal regime, exercised local control. After Duke William conquered England in 1066 and became its king, he and his successors were still vassals of the Capetians for Normandy. But they became so much more powerful than their overlords that they did not hesitate to conduct regular warfare against them. Norman power grew even greater during the early twelfth century, when an English queen married another great vassal of the

French king, the count of Anjou. In the person of their son, King Henry II of England (ruled 1154–1190), England was united with the French fiefs of Normandy, Anjou, Maine, and Touraine in what is sometimes called the Angevin Empire.

But this was not all. King Louis VII of France had married Eleanor, the charming heiress of Aquitaine, a great duchy in the southwest of France. When he got the marriage annulled (1152) for lack of a male heir, Eleanor lost no time in marrying the Angevin Henry II and adding Aquitaine to his already substantial French holdings. So when Henry became king of England in 1154, he was also lord of more than half of France. He added Brittany and still other French territories. This Angevin threat was the greatest danger faced by the Capetian monarchs, and it was their most signal achievement that they overcame it.

The first round in the victorious struggle was the achievement of Philip II, Philip Augustus (ruled 1180–1223), who quadrupled the size of the French royal domain. Shrewd, calculating, bald, one-eyed, and fierce-tempered, Philip first supported Henry II's rebellious sons against him. Then, after Henry's death, Philip plotted with Henry's younger son, John, against John's older brother, Richard the Lionhearted—Philip's former companion on the Third Crusade (see Chapter 9) and now (1191–1194) a captive in Austria. Philip even married a Danish princess with the idea of using the Danish fleet against England and making himself heir to the Danish claims to the English throne. He also divorced her, but the mighty Pope Innocent III was able to force him to take her back in 1198. Even Innocent, however, could not force Philip to accept papal mediation in his English quarrel. When John succeeded Richard in 1199, Philip Augustus supported a rival claimant to the English throne—John's nephew, the young Arthur of Brittany.

Through legal use of his position as feudal suzerain, Philip managed to ruin John. In 1200 John foolishly married a girl who was engaged to somebody else. Her father, vassal of the king of France, complained in proper feudal style to Philip, his suzerain and John's. Since John would not come to answer the complaint, Philip declared his fiefs forfeit and planned to conquer them with young Arthur's supporters. When John murdered Arthur (1203), he played right into Philip's hands, lost his supporters on the Continent, and in 1204 had to surrender Normandy, Brittany, Anjou, Maine, and Touraine to Philip Augustus. Only Aquitaine was now left to the English, who had been expelled from France north of the Loire. In 1214, at the famous battle of Bouvines in Flanders, Philip Augustus, in alliance with Frederick II, now supported by the Pope, defeated an army of Germans and English under the emperor Otto IV, John's ally and former papal protégé. Unable to win back their former French possessions, the English confirmed this territorial settlement by treaty in 1259. England's remaining possessions in France were to be the cause of much future fighting.

But John's great losses were added to the French royal domain. The French kings now had possession of the efficiently run duchy of Normandy, which they could use as a model for the rest of France.

The Albigensian Crusade and the Winning of the South

Next the Capetians moved south to the rich and smiling land of Languedoc and Toulouse, the true Mediterranean south. Its people drew much of their culture from Muslim Spain and spoke a dialect different from that of the north of France. And many of them belonged to the heretical church of the Cathari (Greek for "pure ones"), with its center at the town of Albi.

The Albigensians, as the Cathari were called, believed that the history of the universe was one long struggle between the forces of light (good) and the forces of darkness (evil). The evil forces (Satan) created man and the earth, but Adam had some measure of goodness. Jesus was not born of a woman, nor was he crucified, because he was wholly good, wholly of light. Jehovah of the Old Testament was the God of evil. The Albigensians had an elite of their own ("the perfect") who devoted themselves to pure living. Some of them forbade the veneration of the cross; others forbade infant baptism, the celebration of the Mass, or the holding of private property. Many of them denied the validity of one or more of the sacraments. Some even said the Catholic church itself was Satan's. The Albigensians were strongest among the lower classes, but they often had the support of nobles who adopted their views in order to combat the Church politically.

This heresy, which reminds one of the Gnostics' dualist views, had originated in the third century A.D. in Mesopotamia in the teachings of the Manichaeans, which had so appealed to Saint Augustine in his youth. Though suppressed, dualist doctrines survived. They reappeared in the Byzantine Empire, spread to the Balkans, to northern Italy, and finally to France. The Church proclaimed a crusade against the Albigensians in 1208, after the count of Toulouse had connived at the murder of a papal envoy.

Philip Augustus did not at first participate in the expeditions of his nobles, who rushed south to plunder and kill in the name of the Catholic church. By the year of his death (1223), however, after the war had gone on intermittently for fourteen years, the territorial issue had become confounded with the religious one. Northern French nobles were staking out their claims to the lands of southern French nobles who embraced the heresy; so Philip finally sponsored an expedition led by his son, Louis VIII (ruled 1223–1226). Assisted by a special clerical court called the Inquisition, which was first set up to extirpate this heresy, Louis VIII and his son Louis IX (ruled 1226–1270) carried on the campaign, which by the 1240s had driven the heresy underground. Languedoc itself was almost entirely taken over by the Crown, and it was arranged that the lands of Toulouse would come by marriage to the brother of the king of France when the last count died, as he did in 1249.

Royal Administration

Administrative advance kept pace with territorial gain. Indeed, it is doubtful if Philip Augustus and his successors could have added to the royal domain if they had not overcome many of the disruptive elements of feudalism and if they had not asserted their authority effectively in financial, military, and judicial matters. Philip Augustus systematically collected detailed information on precisely what was owing to him from the different royal fiefs. He increased the number of his own vassals, and he reached over the heads of his vassals to *their* vassals, in an attempt to make the latter directly dependent on him.

He exacted stringent guarantees—such as a promise that if a vassal did not perform his duties within a month, he would surrender his person as a prisoner until the situation was resolved. Moreover, if a vassal did not live up to this agreement, the Church would lay an interdict upon his lands. This dreadful punishment meant that everyone resident on the lands was denied access to most of the sacraments and comforts of religion. The people naturally feared an interdict above all else, since they could not marry, or have their babies baptized, or have their sins forgiven on their deathbeds.

Philip and his officials were alert to increase the royal power by purchasing new estates, by interfering as much as possible in the inheritance of fiefs upon the death of their holders, and by providing suitable husbands of their own choosing for the great heiresses. Since the men of those days led violent lives, a lady would sometimes outlast three or four husbands, inheriting from each, and thus each time becoming a more desirable prize, and offering the king a chance to marry her off with profit to himself.

The local officials of the Crown, the *prévôts*, had regularly been rewarded by grants of land, which, together with the office, tended to become hereditary. The Crown lost both income and power as well as popularity when a local *prévôt* made exactions on his own behalf. Early in his reign, Philip Augustus held an investigation and heard the complaints to which the system had given rise. He appointed a new sort of official, not resident in the countryside, but tied to the court, who would travel about, enforcing the king's will in royal lands, rendering royal justice, and collecting moneys due to the king. This official received no fiefs to tie him to a given region; his office was not hereditary. He was a civil servant appointed by the king, who paid him a salary and could remove him at will. In the north, where this system was introduced, he was called a *bailli* (bailiff), and his territory a *baillage* (bailiwick). In the south, to which the new system was extended, he was called a *sénéchal* (not to be confused

with the old officer of the household), and his district a *sénéchaussée.*

Like any administrative system, this one had its drawbacks: a *bailli* or *sénéchal* far from Paris might become just as independent and unjust as the old *prévôt* had been, without the king's being aware of it. Louis IX (ruled 1226–1270) had to limit the power of these officials in two ways. He made it easy for complaints against them to be brought to his personal attention. And he appointed a new kind of official to take care of the caretakers. These were the *enquêteurs* or investigators, royal officials not unlike Charlemagne's *missi.* The *enquêteurs* had supervisory authority over the *baillis* and *sénéchals,* and traveled about the country inspecting their work. This whole complex of new civil servants introduced in the late twelfth and thirteenth centuries meant that the king was in a position to interfere with almost all local and private transactions, to exact his just due, and to supply royal justice at a price.

Naturally the king's court (*curia regis*) was so swamped with new business that the old haphazard feudal way of attending to it could no longer be followed. To depend, like Hugh Capet, on officers of the household, would have been a little like the United States government of today trying to get along with no filing system except an old chest of drawers belonging to George Washington. The administration of France in the thirteenth century was nowhere near as complicated as that of the United States in the twentieth, and there was plenty of time for gradual experiment and development.

What happened was something like this. The king's household differentiated itself into departments, most of which had little to do with government. Rather, they attended to the needs of the king and the curia regis. This court consisted not only of retainers but of clerics and others who served as advisers on day-to-day problems. When a major policy question affecting the realm was up for decision, or when a major legal case needed to be tried, the king was entitled to summon his vassals (both lay and clerical) for counsel, and those he summoned were obliged to come. They then joined the rest of the curia regis in a kind of enlarged royal entourage.

When the curia regis sat in judgment on a case, it came to be known as the *parlement,* a high judicial tribunal. Naturally, as law grew more complex, trained lawyers had to handle more and more of the judicial business. At first, they explained the law to the vassals sitting in judgment, and then, as time passed, they formed a court of justice and arrived at decisions themselves in the name of the king. By the fourteenth century, this court of justice was called the *Parlement de Paris,* because Paris was its headquarters.

When the curia regis sat in special session on financial matters, auditing the reports of income and expenditure, it acted as a kind of government accounting department. By the fourteenth century, this was called the *chambre des comptes,* or chamber of accounts. Naturally enough, it engaged more and more professional full-time employees, clerks and auditors and the like.

Cash flowed to the Crown from the lands of the royal domain, from customs dues and special tolls, from fees for government services, and from money paid in by vassals in order to avoid rendering such outmoded feudal services as entertaining the king and his court. But, in spite of this variety of revenue, the king of France could not levy regular direct taxes on his subjects. During the twelfth century the regular collection of feudal aids accustomed the nobles to paying money to the Crown. Then a special levy was imposed on those who stayed home from the Crusade of 1145. In 1188, Philip Augustus collected one-tenth of the movable property and one-tenth of a year's income from all who failed to join in a Crusade. These extraordinary imposts, however, never failed to arouse a storm of protest.

Saint Louis

New advances in royal power came with Louis IX (ruled 1226–1270), in many ways the greatest of all medieval kings. Deeply pious, almost monastic in his

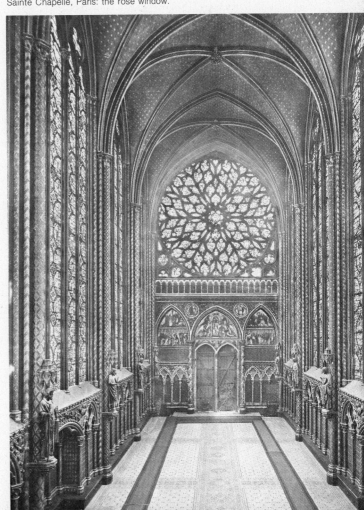

Sainte Chapelle, Paris: the rose window.

personal life, Louis carried his own high standards over into his role as king. He wore simple clothes, gave alms to beggars, washed the feet of lepers, built hospitals, and created in Paris the Sainte Chapelle (Holy Chapel), a small church that is a real jewel-box of glowing stained glass, to hold Christ's Crown of Thorns. The Church made him a saint in 1297, less than thirty years after his death.

One of his knights, the Sieur de Joinville, tells this characteristic story about Saint Louis in his memoirs:

> Of his mouth he was so sober, that on no day of my life did I ever hear him order special meats, as many rich men are wont to do; but he ate patiently whatever his cooks had made ready. . . . In his words he was temperate; for on no day of my life did I ever hear him speak evil of any one; nor did I ever hear him name the Devil—which name is very commonly spoken throughout the kingdom, whereby God, as I believe, is not well pleased.
>
> He put water into his wine by measure, according as he saw that the strength of the wine would suffer it. . . . He asked me why I put no water into my wine; and I said this was by order of the physicians, who told me I had a large head and a cold stomach, so that I could not get drunk. And he answered that they deceived me; . . . if I drank pure wine in my old age, I should get drunk every night, and that it was too foul a thing for a brave man to get drunk.*

Saint Louis was a dutiful husband and an energetic king. During the early years of his reign, when he was still a youth, his very able mother, Blanche of Castile, acted as regent on his behalf and kept the great lords from successful revolt. Louis was grateful to her, yet he resented her attempts to dominate his relations with his wife, Queen Margaret. Joinville recalls:

> The unkindness that the Queen Blanche showed to the Queen Margaret was such that she would not suffer, in so far as she could help it, that her son should be in his wife's company, except at night when he went to sleep with her. The palace where the king and his queen liked most to dwell was at Pontoise, because there the king's chamber was above and the queen's chamber below; and they had so arranged matters between them that they held their converse in a turning staircase that went from the one chamber to the other; and they had further arranged that when the ushers saw the Queen Blanche coming to her son's chamber, they struck the door with their rods, and the king would come running into his own chamber so that his mother might find him there.†

Saint Louis did not let his own devotion to the Church stop him from defending royal prerogatives against every attempt of his own bishops or of the papacy to infringe upon them. For example, when the popes tried to enforce the theory that "all churches belong to the pope," and to assess the churches of

*Joinville's Chronicle of the Crusade of Saint Louis, in Memoirs of the Crusades, Everyman ed. (New York, 1933), pp. 139–140.
†Ibid., p. 288.

France for money and men for papal military campaigns, the king declared that church property in France was "for the requirements of himself and his realm," and was not to be despoiled by Rome (1247). Yet when he himself became deeply interested in the crusading movement (see Chapter 9), he found himself in need of papal support to enable him to tax the French clergy. Indeed, the clergy then complained to the pope concerning the king's exactions.

In the towns, too, those old allies of the Capetian dynasty, there were difficulties during Louis' reign. These difficulties arose in large measure out of internal conflicts between the small upper class of rich merchants, who kept city government a kind of oligarchy, and the lower class of tradesmen and artisans, who felt oppressed and excluded from their own government. When the Crown intervened, it was out of concern not so much for the poor and humble as for the maintenance of order and the continued flow of funds to the royal coffers. Louis began to send royal officials into the towns, and in 1262 issued a decree requiring that the towns present their accounts annually.

This decree itself is a further instance of the king's assertion of royal prerogative. It was a new sort of enactment, the ordonnance, or royal command issued for all of France without the previous assent of all the vassals. Royal power and prestige had now progressed to the point where Louis did not feel the need to obtain all his vassals' consent every time he wished to govern their behavior. Ordonnances signed by some vassals governed all. Examples of Louis' ordonnances are his prohibition of private warfare and his law providing that royal money was valid everywhere in France. Both show his advanced views as well as his determination to strengthen the power of the monarchy.

Royal justice had now become a widely desired commodity, and appeals flowed in to the parlement from the lower feudal courts. The royal court of justice alone came to be recognized as competent to try cases of treason and of breaking the king's peace, and the extension of royal justice to the towns was secured by bringing in to the parlement's deliberations representatives of the middle classes: the king's bourgeois. So fair and reasonable was the king's justice felt to be that his subjects often applied to him personally for it. He made himself available to them by sitting under an oak tree in the forest of Vincennes, near Paris, and listening to the case of anybody, high or low, who wished to tell him his story. He maintained no royal protocol on these occasions, and there were no intermediaries. His justice was prized not only in France but also abroad. He settled quarrels in Flanders, Navarre, Burgundy, Lorraine, and elsewhere. He reached a reasonable territorial settlement with England in 1259, and in 1264 was asked to judge a dispute between King Henry III of England and the English barons.

Remarkable though he was, Louis was simply a remarkable man of the thirteenth century. In his devotion to the crusading enterprise, for instance, he was embracing wholeheartedly the highest ideals of the period. But he never seemed to realize that Crusades were now no longer very practicable (see Chapter 9 for details). Moreover, it cost France dear to have the king delayed abroad for years and to have him languish in captivity from which he was redeemed only at great expense. Yet, for all his human failings, Saint Louis typifies the medieval ideal that the divine law of God's revelation was mirrored in our human law. As God ordered the universe, so human law established the proper relationships of men to one another in society. In human society, the king had his special role, and Saint Louis, in his conception and enactment of that role, reached heights that had not been attained by other monarchs.

The System Hardens: Philip the Fair

After the death of Saint Louis, the French kingship experienced the general change that was coming over the entire world of the Middle Ages during the late thirteenth and fourteenth centuries. Old conventions and forms persisted, but they seemed to be hardening, to be losing the possibility of fresh and vigorous new expression. In the political history of France, these tendencies begin with the reign of Saint Louis's grandson, Philip IV (1285–1314). Called "the Fair" because he was handsome, Philip offered a striking contrast to Louis in personality and in character. Ruthlessly, he pushed the royal power and consolidated the royal hold; the towns, the nobles, and the Church all suffered invasions of their rights from his ubiquitous agents. Against the excesses of Philip the Fair, the medieval checks against tyranny, which had been successful against many other aggressive kings, failed to operate. His humiliation of the papacy alone helped as much as any other event of the Middle Ages to bring an end to the Christian commonwealth to which Saint Louis had been so devoted. The multiplying *gens du roi*, "the king's men," used propaganda, lies, and trickery to undermine all authority except that of the king.

This undermining was a steady war that went on in a series of small engagements in local courts of justice, with the king's lawyers pushing his rights. One of the devices used was *prévention:* a rule that if a case was started in a court, it had to be finished there, no matter what court was properly competent to try it. If the king's agents managed to bring a case into the royal court, it had to be completed there, even if the royal court was not the proper place for it. Another device was *défaute de droit:* a rule that if justice were refused in a lower court, the plaintiff had a right to appeal to his suzerain's court. The king's agents would urge plaintiffs to claim on any and all occasions that they had been denied justice in their lord's court, and to bring the case to the royal court. Still another device was *faux jugement:* a rule that if a man lost a suit he would be entitled to an appeal by challenging the judge, calling him "wicked and false." On the appeal, the judge would be the defendant in the next higher court. By using this device at the high level of the great lords' courts, the king's men would bring appeals into the royal courts. The system of royal justice was gradually swallowing up the system of feudal justice.

And, as the new cases flowed in, the parlement became ever more specialized and professionalized. The *chambre des requêtes* (chamber of petitions) now handled all requests that the royal court intervene. The *chambre des enquêtes* (chamber of investigations) would establish the facts in new cases. In the *chambre des plaids* (chamber of pleas) the lawyers actually argued the cases, and judgments were handed down. Members of the parlement now traveled to the remotest regions of France, bringing royal justice to all parts of the king's own domain, and more and more taking over the machinery of justice in the great lordships.

At the same period, the most intimate advisers of the king in the curia regis, whom he regularly consulted, became differentiated as the "narrow" or "secret" council, while the larger group of advisers, consisting of the remaining lords and high clerics, was called the "full council." In 1302, for the first time, representatives of the towns attended a meeting of this large council. At the moment when townsmen first participate, we are making a transition to a new kind of assembly, the Estates General (though the term would not be used in France for some time). An estate is a social class. Traditionally, the clergy is the first estate, the nobility the second, and the townsmen the third. When all three estates are present, an assembly is an Estates General. Though the clerics and nobles acted as individuals, the townsmen came as chosen delegates from the corporations of their municipalities, and so acted as representatives.

War with England kept Philip pressed for cash during much of his reign. He summoned the estates to explain his need for money and to obtain their approval for his proceeding to raise it. He usually asked for funds in a general way, but did not fix the amount, since the groups whom he was asking to contribute always had the right to bargain. Since the medieval man felt that no action was proper unless it had always been customary, whenever the king wanted to do anything new he had to try to make it somehow seem like something old. A protest that such and such attempt to get money was an *exactio inaudita* (an unheard-of exaction) often was enough to frustrate the king's efforts. Philip tried all the known ways of getting money. One of the most effective was to demand military service of a man, and then permit him to buy himself off by paying a specific amount assessed on his property. When protests arose, the king usually had to swallow them and retreat to more orthodox methods. Requests for revenue that had hitherto been irregular were made regular. Forced loans, debasement of the coinage, additional customs dues, and royal levies on commercial transactions also added to the royal income.

Philip the Fair and the Papacy; The Templars

Although the need for money lay behind the most famous episode of Philip's reign—his fierce quarrel with the papacy—its importance and the significance of its outcome had a major impact on the medieval world. In his papal opponent, Boniface VIII (ruled 1294–1303), Philip was tangling with a fit successor to Gregory VII and Innocent III. A Roman aristocrat and already an old man when elected pope, Boniface suffered from a malady that kept him in great pain and probably partly accounted for his undoubted bad temper and fierce language. In the course of his fight with Philip, for instance, he said that he would rather be a dog than a Frenchman, whereupon Philip's pamphleteers charged Boniface with heresy for implying that Frenchmen, like dogs, had no souls. In his search for cash Philip claimed the right to tax the clergy for the defense of France in his wars against England; but the English monarch was also taxing his clergy on the other side of the Channel to pay for the fight against France. Boniface issued an edict (known as a "bull" from the papal seal on it) declaring that kings lacked the right to tax clerics, and that clerics should disobey them: the bull *Clericis laicos* (1296). Philip the Fair answered not with theory but with action. He clapped an embargo on exports from France of precious metals, jewelry, and currency. The order threatened the elaborate financial system of the papacy so severely that— under pressure from his distressed bankers, and from a hostile group of cardinals who were accusing him of various crimes—the pope retreated, saying in 1297 that in an emergency the king of France could go ahead and tax the clergy without papal consent, and that the king would decide when an emergency had arisen.

But a new quarrel arose in 1301. Boniface had held a Jubilee in Rome in 1300 and felt more confident. Philip ordered a French bishop to be arrested, tried, and convicted of blasphemy, heresy, and treason. He asked for papal approval of the sentence, but Boniface flatly refused, and wrote Philip a letter beginning *Ausculta fili* ("Listen, son"), in which he declared that when a ruler was wicked the pope might take a hand in the temporal affairs of that realm. Philip's agents told the world that the king had replied in scornful and sarcastic language, calling the pope "your fatuousness." When Boniface pushed his claims still further in a still more famous bull (*Unam sanctam*), which declared that it was necessary to salvation for every human creature to be subject to the pope, and when he threatened to excommunicate the king, Philip issued a whole series of extreme charges against Boniface and sent a gang of thugs to kidnap him.

They burst into the papal presence at the Italian town of Anagni (September 7, 1303), and threatened him brutally, but did not dare put through their plan to seize him. Nonetheless, Boniface, who was over eighty, died not long after this humiliation. In 1305, Philip obtained the election of a French pope, who never went to Rome at all. Thus began the "Babylonian captivity" of the papacy at Avignon (1305–1378). Moreover, the French pope issued bulls reversing Boniface's claims and even lifted the sentence of excommunication from Boniface's attackers, and praised Philip the Fair for his piety.

The last installment of the long-continued story that had begun in 1046, when Henry III had installed a reforming pope whose successors fought the German emperors for two centuries, thus took the form of a final quarrel between the pope and the king of France. The efforts of the papacy to use the spiritual authority of the church to govern the policies of national states had failed. In Avignon for three-quarters of a century the papacy instead became a tool of the French monarchy.

In another notorious affair, Philip IV used the docile papacy of Avignon in his attacks on the Knights Templars, a crusading order that had become a rich banking house. He owed them money, and to avoid paying it brought them to trial on a series of charges of vicious behavior. With papal cooperation he used as evidence against them confessions extorted by the Inquisition. In 1312 the order was abolished. Philip did not pay them what he owed, and took over their funds, while a rival order was allowed to annex the Templars' lands. Philip also proceeded against others with money, arresting the Jews, stripping them of their property, and expelling them from France in 1306. In 1311 he expelled the agents of Italian bankers. All debts owing the Jews and Italians were simply collected by royal agents, and the Crown kept the money.

Protest in France

Just before Philip died in 1314, the towns joined with the lords in forming a series of local leagues that staged a taxpayers' strike in protest against the king's having raised money for a war in Flanders and then having made peace instead of fighting. Louis X (ruled 1314–1316) calmed the unrest by revoking the aid, returning some of the money, and making scapegoats of the more unpopular bureaucrats. He also issued a series of charters to several of the great vassals, confirming their liberties. The episode resembled in many ways the protest that had arisen in England a century earlier and had culminated there in one great charter—Magna Carta—as we shall see.

But taxation was still thought of as inseparably connected with military service, and military service was an unquestioned feudal right of the king. So the king was still free to declare a military emergency, to summon his vassals to fight, and then to commute the service for money, just as Philip the Fair had done. For this reason the charters of Louis X did not put an effective halt to the advance of royal power, and there was no committee of barons (as there had been in England) to make sure that the king lived up to his promises. Because the French barons did not defend their corporate interests, the French monarch could continue to enjoy a position unique among the kings of western Europe.

III The Development of England: From the Anglo-Saxons to Edward I

The Norman Conquest

The England that for so long threatened the security of France had first become a major power as the result of the Norman Conquest of 1066. In that year, the Duke of Normandy, William the Conqueror, defeated the Anglo-Saxon forces at Hastings on the south coast of England. The Anglo-Saxon monarchy had since the death of Canute in 1035 fallen more and more prey to faction, and when Edward the Confessor (ruled 1042–1066), a pious but ineffectual monarch, died, his brother-in-law, Harold, half-Danish son of a powerful upstart earl, Godwin, succeeded to the throne. But William of Normandy also had an excellent claim to the English crown.

As we know, pre-conquest England had its witenagemot, its royal tax of the Danegeld, its thirty-four shires each with its sheriff, its system of shire and hundred courts, and its national militia, or *fyrd*. But it had no knights and very few castles; its long-haired and mustachioed warriors still fought with battle-axes instead of swords, and seldom on horseback. Its army was national, not feudal. Though rich from well-managed commerce, and possessed of thriving towns, England was old-fashioned in the eleventh century, without secular cathedral schools. It had been a century since the last monastic revival, so that monastic intellectual influence had waned. Edward the Confessor, who had been brought up in exile in Normandy, felt himself almost an alien in England among the mighty Anglo-Danish earls. Harold seems to have been a rough customer, a contrast, in his fondness for bad language and personal behavior, to the pious Edward.

William, on the other hand, after a troubled minority, had successfully asserted his rights in Normandy over his vigorous and tough Norman nobility, close-cropped and clean shaven. Wielding his rights as feudal overlord with complete assurance in this very feudal land, he allowed no castle to be built without his license, and insisted that, once built, each castle be put at his disposal on demand. Mid-eleventh-century Normandy was a unified duchy, but still overloaded with younger sons, though many of these had gone off on the great south Italian adventure half a century earlier. The Norman cavalry was formidable, and early perfected the technique of charging with the lance held couched, so that all the force of horse and rider was concentrated in the point of the weapon at the moment of shock. Infantry and bowmen supported the charge. As a result of trade with Scandinavia and England, Normandy was prosperous even beyond the norms of

William the Conqueror as depicted in a thirteenth-century manuscript illumination.

the eleventh-century revival, and enjoyed a flourishing agriculture, growing towns, a flowering of monastic learning and church-building under ducal patronage, an effective fiscal administration, and peace and order quite unusual for a feudal principality. William put down private warfare and efficiently dispensed justice.

Facing England across the Channel, Normandy had always maintained contact with the Scandinavian lands of Norman origin; and—after the Danish invasions of England—all three regions were closely involved in commercial relations and often in strife. Emma, daughter of a Norman duke, married first the Anglo-Saxon King Ethelred II (ruled 979–1016), by whom she was the mother of Edward the Confessor, and then the Danish King Canute (ruled 1016–1035), by whom she had a son, Harthacnut (ruled 1040–1042). Wife of two English kings and mother of an English king by each of them, she apparently bossed all four. And she remained close to her Norman ducal relatives. William was her great-nephew. In the tangled skein of English-Danish-Norman royal politics there were dark

A scene from the Bayeux Tapestry, depicting the Norman fleet under Wiliam the Conqueror crossing the English Channel.

crimes, including the murder in 1036 of Edward the Confessor's older brother Alfred: Earl Godwin, Harold's father, was in part guilty, and the Normans at Hastings were in part revenging Godwin's act on his son Harold. It was Norman nobles, favorites of Edward the Confessor, who built the first few castles in England shortly before the conquest; Edward gave important posts in the English church to Norman clerics; and as early as 1051 Edward recognized William as his rightful heir.

Inside England itself pro-Normans and anti-Normans jostled, intrigued, and squabbled for two decades before 1066. Norman sources report that, probably in 1064, Harold himself went to Normandy to reaffirm the promise of William's succession to the English throne, and to swear a personal oath of fealty to him, in exchange for a confirmation of Harold's English lands. So in taking the throne in 1066, Harold was breaking his oath. The cleric who crowned Harold was probably the Archbishop of Canterbury, Stigand, then under papal excommunication. But some Anglo-Saxon sources say that on his deathbed Edward the Confessor made Harold his heir after all. Even if he did, it may have been under duress. And nothing can alter the fact that Harold, though his sister was married to Edward, had himself no drop of royal blood, English or Danish. There was also a third claimant to the English throne, the King of Norway; just before William's victory in 1066 the Norwegians landed and Harold defeated them at Stamford Bridge in Yorkshire.

William's invasion had the blessing of the papacy, which recognized his right to the throne of England. His fleet had to be built in nine months. He had to weld an army of seven thousand men, mostly Norman but including adventurers from many parts of France

and from southern Italy, into a fighting unit. He had to wait for favorable weather. But he landed and established two fortified beachheads on the Sussex coast before Harold could get back from defeating the Norwegians. It was all over in a hard day's fighting. Norman horsemen and bowmen slaughtered Harold's close-packed warriors fighting on foot with battle-axes. The decisiveness of the victory was not fully apparent at the time, and it took William until 1071 before he had fully conquered England.

In three months, he won many submissions in southern and southeastern England, surrounded London, entered it without resistance, and was crowned on Christmas day, 1066, not by the excommunicated Archbishop of Canterbury but by the Archbishop of York. The Norman accounts are full of joy and stress the new master's clemency; the Anglo-Saxon accounts naturally echo the bitterness of defeat and of accepting an alien master, who took vast quantities of loot from the victims and turned them over to his triumphant supporters. Yet William seems to have taken special pains to be just even here, and to allow nothing disorderly. *The Anglo-Saxon Chronicle* itself says of him:

Amongst other things the good security that he made in this country is not forgotten—so that any man could travel over his kingdom without injury, with his bosom full of gold; and no one dared strike another, however much wrong he had done him.*

But that was after William had been able to take possession of the whole of England. This took two cam-

*D. Whitelock, D. C. Douglas, and S. I. Tucker, eds., *The Anglo-Saxon Chronicle* (London, 1961), p. 164.

paigns in the far southwest—Devon and Cornwall (1068, 1069) and expeditions to the north (1069, 1070) in which William punished pro-Danish English rebels by destroying the crops of a large area and precipitating a terrible famine. The last uprising in England came in 1071 in Ely, and in 1072 the Conqueror won the submission of the King of Scotland, who became his vassal. There were political troubles even after this, but the conquest was substantially complete. Each stage was marked by the building of new castles to hold the region and enforce order. The former ruling class of England was replaced now by Norman and French nobles, perhaps a total of ten thousand new rulers in a population of about one and a half million.

All of England belonged to William by right of conquest. He kept about one-sixth as royal domain, gave about half as fiefs to his great Norman barons, and returned to the church the quarter that it had held before. Although many of his barons subinfeudated their lands, their vassals owed military service only to William, and swore primary allegiance to him (Salisbury Oath, 1086), giving him authority that no French king would ever enjoy. The bishops and abbots held of him, and owed him feudal services. He alone claimed all castles, and none could be built without a license from him. He forbade private war and allowed only royal coinage. He continued to levy the Danegeld, to impose judicial fines, and to summon the *fyrd* as well as the feudal array. He kept the Anglo-Saxon system of courts, and bound the sheriffs closely to the Crown by giving them wide local authority at the expense of bishop and earl.

The Conqueror thus maintained old English custom and law, but superimposed the Norman feudal structure, with its mounted knights and castles. The sheriffs provided continuity. The Norman curia regis superseded the Anglo-Saxon witenagemot; it met regularly three times a year, but could be summoned at any time. It gave counsel and tried the cases of the great vassals. Its members could be asked to perform special tasks in the shires. In 1086 William ordered a careful survey of all landed property in England. The record of the survey is the famous Domesday Book, which included for every piece of land a full statement of ownership, past and present, and a listing of all resources, so that the royal administration might ascertain whether and where more revenue could be obtained. Tenants, plows, forest land, fish ponds, all were listed in Domesday Book. Contemporary accounts reveal the thoroughness of William's inquiry and the resentment it caused:

So very narrowly did he have it investigated, that there was no single hide nor a yard of land, nor indeed (it is a shame to relate but it seemed no shame to him to do) one ox nor one cow nor one pig was there left out, and not put down on his record: and all these records were brought to him afterward. . . .

Other investigators followed the first; and men were sent into provinces which they did not know, and where they themselves were unknown, in order that they might be given the opportunity of checking the first survey and, if necessary, of denouncing its authors as guilty to the king. And the land was vexed with much violence arising from the collection of the royal taxes.*

Those who collected the information from the old Anglo-Saxon territorial subdivisions of vill and hundred arranged it under the new Norman divisions of royal demesne and fiefs of the king's tenants-in-chief. Domesday Book, then, was "the formal written record of the introduction of feudal landholding and of feudal law into England." The language of administration was now Latin, as it was on the Continent. No such monumental survey was ever compiled for any other country in the Middle Ages.

With the assistance of the able Italian, Lanfranc, whom he made Archbishop of Canterbury, William established continental practices in the English church. Norman churchmen gradually replaced the English bishops. To commemorate the victory at Hastings, William founded Battle Abbey on the site of the battlefield; and other monastic foundations followed, notably in the north. Norman abbots brought books and learning, and, above all, Latin, from the Continent. For a time vernacular writing in English ceased; England had become "a province of the commonwealth of Latin Europe." William refused the pope's demand that feudal homage be done to him as overlord of England. Rightly maintaining that none of his predecessors on the English throne had ever acknowledged papal suzerainty, he agreed only to pay the accustomed dues to the Church of Rome. The English church recognized no new pope without the king's approval, and accepted no papal commands without his assent. When William died in 1087, the English monarchy was stronger than the French was to be for more than two hundred years.

Henry I and Henry II: Administration and Law

William's immediate successors extended the system. More and more they made their administrators depend upon the king alone by paying them fixed salaries, since payments in land (fiefs) often led the recipient to try to make his office hereditary, and since clerical administrators might feel the rival pull of papal authority. Household and curia regis grew in size, and special functions began to develop. Within the curia regis, the king's immediate advisers became a "small council." The full body met less often. The royal *chancery* or secretariat also grew, since the king was duke of Normandy, and had much business on the Continent.

Henry I (ruled 1100–1135) allowed his vassals to make payments (*scutage*, "shield money") to buy themselves off from military service. He also exempted the

*Ibid., and a note by the Bishop of Hereford in D. C. Douglas and G. W. Greenaway, eds., *English Historical Documents, 1042–1189* (New York, 1953), II, 161, 851.

boroughs from Danegeld but collected still heavier payments from them. To handle the increased income, the first specialized treasury department came into existence, the *exchequer*, so called because the long table on which the clerks rendered to the officers of the curia regis their semiannual audit of the royal accounts was covered with a cloth divided into checkerboard squares representing pounds, shillings, and pence.

Because Henry's only legitimate son died before his father, the succession was disputed between Henry's daughter Matilda, wife of Geoffrey of Anjou, and Henry's nephew Stephen. A period of civil war (1135–1154) between their partisans produced virtual anarchy in England, and showed what could happen when the strong royal hand disappeared from the helm. Yet when the Angevin Henry II (ruled 1154–1189), son of Matilda and Geoffrey, succeeded to the throne, he found the foundations of a powerful monarchy still intact. We have already encountered him as the lord of half of France.

Stormy and energetic, Henry II systematically cut at the roots of the anarchy: he had more than 1,100 unlicensed castles destroyed. From the contemporary *Dialogue Concerning the Exchequer,* written by his treasurer, we learn how the money rolled in: from scutage plus special fees for the privilege of paying it, from fines, from aids, from tallage paid by the boroughs, and from a new tax collected from the knights who did not go on Crusades. Even more important than this reestablishment and strengthening of the financial institutions was Henry's contribution to the law of England, built on that of Henry I.

In our own day, when the making of new laws is something we take for granted, it requires a real effort of the imagination to think of a period in which new law could not, in theory, be made at all. Law was what had always existed, and it was the job of the lawyers and government officials to discover what this was and proclaim it. Henry I and Henry II therefore did not fill whole statute books with new enactments: they could never have dreamed of such a thing. Instead, Henry I claimed that he was ruling in accordance with the law of the Saxon King Edward the Confessor, and the law books issued in his period contain a mixture of Anglo-Saxon and other materials, including, for example, fixed schedules of money payments imposed as penalties for crime. It was not by issuing laws that Henry I and Henry II transformed the legal practices of England. By developing old instruments in new combinations they created the new common law, law common to all of England because it was administered by the royal courts. Though the hundred and shire courts continued to exist, their jurisdiction had been diluted by that of the competing courts, baronial and ecclesiastical. Moreover, only the king could give Englishmen better ways of settling their quarrels among themselves than the old trial by ordeal or trial by battle. The chief royal instruments were writs, juries, and itinerant (that is, traveling) justices.

If, for example, somebody seized a subject's property, by the middle of Henry II's reign the victim could buy quite reasonably a royal writ: an order from the king directing a royal official to give the plaintiff a hearing. The official would assemble a group of twelve neighbors who knew the facts in the case; they took an oath, and were therefore called a jury (from *juré,* "man on oath"); and then they told the truth as they knew it about whether dispossession had taken place, answering yes or no, and thus giving a verdict (from *veredictum,* "a thing spoken truly"). These early juries were *not* trial juries in the modern sense but men who were presumed to be in the best position to know the facts already. By similar machinery of writ and jury, inheritances unjustly detained could be recovered, and a man unjustly held as a serf could win his freedom. Thus, though the use of a jury, or sworn inquest, dated back to the ninth-century Carolingians, and had come to England with the Conqueror, its application to civil cases between individuals was a new procedure, and so was the flexibility permitted by a variety of writs. No matter who won, the royal exchequer profited, since the loser had to pay a fine. Also, judgments rendered by royal judges in effect became new law without any legislation in the modern sense.

Building on the practice begun by Henry I, Henry II also regularly sent itinerant justices out to the shires. On their travels they were instructed in each shire to receive reports from the local officials, and to try all cases pending in the shire court. Moreover, the sheriffs had to bring before the justices from each hundred and township a group of sworn men to report under oath all crimes that had occurred since the last visit of the justices, and to indicate whom they considered to be the probable criminal in each case. This is another use of the jury, the jury of presentment, since it presented the names of suspect criminals. It is the ancestor of the modern grand jury ("grand" simply in the sense of large), consisting of greater numbers of men than the twelve that took part in the petty juries. Again the treasury profited, as the itinerant justices imposed heavy fines. Again blatant innovation was avoided; again refinements and combinations of existing instruments produced new legal conditions. Of course, this was still the Middle Ages. The usual means of proof in a criminal trial was still under Henry II the ordeal by cold water: if the accused, with hands and feet tied, floated in a pool blessed by the Church, he was guilty; if he sank, he was innocent.

Henry II and Becket

Where Henry II failed was in an effort to limit the competing system of canon law. Confident that he would have a pliant assistant, he appointed his friend and chancellor, Thomas à Becket, to be archbishop of Canterbury. But once he had become archbishop, Becket proved inflexibly determined not to yield any of the Church's rights, but rather to add to them whenever he could. The great quarrel between the two broke out over the question of "criminous clerks"—that is, clerics convicted of crime. In publishing a collection of earlier customs relating to the Church (Constitutions of Clarendon, 1164), Henry included one provision that clerics charged with crimes should be indicted in the royal court before being tried by the bishop's court, and then if convicted returned to the royal authorities for punishment. Becket refused to agree to this part of the document and appealed to the pope for support.

Although the issue was compromised after a dispute that lasted six years, Henry, in one of his fits of temper, asked whether nobody would rid him of Becket. Four of his knights responded by murdering Becket in his own cathedral at Canterbury. Henry swore to the pope that he was innocent of complicity in the murder, but he had to undergo a humiliating penance and, more important, he had to yield on the issue. The Church in England won the sole right to punish its clergy—benefit of clergy, the principle was called. Moreover, Henry had to accept the right of litigants in church courts to appeal to Rome direct, without royal intervention or license of any sort. This meant that the papacy had the ultimate say in an important area of English life. It was a severe defeat for Henry's program of extending royal justice. Yet the other clauses in the Constitutions of Clarendon were not challenged, and the king continued to prevent the pope from taxing the English clergy directly. For his part, Becket was made a saint only two years after his death, and pilgrimages to his miraculous tomb at Canterbury became an important part of English life.

Henry's reign was also notable for the reorganization of the old Anglo-Saxon *fyrd* by the Assize of Arms, 1181, which made each free man responsible, according to his income, to maintain suitable arms for the defense of the realm. Forests, floods, the ingredients and prices of bread and beer, and of course the war with France all occupied Henry's attention. Unfortunately, he could not control his own sons, who rebelled against him and made his last years miserable by attacking his possessions on the Continent. When he died, he is said to have turned his face to the wall and said, "Shame, shame on a conquered king!"

Richard I and John

Henry II's son, Richard the Lionhearted (ruled 1189–1199), spent less than six months of his ten-year reign in England. But the country did not revert to the anarchy that had been characteristic of the reigns of Stephen and Matilda. Henry II had done his work too well for that. The bureaucracy functioned without the presence of the king. Indeed, it functioned all too well for the liking of the population. For Richard needed more money than had ever been needed before to pay for his crusade, for his ransom from captivity, and for his wars against Philip Augustus of France. Heavy taxes were levied on income and on personal property; cer-

An Italian depiction of the martyrdom of Thomas à Becket: fresco from SS Giovanni e Paolo, Spoleto.

tain kinds of possessions, including silver plate, were simply confiscated; a large number of charters were sold to cities. Thus it was that Richard's brother, John (ruled 1199–1216), who was clever but unreliable, greedy, and tyrannical, succeeded to a throne whose resources had been squandered. John had the great misfortune to face three adversaries who proved too strong for him: Philip Augustus, whom we have seen expelling the English from France north of the Loire; Innocent III, whom we have also seen in action; and the outraged English baronage.

In 1206 the election to the archbishopric of Canterbury was disputed between two candidates, one of whom was favored by John. The pope refused to accept either, and in 1207 procured the election of a third, Stephen Langton. John exiled the members of the cathedral chapter of Canterbury and confiscated the property of the see. Innocent responded by putting all England under an interdict (1208) and by excommunicating John (1209). He threatened to depose John, and thought of replacing him with a Capetian; he corresponded with Philip Augustus, who prepared to invade

Fourteenth-century manuscript illumination showing King John hunting deer.

one of the most celebrated occasions in all human history. The document that he agreed to send out under the royal seal to all the shires of England had sixty-three chapters, in the legal form of a feudal grant or conveyance, known as Magna Carta, the Great Charter.

Magna Carta was a feudal document, a list of specific concessions drawn up in the interest of a group of great barons at odds with their feudal lord, the king. The king promised reform in his exactions of scutage, aids, reliefs, and in certain other feudal practices. He made certain concessions to the peasantry and the tradesmen (uniform weights and measures, town liberties) and to the Church (free elections to bishoprics and maintenance of liberties).

Why do English and American historians and politicians often call this medieval special-interest document the foundation-stone of our present liberties? Largely because in later centuries some of its provisions could be and have been given new and expanded meanings. For instance, the provision "No scutage or aid, save the customary feudal ones, shall be levied *except by the common consent of the realm*" in 1215 meant only that John would have to consult his great council (barons and bishops) before levying extraordinary feudal aids. Yet this could later be expanded into the doctrine that all taxation must be by consent, that taxation without representation was tyranny, which would have astonished everybody at Runnymede. Similarly, the provision that "No freeman shall be arrested or imprisoned, or dispossessed or outlawed or banished or in any way molested; nor will we set forth against him, nor send against him, unless by the lawful judgment of his peers and by the law of the land" in 1215 meant only that the barons did not want to be tried by anybody not their social equal, and they wished to curb the aggressions of royal justice. Yet it was capable of later expansion into the doctrine of due process of law, that everybody was entitled to a trial ("by his peers").

Although medieval kings of England reissued the charter with modifications some forty times, it was to be ignored under the Tudor monarchy in the sixteenth century, and Englishmen did not appeal to it until the revolt against the Stuarts in the seventeenth century. By then, the Middle Ages had long since been over, and the rebels against Stuart absolutism could read into the medieval clauses of Magna Carta many of the same modern meanings that we, just as inaccurately, see in them at first glance. Thus Magna Carta's lasting importance lies partly in what later interpreters were able to read into its original clauses. It also lies perhaps even more, however, in two general principles underlying the whole document: that the king was subject to the law and that he might, if necessary, be forced to observe it. This is why this document, more than seven centuries old, dealing with a now obsolete social system, still carries vitally important implications for us in the twentieth century.

As soon as John had accepted the charter, he in-

England. Fearing with good reason that his own vassals would not stay loyal in the face of such an invasion, John gave in (1213). Not only did he accept Langton as archbishop of Canterbury and promise to restore Church property and to reinstate banished priests, but he also recognized England and Ireland as fiefs of the papacy, and did homage to the pope for them. In addition, he agreed to pay an annual tribute to Rome. All this of course represented a startling papal victory. From now on, Innocent sided with John in his quarrel with a large faction of the English barons—a quarrel that became acute after the French had won the Battle of Bouvines (1214). "Since I have been reconciled to God, and have submitted to the Roman Church," John exclaimed when the news of Bouvines was brought to him, "nothing has gone well with me."

John and the Barons: Magna Carta

The quarrel with perhaps a third of the English barons arose from John's ruthlessness in raising money for a campaign in France, and from his habit of punishing vassals without trial. At the moment of absolution by the pope in 1213, John had sworn to Stephen Langton that he would "restore the good laws of his predecessors." But he violated his oath. After Bouvines, the barons hostile to John renounced their homage to him and drew up a list of demands, most of which they forced him to accept on June 15, 1215, at Runnymede,

stantly tried to break his promises; the pope declared the charter null and void; and Langton and the barons opposed to John now took the pope's former place as supporters of a French monarchy for England. Philip Augustus' son actually landed in England and occupied London briefly; but John died in 1216 and was succeeded by his nine-year-old son, Henry III (ruled 1216–1272), to whose side the barons rallied. The barons then expelled the French from England. It was not until 1258 that the king found himself again actually at open war with a faction of his own barons. Yet, during the interval, there were warnings of future trouble.

Henry III and the Barons

In Henry's reissue of Magna Carta (1216 and 1217), the clause requiring the great council to approve unusual taxation was omitted. In 1232, Henry appointed a French favorite to the highest post in his administration, replacing a loyal Englishman who had become identified with the barons' revolt. Frenchmen in high places in the state were now added to the host of Italians appointed by the pope to high places in the English church. Since both the French and the Italian appointees were avaricious, many English nobles felt a deep resentment toward these foreigners. Henry's marriage to a French princess (1236) fanned the flames. The great council flatly refused to give Henry money for a campaign in France, and its members discussed plans for limiting the royal power. In 1254 Henry received from the pope the crown of Sicily for his second son, and in 1257 he permitted his brother to seek election as Holy Roman Emperor. This was all part of the last phase of the papal campaign against the Hohenstaufens. For England it was expensive, since Sicily had to be conquered and the empire had to be bought. Things came to a head in 1258, a year of bad harvest, when Henry asked for one-third of the revenues of England as an extra grant for the pope.

Now the barons openly rebelled. They came armed to the session of the great council and secured the appointment of a committee of twenty-four of their number, which then issued a document known as the Provisions of Oxford. This document created a council of fifteen without whose advice the king could do nothing. The committee put its own men in the high offices of state. It also replaced the full great council with a baronial body of twelve. This provision clearly contained the seeds of a baronial tyranny perhaps worse than the king's own. The foreigners were expelled. But the barons could not agree among themselves; the pope declared the Provisions null and void, and Henry III resumed his personal rule. Civil war broke out in 1263 between the king and the baronial party headed by Simon de Montfort. When in the next year Louis IX was called in to arbitrate, he ruled in favor of the king and against the barons. Simon de Montfort, however, would not accept the decision, took arms again, cap-

tured the king in 1264, and set up a regime of his own based on the restoration of the Provisions of Oxford. This regime lasted fifteen months. In 1265, Simon de Montfort called an assembly of his supporters, which, as we shall see, was a step in the evolution of Parliament. But in this same year, the heir to the throne, the lord Edward, defeated and killed Simon de Montfort, and restored his father, Henry III, to the throne. For the last seven years of Henry's reign (1265–1272), as well as for the next thirty-five years of his own rule (1272–1307), Edward I was the real ruler of England.

The Origins of Parliament

The revolts of the thirteenth century had given the barons experience in the practical work of government, and many of their reforms had been accepted by the royal governments that followed. Still more important, during the course of the struggle the local communities of England had emerged as significant elements in the operations of the central administration. Indeed, it is to these years of Henry III that historians turn for the earliest signs of the greatest contribution of the English Middle Ages to mankind: the development of Parliament.

The word *parliament* is French and simply means a "talking" or "parley," a conference of any kind. The French historian Villehardouin refers to a discussion between the French and Venetian leaders in the Fourth Crusade (1204) as a *parlement*. Joinville, the biographer of Saint Louis, refers to his hero's secret conversations with his wife on the palace staircase as *parlement*. And we have already encountered the word as applied in France to that part of the curia regis which acted as a court of justice. In England, during the thirteenth century, the word is found more and more often in reference to the assemblies summoned by the king, especially those that were to hear petitions for legal redress. In short, a parliament in England in the thirteenth century is much like the *parlement* in France: a session of the king's large council acting as a court of justice.

The Anglo-Saxon witenagemot had been an assembly of the great churchmen and laymen of the kingdom who advised the king on taxation and on matters of policy, and who could also act as a supreme court in important cases. In these respects the great council of the Norman and Angevin kings was not much different from the witenagemot. Feudal law simply reinforced the king's right to secure from his chief vassals both aid (that is, military service and money) and counsel (that is, advice on law and custom and a share in judicial decisions). The Norman kings made attendance at sessions of the great council compulsory; it was the king's privilege, not his duty, to receive counsel, and it was the vassal's duty, not his privilege, to offer it.

But by requiring the barons to help govern England, the kings entirely unconsciously, and indeed contrary to their own intentions, actually strengthened the assembly of the vassals, the great council. The feeling gradually grew up that the king *must* consult the council; this feeling is reflected in the scutage and aid provision of Magna Carta. Yet the kings generally consulted only the small council of their permanent advisers; the great council met only occasionally and when summoned by the king. The barons who sat on the great council thus developed a sense of being excluded from the work of government in which they felt entitled to participate. It was this baronial discontent, perhaps as much as the issues we have already considered, that led to the troubles under Henry III. When the barons took over the government in 1258, they determined that the great council should meet three times a year, and they called it a parliament. When Henry III regained power, he continued to summon the feudal magnates to the great council, to parliament.

Knights of the Shire and Burgesses

The increasing prosperity of England in the thirteenth century had enriched many members of the landed gentry who were not necessarily the king's direct vassals, and might occupy a position fairly far down in the feudal pyramid. The inhabitants of the towns had also increased in number and importance with the growth of trade. Representatives of these newly important classes in country and town now began to attend parliament at the king's summons. They were the knights of the shire, two from each shire, and the burgesses of the towns. Accustomed since Anglo-Saxon times to the compulsory participation in their local hundred and shire courts, the knights of the shire were landholders with local standing, and they were often rich men. By the time of Richard the Lionhearted, some were occasionally selected to bring court records to the judges. For other purposes (bringing in accounts or documents to show title) townsmen, too, had been chosen by the towns at royal command to appear before royal justices either on circuit in the shires or in London. In 1213, 1226, and 1227, knights of the shire had been summoned by the king to discuss current problems; in 1254 they were summoned for the first time to a meeting of the great council. Meanwhile, burgesses or townsmen were also being summoned by the king to appear before his justices either on circuit in the shires or in London; they brought accounts or legal documents.

Although controversy on the subject still rages, recent research has made it seem probable that the chief reason for the king's summons to the shire and town representatives was his need for money. By the thirteenth century the sources of royal income, both ordinary and extraordinary, were not enough to pay the king's ever-mounting bills. Thus he was obliged, according to feudal custom, to ask for "gracious aids" from his vassals. These aids were in the form of percentages of personal property, and the vassals had to assent

to their collection. So large and so numerous were the aids that the king's immediate vassals naturally collected what they could from *their* vassals to help make up the sums. Since these subvassals would contribute such a goodly part of the aids, they, too, came to feel that they should assent to the levies. The first occasion when we can be sure that the king summoned subvassals for this purpose was the meeting of the great council in 1254, to which he called the knights of the shire. It should be emphasized that this was not exactly a great innovation; the knights of the shire, as we have seen, were already accustomed to bringing information to the king and speaking on behalf of their shires.

The towns also came to feel that they should be consulted on taxes, since in practice they were often able to negotiate with the royal authorities for a reduction in the levy imposed on them. Burgesses of the towns were included for the first time in Simon de Montfort's "parliament" of 1265. Knights of the shire likewise attended this meeting, because Simon apparently wanted to muster the widest possible support for his program, and believed that an assembly of the direct vassals would not be representative enough. But only known supporters of Simon were invited to attend the parliament.

Scholars no longer believe, as they once did, that de Montfort had a twentieth-century democrat's devotion to representative institutions, or even that he regarded the assembly he was summoning as establishing a precedent for the future. Yet it did prove to be such a precedent, and the simultaneous presence of shire and town representatives made it the first true ancestor of the modern House of Commons. Not all subsequent parliaments had representatives from shire and town, and not all assemblies attended by knights and burgesses were parliaments. Knights and burgesses had no "right" to come to parliament; no doubt, they often felt it a nuisance and an expense to come, and not a privilege. But gradually they came to attend parliament regularly.

Edward I

Edward I, who became an extraordinary legislator, also tried but failed to unite all Britain into a single kingdom. In 1283 he put down a revolt of the Welsh, executed the brother of the last native prince, and proclaimed his own infant son prince of Wales. Ever since, this title has been reserved for the eldest son of the English monarch. In the 1290s a disputed succession to the throne of Scotland, and the formation of a Franco-Scottish alliance, brought Edward to Scotland as invader. Although he declared himself king of Scotland in 1296, and carried off the Stone of Scone, the symbol of Scottish kingship, to Westminster Abbey, William Wallace's rebellion (1297–1305) required a second conquest of Scotland and led to the capture and execution of Wallace. Edward incorporated Scotland with England. However, the celebrated Robert Bruce now rebelled, and Edward I died while on an expedition against him (1307). Edward II (ruled 1307–1327) lost Scotland to Bruce at the Battle of Bannockburn (1314). So it was not until 1603 that England and Scotland were joined under the same king (James I), and he was a Scot who became king of England.

By the late thirteenth century the earlier medieval belief that law is custom, and that it cannot be made, was disappearing. In Edward I England found a lawgiver who enacted a great series of systematizing statutes. Indeed, Edward is sometimes called, a bit misleadingly, "the English Justinian." Edward's statutes were framed by the experts of the small council, who elaborated and expanded the machinery of government, and under whose rule parliament's function was more judicial than legislative or consultative. Each of the statutes was really a large bundle of different enactments. Taken together, they reflect a declining feudalism, and show us an England in which the suzerain-vassal relationship was becoming more and more a mere landlord-tenant relationship, and in which the old duties of fighting were becoming less important than the financial aspects of the matter. The Second Statute of Westminster (1285), for example, was designed to assure the great landowner that an estate granted to a tenant could not be disposed of except by direct inheritance; this is what we would call entail. Similarly, the Statute of Mortmain (1279) prevented transfer of land to the Church without the consent of the suzerain. The Church placed a "dead hand" (*mortmain*) on land and could hold on forever to any land it received; lay landlords, therefore, found it highly unprofitable to see portions of their holdings transferred to clerical hands.

In addition to these statutes, which redounded to the interest of the landlord, Edward I in another statute commanded the barons to show by what authority (*quo warranto*) they held any privilege, such as the right to have their own court of justice. Some privileges (franchises) he revoked, but his chief aim was to assert the principle that all such franchises came from the king, and that what he had given he could take away. Under Edward the business of royal justice increased steadily, and specialized courts began to appear, all of them the offspring of the central curia regis. The Court of Common Pleas, which handled cases that arose between subjects, had begun to take shape earlier, but now crystallized into a recognizable, separate body. The new Court of King's Bench handled criminal and Crown cases, and the special Court of Exchequer dealt with disputes pertaining to royal finance.

Edward I also regularized and improved existing financial and military practices. He made permanent the king's share in export duties on wool and leather, the burden of which fell mostly on foreigners, and in customs dues on foreign merchandise, which soon became the most important single source of royal income, eloquent testimony to the flourishing commerce of the

The Parliament of Edward I. This ancient picture is probably the earliest authentic view in existence of Parliament in session.

period. At the behest of parliament, Edward expelled the Jews from England in 1290; they were not allowed to come back until the mid-seventeenth century. After their expulsion, the Italians assumed the role of moneylenders.

Edward required all freemen to be responsible for military service and to equip themselves appropriately. The less well-off served as foot soldiers. But those with a certain minimum amount of property were compelled to become knights (distraint of knighthood) and serve on horseback, in part for financial reasons: once they had achieved knight's status the king could collect feudal dues from them. Edward's vigorous extension of royal power aroused the same sort of opposition that had plagued John and undone Henry III. In 1297 both the clergy (under the influence of Pope Boniface VIII) and the barons refused to grant the aid that Edward wanted; they were able to make him confirm Magna Carta and promise not to levy any further taxes without first obtaining consent.

Edward I's parliament of 1295 is traditionally called the Model Parliament, because it included all classes of the kingdom, not only barons, higher clergy, knights of the shire, and burgesses, but also representatives of the lower clergy. In the royal summons of 1295 we find a celebrated clause: "What touches all should be approved by all." This echoes a famous provision of Roman law, and pays at least lip service to the principle that consent to taxation was necessary.

The Court of King's Bench in the fifteenth century.

France and England: A Contrast

In France, the Capetian kings, beginning as relatively powerless and insignificant local lords, had by 1300 extended the sway of their royal administration into the lands of their great vassals, and created the institutions of a powerful centralized monarchy. The question of the English claims to large areas on the Continent remained to be settled in the grim struggle of the Hundred Years' War (see Chapter 10). In England, on the other hand, the Norman conquerors proved able to make the most of existing Anglo-Saxon institutions, and to superimpose effective feudal monarchy, while they and their Angevin successors developed the common law, bringing not only money and power to the monarch but security to the subject.

Whereas in France the vassals were unaware of the danger to their position until it was too late, and too divided among themselves to unite in opposition to the monarch's aggressions, in England the vassals early recognized the need for presenting a united corporate opposition if they were to preserve their rights. And out of their opposition emerged the guarantees that limited the king: promises given in the first instance on behalf of the great vassals, but later subject to much broader interpretation. By the early fourteenth century, out of the king's need to obtain assent for taxation and out of the custom of consultation between king and subject, there was beginning to emerge Parliament, "incomparably the greatest gift of the English people to the civilization of the world." Both peoples were now launched upon the contrasting historical trajectories that would carry them toward a point in our own day when the stereotypes with which we began this chapter would at least seem plausible, even if not subject to proof or universally acceptable.

IV Literature in the Medieval West

In literature and the arts, as in the social and economic life of medieval men, the eleventh century provides a convenient turning-point for the student. Latin, as we have abundantly seen, continued to be the language of the Church and of learned communication everywhere in western Europe. In fact, men wrote it far better and more fluently than they did in the earlier Middle Ages, when, with the exception of the Carolingian period, literacy was in some measure kept alive by the half-literate. All the churchmen we have encountered—John of Salisbury, Abelard, Bernard, Aquinas, and the rest—wrote Latin even when corresponding informally with their friends. Schoolboys, often destined for the Church or they might not have been schoolboys at all, began their academic lives by learning it. It was also the language of the law and of politics: all documents, not only important ones like Magna Carta or a royal enactment, or treaty of peace, but private ones like a deed to a piece of property or a letter from one man to another were written in Latin

Again, in 1297, Edward declared that the "good will and assent of the archbishops, bishops, and other prelates, earls, barons, knights, burgesses, and other freemen of our realm" were *essential* to a royal levy of a tax. This principle was frequently reasserted in later years, and parliament sometimes made its confirmation a condition for the grant of money. The regular presence of the knights and burgesses had gradually made them more and more nearly indispensable to the king's business. Unlike the French monarchs, the English had encountered a corporate baronial opposition, which by forcing consultation upon the king had begun to create brand-new institutions.

as a matter of course. Sermons were written and delivered in Latin, hymns were composed and sung in Latin, and much verse was still written in Latin, even extremely colloquial or satirical verse, such as the famous student songs of the twelfth century, still preserved in a single manuscript found in a German monastery.

These songs, all anonymous, are called Goliardic because the authors—mostly, we imagine, wild young renegade clerics wandering about Europe from one lecturer to another—claimed to be in the service of a certain Golias, a kind of satanic figure perhaps deriving originally from the Old Testament giant, Goliath, whom David slew with a stone from his sling. Their verses mocked the form and the values of the serious religious poetry of the time, and goodhumoredly, though very roughly, satirized the clergy and the Church and even the Bible. No doubt the Goliardic verses in praise of wine, women, and song shocked the virtuous, as they were intended to do. Here is the way in which the Confession of Golias, so called, defined the highest good.

> My intention is to die
>   In the tavern drinking;
> Wine must be on hand, for I
>   Want it when I'm sinking.
>
> Angels when they come shall cry,
>   At my frailties winking:
> "Spare this drunkard, God, he's high,
>   Absolutely stinking." *

But if Latin persisted and was widely used for all literary purposes, the period after the eleventh century marks the gradual triumph of the vernacular languages all over Europe for the literature of entertainment, of belles lettres. Whereas *Beowulf*, coming from a Britain never thoroughly Latinized, was our only important literary vernacular poem during the early Middle Ages, now such poems began to appear in ever greater numbers everywhere *except* Britain, when English was in temporary eclipse. A particularly celebrated one is *The Song of Roland*, in Old French, whose earliest surviving manuscript was probably written down a little after the year 1100. It breathes a spirit as heroic as that of *Beowulf*, but it was molded in an environment vastly different from the Scandinavian and Germanic forests and lakes where Grendel and his mother lived.

The poem deals with a historic episode, then already far in the past: the defeat of Charlemagne's rear guard by the Muslims in the year 778, in a mountain pass at Roncevaux in the Pyrenees. Even though our earliest written version dates from after 1100, we know that earlier versions of the story were sung well before

that date: for example, as William the Conqueror's men were about to go into battle at Hastings in 1066, a minstrel sang to them about Charlemagne and Roland and Oliver and the vassals of the great king who died at Roncevaux. We also accept, as some scholars do not, the argument that many of the otherwise incomprehensible names of tribes and persons appearing in one episode of the poem can readily be understood in terms of tribes and persons and place names actually connected with the Normans of southern Italy in their invasion of the Balkan lands of the Byzantine Empire across the Adriatic Sea in 1081–1082.

In *The Song of Roland*, human beings have replaced monsters as the enemy; the landscape has brightened; a more intense Christian piety softens some of the worst violence: Roland sees to it that his comrades slain by the infidel receive a Christian blessing. It is human treachery—by the villainous Ganelon—that brings down tragedy on the heroic forces of Charlemagne, leaving the noble Oliver dead, and Roland and the king grief-stricken. The highest virtue in the poem is loyalty to one's lord: a quality that was the first necessity in a feudal society which only the knight's loyalty to his suzerain saved from anarchy. And, as the knight was always defined as a mounted man, a man on a horse, so the unwritten but generally accepted code that during these centuries came to govern his behavior in more and more elaborate detail as time went on was called *chivalry*, from the word that means a horse: chivalric actions are those knightly deeds to be expected from a mounted man.

In *The Song of Roland* at the very end of its four thousand lines, after the traitor Ganelon has been torn limb from limb by horses, Charlemagne is immediately summoned by a new emergency:

> St. Gabriel came to him with a message from God: "Charles, summon the armies of the empire! By force shalt thou enter the land of Bire and bring succour to king Vivien in his city of Imphe, which the heathen have besieged. The Christians are crying out and calling for thee." The emperor had no wish to go. "God," he said, "how full of toil is my life!" And the tears flowed from his eyes and he tore at his white beard.

The final note, then, is of an old man (for the poet had forgotten that Charlemagne in 778 was not yet old and was not yet even emperor) tormented by the great weight of earthly responsibilities, and tired and human after all, rather than heroic or superhuman. And in Roland's deep loyalty to his lord, Charlemagne, we find something new: a love for "sweet France," a patriotic note of love for country struck at just about the earliest moment that we can speak of Europeans as having a country.

Many other songs were sung about Charlemagne's captains, and stories told about them; and other such "cycles" of stories also evolved at the same period around other great heroes. King Arthur of Britain, far more legendary than Charlemagne, was of course one

---

*From *The Goliard Poets* by George F. Whicher. Copyright 1949 by George F. Whicher. Reprinted by permission of New Directions Publishing Corporation.

of the most famous, and the exploits of his knights were celebrated not only among Arthur's fellow Celts in Wales, Ireland, and Brittany but in France as well, by such poets as Marie de France and Chrétien de Troyes. From France they passed in the thirteenth century into Germany, where Wolfram von Eschenbach wrote a splendid long poem about King Arthur's knight Sir Percival, and gave new impetus to an old tradition that would not culminate perhaps until Wagner's opera of the nineteenth century. If Wagner found inspiration in the Arthurian cycle, so did Tennyson, Edwin Arlington Robinson, and a host of other moderns, always ready to retell a well-known story in a way that would speak afresh to the psychological attitudes of new generations.

Similarly, the men of the thirteenth century rediscovered the story of the Trojan War, itself an event already almost three thousand years in the past. It was of course not yet Homer, himself still unknown in the Latin West, but two rather humdrum summary accounts in Latin supposedly by one Dares the Phrygian and Dictys the Cretan (imaginary figures, both of them) that supplied the impetus to the revival of interest in Troy. And current or recent events, like the Crusades, led to dozens of other poetic narratives of adventure: a *Song of Antioch* (Old French), for example, dealing with the adventures of the Crusaders near that historic Eastern city. To read any large number of these medieval vernacular poems is to encounter again and again the same attitudes toward noble action, and the same chivalric virtues of loyalty and good faith and courage that were celebrated in *Roland*. Collectively these poems, chiefly a northern French phenomenon, are called the *chansons de geste:* songs of deeds, or songs of action.

In southern France before the Albigensian Crusade, things were gentler. No doubt the sunny climate, the greater leisure, and the proximity to the cultivated Muslims of Spain all played a part. Here lyric poetry flourished, with love as its favorite theme. But love in southern France soon had a curious code of its own: *courtoisie,* or courtly love. The singer's lady was never a properly attainable sweetheart, unmarried and perhaps ready to be won. She was always the wife of another; she was worshiped from afar; and the singer celebrated in ecstasy even the slightest kindness she might offer him. Her merest word was a command, and her devoted knight undertook without question even the most arduous mission she might propose to him, without hope of a reward. But a lady who failed to reward him, at least to some degree, was not playing by the rules of this elaborate and artificial game. The twelfth-century troubadours who sang in the southern French language (called Provençal after the large region of Provence, and quite a different dialect from that spoken in the north) were often half-humorous as they expressed their hopeless longings for the unattainable lady.

Aquitaine, the southwestern portion of France, was long a center for this form of lyric poetry. Duke William IX in the early twelfth century was himself a troubadour, and his granddaughter, Eleanor—the wife successively of Louis VII of France and then of Henry II of England—held "courts of love." Here, in sessions patterned mockingly on those of feudal courts of justice, the lovesick troubadours sang their songs and had their cases judged, and petitions from ladies and gentlemen crossed in love received mock-serious attention. So the southern French modified the general feudal attitude toward women as mere breeders of new generations of fighters, and made life more agreeable and far more sophisticated for all who heard the songs of courtly love.

The influence of the troubadours penetrated into Germany, where courtly love was soon called *Minne,* and its celebrants the minnesingers. Needless to say, few medieval nobles behaved according to the code, and yet portions of the conceptions fostered among the troubadours did become part of the developing notions of chivalry. In such a thirteenth-century figure as Saint Louis, we find as nearly a truly chivalrous figure as can have ever existed. His faithful biographer, Joinville, from whom we have already quoted passages illustrating Louis' character, was himself the personification of a loyal vassal, as he accompanied his royal master on his ill-fated Crusades. And Joinville's work is one of the two most important vernacular French prose documents of the thirteenth century, the other being the only slightly earlier account by Villehardouin of the Fourth Crusade and the capture of Constantinople. When historians began to write for their audiences in the language of every day rather than in Latin, the triumph of the vernacular was at hand.

In Italy, the original home of the Latin language, vernacular was somewhat slower to develop. But here too, at the sophisticated and cosmopolitan court of the emperor Frederick II (1215–1250) in Palermo, some of Frederick's chief advisers began to write love poetry in what they themselves called the "sweet new style" (*dolce stil nuovo*), and soon the fashion of writing at least that form of literature in the vernacular spread northward. But it was not until somewhat later, with Dante Alighieri (1265–1321) of Florence, that the vernacular Italian tongue scored its definitive triumph. It is significant to note that Dante himself, among his other books, felt impelled to write—in Latin—a stirring defense of vernacular Italian: *De Vulgari Eloquentia (Concerning the Speech of Every Day)*. And for his own greatest work, *The Divine Comedy*, he himself chose Italian.

Among the writers in the Western tradition, Dante belongs with Homer, Vergil, and Shakespeare as a supreme master; so that it would be absurd to try to "appreciate" him here. Moreover, as a towering intellectual figure he heralds the new age of rebirth at least as loudly as he sounds the familiar medieval note; and we shall be discussing him again when we consider the Renaissance. It would distort our picture, however, not to examine here *The Divine Comedy* as a medieval book, a very long book, perhaps the most celebrated and in some ways the most typical of all medieval books.

Lost in a dark wood, in his thirty-fifth year ("half-way along the road of our human life"), Dante encounters the Roman poet Vergil, who consents to act as his guide through two of the three great regions of the afterlife of man: Hell and Purgatory. Descending through the nine successive circles of Hell, where the eternally damned must remain forever, the two meet and converse with individual souls in torment, some of them historic persons like Judas or Brutus, others recently deceased Florentines of Dante's own acquaintance, about whose sins he knew at first hand. In Purgatory, less sinful human beings are working out their punishment before they can be saved. The souls of the great pagan figures, born too early to have become Christians, are neither in Hell nor in Purgatory but in Limbo, a place on the edge of Hell, where Vergil himself must spend eternity. Here he introduces Dante to the shades not only of such ancients as Homer, Plato, and Socrates, but of characters in ancient myth and poetry such as Hector, Odysseus, and Aeneas. Even the Muslim scholar Averroës and the Muslim hero Saladin are in Limbo, not in Hell.

When the poet comes to the gates of Paradise, Vergil cannot continue to escort him; so the guide to the final region of the afterlife is Beatrice, a Florentine girl with whom Dante himself had fallen desperately in love as a youth but whom he had worshiped only at a distance. Here Dante was consciously transforming one of the central experiences of his own life into literature in accordance with the traditions of the code of courtly love. In Paradise, of course, are the Christian worthies and the saints,—Benedict, Bernard, Aquinas, and others—and at the climax of the poem, a vision of God himself.

This voyage through the afterlife is designed to show in new pictorial vividness an ancient concept: that man's actions in this life determine his fate in the next. From the lost souls in Hell, who have brought themselves to their hopeless position ("Abandon Hope, All Ye Who Enter Here" reads the inscription over the gates of Hell), through those who despite their sufferings in Purgatory confidently expect to be saved and will indeed be saved, to those whose pure life on earth has won them eternal bliss, Dante shows the entire range of human behavior and its eternal consequences. It is a majestic summary of medieval Christian moral and ethical ideas, and has often been compared in its completeness and its masterful subordination of detail to general vision with the philosophical work of Aquinas. *The Divine Comedy* is a poetic and moving *summa*.

In the generation after Dante's death, the Italian authors Petrarch and Boccaccio became the chief intellectual and literary figures of Europe. We will consider them among the forerunners of the Italian Renaissance. Here, however, we must stop to pay tribute to a poet perhaps greater than they, one who knew Petrarch personally and had read many of Boccaccio's works, but who is nonetheless in many ways a medieval figure: Geoffrey Chaucer (1340–1400). In England, by Chaucer's day the vernacular had long since recovered, and the Old English of the pre-conquest period had evolved into a new form of the language usually called Middle English, quite recognizable to most of us today as an archaic version of the language we ourselves speak (although we may sometimes be perplexed by its forms). Chaucer is the supreme poet of Middle English, and surely the most brilliant English literary voice before Shakespeare. Not a scholar but an experienced man of affairs, who made several trips to the Continent on business for the king of England, and who eventually became Controller of Customs and Clerk of the King's Works, Chaucer left behind many literary works, including several allegorical poems, some of which seem to satirize contemporary politics, and a long and moving verse narrative love story full of passion and beauty, *Troilus and Criseyde*, deriving its characters from the Trojan War stories now so fashionable in western Europe.

But of course Chaucer's most celebrated work is *The Canterbury Tales*, and the student sometimes comes to feel that if nothing else had survived of medieval literature, we should still be able to learn most of what we know about it from the *Tales* alone. The tales are told by a group of pilgrims on their way to the tomb of Thomas à Becket, the archbishop of Canterbury murdered under Henry II and now a saint. The pilgrims come from all walks of English life except the high nobility, and include a knight, a squire, a prioress, a clerk, a monk, a friar, a sailor, a miller, and others. In a brilliant prologue, Chaucer, who was himself one of the group, characterizes his fellow pilgrims, each of whom emerges as a living person. On the way from London, each tells at least one story, fully consonant with his personality and experience.

The knight tells a romantic story of chivalric love: two cousins, Palamon and Arcite, both fall in love with a maiden whom they have barely glimpsed from the window of their prison cell. Deadly rivals thereafter, they continue to cherish their mutual strife, in prison and out, without the lady's ever being aware of them. When she learns, she does very little about it, and in the end one kills the other, and wins her as his own. It is indeed a strange story to us: the lady's passivity, the two knights' lovesickness unfed by any encouragement; but it is a true story of courtly love, and befits the experienced warrior who tells it. The miller tells a raw story of a young wife's deception of her elderly husband with a young lover, a barnyard anecdote, in effect, but full of liveliness and good humor. The prioress tells a saint's legend, the squire an (unfinished) story full of semiscientific marvels, and so on. Chaucer does not hesitate to satirize his churchmen: as we shall see, the fourteenth century was a period of much discontent with the English church, and the poet was striking a note that was sure to be popular. The sophistication, delicacy, power, passion, and humor that Chaucer commands put him in the same class with Dante, and with no other medieval writer in any country.

V The Arts

As in literature, so in the arts, the centuries beginning with the eleventh saw notable changes in Europe and in Britain. Evolving from the Ottonian styles of the earlier period, the Romanesque style dominated the eleventh and most of the twelfth centuries. The Gothic style, following it and developing from it, began in the twelfth century and continued to prevail down to the fifteenth. The transition between Romanesque and Gothic is complex; and art historians have recently begun to see the years between about 1180 and about 1220, especially in northern France, as a fairly distinct period which they have labeled transitional.*

*The concept was probably brought closer to general acceptance by an extraordinary exhibition of art called "The Year 1200," held in New York in 1970 to celebrate the hundredth anniversary of the Metropolitan Museum of Art, which concentrated upon the glories and problems of these years.

The Cathedral of Worms, western Germany, begun in the eleventh century.

But the whole matter of terminology is difficult here: the term "Romanesque" is sometimes rather loosely used for buildings as early as the Carolingian and Ottonian periods, but many prefer to use "pre-Romanesque" and "proto-Romanesque" for these, both terms suggesting, quite properly, that we are on our way to something that we have not yet quite reached. Beginning in Lombardy, where the first schools of craftsmen were formed, and from which the builders traveled wherever they were needed and summoned, their skills and styles traveled across southern France to northern Spain: in both regions Catalan craftsmen practiced the art. One of the very earliest Romanesque churches, high up in the French Pyrenees, is St. Martin du Canigou, built in the first quarter of the eleventh century. Like many of these new buildings, it is a monastic church, far larger than most of the churches of the earlier period, and its interior provides examples of two important adaptations of earlier Roman architectural devices: the barrel or tunnel vault, or continuous round-arch roofing, now used for far larger spaces than before; and the groin vault, at first used in crypts only, and then later moved above ground to the main church. To the groin vault ribbing was sometimes added for strengthening. At St. Martin, the tower and cloister and body of the church are in harmonious balance, and all are adapted to the precipitous slope on which the church was built.

Most Romanesque churches had as their fundamental ground plan a Latin cross, with a long staff and shorter cross-arms; the shrine of the church, where stood the altar with the relics of the saint, was at the east end, and usually its walls formed a curved arc: this was the apse. Within this portion of the church also the choir sang. The arms of the cross extended north and south, usually from a point immediately west of the apse; these were the transepts. And the long portion of the cross, extending westward to the west front, was the nave, usually with an aisle at each side. Towers might be built over the crossing of nave and transepts, and at either side of the west front. Some churches had none or only one, some as many as six, if additional ones were built at the ends of the transepts. Around the interior of the apse—sometimes called simply "the choir"—there often opened a series of chapels, usually reflected in the exterior design by smaller arcs emerging from the apse wall, like bulges, little apses, or absidioles, as they are called. Of course, the ground plans varied greatly in detail from church to church, according to the wealth and taste of the community and the length of time that construction took, since as fashions changed, innovations could and would be incorporated in any church that remained a long time in the building.

Among the great Romanesque churches were those built at Mainz, Worms, and Speyer in western Germany by the Holy Roman emperors of the Salian line. Opposite is a view of the exterior of Worms as it is today. Surely one of the best ways to gain an impression of

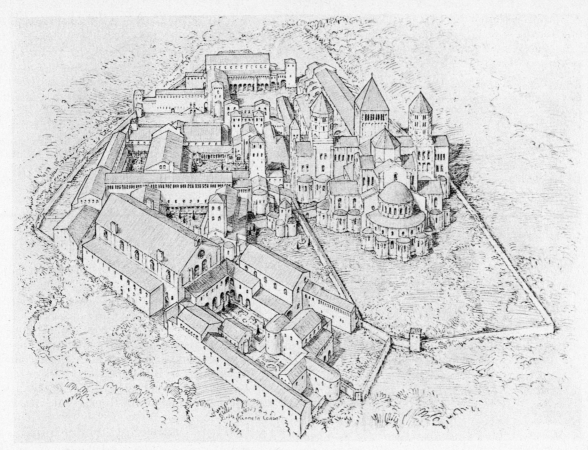

Drawing of a model of the monastery of Cluny as constructed by Professor Conant.

a great Romanesque monastery church, with its surrounding buildings (now so destroyed and rebuilt that no spectator can tell what they once looked like), is to examine the painstaking reconstructions made by a brilliant student of past architecture, Professor K. J. Conant. Here is Conant's drawing of his model of the entire complex of Cluny as it was in 1157. And to be compared with the church at Cluny is a reconstruction of the noble pilgrimage church of St. James (Santiago) at Compostela in far northwestern Spain.

To Compostela from all over western Europe but especially from France there flooded in these years throngs of pilgrims to worship at the shrine of the saint. And along the routes, to accommodate the pilgrims, hospices were built, and monasteries and churches flourished. It has long been realized that Romanesque architecture spread along these routes as well, and "pilgrimage churches," great Romanesque buildings at which the pilgrims would stop to worship along their way, were built in many key centers. The interior of Ste. Foi at Conques in south-central France, with its groin vaulting in the nave, is typical.

Variations on the typical Romanesque church can be seen, for example, in southwestern France, where a group of churches, unlike those anywhere else, have

Santiago de Compostela, the goal of western European pilgrims: a drawing of a restoration to its medieval state.

Angoulême: The nave of a church whose roof is a series of domes.

domed roofs, sometimes with the domes placed in a row above the nave, and, at St. Front of Perigueux, placed in a Greek (equal-armed) cross pattern, with a central dome, surrounded by four side domes, like St. Mark's at Venice, itself an imitation of the (lost) Church of the Holy Apostles in Byzantium. It has long been argued, and cogently, that Greek influence was somehow at work in this corner of France. The effect upon the worshiper standing under a roof made up of a series of domes is entirely different from that produced by the ordinary Romanesque barrel of groin vaulting, a point well illustrated by the interior of the Cathedral of Angoulême. That Romanesque was a truly international style despite its many variations may be seen in further examples, the interiors of two widely separated cathedrals: that of Pisa, in Italy, and that of Durham, in northern England.

A little before the year 1100, there began an extraordinary revival of European sculpture. While the tradition had never been lost, as we know from looking at monuments as late as the early medieval Irish and English crosses, and at the extraordinary figures at Cividale, the finest surviving examples of the art of sculpture before the Romanesque revival were the smaller examples in ivory and in metalwork that we have also noted. But now, quite suddenly, with joy and exuberance, the stones of the Romanesque churches we have been discussing came literally to life. The older classical columns usually had Corinthian capitals with their acanthus leaves. But now capitals began to blossom out with rosettes, palm-leaf ornament, and grapevines, and amidst the foliage there suddenly prolifer-

The nave of Pisa Cathedral, an Italian church of the Romanesque Period.

ated a whole race of marvelous beasts. Some were carved as if they were illustrations to the popular bestiaries (collections of anecdotes about real and mythical animals, usually with a Christian allegorical explanation of the animals' incredible characteristics); some were taken from real life, and some from the teeming imagination of the sculptors. At such places as Chauvigny, in western France, lions and pelicans, horses and elephants, griffins and dragons, and mermaids and other weird monsters, savage harpies attacking each other, all now edified the beholder, or, as Saint Bernard stoutly maintained, distracted him from his real business in church: the capitals at his church of Clermont and at Cîteaux were severely plain.

Of course, scenes from the Bible also appeared on the capitals, and elsewhere in the churches, but now often interpreted with a freedom from the traditional ways of showing such subjects, and with a due consideration for the space available to the artist within the small compass of the top of a column. On some capitals, the three magi (wise men from the East) sleep happily under the same blanket with their crowns on. Judas hangs himself, while terrifying winged demons pull actually and symbolically at each end of the rope. And from the capitals, of course, the sculpture spread to the available large flat and vertical surfaces available to the artist in a Romanesque church: for example, to the arched space over the outside of the front portal, the tympanum, as it is called.

Here Christ himself could be shown enthroned, often with the Virgin and the saints at his side, and surrounding and beneath them a depiction of the Last Judgment, the souls of the damned being eternally rejected at the moment of the Second Coming of the Lord, while those of the blessed rise from the tomb to enjoy their eternal salvation. At Vézelay and Autun in Burgundy, at Conques and Beaulieu and many other Romanesque churches of the pilgrimage routes, such large-scale representations of this complicated composition gave the sculptor scope for his versatility at filling space and portraying what is after all the sublimest moment in the Christian's conception of his universe.

On the doorposts, and in the repeated hollow indented narrow arches around the portals (called *voussures*), sculptured ornament also took over. At Moissac and Souillac in southern France, a frantic series of grotesque beasts, each gripping and eating the next, climbs and struggles its way up an entire vertical column or doorpost. Human and animal heads look out side by side from the voussures surrounding the tympanum. In one region of southwest France, specially noted for its breeding of horses, it is horses' heads alone that ornament the church portals and façades. In the cloister of San Domingo de Silos in northern Spain or in Chichester Cathedral in southern England, one still can see large plaques sculptured with splendid representations of biblical scenes. Romanesque sculpture is almost always in relief rather than in the full round.

Durham Cathedral in northern England: the nave, view toward the east.

In the nature of things, far less survives of Romanesque painting than of Romanesque sculpture. In the first place, when anti-Christian vandals in later periods of revolution set about the business of defacing earlier Christian monuments, they naturally found it somewhat easier to destroy paintings by scraping them off the walls or tearing out illuminations from books than to shatter stone monuments completely. In the second place, a painting on a plaster wall, for example, deteriorates faster with the passage of time than does a piece of sculpture, especially one that is indoors. However, enough survives, often in out-of-the-way places, to show that painting too experienced a revival no less significant than sculpture. In León in northern Spain, in many churches of Catalonia, and in a few places in England, France, and Italy, wall paintings can still be seen from this early period.

Probably the most complete series still visible is in the abbey church of St.-Savin-sur-Gartempe, not far from Poitiers in western France, and only a few moments' drive from the grotesque capitals at Chauvigny. At St.-Savin, the walls and ceiling of the apse and the entire long barrel vaulting of the ceiling of the nave were covered with an elaborate series of paintings, the nave with scenes from the Old Testament: Creation, the murder of Abel, Noah's Ark, the stories of Abraham and Joseph, and the Tower of Babel; and the apse with scenes from the New, including the deposition from the Cross and the Resurrection. One may also consider as a special kind of Romanesque painting the unique and famous Bayeux tapestry (actually an embroidery) commemorating the Norman Conquest of England and made soon afterwards.

Such elaborate "programs" of painting as that at St.-Savin are more familiar to us from the monuments of Italy, where the painting often took the ancient form of mosaic, used by the Romans but perfected for Christian art and for wall decoration by the Byzantines. Just as in the earlier period Eastern influence produced the great mosaics in Ravenna, we find in the Romanesque period especially rich mosaic paintings in the churches of Norman Sicily, always open to Eastern influences, and still inhabited by and visited by many Greeks. In Palermo alone, the chapel of the royal palace of the Norman kings (Capella Palatina), the church of the Martorana, and the magnificent nearby Cathedral of Monreale all display these Byzantine-influenced mosaic paintings against the usual gold ground and present a rich variety of scenes. Not far away at Cefalù is still another large church with mosaic decoration. The earliest surviving mosaics at St. Mark's in Venice—also intimately linked with Byzantium, as we know—date shortly after the beginning of the thirteenth century.

We turn now briefly to the changes that came over the Romanesque beginning in the late twelfth century. In architecture, the arches, from being round, now gradually rose to points at the peak, and similarly the roofs, once barrel-vaulted (or barrel-vaulted with groins and ribs), now also rose more and more sharply, as the smooth flow of the arc was sharply broken, and two loftier curves now met instead at a point. The continuous Romanesque barrel vault pressed down upon its supporting walls with even stress, and the walls had to be made very strong, with few openings, and often with buttresses—stone supports built at right angles to the main wall to take part of the outward push. But the chief feature of the newer medieval architecture always known as "Gothic" was precisely this pointed arch, a new device by which the builder could carry his buildings to soaring heights. The vaulted ceiling now rested upon a series of masonry ribs, in groups of four, two rising from each side of the wall, and each group supported by a massive pillar. Four pillars therefore could now be made to take the place of a whole section of solid Romanesque wall, and the spaces between the pillars could be freed for windows. From the beginning, therefore, Gothic churches were far lighter inside than Romanesque churches.

Outside too, a new effect of increased lightness and soaring height was achieved by moving the vertical buttress of the Romanesque period away from the walls

The west tympanum at Autun.

of the church, and by bridging the gap between buttress and church wall with an arched support that looked as if it were actually flying between the now distant vertical and the lofty masonry wall, part of whose outward thrust it was designed to take. These "flying buttresses" also freed the builder to soar upward. Into the new window spaces made possible by the new architectural devices the craftsmen of the thirteenth century and later fitted a new form of painting: the window in multicolored (stained) glass, glittering with gemlike color in ruby, sapphire, and emerald, and showing biblical episodes or episodes from the life of the saint whose church they illuminated.

Gothic architecture flourished for at least two centuries everywhere in Europe. Its first and perhaps greatest moments came in northern France, with the building—all between the 1190s and about 1240—of the cathedrals of Chartres, Reims, Amiens, Notre Dame of Paris, and other celebrated churches. Sometimes the ambition of a designer extended beyond his control of engineering: the architect of Beauvais, who managed to build the loftiest apse and transepts of any Gothic church, found that he could not get his nave to stand up; so it fell, and what remains still looks like an exercise in defiance of the law of gravity.

Open and vast, but solidly built, soaring upward according to well-worked-out and usually well-understood mathematical architectural proportional formulas, the Gothic cathedral terminates in aerial towers. Though its great windows let in the light, the stained glass keeps the interior dim and awe-inspiring. In England, York and Canterbury, Salisbury and Wells, Ely and Winchester among a good many other cathedrals still stand as the best of island Gothic, fully comparable with the best on the Continent. With the passage of time in the fourteenth and fifteenth centuries ornamentation grew richer, decoration became more intricate, literally flamelike, or "flamboyant," and Gothic architecture on the Continent moved toward its decline. The later tower at Chartres illustrates this overripe look; in England, however, the later richer Gothic has given us such marvels as King's College Chapel in Cambridge and the Henry VII Chapel at Westminster Abbey in London.

Of sculpture in the years between 1180 and 1220 it has been recently said that ". . . for practically the first time since ancient Greek and Roman times, draperies curl and caress the bodies underneath; limbs themselves are proudly and successfully shown as organic entities; strength becomes a thing of muscles rather than size alone; physiques are neither camouflaged nor ignored, but studied and presented to our eyes in an almost overpowering beauty. Faces become truly alive, eyes shine with an inner light, gestures seem to develop an entirely new expressive poetry of their own. Drama is supreme." * Refusing to call this style

*Thomas P. F. Hoving, in his Foreword to *The Year 1200: A Centennial Exhibition at the Metropolitan Museum of Art* (New York: The Metropolitan Museum of Art, 1970), I, vii.

Chartres: figures of Melchizedek, Abraham, and Moses on the north portal.

Amiens: the nave.

King's College Chapel, Cambridge.

Chartres: the facade.

"Style 1200": Two of Nicholas of Verdun's enameled plaques made for the Klosterneuburg altarpiece—Christ enthroned, and the mouth of Hell. In the first, note the folds of the draperies and the genuine bodies beneath.

either Romanesque or Gothic, and discarding even the name "transitional" but preferring simply the slightly awkward term "Style 1200," recent scholars point to the work in metals of Nicholas of Verdun and of sculptors working in the valley of the Meuse, where France, Belgium, Holland, and Germany are close together, as marking the beginning of the new school; but more generally northern France, western Germany, and England all saw its activity.

Gradually during this period, sculpture in the round became more and more common, beginning with figures that were carved fully in the round from the midsections of columns, engaged in the façade or the portal of a church only at the top and at the base. The lifelike representation of drapery, the firm balance of the figures on their feet, are principal characteristics of these new statues, chiefly occurring in northern France. Similar influences are shown elsewhere in metalwork and in manuscript illumination, rather than in monumental sculpture, and it is agreed that the influences from outside that help make the development possible must be sought in Byzantine art, then itself undergoing a kind of classical renaissance, and available to Western eyes through renewed and intensified contacts between East and West by pilgrims, travelers, and warriors during the period of the Crusades. What we have here is an artistic revival more splendid and more complicated even than had hitherto been suspected.

Reading Suggestions on Medieval Western Society: National Monarchy, Secular Literature

General Accounts: France

A. Tilley, *Mediaeval France* (Cambridge Univ., 1922). Political-historical essays.

Special Studies: France

A. Luchaire, *Social France at the Time of Philip Augustus* (Peter Smith, 1929). A well-written account, perhaps overemphasizing the seamy side of life.

A. R. Kelly, *Eleanor of Aquitaine and the Four Kings* (Harvard Univ., 1950; *Vintage). A learned and lively treatment, the best in English.

R. Fawtier, *The Capetian Kings of France* (*Papermac). The most up-to-date account.

J. Evans, *Life in Mediaeval France* (Oxford Univ., 1925). Good picture of French society.

General Accounts: England

A. L. Poole, *From Domesday Book to Magna Carta, 1087–1216* (Clarendon, 1951).

F. M. Powicke, *Mediaeval England, 1066–1485* (Home University Library, 1948) and *The Thirteenth Century, 1216–1307* (Clarendon, 1953).

D. M. Stenton, *English Society in the Early Middle Ages* (*Penguin).

A. R. Myers, *England in the Late Middle Ages* (*Penguin). A useful introduction at the popular level.

H. M. Cam, *England before Elizabeth* (Hutchinson's University Library, 1950). Excellent.

Special Studies: England

G. O. Sayles, *The Medieval Foundations of England* (*Perpetua). Excellent basic study. With H. G. Richardson, Sayles is co-author of *The Governance of Medieval England from the Conquest to Magna Carta* (Edinburgh, 1963), a brilliant and provocative analysis.

D. C. Douglas, *William the Conqueror: The Norman Impact upon England* (*Univ. of California). Scholarly.

F. Barlow, *William I and the Norman Conquest* (English University Presses, 1965). Popular.

R. A. Brown, *The Normans and the Norman Conquest* (*Con- stable). Well-written, authoritative recent introduction to the subject, excellent for the student.

C. A. Hollister, *Anglo-Saxon Military Institutions on the Eve of the Norman Conquest* (Oxford Univ., 1964) and *The Military Organization of Norman England* (Oxford Univ., 1965). Excellent scholarly monographs settling many disputed questions.

B. Wilkinson, *The Constitutional History of England, 1216–1399* (Longmans, 1948–1952). Uses the latest scholarly investigations of a much-debated subject.

F. M. Powicke, *King Henry III and the Lord Edward* (Clarendon, 1947). Scholarly.

G. L. Haskins, *Growth of English Representative Government* (*Perpetua). A clear account of a most difficult and vital subject.

G. C. Homans, *English Villagers of the Thirteenth Century* (Russell & Russell, 1960). Interesting study of social organization and behavior.

Literature

H. Waddell, *The Wandering Scholars* (*Anchor). Lively account.

C. S. Lewis, *The Discarded Image: An Introduction to Medieval and Renaissance Literature* (Cambridge Univ., 1964). Original and provocative.

Note: There are many available translations of Dante and editions and translations of Chaucer into modern English.

Sources

D. C. Douglas and G. W. Greenaway, eds., *English Historical Documents, 1042–1189* (Oxford Univ., 1953). Volume II of a monumental series still in publication.

The Chronicle of Jocelin of Brakelund, trans. H. E. Butler (Nelson, 1949). Medieval monastery life.

Historical Fiction

W. E. Bryher, *The Fourteenth of October* (Pantheon, 1952). A good novel about the Norman Conquest of England.

H. Muntz, *The Golden Warrior* (Scribner's, 1949). Another good novel about the Norman Conquest.

Z. Oldenbourg, *The World Is Not Enough* (Pantheon, 1948). A highly successful effort to recapture in fiction the life, violence and all, of twelfth-century France.

The East

Late Middle Ages

The Main Threads

In the third quarter of the eleventh century, the relations between Roman Christendom, Greek Christendom, and Islam entered upon a long period of crisis. Our first task in this chapter is to deal with the late medieval interaction of these three great societies, particularly in the movement called the Crusades. Next, we shall consider the decline and final collapse of the Byzantine Empire. And, finally, we shall trace the fortunes down to the end of the seventeenth century of the two states that, in different senses, were its successors: the Ottoman Empire, and Muscovite Russia. In this introductory section we shall examine the main pattern of all these developments before discussing them in detail.

By the eleventh century, each of the three societies had well-established relationships with the other two. Byzantium had conducted diplomatic negotiations with many Western monarchs; the papacy had maintained regular official contact with the Byzantines even after the official break in 1054; and southern Italy had been a Byzantine outpost. The Byzantines had been involved in more or less continuous war and diplomacy with the caliphate and the local Muslim dynasties in Syria. Islam had touched Roman Christendom in Spain and Sicily, and Western pilgrims had thronged, as we shall see, to the shrines of Christendom in Muslim Palestine. But after 1071, when the Normans took Bari and drove the Byzantines from Italy, and the Seljuk Turks won at Manzikert and battered their way into the central Byzantine stronghold of Asia Minor, the tempo of the relationship steadily quickened. For the next six centuries, the fate of each society became ever more closely bound up with the fate of the other two.

The Norman assault on the Byzantines now moved eastward from Italy across the Adriatic to the Balkan shores of the empire itself. In order to ward it off, the

neously by the Seljuks, in 1082 made an alliance with the booming port of Venice—once their vassal, now their equal. In exchange for naval assistance, they gave the Venetians commercial concessions in the empire. Permitted to import and export at special tariff rates and given a quarter in Constantinople itself, with warehouses, churches, and dwelling places, the Venetians and later the Genoese joined the sailors of Amalfi and Pisa in taking over the carrying-trade of the eastern Mediterranean.

The Crusades

Meanwhile, the papacy, stimulated by Byzantine appeals for military assistance against the Seljuks, proclaimed a holy war against Islam. This concept had already become familiar in the Byzantine wars against the Muslims and in the Catholic attempts to reconquer Spain and Sicily. In 1095 Pope Urban II launched the great military movement of the Crusade. The recovery of the Holy Sepulcher was the ultimate aim, and the Crusaders fought with the cross as their symbol. They were granted special privileges as soldiers of the Lord. For almost two hundred years, expedition after expedition was hurled against the Muslims, most often in Syria and Palestine, but also in Egypt, North Africa, and even Portugal. The armies were sometimes commanded by kings and emperors, sometimes by lesser nobles. Sometimes they came by sea, sometimes by land, sometimes by a combined land-and-sea route. Sometimes they scored successes, great or small; more often they met with partial or total failure. Reinforcements from the West flowed to the East in an almost continuous stream. Therefore, the common practice of calling certain specific expeditions the Second, Third, or Fourth Crusade, and so on up to the Eighth, is really not very accurate, though it is often

As a result of the First Crusade, the Westerners established in Muslim territory in Syria four independent states of their own, usually called the Latin or Frankish states (to the Muslims all Westerners were "Franks"). These states were ruled by Europeans of various origins, jealous of each other and often at odds. After the First Crusade, many of the later expeditions were directed toward meeting some emergency that had arisen in the Latin states. Here in the East, a new society sprang up, in which Western feudal practice could combine with Muslim local practice. Yet by 1187 the Muslims, overcoming their disunity, had swept away all but a remnant of the Western outposts. After a century of epilogue, the process was complete by 1291.

Thereafter, although the crusading ideal continued to be preached in the West, no major expedition was ever again launched to reconquer the Holy Land, which remained in Muslim hands. In the fourteenth and fifteenth centuries some of the Western expeditions against the Ottoman Turks took on various aspects of a crusade, but they were never the genuine article.

The Downfall of Byzantium

Most of the important crusading expeditions passed through Byzantium. From the first, the emperors were embarrassed by the presence of the often uncontrollable "barbarian" armies in their territory. Naturally, they tried to move the Westerners as quickly as possible on to Muslim soil and into the combat against the infidel for which they had come. But the Westerners tended to regard these precautions as perfidy, and distrusted the Greeks. The vast material wealth of Constantinople appealed greatly to the greedy eyes of the western European military commanders. There were profound religious and social differences between the Greeks and Latins, and the Byzantines hated the Italian merchants resident among them, as well as the Western armies pouring through the capital. Tension mounted throughout the twelfth century. Internal disorder increased, signalized by a great increase in Byzantine feudal decentralization.

Finally, in 1204, the Fourth Crusade, which had set out from Venice by sea to fight in the Holy Land, was diverted for political reasons to Constantinople, and took the city by storm. This was the first time the Byzantine capital had been taken: a landmark in the history of the relations between Eastern and Western Christians. The Westerners set up a "Latin Empire" in Constantinople, gained a foothold in Asia Minor, and founded feudal principalities throughout Greece and in the islands of the Aegean. Meanwhile, the Byzantines, driven from their capital, founded two Greek states in Asia Minor, Trebizond and Nicaea, and one in Europe, Epirus. All three states eventually called themselves empires.

In 1261 the Latins, deprived of help from home, without roots, hated by the Greeks, were driven from Constantinople by the Greek emperor of Nicaea, and

Seventeenth-century Russian woodcut: a Cossack or "free adventurer."

the Byzantine Empire was restored. But from then on for the next two centuries, the empire was merely a shadow of its former self. Though expelled as rulers from the capital, the Westerners remained in Greece and on the islands. Venetians and Genoese retained and strengthened their privileged positions in Constantinople. In the Balkans, the Serbians founded a powerful kingdom and menaced Byzantium itself. It proved impossible to restore the Byzantine military or economic system. Although its pretensions to being the only civilized state in the world and its theoretical aspirations to world empire were never abandoned, Byzantium was now only a Balkan state. And, toward the end of the thirteenth century the Byzantine emperors became aware of how great a danger was presented by a new Turkish people, the Osmanlis, or Ottoman Turks. Muslims like the rest, the Ottoman Turks in only a few generations had been able to consolidate their power in northwestern Asia Minor, opposite Constantinople.

The Ottoman Turks

Themselves a product of a fusion between Greek natives and Turkish invaders, the Osmanlis crossed the Straits into Europe in the mid-fourteenth century, were invited to assist the parties in the ever-growing internal Byzantine strife, and gradually became a European power. They occupied most of the former Byzantine territory, except for the capital itself. A variety of efforts to reunite the Eastern and Western churches and to obtain assistance from the Roman Catholic West for the Byzantines, who were beleaguered by their Muslim enemy, all met with failure. In 1453 the Osmanlis besieged and captured the city of Constantine, and the empire that proudly traced its origins to Augustus finally came to an end.

Yet the end, though definite enough, was in some ways more of an appearance than a reality. The Ottoman Turks by 1453 had become a partly European people, and, though their system had many features that may be considered purely Turkish, they too, like so many of the earlier enemies of the empire, were overwhelmed by their sense of its prestige. With Constantinople as their capital, the Ottoman sultans ruled like Byzantine emperors. Though Muslim, they permitted their Christian subjects to worship in their own way. Christians suffered certain disabilities, but the religious life of the Orthodox continued to be governed by the patriarch of Constantinople, a Greek as always. Byzantine ways persisted throughout the Balkan region. In a sense, the Ottoman Empire, despite its own peculiar institutions, was a successor state to Byzantium, and many of its inhabitants were descendants of the Byzantines.

Extraordinarily successful as a military power, the Turks, during the first two centuries of their domination at Constantinople, repeatedly threatened Europe. Twice they advanced as far as Vienna, and they fought naval wars all over the Mediterranean. Although a new general crusade against them was never launched successfully, many crusades were preached. The West did develop strong defenders, especially the Hapsburg rulers of the Holy Roman Empire, now centered at Vienna, who in the end were able to resist the Ottoman onslaught. And meanwhile, after the end of the sixteenth century, the Ottoman system itself was in full internal decay. The astonishing thing is that it was able to forestall total disruption. By the end of the seventeenth century, European rulers were already beginning to discuss how they should divide the Turkish lands when the empire fell apart. But contrary to all calculations, the Ottoman Empire, perhaps largely because its existence was valuable to some of the European powers, remained as an independent state down to the end of World War I in our own twentieth century.

Post-Kievan Russia

Although the Ottoman Empire represented a kind of successor state to Byzantium, it was still a Muslim state. There was, however, another state, which, though it occupied no Byzantine territory and never included within its borders more than a handful of Byzantine subjects, was also in its way a successor state to Byzantium, and which regarded itself as the new leader of the Orthodox world. This was Russia, whose story we left at the time of the decline of Kiev, when it was torn by internal dissension and was as well a prey to invasion by the Mongol Tatars.

In the thirteenth, fourteenth, and early fifteenth centuries, the extreme western portions of the Kievan state fell under Polish and Lithuanian influence. At the same time, the city of Novgorod in the north continued to develop its trade with the West, chiefly Germany, and its municipal institutions. But the most striking feature of Russian development was the Tatar domination of the entire northeastern and eastern regions. The Tatars exercised their domination from afar, and, except for devastating raids, did not occupy the country, though they did levy a large annual tribute upon the Russians. Not until the fifteenth century were the princes of Moscow, who for a variety of reasons had emerged as the leading power in the region, able to throw off this obligation, and even after this, the Tatars continued to maintain important settlements on Russian soil. The most important effect that the Tatar domination had on the future development of Russia was the cutting off of so vast an area from the West, and the consequent deepening of the cultural lag that we have already observed as one of the consequences of Kievan Russia's having been converted to Christianity from Byzantium.

Moreover, the princes of Moscow, in establishing themselves as supreme over the Russian lands, received from the Orthodox church, which was backing them in their endeavor, a full-fledged ideology: that Moscow was the successor of Byzantium, which had fallen to the Turks, and thus of Rome, which had fallen to the schismatic Roman Catholics. Moscow was thus the third and final Rome, and the rulers of Moscow were the direct heirs of the Byzantine emperors. The importance of this concept for future Russian historical development is sometimes disputed by scholars. Yet it did greatly affect the Russian princes, and it contributed much over the centuries to their absolutist rule.

II The Crusades
The Idea of a Holy War

In 964, when the Byzantine emperor Nicephorus Phocas (ruled 963–969) was about to go to war against the Arabs, he wrote a long letter to the caliph, full of insults, threats, and boasts of his previous victories.

> We have conquered your impregnable fortresses . . . left piles of corpses with blood still pouring from them . . . rendered your peasants and their wives helpless in the very midst of their flocks. Lofty buildings have been destroyed. . . . When the owl hoots there now, echo answers. . . . People of Baghdad, flee at once, and bad luck to you, for your weakened empire will not last. . . . I shall march with all speed toward Mecca, bringing in my train a throng of soldiers black as night. I shall seize that city, and stay there a time at my ease, so that I may establish there a throne for the best of beings: Christ.*

In 975 Nicephorus' assassin and successor, John Tsimisces (ruled 969–976), wrote a letter to his ally, the

*G. L. Schlumberger, *Nicéphore Phocas* (Paris, 1923), pp. 348 ff. Our translation.

king of Armenia, telling of his campaigns of that year against the Muslims in Syria. He had taken Damascus, he wrote, and Nazareth:

> People came from Ramleh and Jerusalem, to beseech our majesty for grace. They asked of us a leader, and declared themselves to be our subjects. We gave them what they asked for. It was our wish to free the holy tomb of Christ from the insults of the Muslims. . . . If those accursed Africans [i.e., Egyptian Muslims] who now live in Caesarea on the seacoast had not taken refuge in the castles along the shore, we should have marched into the holy city of Jerusalem and should have been able to pray in those holy places.*

These two tenth-century Byzantine documents breathe the spirit of the later Western movement known as the Crusades: a holy war against the Muslims for the possession of the Holy Places. Although the Byzantines never were able to fulfill their ambition, they had the will and the intention.

Similarly, in the West, the idea of a holy war was not new in 1095. In Spain, the fighting of Christian against Muslim had been virtually continuous since the Muslim conquest in the eighth century. The small Christian states of the north pushed southward when they could, and retreated again when they had to. Just after the year 1000, the Cordovan Caliphate weakened, and the Spanish Christian princes of the north won the support of the powerful French abbey at Cluny. Under prodding from Cluny, French nobles joined the Spaniards in warring on the Muslims. And soon the pope offered an indulgence to all who would fight for the Cross in Spain. In 1085 the Christians took the great city of Toledo, but a new wave of Muslim Berbers from North Africa set them back for a time. The Christian movement continued during the remainder of the eleventh century, and on into the twelfth. It recovered a large area of central Spain, and it was itself a Crusade: a holy war against the infidel supported by the papacy. So too were the wars of the Normans in southern Italy against the Muslims of Sicily.

Pilgrimages

From the third century on, Christians had visited the scenes of Christ's life. At Jerusalem, Constantine's mother, Saint Helena, discovered the true cross and other relics of the Passion. Her son built the Church of the Holy Sepulcher. Before the Muslim conquest in the seventh century, pilgrims came from Byzantium and the West, often seeking sacred relics for their churches at home. For a while after the Muslim conquest, pilgrimages were very dangerous, and could be undertaken only by the hardiest pilgrims. Saint Willibald, an Englishman who made the journey between 722 and 729, encountered freezing cold and hunger in Asia Minor, captivity and imprisonment as a spy by

*G. L. Schlumberger, *L'Epopée Byzantine* (Paris, 1896), I, 287–288. Our translation.

Muslims in northern Syria, sickness on three different occasions, blindness at Gaza, a savage lion in the olive groves of Esdraelon, severe Muslim customs officers at Tyre (Willibald was smuggling at the time), and a volcanic eruption on an Italian island on the way home.

During the reign of Charlemagne, conditions improved for Western pilgrims, largely because of the excellent relations between Charlemagne and the famous caliph Harun al-Rashid (see Chapter 6). The caliph made Charlemagne a present of the actual recess in which Christ was buried, and allowed him to endow a hostel in Jerusalem for the use of pilgrims. Charlemagne gave a splendid library to the Latin Church of St. Mary, and sent money and bought land to support Christian foundations. So deep was his interest that there sprang up a legend that he had somehow acquired from Harun a "protectorate" over the Holy Land, and another that he had actually made a pilgrimage to the East in person. Neither of these stories is true, but they reflect the importance of the pilgrimage in Charlemagne's period.

In the tenth century, the belief grew that pilgrimage would procure God's pardon for sins. Santiago (St. James) of Compostela in Spain, and of course Rome itself, became favorite places of pilgrimage, but no place could compare in importance with the shrines of Palestine. Large organized groups began to replace the individual traveler. Great lords with suites of followers came, as well as humble clerics from all over Europe. We know of more than one hundred Western pilgrimages during the eleventh century. On one occasion, contemporaries report seven thousand German pilgrims, all traveling together.

The Late-Eleventh-Century Crisis

Stable conditions in both Muslim and Byzantine dominions were essential for the easy and safe continuance of pilgrimages. But in the early eleventh century the half-mad Egyptian ruler of Palestine, Hakim, himself a Muslim heretic, abandoned the tolerant practices of his predecessors, and began to persecute Christians and make travel to the Holy Places unsafe. Moreover, with the death of the last ruler of the Macedonian house in 1057, there began at Byzantium an open struggle between the party of the court civil servants and the military party of the great Asia Minor landowners. Simultaneously came Pecheneg invasions of the Balkans, Norman attacks on Byzantine southern Italy, and the rise in Asia of the Seljuk Turks. By 1050 the Seljuks had created a state centering on Persia. In 1055 they entered Baghdad on the invitation of the Abbasid caliph himself, and became the champions of Sunnite Islam against the Shiite rulers of Egypt. In the 1050s, Seljuk forces appeared in Armenia and Asia Minor; they raided deep into Anatolia, almost to the Aegean. Their advance culminated in the catastrophic Byzantine defeat of Manzikert in 1071, followed by the occupation of most of Asia Minor, and the establishment of a new sultanate with its capital at Nicaea. The Seljuks conquered not only much of Asia Minor but also Syria and Palestine. Jerusalem fell in the very year of Manzikert and Bari, 1071, and became part of a new Seljuk state of Syria.

Amid disorder and palace intrigue, with the empire reduced in territory and the capital in danger, there came to the Byzantine throne in 1081 Alexius I Comnenus, a general and a great landowner, who was to found a dynasty that staved off disaster for over a century. Between 1081 and 1085, he held off the Norman attack on the Dalmatian coast by means of his alliance with Venice. He was at home in the slippery field of intrigue, playing one local Turkish potentate off against another, and slowly reestablishing a Byzantine foothold in Asia Minor. Civil wars among the Turks and the multiplication of brigands on the highways in Anatolia and Syria made pilgrimage in the two decades after Manzikert a dangerous pursuit indeed, despite the relatively decent conditions in Palestine itself.

The schism between Eastern and Western churches provided the papacy with an additional incentive for intervention in the East. The vigorous reforming popes of the later eleventh century felt that the disunity of Christendom was intolerable, the rending of a seamless garment. In 1073 Pope Gregory VII (Hildebrand) sent an ambassador to Constantinople, who reported that the emperor was anxious for a reconciliation, and emphasized the dreadful conditions brought about for travelers by the Turkish conquests in Asia Minor. Gregory VII planned to extend the holy war from Spain to Asia by sending the Byzantines an army of Western knights. Even more striking, he intended to lead them himself, and thus put himself in a position to bring about a reunion of the churches. It was only the quarrel over investiture with the German emperor (see Chapter 7) that prevented the pope from carrying out this plan. But here, more than twenty years before the opening of the first Crusade, all the necessary ingredients were already present: a holy war, to be fought in alliance with the Greeks against the Muslims in Asia, under the direct sponsorship of the papacy.

The First Crusade

Pope Urban II (1088–1099) carried on the tradition of Gregory VII. To his Council of Piacenza in 1095 came envoys from Alexius, who asked for military help against the Turks. Turkish power was declining, and now would be a good time to strike. The Byzantine envoys also seem to have stressed the sufferings of the Christians in the East. Eight months later, at the Council of Clermont, Urban preached to a throng of the faithful. He emphasized the appeal received from the Eastern Christians, brothers in difficulty, and painted in dark colors the hardships that now faced pilgrims to Jerusalem. He summoned his listeners to form themselves, rich and poor alike, into an army, which God would assist. Killing each other at home should give way to fighting a holy war. Poverty at home would yield to the riches of the East (a theme especially important in view of the misery in which so many Europeans lived). If a man were killed doing this work of God, he would automatically be absolved of his sins and assured of salvation. The audience greeted this moving oration with cries of "God wills it." Throngs of volunteers took a solemn oath, and sewed crosses of cloth onto their garments. Recruitment was under way. The First Crusade had been launched.

On the popular level, a certain Peter the Hermit, an unkempt, barefoot old man, who lived on fish and wine and was a moving orator, proved the most effective preacher of the Crusade. Through France and Germany he recruited an undisciplined mob of ignorant peasants, including women and children, many of them serfs living wretched lives, suffering near-starvation as a result of crop failure. Often they believed that Peter was leading them straight to heaven, the New Jerusalem, flowing with milk and honey, which they confused with the Jerusalem on earth. People less well fitted for the tasks of the holy war can hardly be imagined.

In two installments, the rabble poured up the Rhine, across Hungary, where four thousand Hungarians were killed in a riot over the sale of a pair of shoes, and into Byzantine territory at Belgrade. The Byzantines, who had hoped for the loan of a few hundred well-trained knights, were appalled at the prospect of the enormous armies of human locusts about to descend on them from the West. They proceeded to arrange military escorts and to take all precautions against trouble. Despite their best efforts, the undisciplined Crusaders burned houses and stole everything that was not chained down, including the lead from the roofs of churches.

Once in Constantinople, they were graciously received by Alexius Comnenus, who shipped them across the Straits as quickly as possible. In Asia Minor they quarreled among themselves, murdered the Christian inhabitants, scored no success against the Turks, and were eventually massacred. The trouble brought upon the Byzantines by this first mob of Crusaders was a symbol of future difficulties.

Meanwhile, at the upper levels of Western society, no kings had enlisted in the Crusade, but a considerable number of great lords had been recruited, including a brother of the king of France, the duke of Normandy, and the count of Flanders. The most celebrated, however, were Godfrey of Bouillon (duke of Lower Lorraine), and his brother Baldwin, Count Raymond of Toulouse, Count Stephen of Blois, and Bohemond, a Norman prince from southern Italy. Better equipped and better disciplined, the armies led by these lords now began to converge on Constantinople by different routes, arriving at intervals. Still, there was plenty of trouble for the people on the routes. "My lips are tight,"

The Advance of the Ottoman Turks

It was the Ottoman Turks, however, who gave the empire the final blow. These Turks were the ablest and luckiest of the groups to whom the Seljuk Empire in Asia Minor was now passing as it disintegrated. We find them in the last quarter of the thirteenth century settled on the borders of the province of Bithynia, across the Straits from Constantinople. This region had been the center of Greek resistance to the Latins during the Latin Empire and the base for the reconquest of the capital by the empire of Nicaea. Economic and political unrest led the discontented population of this region to turn to the Ottomans in preference to the harsh and ineffectual officials of the Byzantine government. As a whole, the Turks were not fanatical Muslims, and they had no racial distaste for the Greek population, from whom, in fact, they were anxious to learn.

The Ottoman conquest of Bithynia was a kind of gradual penetration, beginning with cattle raids and continuing with the acquisition of land. The farmers willingly paid tribute to the Turks, and as time went on many of them were converted to Islam in order to avoid the payment. They learned Turkish, and taught the nomadic Turkish conquerors some of the arts of a settled agricultural life; the Turks, in turn, adopted Byzantine practices in government. One interesting institution that probably speeded the process of assimilation of the two peoples was the Ottoman corporations of the Akhis, a curious combination of craft guild, monastic order, and social service agency. Highly tolerant, the Akhis were organized according to the craft or trade of their members. They were intensely pious Muslims who were determined to fight tyrannical government. In the towns of Anatolia they built hostels for travelers, where they gave religious dances and read the Koran. They presented Islam at its most attractive. Within a generation or two it is likely that the original Ottoman Turks had become very highly mixed with the native Greeks of Anatolia.

Even before this process had got very far the Turks had begun to conquer the cities of Bithynia, and to engage in open warfare with the Byzantines. The Turks built a fleet and began raiding in the Sea of Marmora and the Aegean. It was not long before they were invited into Europe by one of the rival claimants to the Byzantine throne, who in 1354 allowed them to establish themselves in the Gallipoli peninsula. Soon they were occupying much of the neighboring province of Thrace. In 1363 they moved their capital to the city of Adrianople, on the European side of the Straits. Constantinople was now surrounded by Turkish territory, and could be reached from the west only by sea. In order to survive at all, many of the later emperors had to reach humiliating arrangements with the Turkish rulers—in some cases becoming their vassals.

The Byzantine Empire survived down to 1453. But its survival was no longer in its own hands. The Turks chose to conquer much of the Balkan region first, putting an end to the independent Bulgarian and Serbian states in the 1370s and 1380s. The final defeat of the Serbs at the battle of Kossovo on June 28, 1389, has long been celebrated by the defeated Serbs themselves in poetry and song. June 28, Saint Vitus' day, is their national holiday, and the day on which the archduke Franz Ferdinand was assassinated by the Serb nationalists in 1914. A European "crusade" against the Turks was wiped out at Nicopolis on the Danube in 1396.

But Turkish conquests were delayed for half a century when a new wave of Mongols under Timur (celebrated in our literature as Tamerlane) emerged from central Asia in 1402 and defeated the Ottoman armies at Ankara in the Anatolian plateau, the present-day capital of Turkey. Like most Mongol efforts, this proved a temporary one, and the Ottoman armies and state recovered. In the 1420s and 1430s, the Turks moved into Greece; and the West, now thoroughly alarmed at the spread of Turkish power in Europe, tried to bolster the Byzantine defenses by proposing a union of the Eastern and Western churches in 1439 and by dispatching another "crusade" to Bulgaria in 1444. Both efforts proved futile.

With the accession of Muhammad II to the Ottoman throne in 1451, the doom of Constantinople was sealed. His skillful Hungarian engineer cast for him an enormous cannon that fired great stone balls. It took two months to drag the cannon from Adrianople to the walls of Constantinople. New Turkish castles on the Bosporus were able to prevent ships from delivering supplies to the city. In 1453 strong forces of troops and artillery were drawn up in siege array, and at one moment the Turks dragged a fleet of small boats uphill on runners and slid them down the other side into the Golden Horn itself. As final defeat grew more and more inevitable, the Greeks and Latins inside the city took communion together inside Hagia Sophia for the last time, and the last emperor, Constantine XI, died bravely defending the walls against the Turkish onslaught.

On May 29, 1453, with the walls breached and the emperor dead, the Turks poured into the city. Muhammad II, the Conqueror, gave thanks to Allah in Hagia Sophia itself and ground the altar of the sanctuary beneath his feet. Thenceforth it was to be a mosque. When he passed through the deserted rooms of the imperial palace, he is said to have quoted a Persian verse on the transitoriness of human power: "The spider has become the chamberlain in the palace of Afrasiab, and has woven her curtain before the door; the owl is now the trumpeter upon the battlements thereof." Shortly thereafter, he installed a new Greek patriarch, and proclaimed himself protector of the Christian church. On the whole, during the centuries that followed, the Orthodox church accepted the sultans as successors to the Byzantine emperors.

Interior of Hagia Sophia, with the Turkish medallions installed after the capture of Constantinople.

IV   The Ottoman Successor-State, 1453–1699

Part of the Ottomans' inheritance no doubt came from their far-distant past in central Asia, when, like other Turks, they had almost surely come under the direct or indirect influence of China, and had lived like other nomads of the steppes. Their fondness and capacity for war and their rigid adherence to custom may go back to this early period, as did their native Turkish language. From the Persians and the Byzantines, who themselves had been influenced by Persia, the Turks seem to have derived their exaltation of the ruler, their tolerance of religious groups outside the state religion, and their practice of encouraging such groups to form independent communities inside their state. Persian was always the literary language and the source of Turkish literature, both in form and in content. From Islam, the Turks took the sacred law and their approach to legal problems, the Arabic alphabet in which they wrote their Turkish tongue, and the Arabic vocabulary of religious, philosophical, and other abstract terms. All the wellsprings of their inheritance—Asiatic, Persian-Byzantine, and Muslim—tended to make them an exceptionally conservative people.

The Ottoman System

Fortunate in finding their neighbors weak as they themselves grew in strength, and fortunate in their geographic position as near neighbors to the Byzantines, the Ottomans allowed the peoples that they conquered to pass through a stage of vassalage rather than insisting upon immediate annexation by force. Until the sixteenth century they showed tolerance to their infidel subjects, permitting Christians and Jews to serve the state, and allowing the patriarch of Constantinople and the Grand Rabbi to act as leaders of their own religious communities, or *millets*. The religious leader not only represented his flock in its dealings with the Ottoman state but also had civil authority over them in civil, judicial, and financial matters that affected them alone. Non-Muslims paid a head-tax and lived in peace. The patriarch of Constantinople exercised far more power than he ever had under the Byzantines.

From 1280 to 1566, ten successive able sultans ruled the Ottomans. They received early training in administration, and were expected on their accession to kill off all their brothers—on one occasion there were nineteen victims—in order to forestall civil strife. In theory, the sultan possessed the entire wealth of his dominions, and his object was to exploit it to the full. To do so he maintained an elaborate system of administrators whose lives and property belonged absolutely to him, all of whom were slaves (*kullar*), and at the same time members of the ruling class (Ottomans). To belong to the ruling class a man had to be loyal to the sultan, a Muslim, and a true Ottoman: that is, he had to

Sultan Muhammad II (ruled 1451–1481): a painting by Gentile Bellini.

master the "Ottoman way" of speaking and behaving. All those who lacked one or more of these attributes were not members of the ruling class, but subjects (*raya*, literally "cattle"). Any raya could become an Ottoman by acquiring the three necessary attributes. Beyond the activities of collecting, spending, and increasing the imperial revenues, and defending and adding to the imperial possessions, the Ottomans had no duties, and rayas could, in their own millets, take care of everything else.

The Ottoman ruling class included four subdivisions, the "men of the emperor," the "men of the sword," the "men of the pen," and the "sages." The first—the imperial class—comprised an inner service, embracing the sultan himself and his wives, sons, servants, private purse, and palace attendants, including the entire harem; and an outer service, including the grand viziers and the other highest officers of the state, those who directed all the other branches of the service. In the early days of the Ottoman Empire, the Turkish princely families from Anatolia virtually monopolized both the inner and the outer services of this imperial class. But as early as the fourteenth century, and even more markedly in the fifteenth, the sultans learned to balance their influence by recruiting new talent from among the newly acquired Christian subjects. Some entered the system as prisoners of war; some the sultan bought or received as presents. But most he obtained through the regular levying of the *devshirme,* or tribute of children.

Every four years until sometime in the seventeenth century, specially trained officers, each with a quota of places to fill, visited the Balkan and Anatolian villages and selected and took away the strongest and ablest-appearing unmarried Slavic or Albanian or Greek youths, between the ages of ten and twenty, especially those between fourteen and eighteen. Christian families naturally hated and feared the practice. Yet it did hold out to the luckiest and most intelligent unlimited opportunities for advancement. The recruits had to accept Islam, and though we know of a few cases of resistance or escape, most seem to have become good Muslims, or at least indifferent to religious matters. All then received a systematic education, perhaps a tenth of the group every year going on to higher studies, and the very cream of the crop attending the sultan's own palace school as pages in his household. Here they studied languages, Muslim and Turkish law, ethics, and theology, as well as horsemanship and military science. Each year the state increased their allowance and reviewed their progress. If a man who had not at first been selected for one of the higher schools proved unexpectedly able, he would be transferred to one.

All left school at the age of twenty-five, and the top men received posts in the imperial class. One sixteenth-century Slav graduated from the page corps as a gatekeeper, advanced to chief taster to the sultan, moved to the cavalry and became a general, then equerry, then commander of the picked infantry corps, governor of Egypt, and finally passed through the three grades of vizier, finishing his career as grand vizier, the very top officer of the state. So the devshirme recruits, all originally Christian, competed with the older Turkish aristocratic families for the honor of staffing the imperial class. A grand vizier presided over the council of state, and if the sultan trusted him might exercise great influence. If not, the sultan would depose or kill him: as a slave, the vizier was completely subject to the sultan's whim.

The "men of the sword" included all those connected with the Ottoman armies. In addition to the usual irregular troops and the garrison forces, these were the cavalrymen, or *spahis,* who predominated in the early centuries of Ottoman history. They received fiefs of land, (*timars,* or in the case of big fiefs, *ziamets*) in exchange for service, and could administer these fiefs as they wished, collecting taxes from their tenants and keeping order and justice among them. The infantrymen, at first far less important, received fixed salaries from the treasury. But with the introduction of gunpowder and the development of artillery and rifles, the Ottomans founded a special new corps to use these weapons, the *yeni cheri* (new troops, janissaries). Most of the janissaries came from the devshirme recruits who were not selected for training for the imperial class. The janissaries lived in special barracks in the capital and enjoyed special privileges. A source of strength, they also posed a constant potential danger to the state.

At the height of Turkish military successes, the sultans could put into the field formidable armies, sometimes amounting to more than a quarter of a million men on the march. They were absolutely fearless in battle and were the terror of all opponents. An ambassador from the Hapsburgs who spent eight years in Constantinople between 1554 and 1562 compares their endurance favorably with that of European troops. The Turks, he says:

> . . . take out a few spoonfuls of flour and put them into water, adding some butter, and seasoning the mess with salt and spices; these ingredients are boiled and a large bowl of gruel is thus obtained. Of this they eat once or twice a day. . . . It is the patience, self-denial, and thrift of the Turkish soldier that enable him to face the most trying circumstances and come safely out of the dangers that surround him. What a contrast to our men! Christian soldiers on a campaign refuse to put up with their ordinary food and call for thrushes, and other such like dainty dishes. . . . It makes me shudder to think what the result of a struggle between such different systems can be. . . .*

The "men of the pen" performed the other duties of government, striving to see that all land was tilled and all trade carried on as profitably as possible so that the sultan might obtain his share in taxes. Once the money came in, these officials spent it on the necessary expenses of state, including all salaries for troops and other employees. To keep an official honest and zealous, the Ottoman system often rewarded him by giving him in lieu of salary a portion of the sultan's property to exploit for himself, a kind of fief, from which he might make as much money as he could by administering it. Sometimes he had to turn in a portion of his proceeds as revenue to the sultan, and more rarely he received a salary and had to turn in all the proceeds. In the countryside every farm and village, in town every business and trade, in the government every job thus became a kind of fief. As the Ottoman system declined in the seventeenth and eighteenth centuries, the transformation of these fiefs in land or money into private possessions without obligations signalized the loss by the sultan's administration of its former power to extract wealth from all its resources.

*O. G. Busbecq, *Turkish Letters,* trans. C. T. Forster and F. H. B. Daniell (London, 1881), I, 220–221.

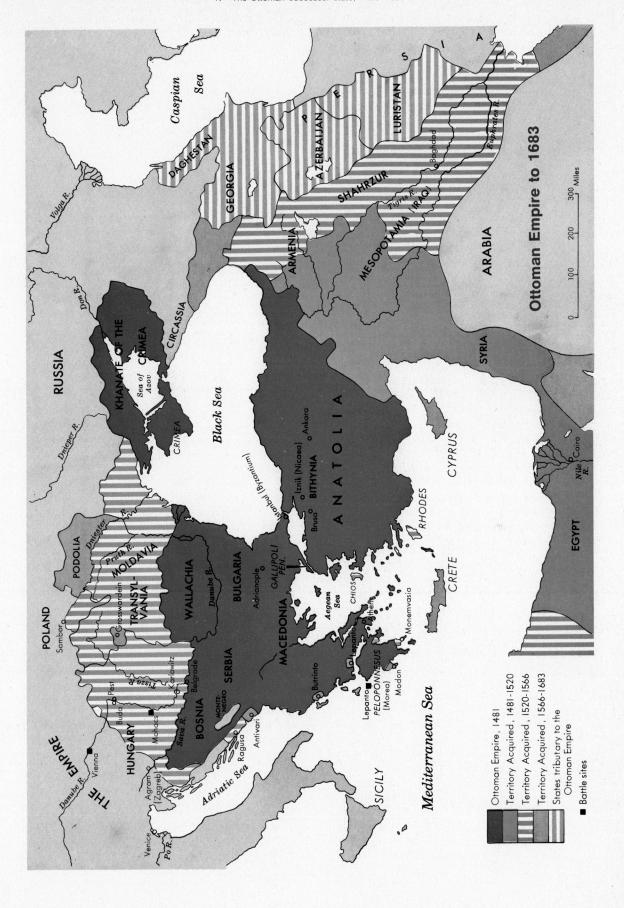

Ottoman Empire to 1683

Miles
0   100   200   300

Caspian Sea

PERSIA

DAGHESTAN

GEORGIA

AZERBAIJAN

LURISTAN

SHAHRZUR

Baghdad

Euphrates R.

ARMENIA

MESOPOTAMIA (IRAQ)

Tigris R.

ARABIA

Volga R.

RUSSIA

Don R.

CIRCASSIA

KHANATE OF THE CRIMEA

Sea of Azov

CRIMEA

Black Sea

Dnieper R.

POLAND

Dniester R.

Prut R.

PODOLIA

MOLDAVIA

TRANSYL-VANIA

Groswardein

Sambor

THE EMPIRE

HUNGARY

Vienna

Danube R.

Buda

Pest

Tisza R.

Karlowitz

Belgrade

Mohacs

Agram (Zagreb)

Sava R.

BOSNIA

MONTE-NEGRO

SERBIA

WALLACHIA

Danube R.

BULGARIA

Adrianople

MACEDONIA

Venice

Po R.

Adriatic Sea

Ragusa

Antivari

Burinto

Lepanto

PELOPONNESUS (Morea)

Modon

Athens

Monemvasia

GALLIPOLI PEN.

Istanbul (Byzantium)

Iznik (Nicaea)

Brusa

BITHYNIA

Ankara

ANATOLIA

Aegean Sea

CHIOS

CRETE

RHODES

CYPRUS

SICILY

Mediterranean Sea

SYRIA

EGYPT

Nile R.

Cairo

Ottoman Empire, 1481
Territory Acquired, 1481–1520
Territory Acquired, 1520–1566
Territory Acquired, 1566–1683
States tributary to the Ottoman Empire
■ Battle sites

Mosque of the emperor Suleiman the Magnificent, Istanbul, sixteenth century.

The "sages" (*ulema*) included all those connected with religion: the judges who applied Muslim law in the courts, the teachers in the schools, and the scholars of the Koran and the holy law (*Shariya*), the *muftis*.

The muftis, or jurists, answered questions that arose in the course of lawsuits and that were submitted to them by the judges. It was their function to apply the sacred law of Islam, and they usually gave short replies, without explanation. These replies settled the case. The grand mufti in Istanbul, whom the sultan himself consulted, was known as the *Sheikh-ul-Islam*, the ancient or elder of Islam, and outranked everybody but the grand vizier. Since he could speak the final word on the sacred law, he may even be said to have exercised a kind of check on the absolute power of the sultan himself. He alone could proclaim the beginning of war, or denounce a sultan for transgression of the sacred law, and summon his subjects to depose him. The opinions of the muftis were collected as a body of interpretative law, lying between the changeless, age-old sacred law of Islam and the current enactments of the sultans. The general acceptance by all Muslims of the supremacy

of the sacred law and the reluctance of the muftis to accept change were two of the factors that accounted for the failure of the Ottoman system to develop with the times. There are no "reformations" in Turkish history until the twentieth century.

The effectiveness of this entire structure depended upon the character of the sultan himself. After the mid-sixteenth century, all were brought up in the stifling seclusion of the harem, with its constant quarrels and intrigues between rival concubines, and its often debilitating pleasures. After the first ten generations, the sultans mostly were weaklings, drunkards, debauchees, and men of little experience or political understanding. Harem intrigue played a great role in the state. But in its earlier centuries the Ottoman system flourished and its territories grew.

Ottoman Expansion to 1566

By the end of the 1460s most of the Balkan peninsula had been consolidated under Turkish rule, except for the tiny Slavic mountain region of Montenegro, which maintained a precarious independent existence. Thus the core of the new Ottoman state was Asia Minor and the Balkans, the same core around which the Byzantine Empire had been built. From this core before the death of Muhammad II in 1481, the Turks expanded across the Danube into modern Romania, seized the Genoese outposts in the Crimea, and made this southern Russian region a vassal state under its Tatar rulers. They also fought against the Venetians, and even landed forces in Italy. The limits of their expansion were marked by the great Hungarian fortress of Belgrade, key to a farther advance into central Europe, and the island fortress of Rhodes in the Mediterranean, stronghold of the Hospitalers and key to a farther naval advance westward.

Sultan Selim I (1512–1520) nearly doubled the territories of the empire, but almost exclusively in Asia, at the expense of the Persians, and in Africa, where Egypt was annexed in 1517 and the rule of the Mamluks ended. From them the sultan inherited the duty of protecting Mecca and Medina. He also assumed the title of caliph, with the sacred insignia of office. It is doubtful whether this alone greatly enhanced his prestige, since the title had for centuries been much abused. At one moment in his reign, Selim contemplated a general massacre of all his Christian subjects. Only the refusal of the Sheikh-ul-Islam to grant his consent saved the Christians. This episode vividly illustrates the precariousness of Christian life under the Turks. It also demonstrates that the character of the Ottoman state was substantially altered by the acquisition of so much territory. It was now no longer necessary to appease the Christians by generous treatment, because the overwhelming majority of the population was Muslim. Moreover, most of the newly acquired Muslims were Arabs, more fanatical than the Ottoman Turks had hitherto been.

Suleiman the Magnificent (1520–1566), contemporary of the Western emperor Charles V and of Francis I of France and Henry VIII of England, resumed the advance into Europe. Indeed, the Ottoman Empire now became deeply involved in western European affairs. It participated in the dynastic wars between the imperial house of Hapsburg and the French Valois, and affected the course of the Protestant Reformation in Germany by the threat of military invasion from the southeast. The newly consolidated national monarchies of the West had begun to outclass the old European enemies of the Turks, the Venetians and the Hungarians. Charles V had inherited Spain and now had to face the naval attacks of the Ottoman fleets. His younger brother, Ferdinand, as ruler of the Austrian and later the Hungarian territories, bore the brunt of the Turkish attacks on land. Cheering the Turks on were the French. Even though their king was the eldest son of the Church, their wars against the Hapsburgs came first.

In 1521 Suleiman took Belgrade, and in 1522

The emperor Charles V shown victorious over Suleiman in a sixteenth-century painting ascribed to Cornelius Cornelisz.

Rhodes, thus removing the two chief obstacles to westward advance. In 1526, at Mohács in Hungary, he defeated the Christian armies, and the Turks entered Buda, the Hungarian capital on the middle Danube. In September 1529 Suleiman besieged Vienna itself, posing a threat to Christendom greater than any since Leo III and Charles Martel had defeated the advance guard of the Arabs in the early eighth century. But the Turkish lines of communication were greatly overextended; Suleiman had to abandon the siege after two weeks. Finally, in 1533, Ferdinand recognized Suleiman as overlord of Hungary. In the years that followed, Suleiman made good his claim to actual control over the south-central portion of Hungary, and added other lands north and east of the Danube. In North Africa he acquired Algeria, which remained an Ottoman vassal state in the western Mediterranean until the nineteenth century. In Asia he defeated the Persians, annexed modern Iraq, including Baghdad itself, and secured an outlet on the Persian Gulf. He even fought naval wars against the Portuguese in the Persian Gulf and the Indian Ocean.

In 1536 a formal treaty was concluded between France and the Ottoman Empire, the first of the famous "capitulations." It permitted the French to buy and sell throughout the Turkish dominions on the same basis as any Turk. They could have resident consuls with civil and criminal jurisdiction over Frenchmen in Turkey. In Turkish territory, Frenchmen were to enjoy a complete religious liberty, and were also granted a protectorate over the Holy Places, the old aim of the Crusades. This was a great advance in prestige for the Roman Catholic church. The Orthodox church never accepted this settlement, and the same old dispute helped touch off the Crimean War in the nineteenth century. These "capitulations" gave the French a better position in the Ottoman Empire than that of any other European power and thus contributed to the wealth and prestige of France. They also brought the Turks into the diplomatic world of western Europe. And they are particularly interesting as parallels to the earlier Byzantine trade treaties with Venice and Genoa, who had received virtually the same privileges beginning at the end of the eleventh century. In this respect, as in so many others, the Ottoman sultans were behaving as the successors of the Byzantine emperors.

Ottoman Decline, 1566-1699

After Suleiman, the Ottoman system, already manifesting signs of weakness, deteriorated despite occasional periods of Turkish success. The Ottoman capture of Cyprus in 1571 led to the formation of a Western league against the Turk, headed by the pope, an enterprise as near to a crusade as the sixteenth century could produce. In 1571 the league won the great naval battle of Lepanto, off the Greek coast. It destroyed the Ottoman fleet, but failed to follow up the victory, permitting the Turks to recover.

By the end of the century, the sale of government offices had become a regular practice, and the repeated rebellions of janissaries were jeopardizing the sultan's position. In 1606, a peace was signed that put an end to one of the perennial wars with the Hapsburgs. Previously, all treaties with Western states had been cast in the form of a truce granted as a divine favor from the sultan to a lesser potentate, and had been accompanied by a provision that the other party would pay tribute as part of the settlement. This time the Turks had to negotiate as equals. They gave the Hapsburg emperor his proper title, and were unable to demand tribute.

Indeed, had it not been for the convulsion of the Thirty Years' War, which preoccupied the states of western Europe (see Chapter 13), the Ottoman Empire might have suffered even more severely in the first half of the seventeenth century than it did. As it was, internal anarchy rent the state; troops rioted, and several

sultans were deposed within a few years; the Persians recaptured Baghdad; and rebellion raged in the provinces. In 1622, the British ambassador wrote to his government:

> The Empire has become, like an old body, crazed through many vices. All the territory of the Sultan is dispeopled for want of justice, or rather by reason of violent oppression: so much so that in his best parts of Greece and Anatolia a man may ride three, four, and sometimes six days, and not find a village to feed him and his horse. The revenue is so lessened that there is not wherewithal to pay the soldiers and maintain the court.*

Here we are already encountering what nineteenth-century statesmen two hundred years later were still calling the "sick man of Europe."

Yet a firm sultan, Murad IV (1623-1640), temporarily restored order through the most brutal means. Despite a temporary retrogression after his death, what looked like a real revival began with the accession to power of a distinguished family of viziers, the Köprülü. The first Köprülü ruthlessly executed thirty-six thousand people in a five-year period (1656-1661), hanged the Greek patriarch for predicting in a private letter that Christianity would defeat Islam, rebuilt the army and navy, and suppressed revolt. Between 1661 and 1676 the second Köprülü led the Ottoman navies to a triumph in Crete, which they took from Venice. The Turks temporarily won large areas of the Ukraine from the Russians and Poles, only to lose them again in 1681. In 1683 the Turks again penetrated the heart of Europe, and for the last time Vienna was besieged, with all Europe anxiously awaiting the outcome. For the second time in two centuries, the Turkish wave was broken, and now Europe began a great counteroffensive against the Turks. Although the Köprülü had galvanized the warlike Ottoman armies into a last successful effort, they did not touch and could not touch the real evils of the Ottoman system.

The End of an Era

Now the Hapsburgs drove the Turks out of Hungary, and the Venetians seized the Greek Peloponnesus. The Turks needed peace. In 1699, after an international congress at Karlovitz on the Danube, most of the gains of the European counteroffensive were recognized, including those of the Austrians, Poles, Venetians, and Russians. The Russians had appeared for the first time since the Tatar invasion on the shores of the Sea of Azov, which opens into the Black Sea. The extensive territorial losses suffered by the Turks, the strengthening of the Hapsburgs to the east, and the appearance of Russia as an important enemy of the Turks all mark

*Quoted in E. S. Creasy, *History of the Ottoman Turks* (London, 1854), I, 392-393.

this settlement as a landmark. From now on the western European powers could stop worrying about the Ottoman menace, which had preoccupied them ever since the fourteenth century, and which had replaced the Crusades as a great cause for which Christendom could occasionally be united. From now on, the importance of Turkey is no longer its military potential, but its diplomatic position as a power in decline over whose possible disintegration and division the states of Europe might squabble and negotiate. With Karlovitz, what we call the "Eastern question" may be said to have begun.

With this shift from the military offensive, which had been their only policy since their arrival in Bithynia in the thirteenth century, to a new enforced policy of defensive diplomacy, the Ottoman Turks were forced to go outside their slave-family for administrators. Nobody trained in the old way had the proper equipment to act in the new. Thus it was that during the eighteenth century the Turks were forced, against their will, to rely more and more upon Christian Greeks to fill certain high offices of state. Born negotiators with centuries of experience in commerce, and perhaps retaining the talents of their Byzantine ancestors, the Greeks now appear as the chief Ottoman diplomats. It is striking that the Turkish representative at Karlovitz should have been a Greek named Mavrogordato, from the island of Chios, who is said to have settled the disturbing question of protocol and precedence at the peace conference by inventing a round chamber with a door for each delegate, in the middle of which stood a round table. Each delegate could enter by his own door at the same moment, and sit in his own place at the round table with no question of higher and lower stations. This was a typically Greek idea, which no Turk could have had, and it may serve as a convenient symbol for the opening of a new era in administration and diplomacy.

V Russia from the Thirteenth to the End of the Seventeenth Century

With the collapse of Kievan Russia about the year 1200, Russian development entered upon a confused and difficult period of about two hundred and fifty years. During this time, even the shrewdest contemporary observer would have been hard pressed to predict the future course of Russian history, or even the likely center for a future Russian state. There were at least four main centers of Russian national life, exposed to different enemies, undergoing different internal stresses, and shaping themselves in different ways.

The Western Lands

The southwestern portion of Russian territory, including the old capital at Kiev, became a virtually inde-

pendent principality during the thirteenth century. It was distinguished by a particularly unruly nobility, which hampered all efforts of the princes to achieve consolidation in the face of the constant pressure from their Polish and Lithuanian neighbors. A parallel development occurred in the northwest portion, centering around the cities of Polotsk and Smolensk. No Russian prince after the end of the thirteenth century was able to maintain himself in the face of these pressures.

By the early fourteenth century, the grand duke of Lithuania, with his capital at Vilna, ruled nominally over most of the western Russian lands. The Lithuanians, still mostly pagan, gradually took over the language and manners of their more advanced Russian vassals. But in 1386, a celebrated dynastic marriage united Lithuania to Poland instead of to Russia. As a result, the Polish Roman Catholic church and the Polish nobility now came to the fore. Had it not been for the antagonism between Orthodox Russians and Catholic Poles, and for the conflicting interests of the nobles of different religions and languages, the original Lithuanian-Russian combination might just possibly have proved to be the center around which Russia could reunite. Yet even before the addition of the largely unassimilable Polish element, this region had become so feudal in character that its potential ability to unify Russia is extremely doubtful. Even under the grand duke of Lithuania, most of the lands nominally affiliated with his duchy were ruled without interference by local nobles bound to him only by an oath of fealty and by their obligations to render military service. A parliament of nobles also limited the political authority of the grand duke. As in the West, the economic basis of the society in the western Russian lands was manorial. We find restrictions on the movement of the peasant farmer here long before we find them elsewhere in Russia.

The North

The northern regions of Russia, between the Baltic shore and Lake Ilmen, stretching far away to the north and northeast all the way to the Arctic Ocean and nearly to the borders of Siberia, were distinguished in this period by the growth of the town commonwealth of Novgorod (Newtown). This city, spread out along the banks of the Volkhov River where it flows out of Lake Ilmen, came to rule over the vast, empty, infertile northern regions, which were explored by armed merchants and pioneers in search of furs and other products of the forests and tundra.

In Novgorod even before the collapse of Kiev there grew up a tradition of municipal independence. The town council, or *veche* (pronounced *vyé-che*), became very strong. The lifeblood of the city was its trade with the West: Russian furs, wax, honey, tar, and tallow were exchanged for German cloth and metalwork. The Germans had their own quarter in Novgorod, which they

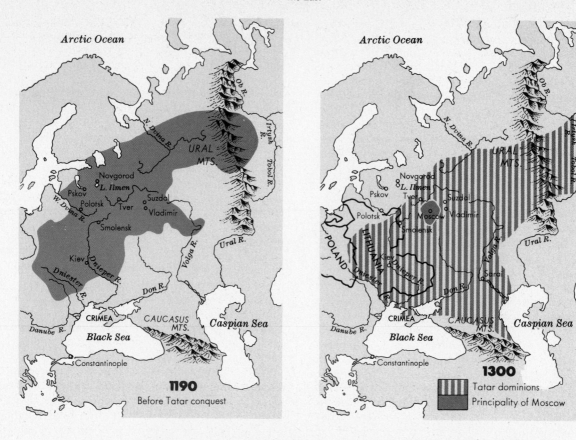

Medieval and Early Modern Russia, 1190–1689

1190
Before Tatar conquest

1300

Tatar dominions

Principality of Moscow

1505
At death of Ivan III

1689
At accession of Peter the Great

maintained for several centuries despite constant friction with the Russians. The town grew rich and strong. One might have expected this city to serve as the agent to reunify Russia, although its territory was exposed to and suffered attack by the Teutonic Knights and the Swedes.

But internally Novgorod had an extremely rigid class system. The representatives of the richer merchants came to control the veche. A few powerful families concentrated the city's wealth in their hands and disputed with each other for political power. Economic discrepancies between rich and poor grew very wide. A man who could not pay his debts would be made a slave, and slaves frequently revolted and became brigands. Because the surrounding countryside had little good soil, the city depended upon the region to the southeast, around Moscow, for its grain. Yet its rulers did not have the sense to realize that Moscow possessed this weapon against them. When in the fifteenth century the Polish-Lithuanian state and the state of Moscow were competing, the class struggle inside

Novgorod was reflected in the allegiances of the population. The upper classes favored the Poles and Lithuanians, the lower favored Moscow. In 1478 the ruler of Moscow conquered the city, took away the bell, the symbol of its independence, and wiped out the upper classes. Novgorod may be compared with Venice and with other commercial patrician oligarchies in the West. But its inability to solve its own internal problems deprived it of its chance to unify Russia.

The Northeast: Moscow and the Tatars

Thus both Western feudalism and Western urban commercial development had their counterparts on Russian soil during the period after the collapse of Kiev. But it was the principality of Moscow, northeast of Kiev, east of Smolensk, and southeast of Novgorod, that succeeded where the other regions failed. Here neither feudality nor commercial oligarchy triumphed. This was the region where the prince was strong.

At the end of the Kievan period, the region of

The thirteenth-century Kremlin at Pskov.

Moscow was still a frontier area, newly settled. Agriculturally poorer than the fertile southeast, it was richer than the north, could provide food enough for its people, and had flourishing forest industries. The cities remained small, and the pioneers turned neither to the nobility nor to the veche, since neither existed to any notable extent. Instead, they turned to the prince. This was also the region most exposed to the Tatar conquests of the thirteenth century.

By the early years of the thirteenth century, the celebrated Genghis Khan had succeeded in consolidating under his command a large number of those Mongolian nomads of central Asia who before, as Huns, Avars, and Polovtsy, had repeatedly erupted into Europe. Having conquered northern China and Asia from Manchuria to the Caspian Sea, Genghis Khan led his savage Tatars across the Caucasus and into the steppes of southern Russia, defeating Russians and Polovtsy together in 1223, but then retreating to Asia, where he died in 1227. His nephew Baty brought the Tatar hordes back again in the 1230s, sacked Moscow in 1237 and Kiev in 1240, and moved into the western Russian regions and into Poland, Hungary, and Bohemia, Everywhere the Tatars went, devastation and slaughter marked their path.

Their success seems to have been due to their excellent military organization: unified command, general staff, clever intelligence service, and deceptive battle tactics. Though Baty defeated the Poles and the Germans in 1241, political affairs in Asia drew him eastward again, and the Tatars never again appeared so far to the west. Baty retreated across Europe, and at Sarai, near the great bend of the Volga, close to modern Volgograd (formerly Stalingrad), he founded the capital of a new state. This was the Golden Horde, which accepted the overlordship of the far-off central government of the Mongols, in Peking.

Other Mongol leaders were responsible for ending the Abbasid Caliphate in 1258 and were defeated by the Mamluks in 1260. The enmity between Mongols and Muslims led the popes, Saint Louis, and other leaders of western Europe to hope that they could bring the Mongol rulers into an alliance directed against the Muslims, and so crush the opponents of Christianity between Eastern and Western enemies. The existence of various Christian sects in distant Asia lent strength to the hope that the khan himself could be converted. Considerable diplomatic correspondence was exchanged, and several embassies were sent to Mongolia and China during the thirteenth and fourteenth centuries with this end in view. But nothing ever came of all this, except a great increase in geographical knowledge derived from the extraordinarily interesting accounts of the European ambassadors, who were usually Franciscans or Dominicans. Their reports of their journeys into Asia and of their varied receptions at the court of the Mongol rulers rival any travel books ever written.

The most lasting effect on Europe of the Tatar invasions is found in Russia. Here the Tatars' main purpose was the efficient collection of tribute. Although they laid waste the territory while they were in the process of conquering it, after the conquest had been achieved they shifted to a policy of exploitation. They took a survey of available resources and assessed tribute at the limit of what the traffic would bear. It was not to their interest to disturb economic life, so long as their authority was recognized. They did draft Russian recruits for their armies, but after a while they made the local Russian princes responsible for the deliveries of men and money, and stayed out of Russian territory except occasionally to take censuses, survey property, and punish the recalcitrant. They had to confirm their tributary Russian princes, each of whom traveled to Sarai on his election to do homage. Some of them had to go all the way to China. Although no part of Russia was exempt from Tatar attacks during the period of conquest, thereafter the expensive burden of tribute and the humiliating sense of subservience fell most heavily upon the region of Moscow.

Toward the end of the fourteenth century, as the Mongol Empire itself grew feebler, the Russians became emboldened. The first Russian victories over the Tatars, scored by a prince of Moscow in 1378 and 1380, were fiercely avenged. Yet they served to show that the Tatars could be attacked and defeated. The Golden Horde did not disintegrate until the early fifteenth century, and even then the Tatars did not disappear from Russian life. Three separate khanates, or Tatar states, were formed from the debris of the Golden Horde: one at Kazan on the middle Volga, where it blocked the course of the river for another century and a half to Russian trade; one at Astrakhan at the mouth of the Volga on the Caspian; and one in the Crimea, where it later became a vassal of the Ottoman sultan.

Tatar Impact on Russian Civilization

Historians have long debated the effect upon Russia of the "Tatar yoke"; one school has recently argued that the experience was somehow beneficial, because it eventually enabled the centralizing influence of the prince of Moscow, successor of the Tatar khan, to prevail. They add that trade with Asia helped Russia. They minimize the devastation wrought by the Tatar forces, and emphasize the fact that except for an occasional punitive expedition the Russian people never saw a Tatar after the conquest itself was over.

Yet it seems sure that the Tatar conquest also had a very serious negative effect on Russia. As the great nineteenth-century Russian poet Pushkin remarked, the Tatars brought to the Russians "neither algebra nor Aristotle." By this he meant to contrast the cultural impact of the Tatars on Russia with that of the Muslims on, let us say, Spain. Rule by an alien power is sometimes tolerable if the aliens are the bearers of a higher culture. But the Tatars, despite their military efficiency, were bearers of a lower culture than the Russians of the Kievan period had already achieved.

As we have seen (Chapter 6), there was no inherent reason why Russia in the late twelfth century should not have developed as a European state with highly individual characteristics of its own. After two centuries of Tatar domination, however, it had not advanced; rather, it had gone backward. Contemporaries felt that the Tatar yoke was a calamity, and historians have yet to demonstrate convincingly that it was anything else. When the Tatar power was finally shattered in the fifteenth century, Russian civilization was far behind that of the West. To the retarding effect of Byzantine Christianity there had been added the tremendous handicap of two centuries of cultural stagnation.

The Development of the Muscovite State

During these two centuries, the princes of Moscow asserted themselves and assumed leadership. Moscow had a favorable geographical position, near the great watershed from which the Russian rivers, always the great routes for trade, flow north into the Baltic or south into the Black Sea. Thus, when the Tatar grip relaxed, and trade could begin again, Moscow was advantageously located. Moreover, Moscow was blessed with a line of remarkably able princes, not so much warriors as grasping, shrewd administrators, anxious to increase their holdings and to consolidate their own authority within the steadily expanding borders of their principality. They married into powerful families, acquired land by purchase and by foreclosing mortgages, and inherited it by will. They established the principle of seniority, so that their domain was not divided among their sons in each generation, and the tragedy of Kiev was not repeated.

Then too, they developed useful relations with their Tatar overlords. It was the princes of Moscow whom the Tatars chose to collect the tribute from other neighboring princes, and to deliver it at Sarai. Thus the princes were able to point to their success in excluding the Tatar agents from Russia, and to attract settlers to their lands. They were enabled to keep a close watch on the Tatars, so that when the moment of Tatar weakness came, it was they who could take advantage of it and marshal armies against them. They scored the first victories over the Tatars, and could truthfully claim to be the agents of liberation and the champions of Russia.

Finally, and very possibly most important, the princes of Moscow secured the support of the Russian church. In the early fourteenth century, the metropolitan archbishop transferred his see to Moscow, and made it the ecclesiastical capital of Russia. When the effective line of Muscovite princes faltered temporarily,

it was the metropolitan who administered the principality loyally and effectively until the royal house recovered. Thus the Russian church deliberately bet on Moscow, and consciously decided to throw in its lot with the Muscovite house rather than with any other. The metropolitan who first moved to Moscow is said by his biographer to have advised the prince as follows:

> If you build a church of the Virgin in Moscow, my son, and bury me in this city, so will you yourself become famous above the other princes, and also your sons and grandchildren from generation to generation. And this city will become celebrated above all the other Russian cities, and bishops will live here, and they will turn the city's forces against your enemies, and will praise God here.*

The Autocracy

By the middle of the fifteenth century, Moscow was a self-conscious Russian national state that was able to undertake successful wars against both the Polish-Lithuanian state and the Tatars. Ivan III (ruled 1462–1505) put himself forward as the heir to the princes of Kiev, and declared that he intended to regain the ancient Russian lands that had been lost to foreign Poles and Tatars—a national appeal, although a purely dynastic one. Many nobles living in the Western lands came over to him with their estates and renounced their loyalties to the Lithuanian-Polish state. In 1492, the Prince of Lithuania was forced to recognize Ivan III as sovereign of "all the Russias." This new national appeal was fortified by a religious appeal as well, for in addition to being sovereign Ivan was also the champion of Orthodoxy against the Catholic Poles and the Muslim Tatars. His wars took on the character of a purely Russian crusade. But he felt himself to be much more than a mere Russian prince.

In 1472 Ivan had married the niece of the last Byzantine emperor, Constantine XI, who had been killed fighting against the Turks on the battlements of Constantinople in 1453. Ivan adopted the Byzantine title of *autocrat*, used the Byzantine double eagle as his seal, and began to behave like a Byzantine emperor. He sometimes used the title *czar* (caesar). He no longer consulted his nobles, but reached decisions in solitude. Italian architects built him an enormous palace, the Kremlin, a building set apart, like the one at Byzantium. When the Holy Roman emperor in the 1480s decided to make an alliance with Ivan III and to arrange for a dynastic marriage, Ivan responded:

> By God's grace we have been lords in our land since the beginning of time, since the days of our earliest ancestors. God has elevated us to the same position which they held, and we beg him to grant it to us and our children.

*E. Golubinsky, *Istoriya Russkoi Tserkvi*, 2nd ed. (Moscow, 1901–1911), II, 144. Our translation.

We have never desired and do not now desire confirmation of this from any other source.*

Here is the claim to unlimited power derived directly from God that the Byzantine emperor had been accustomed to make.

When a rebellious noble fled Russia under the reign of Czar Ivan IV, the Terrible (1534–1584), he wrote the czar from abroad, denouncing him for failing to consult his nobles on important questions, as had been the custom in the days of Kievan Russia. Ivan replied that he was free to bestow favors on his slaves or inflict punishment on them as he chose. The czar thought of Russian nobles as his slaves. He scorned Queen Elizabeth I of England for living among merchants, whom she permitted to influence her. In short, from the late fifteenth century on, we find the czars calling themselves autocrats and acting like autocrats.

Part of the explanation for the immensely rapid growth of an autocratic theory and practice lies in the fact that Russia lived in a constant state of war or preparation for war. A national emergency prolonged over centuries naturally led to a kind of national dictatorship. Perhaps more significant is the fact that in Moscow's lands feudalism had not, as it had in the West, developed a united class of self-conscious nobles who would fight for the rising monarchy for their privileges. Instead of uniting against the pretensions of the monarch, the Muscovite nobility produced various factions, with which the monarch could deal individually. Moreover, the absolutism of the Tatar khans probably helped furnish a model.

But most important of all was the ideology supplied by the Church and taken over largely from Byzantium. In the West, the Church itself was a part of feudal society, and jealous of its prerogatives. In Russia, as we have seen, it became the ally of the monarchy and something like a department of state. Russian churchmen were entirely familiar with Rome's claim to world empire, and to Constantinople's centuries-long position as "new Rome." They knew many written Byzantine claims to world domination, and they were conscious of many historical legends that could be useful to them. With the fall of Constantinople (Czargrad) to the Turks, they elaborated a famous theory that Moscow was the successor to the two former world capitals:

The Church of Old Rome fell because of its heresy; the gates of the Second Rome, Constantinople, have been hewn down by the axes of the infidel Turks; but the Church of Moscow, the Church of the New Rome, shines brighter than the Sun in the whole Universe. . . . Two Romes have fallen, but the Third stands fast; a fourth there cannot be.†

*F. Adelung, *Kritisch-literarische übersicht der Reisenden in Russland* (St. Petersburg and Leipzig, 1846), I, 153. Our translation.

†Quoted in A. J. Toynbee, *Civilization on Trial* (New York, 1948), p. 171.

Russian churchmen spread the story that Rurik, the first political organizer of Russia, was descended from the brother of Augustus. They claimed that the Russian czars had inherited certain insignia and regalia not only from the Byzantines but even from the Babylonians. All the czars down to the last, in 1894, were crowned with a cap and clothed with a jacket that were actually of Byzantine manufacture, though of uncertain history. Thus the Church supplied the state with justification for its behavior. Imperial absolutism became one of the chief political features of modern Russia.

Nobles and Serfs

Between the accession of Ivan III in 1462 and the accession of Peter the Great in 1689, the autocracy succeeded in overcoming the opposition of the old nobility. This was done in part by virtually creating a new class of military-service gentry who owed everything to the czar. Their estates (*pomestie*), at first granted only for life in exchange for service, like the Byzantine pronoia, eventually became hereditary, like the western European fief. The estates of the old nobility (*vochina*), which had always been hereditary but for which they had owed no service, became service-estates, and thus like fiefs too. By the end of the period, the two types of noble and the two types of estate had by a gradual process become almost identical. The hereditary nobles often owed service. The military-service nobles often had hereditary land. Under Peter the Great (1689–1725) this process was to be completed and state service was to become universal. A central bureau in Moscow kept a census of the "service" men and of their obligations in time of war.

This tremendously important social process was accompanied by another, which is really the other side of the coin—the growth of serfdom. In a fashion familiar to us from our study of the West and of Byzantium, economic factors and political unrest in Russia had forced more and more peasants to seek out large landowners for dependence. The peasants would accept contracts that required rent in produce and service on the landlord's own land, and that involved the receipt of a money loan which had to be repaid over a period of years with interest or in the form of extra services. By the early seventeenth century it had become customary that the peasant could not leave his plot until he had paid off his debt. Since the debt was often too big for him to repay, he could in practice never leave.

The process was enormously speeded up when the czars gave estates to the new military-service gentry. An estate was not much good unless there was farm labor to work it. In periods of bitter agrarian and political crisis such as the sixteenth and seventeenth centuries, it became advisable for the government to help the service gentry to keep their farmers where they were. And, since the peasants paid most of the taxes, it was easier for the government to collect its own revenues if it kept the peasants where they were. Gradually it was made harder and harder for a tenant to leave his landlord, until by 1649 the avenues of escape were closed, and the serf was fixed to the soil. The landlord administered justice, and had police rights on the estate. He collected the serfs' taxes. He himself could sell, exchange, or give away his serfs. And the serf status became hereditary; children of serfs were enrolled on the estate's census books as serfs like their fathers.

The Russian serfs were not emancipated until 1861. Together with the absolute autocracy, the institution of serfdom is the most characteristic feature of Russian society. It affected every Russian, whether landowner, serf, or neither, for all the centuries it existed. In a very real sense, the consequences of Russian serfdom are still with us today, posing a serious problem not only for the rulers of the Soviet Union but for all the world that has to deal with them. Russian serfdom became a fixed custom far later in time than did western European serfdom. In fact, it was most widely extended during the eighteenth century, at a moment when the serfs in western Europe had long been on their way to complete liberation. This is another illustration of the fact that Russia went through many of the same processes as the West, but with greater intensity and at a later time.

A contemporary portrait of Ivan the Terrible.

The Reign of Ivan the Terrible

Most of the disorders that characterize Russian history in the sixteenth and seventeenth centuries have their origin in the long reign (1534–1584) of Ivan IV, the Terrible. Pathologically unbalanced, Ivan succeeded to the throne as a small child. He experienced helplessly the indignities inflicted on him by the various rival groups of nobles who were maneuvering and intriguing for power. Devoted to the rites of the Church, and fancying himself as a theologian, Ivan was nonetheless horribly cruel. He had perhaps as many as seven wives; he murdered his own son in a fit of lunatic rage. Soviet historians have tried to turn him into a hero by explaining that his wrath was directed against the selfish nobles who were conspiring to take over Russia. But, though the nobles were selfish enough, the danger of their intrigues was surely hugely exaggerated by the czar.

When Ivan finally was strong enough, in 1547, to assume the crown and throw off the tutelage of the boyars, he embarked upon a period (1547–1560) usually regarded as one of sound government and institutional reform. He regulated the rapacity of the imperial administrators in the provinces, who had oppressed the population. He also convoked the first *zemski sobor* (land assembly), a consultative body consisting of nobles, clerics, and representatives from the towns, to assist with the imperial business, particularly with important questions of war and peace. Though comparable in its social composition to the various assemblies of the medieval western European world, the zemski sobor under Ivan seems to have met only once, and can in no sense be regarded as a parliamentary body.

When Ivan fell ill in 1553, the nobles refused to take an oath of allegiance to his son. This action apparently reawakened all his savagery, and upon his recovery he created a fantastic new institution: the *oprichnina,* or "separate realm," to belong to him personally, while the rest of Russia continued to be administered as before. The men whom Ivan now appointed to run the oprichnina (called oprichniks), grimly dressed in black and riding black horses, bore on their saddlebows a dog's head (for vigilance) and a broom (symbolizing a clean sweep). They were the forerunners of the grim secret police forces that have long characterized Russian society. They waged a fierce, relentless war on the nobles, confiscating their estates, exiling them, killing them off. The czar, as was said, had divided his realm in two, and had set one part of it warring on the other. And in the diary of one oprichnik we find this revealing entry: "Today I did no harm to anyone: I was resting." The oprichniks took over the old estates of the men whom they were destroying. By the time of Ivan's death, many of the oprichniks themselves had been murdered at his orders, and Russian administration had degenerated to a state approximating chaos. Yet Ivan was able to extend Russian authority far to the east against the Kazan and Astrakhan Tatars, thus for the first time opening the whole Volga waterway to Russian commerce, and facilitating expansion farther east, into Siberia.

The Time of Troubles

Though the territory was wide and the imperial rule absolute, ignorance, illiteracy, and inefficiency weakened the structure of Russian society. The few foreign observers who knew the Russia of Ivan could foresee chaos ahead. And the czar himself had his own dire forebodings: "The body is exhausted, the spirit is ailing, the spiritual and physical wounds multiply, and there is no doctor to cure me," * he wrote in his last will. Though the old nobility had been dealt a series of blows, the new gentry had as yet no sense of corporate entity and therefore was not firmly in control of the machinery. Ivan's son and heir, Fëdor (1584–1598), was an imbecile, and with his death in 1598 the Moscow dynasty, descended from the rulers of the former Kievan state, died out. The cliques of rival nobles intrigued for power. Fëdor's brother-in-law, Boris Godunov, emerged as the dominant figure in the state.

Though Boris Godunov was probably a man of talent, he could not overcome his handicaps: Ivan's legacy of disorder, the intrigues of the nobility, and the famine and plague that began in 1601. Bands of brigands roamed the countryside, and when in 1603 a pretender arose under the protection of the king of Poland and declared that he was a son of Ivan the Terrible—who had in fact died long before—he was able to capture the support of many of the discontented. Russia was launched on the decade known as the Time of Troubles (1603–1613).

After Boris Godunov's death (1605), the pretender ruled briefly as czar. But within a year he was murdered, and was succeeded by a certain Shuiski, a representative of the ancient aristocracy. But new pretenders arose; the mobs of peasants and brigands were rallied once again; civil war continued, as Poles and Swedes intervened. Shuiski fell in 1610, and was succeeded by no one czar but by a small group of nobles who planned that the heir to the Polish throne would become czar of Russia.

Polish forces took over in Moscow, and it soon appeared that the king of Poland intended not to turn over the power to his son but to reign in Russia himself. It was this specter of a foreign and Catholic domination that aroused the national sentiments of the Russians. In answer to a summons from the patriarch, there assembled a kind of national militia, drawn largely from the prosperous free farmers of the middle Volga region, organized by a butcher named Kuzma Minin, and led by a nobleman named Dmitri Pozharski. These two are the national heroes of the Time of Troubles. Under their command the militia won the support of other rebellious elements and drove the Poles from Moscow in 1613.

The Role of the Zemski Sobor

A zemski sobor now elected Czar Michael Romanov. From the election of Michael in 1613 to the Russian Revolution of 1917, the Romanov dynasty held the throne. Michael succeeded with no limitations placed upon his power by the zemski sobor or by any other body; he was that curious anomaly, an elected autocrat. For the first ten years of the reign of Michael Romanov, the zemski sobor stayed in continual session. Since it had picked the new czar in the midst of crisis, it had indeed performed a constitutional function. It even included some representatives of the free peasantry. It assisted the uncertain new dynasty to get under way by endorsing the policies of the czar and his advisers, and thus lending them the semblance of popular support. One might have supposed that this would be the beginning of a new kind of partnership, and that, as had sometimes happened in the West, representatives of the various social classes would gain more and more political self-confidence and power, and might even transform the zemski sobor from a consultative to some sort of legislative assembly, a parliament.

But this was not to be. After 1623, the zemski sobor was summoned only to help declare war or make peace, to approve new taxation, and to sanction important new legislation. It endorsed the accession of Michael's son Alexis (ruled 1645–1676), and in 1649 confirmed the issuance of a new law code, summarizing and putting in order past statutes. After 1653 Alexis did not summon it again, nor did his son and successor, Fëdor (ruled 1676–1682). Its last meetings were in 1682.

No law abolished the zemski sobor. None had created it. The dynasty was entrenched and no longer needed it. Czardom, autocratic czardom, was taken for granted. No czar needed to consult with any of his subjects unless he felt the need to do so. No subject had the right to insist on being consulted, though all subjects had the duty to give advice when asked for it. As the Romanovs became entrenched, they no longer felt the need to consult anybody's wishes except their own and those of their court favorites.

Individually, the early Romanovs were neither distinguished nor talented. The central government consisted of a number of bureaus or ministries or departments (*prikazy*), often with ill-defined or overlapping areas of competence. Provincial governors continued to milk the long-suffering population, and local efforts at self-government were in practice limited to

*Quoted in M. T. Florinsky, *Russia: A History and an Interpretation* (New York, 1953), I, 208.

the choice of officials obliged to collect and hand over taxes to the central authorities. Opposition to the system there certainly was, but it came not from articulate or literate citizens offering criticism or suggestions for improvement. It came from below, from the oppressed and hungry peasantry. And it expressed itself in the only form of action the serf knew: large-scale or small-scale revolt, the burning of the manor house, the slaughter of the landlord or the tax collector, the ill-directed march about in the vast flat countryside. Such affairs were a matter of yearly occurrence, the largest and most famous being that of Stenka Razin (1676), the "Russian Robin Hood." Such uprisings were almost never directed against the czar but against the landlords and officials, of whose misdeeds the czar was supposed not to know. Often indeed the peasant leaders would arouse their followers *in the name* of the czar. Sometimes, as during the Time of Troubles, the leaders pretended to be czars in order to obtain more followers.

The Role of the Church

The Church remained the partner of the autocracy. The czar controlled the election of the Metropolitan of Moscow, and after 1589 he controlled the election of the newly proclaimed patriarch of Moscow, a rank to which the Metropolitan was elevated. In the seventeenth century there were two striking instances when a patriarch actually shared power with the czar. In 1619 the father of Czar Michael Romanov, Filaret, who had become a monk, became patriarch and was granted the additional title of "great sovereign." He assisted his son in all the affairs of state. In the next generation Czar Alexis (ruled 1645–1676) appointed a cleric named Nikon to the patriarchal throne and gave him the same title and duties. Nikon proved so arrogant that he aroused protests from clergy as well as laity. He also seriously put forth the theory that the authority of the patriarch in spiritual affairs exceeded that of the czar, and that, since the spiritual realm was superior to the temporal, the patriarch was actually superior to the czar. This was a claim parallel to the one that was regularly made in the West by the more powerful popes but that was almost never advanced in Byzantium or in Russia. In 1666 a Church council deposed Nikon, who died a mere monk. These two experiments with two-man government (dyarchy, it was called, in contrast with monarchy) were never repeated, and they are interesting because they are the exceptions that prove the rule in Russia: the Church depends upon the state. Peter the Great was to abolish the patriarchate largely because he did not wish Nikon's claims ever to be repeated.

As in the Byzantine Empire, so in Russia, monasteries became immensely rich. By 1500 it is estimated that they owned more than a third of the land available for cultivation. Opposition to monastic worldliness arose within the Church itself, and one might have supposed that the government would have supported this movement. But those who favored monastic poverty also wished to enforce the noninterference of the state in monastic affairs. To preserve their right to control the monasteries in other respects, the government of the czar was obliged to oppose this reforming movement with respect to monastic property.

The Church, almost alone, inspired the literature and art of the Muscovite period. History was written by monks, in the form of chronicles. Travel literature took the form of accounts of pilgrimages to the Holy Land, although we have one secular travel book, a report by a Novgorod merchant who went to India on business. A handbook of etiquette and domestic economy, called *Household Management,* advises how to run a home and how to behave in company, revealing a conservative, well-ordered, solid, and smug society. Theological tracts attack the Catholics, and also the Protestants, whose doctrines were known in the western regions. This literature is limited, and it was still dominated by the Church several centuries after the West had made the break. Almost all of it was written in Old Church Slavonic, the language of the liturgy and not the language of everyday speech. Though stately and impressive, Old Church Slavonic was not an appropriate vehicle for new ideas. There was no secular learning, no science, no flowering of vernacular literature, no lively debate on the philosophical level in the field of theology.

The Expansion of Russia

The sixteenth and seventeenth centuries saw the tremendous physical expansion of the Russian domain. Russian pioneers, in search of furs to sell and new land to settle, led the way, and the government followed. Frontiersmen in Russia were known as Cossacks (*kazakh* is a Tatar word meaning "free adventurer"). It is a common error to suppose that they were somehow racially different from the mass of Russians. They were not; they were simply Russians living on the frontiers, organizing themselves for self-defense against the Tatars as our American pioneers did against the Indians. The Cossack communities gradually grew more settled, and two Cossack republics, one on the Dnieper, the other on the Don, were set up. These republics lived in a kind of primitive democracy relatively independent of Moscow; they fought Tatars and Turks quite at their own free will. As time passed, more Cossack groups formed in the Volga, in the Urals, and elsewhere.

The expansion movement took the Russians eastward into the Urals and on across Siberia—one of the most dramatic chapters in the expansion of Europe. Far more slowly, because of Tatar, Turkish, and Polish opposition, the Russians also moved southeast toward the Caucasus and south toward the Black Sea. Repeated wars were fought with Poland over the old west-Russian territory of the Ukraine. Sometimes the Cossacks favored the Poles, and sometimes the Russians. But by 1682 the Poles were weakening, and were soon to yield. On the European frontiers it was the Swedes, still blocking the Baltic exit, against whom Russia's future wars would be fought. The struggle with the Tatars of the Crimea, whose lands extended far north of the peninsula, was also a constant feature. The Ottoman Turks, overlords of the Tatars, held the key fort of Azov, controlled the Black Sea, participated in the wars over the Ukraine, and now for the first time became perennial enemies of the czars.

Russia and the West

A final development of these two centuries was to prove of the utmost importance for the future Russia. This was the slow and gradual penetration of foreigners and foreign ideas, a process warmly welcomed by some Russians, deeply deplored by others, and viewed in a rather mingled light by still others, who prized the technical and mechanical learning they could derive from the West but feared Western influence on Russian society and manners. This ambivalent attitude toward Westerners and Western ideas became characteristic of later Russians: they loved what the West could give, but they often feared and even hated the giver.

St. Basil's Cathedral, Red Square, Moscow, built 1554–1560.

The first foreigners to come were the Italians, who helped build the Kremlin at the end of the fifteenth century. But they were not encouraged to teach Russians their knowledge, and failed to influence even the court of Ivan III in any significant way. The English, who arrived in the mid-sixteenth century as traders to the White Sea, were welcomed by Ivan the Terrible, who had tried to attract German and other artisans, but who had been blocked by Swedish control of the Baltic shore. He gave the English valuable privileges and encouraged them to trade their woolen cloth for Russian timber and rope, pitch, and other naval supplies. These helped build the great Elizabethan fleets that sailed the seas and defeated the Spanish Armada. The English were the first foreigners to penetrate Russia in any numbers and the first to teach Russians Western industrial techniques. They got along well with the Russians and supplied a large number of officers to the czar's armies, mostly Scotsmen. Toward the middle of the seventeenth century, the Dutch were able to displace the English as the most important foreign group engaged in commerce and manufacturing. The Dutch had their own glass, paper, and textile plants in Russia.

After the accession of Michael Romanov in 1613, the foreign quarter of Moscow, always called "the German suburb," grew rapidly. Foreign technicians of all sorts—textile weavers, bronze founders, clockmakers—received enormous salaries from the state. Foreign merchants sold their goods, much to the distaste of the native Russians, who begged the czars to prevent the foreigners from stealing the bread out of their mouths. Foreign physicians and druggists became fashionable, though always suspected by the superstitious common people of being wizards. By the end of the seventeenth century, Western influence is apparent in the life of the court. The first play in Russia was performed in 1672, and although it was a solemn biblical drama about Esther, it was at least a play. A few nobles began to buy books and form libraries, to learn Latin and French and German. People were eating salad and taking snuff, and shyly beginning to try their skills at some of the social arts, such as conversation. A few Russians went abroad to travel, and, of these few, all who could refused to go back.

The people, meanwhile, distrusted and hated the foreigners, looted their houses when they dared, and jeered at them in the street. As one intelligent writer of the seventeenth century put it:

> Acceptance of foreigners is a plague. They live by the sweat and tears of the Russians. The foreigners are like bear-keepers who put rings in our noses and lead us around. They are Gods, we fools, they dwell with us as lords. Our Kings are their servants.

The most dramatic outbreak of anti-foreign feeling took place, as might have been expected, in the field of religion. Highly educated clerics from the western lands (the Ukraine) and Greek scholars recommended to Patriarch Nikon that the Holy Books be revised and corrected in certain places where the texts were not sound. Resentment against this reform took the form of a great schism in the Russian church itself. Given the deep Russian regard for the externals, the rite, the magic, rather than for the substance of the faith, we must not be surprised at the horror that was aroused when the Russians were told that for centuries they had been spelling the name of Jesus incorrectly and had been crossing themselves with the wrong number of fingers. As at Byzantium, the religious protest reflected a deep-seated hatred of change, particularly change proposed by foreigners. Declaring that the end of the world was at hand (since Moscow, the Third Rome, had now itself become heretical), about twenty thousand of the schismatics shut themselves up in their huts and burned themselves alive. When the world did not end, those schismatics who survived, always known as the Old Believers, settled down and became sober, solid Russian citizens, many of them merchants and well-to-do peasants. Some later governments persecuted them; most did not. But, whatever the policies of the state might be toward them, the Russian church itself was weakened as a result of the schism.

Peter the Great is usually thought of as the initiator of westernization for Russia. But before he had ever come to the throne, Russian society had been profoundly split at its heart, the Church, by the influx of foreigners and foreign ways during the sixteenth and seventeenth centuries.

VI Conclusion

In this complex chapter we have handled as a unit events whose relationship is not often recognized by historians. Yet is has seemed to us that their true significance is comprehensible only if some of the more conventional dividing lines are disregarded. We have seen how, beginning in the last quarter of the eleventh century, the medieval West undertook a prolonged onslaught against the Muslim and Orthodox East. The crusades against Islam, the Norman and Hohenstaufen attacks on Byzantium, the ambitions of the Italian cities, the Western distaste for the schism between the churches—all came together in the attack on Constantinople in 1204 and in the collapse of the Byzantine Empire, already deeply penetrated by the West. Yet the Crusader states founded on Syrian and Greek soil proved ephemeral. In Syria the Muslims had put an end to them by the close of the thirteenth century. In the Byzantine world, though the empire was reestablished in 1261, the future lay with the Osmanli Turks, whose long slow rise to supremacy forms the central theme of the later Middle Ages in the southeast. Dominating the old Byzantine and Islamic worlds down to the end of the seventeenth century, the Ottoman empire was the successor-state to both. Meanwhile, Orthodox Russia—forced by the Tatar invasion to remain medieval long after the western European world had emerged into a new period—took its character from Moscow, the Third Rome, and in its way proved itself also the heir of the Byzantine heritage. In dealing with the East, we perceive the fundamental continuities only by disregarding the conventional periods that are useful for the West: long after the West had emerged from the Middle Ages—in fact, down to the end of the seventeenth century—the Ottoman Empire and Russia were still medieval.

Reading Suggestions on the East in the Late Middle Ages

(See also the listings for Chapter 6).

General Accounts

A History of the Crusades, Vol. I: *The First Hundred Years,* ed. M. W. Baldwin; Vol. II: *The Later Crusades, 1189–1311,* ed. R. L. Wolff and H. W. Hazard (2nd ed., K. M. Setton, general ed., Univ. of Wisconsin, 1969). Collaborative work with authoritative contributions by many scholars; good bibliographies.

S. Runciman, *A History of the Crusades,* 3 vols. (Cambridge Univ., 1951–1954). The fullest treatment of the subject by a single scholar.

E. S. Creasy, *History of the Ottoman Turks,* 2 vols. (1854–1856), new ed., intro. Z. Zeine (Beirut Khayats, 1961). Despite its age, still the only good general account in English based on a ten-volume German work.

Special Studies

J. L. LaMonte, *Feudal Monarchy in the Latin Kingdom of Jerusalem* (Mediaevel Academy, 1932). A study of the institutions of the Crusader states in the Levant.

Joshua Prawer, *The Crusaders' Kingdom* (Praeger, 1972). A fine study of the Crusader states as European colonies.

W. Miller, *The Latins in the Levant: A History of Frankish Greece (1204–1566)* (John Murray, 1908) and *Essays on the Latin Orient* (Cambridge Univ., 1921). Now somewhat dated.

C. M. Brand, *Byzantium Confronts the West, 1180–1204* (Harvard Univ., 1968). Scholarly study of the diplomacy of an important period.

J. W. Barker, *Manuel II Palaeologus, 1391–1425* (Rutgers Univ., 1969). Good monograph on a late Byzantine emperor.

A. S. Atiya, *The Crusade in the Later Middle Ages* (Methuen, 1938). A study of the propaganda and the expeditions that marked the decline of the crusading movement.

E. Pears, *The Destruction of the Greek Empire and the Story of the Capture of Constantinople by the Turks* (Longmans, 1903). A solid work not superseded by more recent studies.

H. A. Gibbons, *The Foundation of the Ottoman Empire* (Century, 1916). An older work whose conclusions are again finding favor.

P. Wittek, *The Rise of the Ottoman Empire* (Royal Asiatic Society, 1938). A suggestive essay on the elements that helped to advance the Ottoman state.

A. H. Lybyer, *The Government of the Ottoman Empire in the Time of Suleiman the Magnificent* (Harvard Univ., 1913). A pioneering work on Ottoman institutions, now out of date in some details.

H. A. R. Gibb and H. Bowen, *Islamic Society and the West,* Vol. I, Parts 1 and 2 (Oxford Univ., 1950, 1956). The most authoritative survey of Ottoman institutions.

C. Cahen, *Pre-Ottoman Turkey* (Sidgwick & Jackson, 1968). The only recent work in English on the subject; by the leading authority on the period before 1330.

S. Vryonis, *The Decline of Medieval Hellenism in Asia Minor and the Process of Islamization from the Eleventh through the Fifteenth Century* (Univ. of California, 1971). The title well describes the subject of this massive, recent, scholarly study.

N. Itzkowitz, *Ottoman Empire and Islamic Tradition* (*Knopf). Excellent brief introduction covering the period to the end of the eighteenth century.

H. Inalcik, *The Ottoman Empire: The Classical Age, 1300–1600* (Weidenfeld & Nicolson, 1973). Recent monograph by a distinguished Turkish scholar, disappointingly lacking in interpretation.

B. Miller, *Beyond the Sublime Porte* (Yale Univ., 1931), and *The Palace School of Mohammed the Conqueror* (Harvard Univ., 1941). Studies of the Ottoman imperial palace and the Ottoman educational system, respectively.

D. M. Vaughan, *Europe and the Turk: A Pattern of Alliances, 1350–1700* (Liverpool Univ., 1954). Role of the Ottoman Empire in European diplomacy.

G. Vernadsky, *The Mongols and Russia* (Yale Univ., 1953). Volume III of the Yale History of Russia.

J. L. I. Fennell, *Ivan the Great of Moscow* (Macmillan, 1961). Valuable monograph.

Sources

Anna Comnena, *The Alexiad,* trans. E. A. S. Dawes (Kegan Paul Trench, Trübner, 1928). The life and reign of Emperor Alexius Comnenus (1081–1118), by his daughter.

Fulcher of Chartres, *Chronicle of the First Crusade,* trans. M. E. McGinty (Univ. of Pennsylvania, 1941).

An Arab-Syrian Gentleman and Warrior in the Period of the Crusades: Memoirs of Usamah ibn-Munqidh, trans. P. K. Hitti (Columbia Univ., 1929).

William, Archbishop of Tyre, *A History of Deeds Done beyond the Sea,* trans. E. A. Babcock and A. C. Krey, 2 vols. (Columbia Univ., 1943). The greatest of the contemporary accounts of the Crusaders' Levant.

Memoirs of the Crusades, including Villehardouin's chronicle of the Fourth Crusade and Joinville's of the Crusade of Saint Louis, trans.

F. T. Marzials (*Dutton). Eyewitness accounts by prominent participants.

Robert of Clari, *The Conquest of Constantinople,* trans. E. H. McNeal (Columbia Univ., 1936). Eyewitness account by a humble participant in the events of 1204.

P. W. Topping, *Feudal Institutions as Revealed in the Assizes of Romania, The Law Code of Frankish Greece* (Univ. of Pennsylvania, 1949).

Kritovulos, *History of Mehmed the Conqueror,* trans. C. T. Riggs (Princeton Univ., 1954). A Greek life of Muhammad the Conqueror.

The Life and Letters of Ogier Ghiselin de Busbecq, ed. C. T. Forster and F. H. Blackburne Daniell, 2 vols. (C. K. Paul, 1881). Perceptive and amusing reports of a Hapsburg ambassador to Suleiman the Magnificent.

The Correspondence between Prince A. M. Kurbsky and Tsar Ivan IV of Russia, 1564–1579, ed. and trans. J. L. I. Fennell (Cambridge Univ., 1955), and *Kurbsky's History of Ivan IV,* ed. and trans. J. L. I. Fennell (Cambridge Univ., 1965). Hitherto regarded as fundamental sources for the political theories of the czar and his noble opponents. The most recent scholarship casts grave doubt on their authenticity. See E. L. Keenan, *The Kurbskii-Groznyi Apocrypha* (Harvard Univ., 1971).

G. Fletcher, *Of the Russe Commonwealth,* ed. R. Pipes and J. Fine (Harvard Univ., 1966). A splendid traveler's account of 1591, reproduced in its original form with a good introduction.

The West

I Introduction:
The Passage from Medieval to Modern

In eastern Europe, as the last chapter showed, medieval institutions continued to flourish long after the Turks captured Byzantium in 1453, the date often cited as the turning point from medieval to modern. Indeed, in Russia the Middle Ages ended comparatively recently, with the emancipation of the serfs in 1861. In western Europe, by contrast, the Middle Ages really did come to an end about five centuries ago. No one year or one event can be singled out; rather, a series of crucial developments took place over the span of half a century in the later 1400s and early 1500s—the consolidation of royal authority in the national monarchies of France, England, and Spain; the discovery of America; the virtual disappearance of serfdom in the West; and the revolt of Martin Luther against the medieval church. This chapter surveys the political, economic, and social forces that destroyed feudal and manorial society. Succeeding chapters examine the famous twin movements of the Renaissance and the Reformation that disrupted the Christian cultural synthesis and the religious unity of the Middle Ages.

During the fourteenth and fifteenth centuries old forms and attitudes persisted in Western politics but, in a manner characteristic of an era of decline, became more rigid and less flexible, more sterile and less creative. Political leaders sometimes acted as though they were living centuries earlier: the Holy Roman emperor Henry VII in the early 1300s sought to straighten out the affairs of Italy in the old Ghibelline tradition, even though he had few of the resources that had been at the command of Frederick Barbarossa a century and a quarter before. The nobles of France and England, exploiting the confusion of the Hundred Years' War, built again the private armies and the great castles of the feudal heyday and attempted to transfer power back from the monarch to themselves. Their movement has been called "bastard feudalism," for service in these neofeudal armies hinged upon money, not upon the genuinely feudal elements of personal loyalty and mutual respect and guarantees.

Manifestations like these have been interpreted as symptoms of senility, a hardening of the arteries of the body politic, and so in some senses they were. But they may also be viewed as expedients or experiments in the adjustment of old institutions to new demands. The nobles who practiced bastard feudalism were not only taking selfish advantage of a prolonged war but also putting soldiers in the field at a time when neither the French nor the English monarchy could sustain a military effort decade after decade. The importance of the monetary factor—the soldier hired for money, the ex-serf paying rent in money, the banker earning his livelihood handling money—was characteristic of the passage from medieval to modern.

By the close of the fifteenth century it was evident that the future lay not with neofeudal lords but with the so-called new monarchs, who had little interest in reviving faded glories and were very much committed to what we know as power politics. While politics and power had always gone hand in hand, what distinguished the "new" monarchs from their predecessors was the candor and the professionalism of their operations. They made no bones about the pursuit of power naked and unadorned with medieval trappings; and they were served by better instruments of government, better soldiers, diplomats, and bureaucrats. Outstanding representatives of the new professionalism were Louis XI of France, Henry VII of England, and Ferdinand and Isabella of Spain, all of them monarchs of developing national states. On a local or regional scale, the princes of the various German states and the despots of the Italian city-states also often exemplified the new businesslike political behavior.

Meanwhile, the economy and society of western

Europe had been undergoing even more strain and upheaval than its political institutions had experienced. In the countryside the traditional patterns of manorialism, serfdom, and payment in kind coexisted with new patterns of a free peasantry producing for the cash market and paying rents and taxes in cash. The economy and society showed some of the same symptoms of rigidity and senility affecting political life. Former serfs, for example, who thought they were now legally free peasants, often found that a lord could still oblige them to use his bake oven or flour mill or wine press and pay a stiff fee for the privilege. They also found that they could no longer turn to a lord for protection in time of trouble. The uncertainty and insecurity of a world no longer wholly medieval nor yet wholly modern underlay the numerous outbreaks of agrarian violence in the fourteenth century, such as the French Jacquerie or the English Peasants' Revolt. Crises also convulsed urban life in the 1300s. Civil war broke out in the prosperous woolen-manufacturing towns of Flanders, and chronic strife developed between the wealthy and poorer classes in another woolen center, Florence, where the rigid old institution was the guild and the unsettling new element was the aggressive entrepreneur.

Two social traumas particularly undermined the morale and resiliency of fourteenth-century Europe. The first was the great famine of 1315–1317, probably caused by the conjunction of a protracted spell of bad weather and the gradual termination of the long medieval process of clearing forests and draining marshes for new farmland. With Europe unable to grow enough grain to supply its population with bread, then the mainstay of the diet, starvation was widespread. For example, about 10 percent of the inhabitants of the Flemish town of Ypres died in one six-month period. The second and greater trauma was the Black Death of 1347–1350, which is estimated to have killed between one-third and one-half of the European population. This ghastly epidemic apparently marked the first appearance in Europe of bubonic plague, introduced by ships coming from the Near East. A major social consequence of the plague was a severe shortage of labor, which depressed the economy for several decades and emboldened the peasants and workers who had survived the epidemic to press for greater rights, usually with only transient success.

II The Emerging National Monarchies

At the death of Philip the Fair in 1314 the Capetian monarchy of France appeared well on the way to evolving into the kind of new professional institution manned by efficient and loyal bureaucrats described above. Philip Augustus, Louis IX, and Philip the Fair had all consolidated the royal power at the expense of their feudal vassals, who included the kings of England. Soon, however, France became embroiled in a pro-

tracted conflict with England—the Hundred Years' War, 1337–1453—that crippled the monarchy for more than a century.

The Outbreak of the Hundred Years' War

The nominal cause of the war was a dispute over the succession to the French throne. For more than three hundred years, ever since Hugh Capet had been succeeded by his son, son had followed father as king of France. This remarkable streak of good fortune ended with the three sons of Philip the Fair, who ruled in turn between 1314 and 1328 and none of whom fathered a son who survived infancy. The crown then passed to Philip of Valois, Philip VI (1328–1350), a nephew of Philip the Fair and the first cousin of his sons. But the king of England, Edward III (1327–1377), whose mother Isabella had been a daughter of Philip the Fair, challenged the Valois succession, claiming that as the nephew of the last Capetian kings he had a better right to succeed than their first cousin, Philip of Valois. To settle the question, French lawyers went all the way back to the Frankish Salic law of the sixth century, which said that a woman could not inherit land. Although the Salic law had not applied in France for centuries, the lawyers now interpreted it to mean that a woman could not transmit the inheritance to the kingdom. This legal quibble was to serve Edward III as pretext for beginning the Hundred Years' War.

Edward's claim to the French throne was not the only reason for the outbreak of war. England's continued possession of the rich duchy of Aquitaine, with its lucrative vineyards and its prosperous wine-shipping port of Bordeaux, was an anomaly in an increasingly unified France. As suzerains over Aquitaine, the kings of France encroached upon the feudal rights of the kings of England; the English, for their part, wished not only to keep what they had, but to regain Normandy and the other territories they had lost to Philip Augustus.

The most pressing issue arose farther north, in Flanders. This small but wealthy area, which today straddles the frontier between Belgium and France, was ruled in medieval times by the count of Flanders, a vassal of the king of France. The thriving Flemish cloth manufacturers bought most of their wool from England and sold much of their finished cloth there; the English crown collected taxes both on the exported wool and on the imported woolens. Inside Flanders, the artisans and tradesmen of the towns were in almost constant conflict with the rich commercial ruling class. The rich sought the backing of their lord, the count of Flanders, and he in turn sought that of his overlord, the king of France; the workers got the help of the English, who feared the disruption of their lucrative trade. Warlike incidents multiplied during the early fourteenth century, culminating in a victorious invasion of Flanders by French armies. Edward III thereupon allied himself with a Flemish merchant, Jacob van Artevelde, who expelled both the ruling Flemish oligarchy and the French, and organized his own government of Flanders. It was in response to pressure from these Flemish allies that Edward III put forth his claim as king of France and precipitated war in 1337.

The war dominated the history of France for a troubled century. The Valois kings, with the notable exception of Charles V, the Wise (1364–1380), were far less effective rulers than the Capetians had been. The English won the main battles and gained by treaty huge amounts of French territory. France was racked by the Black Death and swept by social crisis and civil war. Yet the English were overextended, and the French ultimately drove them out and completed the unification of their country under a strong national monarchy. Necessity obliged the Valois kings to develop a standing army, finance it from a system of direct taxation, and enlist the support of the middle classes, on whose assistance, indeed, the whole accomplishment depended.

The first major operation of the war was an English naval victory at Sluys (1340), which gave the English command of the Channel for many years. When their Flemish ally, Van Artevelde, was killed in 1345, the English invaded northern France and gained a great victory at Crécy in 1346. Despite inferior numbers, the English profited by the incompetent generalship of the French and by their own successful—and very unfeudal—experiments in relying upon large numbers of infantrymen, armed with the longbow. From higher ground English archers poured arrows down on a confused crowd of mounted French knights and of mercenaries armed with the crossbow, a cumbersome weapon rather like a giant slingshot. Next the English took Calais, which gave them a port in France. When open warfare was resumed after the Black Death, the English not only defeated the French again, at Poitiers in western France (1356), but also captured the French king, John (1350–1364), and carried him off to a luxurious captivity in England. John's son, Charles, the future King Charles the Wise, became regent for his father in France.

The Estates General and Charles the Wise

In these years the French monarchy faced increasingly hostile criticism at home, focused in the central representative assembly. This assembly was the Estates General, to which the three estates or social classes of the realm—the clergy, the first estate; the nobles, the second; and the commoners, the third—sent deputies. Since the French word *état* means state as well as estate, older books often call the assembly the States General (*Etat* and the English *status, standing, state,* and *estate* are all derived from the Latin verb *stare,* to stand). When summoned in 1355 to consent to a tax, the Estates General insisted on fixing its form—a general levy on sales and a special levy on salt—and demanded also that their representatives rather than those of the Crown act as collectors. Moreover, the Estates for the first time scheduled future meetings "to discuss the state of the realm." After the defeat at Poitiers, they demanded that the regent, Charles, dismiss and punish the royal advisers and substitute for them twenty-eight delegates chosen from the Estates. When Charles hesitated, the leader of the Estates, the Paris merchant Etienne Marcel, led a general strike and revolution in the capital, the first of many in French history, and forced the regent to consent.

But this was as far as the success of the Estates went. Marcel made two cardinal mistakes. He allied himself with a rival claimant to the throne, and he assisted a violent peasant revolt, the Jacquerie (so called from the popular name for a peasant, Jacques Bonhomme—James Goodfellow). Already harrowed by the Black Death, the peasants endured fresh suffering from bands of soldiers living off the land, and from demands for more taxes and also for money to pay the ransom of nobles taken prisoner along with King John. In desperation they rose up in 1358, without a specific program or effective leadership, murdering nobles and burning châteaux. The royal forces, in disarray though they were, put down and massacred the peasants (the death toll has been estimated at twenty thousand). The outcome of the Jacquerie showed that, put to the test, the country failed to support the more radical Parisians—this, too, was to be a familiar pattern in later French history. In the final flare-up, Marcel was killed, and Charles won his struggle.

Manuscript illumination shows victims of the Black Death being buried in mass graves at Tournai, Belgium, in 1349.

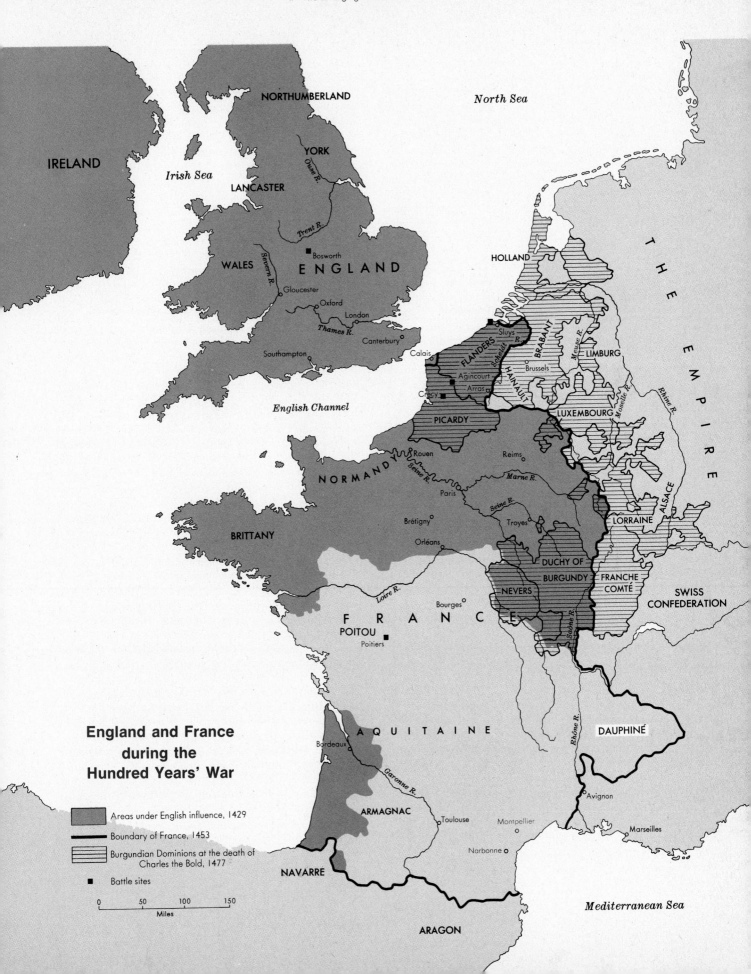

England and France during the Hundred Years' War

Areas under English influence, 1429

Boundary of France, 1453

Burgundian Dominions at the death of Charles the Bold, 1477

■ Battle sites

0   50   100   150

Miles

Although the Estates had in effect run France for two years (1356 and 1357), they had imposed no principle of constitutional limitation upon the king. With the country in chronic danger of invasion, even rebellious Frenchmen wished to meet the emergency by strengthening rather than weakening their monarchy. They were willing to criticize its methods but not to limit them. Moreover, the opponents of the Crown—clergy, nobles, townsmen—came from all three estates and mistrusted one another because of conflicting class interests; even members of a single estate were divided by the differing interests of the provinces from which they came. Charles the Wise was quick to exploit the advantages that these class and local antagonisms gave the Crown. As early as 1358 the reasons were clear why the Estates General would never become in France what Parliament was in England.

In 1360 the Hundred Years' War entered another pause when by treaty Edward III renounced his claim to the French crown in exchange for all southwestern France and lands bordering the Channel near Calais. When the war was resumed in 1369, the French made impressive gains under Charles the Wise and his capable middle-class advisers. By his death in 1380, they had driven the English from French soil except for a string of seaports, including Bordeaux and Calais. For the first time since the beginning of the war, the French fleet was able to sail freely in the Channel and raid the English coasts. At home, Charles kept the upper hand over the Estates General, securing their agreement that existing taxes would be made permanent and not require further approval by the Estates.

Burgundians and Armagnacs

Instead of initiating a period of reconstruction and recuperation, the successes of Charles the Wise were the prelude to a period of still worse suffering. The new king, Charles VI (1380–1422), was a feeble ruler who became insane. During his reign the monarchy was threatened by the disastrous results of the earlier royal policy of assigning provinces called *apanages* to a king's younger sons. Such a son might himself be loyal, but within a generation or two his heirs would be remote enough from the royal family to become its rivals. It was essentially this pattern that had ruined the Carolingians. In 1363, King John revived the practice and opened the door to bastard feudalism by making the important duchy of Burgundy the apanage of his youngest son, Philip. Charles the Wise compounded the danger by giving the duchy of Orléans as an apanage to his younger son, Louis.

During the reign of Charles VI the two dukes, who were the king's uncle and brother, respectively, engaged in a bitter rivalry for influence and power, which was continued by their successors in the duchies. In 1407 John, who followed his father, Philip, as Duke of Bur-

gundy, arranged the assassination of Louis, Duke of Orléans. All France was now torn by the factional struggle between the Burgundians and the Orléanists, who were called Armagnacs after their leader, Count Bernard of Armagnac, the father-in-law of the new Duke of Orléans. The Armagnacs commanded the loyalty of much of southern and southwestern France, while the Burgundians controlled the north and east. The Armagnacs were strongest among the great nobles, and were professedly anti-English; the Burgundians, whose duke had inherited Flanders and had thus become immensely rich, were pro-English, and had the support of the upper bourgeoisie in the towns. The English king Henry V (1413–1422) reopened the war in alliance with the Burgundians and won the battle of Agincourt (1415), where the heavily armored French knights were mired in the mud. The Burgundians took over in Paris, massacring partisans of the Armagnacs, whose faction fled south of the Loire to set up a rival regime. When the English took the capital of Normandy, Rouen (1419), the alarmed Burgundians tried to patch up a truce with the Armagnacs, but John, the duke of Burgundy, was assassinated to avenge the murder of the duke of Orléans a dozen years earlier.

Next, the unstable Charles VI declared his own son, the dauphin, to be illegitimate (the title of dauphin and the right to hold the province of Dauphiné, in southeastern France, were reserved for the eldest son of the king). By the Treaty of Troyes (1420), Charles adopted Henry V of England as his heir and made him his regent during his lifetime. Henry married Charles' daughter and was allowed to retain the conquests he had made north of the Loire until he should inherit all of France on the death of Charles. This fantastic settlement, which threatened to extinguish French national sovereignty, was supported by the Burgundians, the Estates General, and the University of Paris. Had Henry V lived, it is possible that the entire future of France might have been changed. But in 1422 both Charles VI and Henry V died, the English crown passed to the infant Henry VI, and England, too, was torn with faction and was not able to supply enough troops to hold down conquered northern France.

In France, the dauphin, excluded from Paris by the Burgundians, ruled at Bourges in central France as King Charles VII (1422–1461) with Armagnac support. When the regent for Henry VI of England prepared to move south against Charles, the miracle of Joan of Arc saved France. The demoralized forces of Charles VII were inspired by the visionary peasant girl from Lorraine who reflected the deep patriotism of the French at a moment when all seemed lost. The story is well known: how saints and angels told Joan that she must bring the pitiful Charles VII to be crowned at Reims, traditional coronation place for the kings of France; how she was armed and given a small detachment that drove the English out of Orléans on the north bank of the Loire; how the king was crowned, Joan taken prisoner by the Burgundians, sold to the English, turned over to the French Inquisition, and burned at Rouen (1431). The papacy itself undid the verdict against her in 1456 and made her a saint in 1919.

Against heavy odds the French monarchy managed to sustain the impetus provided by the martyred Joan. In 1435, Charles VII and Burgundy concluded a separate peace that made it impossible for the English to win the war. While Charles now recovered Paris, for ten years the countryside was ravaged by bands of soldiers known as *écorcheurs* ("flayers"), a term indicating vividly their mode of treating the peasantry. Moreover, leagues of nobles, supported by the new dauphin, the future Louis XI, revolted in 1440. Fortunately for the Crown, the Estates General in 1439 granted the king the permanent right to enjoy two essential nonfeudal resources—to keep a standing army, and to levy the *taille* (from a French word meaning "cut"), a tax paid directly by individuals and collected by royal agents.

With these instruments ready to his hand, with additional financial aid from the great merchant prince Jacques Coeur, and with assistance from professional experts, Charles VII embarked on reforms that at last supplanted the inadequate military arrangements of the Middle Ages. Twenty companies of specialized cavalry were organized, 1,200 to a company, under commanders of the king's personal choice. These companies, which supplanted the contingents of écorcheurs, were assigned to garrison the towns. Professionals supervised the introduction of artillery, which became the best in Europe. The new French force drove the English out of Normandy and Aquitaine (1449–1451) so that Calais alone in France remained in English hands when the Hundred Years' War finally ended in 1453. The standing army, based on direct taxation that had been granted by the Estates as a royal right, had enabled France to overcome the English threat.

Meantime, Charles had scored against another institution that might have weakened the Crown. In 1438, he regulated church-state relations by the Pragmatic Sanction of Bourges (the term refers to a solemn royal pronouncement), which laid down the policy known as Gallicanism, claiming for the Gallican, or French, church a virtually autonomous position within the Church Universal. It greatly limited papal control over ecclesiastical appointments and revenues in France and asserted the superiority of church councils over popes.

The Burgundian Threat and King Louis XI

Against one set of enemies, however, Charles VII was not successful—his rebellious vassals, many of them beneficiaries of the new bastard feudalism, who still controlled nearly half of the kingdom. The most powerful of these vassals was the duke of Burgundy, Philip the Good (1419–1467), whose authority reached far beyond the duchy of Burgundy in eastern France and the adjoining Franche-Comté (Free County of Burgundy— still technically part of the Holy Roman Empire) and extended to Flanders and other major portions of the Low Countries. This sprawling Burgundian realm almost deserved to be called an emerging national state. But it was a divided state. The two main territorial blocs in eastern France and the Low Countries were separated by the non-Burgundian lands of Alsace and Lorraine. And it was a personal state, for Duke Philip had assembled it as much by good luck as by good management, inheriting some lands and acquiring others by conquest or negotiation. Yet it was also a menacing state, which might have interposed itself permanently as a middle kingdom between France and Germany. Philip had defied Charles VII by allying with the English in the Hundred Years' War and behaved in general as though he were a monarch of the first magnitude. The wealth of the Flemish and Dutch towns enabled him to maintain the most lavish court in Europe, and his resources at least equaled those of his feudal overlords, the king of France and the Holy Roman emperor.

The decisive trial of strength between France and Burgundy took place under the successors of Charles VII and Philip the Good—King Louis XI (1461–1483) and Duke Charles the Bold (1467–1477). Although the new French king had repeatedly intrigued against his

Charles VII of France presiding over the Court of Parlement, 1458: a painting attributed to Jean Fouquet.

father while he was dauphin, he now pursued energetically the policies that Charles VII had initiated. At his accession Louis was already a crafty and practiced politician, who despised the pageantry of kingship, liked a simple tavern meal better than elaborate royal fare, and preferred secret diplomacy to open war. One of his aides, Philippe de Commynes (or Comines, 1447–1511), drew a notable portrait of him:

> Amongst all those I have ever known, the most skillful at extricating himself out of a disagreeable predicament in time of adversity was King Louis XI . . . , the most humble person in terms of speech and manner and the prince who worked more than any other to gain to his cause any man who could serve him or who could be in a position to harm him. And he was not discouraged if a man he was trying to win over at first refused to cooperate, but he continued his persuasion by promising him many things and actually giving him money and dignities which he knew the other coveted. . . .
>
> He was naturally a friend to those of middle rank and an enemy of all the powerful lords who could do without him. No man ever gave ear to people to such an extent or inquired about so many matters as he did, or wished to make the acquaintance of so many persons. For indeed he knew everyone in a position of authority and of worthy character who lived in England, Spain, Portugal, Italy, in the territories of the Duke of Burgundy, and in Brittany, as well as he knew his own subjects. These methods and manners . . . saved the crown for him, in view of the enemies he had acquired for himself at the time of his accession to the throne.*

Louis returned to the strong monarchical tradition of Philip Augustus and Philip the Fair. He forced his protesting subjects to pay higher taxes but gave men of the middle class responsible posts in his administration. He propitiated the pope by withdrawing the Pragmatic Sanction of 1438 but in practice continued most of its restrictions on papal control over the Gallican church. He enlarged the army bequeathed him by his father yet conserved its use for the direst emergencies only.

Where Louis XI was cautious, Charles the Bold was audacious to the point of folly. His temperament and policies were nicely assessed by Commynes, who had served Charles before he shifted his allegiance to Louis:

> I have not seen any reason why he should have incurred the wrath of God, unless it was because he considered all the graces and honors which he had received in this world to have been the result of his own judgment and valor, instead of attributing them to God, as he should have. For indeed he was endowed with many good qualities and virtues. No prince ever surpassed him in eagerness to act as patron to great men. . . . No lord ever granted audi-

*Samuel Kinser, ed., *The Memoirs of Philippe de Commynes,* trans. Isabelle Cazeaux (Columbia, S. C., 1969), 1:130–131. Reprinted by permission of the University of South Carolina Press.

ence more freely to his servants and his subjects. . . . He was very ostentatious in his dress and in everything else—a little too much. He was very courteous to ambassadors and foreigners; they were well received and lavishly entertained. . . . He desired great glory, and it was that more than anything else which made him engage in these wars.*

Charles determined to build a true middle kingdom by bridging the gap between Burgundy and the Low Countries and seizing Lorraine and Alsace. Since Alsace was a confused patchwork of feudal jurisdictions overlapping northern Switzerland, his designs threatened the largely independent Swiss confederation. Subsidized by Louis XI, the Swiss defeated Charles three times in 1476 and 1477; in the last of the battles Charles was slain.

Since Charles left no son, his lands were partitioned. The Duchy of Burgundy passed permanently, and the Franche-Comté temporarily, to France. The Low Countries went to Mary, the daughter of Charles, who married Maximilian of Hapsburg, later Holy Roman emperor. Their son was to marry the daughter of Ferdinand and Isabella of Spain, and their grandson, the emperor Charles V, was to rule Germany, the Low Countries, and Spain, and to threaten France with hostile encirclement.

Though Louis XI did not keep all the Burgundian inheritance out of the hands of potential enemies, he shattered the prospect of a middle kingdom. He broke the strength of the Armagnac faction as well, recovered most of the territory held as apanages and doubled the size of the royal domain. At his death, French bastard feudalism was virtually eliminated. The only major region still largely independent of the Crown was the Duchy of Brittany, and this passed to royal control during the reign of his son. The France of Louis XI was not yet a full-fledged national monarchy, but by his consolidation of territory and by his competent central administration, Louis laid the foundations for a proud, cohesive, confident nation in subsequent centuries.

England: Edward II and Edward III

England, too, was emerging as a national monarchy. Here too, social and political dissension had accompanied the Hundred Years' War, and bastard feudalism flourished until Edward IV and Henry VII reasserted the royal power in the later fifteenth century, much as their contemporary, Louis XI, did in France. But, however close the parallels between the two countries, there was also an all-important difference. Whereas in France the Estates General was becoming the docile servant of the monarchy, the English Parliament was slowly setting the precedents and acquiring the powers that would one day make it the master of the Crown.

*Ibid., 1:135.

In England, after the death of the strong and successful Edward I in 1307, the political tide turned abruptly against the monarchy. His son, Edward II (1307–1327), was a weak and inept ruler, dominated by his favorites and by his French queen, Isabella. In 1314 he lost the battle of Bannockburn to the Scots, and with it the short-lived English hegemony over Scotland. Meantime, Edward II faced baronial opposition much like that which had harassed his grandfather, Henry III. In the Ordinances of 1311, the barons set up as the real rulers of England twenty-one "lords ordainers" who had to consent to royal appointments and to declarations of war. Like the barons of Henry III, the barons of Edward II were as selfish as the king's bureaucrats had been, and Parliament repealed the ordinances in 1322. Noble malcontents then gathered around Queen Isabella, who led a revolt against her husband. Imprisoned, then murdered, Edward II was succeeded on the throne by his fifteen-year-old son, Edward III, a knightly and vigorous figure.

The reign of Edward III (1327–1377) was marked by the stunning English victories in the early campaigns of the Hundred Years' War and by the great economic crisis following the Black Death. The plague created a terrible shortage of manpower; crops rotted in the fields for lack of harvesters, and good land dropped out of cultivation. Agricultural laborers of England, aware of their suddenly increased bargaining power, and of the wealth gained by their masters from the French war, demanded better working conditions, or left home and flocked to the towns. In 1351, Parliament passed the Statute of Laborers, forbidding workmen to give up their jobs and attempting to fix wages and prices as they had been before the plague. The law was not a success, and the labor shortage hastened the end of serfdom and paved the way for the disorders that took place under Edward's successor. The cause of the peasants was defended most effectively in a striking verse satire of Edward's reign called *The Vision Concerning Piers Plowman,* which denounced the corruption of officials and of the clergy.

The attempts to enforce the Statute of Laborers were made by the justices of the peace, a notable English institution first appearing under Edward III. The justices were all royal appointees, selected in each shire from the gentry, who were substantial landholders and accustomed to exercising local leadership. Since they received no pay, they accepted office from a sense of duty or from a fondness for prestige. As the old shire and hundred courts disappeared, the justices of the peace became the chief local magistrates and the virtual rulers of rural England almost to our own day.

The reign of Edward III also witnessed the growth of English national feeling, fostered by the long war with France. The fact that the popes now resided at Avignon and were thought to be under the thumb of the French made the papacy a particular target of nationalist suspicion. In 1351, Parliament passed the Statute of Provisors restricting the provision (that is, the appointment) of aliens to church offices in England. Two years later, Parliament checked the appeal of legal cases to the papal curia by the Statute of Praemunire (the Latin term refers to the prosecution of a legal case). Meantime, increased use of the English language reflected the developing sense of national identity. In 1362, Parliament declared English the official language of the courts, although the Norman French of the old ruling classes persisted in some legal documents. As the years passed, English was taught in the schools and in 1399 was used to open Parliament.

Nationalism, the dislike of the papacy, and the widespread social and economic discontent were all involved in England's first real heresy, which was preached during the last years of Edward's reign by John Wycliffe (or Wiclif), an Oxford scholar who died in 1384. Advocating a church without property, in the spirit of the early Christians, Wycliffe called for the direct access of the individual to God without the priest as intermediary and for the weakening of many other priestly functions. He denied that in the Mass the bread was miraculously transubstantiated into the body of Christ. He and his followers were also responsible for an English translation of the Bible, despite the Church's insistence that the Scriptures should be read only in the Latin of the Vulgate and not in the vernacular.

The most significant constitutional development of Edward III's long reign was the evolution of Parliament. The division of Parliament into two houses was beginning to appear in the fourteenth century, although the terms "House of Commons" and "House of Lords" were not actually used until later. Edward I's Model Parliament of 1295 had included representatives of the lower clergy as well as the higher clergy, barons, knights of the shire, and burgesses. While the lower clergy soon dropped out, preferring to limit their attendance to the assembly of the English church known as Convocation, all the other groups present in 1295 continued to appear. The higher clergy, the lords spiritual, who also attended Convocation, had to come to Parliament as vassals of the king. In time, the lords spiritual coalesced with the earls and barons, the lords temporal, to form the nascent House of Lords; the knights of the shire and the burgesses coalesced to form the nascent House of Commons.

The gradual coalescence of knights and burgesses was an event of capital significance—an event that laid the social foundation of the future greatness of the House of Commons. It brought together two elements, the one representing the gentry, the lower level of the second estate, and the other representing the third estate, which always remained separate in the assemblies of the continental monarchies. Little is known about the precise reasons for this momentous development. We do know that in the fourteenth century the knights of the shire had little sense of social unity with the burgesses and they felt closer to the great lords, with whom they had many ties of blood and common interests. But we also know that some of the smaller boroughs were represented by knights from the countryside nearby. By the end of the fourteenth century, the important office of Speaker of the House was developing, as the Commons chose one of their members to report to the king on their deliberations. The parliamentary coalition of knights and burgesses evidently came into existence well before their sense of social closeness.

Meantime, the political foundations of the future greatness of the House of Commons were also being laid. In the fourteenth century the chief business of Parliament was judicial. From time to time, the knights and burgesses employed the judicial device of presenting petitions to the king; whatever was approved in the petitions was then embodied in statutes. This was the faint beginning of parliamentary legislative power. The growth of parliamentary power was further stimulated by Edward III's constant requests to Parliament for new grants of money to cover the heavy expenses of the Hundred Years' War. More and more, Parliament took control of the purse strings, while Edward, who had little interest in domestic affairs other than finances, let the royal powers be whittled away imperceptibly. Significantly, the responses to the major economic and nationalistic grievances of the mid-fourteenth century took a parliamentary form—the Statutes of Laborers, Provisors, and Praemunire.

Richard II and Bastard Feudalism

When Edward III died, his ten-year-old grandson succeeded as Richard II (1377–1399). Richard's reign was marked by mounting factionalism on the part of royal relatives and their noble followers and by an outbreak of peasant discontent. Both conflicts strongly resembled their French counterparts, the strife between Burgundy and Armagnac, and the Jacquerie of 1358.

The social disorders arose out of protests against the imposition of poll (head) taxes, which fell equally upon all subjects; the poorer classes bitterly resented paying their shilling a head for each person over fifteen. Riots provoked by attempts to collect the tax led to the Peasants' Revolt of 1381. The peasants burned manor records to destroy evidence of their obligations, murdered the archbishop of Canterbury, and demanded the ending of serfdom and the seizing of clerical wealth—a program that showed the widespread influence of Wycliffe's teaching. When they marched on London, the fifteen-year-old king promised to settle their grievances and saved his own life by offering to lead the peasants himself. But Richard failed to keep his promises and permitted severe reprisals against the rebels; indeed, king and Parliament would have restored serfdom had it been economically possible.

Under Richard II and his successors, factional strife assumed critical dimensions as a result of the new bastard feudalism. During the fourteenth century the baronage had become a smaller and richer class of great magnates, whose relationship to their vassals grew to be based more on cash and less on military service and protection. These great lords recruited the armed following they still owed to the king, not by bringing into his increasingly professional army their tenants duly equipped as knights, but by hiring little private armies to go to war for them. Soldiers in these armies, while often members of the country gentry, were bound not by the old feudal ties but by "written indenture and a retaining fee." The custom was known as "livery and maintenance," since the lord provided uniforms for his retainers, who, in turn, "maintained" the lord's cause, especially in legal disputes. Though forbidden by statute in 1390, this practice continued to flourish. The danger from private armies became greater during each interlude of peace in the war with France, as mercenaries used to plundering in a foreign country were suddenly turned loose in England.

The trouble had begun during the last years of Edward III, when effective control of the government passed from the aging king to one of his younger sons, John of Gaunt, duke of Lancaster, and his corrupt entourage. John of Gaunt could mobilize a private army of fifteen hundred men, and his faction persisted after the accession of Richard II; and new factions also appeared, centered on two of the king's uncles, the dukes of York and Gloucester. After defeating Richard II's supporters in battle, Gloucester had royal ministers condemned for treason in a packed Parliament (1388), which was called either "wonderful" or "merciless," depending on one's factional ties. The baronage put its own people onto royal administrative commissions and seemed to control the Crown. Richard II waited a few years and then in 1397 arrested Gloucester and moved against his confederates. The king packed Parliament in his own favor, had it pass retroactive laws against treason, and also imposed heavy fiscal exactions on his subjects. Richard's confiscation of the estates of his first cousin, Henry of Bolingbroke, son of John of Gaunt, precipitated a revolution. Its success rested not so much on the popularity of the exiled Bolingbroke as on the great alarm created by Richard's doctrine that the king could control the lives and property of his subjects. After Bolingbroke's landing in England, Richard was defeated, was forced to abdicate in 1399, and was later murdered; Bolingbroke became Henry IV (1399–1413), first monarch of the House of Lancaster.

Lancaster and York

To recover from the upheavals of Richard II's reign and to check the growth of bastard feudalism, England badly needed a long period of stable royal rule. But

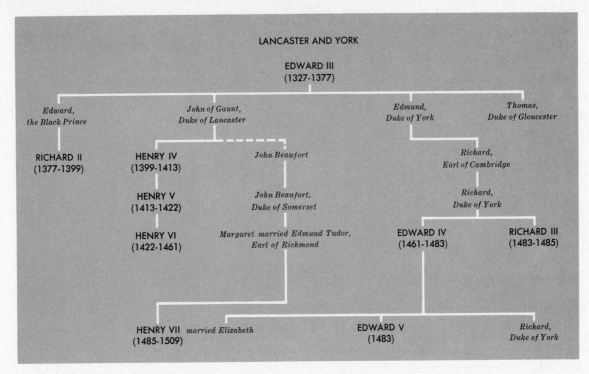

LANCASTER AND YORK

EDWARD III
(1327-1377)

Edward,
the Black Prince

John of Gaunt,
Duke of Lancaster

Edmund,
Duke of York

Thomas,
Duke of Gloucester

RICHARD II
(1377-1399)

HENRY IV
(1399-1413)

John Beaufort

Richard,
Earl of Cambridge

HENRY V
(1413-1422)

John Beaufort,
Duke of Somerset

Richard,
Duke of York

HENRY VI
(1422-1461)

Margaret married Edmund Tudor,
Earl of Richmond

EDWARD IV
(1461-1483)

RICHARD III
(1483-1485)

HENRY VII married Elizabeth
(1485-1509)

EDWARD V
(1483)

Richard,
Duke of York

this the Lancastrian dynasty was unable to provide. Henry IV owed his position in part to confirmation by Parliament, and Parliament in turn, mindful of its experience with Richard II, was very sensitive about allowing any assertion of the royal authority. Moreover, Henry faced a whole series of revolts—by dispossessed supporters of Richard, by the Welsh aristocracy, and by the great family of the Percies in Northumberland, on the Scottish border. The last years of his reign were troubled by his own poor health and by the hostility of his son, the "Prince Hal" made famous by Shakespeare. The son came to the throne as King Henry V (1413–1422), who renewed the Hundred Years' War with spectacular victories and embarked at home on a course of royal assertiveness, tempered by his need to secure parliamentary support in financing his French campaigns. He also persecuted vigorously the followers of Wycliffe in an attempt to suppress the social and religious discontent evidenced in the Peasants' Revolt.

The untimely death of Henry V in 1422 ended the brief period of Lancastrian success, for it brought to the throne Henry VI (1422–1461), an infant nine months old, who proved mentally unstable as he grew up. The reign of this third Lancastrian king was a disaster for England. Her forces went down to defeat in the last campaigns of the Hundred Years' War, and, while the feebleness of Henry VI did strengthen the hand of Parliament, it strengthened still more the power of bastard feudalism. As corrupt noble factions competed for control of government, a quarrel broke out between Henry VI's queen, Margaret of Anjou, and

her English allies on the one side, and, on the other, Richard, duke of York, a great-grandson of Edward III and heir to the throne. The quarrel led directly to the Wars of the Roses (1455–1485), named for the red rose, the badge of the House of Lancaster, and the white rose, the badge of the House of York.

In thirty years of sporadic fighting, Parliament became the tool of rival factions, and the kingdom itself changed hands repeatedly. In 1460 Richard of York was killed, and the ambitious Earl of Warwick, the "kingmaker," took over the leadership of the Yorkist cause. Warwick forced the abdication of Henry VI and placed on the throne the son of Richard of York, Edward IV (1461–1483). The king and the kingmaker soon fell out, and Warwick briefly restored Henry VI to the throne (1470–1471). Edward IV quickly regained control, and Henry VI and Warwick were killed. With Edward securely established, firm royal government returned to England, seemingly on a permanent basis.

Again, however, the prospect of stability faded, for Edward IV died in 1483 at the threshold of middle age. The crown passed momentarily to his twelve-year-old son, Edward V, who was soon pushed aside by his guardian and uncle, brother of the older Edward, Richard III (1483–1485), last of the Yorkist kings. Able, courageous, and ruthless, Richard III may not have been quite the villainous figure indelibly imprinted on history by Shakespeare's play. There is still controversy over whether he was responsible for the death of the "little princes of the Tower"—Edward V and his younger brother. In any case, factional strife flared up again as Richard's opponents found a champion in the Lancastrian leader, Henry Tudor. In 1485, on Bosworth Field, Richard III was slain, and the Wars of the Roses at last came to an end. The battle gave England a new monarch, Henry VII, and a new dynasty, the Tudors.

Henry VII

Henry VII (1485–1509) was descended from a bastard branch of the Lancastrian family (his great-grandfather was the illegitimate son of John of Gaunt). His right to be king, however, derived not from this tenuous hereditary claim but from his victory at Bosworth and subsequent acceptance by Parliament. The new monarch had excellent qualifications for the job of tidying up after the dissipations of civil war. Shrewd, able, working very closely with his councillors, waging foreign policy by diplomacy and not by war, Henry VII had a good deal in common with Louis XI of France. Unlike Louis, however, Henry was devout and he was generous, maintaining a lavish court and endowing at Westminster Abbey the magnificent chapel, in the elaborate late Gothic style, that bears his name.

Henry formally healed the breach between the houses of the rival roses by marrying the Yorkist heiress Elizabeth, daughter of Edward IV. When some of the magnates supported Perkin Warbeck, an imposter who claimed to be Elizabeth's brother, the younger of the "little princes of the Tower," Henry dealt very firmly with the rebels. He deprived the nobles of their private armies by forbidding livery and maintenance, and also banned the nobles' interference in the royal courts to intimidate litigants. While measures like these had been tried by Henry's predecessors and had ultimately failed for lack of enforcement, Henry enforced his policies so vigorously that he has sometimes been nicknamed "the

A silver groat, ca. 1500, with a likeness of King Henry VII.

Big Policeman." In 1487 a parliamentary statute charged a special committee of the king's council with the task of seeing that the apparatus of the law should not be used to back up factional interests or juridical abuses. The new committee became the administrative court known as the Star Chamber, from the star-painted ceiling of the room in which it met. While its operations were sometimes arbitrary, it had no direct connection with the later court of the same name, under the seventeenth-century Stuart kings, which made the term *star chamber proceedings* synonymous with abuse of judicial authority. In fact Henry VII abandoned the experiment with the Star Chamber after a few years and relied on the ordinary courts, particularly those of the justices of the peace.

While Henry depended heavily on the country gentry and other traditional mainstays of monarchical government, he also welcomed new men, from the prosperous urban merchant class or from the ranks of churchmen who had worked their way up and owed their careers to him, like the able lawyer Morton, who became archbishop of Canterbury. Henry rewarded many of his advisers with lands confiscated from his opponents at the end of the Wars of the Roses. Also, the king and his councillors more than doubled the revenues of the central government, partly by using such high-handed methods as "Morton's Fork," attributed (probably unfairly) to Archbishop Morton. When prelates were summoned to make special payments to the king, those who dressed magnificently in order to plead exemption on the grounds of the cost of high ecclesiastical office were told that their rich apparel argued their ability to make a large payment. The other tine of the fork caught those who dressed shabbily to feign poverty, for their frugality argued that they, too, could afford a large contribution. These practices enabled Henry to avoid a clash with Parliament, because he seldom needed taxes requiring its sanction. The king's obvious efficiency, his avoidance of costly wars, and his assistance to English merchants in gaining trading privileges abroad won him support in the increasingly significant business community.

Henry VII reestablished prosperity as well as law and order in an England weary of rebellion and civil war. His policies set the stage for the more dramatic reigns of his successors, Henry VIII and Elizabeth I. He restored the prestige of the monarchy, made it the rallying point of English nationalism, and fixed the pattern for the Tudor policy toward Parliament, a policy often given the misleading label of "Tudor absolutism." While Henry VII and his successors were indeed strong monarchs, they were not absolute in the sense that they attempted to trample over Parliament or to ignore it. Henry, as we have just seen, asked Parliament for money as infrequently as possible; during the last dozen years of his reign he had to summon only one Parliament, which met for a few weeks in

1504. Even so, when it refused to give him all the monies he wanted, he yielded gracefully and avoided a confrontation. Henry VII was well aware that precedents for limiting a monarch's authority lay at hand ready for use against an arbitrary ruler.

Spain

The accomplishments of Henry VII and Louis XI, impressive though they were, were overshadowed by those of their Spanish contemporaries, Ferdinand and Isabella. Henry and Louis ruled kingdoms that, however racked by internal dissensions, had long been well-defined states with established central institutions. Ferdinand and Isabella inherited a Spain that had never really been united; they had to build the structure of central government from the very foundations.

The decisive event in the early medieval history of the Iberian peninsula was the conquest by the Muslims, who brought almost the whole of the peninsula under their control. In the eighth and ninth centuries, Christian communities free of Muslim domination survived only in the extreme north—the Carolingian march of Catalonia and the tiny states of Galicia, the Asturias, León, and Navarre. From the ninth century through the fifteenth, the Christian states of the north pressed southward until the last Muslim stronghold at Granada fell in 1492. This slow expansion by Catholic Spaniards has often been likened to a crusade more than five hundred years long. It was indeed a crusade, and the proud and militant spirit of the crusader left a permanent mark upon the Spanish "style." The reconquest of Spain, however, like the great Crusades to the Holy Land, was a disjointed movement, undertaken in fits and starts by rival states that sometimes put more energy into combating each other than into fighting the Muslim.

Three Christian kingdoms dominated the Iberian peninsula in the middle of the fifteenth century. Castile,

the largest and most populous, occupying the center of the peninsula, had originated as a frontier province of León and had assumed the leadership of the reconquest. The capture of Toledo in central Spain (1085) and the great victory over the Muslims at Las Navas de Tolosa (1212) were landmarks in its expansion southward. But the power of the Castilian kings did not grow in proportion to their territory. The powerful organization of sheep-ranchers, the *Mesta*, controlled vast stretches of Castilian territory and constituted a virtual state within the state. Both the nobility and the towns, which played a semi-independent part in the reconquest, maintained many rights against the royal authority. Both were represented, together with the clergy, in the Cortes, the medieval Castilian counterpart of the English Parliament and the French Estates General, which had become largely powerless by the fifteenth century.

To the west of Castile, along the Atlantic coast, lay the second Christian kingdom, Portugal, a former Castilian province that had won independence in the twelfth century. Though still retaining close links with Castile, the Portuguese developed their own distinctive language and pursued their own particular national interests, especially in exploration and commerce overseas.

The third kingdom, located in northeastern Spain, was Aragon, which was as much a Mediterranean power as a Spanish one. Its kings controlled the Balearic Islands, ruled lands along the Mediterranean on the French side of the Pyrenees, and had an important stake in southern Italy. In the breakup of the Hohenstaufen Empire Aragon took the island of Sicily (1282); later, King Alfonso the Magnanimous (1416–1458) added the mainland territories of Naples. In Aragon, as in Castile, the oldest established political institutions were those limiting the Crown—the nobility, the towns, and the Cortes, which was much more powerful here than in Castile. Moreover, two territories of the Crown

Christian Conquest of Spain

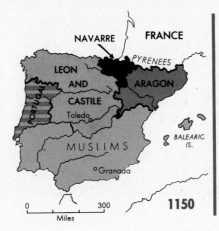

of Aragon on the Spanish mainland had Cortes of their own and so many other autonomous privileges that they were in effect separate states. These were Valencia, dominated by the city of the same name on the Mediterranean, and, farther north, Catalonia, centered on the prosperous port of Barcelona.

Ferdinand and Isabella

In 1469, Ferdinand, later king of Aragon (1479–1516), married Isabella, later queen of Castile (1474–1504), and thus made the dynastic alliance that eventually consummated the political unification of Spain. The obstacles confronting them were enormous. Not only was the royal power weak in both states; the inhabitants of Castile and Aragon did not always speak the same language, a difference still evident today in the distinction between the Castilian Spanish spoken in Madrid and the Catalan of Barcelona, whose closest linguistic relative is the Provençal once spoken in the south of France. Aragon looked toward the Mediterranean, Castile toward the Atlantic so that the union of Castile with Portugal might have been more natural.

Even today, Spanish nationalism is diluted by strong regional loyalties, especially in Catalonia.

Ferdinand and Isabella made an impressive beginning on the very long task of forging a single Spanish nation. Though very different in personality, they made a good political partnership. He was a wary realist of the stamp of Louis XI and an ardent promoter of Aragon's interests in Italy; though given the honorific title of "The Catholic" by the pope, he was skeptical and tolerant in religion. Isabella, on the other hand, was devout to the point of fanaticism, adored the pomp and circumstance of the throne, and in politics was wholly absorbed in the consolidation of her authority in Castile. She vested much authority in a potent new instrument of absolutism staffed by royal appointees, the Council of Castile. She allied herself with the middle class of the towns against the nobles and drew military support from town militias rather than from feudal levies. Finding her sovereignty weakened by three large military brotherhoods founded in the twelfth century to advance the reconquest and controlled by the Castilian nobility, she insisted that Ferdinand become head of each brotherhood. Toward the

This eighteenth-century print, published in London, was captioned "View of the Principal Place & manner of Execution of Persons condemned by the inquisition of Spain."

Mesta Isabella was more indulgent, since payments made by the sheep interests were the mainstay of royal revenue until the wealth of the New World began to pour in.

Ferdinand and Isabella relied heavily on the Church in advancing the royal power. Though pious, the Queen was determined to bring the Church under royal discipline and prescribed a much-needed purge of ecclesiastical corruption. The Spanish monarchs also obtained from the papacy the right to make appointments to high offices in the Spanish church and to dispose of parts of its revenue. Like the Gallican church, the Spanish church was half-independent of Rome; far more than the Gallican church, it was the prop of royal absolutism. The ranking Spanish prelate, Cardinal Jiménez (or Ximenes, 1436–1517), the archbishop of Toledo, became Isabella's chief minister and executed her policies of purifying the Church, curbing the aristocracy, and courting the towns.

When the Inquisition was introduced into Spain in 1478, it was from the first a royal rather than a papal instrument. The Spanish Inquisition sought to promote Spanish nationalism by enforcing universal Catholicism, and to create loyal subjects of the Crown by obliging men to be obedient children of the Church. Its chief targets were two religious minorities—the Muslims and the Jews—which long enjoyed toleration and owned some of the most productive farms and businesses in Spain. The Jews, because of their economic capacity and political reliability, were favorite agents of the Crown until Isabella's alliance with the Christian townsmen. Earlier, however, fear and envy of Jewish success had promoted popular anti-Semitic outbreaks that led many Jews to become converts to Christianity. It was in order to check backsliding among these New Christians that the Inquisition was established. The persecution was so menacing, with its tortures and burnings at the stake, that more than one hundred thousand New Christians fled the country. In 1492 unconverted Jews were confronted with the alternatives of immediate baptism or immediate exile with the loss of their property; about one hundred fifty thousand chose exile. Ten years later it was the turn of the Muslims, who received no choice except baptism. Catholicism thereby won many nominal new adherents who conformed only because they dreaded what the Inquisition had in store for those who wavered in their new faith. Isabella and Jiménez had secured religious uniformity but had alienated some of the most productive groups in Spanish society.

The year 1492, accordingly, may be viewed as the most crucial date in the whole of Spanish history. It began, on January 2, with the triumphal entry of Ferdinand and Isabella into the Alhambra at Granada, marking the conquest of the last fragment of independent Muslim Spain. Later in the year, the way was opened for immense new conquests when Columbus

Illustrations from the fourteenth-century "Mirror of Saxony" ("Der Sachsenspiegel"). Top: The pope (center) receives the key from Saint Peter; the emperor is at the left. Center: The pope and emperor embrace, symbolizing the coordination of spiritual and temporal power. Bottom: The pope consecrates the emperor; six electors look on at the left.

sailed from a Castilian port on the first of his voyages to the New World. But in the same year persecution on a grand scale was confirmed as national policy. The new Spanish monarchy already bore the stamp of the intolerant nationalism that was to be at once its strength and its weakness in generations to come.

III Particularism in Germany and Italy
The Princes and the Empire

In contrast to the new monarchies of western Europe, Germany had monarchs but no national monarchy, as power shifted steadily from the emperor to the princes of the particular states. Once, indeed, for a span of almost two decades there was no emperor at all—the

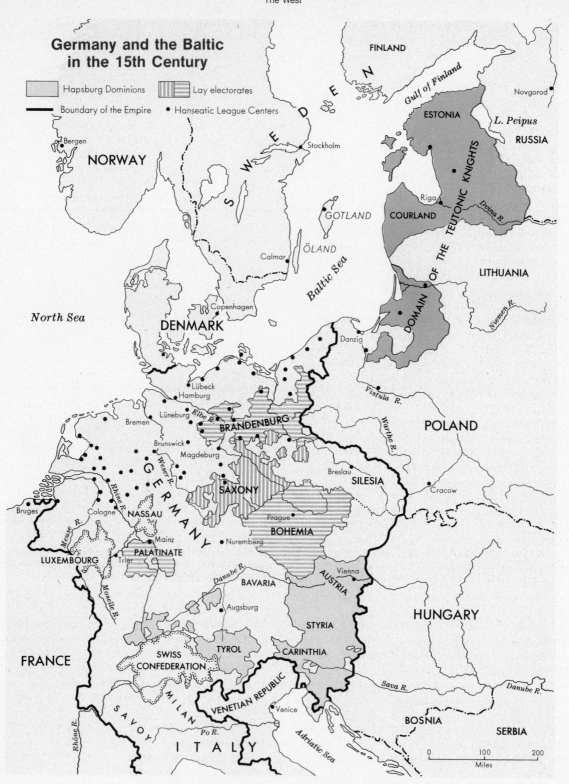

Germany and the Baltic in the 15th Century

Hapsburg Dominions

Lay electorates

Boundary of the Empire

Hanseatic League Centers

FINLAND

Gulf of Finland

Novgorod

ESTONIA

L. Peipus

RUSSIA

NORWAY

Bergen

S W E D E N

Stockholm

GOTLAND

ÖLAND

Calmar

Baltic Sea

Riga

Dvina R.

COURLAND

DOMAIN OF THE TEUTONIC KNIGHTS

LITHUANIA

Niemen R.

North Sea

DENMARK

Copenhagen

Danzig

Vistula R.

POLAND

Lübeck

Hamburg

Lüneburg

Elbe R.

BRANDENBURG

Warthe R.

Bremen

Brunswick

Magdeburg

G E R M A N Y

Weser R.

SAXONY

Breslau

SILESIA

Cracow

Bruges

Rhine R.

Cologne

NASSAU

Prague

BOHEMIA

Meuse R.

Mainz

Nuremberg

PALATINATE

LUXEMBOURG

Trier

Moselle R.

Danube R.

BAVARIA

Vienna

AUSTRIA

HUNGARY

Augsburg

STYRIA

FRANCE

SWISS CONFEDERATION

TYROL

CARINTHIA

Sava R.

Danube R.

SAVOY

MILAN

VENETIAN REPUBLIC

Venice

BOSNIA

SERBIA

Rhône R.

Po R.

I T A L Y

Adriatic Sea

0   100   200

Miles

1300 to 1715

The Renaissance

Introduction

Renaissance—"rebirth"—is the name traditionally bestowed upon the remarkable outpouring of intellectual and artistic energy and talent that accompanied the passage of Europe from the Middle Ages to the modern epoch. The term is often extended to politics and economics. The preceding chapter has described the acceleration of political change, especially toward the close of the last medieval century, the fifteenth. The present chapter examines first the emergence of capitalism and banking and the sometimes revolutionary impact of these powerful new forces on agriculture, industry, and trade. It turns next to the rise of vernacular literatures and of humanistic philosophy, to the contemporaneous quickening of science and religion, and then to the fine arts, the highest expression of Renaissance genius. The chapter concludes with an attempt to identify some of the distinctive features of Renaissance life.

Throughout the chapter we confront the basic problems that the Renaissance raises for the historian. Relatively little difficulty arises in ascertaining when and where the Renaissance began, how far it spread, and for how long it continued. It started in Italy around 1300 and continued for three centuries, in the course of which the economic, intellectual, and cultural currents flowing from its homeland eventually reached France, the Low Countries, Germany, and England and also, though with diminished force, Spain and Portugal. By 1600, with Europe increasingly preoccupied by the great Protestant-Catholic antagonism issuing from the Reformation, it had virtually come to an end, giving way to the culture called baroque.

What has been much more difficult to establish and has aroused lively controversy among scholars is the degree to which the term *Renaissance* should be interpreted literally. Were the classical values of ancient Greece and Rome in fact reborn at the close of the Middle Ages? Could such a rebirth alone possibly account for the extraordinarily productive careers of Renaissance writers, sculptors, painters, architects, musicians, and scientists? Until the middle of the nineteenth century most educated people would have given a simple affirmative response to both questions. The chief reason for the classical revival appeared to be the capture of Constantinople by the Turks in 1453 and the subsequent flight of Greek scholars to Italy and other countries of western Europe. The manner in which the eighteenth-century historian Edward Gibbon saluted the event is indicative:

> Before the revival of classical literature, the barbarians in Europe were immersed in ignorance; and their vulgar tongues were marked with the rudeness and poverty of their manners. The students of the more perfect idioms of Rome and Greece were introduced to a new world of light and science; to the society of the free and polished nations of antiquity; and to a familiar converse with those immortal men who spoke the sublime language of eloquence and reason. . . . As soon as it had been deeply saturated with the celestial dews, the soil was quickened into vegetation and life; the modern idioms were refined; the classics of Athens and Rome inspired a pure taste and a generous emulation; and in Italy, as afterwards in France and England, the pleasing reign of poetry and fiction was succeeded by the light of speculative and experimental philosophy.*

Today, these simple answers no longer suffice. We know that long before 1453 knowledge of Greek writings was filtering into the West from Muslim Spain, from Sicily, and from Byzantium itself. Moreover, Greek influence was by no means the only catalyst of the Renaissance. In an influential study first published in 1860, Professor Jacob Burckhardt of the University of Basel in Switzerland insisted that much of the credit for Renaissance productivity must go also to the genius

*E. Gibbon, *The Decline and Fall of the Roman Empire*, chap. 66.

and individualism of Italians. Burckhardt, however, accepted the traditional contrast between medieval darkness and Renaissance light that had first been drawn by the men of the Renaissance themselves and that Gibbon expressed so extravagantly. Today, of course, it is almost universally agreed that a great Christian civilization had in fact come to maturity during the Middle Ages, and that the cultural heritage from classical antiquity had never actually disappeared from the medieval West. Some historians have contended that the cultural rebirth had occurred much earlier than the fourteenth or fifteenth century, in the "Carolingian Renaissance" or the "Renaissance of the twelfth century" centered at the court of Eleanor of Aquitaine.

But to find that the germ of the Renaissance had been planted and had sprouted long before 1300—to deny any originality to the Renaissance, as a few historians do—is to swing the pendulum of reinterpretation too far. The intellectuals and artists of the Renaissance owed a substantial debt to their medieval predecessors, and they were often as religious, as credulous, as caste-conscious and "feudal" as their forebears. Yet they were also materialistic, skeptical, and individualistic to a degree almost unknown in the Middle Ages. The distinguished Italian historian Federico Chabod has observed that the new secular credo could be summed up as "art for art's sake, politics for politics' sake, science for science's sake."[*] Men were attempting to create things, to do things, and to study things as ends in themselves rather than as the means to the glorification of God and to salvation, much as Machiavelli divorced political thought from theology or as Machiavellian rulers cultivated power politics.

II A Money Economy
Trade

During the Renaissance the more developed areas of Europe that are loosely termed the West—that is, the areas to the west of the Adriatic Sea and the Elbe River—were taking giant steps along the road from the subsistence economy of the early Middle Ages to a money economy. But it was also a long and uneven road from an economy based on home-grown produce paid for in kind to one relying heavily on imports paid for in money. By the fifteenth century the West had long been importing salt, from the salt mines of Germany or the sea-salt pans of the Atlantic coast, in order to preserve food. To make food tasty if it had begun to spoil, the West had long sought the spices of the East; and to wash it down western Europeans had already developed a taste for the wines of the Rhine, of Burgundy, and of Bordeaux. The furs of eastern Europe, the wool of England and Spain, and the woolen cloth of Flanders and Italy all commanded good markets

[*]F. Chabod, *Machiavelli and the Renaissance* (London, 1958), p. 184.

among the residents of chilly medieval buildings. At the close of the Middle Ages, supplies of palatable food and warm clothing were steadily increasing. Salt fish, for example, was cheap and did not spoil. In the fourteenth century, such a boom occurred in the herring fisheries along the narrow Baltic waters between Denmark and Sweden that, according to the inflated report of one traveler, the Baltic fisheries employed three hundred thousand people in catching fish, salting them down, and making the barrels to pack them in.

Trade slumped during the serious economic depression of the early 1300s and the prolonged aftermath of the Black Death and the Hundred Years' War. Recovery came in the fifteenth century, and by the later 1400s the trade of the West could for the first time be compared in volume and variety with that of Rome in the days of the empire, of Byzantium at its tenth-century peak, and of Norman and Hohenstaufen Sicily. Meantime, Western merchants developed more elaborate commercial procedures and organizations, of which the Hanseatic towns of the Baltic and the trading cities of Italy provide the most telling illustrations.

In the fourteenth and fifteenth centuries the membership of the Hanse (the German word means "league") included almost a hundred towns, among which Lübeck, Hamburg, Bremen, and Danzig were the leaders. The weakness of the Holy Roman Empire and the fact that many of the Hanseatic towns began as autonomous frontier outposts east of the Elbe in the course of the *Drang nach Osten* ("the push to the East") enabled the Hanse to play an independent political and military role in addition to exercising widespread economic power. Its policies were determined by meetings of representatives from the member towns, held usually at Lübeck.

The Hanse was not the first important confederation of commercial towns in Europe, nor was it the first to resist control by a higher political authority. Alliances of communes in Lombardy and in Flanders had blocked the ambitions, respectively, of Hohenstaufen emperors and French kings. The Hanse, however, operated on a grander scale. Its ships carried Baltic fish, timber, grain, furs, metals, and amber to western European markets and brought back cloth, wine, and spices; for a time, Hanseatic vessels controlled the lucrative transport of wool from England to Flanders. Hanseatic merchants, traveling overland with carts and pack trains, took their Baltic wares to Italy. The Hanse maintained especially large depots at Venice, Bruges, London, Novgorod (in northwestern Russia), and Bergen, on the Norwegian coast, where the Hanseatic colony was said to number three thousand. These foreign establishments enjoyed so many special rights of maintaining their own German officials and laws that they were colonial outposts of a Hanseatic empire. The Hanse itself had its own legal code (the Law of Lübeck), its own diplomats, and its own flag. It made treaties, declared war, and sometimes resorted to undeclared war; in 1406, to teach a forceful lesson to

English vessels poaching on fishing grounds off Norway, Hanseatic captains seized ninety-six English seamen, bound them hand and foot, and cast them overboard.

After 1500 the fortunes of the Hanse declined rapidly. The shifting of trade routes from the Baltic to the Atlantic ended the prosperity of many Hanseatic towns to the advantage of Holland and England. The loosely organized Hanse was no match for the stronger monarchical governments growing up along the rim of its Baltic preserve in Sweden, Russia, and some of the German princely states. Internally, the Hanse was weakened by the mounting conservatism and restrictiveness of its merchants and by rivalries among member towns and competing merchant families. Only a minority of the member towns usually sent representatives to the deliberations in Lübeck, and very few of them could be counted on for men and arms in an emergency. Moreover, Hanseatic trading activities were carried on in a relatively primitive fashion by a multitude of individual merchants who entered temporary partnerships for a single venture rather than establishing permanent firms.

The truly big business of the last medieval centuries was to be found not along the Baltic but in the cities of the Mediterranean, many of which were already thriving veterans of trade, enriched and toughened by the Crusades—in Italy, Venice, Genoa, Pisa, Lucca, Florence, Milan, and a dozen others; in France, Marseilles, Montpellier, and Narbonne; and in Spain, Barcelona. Venice furnishes an excellent case study. It was the East-West trade that brought wealth to Venetian merchants—from the East, spices, silk, cotton, sugar, dyestuffs, and the alum needed to set colors, and from the West, wool and cloth. The area of Venetian business was enormous, from England and Flanders to the heart of Asia, which the thirteenth-century Venetian Marco Polo traversed to reach China.

The main carrier of Venetian trade was the galley. By 1300, the designers of the arsenal, the government-operated shipyard, had improved the traditional long, narrow, oar-propelled galley of the Mediterranean into a swifter and more capacious merchant vessel, relying mainly on sails and employing oarsmen chiefly for getting in and out of port. In the fifteenth century, these merchant galleys had space for 250 tons of cargo—a capacity that seems ridiculously small by present-day standards but commodious enough for lucrative shipments of spices and other items small in bulk and large in value. Records from the early fifteenth century show approximately forty-five galleys sailing annually, among them four to Flanders, two to southern France, three to the Black Sea, three to Alexandria, four to Beirut, and two or three transporting pilgrims to Jaffa in the Holy Land. The Flanders fleet, which touched also at London and Southampton, was a very important economic institution because from its initiation in 1317 it provided a service between Italy and northwestern Europe that was cheaper and more secure than the older overland route.

Fifteenth-century Hanseatic merchants.

The state supervised the activities of these galleys from the cradle to the grave. Since the average life of galleys was ten years, government experts tested their seaworthiness periodically, and the arsenal made needed replacements. The government provided for the defense of the galleys and their cargoes by requiring that at least twenty of the crew be bowmen. The captains of the Flanders galleys were directed to protect the health of the crew by enlisting a physician and a surgeon, and to maintain the prestige of the city with two fifers and two trumpeters. For the Flanders fleet the government also laid down the policies of the captains (get to Bruges before the Genoese, and avoid "affrays and mischiefs" in English ports, even if the crew have to be denied shore leave). The republic also maintained an ambassador in England to smooth the way for its merchants.

Industry

The expansion of trade stimulated the industries that furnished the textiles, metals, and ships required by merchants. The towns of Flanders and Italy developed the weaving of woolen cloth into a big business, with many workmen and high profits for a relatively few entrepreneurs. In the early fourteenth century, it is estimated, two hundred masters controlled the wool guild of Florence, which produced nearly one hundred thousand pieces of cloth annually and employed thirty thousand men. By and large, only the two hundred had the capital—the saved-up funds—to finance the importation of raw wool from England and put it through the long process that ended with the finished cloth. The earlier practice of grouping in a single guild all artisans engaged in making a single product was giving way to the modern division—and tension—between capital and labor, and, within the ranks of labor, between the highly skilled and the less skilled. The preceding chapter noted the strife in late fourteenth-century Florence among the seven great guilds, the fourteen lesser guilds, and the Ciompi, the workers excluded from guild membership.

Despite the growth of capitalism, Europe had not yet experienced a true industrial revolution, and manufacturing continued to be what the Latin roots of the word suggest that it was—making by hand—though many hand tools were ingenious and efficient. The modern aspects of late medieval industry, confined largely to a few advanced crafts, were the increase in output, the mass production of standardized articles, and the specialization of the labor force. In Lübeck, Hanseatic capitalists promoted the mass output of rosaries by hiring beadmakers and supplying them with materials. In the Hapsburg lands of central Europe, the silver mines inaugurated round-the-clock operation by dividing their labor force into three parts, each working an eight-hour daily shift. In Florence, twenty or more different specialized crafts participated in woolen production—washing, combing, carding, spinning, weaving, dyeing, and so forth. But the actual work was subcontracted, in effect, to small domestic shops according to the "put-out system": instead of the worker's going to a mill or a factory, the work went to the worker in his home.

The largest industrial establishment in Europe was probably the Venetian arsenal, which normally employed a thousand men and during emergencies many more. These workmen, called arsenalotti, formed a pyramid of skills, with stevedores and other unskilled laborers at the bottom; at the next level, the sawyers, who cut the timbers for the galleys, and the caulkers, who made the wooden hulls seaworthy; then the pulley-makers and mastmakers; and at the top, the highly skilled carpenters, who shaped the lines of the hull. Supervisors, like modern foremen, disciplined the arsenalotti, checking on their presence at their posts during the working day; anyone who reported late, after the arsenal bell had ceased tolling its summons to work, forfeited a day's pay. By the sixteenth century, the process of adding a superstructure to the hull and outfitting the vessel was so efficient that it took the arsenalotti only two months to complete and equip a hundred galleys for a campaign against the Turks.

Banking

The expansion of industry and trade promoted the rise of banking, as merchants invested their accumulated capital in trading enterprises. In addition, kings, popes, and other rulers borrowed money to meet the expenses of war and administration. The risks of lending were great—rulers, in particular, were likely to repudiate their debts—but so too were the potential profits. Florentine bankers were known to charge 266 percent annual interest on an especially risky loan, and in 1420 the Florentine government vainly tried to put a ceiling of 20 percent on interest rates. Bankers were money-changers as well as moneylenders, for only experts could establish the relative value of the hundreds upon hundreds of coins in circulation, varying enormously in reliability and precious metallic content and minted by every kind of governmental unit from the national monarchy down to the small city and the tiny feudal principality.

Bankers also facilitated the transfer of money over long distances. Suppose an English exporter, A, sold wool to an Italian importer, Z; it would be slow and dangerous for Z to pay A by shipping coins to him. Now suppose that two others entered the transaction: Y, an Italian woolen manufacturer who sold cloth to B, an English importer. It was safer and speedier if Z paid Y in Italy what he really owed to A in England, and if B paid A what he really owed Y. This sort of transaction was facilitated by bills of exchange, which bankers bought and sold.

The great European bankers were Italians, the "Lombard" bankers, though many of them came not from Lombardy but from Florence, Siena, and other towns in Tuscany. By the late 1200s, Italian bankers had become the fiscal agents of the pope, charged with the transfer of papal revenues from distant countries to Rome. The beautiful florins minted by Florence were the first gold coins made outside Byzantium to gain international currency because of their reliability. The great Florentine banking families of the Bardi and the Peruzzi financed imports of English wool and the export of finished cloth. Both firms advanced large sums to the kings of England and France at the outbreak of the Hundred Years' War, and both failed in the 1340s when Edward III defaulted on his debts. The repercussions of the failure, felt for more than a generation, included new attempts to democratize the Florentine government and the revolt of the Ciompi in 1378. Florentine banking rallied in the fifteenth century under the dynamic Cosimo de' Medici, whose activities involved companies for woolen and silk manufacture as well as the Medici bank and branch firms in Venice, Milan, Rome, Avignon, Geneva, Bruges, and London. However, the inefficiency of branch managers together with the extravagance of Lorenzo the Magnificent caused the failure of the Medici bank before the century was out.

The house of Jacques Coeur in Bourges, France (fifteenth century).

Meanwhile, money and banking were thriving elsewhere. The golden ducats of Venice joined the florins of Florence in international popularity, and the Bank of Saint George, founded at Genoa in 1407, eventually took over much of the Mediterranean business done by Spanish Jews before their persecution in the late 1400s. In London, the celebrated merchant and moneylender Sir Richard (Dick) Whittington served as lord mayor for three terms around 1400. In France, Jacques Coeur of Bourges (1395–1456) used private wealth to secure public office, and public office to augment his private wealth.

Coeur made a fortune by trading with the Muslim Near East and transporting pilgrims to the Holy Land. King Charles VII of France sent him on diplomatic missions, made him the chief royal fiscal agent, and placed him in charge of the royal mint; Coeur financed the final campaigns of the Hundred Years' War. Aided by the royal favor, Coeur acquired a string of textile workshops and mines, bought landed estates from impoverished nobles, lent money to half the dignitaries of France, and obtained noble husbands and high church offices for his own middle-class relatives. At Bourges he met the cost of embellishing the cathedral and built himself an elegant palace. While Coeur thus demonstrated the eminence that a bourgeois could reach, too many highly placed people owed him too much money. He was disgraced by Charles VII, who trumped up a charge against him to avoid repaying loans.

In Germany, powerful banking families flourished in the small Bavarian cities of Augsburg and Nuremberg; the most famous was the Fugger family of Augsburg. The founder of Fugger prosperity was a linen weaver and trader in the late fourteenth century. His sons and grandsons imported textiles and luxuries from Venice and began buying up silver and lead mines. In the late 1400s, the Fuggers became bankers to the Hapsburgs and, after the failure of the Medici bank, to the papacy as well. With the Fuggers, as with Jacques Coeur, wealth bred more wealth, power, and eventual ruin. Through Hapsburg favor they secured silver, iron, and copper mines in Hungary and the Tyrol, and in the 1540s the family fortune is estimated to have exceeded a quarter of a billion of our present-day dollars. Thereafter it dwindled as the flood of gold and silver from America ended the central European mining boom, and as the Fuggers themselves made extensive loans to the Hapsburg Philip II of Spain who went through repeated bankruptcies. In 1607, the family firm went bankrupt.

Two quotations convey something of the personality of these German bankers. Here is the epitaph that Jacob Fugger, a grandson of the founder, composed for his own tomb in the early sixteenth century:

> To the best, greatest God! Jacob Fugger of Augsburg, the ornament of his class and people, imperial councillor under Maximilian I and Charles V, who was behind no one in the attainment of extraordinary wealth, in generosity, purity of morals, and greatness of soul, is, as he was not comparable with anyone in his lifetime, even after death not to be counted among the mortals.*

But the haughty Fuggers were not just "robber barons"; here is the inscription at the entrance to the Fuggerei, a garden village that they built for the poor of Augsburg:

> Ulrich, George, and Jacob Fugger of Augsburg, blood brothers, being firmly convinced that they were born for the good of the city, and that for their great prosperity they have to thank chiefly an all-powerful and benevolent God, have out of piety, and as an example of special generosity founded, given, and dedicated 106 dwellings, both buildings and furnishings, to those of their fellow citizens who live righteously, but are beset by poverty.†

Town and Countryside

While Augsburg, with its special housing development for low-income families, may appear to have resembled a modern metropolis, its total population at the zenith of Fugger power probably never exceeded twenty thousand. In fact, none of the centers of international economic life five or six hundred years ago was really a big city at all. One set of estimates for the fourteenth century puts the population of Venice, Florence, and Paris in the vicinity of one hundred thousand each; that

*M. Beard, *A History of the Business Man* (New York, 1938), pp. 239–240.
†J. Strieder, *Jacob Fugger the Rich* (New York, 1931), p. 176.

of Genoa, Milan, Barcelona, and London at about fifty thousand; and that of the biggest Hanseatic and Flemish towns between twenty and forty thousand. Most Europeans still lived in the countryside.

The urban minority, however, was beginning to bring important changes to the life of the rural majority. Ties between town and countryside were especially close in areas where towns were numerous—Lombardy, Tuscany, Flanders, the Rhine Valley, and northern Germany. Merchants often invested their wealth in farm properties, nobles who acquired interests in towns usually retained their country estates, and peasants often moved to town as workmen or became artisans on the farm itself under the put-out system. Rural laborers made prayer beads for the capitalists of Lübeck and spun woolen yarn for the guild masters of Florence. Town governments sometimes improved adjacent farmland on the pattern established by the medieval communes of Milan and Siena, which had drained nearby marshes to increase the amount of cultivable land.

The development of a money economy greatly altered the agrarian institutions of the West. Many manors now specialized in a single crop, like grain or wool, olives or grapes, and therefore purchased items that they themselves no longer produced. The lords of these one-crop manors, depending increasingly on a monetary income, became capitalists on a modest scale. The more enterprising wanted to sweep away what seemed to them inefficient medieval survivals, demanding that their peasants pay rent in money rather than in commodities or in work on the demesne land. The sheep-raising capitalists of sixteenth-century England got the right of enclosure, of fencing off for their own flocks common lands where peasants had traditionally pastured their own livestock. In Spain, the great guild of sheep-raisers, the Mesta, secured comparable exclusive rights to vast tracts of pasture. Urban businessmen wanted property in a form that they might readily buy and sell, free from the restrictions of feudal tenure; they wanted laborers whom they could hire and fire, free from the restrictions of serfdom. All these forces, together with the labor shortage and peasant unrest created by the Black Death, precipitated the end of serfdom, which virtually disappeared in most areas of western Europe by 1500.

Thus, at the heart of economic and social relationships, the cash nexus of the capitalist was beginning to replace the medieval complex of caste and service. These new developments blurred the old lines between classes. The ordinary individual very probably made a gain in real income by becoming a wage-earning worker or rent-paying tenant farmer instead of a serf. Yet he also lost something—the security, the inherited job, the right to certain lands—which he had possessed in the days of manorialism. Despair and discontent came to the surface in the Jacquerie and the English peasant uprising of 1381 and continued as undercurrents in the more prosperous Europe of the fifteenth century. In towns and cities, too, pressures mounted, as the guilds became more exclusive and the separation between the wealthy master and the ordinary workman widened. In Venice, pressures were kept under control, but elsewhere they sometimes exploded, as in the Flemish towns on the eve of the Hundred Years' War and in the revolt of the Florentine Ciompi.

A very important political result of the economic changes we have been surveying was the expanded role of the business class, the bourgeoisie. Sometimes the bourgeois themselves ruled, as did the Medici in Florence and the merchants of Venice and the Hanse. Sometimes they provided monarchs with the money or the professional skills to further dynastic and national interests. Archbishop Morton helped Henry VII to bring law and order back to England; Fugger money supported the Hapsburgs; Charles VII could not have brought France successfully out of the Hundred Years' War without the support of Jacques Coeur. Yet Coeur's disgrace underscored the fact that, while holders of political power were beholden to the wielders of economic power, the reverse was also true.

The economic leaders made their mark not only on politics but on the whole style of the age. No medieval man, apart from such a rare specimen as the emperor Frederick II, would have manifested the presumptuousness, the lack of humility, found in the epitaph of Jacob Fugger. The bourgeois were beginning to invade the Church's near-monopoly of the support of culture. The Medici, the Fuggers, Coeur, and the well-to-do generally supported the patronage of art and learning and the financing of public monuments. The palace or the library of the rich man challenged the monastery or the church-dominated university as a center of scholarship. In the late fifteenth century, we shall shortly see, the intellectual life of Florence revolved around the Platonic Academy subsidized by Lorenzo the Magnificent. Finally, there was little to distinguish the rich and cultivated prelate from the rich and cultivated layman. Such Renaissance popes as Sixtus IV, Alexander VI, and Julius II, like their contemporaries in the business world, were great admirers and amassers of material wealth and great connoisseurs of art.

III Literature and Thought

The burgeoning capitalism and secularism of the Renaissance centuries did not mean that all medieval values were rejected or all medieval customs supplanted. A good case in point is linguistic: the new vernaculars, the "native" or "local" languages, became important media of literary expression without seriously undermining the traditional preeminence of Latin in the realm of learning. Linguistically, the Renaissance had a kind of split personality or dyarchy (dual rule), with the vernaculars dominating the world of popular culture and Latin that of "serious" thought.

The Vernaculars

The vernaculars of the western European countries emerged gradually, arising deep in the Middle Ages as the spoken languages of the people, then becoming vehicles for popular writing, and finally achieving official recognition. Many vernaculars—Spanish, Portuguese, Italian, and French—developed from Latin; these were the Romance (Roman) languages. Castilian, the core of modern literary Spanish, attained official status in the thirteenth century when the king of Castile ordered that it be used for government records. In Italy, the vernacular scarcely existed as a literary language until the eve of the Renaissance when Dante employed the dialect of his native Tuscany in the *Divine Comedy,* and it was not until the early sixteenth century that Tuscan Italian won out over the rival dialect of Rome as the standard medium for vernacular expression.

In medieval France, two families of vernaculars appeared. Southern Frenchmen spoke the *langue d'oc,* so called from their use of *oc* (the Latin *hoc*) for "yes"; their northern cousins spoke the *langue d'oïl,* in which "yes" was *oïl,* (the modern *oui*). The epic verses of the *Song of Roland,* the rowdy *fabliaux,* and the chronicles of Villehardouin and Joinville were all composed in the *langue d'oïl,* while the troubadours at the court of Eleanor of Aquitaine sang in Provençal, a variety of the *langue d'oc.* By 1400, the *langue d'oïl* of the Paris region was well on its way to replacing Latin as the official language of the whole kingdom, though a century later champions of this French tongue were complaining that it was used only for frivolous writing. Provençal eventually died out; however, another offshot of the *langue d'oc* survives in Catalan, used in both Spain and France at the Mediterranean end of the Pyrenees, and the name *Languedoc* is still applied to southern France west of the Rhone.

In Germany and in England, the vernaculars were derived ultimately not from Latin but from an ancient Germanic language. The minnesingers of thirteenth century Germany composed their poetry in Middle High German, the predecessor of modern literary German. The Anglo-Saxons of England had spoken a dialect of Low German which incorporated some words of Scandinavian or Celtic origin and later added many borrowings from Norman French and Latin to form the English vernacular. As we have already noted, English achieved official recognition in the fourteenth century; meantime, it was also coming into its own as a literary language with such popular works as *Piers Plowman* and Chaucer's *Canterbury Tales.*

Use of a common language undoubtedly heightened among Englishmen a common sense of national purpose and a common mistrust of foreigners who did not speak the King's English. The vernaculars also accelerated the emergence of distinctive national styles in France and in Spain. Yet the triumph of particularism in fifteenth-century Germany and Italy demonstrated that the vernaculars could not by themselves create national political units. Nor did the vernaculars divide Western culture into watertight national compartments. Translations kept ideas flowing across national frontiers, and some of the vernaculars themselves became international languages. In the Near East, the Italian that had been introduced by the Crusaders was the *lingua franca*, the Western tongue most widely understood.

Humanism

Meantime, Latin remained the international language of the Church and of the academic world. Scholars worked diligently to perfect their Latin and, in the later Renaissance, to learn at least the rudiments of Greek and sometimes of Hebrew too. They called themselves humanists, that is, devotees of what Cicero had termed *studia humanitatis*, or humane studies. While these were more restricted than the "humanities" or "liberal arts" of modern higher education, they usually included rhetoric, grammar, history, poetry, and ethics. Humanism was far more than a linguistic term, and the humanist was usually much more than a philologist. His studies of the great men and great ideas of the classical past led him to cherish the values of antiquity, pagan though they might be. Machiavelli, as the preceding chapter noted, found greater virtue in pre-Christian Greece and Rome than he did in the nominally Christian society of his own day. Other humanists, we shall

find, sought a kind of highest moral denominator in the best ancient doctrines and in the loftiest Christian aspiration.

Altogether, humanism revolutionized men's attitudes toward the classical heritage. The medieval schoolmen had not disdained this heritage; they admired and copied its forms but transformed or adapted its ideas to fortify their own Christian views. They found in Vergil's *Aeneid*, for instance, not only the splendor of epic poetry but also an allegory of man's sojourn on earth. The humanists of the Renaissance, in turn, transformed their medieval heritage in the more secular spirit of their own age and in the light of their own more extensive knowledge of the classics. They revered both the style and the content of the classics and began to study them for their own sake, not to strengthen or enrich their faith. Reverence for the classics did not prevent some humanists from becoming enthusiastic advocates of the vernacular; the reverse was also true, as vernacular writers acquired the habit of studying Cicero and other classical masters to improve their own style (the passage from Gibbon quoted in the introduction to this chapter is a good specimen of Ciceronian English).

Writers of the Early Italian Renaissance

Dante Alighieri (1265–1321) was the first major Italian writer to embody some of the qualities that were to characterize Renaissance literature. As an earlier chapter has already noted, much of Dante's writing and outlook bore the stamp of the Middle Ages. The grand theme of the *Divine Comedy* was medieval, and the chivalric concept of disembodied love inspired his devotion to Beatrice, whom he seldom saw. His hostility to the political ambitions of Boniface VIII did not express a Machiavellian anticlericalism but the reaction of a good Christian who wanted the pope to keep out of politics. Yet Dante not only chose the vernacular for the *Divine Comedy* but also wrote a treatise in Latin urging others to follow his example. He modeled the style of the *Comedy* on the popular poetry of the Provençal troubadours rather than on the epic verse of the ancients. He gave the classics their due by including among the characters of the *Comedy* a host of figures from antiquity, both real and mythological. The Trojan Hector, Homer, Vergil's Aeneas. Vergil himself, Euclid, Plato, Socrates, Caesar, and other virtuous pagans dwell forever in Limbo on the edge of Hell, suffering only the hopelessness of the unbaptized who can never reach God's presence. Significantly, Dante also placed in Limbo the Muslims Saladin and Averroës.

The concerns of this world are constantly with Dante in the other world. The lost souls in Hell are real people, from Judas through corrupt medieval clerics down to Dante's own fellow Florentines. Dante was not one of the medieval intellectuals who withdrew from society to the sanctuary of holy orders. Deeply involved in Florentine politics, he became a refugee

Portrait of Dante, attributed to the school of Giotto.

from Guelf factionalism, and adopted the good Renaissance expedient of obtaining the patronage of the despot ruling Verona. As a man of letters, he achieved a remarkable popular success during his own lifetime. Half a century after his death, a group of Florentine citizens honored the memory of their exiled compatriot by founding a public lectureship for a person "well trained in the book of Dante."

Popular fame and classical enthusiasm obsessed the next important Italian literary figure, Petrarch (Francesco Petrarca, 1304–1374). Since his father was a political exile from Florence, the young Petrarch lived for a time at the worldly papal court in Avignon and attended the law school at the University of Bologna. As a professional man of letters, he collected and copied the manuscripts of ancient authors, produced the first accurate edition of the Roman historian Livy, and found in an Italian cathedral some forgotten letters by Cicero that threw new light on Cicero's political activities. Petrarch so admired the past that he addressed a series of affectionate letters to Cicero and other Roman worthies; he also composed a Latin epic in the style of the *Aeneid* to celebrate Scipio Africanus, the hero of the Second Punic War. He tried to learn Greek and failed, but at least he could gaze reverently at his manuscripts of Homer and Plato.

Petrarch's attainments led the Senate of Rome (then a kind of municipal council) to revive the Greco-Roman recognition of excellence and crown him with a wreath of laurel in an elaborate ceremony. The new laureate reveled in the honor, for he longed to be ranked with the ancient Romans to whom he addressed his letters. Ironically, the writings of Petrarch most admired in modern times are not those in his cherished Latin but those he esteemed the least, the vernacular love poems he addressed to his adored Laura, whom he courted in vain until she died during the Black Death. In these lyrics, Petrarch perfected the verse form known as the Italian sonnet, fourteen lines long, divided into one set of eight lines and another of six, each with its own rhyme scheme. The word "sonnet" means "little song," and Petrarch developed his sonnets from vernacular folk songs. Almost despite himself, therefore, he proved to be one of the founders of modern vernacular literature.

Petrarch is an excellent instance of the intermixture of old and new in the Renaissance. He exemplified emerging humanism by his devotion to the classics and his deep feeling for the beauties of this world; for him Laura was a real woman, not a disembodied chivalric heroine. He criticized medieval Schoolmen because of their rationalism, their dependence on Aristotle as an infallible authority, and their preoccupation with detail, all of which led them, in his judgment, to miss the true spirit of Christianity in their concern with its letter. But he admired Augustine almost as much as he admired Cicero, believing that the religious teachings of the one and the Stoic morality of the other could counter the materialism he observed around him. "I am filled with bitter indignation against the mores of today," he wrote in a letter to Livy, "when men value nothing except gold and silver and desire nothing except sensual pleasures." * We shall encounter other humanists who shared Petrarch's low estimate of existing society and his belief that classical learning and Christian precepts could both contribute to ennoble the human spirit.

Petrarch's friend and pupil, Giovanni Boccaccio (1313–1375), shared his master's estimate of mankind but not his confidence in the possibility of human improvement. Boccaccio, who was the son of a Florentine banker, spent part of his youth at the frivolous court of the Angevin kings of Naples, and turned to letters after his apprenticeship in banking left him disillusioned by the sharp business practices of wealthy Florentines. He became a humanist scholar and eventually held the Dante memorial lectureship at Florence; meantime, he went Petrarch one better by learning Greek, and aided his master in tracking down old manuscripts, once finding a copy of Tacitus in the Benedictine abbey on Monte Cassino. His distress at the negligence of the clergy in conserving manuscripts together with his observation of clerical corruption made him strongly anticlerical.

Anticlericalism is a recurrent theme in his *Decameron*, the first major prose work in the Italian vernacular, which recounts the stories told by a group of young Florentines who have moved to a country villa during the Black Death. Most of the plots in the *Decameron* were not original with Boccaccio, who borrowed freely from classical and Eastern sources and from the bawdy *fabliaux* of medieval France, particularly those exposing clerical peccadilloes. He retold these earthy tales in a graceful and entertaining way, and with a lighthearted disenchantment based on his own worldly experience. Here is the gist of one of the stories:

> You must know, then, that there was once in our city a very rich merchant called Arriguccio Berlinghieri, who . . . took to wife a young gentle woman ill sorting with himself, by name Madam Sismonda, who, for that he, merchant-like, was much abroad and sojourned little with her, fell in love with a young man called Ruberto.†

Arriguccio discovers his wife's infidelity and gives her the beating of her life—or so he thinks. The beating occurs in a darkened room, Sismonda has directed her maid to take her place, and it is actually the maid whom Arriguccio had thrashed. Unaware of the deception, he summons Sismonda's brothers to witness her disgrace. "The brothers,—seeing her seated sewing with no sign of beating on her face, whereas Arriguccio avouched that he had beaten her to a mummy,—began to marvel." Sismonda immediately accuses her hapless husband of "fuddling himself about the taverns, fore-

*M. P. Gilmore, *Humanists and Jurists* (Cambridge, Mass., 1963), p. 6.
†This and the following quotations are from the eighth story of the seventh day, as translated in the Modern Library edition of the *Decameron*.

gathering now with this lewd woman and now with that and keeping me waiting for him . . . half the night." The result: the brothers give Arriguccio a thorough beating. And Boccaccio's moral:

> Thus the lady, by her ready wit, not only escaped the imminent peril but opened herself a way to do her every pleasure in time to come, without evermore having any fear of her husband.

Classical Scholarship

The men of letters who followed Petrarch and Boccaccio may be divided into three groups. First, there were the conservers of classical culture, the bookworms, scholars, cultivated despots and businessmen, all the heirs of Petrarch's great humanistic enthusiasm for classical antiquity. Second were the vernacular writers—many of them not Italians—who took the path marked out by the *Decameron*, from Chaucer at the close of the fourteenth century down to Rabelais and to Cervantes in the sixteenth. And third there were the synthesizers, headed by Pico della Mirandola and Erasmus, who endeavored to fuse Christianity, classicism, and other elements into a universal philosophy of man.

The devoted antiquarians of the fifteenth century uncovered a really remarkable number of ancient manuscripts. They ransacked monasteries and other likely places, in Italy and Germany, in France and Spain. They pieced together the works of Cicero, Tacitus, Lucretius, and other Latin authors. Collecting Greek manuscripts became a regular business, transacted for Italian scholars and patrons by agents in Constantinople both before and after 1453. They did their work so thoroughly that almost all the Greek classics we now possess reached the West before 1500. To preserve, catalog, and study these literary treasures, the first modern libraries were created. Cosimo de' Medici supported three separate libraries in and near Florence and employed forty-five copyists. Humanist popes founded the library of the Vatican, today one of the most important collections in the world, and even the minor duchy of Urbino in northern Italy had a major library, assembled by its cultivated duke.

Greek scholars as well as Greek manuscripts made the journey from Byzantium to Italy. One of the earliest of them, Manuel Chrysoloras (1368–1415) came to Italy to seek help for the beleaguered Byzantines against the Turks and remained to teach at Florence and Milan. He did literature a great service by insisting that translations into Latin from the Greek should not be literal, as they had been in the past, but should convey the message and spirit of the original. The revival of Greek studies reached maturity in the 1460s with the emergence of the informal circle of Florentine humanists known as the Platonic Academy. The Greek language, however, never equaled Latin in popularity because of its difficulty, a fact that discouraged interest in the Greek drama and led most humanists to study Plato in Latin translation.

The classicists of the fifteenth century made a fetish of pure and polished Latin. The learned composed elaborate letters designed less for private reading than for the instruction of their colleagues. Papal secretaries began to make ecclesiastical correspondence conform to what we should call a manual of correct style. At their worst, these men were pedants, exalting manner over matter, draining vitality from the Latin language. But at their best, they were keen and erudite scholars who sifted out the inaccuracies and forgeries in defective manuscripts to establish definitive texts of ancient writings.

Lorenzo Valla (1407–1457) represented classical scholarship at its best. One of the few important figures of the Italian Renaissance not identified with Florence, Valla was reared in Rome and passed much of his adult life there and at Naples. Petty and quarrelsome, fond of exchanging insults with rival humanists, he also commanded both immense learning and the courage to use it against the most sacred targets. He even criticized the supposedly flawless prose of Cicero and took Thomas Aquinas to task for his failure to know Greek. His own expert knowledge of the language led him to point out errors and misinterpretations in the Vulgate, as compared to the Greek New Testament, and thereby to lay the foundation for humanist biblical scholarship.

Valla's fame rests above all on his demonstration that the Donation of Constantine, long a basis for justifying papal claims to temporal dominion, was actually a forgery. He proved his case by showing that both the Latin in which the Donation was written and the events to which it referred dated from an era several centuries after Constantine, who had been emperor in the early fourth century. When Valla published this exposé in 1440, he was secretary to Alfonso the Magnanimous, king of Aragon, whose claim to Naples was being challenged by the papacy on the basis of the Donation itself. The pope might well have been expected to condemn Valla as a heretic. Nothing of the kind occurred, and Valla soon accepted a commission to translate Thucydides under papal auspices.

Chaucer and Rabelais

The second group of literary men, the vernacular writers, illustrate once again the broad range of the Renaissance. Geoffrey Chaucer, like Dante, belongs both to the Middle Ages and to the Renaissance. As an earlier chapter has noted, his *Canterbury Tales* have a medieval setting; they are told by pilgrims on their way to the shrine of the martyred Becket, not by the secular young people of the *Decameron*. Yet Chaucer's tales are not unlike Boccaccio's; he, too, used the vernacular and borrowed stories from the *fabliaux*. Although Chaucer apparently had not actually read the *Decameron*, he was familiar enough with other writings of Boccaccio to use the plot of one for his Knight's Tale and of another for *Troilus and Criseyde*, the long narrative poem about two lovers in the Trojan War. The Clerk's

Tale, he reveals, "I Lerned at Padowe of a worthy clerk . . ., Fraunceys Petrark, the laureat poete," and the Wife of Bath mentions "the wyse poete of Florence That Highte Dant."

Chaucer came to know Italian literature in the course of several trips to Italy on official business for the English king. He led a busy and prosperous life in the thick of politics, domestic and international. Coming from a family of well-to-do London merchants, he was a justice of the peace in Kent, represented the county in the House of Commons, and filled important royal posts. Chaucer showed that the English vernacular was coming of age and that in England, as in Italy, the profession of letters was no longer a clerical monopoly.

The medieval values still evident in the writings of Chaucer had largely vanished a century and a half later in the works of the Frenchman François Rabelais (ca. 1494–1553). Rabelais contributed far more to literature than the salacious wit for which he is famous. He studied the classics, particularly Plato and the ancient physicians; practiced and taught medicine; and created two of the great comic figures of letters, Gargantua and his son Pantagruel. The two are giants, and everything they do is of heroic dimensions. The abbey of Theleme (the Greek word for "will"), which Gargantua helps to found, permits its residents a wildly unmonastic existence:

> All their life was spent not in lawes, statutes or rules, but according to their own free will and pleasure. They rose out of their beds, when they thought good: they did eat, drink, labour, sleep, when they had a minde to it and were disposed for it. . . . In all their rule, and strictest tie of their order, there was but this one clause to be observed,
>
> DO WHAT THOU WILT.*

To Rabelais free will meant self-improvement on a grand scale. Gargantua exhorts Pantagruel to learn everything: he is to master Arabic in addition to Latin, read the New Testament in Greek and the Old in Hebrew, and study history, geometry, architecture, music, and civil law. He must also know "the fishes, all the fowles of the aire, all the several kinds of shrubs and trees," "all the sorts of herbs and flowers that grow upon the ground: all the various metals that are hid within the bowels of the earth." "In brief," Gargantua concludes, "let me see thee an Abysse, and bottomless pit of knowledge."† Both his insatiable appetite for knowledge and the exuberance with which Rabelais wrote about it represent important aspects of the Renaissance style.

The Philosophical Humanists

Another facet of the Renaissance style was highlighted by the third group of writers, the philosophical human-

ists, who aspired not only to universal knowledge but also to a universal truth and faith. They were centered first at Florence, attracted by the Platonic Academy founded in 1462 by Cosimo de' Medici, two years before his death, when he decided to underwrite the translation of Plato's works into Latin. He entrusted the commission to Marsilio Ficino (1433–1499), a medical student turned classicist, who translated not only the whole body of Plato's writings but some of the Neoplatonists' works as well. These followers of Plato, who flourished in the third century A.D. and later, long after the master, cultivated the search for God through mystical experiences. The opportunity for stressing the compatibility of Neoplatonism with Christianity exerted a strong attraction on Ficino and his circle.

Ficino, who was also a priest, argued that religious feeling and expression were as natural to man as barking was to dogs or neighing to horses. Man, he wrote, has the unique faculty called intellect, which he described as an "eye turned toward the intelligible light" or God. He coined the term "platonic love" to describe the love that transcends the senses and may also lead man to mystical communion with God. He supported his arguments with appeals to a wide range of authorities—the wise men of the ancient Near East, the prophets of the Old Testament, the apostles of the New, and the Greek philosophers, including Pythagoras and Aristotle in addition to Plato. Ficino seemed to be attempting a synthesis of all philosophy and religion.

The attempt was pressed further by Ficino's pupil, Pico della Mirandola (1463–1494). Pico crowded much into his thirty-one years and would have delighted Rabelais's Gargantua, for he knew Arabic and Hebrew in addition to Greek and Latin and studied Jewish allegory, Arab philosophy, and medieval Scholasticism, which, almost alone among humanists, he respected. Pico's tolerance was as broad as his learning. In his short *Oration on the Dignity of Man*, he cited approvingly Chaldean and Persian theologians, the priests of Apollo, Socrates, Pythagoras, Cicero, Moses, Paul, Augustine, Muhammad, Saint Francis, Thomas Aquinas, and many others.

In all the varied beliefs of this galaxy, Pico hoped to find the common denominator of a universal faith. This process of syncretism, of borrowing and assimilating from many sources, he was unable to complete, but, together with Ficino, he helped to found the great humane studies of comparative religion and comparative philosophy. And he reaffirmed and strengthened Ficino's idea that man was unique, the link between the mortal physical world and the immortal spirtual one, the hinge of the universe, so to speak. This concept of the uniqueness of man and his central position in the universe lay at the core of the Renaissance style. Yet among the Platonic humanists, the medieval element also remained strong; Pico, in his final years, gave away his worldly possessions and became an ardent supporter of the fanatical preacher Savonarola.

The "Prince of Humanists," the man who gave the

---

*F. Rabelais, *Gargantua and Pantagruel*, Urquhart trans. (New York, 1883), book I, chap. 57.
†Ibid., book I, chap. 8.

Hans Holbein's portrait of Erasmus.

those who claim to be wise. Erasmus mocked any group inflated by a sense of its own importance—merchants, churchmen, scientists, philosophers, courtiers, and kings. In *The Praise of Folly* he also punctured the pretensions of nations:

And now I see that it is not only in individual men that nature has implanted self-love. She implants a kind of it as a common possession in the various races, and even cities. By this token the English claim . . . good looks, music, and the best eating as their special properties. The Scots flatter themselves on the score of high birth and royal blood, not to mention their dialectical skill. Frenchmen have taken all politeness for their province. . . . The Italians usurp *belles lettres* and eloquence; and they all flatter themselves upon the fact that they alone, of all mortal men, are not barbarians. . . . The Greeks, as well as being the founders of the learned disciplines, vaunt themselves upon their titles to the famous heroes of old.*

In appraising human nature, in general, Erasmus tempered criticism with geniality. In what proportions, asks an ironic passage in *The Praise of Folly,* did Jupiter supply men with emotion and reason?

Well, the proportions run about one pound to half an ounce. Besides, he imprisoned reason in a cramped corner of the head, and turned over all the rest of the body to the emotions. After that he instated two most violent tyrants, as it were, in opposition to reason: anger, which holds the citadel of the breast, and consequently the very spring of life, the heart; and lust, which rules a broad empire lower down. . . .†

So, Erasmus concludes, we must cherish particularly the few outstanding individuals who have led great and good lives. Christ heads his list of great men; Cicero and Socrates rank very high. Plato's account of the death of Socrates moved Erasmus so deeply that he wanted to cry out, "Pray for us, Saint Socrates."

Erasmus possessed most of the main attributes of Renaissance humanism. He coupled a detached view of human nature with faith in the dignity of man or at least of a few individuals. He joined love of the classics with respect for Christian values. While he was both testy and vain, he had little use for the fine-spun arguments of Scholasticism and was a tireless advocate of what he called his "philosophy of Christ," the application of the doctrines of charity and love taught by Jesus. Yet, although Erasmus always considered himself a loyal son of the Church, he nevertheless helped to destroy the universality of Catholicism. His edition of the Greek New Testament raised disquieting doubts about the accuracy of the Latin translation in the Vulgate and therefore of Catholic biblical interpretations. His repeated insistence on elevating the spirit of piety above the letter of formal religious acts seemed to diminish the importance of the clergy, and his attacks on clerical laxity implied that the wide gap

most mature expression of the impulse to draw on all wisdom, was not Italian but Dutch—Desiderius Erasmus (1466–1536). He might also be called the foremost citizen of the Republic of Letters, for he studied, taught, and lived at Oxford and Cambridge, at Paris, and in Italy, and he particularly relished the free atmosphere of "mini" city-states like Louvain in the Low Countries, Basel in Switzerland, and Freiburg in the Rhineland. Building on Valla's scholarship, Erasmus published a scholarly edition of the Greek New Testament. He carried on a prodigious correspondence in Latin and compiled a series of *Adages* and *Colloquies* to give students examples of good Latin composition. Because Erasmus never regarded elegance of style as an end in itself, he assailed the "knowledge factories" of the grammarians:

As for those stilted, insipid verses they display on all occasions . . ., obviously the writer believes that the soul of Virgil has transmigrated into his own breast. But the funniest sight of all is to see them admiring and praising each other, trading compliment for compliment, thus mutually scratching each other's itch.*

This passage is from the satirical *Praise of Folly,* in which Erasmus employed the female Folly, as many of his contemporaries used the jester or fool, to contrast the spontaneous natural reactions of the supposedly foolish with the studied and self-serving artificiality of

*Desiderius Erasmus, *The Praise of Folly,* trans. Hoyt Hopewell Hudson (copyright 1941, © 1969 by Princeton University Press, Princeton Paperback, 1970), p. 71. Reprinted by permission of Princeton University Press.

*Ibid., p. 61.
†Ibid., p. 23.

between the lofty ideals and the corrupt practices of the Church could not long endure. A famous sixteenth-century epigram states: "Where Erasmus merely nodded, Luther rushed in; where Erasmus laid the eggs, Luther hatched the chicks; where Erasmus merely doubted, Luther laid down the law." When Luther did lay down the law in the Protestant revolt, however, the growing dogmatism and belligerence of the rebels soon alienated Erasmus. Both his fidelity to the Christian tradition, as he understood it, and his humanist convictions committed Erasmus to the position that the only weapons worthy of man were reason and discussion.

IV Science and Religion
An Age of Preparation

Humanism both aided and impeded the advance of science, so that the Renaissance centuries did not witness a dramatic rebirth of this discipline but rather constituted an age of preparation for the scientific revolution that was to come in the seventeenth century of Galileo and Newton. To this preparation the major contribution of the humanists was increased availability of ancient scientific authorities, as works by Galen, Ptolemy, Archimedes, and others were for the first time translated from Greek into the more accessible Latin. But an important contribution also came from the Scholastic tradition, which survived robustly throughout the Renaissance centuries, notably at the universities of Paris and Padua, despite the scorn the humanists heaped upon it. The Scholastics' insistence on systematic work habits and their enthusiasm for Aristotle promoted scientific studies.

Where humanism thwarted the advancement of science was its disposition to put old authorities high on a pedestal, beyond the reach of criticism. Few men of the Renaissance believed it possible to improve on the astronomy taught by Ptolemy during the second century A.D., or on the medicine taught by Galen in the same century. Galen, for example, had advanced the erroneous theory that the blood moved from one side of the heart to the other by passing through invisible pores in the thick wall of tissue separating the two sides of the organ. Actually, as Harvey was to discover in the seventeenth century, the blood gets from the one side to the other by circulating through the body and lungs. Galen's theory of invisible pores kept Leonardo da Vinci from anticipating Harvey; when the great artist's anatomical investigations led him to the brink of discovery, he backed away because he could not believe that Galen might have erred.

Da Vinci (1452–1519) exemplifies both the shortcomings and the achievements of Renaissance science. Taking notes in a hit-or-miss fashion, and in a secretive left-handed writing that must be held up to a mirror to be read, he did not have the modern scientist's concern for the systematic cataloging of observations and the frequent publication of findings and speculations. Yet Leonardo also showed remarkable inventiveness, drawing plans for lathes, pumps, war machines, flying machines, and many other contraptions, not all of them workable, but all highly imaginative. He had a passionate curiosity for anatomy and proportions, and for almost everything about man and nature. His accurate drawings of human embryos differed radically from the older notion of the fetus as a perfectly formed miniature human being. Moreover, Leonardo did not always bow before established authority, as he did before Galen. His geological studies convinced him that the earth was far older than the men of his time thought it to be. The Po River, he estimated, must have been flowing for two hundred thousand years to wash down the sediments forming its alluvial plain in northern Italy.

Invention and Technology

The best-known invention of the Renaissance—the printed book—furnishes an instructive case history of the way in which many technological advances contributed to the end result. The revolution in book production began in the twelfth century when Muslims in Spain introduced a technique first developed by the Chinese and began to make paper by shredding old rags, processing them with water, and then pressing the liquid out of the finished sheets. The cost of the new product was only a fraction of that of the sheepskin parchment or calfskin vellum theretofore employed for manuscripts. The next step came when engravers, adapting another Chinese technique, made a mirror image of a drawing on a woodblock or copper plate that could make many identical woodcuts or engravings. Sentences were then added to the plates or blocks to explain the drawings. Finally, movable type was devised, each piece representing a single letter on a minute bit of engraving that could be combined with other pieces to form words, sentences, a whole page, and then salvaged to be used over and over again. This crucial invention was perfected during the 1440s, almost certainly in the German Rhineland; Johann Gutenberg, who used to receive the credit for it, has been the focus of a scholarly controversy that has deflated his old heroic reputation.

The new invention gained wide popularity because printed books were not only much cheaper than manuscripts but also less prone to copyists' errors, which pyramided over the years because a copyist often failed to correct the mistakes in the manuscript he was following and made fresh ones of his own. By 1500 the total number of volumes in print had reached the millions, and Italy alone had some seventy-three presses employing movable type. The most famous of them, the Aldine Press in Venice (named for its founder, Aldus Manutius, 1450–1515), sold inexpensive, scholarly editions of the classics printed in a beautiful typeface that was said to be modeled on the handwriting of Petrarch and is the source of modern italics. Without the perfection of printing, Erasmus might not have become the acknowledged arbiter of European letters. Without it, Luther could not have secured the rapid distribution of his antipapal tracts, and the Protestant Reformation might not have rent Christian Europe asunder.

Although no other single invention can be compared with printing on the score of quick and decisive effects, many innovations ultimately had comparable influence. Gunpowder, for example, brought from China to medieval Europe, was used in the later campaigns of the Hundred Years' War. Improved firearms and artillery were to doom both the feudal knight and the feudal castle, for both were vulnerable to the new weapons. In navigation, as we have seen, the Venetians made galleys swifter, more capacious, and more seaworthy. At the same time, important marine aids came into general use, particularly the magnetic compass and the sailing charts, which, at least for the Mediterranean, established a high level of accuracy. By the close of the fifteenth century, Europeans possessed the equipment needed for the oncoming age of world discovery.

On land, the mining industry scored impressive technological advances. The engineers of the late medieval centuries solved some of the problems of extracting and smelting silver, iron, and other ores. Then, in 1556, a German physician and mining expert published a comprehensive treatise on the practices of the industry—*De re metallica* (All about Metals), which was translated from Latin into English in 1912 by an American mining engineer and his wife, the future President Hoover. Following the sixteenth-century custom, the author called himself Agricola, a Latinized version of his German name, Bauer ("peasant"). Agricola's treatise was an early specimen of those handbooks that are indispensable to the engineer, and its detailed observations on soil structures made it a pioneer study in geology as well.

Medicine

The wide dissemination of printed books with clear anatomical illustrations advanced medical skills, which were also improved by the partial lifting of the old ban against dissection of human cadavers. Pharmacology also progressed, thanks to experiments with the chemistry of drugs made by the eccentric Swiss physician Paracelsus (Theophrastus Bombastus von Hohenheim, 1493–1541). Despite his classical name, Paracelsus delighted in iconoclastic gestures, such as insisting on lecturing in German and burning the works of Galen to show his contempt for classical authority. The French surgeon Ambroise Paré (1517–1590), who also had little reverence for antiquity, laid the foundations for modern surgery by developing new techniques, notably that of sewing up blood vessels with stitches rather than cauterizing them with a hot iron. Yet many so-called physicians were quacks, and many teachers of medicine merely repeated the demonstrations that

Galen had made more than a thousand years earlier without attemtping to confirm the validity of his findings.

A striking exception to this rule was furnished by the physicians and scholars of the University of Padua. Protected against possible ecclesiastical censorship by the overlordship of Venice, which controlled the city, they maintained a lively tradition of scientific inquiry that presaged the seventeenth-century triumphs of the experimental method. In 1537, a young Belgian named Vesalius (1514–1564), trained at Paris, took a teaching post at Padua. Vesalius repeated the dissections of Galen, but watched for possible errors; thus he rejected Galen's notion of invisible pores in the wall of tissue within the heart because he could not find such pores. In 1543, Vesalius published *De humanis corporis fabrica* (Concerning the Structure of the Human Body), prepared with admirable concern for anatomical accuracy and detail, and illustrated with elaborate woodcuts.

Astronomy

The year 1543 marked not only the appearance of Vesalius' treatise but also the launching of modern astronomical studies with the publication of Copernicus' *De revolutionibus orbium coelestium* (Concerning the Revolutions of Heavenly Bodies). Born in Poland, of German extraction, Nicolaus Copernicus (1473–1543) studied law and medicine at Padua and other Italian universities, and spent thirty years as canon of a cathedral near Danzig. His work in mathematics and astronomy led him to attack the hypothesis of the geocentric (earth-centered) universe derived from Ptolemy and other astronomers of antiquity. In its place, he advanced the revolutionary new hypothesis of the heliocentric (sun-centered) universe.

The concept of the geocentric universe generally accepted in the sixteenth century included an elaborate system of spheres. Around the stationary earth there revolved some eighty spheres, each, as it were, a separate sky containing some of the heavenly bodies, each moving on an invisible circular path, each transparent so that we mortals could see the spheres beyond it. This imaginative and symmetrical picture of the universe had already come under attack before Copernicus, for observers could not make it tally with the actual behavior of heavenly bodies. Copernicus used these earlier criticisms and his own computations to arrive at the heliocentric concept, which required that the earth move around the sun rather than remain stationary.

The Copernican hypothesis had quite radical implications. It destroyed the idea of the earth's uniqueness by suggesting that it acted like other heavenly bodies, and thus opened the way to attacks on the uniqueness of the earth's human inhabitants. Nevertheless, once Copernicus had reversed the roles of the sun and the earth, his universe retained many Ptolemaic characteristics. Its heavens were still filled with spheres revolving along invisible orbits; only they now moved about a stationary sun, instead of the stationary earth, and Copernican astronomy required thirty-four of them, not eighty. The revolution in astronomy begun by Copernicus did not reach its culmination for a hundred and fifty years. The circular orbits of Copernicus had to yield to elliptical orbits; the scheme of thirty-four spheres had to be modified; and a theory explaining the forces that kept the universe together had to be put forward. And all these developments had to await the genius of Galileo and Newton and the observations made possible by the invention of the telescope.

Music

In the medieval curriculum music was part of the quadrivium, the fourfold way to knowledge, along with astronomy, arithmetic, and geometry. The bracketing of music with the sciences is not too surprising, since a great deal of mathematics underlies musical theory and notation. The mainstay of medieval sacred music was the Gregorian chant or plainsong, which relied on a single voice and thus did not involve the harmonizing of two or more voices. At the close of the Middle Ages more intricate innovations appeared. Musicians in the Burgundian domains of the Low Countries and northern France developed the technique of polyphony (from the Greek, "many voices"), which combined several voices in complicated harmony. When French and Flemish musicians journeyed to Italy in the fifteenth century, they introduced polyphonic music and borrowed in return the simple tunes of the dances and folksongs they encountered in southern Europe. Flemish composers even based masses on rowdy popular tunes. The end products of the interaction were the sacred and secular polyphonic compositions of the internationally renowned Fleming Josquin des Pres (ca. 1450–1521) and the hundred-odd masses of the Italian Palestrina (ca. 1526–1594). In spite of the popular borrowings much of this music sounds quite otherworldly today, since it lacks the dissonances and the strong rhythms and climaxes to which we are accustomed.

The secularism and individualism of the Renaissance and its taste for experimentation also affected music. New instruments were developed or imported—the violin, doublebass, and harpsichord; the organ, with its complement of keyboards, pedals, and stops; the kettledrum, which was adopted from the Polish army; and the lute, which originated in medieval Persia and reached Italy by way of Spain. Composers and performers began to lose the anonymity associated with the Middle Ages, although the era of prima donnas and other "stars" had not quite arrived. Paid professional singers staffed the famous choirs of Antwerp cathedral and of the Vatican. Josquin des Pres found patrons at the courts of Milan, Rome, and Paris, and both the pope and various cardinals commissioned Palestrina to write masses. A retinue of musicians became a fixture of court life, with the dukes of Burgundy, Philip the Good, and Charles the Bold, leading the way. Lower down the social scale, German artisans, calling themselves mastersingers, organized choral groups; the most

famous of them, Hans Sachs, a cobbler in Nuremberg in the 1500s, was later immortalized in Wagner's opera *Die Meistersinger*.

The Renaissance and the Church

While the relations between musicians and the Church were generally harmonious, Renaissance science as a whole sometimes aroused discord. Even though Copernicus dedicated his great book to the pope, Christendom did not welcome a theory that questioned the belief in an earth-centered and man-centered universe. By 1543, however, Western Christendom was preoccupied by its division into the warring factions of Catholic and Protestant. To what extent was the Renaissance responsible for the shattering religious crisis of the Reformation? A more detailed examination of the causes of the Reformation will be found in the next chapter; here a few generalizations about the relationship between the Renaissance and the church may be suggested.

First, the Renaissance did not make the Reformation inevitable. It is an oversimplification to suppose that the religious individualism of Luther arose directly out of the more general individualism of the Renaissance. Looking back over the checkered culture of the age, one can find many elements—materialism, self-indulgence, power politics—that are hard to reconcile with traditional Christian values. If pushed to extremes, these elements could indeed become anti-Christian—but they were seldom pushed to extremes. Even the most ruthless condottieri of politics and business, men like Cesare Borgia and Jacob Fugger, remained nominal Christians. Also, a pronounced anticlerical like Machiavelli reserved his most stinging criticism for the pope's claim to temporal authority, not his claim to ecclesiastical supremacy.

Second, the most characteristic intellectual movement of the Renaissance—humanism—did not propose the abandonment of traditional Christian values. Men such as Pico and Erasmus proposed to enrich or purify Christianity; they did not intend to subvert it. As a matter of fact, the Neoplatonic doctrines cherished by Pico and the Platonic Academy had long been identified with the mystical aspects of the Catholic faith. Erasmus, perhaps the most representative thinker of humanism, was too strongly attached to Catholicism and too moderate in temperament to be a revolutionary.

Finally, a religious crisis was indeed gathering during the Renaissance, but it was more internal than external. That is, the Church was only to a limited extent the victim of outside forces operating beyond its control, like the challenge presented to its old international dominion by the new national monarchies. If the Church of the 1400s had been strong and healthy, it might have met such external challenges successfully. Except in Spain, however, the Church set a flabby and unedifying example by and large, although many honorable exceptions to the prevailing laxity and backwardness could be found. Priests were often illiterate, untrained, underpaid, and immoral; many bishops—following good medieval precedent, it must be admitted—behaved as politicians, not as churchmen.

Perhaps the worst shortcomings existed at the top, in the papacy itself. In the fourteenth and early fifteenth centuries, the papacy experienced the crises of Babylonian Captivity, the Great Schism, and the Conciliar Movement. It emerged from the ordeal with its power reinvigorated, notably by its victory over the reformers who sought to make church councils a check against unlimited papal absolutism. But the triple crisis gravely damaged the spiritual prestige of the office, since such Renaissance popes as Sixtus IV, Alexander VI, and Julius II did little to repair the damage. For three-quarters of a century after 1450 the see of Peter was occupied by men who scored political and military successes and lavished money on learning and on the arts. They bequeathed to posterity, among other treasures, the Vatican Library, the Sistine Chapel, and the early parts of the Basilica of Saint Peter. But this munificence increased the burden of ecclesiastical taxation and other fiscal demands, and increased also the resentment that higher levies usually arouse. Papal indifference to spiritual functions enfeebled the Church at a time when it needed firm and dedicated control. The Church was ruled by connoisseurs and condottieri when it needed reformers.

Intellectually, too, the clergy were losing the vitality they had possessed in the age of Abelard and Aquinas. Some of the monks and friars on university faculties hardly qualified as teachers; they blindly defended a decadent Scholasticism against the new humanist studies and provoked a blistering satire, *The Letters of Obscure Men.* The story began when Johann Reuchlin (1455–1522), a German humanist working with Pico at Florence, learned Hebrew in order to read the great books of Judaism. On returning to Germany, he aroused the wrath of theological faculties by suggesting that a knowledge of the sacred Jewish writings might enable a man to be a better-informed Christian. Arraigned in an ecclesiastical court, Reuchlin, who was a layman, assembled in his defense testimonials from leading humanists, *The Letters of Eminent Men.* Then, in 1516 and 1517, a couple of his friends published *The Letters of Obscure Men,* supposedly exchanged between Reuchlin's clerical opponents but actually a hoax designed to laugh the opposition out of court by mocking the futility of theological hair-splitting. One of the "obscure men" related an experience in a Roman tavern:

> For you must know that we were lately sitting in an inn, having our supper, and were eating eggs, when on opening one, I saw that there was a young chicken within.
>
> This I showed to a comrade; whereupon quoth he to me, "Eat it up speedily, before the taverner sees it, for if he mark it, you will have to pay for a fowl."
>
> In a trice I gulped down the egg, chicken and all.

> And then I remembered that it was Friday!
>
> Whereupon I said to my crony, "You have made me commit a mortal sin, in eating flesh on the sixth day of the week!"
>
> But he averred that it was not a mortal sin—nor even a venial one, seeing that such a chickling is accounted merely as an egg, until it is born.
>
> Then I departed, and thought the matter over.
>
> And by the Lord, I am in a mighty quandary, and know not what to do.
>
> It seemeth to me that these young fowls in eggs are flesh, because their substance is formed and fashioned into the limbs and body of an animal, and possesseth a vital principle.
>
> It is different in the case of grubs in cheese, and such-like, because grubs are accounted fish, as I learnt from a physician who is also skilled in Natural Philosophy.
>
> Most earnestly do I entreat you to resolve the question that I have propounded. For if you hold that the sin is mortal, then, I would fain get shrift here, ere I return to Germany.*

Although Reuchlin lost his case and was sentenced to pay the costs of the trial, he managed to avoid making any payment.

Attempts at Renewal and Reform

Dedicated Christians, both lay and clerical, were aware that the Church needed a thorough cleansing. Papal opposition, however, blocked fresh attempts within the ecclesiastical hierarchy to increase the powers of representative church councils. And the great renovation fostered by Queen Isabella and Cardinal Jiménez was restricted to Spanish lands. Meantime, a quiet Catholic renewal had been advanced by the activities of the Brothers and Sisters of the Common Life. Founded in the Low Countries in the 1370s, they consisted of lay people who pooled their resources in communal living and followed the spiritual discipline of a monastic order without, however, taking religious vows. They also emphasized service to one's fellow man as a way of practicing the ideals of Christianity. Opposed to Scholasticism, the Brethren of the Common Life started schools of their own, which had a high reputation in fifteenth-century Europe. Erasmus, who was educated in one of them, complained that the curriculum was too orthodox and rigid, yet he adopted the goals of the Brethren in his own "philosophy of Christ," with its belief that the example of Jesus should guide men in their daily lives. A similar theme, expressed in more mystical terms, ran through the enormously popular *Imitation of Christ,* written by Thomas à Kempis, one of the Brethren. Its message, like that of the Common Life movement, was addressed to the inner life of the individual rather than to the reform of the Christian community or its institutions.

A more radical and sweeping reform movement

*Adapted from F. G. Stokes, ed., *Epistolae obscurorum virorum* (New Haven, 1925), pp. 445–447.

was launched by the Dominican friar Savonarola (1452–1498), who won the favor of the Medici through the influence of Pico. His eloquent sermons and reputed gift of predicting the future soon made him the most popular preacher in Florence. Sparing no one in his denunciations of un-Christian conduct he delivered this typical tirade:

> You Christians should always have the Gospel with you, I do not mean the book, but the spirit, for if you do not possess the spirit of grace and yet carry with you the whole book, of what advantage is it to you? And again, all the more foolish are they who carry round their necks Breviaries, notes, tracts and writings, until they look like pedlars going to a fair. Charity does not consist in the writing of papers. The true books of Christ are the Apostles and saints, and true reading consists in imitating their lives. But in these days men are like books made by the Devil. They speak against pride and ambition and yet they are immersed in them up to their eyes. They preach chastity and maintain concubines. They enjoin fasting and partake of splendid feasts. . . . Only look to-day at the prelates. They are tied to earthly vanities. They love them. The cure of souls is no longer their chief concern. . . . In the Primitive Church the chalices were made of wood and the prelates of gold—today—chalices of gold, prelates of wood!*

He particularly abominated Pope Alexander VI, whom he cursed for "a devil" and "a monster" presiding over a "ribald" and "harlot" church.

In the political confusion following the death of Lorenzo the Magnificent (1492), Savonarola gained power and prestige in Florence, attracting many enthusiastic supporters, including Pico and the artists Botticelli and Michelangelo. By 1497, he was virtual dictator of the Florentine republic and organized troops of boys and girls to tour the city, collect all "vanities," from cosmetics to pagan books and paintings, and burn them on public bonfires. This hysterical pitch of zeal could not be sustained for long, and when Alexander VI placed Florence under an interdict and excommunicated Savonarola, his popular following began to disperse, especially after he had failed in his promise to bring a miracle to pass. Savonarola was condemned for heresy; on May 23, 1498, he was hanged and his body was burned. Savonarola perished not only at the hands of his political and ecclesiastical enemies but also through his own fanaticism. Like most extreme puritans, he did not realize that morals could not be transformed overnight; he was in a sense too unworldly to survive. But the church that he sought to purge was too worldly to survive without undergoing the major crisis of the Reformation.

V The Fine Arts

Even more than the writers and preachers of the Renaissance its artists displayed an extraordinary range of interests and talents. They found patrons both among the princes of the church and among merchant princes, condottieri, and secular rulers. They took for subjects their own patrons and the pagan gods and heroes of antiquity as well as Christ, the Virgin, and saints. Although their income was often meager, they enjoyed increasing status both as technicians and as creative personalities; they boasted of their skills and attainments, for in the arts, too, the anonymous or community stamp of medieval culture was yielding to the ego-trip of the individual.

The artists liberated painting and sculpture from subordination to architecture, which had been the "queen of the arts" during the Middle Ages. The statues, carvings, altarpieces, and stained glass contributing so much to Romanesque and Gothic churches had seldom been entities in themselves but only parts of a larger whole. In the Renaissance the number of freestanding pictures and sculptures—each one an independent aesthetic object—steadily increased.

In painting important advances came with the development of *chiaroscuro* (Italian, "bright-dark"), stressing contrasts of light and shade, and with the growing use of perspective, both of which enhanced the three-dimensional quality of a picture. In the early Renaissance, painters worked in fresco or tempera: fresco involved the application of pigments to the wet plaster of a wall, and painters had to work swiftly before the plaster dried; in tempera they mixed pigments with a sizing, often of eggs, which allowed them to work after the plaster had dried but gave the end-product a muddy look. Oil paints, developed first in Flanders and brought to Italy in the last half of the fifteenth century, overcame the deficiencies of fresco and tempera by permitting leisurely, delicate work and ensuring clearer and more permanent colors.

The Flemish origin of oil paints serves as a reminder that modern scholarship has exploded the old idea that the artistic Renaissance was exclusively an Italian phenomenon existing in splendid isolation and impervious to influences from other quarters of Europe or from the preceding medieval centuries. An older Gothic strain persisted even in Italy, evident in Milan where throughout the Renaissance centuries much money and energy went into building the cathedral, a celebrated specimen of the Gothic "wedding-cake" style. Late Gothic artists, especially those in the Low Countries during the Burgundian ascendancy of the fourteenth and fifteenth centuries, contributed to the Renaissance not only by introducing oil paints but also by stressing decorative richness and an almost photographic realism in depicting the details of nature. Botanists can identify dozens of flowers and plants in the famous Ghent altarpiece (*The Adoration of the Lamb*) of the Van Eyck brothers, who worked in the early fifteenth century. The commercial links between Flemish and Italian cities promoted cultural interchange, and Italians were eager to buy paintings by the Van Eycks and other Flemish masters and also admired the tapes-

*P. Misciatelli, *Savonarola* (New York, 1930), pp. 60–61.

tries, the music, and the fashions of the opulent Burgundian court.

Yet, in spite of these qualifications diluting the unique Italian quality of Renaissance art, it is evident that without Giotto, Masaccio, Leonardo, Michelangelo and other Italian men of genius the Renaissance could never have become one of the very great ages in the history of art. In sculpture it rivaled the golden centuries of Greece, and in painting it was more than a rebirth, for it transformed a rather limited medium into a dazzling new aesthetic instrument. It is no wonder that historians in general often adopt the Italian custom of calling these centuries trecento, quattrocento, and cinquecento (literally, "300s," "400s," and "500s," in abbreviated reference to the 1300s, 1400s and 1500s).

Painting in Italy

Prior to the trecento, Italian artists were much influenced by the Byzantine tradition and produced two-dimensional paintings lacking in depth or movement. Giotto (1276–1337), the father, or perhaps grandfather, of Renaissance painting, though often following Byzantine models, sought to make his paintings less stiff and austere and more lifelike and emotional. He learned much from the realistic statues of Italian sculptors who had studied the striking sculptures on the portals of Gothic cathedrals such as Chartres. Perhaps the best place to view Giotto's achievement is the Arena Chapel at Padua, near Venice, where he executed a series of frescoes creating the illusion of three dimensions by his use of foreshortening and perspective. *Joachim and the Shepherds* shows the pious Joachim returning to his sheepfold after being excluded from the temple because his failure to beget children was taken as a sign that he was accursed by God. His entry from the left of the fresco heightens its drama as the viewer's eyes, in the left-to-right movement of reading, go from Joachim to his dog, with right paw raised in greeting, and then to the lively-looking sheep. Joachim seems downcast by his unjust exclusion, while the *chiaroscuro* on the folds of his cloak suggests the substantial body underneath. In the *Lamentation,* also in the Arena Chapel, the emotional intensity surrounding the burial of Christ is conveyed by the angels who seem to be beating their wings in anguish as they fly above the mourners.

As a person, Giotto exemplified the versatile Renaissance individual, hungry for fame and success. He was no anonymous craftsman, content to work in obscurity, and added to his income from lucrative art commissions by lending money, running a debt-collection service, and renting looms at high fees to weavers in the woolen trade. The richest man in Padua, Enrico Scrovegni, commissioned Giotto to decorate the Arena Chapel on behalf of the soul of his father, whom Dante's *Divine Comedy* placed in hell because he had been a notorious usurer. In Florence, the great banking families of Bardi and Peruzzi employed Giotto to execute frescoes in the Church of Santa Croce.

The example of the Bardi and Peruzzi was followed by many later rich Florentines whose patronage made their city the artistic capital of the Renaissance. Lorenzo the Magnificent, for example, subsidized the painter Botticelli (1445–1510) as well as the humanists of the Platonic Academy. Court painters were commonplace in other states, both in Italy and elsewhere. In Milan the Sforza usurper, Il Moro, made Leonardo da Vinci in effect his minister of fine arts and director of public works; after Il Moro's fortunes collapsed, Leonardo found new patrons in Cesare Borgia, the pope, and the French kings Louis XII and Francis I. The Renaissance popes, who also employed Botticelli, Raphael, Michelangelo, and other luminaries, had a keen aesthetic appreciation coupled with a determination to have Rome surpass Florence in artistic eminence.

The mixture of worldly and religious motives among patrons also characterized the works they commissioned. Artists applied equal skill to scenes from classical mythology, to portraits of their secular contemporaries, and to such Christian subjects as the Madonna, the Nativity, and the Crucifixion. Often the sacred and the secular could be found in the same picture. In the *Last Judgment,* in the Arena Chapel, Giotto portrayed Scrovegni, the donor, on the same scale as the saints, and in the Peruzzi Chapel he framed religious frescoes with medallions depicting the members of the endowing family. Giotto's successors sometimes brought the whole family of the donor into the picture, as in Botticelli's *Adoration of the Magi,* which shows Cosimo and Lorenzo de' Medici as well as the artist himself.

Renaissance artists at first made classical and pagan subjects like Jupiter or Venus just another lord and lady of the chivalric class. Later they restored the sense of historical appropriateness by using classical settings and painting the figures in the nude; at the same time, however, they also created an otherworldly quality. When Botticelli was commissioned by the Medici to do *The Birth of Venus,* he made the goddess, emerging full-grown from a seashell, more ethereal than sensual, and he placed the figures in the arrangement usual for the baptism of Christ. In *Primavera,* Botticelli's allegory of spring, the chief figures—Mercury, Venus, The Three Graces, Flora (bedecked with blossoms), and Spring herself (wafted in by the West Wind)—are all youthful, delicate, and serene, as if this were the Platonic idea of springtime. Botticelli seems to have moved in the circle of Pico della Mirandola and the Florentine Neoplatonists, and his paintings often suggest an aspiration to some mystic Platonic realm.

Botticelli used line and color to achieve artistic effects; in contrast, Masaccio (1401–1428), a talented Florentine of an earlier generation, relied on mass and perspective. In painting the *Expulsion from Eden* for a

Florentine chapel, Masaccio intensified the sense of tragedy by bold *chiaroscuro* treatment of the bodies of Adam and Eve, who appear to be overwhelmed by shame and sorrow. Masaccio, who was called "Giotto reborn," anticipated some of the achievements of the Italian "High Renaissance," the last decades of the quattrocento and the first five or six of the cinquecento. The High Renaissance is studded with so many important names—Raphael, Giorgione, Carpaccio, Tintoretto, Veronese—that we can only sample its brilliance by examining three of its leading masters, Leonardo, Michelangelo, and Titian.

Leonardo da Vinci (1452–1519) completed relatively few pictures, since his scientific activities and innumerable odd jobs for his patrons consumed much of his energy. In addition, his celebrated fresco, *The Last Supper,* began to deteriorate during his own lifetime because the mold on the damp monastery wall in Milan destroyed the clarity of the oil pigments he used. Luckily, Leonardo's talent and his extraordinary range of interests may also be studied in his drawings and notebooks. The drawings include preliminary sketches of paintings, fanciful war machines, and mere doodles along with remarkably realistic portrayals of human embryos and of deformed or suffering individuals. Leonardo combined a zeal for scientific precision with a taste for the grotesque that recalls the gargoyles of a Gothic cathedral.

From his intensive study of human anatomy Leonardo drew up rules for indicating the action of human muscles and for the proportions among the various parts of the human body. When he applied his own rules with the brush, he sought not only to render nature faithfully but also to show people in motion rather than in static repose. In *The Madonna of the Rocks,* the Virgin extends her left hand over the Christ child, who raises the fingers of his right hand in a gesture of blessing; the angel supports the child and points a finger toward the infant Saint John, whose hands are clasped in prayer. The arrangement of the four figures in a pyramid, the foreshortening of the arms, the careful painting of hair and clothing, and the details of plants and flowers in the background all reveal Leonardo's sense of geometry and passion for accuracy.

In composing the *Last Supper* Leonardo departed dramatically from previous interpretations, which depicted the solemn moment of the final communion, with the treachery of Judas suggested only by placing him in isolation from the others, who often looked, it has been observed, as though they were sitting for a group portrait. Leonardo divided the apostles into four groups of three men each around the central figure of Christ—an innovation that was most effective psychologically, even though it would have been physically impossible for the thirteen men to have eaten together at the small table depicted. Leonardo's second departure was to choose the tense moment when Jesus announced the coming betrayal and to place Judas

Self-portrait of Leonardo da Vinci.

among the apostles, relying on facial expression and bodily posture to convey the guilt of the one and the consternation of the others.

Michelangelo Buonarotti (1475–1564), though best known as a sculptor, ranks among the immortals of painting as a result of one prodigious achievement—the frescoes he executed for the Sistine Chapel in the Vatican. Pope Sixtus IV had built the chapel and his nephew, Pope Julius II (1503–1513), entrusted the commission of decorating its walls and ceiling to Michelangelo. He covered a huge area (54 by 134 feet) with 343 separate figures and spent four years working almost single-handed, assisted only by a plasterer and a color mixer, painting on his back atop a scaffold, sometimes not even descending for his night's rest and arguing with the impatient pope from his lofty perch. Michelangelo depicted the grandest scenes from the

Titian's portrait of his friend, Pietro Aretino (1492–1556), author of ribald satirical comedies.

in a mantle, an ever-changing patriarch: hovering over the waters, he is benign; giving life to the motionless Adam or directing Eve to arise, he is gently commanding; creating the sun and the moon, he is the formidable all-powerful deity. In this vast gallery of figures, nude and draped, Michelangelo summed up all that the Renaissance had learned about perspective, anatomy, and motion.

Both Michelangelo and Leonardo had received their artistic training in Florence; Titian (1477–1576) was identified with Venice, and the rich reds and purples that are his hallmark exemplify the flamboyance and pageantry of the city. Titian's longevity, productivity, and success were extraordinary. At the start, he was engaged to do frescoes for the Venetian headquarters of German merchants, and he went on to do portraits of rich merchants, provide *Madonna*s and altarpieces for churches and monasteries, and execute a battle scene for the palace of the doge. In the middle decades of the sixteenth century he was offered commissions by half the despots of Italy and crowned heads of Europe. A gallery of Titian's portraits makes a fine introduction to the high politics of the cinquecento—a condottiere, shrewd, cultivated and worn from the della Rovere family that had produced Sixtus IV and Julius II; Paul III, one of the last of the Renaissance popes, crafty, bent with age, and flanked by his grandsons, one watchful, the other buttering up the old man; and, finally, the emperor Charles V, burdened with all the problems of the vast Hapsburg domains.

Book of Genesis, which he placed in a sequence that reflected a Neoplatonic belief in the ascent from the fleshly to the sublime. He began over the chapel entrance with *The Drunkenness of Noah* and ended over the altar with *The Creation.* God appears repeatedly, draped

Dürer's self-portrait of 1500.

Painting in Northern Europe

In northern Europe the masters of the cinquecento were influenced by their native Gothic traditions as well as by Titian and other Italians. The ranking northern painters included two Germans, Dürer (1471–1528) and Holbein (1497–1543), and two from the Low Countries, Bosch (1462–1516) and Pieter Brueghel (1520–1569). Dürer received commissions from the emperor Maximilian (the grandfather of Charles V), and Brueghel from wealthy businessmen of Antwerp and Brussels. Holbein, who was armed with an introduction from Erasmus when he went to England, executed portraits of Henry VIII and his courtiers as well as a likeness of Erasmus that catches the humanist's wit and intelligence.

Dürer, who became identified with Lutheranism in his later years, created what has been termed the first great Protestant art, in which he simplified traditional Christian themes by pruning them of what Lutherans regarded as superfluous Catholic trimmings. But this was only one facet of Dürer's many-sided talent. His fascination with nature led him to include rather docile wild creatures in many pictures, notably the Virgin in the unusual pose of *The Madonna with Many Animals.* His realistic and compassionate portrait of his aged mother might almost have been taken from

Leonardo's notebooks. And his improvements in the techniques of woodcuts and engravings enabled him to mass-produce his own drawings as illustrations for printed books. Dürer was the first artist in history to become a bestseller.

Northern art retained the medieval fascination with the monstrous and supernatural. Dürer showed this Gothic strain in a series of woodcuts depicting the Four Horsemen and other grim marvels of the Apocalypse. Bosch, who reflected the piety and reforming spirit of the Brethren of the Common Life, made his paintings graphic sermons filled with nightmarish apparitions illustrating the omnipresence of sin and evil and foreshadowing the techniques and effects of the surrealists of our own century. Brueghel's works contain coats-of-arms that actually fight, shellfish that fly, and monstrous hybrids that have insect wings, artichoke bodies, and flower heads. Other paintings of Brueghel are realistic and sensitive comments on human misery, such as *The Blind Leading the Blind* with its file of wretches falling down. Brueghel also favored two types of painting otherwise neglected in the cinquecento. One was the landscape: his series illustrating farming activities through the year was somewhat in the tradition of late medieval books of hours but with new attention to the changing light and atmosphere of the seasons. The other was the densely populated scene of everyday life—children's games and peasant weddings, dances and festivals, depicted with Rabelaisian gusto yet suggesting that people are doomed to repeat endlessly the same simple pleasures and obvious follies. On the whole, northern art was more didactic, more concerned with moralizing, than its Italian counterpart.

Sculpture

In the Renaissance, sculpture and painting enjoyed a close organic relationship, and Italian pictures owed some of their three-dimensional quality to the artists' study of the sister discipline. Leading painters like Michelangelo and Leonardo were accomplished sculptors, the latter, for example, producing miniature anatomical horses stripped of their hides to show the bones and muscles. The first major Renaissance sculptor was Donatello (1386–1466), whose statue of the condottiere Gattamelata in Padua is a landmark in the history of art. The subject is secular, the treatment classical (Gattamelata looks like the commander of a Roman legion), and the medium bronze, not the stone of medieval sculpture. Donatello created the first statue of a nude male since antiquity, a bronze David who, however, looks more like a handsome youth than the inspired slayer of Goliath. Yet Donatello's wooden statue of Mary Magdalen, all lank hair and skin and bones, though criticized as "an emaciated monster," is a saint who really looks the part.

Still another gifted Florentine, Verrocchio (1435–1488), extended the concern for social and political realism. His *David* looks like a plebeian lad, and his statue of the condottiere Colleoni in Venice, mounted on a muscular horse, is tougher and rougher than Donatello's Gattamelata. Painter, goldsmith, teacher of Leonardo, and student of architecture, geometry, music, and philosophy, Verrocchio ranked among the universal men of the Renaissance. So did Cellini (1500–1571), goldsmith, engraver, devotee of high living, and author of a famous egotistical autobiography. Cellini boasted as patrons two popes as well as King

Pieter Brueghel the Elder's "The Blind Leading the Blind," 1563.

Brunelleschi's dome for the Cathedral in Florence.

Though he died long before the great basilica was completed in 1626, and though his successors altered many details of his plan, the huge dome, which was the key feature of the whole structure, followed his basic design. Saint Peter's exemplifies many of the features that distinguish Renaissance architecture from Gothic. Gothic cathedrals are topped by great spires and towers; Saint Peter's is crowned by Michelangelo's massive dome, which rises 435 feet above the floor below yet is almost dwarfed by the massive structure underneath. Gothic buildings, with their great windows, pointed arches, and high-flung vaults, create an impression of strain and instability; Saint Peter's appears indestructible because of its heavier walls, stout columns, and round arches.

Michelangelo modelled the dome on the one completed a century earlier by Brunelleschi (1377–1446) for the cathedral in Florence, itself a monumental achievement. Covering a space 350 feet wide by 300 high, beautifully proportioned, shaped more like a cup than a bowl and with greater stress on the vertical than the domes of antiquity, Brunelleschi's dome required 25,000 tons of stone, which were hoisted into place without immense scaffolding in a tour de force of engineering. It earned its designer a place as an architectural innovator comparable to that of Giotto in painting.

Renaissance architects shared the humanists' enthusiasm for Platonic and Pythagorean concepts of perfect ideas and perfect geometrical forms. Palladio (1518–1580), the leading architectural theorist of the *cinquecento*, stressed the symbolic value of designing churches on the plan of the Greek cross, which had four arms of equal length in contrast to the Latin cross used in Gothic churches, which had one long arm forming the nave. If the ends of the arms of the Greek cross were rounded and the spaces between the arms filled with rounded chapels, then the structure became a circle. Some scholars have interpreted the new popularity of the Greek-cross design as a shift from the medieval emphasis on the sacrifice of Christ to the Renaissance celebration of the perfection of God. Palladio himself designed many elegant structures—the much-photographed Church of San Giorgio Maggiore on an island at the mouth of the Grand Canal in Venice, and palaces, public buildings, villas, and a theater in the area of Vicenza, his home town, in the hinterland of Venice.

In Renaissance Europe private individuals had the wherewithal for lavish residences, and the increasing prevalence of law and order meant that a man's home no longer needed to be a fortress. Elaborately symmetrical villas dotted the Italian countryside, and in the cities the characteristic structure was the *palazzo*, not necessarily a ruler's palace but an imposing townhouse combining business offices and residential apartments; many examples survive today in Rome, Florence, Venice, and other Italian cities. The palazzo was generally three-storied and rectangular, with windows ar-

Francis I of France and the Medici grand duke of Tuscany, the last of whom commissioned his elegant statue of Perseus holding aloft the head of Medusa, which today commands a place of honor overlooking a central square in Florence.

On the same piazza is a replica of Michelangelo's colossal statue of David, a ham-handed muscular nude more than sixteen feet high, fashioned from an enormous block of marble abandoned by another sculptor. Michelangelo went on to carry sculpture to a summit it had not attained since the age of Pericles, perhaps to the highest peak in its whole history. Michelangelo showed his ingenuity in solving technical problems with the world-famous *Pietà*, now in Saint Peter's, which shows the Virgin mourning the dead Christ. It was exceedingly difficult to pose a seated woman with a limp adult body across her lap, yet Michelangelo succeeded triumphantly. The face of Mary is sorrowful yet composed and younger than that of Christ, for Michelangelo explained that she is the eternal Virgin, always youthful, and would not grieve as an earthly mother would. In a statue of Moses, commissioned by Julius II for his tomb, Michelangelo made one side of the prophet's face show compassion and the other reveal the stern lawgiver, somewhat as he depicted the varying aspects of God on the Sistine ceiling.

Architecture

In 1546, at the age of seventy, Michelangelo agreed to become the chief architect of Saint Peter's in Rome.

ranged in symmetrical rows and the monotony of regularity relieved by such devices as pillars, pilasters and cornices and by the use of different finishes of stone, rough or smooth, for different stories. The fame of Italian builders spread far afield, and in Moscow Italian experts supervised the remodeling of the Kremlin for Ivan III. Often the Italian style was combined with older native architecture to produce striking hybrid designs, such as the great châteaux built in the Loire valley of France during the sixteenth century, which combined elements from the feudal castle, the Gothic church, and the Italian palazzo.

VI   The Art of Daily Living

Indoors, Renaissance buildings reflected the improving standard of life among the well-to-do. The small classical rooms were easier to heat than the vast drafty halls of the Middle Ages, and items of furniture began to multiply beyond the spartan medieval complement of built-in beds, benches, cupboards, and tables. Although chairs were still largely reserved for the master of the house and important guests, the variety of chests, benches, or stools on which people could perch was increasing. Chests, which were used not only for storage and sitting but also as trunks on a journey, were usually elaborately painted or carved, sometimes on the model of ancient sarcophagi—one more instance of the Renaissance passion for the classical. New articles of furniture served more specialized purposes: the bookcase to house the new printed books (medieval manuscripts had been kept in chests); the writing desk or bureau (a name derived from *burrus,* the red color of the felt used to protect its surface from the counters used in calculations); and the jewel cabinet, a miniature chest on high legs often encrusted with ivory or inlaid work.

The popularity of brooches, pendants, and other forms of jewelry with intricate gold settings attested both to the affluence and to the discriminating taste of Renaissance men and women. The fact that silversmiths made elaborately etched helmets, shields, and suits of armor better fitted for show than for military use was a sign of the vanishing medieval preoccupation with security. Along with gold and silver work fine glass was highly esteemed, particularly the elaborate and delicate work of Venetian craftsmen. Families in moderate circumstances as well as the rich had embroidered household linens and handsome brass and pewter utensils. One real luxury, however, was a mirror, small and made of polished metal, for mirror glass had not yet been perfected.

What the Italian man of the Renaissance saw when he looked into the mirror was a basic gown or tunic surmounted by a cape or cloak, the whole made of increasingly colorful and elegant material. Personal cleanliness advanced with the custom of the weekly bath and change of body linen; bodily wastes were disposed of in the outside privy or in a "close-stool"

Michelangelo's marble statue of David, 1501–1504.

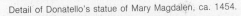

Detail of Donatello's statue of Mary Magdalen, ca. 1454.

Palladio's Palazzo Chiericati, Vicenza.

(commode) indoors. In Italy table manners made a real breakthrough with the substitution of the fork for the fingers, the fading of the old habit of tossing bones and other debris from a meal onto the floor beneath the table, and the use of easily cleaned tiles or mosaics for flooring. Elsewhere progress was slower: in England the fork was not in common use until the seventeenth century (witness Henry VIII tackling a chicken with his bare hands), and the floor of the great hall in many a house was still covered with rushes, "sweetening the rushes" being the putting of a fresh layer of rushes on top and sprinkling fragrant herbs to counter the stench from the lower layers.

Castiglione's *Courtier*

The changing values and ideals of Renaissance men and women, living as they did in a world no longer medieval but not yet fully modern, may be studied in *The Courtier,* a dialogue on manners published by the Italian Castiglione in 1528. Castiglione knew his subject: himself an elegant aristocrat, he had spent years on diplomatic missions and at the highly civilized court of Urbino. He begins his delineation of the ideal cour-

tier with a group of traits differing very little from those commended in the paladins of medieval chivalry:

> I will have this our Courtier to be a gentleman born and of a good house. For it is a great deal less dispraise for him that is not born a gentleman to fail in the acts of virtue than for a gentleman.
>
> I will have him by nature to have not only a wit and a comely shape of person and countenance, but also a certain grace . . . that shall make him at the first sight acceptable and loving unto who so beholdeth him.
>
> I judge the principal and true profession of a Courtier ought to be in feats of arms, the which above all I will have him to practise lively.*

The chivalry of Castiglione has all the patronizing attitude of the patrician toward the plebeian, yet it never gets out of hand; it is restrained by the sense of balance and grasp of reality that we have already found in some of the humanists. In love, the perfect gentleman should adore in his lady "no less the beauty of the mind than of the body." In duels and private quarrels, he

*Adapted from B. Castiglione, *The Courtier,* trans. T. Hoby, modernized (1907), pp. 21, 23, 26.

should be far more moderate than the medieval knight thought to be honorable. He should excel in sport, like the knight of old, should hunt, wrestle, swim, "play at tennis." He should also receive a good education

> . . . in those studies which they call Humanity, and . . . have not only the understanding of the Latin tongue, but also of the Greek, because of the many and sundry things that with great excellency are written in it. Let him much exercise himself in poets, and no less in orators and historiographers, and also in writing both rhyme and prose, and especially in this our vulgar tongue.*

Here in *The Courtier* we encounter once again the celebrated Renaissance concept of the universal man that we have already met in the writings of Pico and Rabelais.

Finally, when Castiglione praises the beauty of the universe (which is, of course, Ptolemaic, not Copernican), he puts into words more eloquently than any of his contemporaries the style of the Renaissance:

> Behold the state of this great engine of the world, which God created for the health and preservation of everything that was made: The heaven round beset with so many heavenly lights; and in the middle the Earth environed with the elements and upheld with the very weight of itself. . . . These things among themselves have such force by the

*Ibid., p. 70.

knitting together of an order so necessarily framed that, with altering them any one jot, they should all be loosed and the world would decay. They have also such beauty and comeliness that all the wits men have can not imagine a more beautiful matter.

> Think now of the shape of man, which may be called a little world, in whom every parcel of his body is seen to be necessarily framed by art and not by hap, and then the form altogether most beautiful. . . . Leave Nature, and come to art. . . . Pillars and great beams uphold high buildings and palaces, and yet are they no less pleasureful unto the eyes of the beholders than profitable to the buildings. . . . Besides other things, therefore, it giveth a great praise to the world in saying that it is beautiful. It is praised in saying the beautiful heaven, beautiful earth, beautiful sea, beautiful rivers, beautiful woods, trees, gardens, beautiful cities, beautiful churches, houses, armies. In conclusion, this comely and holy beauty is a wondrous setting out of everything. And it may be said that good and beautiful be after a sort one self thing. . . .*

A medieval man might also have coupled the good and the beautiful, but he would have stressed the good, the mysterious ways in which God led man to righteousness. Medieval man had a vision of God's world. The age of humanism, which Castiglione interpreted so faithfully, had a vision not only of God's world but also of nature's world and man's world.

*Ibid., pp. 348–349.

Reading Suggestions on the Renaissance
General Accounts

E. P. Cheyney, *The Dawn of a New Era, 1250–1453,* and M. P. Gilmore, *The World of Humanism, 1453–1517* (*Torchbooks). The first two volumes in an important series, The Rise of Modern Europe. Gilmore's is particularly informative on the topics considered in this chapter.

The New Cambridge Modern History. Vol. 1: *The Renaissance* (Cambridge Univ., 1957). Chapters by experts in many fields; uneven but useful for reference.

J. R. Major, *The Age of the Renaissance and Reformation* (*Lippincott), and E. F. Rice, Jr., *The Foundations of Early Modern Europe, 1460–1559* (*Norton). Up-to-date general introductions.

J. H. Plumb, *The Italian Renaissance* (*Torchbooks). Concise historical and cultural survey.

D. Hay, *The Renaissance in Its Historical Background* (*Cambridge Univ.). Valuable treatment of the topic by a British scholar.

G. Mattingly et al., *Renaissance Profiles* (*Torchbooks). Lively sketches of nine representative Italians, including Petrarch, Machiavelli, Leonardo, and Michelangelo.

Interpretations

J. Burckhardt, *The Civilization of the Renaissance in Italy,* 2 vols. (*Torchbooks). The classic statement of the view that the Renaissance was unique and revolutionary.

W. K. Ferguson, *The Renaissance in Historical Thought: Five Centuries of Interpretation* (Houghton, 1948). Valuable and stimulating monograph. Ferguson has edited two useful collections of essays: *Renaissance Studies* (Univ. of Western Ontario, 1963) and *Facets of the Renaissance* (*Torchbooks).

D. Hay, ed., *The Renaissance Debate* (*Holt). Excerpts illustrating contrasting points of view.

F. Chabod, *Machiavelli and the Renaissance* (*Torchbooks). The chapter "The Concept of the Renaissance" is most suggestive.

L. Olschki, *The Genius of Italy* (Cornell Univ., 1954). Scholarly essays on many aspects of the Renaissance.

The Economy

The Cambridge Economic History of Europe. Vol. 2: *Trade and Industry in the Middle Ages;* Vol. 3: *Economic Organization and Policies in the Middle Ages* (Cambridge Univ., 1954, 1965). Advanced scholarly work and a mine of information.

F. C. Lane, *Venetian Ships and Shipping of the Renaissance* (Johns Hopkins Univ., 1934). Unusually interesting monograph.

A. W. O. von Martin, *Sociology of the Renaissance* (*Torchbooks). Instructive study of Italian society in the fourteenth and fifteenth centuries.

M. Beard, *A History of Business,* 2 vols. (*Ann Arbor). With thumbnail sketches of Renaissance millionaires (formerly entitled *A History of the Businessman*).

R. de Roover, *Rise and Decline of the Medici Bank, 1397–1494* (*Norton). Case history of the profits and pitfalls of Renaissance finance.

R. Ehrenberg, *Capital and Finance in the Renaissance: A Study of the Fuggers and Their Connections* (Harcourt, 1928). Another instructive case history.

Literature and Thought

P. O. Kristeller, *Renaissance Thought*, 2 vols. (*Torchbooks). Valuable study, stressing its diversity, by a ranking scholar.

E. Garin, *Italian Humanism* (Blackwell, 1965). Good scholarly survey.

R. Weiss, *The Spread of Italian Humanism* (Hutchinson's University Library, 1964). Lucid, brief introduction.

R. R. Bolgar, *The Classical Heritage and Its Beneficiaries from the Carolingian Age to the End of the Renaissance* (*Torchbooks). The last third of this scholarly study treats the Renaissance.

G. Highet, *The Classical Tradition: Greek and Roman Influences on Western Literature* (*Galaxy). Lively general survey.

M. P. Gilmore, *Humanists and Jurists* (Belknap-Harvard Univ., 1963). Six essays; especially instructive on Erasmus.

G. Holmes, *The Florentine Enlightenment, 1400–1450* (*Pegasus). Informative monograph on humanists obsessed with classicism.

N. A. Robb, *Neoplatonism of the Italian Renaissance* (Allen & Unwin, 1953). Good solid treatment of an intellectual common denominator of the age.

J. Huizinga, *Erasmus and the Age of the Reformation* (*Torchbooks). Excellent analysis by a distinguished Dutch scholar.

W. Kaiser, *Praisers of Folly* (Harvard Univ., 1963). Folly and fools in the writings of Erasmus, Rabelais, and Shakespeare.

Science

M. Boas, *The Scientific Renaissance, 1450–1630* (*Torchbooks). Helpful detailed account.

H. Butterfield, *The Origins of Modern Science, 1300–1800*, rev. ed. (*Free Press). A controversial interpretation, minimizing the scientific contribution of the Renaissance.

A. C. Crombie, *Medieval and Early Modern Science*, 2nd ed. (Harvard Univ., 1963). Volume 2 of this standard survey treats the Renaissance.

G. Sarton, *Six Wings: Men of Science in the Renaissance* (Indiana Univ., 1956), *The Appreciation of Ancient and Medieval Science during the Renaissance* (*A. S. Barnes), and *The History of Science and the New Humanism* (*Indiana Univ.). Clear studies by a pioneering historian of science.

L. Thorndike, *Science and Thought in the Fifteenth Century* (Columbia Univ., 1929). By a specialist on medieval science.

C. Singer et al., *A History of Technology* (Clarendon, 1954–1958). Volumes 2 and 3 relate to the Renaissance. Singer has also written *A Short History of Anatomy and Physiology* (*Dover).

A. Castiglioni, *A History of Medicine*, 2nd ed., rev. (Knopf, 1958). An excellent manual.

E. Garin, *Science and Civic Life in the Italian Renaissance* (*Anchor). A helpful scholarly survey.

Music

E. J. Dent, *Music of the Renaissance in Italy* (British Academy, 1954). Meaty lecture by a great authority.

G. Reese, *Music in the Renaissance* (Norton, 1954). Detailed study.

Religion

A. Hyma, *The Christian Renaissance* (Shoe String, 1965). Reprint of an older work stressing an aspect of the Renaissance often neglected.

R. Ridolfi, *Savonarola* (Knopf, 1959). Biography of the famous Florentine preacher-dictator.

Fine Arts

C. Gilbert, *History of Renaissance Art throughout Europe* (Abrams, 1973). Comprehensive and profusely illustrated introduction.

More detailed scholarly accounts may be found in various volumes of the "Pelican History of Art" (Penguin): J. White, *Art and Architecture in Italy, 1250–1400* (1966); L. Heydenreich and W. Lotz, *Architecture in Italy, 1400–1600* (1974); C. Seymour, *Sculpture in Italy, 1400–1500* (1966); S. J. Freedberg, *Painting in Italy, 1500–1600* (1971); and A. Blunt, *Art and Architecture in France, 1500–1700* (1953).

M. Levey, *The Early Renaissance* (*Penguin). Stressing the interrelations of art and civilization in general.

H. Wölfflin, *Classic Art: An Introduction to the Italian Renaissance*, 3rd ed. (*Phaidon). An older and still very useful interpretation.

F. Antal, *Florentine Painting and Its Social Background* (Kegan, Paul, 1948). Suggestive attempt to relate art to social and economic currents.

E. Panofsky, *Renaissance and Renascences in Western Art* (*Torchbooks); *Studies in Iconology: Humanistic Themes in the Renaissance* (*Torchbooks); *The Life and Art of Albrecht Dürer* (*Princeton Univ. Press). Stimulating studies by an eminent scholar.

K. M. Clark, *Leonardo da Vinci* (*Penguin). Lively and perceptive assessment of his art.

O. Benesch, *The Art of the Renaissance in Northern Europe* (Harvard Univ., 1945). Examines the interrelations of art, religion, and intellectual developments.

R. Wittkower, *Architectural Principles in the Age of Humanism* (*Norton). Important study of the links between humanism and design.

B. Lowry, *Renaissance Architecture* (*Braziller). Brief introduction.

Detroit Institute of Arts, *Decorative Arts of the Italian Renaissance* (Detroit, 1958). Informative illustrated catalogue of a comprehensive exhibition.

Sources and Fiction

J. B. Ross and M. M. McLaughlin, *The Portable Renaissance Reader* (*Viking).

W. L. Gundesheimer, ed., *The Italian Renaissance* (*Prentice-Hall). Selections from eleven representative writers, including Valla, Pico, Leonardo, and Castiglione.

E. Cassirer et al., *The Renaissance Philosophy of Man* (*Phoenix). Excerpts from Petrarch, Pico, Valla, and other humanists, with helpful commentary.

Erasmus, *The Praise of Folly* (*Princeton Univ.).

S. Putnam, ed., *The Portable Rabelais: Most of Gargantua and Pantagruel* (*Viking).

T. B. Costain, *The Moneyman* (Doubleday, 1947). Good novel about Jacques Coeur.

The Protestant Reformation

I Introduction

In October 1517, at Wittenberg in the German electorate of Saxony, the Augustinian monk Martin Luther drew up ninety-five theses for theological disputation, and thereby touched off the sequence of events that produced the Protestant Reformation. The long-accepted fact that Luther inscribed his theses on a large placard that he affixed to the door of the court church at Wittenberg on October 31 has recently been challenged as inaccurate.* The challenge has provoked a debate among scholars, the majority of whom apparently continue to regard the traditional account of the posting of the theses as authentic. Whatever the actual details may have been, they are in a sense unimportant, for the central historical fact remains that Luther's provocative theses were soon translated from Latin into German and were read and debated far beyond the local academic and religious community for which they had originally been intended.

The term "Protestant" dates from 1529, when a meeting of the Diet of the Holy Roman Empire at Speyer rescinded a grant of toleration to Lutherans it had made three years earlier. A minority of delegates—six Lutheran princes and fourteen Lutheran city delegates—thereupon lodged a formal "protest" with the Diet. In Europe the term "Reformed" is often used synonymously with "Protestant," and "Reformation" is the accepted word for the Protestant movement everywhere except in Catholic tradition, which refers to the Protestant "revolt." The difference is significant, because early Protestant leaders like Luther and Calvin did not conceive of themselves as rebels or initiators, beginning new churches, but as returning to the true old Church.

In fact, however, the Protestant leaders did prove to be revolutionaries. The Reformation not only created a major schism in the Church but also constituted a

*E. Iserloh, *The Theses Were Not Posted* (New York, 1968).

major social, economic, and intellectual revolution. In the Middle Ages the Catholic church had faced many reform movements—the Cluniac, the Cistercian, the Franciscan, and, in the century or so before Luther, movements like those of Wycliffe and Hus that anticipated Protestant doctrines and had almost ended by setting up separate or schismatic religious bodies. The Reformation came in a time when the authority of the pope was no longer automatically accepted but had been brought under open discussion by the Conciliar Movement, though the movement itself had failed to set general church councils above the pope.

More important, the Reformation came in a time when men were still groping to replace the old values and institutions being dissolved by the Renaissance. It came in a time of great religious ferment, of economic change, of violence, uncertainty, even a sense of doom—in a time well described by the phrase of the Dutch historian Huizinga as "the autumn of the Middle Ages." Men everywhere were seeking something, not usually specific political or economic reforms, but something less definite—spiritual salvation, renewal, the better world of Christian promise. Luther, notably, appealed from what he held to be existing evil to a good already in men's souls or at least potentially present in them. Hence the Lutheran appeal from *works*, the established conventions of religion, to *faith*, to something not evident to the outward eye but inside us all, if we could but see it.

Although Luther, when he drew up his theses, had no clear intention of setting up a separate religious body, he soon participated in organizing a church outside the Catholic communion. The Lutheran Church proved to be the first of many Protestant churches—Anglican, Calvinist, Anabaptist, and dozens more. By the middle of the sixteenth century the medieval unity of Catholic Christendom had given way to the multiplicity of "denominations" we know so well.

II Protestant Founders: Martin Luther

Luther's Spiritual Crisis

Martin Luther (1483–1546) was a professor of theology at the University of Wittenberg. In 1517, he was undergoing a great religious awakening, in effect a conversion, after a long period of spiritual despair. Luther's parents were of peasant stock; his father, authoritarian in discipline as medieval fathers seem to have been, became a miner and in time a prosperous investor in a mining enterprise. Very ambitious for his son, he was able to send him to the University of Erfurt, then the most prestigious in Germany, for the study of law as preparation for a professional career. The young man, however, yearned instead to enter the religious life and took the decisive step in 1505 as a result of a traumatic experience. On his way back to Erfurt he was terrified by a severe thunderstorm and prayed to the patron saint of miners—"Help, Saint Anne, I will become a monk!" ("I want to become a monk" is another translation.) Against his father's opposition, Luther joined the

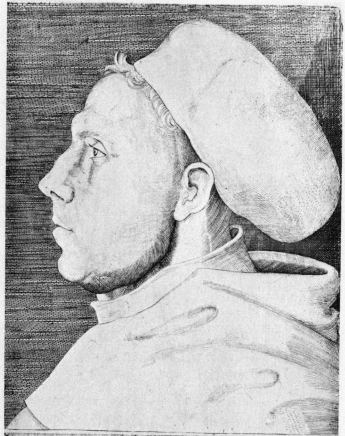

Martin Luther, by Lucas Cranach the Elder.

LVCAE ◦ OPVS ◦ EFFIGIES ◦ HAEC ◦ EST ◦ MORITVRA ◦ LVTHERI ◦
AETHERNAM ◦ MENTIS ◦ EXPRIMIT ◦ IPSE ◦ SVAE ◦
M · D · X · X · I ·

Augustinian friars (or canons), an elite order both socially and intellectually.

While Luther's lifelong enthusiasm for music found satisfaction in the Augustinian devotion to psalm-singing, he underwent a prolonged and intense personal crisis. Luther was convinced that he was lost—literally lost, for as the psychoanalyst Erik Erikson points out in his *Young Man Luther,* modern depth psychology calls his predicament an identity crisis. None of Luther's good works, neither the monastic discipline of his order nor his pilgrimage in 1510 to Christian shrines in Rome, could free him of the gnawing feeling that he could not attain God's grace and was destined for the hell of lost souls. Finally, a wise confessor advised the desperate young man to study the Bible and to become a teacher of Scripture. Through his reading in the Epistles of Paul and the writings of Augustine, Luther gradually found a positive answer to his anxiety. The answer was that man should have faith in God, faith in the possibility of his own salvation. This answer had indeed long been the answer of the Roman church; what later separated Luther doctrinally from this church was his emphasis on faith alone, to the exclusion of works.

The Attack on Indulgences

Fortified by his intense conviction of the great importance of faith, Luther questioned Catholic practices that in his view were abuses and tended to corrupt or weaken faith. He cast his questions in the form of ninety-five theses, written in the manner of medieval Scholasticism as a challenge to academic debate. The specific abuse that the Ninety-five Theses sought to prove un-Christian was what Luther called the "sale" of indulgences, and in particular the activities of a talented ecclesiastical fundraiser, a Dominican named Tetzel. Tetzel was conducting a "drive" for voluntary contributions to help fill the treasury of a great institution that could not extend its taxing powers sufficiently to keep up with the rising costs of an era of inflation and luxurious living. Tetzel was raising money to rebuild Saint Peter's in Rome, and he had papal authorization for his campaign. One of the great German ecclesiastical princes also had a stake in the indulgences. This was Albert, brother of the elector of Brandenburg, who held two major sees, the archbishopric of Mainz and that of Magdeburg, and had paid a very large sum to the papacy for a dispensation permitting him to do so. In order to get the money, he had borrowed heavily from the Fuggers, and to repay them, he would use his share in the proceeds of the indulgences.

Indulgences made possible remission of the punishment for sins. Only God can forgive a sin, but the repentant sinner also has to undergo punishment on earth in the form of penance and after death in purgatory, where he atones by painful but temporary punishment for his sins and is prepared for heaven. Indulgences could not assure the forgiveness of sins, according to the theory advanced by the medieval Schoolmen, but they could remit penance and part or all of the punishment in purgatory. The Church claimed authority to grant such remission by drawing on the Treasury of Merit, a storehouse of surplus good works accumulated by the holy activities of Christ, the Virgin, and the saints. Only the priest could secure for a layman a draft, as it were, on this heavenly treasury. The use of the word *sale* in connection with indulgences became a form of Protestant propaganda; the Catholics insisted that an indulgence was not sold, that it was "granted" by the priest and any monetary contribution made by the recipient was a freewill offering.

The doctrine of indulgences was too complex for the ordinary layman to grasp completely. To the man in the street it must have looked as though a sinner could obtain forgiveness of sin as well as remission of punishment if only he secured enough indulgences. A man such as Tetzel, by making extravagant claims for the power of his indulgences, strengthened the popular feeling summed up in the saying, "The moment the money tinkles in the collection box, a soul flies out of purgatory." * In the Ninety-five Theses Luther vehemently objected to the whole procedure and the doctrine behind it:

23. If any remission of all penalties whatsoever can be granted to anyone, it can only be to those who are most perfect, in other words to very few.

24. It must therefore follow that the greater part of the people are deceived by that indiscriminate and high-sounding promise of freedom from penalty.†

At the theological level Luther's quarrel with his ecclesiastical superiors was over one of the oldest and most abiding tensions of Christian thought, the tension between faith and good works. Faith is inward and emotional belief, and good works are the outward demonstration of that belief expressed by the individual's good deeds, his partaking of the sacraments, and his submitting to the discipline of penance. Indulgences held out the promise that men might secure extra good works by drawing on those stored up in the Treasury of Merit. While Christian practice usually insists on the need for both faith and works, in times of crisis men tend to pursue one extreme or the other. In response to the Ninety-five Theses, the challenged papal party stiffened into a resistance that in turn drove the Lutherans into further resistance. Moreover, Luther's own increasing hostility to things-as-they-were in Germany drove him to emphasize things-as-they-ought-to-be. He was driven to minimize the use of works and, at his most excited moments, to deny their validity altogether. In the Ninety-five Theses he attacked not all works but only those, like indulgences, that he felt to be wrong. Yet in his theses he also made some very harsh statements about the pope, and soon thereafter, under pressure of combat, Luther rejected works entirely and declared that men are saved by faith alone. He went on to deny that priests are necessary intercessors and to affirm the priesthood of all true believers, "every man his own priest."

*O. Chadwick, *The Reformation* (Grand Rapids, Mich., 1965), p. 42.
†E. G. Rupp and B. Drewery, eds., *Martin Luther* (New York, 1970), p. 20.

The sixteenth century German Dominican monk Johann Tetzel riding on an ass selling indulgences.

The Defiance of Papacy and the Empire

The Roman church was quickly alerted to the high importance of the issues that Luther had raised. Tetzel had aroused such indignation that he dared not appear in public, and the archbishop of Mainz complained to the pope of the disastrous financial implications. Pope Leo X (1513–1521), a Medici and the son of Lorenzo the Magnificent but possessing little of the family's intelligence or decisiveness, soon had to give up the pretense that the storm over the Ninety-five Theses was a tempest in a teapot. Accordingly, in 1518, at Augsburg, Luther was summoned before the papal legate, and general of the Dominican order, Cardinal Cajetan, and was directed to recant some of his propositions on indulgences; Luther quietly defied Cajetan. In 1519, at Leipzig, a learned theologian, John Eck, taxed Luther in debate with disobeying the authoritative findings of popes and church councils. Luther denied that popes and councils were necessarily authoritative and, carrying his revolt further, explicitly declared adherence to some of Hus's teachings that had been declared heretical by the Council of Constance a century earlier. In 1520, Luther brought his defiance to its highest pitch by publishing a pamphlet, *To the Christian Nobility of the German Nation on the Improvement of the Christian Estate,* which stated in part:

> It has been devised that the Pope, bishops, priests and monks are called the spiritual estate; princes, lords, artificers and peasants are the temporal estate. This is an artful lie and hypocritical device, but let no one be made afraid by it, and that for this reason: that all Christians are truly of the spiritual estate, and there is no difference among them, save of office alone. As St. Paul says (*I Corinthians XII*), we are all one body, though each member does its own work, to serve the others. This is because we have one baptism, one Gospel, one faith, and are all Christians alike. . . .*

Luther's adherence to justification by faith alone had led him to reject the central Catholic doctrine of works, that only the priest had the God-given power to secure for the layman remission of punishment for sin. In his appeal, *To the Christian Nobility,* he declared the priesthood of all believers by sweeping aside the distinction between clergy and laity. The complete break between the rebel and the Church was now at hand. Late in 1520, a papal bull condemned Luther's teachings, and Luther burned the bull; in January 1521, he was excommunicated; and in April 1521, after a most dramatic session of the imperial Diet at Worms, the emperor Charles V placed him under the ban of the empire, which made him an outlaw and was the civil consequence of excommunication. Shortly before the ban was imposed, Luther was asked in front of the Diet if he would recant. He replied:

> Since your serene Majesty and your lordships request a simple answer, I shall give it, with no strings and no catches. Unless I am convicted by the testimony of scripture or plain reason (for I believe neither in Pope nor councils alone, since . . . they have often erred and contradicted themselves), I am bound by the scriptures I have quoted, and my conscience is captive to the Word of God. I neither can nor will revoke anything, for it is neither safe nor honest to act against one's conscience. Amen†

The famous words credited to Luther at the very close of his statement—"Here I stand. I can do no other. God help me."—are not included in the earliest known document containing Luther's statement at Worms, but they are entirely in harmony with what we are sure he actually said.

The empire and the papacy took their drastic actions in vain. Luther was already gathering a substantial following and becoming a national hero. He had the protection of the ruler of his own German state, the elector Frederick the Wise of Saxony (1463–1525), and was soon to secure the backing of other princes. Frederick arranged to "kidnap" the outlaw on his way back from Worms, and Luther vanished into seclusion at the castle of the Wartburg, where he began work on his celebrated translation of the Bible into vigorous and effective German. In the next year, Luther returned to Wittenberg and remodeled the church in Saxony.

The Reasons for Luther's Success

More than theology was at issue in Luther's revolt and its success. The Church that he attacked was, especially in Rome, under the influence of the half-pagan Renaissance, with its new wealth and new fashion of good living. The papacy, triumphant over the councils, had become embroiled in Italian politics. The Rome Luther visited as a young man, when the warlike Julius II was pope, presented a shocking spectacle of intrigue, ostentation, and corruption. One part of Luther's success was his attack on practices abhorrent to decent men; another part was his particular attack on the exploitation of Germans by Italians and by Tetzel and other Italianate Germans. In *To the Christian Nobility* he claimed:

> For Rome is the greatest thief and robber that has ever appeared on earth, or ever will. . . . Poor Germans that we are—we have been deceived! We were born to be masters, and we have been compelled to bow the head beneath the yoke of tyrants. . . . It is time the glorious Teutonic people should cease to be the puppet of the Roman pontiff.*

While the nationalistic and economic factors present in the Lutheran movement help explain its success, they do not wholly account for it. As always in human affairs, ideas and ideals worked together with material interests and powerful emotions such as patriotism to move the men of the Reformation. The princes who supported Luther stood to gain financially, not only by the cessation of the flow of German money to Italy, but by the confiscation of Catholic property, especially monastic lands, which was not needed for the new Lutheran cult. Luther gave them a new weapon in their eternal struggle against their feudal overlord, the emperor. The princes were also moved by Luther's German patriotism, and some, like Frederick the Wise of Saxony, sympathized with many of his ideas. Philip of Hesse, who had both an amorous disposition and a sensitive conscience, found Luther obliging enough to condone bigamy when he took a second wife without divorcing the first.

*Ibid., p. 43.
†Ibid., p. 60.

*H. S. Bettenson, ed., *Documents of the Christian Church* (New York, 1947), pp. 278–279.

It is true that what Luther started was soon taken out of his hands by princes who joined the reform movement to strengthen their political power and fill their treasuries. Yet Lutheranism without Luther is inconceivable. He wrote the pamphlets that did for this revolution what Tom Paine and the Declaration of Independence did for the American Revolution. Earlier, Luther had been dismayed when his Ninety-five Theses were translated into German without his authorization; now he deliberately wrote *To the Christian Nobility* in the vernacular to reach the largest possible number of readers. That his expectations were fulfilled is one more demonstration of the combined power of the vernacular and the printing press. Luther's defiance of the papal legate Cajetan, of the papal champion Eck, and of the pope himself were well known among Germans, deepening their nationalistic emotions. His marriage to a former nun and their rearing of a large family dramatized the break with Rome. His translation of the Scriptures and the hymns he composed—"Ein Feste Burg" (A Mighty Fortress), above all—became a part of German life and made Luther's language one of the bases of modern literary German. The power and intensity of his language may still be sensed over the centuries—as Erik Erikson relates in his *Young Man Luther:*

> In my youth, as a wandering artist I stayed one night with a friend in a small village by the Upper Rhine. His father was a Protestant pastor; and in the morning, as the family sat down to breakfast, the old man said the Lord's Prayer in Luther's German. Never having "knowingly" heard it, I had the experience, as seldom before or after, of poetry fusing the esthetic and the moral: those who have once suddenly "heard" the Gettysburg Address will know what I mean.*

And back of all this was Luther's conviction that he was doing what he had to do.

Moreover, Luther's doctrine of justification by faith alone has been attractive to many religious dispositions, responding in a more general way to the same needs that the Brethren of the Common Life had tried to meet. Saint Paul at the very beginnings of Christianity set up the contrast between the Spirit—invisible, in a sense private to the believer—and the Letter—only too visible, only too public. Established churches have always tended to balance spirit and letter, invisible and visible, internal and external, faith and works. But to the ardent, crusading Christian even a successful balance of this sort seems a surrender to materialism: he will have none of this compromise, but will imperiously assert the primacy of the spirit. In Luther's day, the established Roman church had lost its medieval balance; the world was too much with it. The Lutheran felt the new church offered him something he could not get in the old.

A final reason for Luther's success applies to many other revolutionary movements as well: the relative

*E. H. Erikson, *Young Man Luther* (London, 1958), p. 10.

weakness of the forces opposing him. Religious opposition centered in the top levels of the Catholic bureaucracy; Pope Leo X did not so much head it as prove its willing instrument. But there were many moderate Catholics, anxious to compromise and avert a schism, both within the Church and on its margin among the humanist scholars, notably Erasmus. The great liberal Catholic historian, Lord Acton, later claimed that if the Catholic church had been headed by a pope willing to reform in order to conserve even Luther might have been reconciled. Luther's ablest associate, Melancthon, was a moderate and a humanist (his great uncle was John Reuchlin, the "hero" of *The Letters of Obscure Men*). Yet, once Luther had been excommunicated and outlawed and had gained powerful political backing, the way to compromise was probably blocked, for Luther's associates could have been won away from him only by concessions too great for a Catholic to make.

Politically, the opposition was centered in the youthful Charles V, who became the Holy Roman emperor in 1519. The combined inheritance of his Austrian Hapsburg father and his Spanish mother made Charles ruler not only of the German empire but also of Hungary, the Low Countries, Spain, Spanish America, and parts of Italy. On the map this looked like the nearest thing to a European superstate since the days of Charlemagne, and Charles wanted very much to make it such a state in reality. The activity of Luther's princely supporters in Germany threatened Charles' power there and might of itself have sufficed to turn him against Luther. But he was also a cautious, conventional Catholic and not ready to exert his great influence on the side of the moderate Catholics. Instead of seeking a compromise, he decided to fight the Lutherans.

But he did not lead the fight personally. Though Charles bore the Hapsburg name, there was little of the German about him: he spoke French, not German, and felt most at home in Ghent and Brussels in the Belgian lands of his Burgundian grandmother. In 1521 he entrusted the government of Germany to his younger brother, Ferdinand, who formed alliances with Bavaria and other Catholic German states to oppose the Lutheran states. Thus began a long series of alliances, the fruits of which were the religious wars of the next few generations, and the division of Germany into, roughly, a Protestant north and east and a Catholic south and west, which has endured to this day. In addition, Charles had too many other fights on his hands to concentrate on Germany. Spanish cities rose in revolt early in his reign, the Low Countries were chronically restless, and the Ottoman Turks, who annexed most of Hungary in the 1520s and then besieged Vienna, continued to threaten Charles' frontiers in central Europe and his lines of communication on the Mediterranean. Above all, Charles' huge inheritance encircled the only remaining great power on the Continent, France, which was already engaged with the Hapsburgs in a struggle for control of Italy. The struggle broadened into an

The emperor Charles V, by Titian.

intermittent general war between Charles V and the French king, Francis I (1515–1547), which outlasted both monarchs and prevented any sustained pressure on the German Protestants by imperial Hapsburg power.

The military arm of the Protestants was the League of Schmalkalden (named for the town where it was founded in 1531), linking cities and princes, with Philip of Hesse in the van. When Charles finally crushed the league with Spanish troops in 1547, his victory was short-lived because it threatened to upset the balance of power and alarmed both the papacy and the German princes, Catholic as well as Protestant. In 1555, in the twilight of his reign, Charles felt obliged to accept the Peace of Augsburg, a religious settlement negotiated by the German Diet.

The peace formally recognized the Lutherans as established in the German states where they held power at the time. Its guiding principle was expressed in the Latin "cuius regio eius religio" (he who rules establishes the religion), which meant in practice that, since the elector of Saxony was Lutheran, all his subjects should be too, whereas, since the ruler of Bavaria was Catholic, all Bavarians should be Catholic. No provision was made for Catholic minorities in Lutheran states, or Lutheran minorities in Catholic. The settlement also fell short of full toleration by failing to recognize any Protestants except Lutherans; the growing numbers of Calvinists and still more radical Protestants were bound to press for equal treatment in the future. More trouble was also bound to arise from the failure to deal with the question of "ecclesiastical reservation," that is, what disposition should be made of Church property in a German state headed by a prelate who had turned Protestant. Yet with all these deficiencies the Peace of Augsburg did make possible the permanent establishment of Protestantism on a peaceful basis in Germany.

A Conservative Revolutionary

While Luther was a great revolutionary, he was also in some respects a staunch conservative. For example, he did not push his doctrines of justification by faith and the priesthood of all believers to their logical extreme of anarchy. If religion is wholly a matter between man and his maker, an organized church is unnecessary. When radical reformers inspired by Luther attempted to apply these anarchical concepts to the churches of Saxony in the early 1520s, they created immense confusion and popular unrest, which resulted in riots and vandalism. Luther, who had no sympathy with such experiments, left his sanctuary in the Wartburg and returned to Wittenberg to drive out the radicals. He and his followers then organized a Saxon church that permitted its clergy to marry and put increased stress on sermons but that also possessed ordained clergymen, ritual, dogmas, even some sacraments—a whole apparatus of good works.

The Lutherans did not found their church as an alternative to the Roman Catholic but as the one true church. Where a Lutheran church was founded, a Catholic church ceased to be; the Lutherans commonly just took over the church building. Stimulated by Luther and his clerical and academic disciples, this process at first went on among the people of Germany without the intervention of political leaders. But very soon the lay rulers of certain states took a hand. In Saxony, Hesse, Brandenburg, Brunswick, and elsewhere in northern Germany, princes and their administrators superintended and hastened the process of converting the willing to Lutheranism and evicting the unwilling. Much excitement was caused in 1525 when the head of the Teutonic Knights, the crusading order controlling Prussia at the eastern corner of the Baltic, turned Lutheran, dissolved the order, and became the first duke of Prussia. Meantime, many of the free cities also opted for Lutheranism, usually not on the initiative of the municipal government but as a result of pressure from the guilds.

Still other social groups took the occasion of the Lutheran revolt to assert themselves. Just beneath the princes, lay and ecclesiastical, in the German social pyramid and like them a legacy of the Middle Ages were the knights, the lesser nobility. Some of them held a castle and a few square miles direct from the emperor, and were in theory as sovereign as the elector of a substantial state such as Saxony or Brandenburg; others were simply minor feudal lords. Many knights were younger sons, without land but nevertheless gentlemen, whose only career could be that of arms. The knightly class as a whole was losing power to the princes and was caught in the squeeze of rising prices and the need to maintain an aristocratic life style. Luther's challenge to the established order, and the opportunity it gave to take over ecclesiastical holdings, was too good a chance to be missed. The knights rose in 1522 and were eventually put down by the bigger lords, but only after a struggle.

The really bitter social conflict of the early German Reformation, however, was not this Knights' War but the Peasants' Rebellion of 1524–1525. In many ways it resembled the peasant revolts of the fourteenth century in England and France. It resisted attempts by money-hungry lords, lay and ecclesiastical, to increase manorial dues; it lacked coordination and effective military organization; it was cruelly put down by the possessing classes; and it was a rising, not of the most oppressed peasants, but of those who were beginning to enjoy some prosperity and who wanted more. In Germany the Peasants' Rebellion centered not in the east, where serfdom was most complete and the status of the peasant the lowest, but in the south and southwest, where the peasantry were beginning to emerge as free, landowning farmers. Yet in one very important respect this sixteenth-century German uprising looks more modern, more democratic, than its medieval counterparts in western Europe. Even more clearly than the English Peasants' Revolt, which had been influenced by Wycliffe and his followers, it was led by educated men who were not themselves peasants and who had a program, a set of revolutionary ideas of what the new social structure should be. Their leaders drew up a series of demands known as the Twelve Articles, which were couched in biblical language (thus showing their relation to the Reformation) and demanded that each parish have the right to choose its own priest, that the tithes paid to the clergy and the dues paid to the lord be reduced, and that the peasants be allowed to take wood and game from the forests.

Although the Twelve Articles were relatively moderate, Luther was horrified at what the peasants' leaders had found in the Bible he had translated into German so that they might read it. He burst into impassioned abuse that sounds even stronger than his abuse of the Catholics, writing a tract entitled *Against the Murdering Thieving Hordes of Peasants*. From this time on, Luther turned definitely to the princes, and the church he founded became itself an established church, respectful toward civil authority. He is quoted as saying: "The princes of the world are gods, the common people are Satan." In fairness to Luther, it may be pointed out that his conservatism in social, economic, and political matters was by no means inconsistent with his fundamental spiritual position. For if the visible, external world is really wholly subordinate to the invisible, spiritual world, the most one can hope for in the world of politics is that it be kept in as good order as possible,

so that the spiritual may thrive. Authority, custom, law, existing institutions combine to provide this orderliness. Kings and princes are better for this wretched world than democratically chosen representatives of the people; obedience is better than discussion.

Luther's conservative views brought him increasing support from kings and princes. By the mid-sixteenth century, Lutheranism had become the state religion in most of the principalities of northern Germany and in the kingdoms of Sweden and Denmark, together with the Danish dependencies of Norway and Iceland, and the Swedish province of Finland. The Scandinavian monarchs, in particular, appear to have been attracted to the Reformation for secular reasons, for the opportunity to curb unruly bishops and to confiscate monastic wealth. Because of this as well as Luther's increasing conservatism it is hardly surprising that the initiative in the Reformation was soon transferred from the Lutherans to other Protestant founders.

III Zwingli, Calvin, and Other Founders
Zwingli

Among the other founders of Protestantism the first in importance is Calvin, but the first in time was Ulrich Zwingli (1484–1531). Almost contemporaneously with Luther's spectacular revolt, Zwingli, a German, began in the Swiss city of Zurich a quieter reform that soon spread to Bern and Basel in Switzerland and to Augsburg and other south German cities. His movement produced no great single organized church, and when it was only a decade old its founder died in battle against the staunchly Catholic forest cantons of Switzerland. Zwingli's reform proved significant because it extended and deepened some of the fundamental theological and moral concepts of Protestantism, and had a wide influence on some of its less conservative and more austere forms. Zwingli was a scholarly humanist trained in the tradition of Erasmus. Like Luther, he sought to combat what seemed to him the perversion of primitive Christianity that endowed the consecrated priest with a miraculous power not shared by the laity. But, where the doctrine of the priesthood of the true believer drove the emotional Luther to the edge of anarchism, the humanistic Zwingli preached that individuals might achieve a community discipline that would promote righteous living. This discipline would arise from the social conscience of enlightened and emancipated people led by their pastors.

Zwingli believed in a personal God, powerful and real yet transcendental in the sense of being far above the petty world of sense experience. Because his God was not to be approached by mere sacraments, Zwingli was more hostile to sacraments than Luther was. He distrusted what many Protestants feel is the continuous Catholic appeal to "superstition," to belief in saints, and to the use of images, incense, and candles. In the

Ulrich Zwingli: a contemporary painting.

early 1520s, Zwingli began the process of abolishing the Catholic liturgy, making the sermon and a responsive reading the core of the service, and simplifying the church building into an undecorated hall, in which a simple communion table in the midst of the congregation replaced the elevated altar of the Catholics. He thus started on the way toward the puritanical simplicity of the later Calvinists.

A good example of Zwingli's attitude is his view of communion. The Catholic doctrine of transubstantiation holds that by the miraculous power of the priest the elements in the Eucharist, the bread and the wine, become in substance the body and blood of Christ, although their "accidents," their chemical makeup, remain those of bread and wine. Luther refused to eliminate the miraculous completely and, in an acrimonious meeting with Zwingli, insisted that Christ had meant himself to be taken literally when he offered bread to his disciples and said, "This is my body." In rejecting transubstantiation, Luther put forward a difficult doctrine called consubstantiation, which states that in communion the body and blood are mysteriously present in the bread and wine. Zwingli, however, went all the way to what is now the usual Protestant position, that partaking of the elements in communion commemorates Christ's last supper in a purely symbolic way. It is not sharing in a sacrament through a miracle, but simply sharing anew the memory of Christ's stay on earth.

John Calvin in 1534.

Calvin

In addition to German-speaking Zurich, Bern, and Basel, another Swiss city ripe for Protestant domination was French-speaking Geneva, where the citizens in 1536 won a ten-year struggle with their Catholic bishop, who was also their political ruler. A new religious and political regime developed there under the leadership of the French-born Jean Cauvin—John Calvin (1509–1564). Calvin shaped the Protestant movement as a faith and a way of life in a manner that gave it a European and not merely a German and Scandinavian basis. Particularly in early Protestant history, *Reformed* meant Calvinist as opposed to the more conservative Lutheran.

Calvin's career had many parallels with Luther's. Both men had ambitious fathers who had made their way up the economic and social ladder; the senior Calvin had risen from an artisan to perform clerical and legal services for the municipal and ecclesiastical authorities in a French town and had eventually gained the considerable distinction of admission to citizenship in the town. Both fathers gave their sons superior education; the young Calvin studied theology and, in deference to his father, law. Both young men experienced spiritual crises, Calvin's resulting in his conversion to Protestantism in his early twenties, though apparently with little of the storm and stress experienced by Luther. Both men took wives (as Zwingli did, too). In temperament, however, the two men differed markedly:

in contrast to the emotional, outgoing Luther, Calvin was a very private person, an intellectual, a humanist scholar much interested in Roman Stoic philosophy with its puritanical morality, an austere man, earnest, high-minded, very certain of his convictions and of his vocation in persuading others to accept them.

In 1536 Calvin published his *Institutes of the Christian Religion*, which laid the doctrinal foundation for a Protestantism that, like Zwingli's, broke completely with Catholic church organization and Catholic ritual. The very title, *Institutes,* suggested Justinian's code; and Calvin's system, reflecting his legal training, had a logical rigor and completeness that gave it great conviction. (Fuller discussion of Calvin's moral and theological ideas may be found in the next section of this chapter.) Also in 1536, while on a journey, Calvin happened to pass through Geneva and was invited to remain. There he organized his City of God and made Geneva a Protestant Rome, a magnet for Protestant refugees from many parts of Europe who received indoctrination in Calvin's faith and then returned, sometimes at the risk of their lives, to spread the word in their own countries. Within a generation or two, Calvinism had spread to Scotland, where it was led by a great preacher and organizer, John Knox; to England, whence it was brought to Plymouth in New England; to parts of the Rhineland; to the Low Countries, where it was to play a major role in the Dutch revolt against Spanish rule; and even to Bohemia, Hungary, and Poland.

In France, where concern over the worldliness of the Catholic church was very great, Calvin's ideas found ready acceptance. Soon there were organized Calvinist churches, especially in the southwest, called Huguenot (probably from the German *Eidgenossen,* "covenanted"). But France was a centralized monarchy, and King Francis I was not eager, as so many of the German princes were, to stir up trouble with Rome. In 1516, he had signed with the pope the Concordat of Bologna, which increased the royal authority over the Gallican church. In the mid-sixteenth century only a few intellectuals could conceive of the possibility of subjects of the same ruler professing and practicing differing religious faiths. In France, therefore, Protestantism had to fight not for toleration but to succeed Catholicism as the established faith. The attempt failed, but only after wars of religion lasting for a generation in the later 1500s, as the next chapter will show, and after Calvinism had left its mark on the French conscience.

Henry VIII

In England, by contrast, the established church became Protestant. The signal for the English Reformation was the desire of King Henry VIII (1509–1547) to put aside his wife, Catherine of Aragon, because she had not

given him the male heir he felt that the recently arrived Tudor dynasty required. In 1529 Henry decided to rest his case on the grounds that Catherine had been married first to his deceased brother Arthur, and that marriage with the widow of a brother was against canon law. But Henry's case was hardly strengthened by the circumstance that he had taken twenty years to discover the existence of this impediment. Moreover, Catherine was the aunt of the emperor Charles V, whom the pope could scarcely risk offending by granting an annulment, the more so since Charles' troops had staged the terrible sack of Rome in 1527. Nevertheless, Henry pressed his case hard through his minister, Cardinal Wolsey, whom he finally dismissed in disgrace for his failure. In 1533 Henry married Anne Boleyn, whom he had made pregnant; Cranmer, the obliging archbishop of Canterbury recently appointed by Henry, pronounced the annulment of the marriage with Catherine. When the pope excommunicated Henry and declared the annulment invalid, Henry's answer was the Act of Supremacy (1534), which made the king supreme head of the church in England.

Much more than the private life of Henry VIII was involved in the English Reformation. Henry could not have secured the Act of Supremacy and other Protestant legislation from Parliament if there had not

Henry VIII and Catherine of Aragon.

been a considerable body of opinion favorable to the breach with Rome, particularly among the prosperous middle classes. Many English scholars were in touch with reformers on the Continent, and one of them, Tyndale, studied with Luther and published an English translation of the New Testament (1526). Antipapal sentiment, which was an aspect of English nationalism, had long existed; it had motivated the fourteenth-century statutes of Provisors and Praemunire, which limited the right of the pope to intervene in the affairs of the English church. Anticlericalism went back to the days of Wycliffe; in the days of Henry VIII it was aimed particularly at the monasteries, which were still wealthy landowners but had degenerated since their great medieval days. In the eyes of many Englishmen, the monasteries had outlived their purpose and needed to be reformed or abolished. Between 1535 and 1540 Henry VIII closed the monasteries and confiscated their property; the larger establishments were not directly suppressed but persuaded to "dissolve" voluntarily. During the 1540s the Crown sold much of the land, usually at a price twenty times its yearly income. The principal purchasers, aside from short-term speculators, were members of the rising merchant class, of the nobility, and, above all, of the country gentry or "squirearchy." The dissolution of the monasteries, by increasing the wealth of the landed gentry, amounted to a social and economic revolution; it contributed to the high rate of economic growth in Tudor England and also to the social dislocations accompanying that growth. It is another illustration of how closely the religious and the secular threads were interwoven in the Reformation.

Yet Henry VIII, though he must be numbered among the founders of Protestantism, did not really consider himself a Protestant. The Church of England set up by the Act of Supremacy was in his eyes—and remains today in the eyes of some of its communicants, the High Church Anglicans—a Catholic body. Henry hoped to retain Catholic doctrines and ritual, doing no more than abolish monasteries and deny the pope's position as head of the church in England. Inevitably, his policies aroused opposition, in part from Roman Catholic Englishmen who greatly resented the break with Rome, but still more from militant Protestants. Henry had hardly given the signal for the break with Rome when Low Church Anglicans began to introduce within the Church of England such Protestant practices as marriage of the clergy, use of English instead of Latin in the ritual, and abolition of auricular confession and the invocation of saints.

Henry used force against the Catholic opposition and executed some of its leaders, notably John Fisher, a cardinal and bishop of Rochester who had stoutly defended Catherine of Aragon, and Sir Thomas More, author of *Utopia*, who had succeeded Wolsey as chancellor. Henry tried to stem the Protestant tide by appealing to a willing Parliament, many members of which had already been enriched by the spoliation of

the Catholic church. In 1539, Parliament passed the statute of the Six Articles, reaffirming transubstantiation, celibacy of the priesthood, confession, and other Catholic doctrines and ritual, and making their denial heresy. By this definition, there were far too many heretics to be repressed, for the patriotic Englishman was against Rome and all its works. England from now on was to be a great center of religious variation and experimentation, and the Anglican church, substantially more Protestant than Henry had intended, became a kind of central national core of precarious orthodoxy.

Anabaptists and Other Radicals

One major item is left to consider in this survey of Protestant origins. Socially and intellectually less "respectable" than the soon-established Lutheran and Anglican churches, or the sober Calvinists, was a whole group of radical sects, the left wing of the Protestant revolution. In the sixteenth century, most of them were known as Anabaptists, from the Greek for "baptizing again." Some of Zwingli's followers had come to hold that the Catholic sacrament of baptism of infants had no validity, since the infant was too young to "believe" or "understand." Here again Luther's doctrine of faith as a direct relation between the believer and God is involved—only for the Anabaptist it is a relation of rational understanding by the believer. Here also is a characteristic Protestant appeal to individual understanding or conscience, closer to the "right reason" of the Schoolmen than to the scientific or commonsensible reason that was to prevail in the eighteenth-century Enlightenment.

The Anabaptists at first baptized again when the believer could hold that he was voluntarily joining the company of the elect. Later generations were never baptized until they came of age, so the prefix *ana-* was dropped, and we have the Baptists of our time. The assumption that the beneficiaries of adult baptism were in effect "saved" could lead to exclusiveness and smugness, a kind of spiritual snobbery that brought accusations of self-righteousness against radical congregations.

Baptism, however, was but one of many issues separating the radicals from other Protestants. A modern scholar defines Anabaptists as those "who gathered and disciplined a 'true church' upon the apostolic pattern as they understood it." * The issue of what the primitive church had been like in the days of the apostles had been joined as early as 1521 when the extremists tried to impose their convictions on the church at Wittenberg during Luther's absence in the Wartburg. Anabaptist preaching of the need to reform both Church and society contributed to the demands put forward by the rebellious German peasants in 1524–1525 and also to the violence sometimes employed by the rebels and always used by those suppressing them.

*F. H. Littell, *The Anabaptist View of the Church* (Boston, 1958), p. xvii.

The Anabaptists split under the pressure of persecution and with the spread of private reading and interpretation of the Bible. For some Catholic observers, the proliferation of Protestant sects seems due inevitably to the Protestant practice of seeking in the Bible for an authority they refused to find in the established dogmas of Catholic authority. The Bible contains an extraordinary variety of religious experience from rigorous ritual to intense emotional commitment and mystical surrender. Especially the apocalyptic books of the Old Testament and the Revelation of Saint John the Divine of the New can be made to yield almost anything a lively imagination wants to find. Many of the leaders of these new sects were uneducated men with a sense of grievance against the established order, who were seeking to bring heaven to earth, quickly. They were in large part landowning farmers, miners, artisans yet felt themselves to be "have nots," almost proletarians, because they were pinched by inflation.

The most spectacular manifestation of extreme Anabaptism gave the conservatives and moderates as great a shock as had the German Peasants' Rebellion. In the mid-1530s, a group of Anabaptists led by John of Leiden, a Dutch tailor, got control of the city of Münster in northwest Germany, expelled its prince-bishop, and set up a biblical utopia. We know about them chiefly from their opponents, who surely exaggerated their doctrines and practices. Still, even allowing for the distortions of propaganda, it seems clear that the Anabaptists of Münster were behaving in ways contrary to Western traditions. For one thing, they preached, and apparently practiced, polygamy; John of Leiden was reported to have taken sixteen wives, one of whom he later decapitated in public when she displeased him. They pushed the Lutheran doctrine of justification by faith to its logical extreme in anarchism, or, in theological language, antinomianism, from the Greek "against law." Each man was to be his own law, or rather, to find God's universal law in his own conscience, not in written law and tradition. They did not believe in class distinctions or in the customary forms of private property. They were disturbers of an established order that was strong enough to put them down by force; their leaders were executed and the rank and file either slain or dispersed.

The great majority of Anabaptists were very far removed from the men of Münster. Many sought to bring the Christian life to earth in quieter and more constructive ways. They established communities where they lived as they thought the primitive Christians had lived, in brotherhood, working, sharing, and praying together. These communities bore many resemblances to monasteries, though their members had taken no vows and did not observe celibacy. This sober majority of Anabaptists, too, met violent persecution in the sixteenth century but survived thanks to the discipline and to the repeated Christian turning of the other cheek insisted upon by their gifted leader, Menno Simons, a Dutch ex-priest. Something of their spirit lives on today in such diverse groups as the Baptists, the Friends, the Hutterites of Canada, and the Mennonites and Amish among the "Pennsylvania Dutch."

Two other radical strains in Protestantism were the mystical and the Unitarian. The former was exemplified by one of the few aristocratic reformers, Caspar von Schwenkfeld, a former Teutonic Knight and a convert to Lutheranism, who believed that the true church was to be found not in any outward observances but solely in the inner spirit of the individual. His stress on the spiritual and the mystical and his antagonism toward formalistic religion contributed later to the development of German pietism in reaction to the established Lutheran church. Some of his eighteenth-century followers settled in eastern Pennsylvania, where there are still Schwenkfelder churches.

Unitarianism today is usually identified with rejection of the Trinity as an irrational concept and the view that Christ was simply an inspired human being. But this version of Unitarianism derives largely from the rationalistic Enlightenment of the eighteenth century; sixteenth-century Unitarianism was a very different matter and much more mystical in outlook. Its most famous advocate, the Spanish physician Servetus (1511–1553), believed that Christ was the Son of God yet at the same time denied the existence of the Trinity and its doctrine that Father and Son were coeternal. Thereby Servetus hoped to make it easier for humanity to acquire a mystic identification with Christ; he also hoped that it would be possible to reconcile the Jewish and Muslim traditions of Spain with the Christian. His teachings, and the uncompromising way he presented them, greatly alarmed many Protestants as well as Catholics; he was prosecuted for heresy at Geneva by Calvin himself and burned at the stake in 1553. Other Unitarian victims of persecution were the Socinians, named for the Italian theologian Fausto Sozzini (Socinus in Latin, 1539–1604), who preached in eastern Europe. The Socinians were mainly in Poland, Hungary, and Transylvania, areas where the weakness of central government and the power of local landlords had permitted Protestantism to make great inroads before the Catholic Counter-Reformation was launched.

IV Protestant Beliefs and Practices
Common Denominators

The most obvious characteristic of the Protestant churches, especially in their formative period, was the wide gap that separated one from another, Anglican from Calvinist, Lutheran from Anabaptist. Yet there were certain common beliefs and practices that linked all the Protestant sects and set them apart from Catholicism. The first of these common denominators was the Protestant repudiation of Rome's claim to be the one true faith. The difficulty here was that each Protestant sect initially considered itself to be the one true faith, the legitimate successor to Christ and his apostles. Some early Protestants were confident that their particular belief would eventually prevail through the slow process of education and conversion. Others, however, could not wait and, though they had once been persecuted themselves, did not hesitate to persecute in their turn when they rose to power; witness Calvin's condemnation of Servetus. The humanist Castellio (or Châteillon) attacked Calvin's action in a book on "whether heretics are to be persecuted" (1554), which asserted that coercion should not be used to change man's religious ideas. While many other humanists shared Castellio's opposition to enforced conformity with an established church, they expressed a minority opinion. In the sixteenth and seventeenth centuries relatively few Europeans accepted what we take for granted today: the separation of church and state and the peaceful coexistence of many creeds all tolerated by an impartial government. The doctrine of religious toleration would emerge into full prominence only with the eighteenth-century Enlightenment.

A second common denominator of Protestantism was the fact that all its churches, even the conservative Anglican and Lutheran, made certain reductions in organization, ritual, and other religious externals. All the sects relaxed the requirement of clerical celibacy and either banned or sharply curtailed monasticism. All reduced somewhat the seven sacraments; a general Protestant minimum was to retain baptism and communion. But theological justifications of these sacraments ranged widely, from Lutheran consubstantiation to the view of the Eucharist as purely symbolic. Veneration of saints, pilgrimages, and the use of rosaries and amulets disappeared among all Protestants; the more radical also banished musical instruments (if not singing), sculptures, paintings, and stained glass, indeed all the arts except the oratorical.

Beneath these outward signs Protestants were linked by the fact that they were all rebels in origin. They had almost always protested in the name of a purer, primitive church, maintaining that Rome was the wicked innovator. (This appeal of the rebel to the past in order to legitimatize his revolt often recurs in Western history.) The Protestants turned from a corrupt established order to seek refuge in a higher law; all of them had at least a tinge of Luther's recourse to individual judgment. This individualism is an important legacy of Protestantism to the modern world.

The Conservative Churches

The divergent beliefs and practices that separate the Protestant churches one from another may be arranged most conveniently in order of their theological distance from Catholicism, beginning with those nearest to it. The Church of England has managed to contain elements from almost the whole Protestant range, from High Churchmen all the way to extreme Low Church-

men who come close to being Unitarians. It permits its clergy to marry and, although it does have some religious orders today, it does not put anything like the Catholic emphasis on the regular clergy. Yet the Church of England does keep a modified form of the Catholic hierarchy, with archbishops and bishops, though without acknowledging the authority of the pope. Perhaps the central core of Anglicanism has been a tempered belief in hierarchy and authority from above, a tempered ritualism, and a tempered acceptance of this imperfect world—a moderate attitude not far from the outlook of Thomas Aquinas. Indeed, Richard Hooker, who wrote a great defense of the Anglican church in the 1590s (*The Laws of Ecclesiastical Polity*), relied heavily on Aquinas; he is usually called "the judicious Hooker" because of his efforts to reconcile divergent points of view.

But there has also been a strong puritanical current in the broad stream of Anglicanism and its American counterpart, Episcopalianism. Puritanism, which may be defined as a combination of plain living and high thinking with earnest evangelical piety, was an important variant of the Low Church attitude. While some Puritans reluctantly left the Anglican communion in the late sixteenth and early seventeenth century, many others remained within it.

The Church of England assumed its definitive form during the reign of Elizabeth I (1558–1603), daughter of Henry VIII and Anne Boleyn. The Thirty-nine Articles enacted by Parliament in 1563 were a kind of constitution for the church. The articles rejected the more obvious forms of Romanism—the use of Latin, auricular confession, clerical celibacy, the allegiance to the pope. They also affirmed the Protestant stand on one of the great symbolic issues of the day—the Eucharist—by giving both the bread and the wine to communicants, as the reformers had long demanded, in contrast to the Catholic custom of giving only the wafer. In interpreting the Lord's Supper the articles rejected both Catholic transubstantiation and Zwinglian symbolism and attempted to find a compromise somewhere in between. Finally, the Thirty-nine Articles sought very emphatically to void the anarchistic dangers implicit in the doctrines of justification by faith and the priesthood of the believer.

The Church of England has always seemed to its enemies, and even to some of its friends, a bit too acquiescent in the face of civil authority. In what was once a word of abuse, the Church of England has seemed Erastian, so called after Erastus, a sixteenth-century Swiss theologian and a disciple of Zwingli who objected to the theocratic practices of the Calvinists. To check abuses by the religious authorities Erastus wanted to increase the power of the political authorities. The term *Erastianism*, however, has come to imply that the state is all-powerful against the church and that the clergy should be simply a moral police force. While Anglicanism seldom went this far in practice, a touch of subservience to the political powers that be, a modified Erastianism, does remain in the Church of England, and we shall encounter it in the English civil and religious strife of the seventeenth century.

To outsiders the Lutheran church has appeared even more Erastian than the Anglican. As the state church in much of northern Germany and in Scandinavia, it was often a docile instrument of its political masters. And in its close association with the rise of Prussia, though Prussia's Hohenzollern rulers later became Calvinist, it was brought under the rule of the strongly bureaucratic Prussian state.

Luther, like so many others upon whom character and fate have thrust rebellion, was at heart a conservative about things of this world, as we have seen. He wanted the forms of Lutheran worship to recall the forms he was used to. Once it had become established, Lutheranism preserved many practices that seem Catholic in origin but that to Luther represented a return to early Christianity before the corruption by Rome. Lutheranism preserved the Eucharist, now interpreted by the doctrine of consubstantiation, and it also preserved bishops, gowns, and something of the plastic arts. The tradition of good music in the church was not only preserved but greatly fortified. The Lutheran church, however, had a strong evangelical party, the germ of the later pietist movement, as well as a conservative High Church party.

Calvinism

For Calvinists the main theological concern is not so much Luther's problem of faith against good works as the related problem of predestination against free will. The problem is an old one in Christianity, already evident in the fifth-century struggle over the heresy of Pelagius, who believed in human goodness and in complete free will, whereas his opponents stressed man's sinfulness and God's goodness. To the logical mind, the problem arises from the concept that God is all-powerful, all-good, all-knowing. If this is so, he must determine everything that happens, even willing that the sinner must sin. For if he did not so will, the individual would be doing something God did not want him to do, and God would not be all-powerful. There is a grave difficulty here: if God wills that the sinner sin, the sinner cannot help himself or be blamed for his sin. We seem to be at a dead end, where the individual can always claim, no matter what he does, that he is doing what God makes him do. We seem to have cut the ground from under individual moral responsibility, just as John of Leiden and his Antinomians did when they took several wives at once and argued that God must want them to, since they wanted to. The dilemma is clear. If the individual has free will to choose for himself between good and evil acts, to do what God does not want him to do, then it looks as though God is not all-powerful. If he has no such choice because his acts are subject to predestination, then it looks as though the individual were morally irresponsible.

At least to an outsider, it may seem that Christians solved the dilemma most frequently by embracing both horns at once—by holding that God determines every human act, and yet that human beings may do things God does not want them to do. Theologians do not of course put the matter this way. Most of their basic solutions preserve the moral responsibility of the individual by asserting the profound distance between God and man, a distance that the miracle—the grace—of faith alone can bridge. This means that for the individual to claim that whatever he does is what God wants him to do is to make the incredibly presumptuous claim that he knows God's will, that his petty human understanding is on a par with God's. The individual can never be certain that what he wants to do is what God wants him to do. Therefore he should look about him and see what signs he can, limited though his vision be, of God's intentions. These he will find in Christian tradition and Christian history. To be concrete: if the individual is tempted to commit adultery, he will not follow the Antinomian and say that God wants him to do so; he will follow Christian tradition and recognize the adulterous desire as an indication that he is being tempted to do wrong and that if he does it he will not be saved, but damned.

Calvin himself, though he would certainly not have put it this way, would have reached the same conclusion. But he was, as we have noted, a logician. Both his temperament and his environment led him to reject what he believed to be the Catholic emphasis on easy salvation by indulgences and the like. He put his own emphasis on the hard path of true salvation, on the majesty of God and the littleness of man. He evolved therefore an extreme form of the doctrine of predestination.

In Calvin's system, Adam's original sin was unforgivable. God, however, in his incomprehensible mercy, sent Jesus Christ to this earth and let him die on the cross to make salvation possible for some—but emphatically not all, nor by any means a majority—of Adam's progeny, stained though they were by original sin. Very few—in fact, only the elect—could attain this salvation, and that through no merit of their own, and certainly not on the wholesale scale the Roman Catholic church of the sixteenth century was claiming. The elect were saved only through God's free and infinite grace, by means of which they were given the strength to gain salvation. Grace is not like anything else that touches human life on earth. It is not of a piece with law, morals, philosophy, and other human ways of relating man to his environment—to hold that it is was to Calvin one of the errors of the Catholic church. But it is not wholly divorced from these earthly relations—to hold that it is the error of the Antinomian. The elect actually tend to behave in a certain way, an identifiable way, a way not wholly misrepresented if it is called puritanical.

Our modern world has exaggerated the gloom of Calvinist puritanism, and the spiritual pride and exclusiveness of its adherents. Yet where the Calvinists were in complete control of an area (as in sixteenth-century Geneva) or in partial control of larger areas (as in England, Scotland, the Netherlands, or puritan Massachusetts), they censored, forbade, banished, and punished. Particularly in Geneva, where all trace of the Roman hierarchy had vanished along with the prince-bishop, the local Catholic tradition of scrutinizing the morals of the populace continued on an intensive scale. Every week a consistory composed of pastors and of lay elders appointed by the city council met and passed judgment on all accused of improper behavior. Though the consistory sometimes failed to get its decisions enforced, its activities were tantamount to a Protestant inquisition. In their own minds the members of the Geneva consistory and other representatives of the puritan spiritual police were God's agents, doing God's work. These firm believers in the inability of human efforts to change anything were among the most ardent of workers toward getting men to change their behavior. To an amazing extent, they succeeded, and they helped make the Industrial Revolution and the modern world.

The note of Christianity the Calvinists most clearly emphasized is not so much asceticism or otherworldliness as austerity. The Calvinist did not seek to annihilate the senses but sought rather to select among worldly desires those that would further man's salvation, and to curb or suppress those that would not. This world is for most of us, the Calvinist believed, an antechamber to hell and eternal suffering; if you really feel this, you are not likely to be much amused. The Calvinist thought that human pleasures—music, dancing, gambling, fine clothes, drinking, playgoing, and fortune-telling, among others—were the kind of thing Satan liked. Although the Calvinist did not hold that all sexual intercourse is sinful, he believed firmly that the purpose God had in mind in providing sex was the continuation of the race, and not the sensuous pleasures of the participants. Those pleasures are all the more dangerous since they may lead to extramarital indulgence, which is a very great sin.

Calvinism also sounded very loudly the ethical note of Christianity. The Calvinist had a high moral code; he was always trying to live up to his code, and to see that other people did so too. Both inward and outward directions of this effort are important. The Calvinist certainly felt the "civil war in the breast," the struggle between what has become famous as the puritan conscience and the temptations of this world. This notion of a higher part of human consciousness that can and should censor and suppress the promptings of a lower part has left a firm imprint on the West. In its outgoing direction, this Calvinist ethical concern has taken many forms other than that of the total, police-enforced prohibition. The Calvinist also believed in persuasion; he made the sermon a central part of his worship. He believed in hellfire and in the moral uses of fear of hellfire, he believed in emotional conversion, and he was a good missionary, though not at his best among primitive peoples.

Calvinism appears in pure or diluted form in many sects, Presbyterian and Congregational in Britain, Reformed on the Continent; it influenced even the Anglicans and the Lutherans. Theologically, its main opponent is a system of ideas called Arminianism, from Jacob Arminius, a late-sixteenth-century Dutch divine. Arminianism may be classified among the freewill theologies, for Arminius held that election (and of course damnation) were conditional in God's mind—not absolute as Calvin had maintained—and that therefore what a man did on earth could change his ultimate fate. Generally, Arminianism was more tolerant of the easy ways of this world than Calvinism, less "puritanical," more Erastian. Though at first condemned by the Dutch Reformed Church, it later exerted a strong influence on other Protestant churches, notably the Baptist and the Methodist.

Calvinism can hardly be accused of being Erastian. Where it did become the established state church—in Geneva, in the England of the 1650s, in Massachusetts, for instance—the Calvinist church ran or tried to run the state. This theocracy was never fully realized, even in Geneva, where the city council refused to surrender all its prerogatives. Where Calvinism had to fight to exist, it preached and practiced an ardent denial of the omnipotence of the state over the individual. Later generations turned these affirmations of popular rights to the uses of their own struggles against kings—and churchmen. In this sense, Calvinism helped create modern democracy. Its basic original concepts are not, however, democratic, if democracy is based, as we think it is, on equalitarian principles and on a generally compassionate and hopeful view of human beings, a minimizing of the legacy of original sin. But Calvin might not recognize his twentieth-century children, for Calvinism today is no longer the vigorous, fundamentalist, fighting creed it was in the sixteenth century. Its churches almost everywhere take a kindlier view of human nature and human potential and have moderated their reforming zeal.

The Radicals

The radical Protestant sects were usually greatly influenced by Calvinist theology and Calvinist example. Their practices, however, varied widely: sometimes the congregation shouted and danced and sang hymns with great fervor; yet the Mennonites put great stress on silent prayer and meditation. Among the radicals, preaching was even more important than in other forms of Protestantism, and more emotionally charged with hopes of heaven and fears of hell. Many sects were vigorously chiliastic—that is, they expected an immediate Second Coming of Christ and the end of this world. Many were in aim, and among themselves in practice,

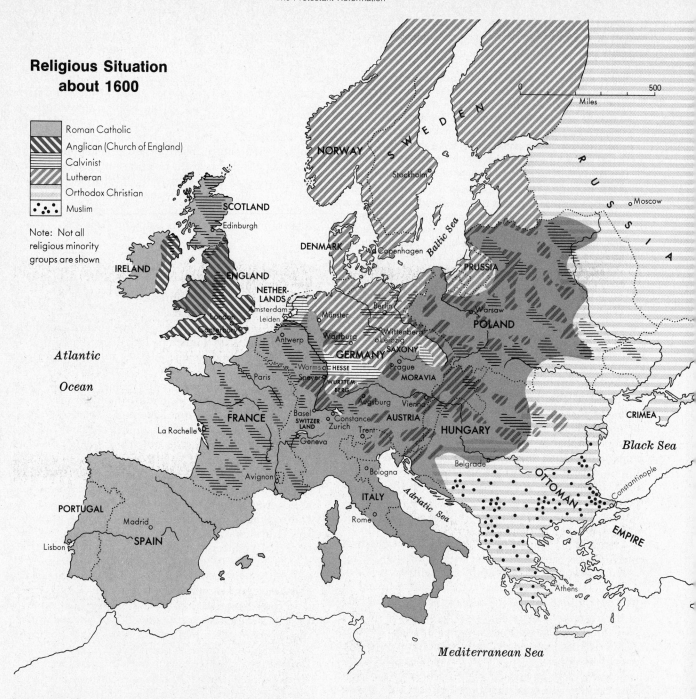

Religious Situation about 1600

- Roman Catholic
- Anglican (Church of England)
- Calvinist
- Lutheran
- Orthodox Christian
- Muslim

Note: Not all religious minority groups are shown

as Magna Carta in the thirteenth century looks quite different from Magna Carta viewed from the twentieth. First, sixteenth-century Protestants were not rationalists; they were almost as "superstitious" as the Catholics. Luther threw his ink bottle at the devil, or so they tell the tourists at the castle of the Wartburg where they point out the dark patch on the wall where the bottle struck; the Calvinists burned witches, or at any rate hanged them. To put the matter more positively, the Protestants for the most part shared with their Catholic opponents very fundamental Christian conceptions of

original sin, the direct divine governance of the universe, the reality of heaven and hell, and—most important—they did not have, any more than the Catholics did, a general conception of life on this earth as capable of progressing toward a better life for future generations.

Second, the early Protestants were by no means tolerant, by no means believers in the separation of church and state. When they were in a position to do so, they used governmental power to prevent public worship in any form other than their own. Many of

The Renaissance

Donatello's statue and the four following color plates may suggest the extraordinary range and innovativeness of Renaissance art. Although three of the works illustrate traditional religious subjects, all three break with medieval artistic conventions in their treatment. Donatello's John the Baptist can function as a freestanding work rather than as a small part of a larger architectural ensemble, which had been characteristic of medieval sculpture. Giotto's *Lamentation* and Michelangelo's *David and Goliath,* while they are units in a whole series of paintings, show how Renaissance artists applied new techniques to heighten dramatic effect—*chiaroscuro* in the case of Giotto, and oil paints in that of Michelangelo.

Leonardo's portrait of Ginevra de' Benci marks a still greater departure from earlier artistic norms: the subject is secular, and both the lady's hair and the foliage of the background are painted with the meticulous care of a great scientist. Finally, the hardworking peasants in Brueghel's *Harvesters* show that the commissions of Renaissance artists were not limited to grand biblical themes or to the glorification of well-to-do patrons.

Saint John the Baptist, by Donatello.
European Art Color, Peter Adelberg, N.Y.C.

The Lamentation, by Giotto: detail.
Scrovegni Chapel, Padua. Scala.

Ginevra de' Benci, by Leonardo da Vinci.
National Gallery of Art, Washington. The Granger Collection.

Pendentive, west wall, the Sistine Chapel: David and Goliath, by Michelangelo.

The Harvesters, by Pieter Brueghel the Elder: detail.
The Metropolitan Museum of Art, Rogers Fund, 1919.

The Seventeenth Century

In contrast to Donatello's John the Baptist, whose saintly quality is emphasized by his emaciated body and crude garments, Bernini's St. Sebastian is a martyr in his physical prime. Fashioned when the sculptor was still in his teens and influenced by Michelangelo, it is a rather mild example of the melodramatic qualities that earned seventeenth-century art the label of *baroque,* a word derived from the term for a large irregular pearl. The exaggerations of baroque art have led some critics to compare it unfavorably with the classical restraint of Renaissance art, citing particularly some of Bernini's later sculptures and the two extravagant constructions—the baldachin and "St. Peter's chair"—that he designed for the interior of St. Peter's in Rome.

Yet Bernini himself continued the Renaissance tradition of versatility in a distinguished career as sculptor, architect, and urban planner. And, as the paintings in the two succeeding plates show, baroque masters could be as subtle as their Renaissance predecessors. Velásquez, the court painter of the Spanish Hapsburgs, made the princess Maria Theresa (the future queen of Louis XIV) look reasonably regal without concealing her ugly thick Hapsburg lips. The Dutch Rembrandt, who shared his countrymen's fascination with light, imparted a golden glow to many of his paintings including the portrait of his son.

Saint Sebastian, by Gianlorenzo Bernini.
European Art Color, Peter Adelberg, N.Y.C.

The Infanta Maria Theresa, by Diego Velásquez.
The Metropolitan Museum of Art, the Jules S. Bache Collection, 1949.

The Artist's Son, Titus, by Rembrandt.
The Metropolitan Museum of Art, bequest of Benjamin Altman, 1913.

them persecuted those who disagreed with them, both Protestants of other sects and Catholics—that is, they banished them or imprisoned them or even killed them.

Third, the early Protestants were hardly democratic, at least in the sense that the word has for twentieth-century Americans. Logically, the Protestant appeal from the authority of the pope backed by Catholic tradition to the conscience of the individual believer fits in with such notions as "individualism," "rights of man," and "liberty." Some historians have even found a correlation between the Protestant appeal to the authority of the Bible and the later American appeal to the authority of a written constitution. But most of the early Protestant reformers certainly did not hold that all men are created equal; rather, they believed in an order of rank, in a society of status. Lutheranism and Anglicanism were clearly conservative in their political and social doctrines. Calvinism can be made to look very undemocratic indeed if we concentrate on its conception of an elect few chosen by God for salvation and an unregenerate majority condemned to eternal damnation. And in its early years in Geneva and in New England, Calvinism came close to being a theocracy, an authoritarian rule of the "saints."

In the long run, however, Calvinism favored the domination of a fairly numerous and prosperous middle class. As we shall see shortly, the most persuasive argument for a causal relation between Protestantism and modern Western democratic life does not proceed directly from the ideas of the early Protestants about men in society, but from the way Protestant moral ideals fitted in with the strengthening of a commercial and industrial middle class. Finally, among the Anabaptists and other radical sects, we do find even in the sixteenth century demands for political, social, and economic equality. But where these demands are made, they are cast in biblical language and rest on concepts of direct divine intervention quite strange to us. Moreover, many of these sects tended not so much toward active social revolt to improve earthly standards of living as toward a peculiarly Protestant form of withdrawal from things of this earth, toward pacifism, mysticism, and a spiritual exclusiveness quite compatible with leaving the unregenerate majority in possession of this unworthy physical world.

The Protestant Reformation, then, did not create modern society single-handedly. But it did challenge those in authority in many parts of Europe and did start all sorts of men, some of them in humble circumstances, thinking about fundamental problems of life in this world as well as in the next. Its educators and propagandists, using the new weapon of the printing press, began the drive toward universal literacy. It was one of the great destroyers of the medieval synthesis. Its most important positive action can best be traced through its part in forming the way of life of the middle classes who were to lay the foundations of modern Western democracy.

The Weber Thesis

The German sociologist Max Weber explored this question in *The Protestant Ethic and the Spirit of Capitalism,* first published in 1904. The thesis that he advanced has aroused a storm of controversy, in part because he touched on the sensitive area of religion and in part because a mere sociologist dared to invade the sensitive province of the historian. Though many historians nowadays reject his conclusions, the Weber thesis remains a stimulating and suggestive contribution to the ventilation of an issue that can never be fully resolved.

What started Weber's exploration was evidence suggesting that in his own day German Protestants had a proportionately greater interest in the world of business, and German Catholics a proportionately smaller interest, than their ratio in the German population would lead one to expect. Why was this so? Weber's answer—his celebrated thesis—may be summarized as follows. The accumulation of capital requires some abstention from immediate consumption; the entrepreneur, if he is a true capitalist, must plow some of his profits back into his enterprise so that he produces still more and makes higher profits, with a higher potential for future capital. To achieve this a businessman must not only curb his expenditures but also work very hard; he must spend the bulk of his time making money.

Weber argued that Protestantism, especially in its Calvinist form, encouraged this sort of life. It encouraged hard work because, as the maxim put it, "The devil lies in wait for idle hands." Work keeps a man from temptation to run after women, or play silly games, or drink, or do many other things unpleasing to the Calvinist God. More, work is positively a good thing, a kind of tribute we pay to the Lord. Luther, too, glorified work of all kinds and preached the doctrine of the dignity of the vocation a man is called to, be it ever so humble. In almost all forms of Protestantism we find this feeling, so contrary to the contempt for work of the field and countinghouse evident in the tradition of chivalry.

So much for work, the positive side of the equation. But on the negative side, Protestantism, and in particular Calvinism, discouraged many kinds of consumption that took energies away from the large-scale production that is the essence of the modern economic system. The Calvinist, to put it mildly, discouraged the fine arts, the theater, the dance, expensive clothes, what the American economist Veblen called "conspicuous consumption" generally. But he did not discourage—in fact he encouraged by his own way of living—the satisfaction of the simple needs of solid, substantial food and adequate shelter and clothing and the like, all needs most readily supplied by large-scale industry serving a mass demand. The Calvinist represents a new development of the perennial Christian ascetic tradition.

A society with many Calvinists tended to produce

much, to consume solidly but without waste or ostentation. Therefore, under competitive conditions, its business leaders accumulated capital, which they could invest in the methods of production that have so enriched the West. All work and no play—well, not much—made the Calvinist society an economically prosperous one.

The Scots, the Dutch, the Swiss, the Yankees of New England—all of them markedly Calvinistic peoples—have long had a popular reputation for thrift, diligence, and driving a hard bargain. And it is surprising how many concrete bits of evidence reinforce the Weber thesis. The Protestant societies at once cut down the number of holy days—holidays without work. They kept Sunday very rigorously as a day without work, but the other six were all work days. The Calvinists even eliminated Christmas, and, since there were as yet no national lay equivalents of the old religious festivals, no Fourth of July or Labor Day, the early modern period in most Protestant countries had a maximum of work days per year. This is a marginal matter, but it is in part by such margins that economic growth is won. Many Protestant theologians rejected the medieval Catholic doctrine that regarded interest on investments beyond a low, "just" rate as usury, and they also rejected most of the medieval attitudes suggested by the term "just price" in favor of something much closer to modern ideas of free competition in the market. In the market, God would certainly take care of his own!

Finally, the firm Calvinist retention of the other world as the supreme, but for the individual never certain, goal helped shield the newly rich from the temptation to adopt the standards of a loose-living, free-spending upper class. Prosperity might be a token that a man was predestined to election, but so, too, was the cautious way he husbanded his profits. Among Calvinists, family fortunes founded by hard work and inconspicuous consumption tended to hold together for several generations at least.

Weber's thesis must not be taken as the sole explanation of capitalism in early modern times, for it is but one of many variables in a complex situation. The stirrings of modern economic life far antedated Luther and Calvin and were first evident in regions that were never won over to Protestantism—Italy, southern Germany, Belgium. Banking began in Florence and other northern Italian cities under Catholic rulers in an era when usury was still prohibited, at least in theory. Almost certainly rules against usury would have been relaxed with the sanction of the Catholic church even if there had been no Protestant Reformation. Moreover, there is no perfect coordination between Protestantism and industrial development on the one hand and Catholicism and industrial backwardness, or notably slower development, on the other. Belgium, the German Rhineland, Piedmont, and Lombardy are striking examples of Catholic regions that have kept well up to the fore in general productiveness and prosperity. Finally, no sensible explanation of the rise of a modern industrial economy can neglect the simple facts of geography and natural resources. Even if Italy had turned Calvinist, it still would not have enjoyed the coal and iron deposits that contributed to Protestant Britain's headstart in industrialism.

Yet the Protestant ethic did perhaps provide the extra fillip that started the West on its modern path—along with the expansion of Europe, which helped the Atlantic nations over the Mediterranean nations; along with the natural resources of northern and western Europe; along with the damp, temperate climate that made hard work easier than in the Mediterranean; along with free enterprise, freedom for science and invention, relatively orderly and law-abiding societies, and whatever else goes to produce that still not fully understood phenomenon, economic growth.

The Reformation and Nationalism

One final generalization about the Reformation is much less disputable than attempts to tie Protestantism in with modern individualism, democracy, and industrialism. After the great break of the sixteenth century, both Protestantism and Catholicism became important elements in the formation of modern nationalism. Here again the trap of one-way causation must be avoided. Neither Protestants nor Catholics were always patriots: French Huguenots sought help from the English enemy, and French Catholics from the Spanish enemy. But where a specific form of religion became identified with a given political unit, religious feeling and patriotic feeling each reinforced the other. This is most evident where a political unit had to struggle for its independence. Protestantism heightened Dutch resistance to the Spaniard; Catholicism heightened Irish resistance to the Englishman. But even in states already independent in the sixteenth century, religion strengthened patriotism. England from Elizabeth I on has, despite the existence of a Catholic minority, proudly held itself up as a Protestant nation; Spain has with equal pride identified itself as a Catholic nation. In the great wars to which we now turn, religion and politics were inextricably combined.

Reading Suggestions on the Protestant Reformation

General Accounts

O. Chadwick, *The Reformation* (*Penguin). A comprehensive survey addressed to the general reader.

R. H. Bainton, *The Reformation of the Sixteenth Century* (*Beacon). Excellent introduction by a Protestant scholar, who has written several more specialized works on the period.

E. H. Harbison, *The Age of Reformation* (*Cornell Univ.). A brief, perceptive introduction.

G. R. Elton, *Reformation Europe, 1517–1559* (*Torchbooks). A lively survey summarizing many of the findings in the more ponderous *New Cambridge Modern History,* Vol. 2: *The Reformation* (Cambridge Univ., 1958), which Elton edited.

A. G. Dickens, *Reformation and Society in Sixteenth-Century Europe* (*Holt). Informative, broad survey, with many illustrations.

H. G. Koenigsberger and G. L. Mosse, *Europe in the Sixteenth Century* (*Holt). Up-to-date, scholarly survey, with excellent bibliographies.

E. F. Rice, Jr., *The Foundations of Early Modern Europe, 1460–1559* (*Norton). Recent brief introduction.

J. Huizinga, *Erasmus and the Age of Reformation* (*Torchbooks). By a celebrated Dutch historian.

Luther

R. H. Bainton, *Here I Stand: A Life of Martin Luther* (*Mentor). Sympathetic, scholarly, readable.

E. H. Erikson, *Young Man Luther* (*Norton). Luther's "identity crisis" persuasively presented.

H. Grisar, *Martin Luther: His Life and Works* (Herder, 1930). From the Catholic point of view.

E. G. Schwiebert, *Luther and His Times* (Concordia, 1952). From the Lutheran point of view; particularly useful for the setting and the effects of Luther's revolt.

K. Brandi, *The Emperor Charles V* (*Humanities). Comprehensive study of Luther's antagonist.

H. Holborn, *A History of Modern Germany,* Vol. 1: *The Reformation* (Knopf, 1959). Scholarly and readable.

The Other Founders

J. Courvoisier, *Zwingli: A Reformed Theologian* (*John Knox). Good study of an important and often neglected figure.

F. Wendel, *Calvin: The Origins and Development of His Religious Thought* (Harper, 1963). Translation of a solid study by a French scholar.

G. Harkness, *John Calvin: The Man and His Ethics* (*Apex). A good short introduction.

J. Mackinnon, *Calvin and the Reformation* (Longmans, 1936). Substantial longer study.

J. J. Scarisbrick, *Henry VIII* (*Univ. of California). The first major scholarly assessment since A. F. Pollard, *Henry VIII* (*Torchbooks), which appeared early in this century.

A. G. Dickens, *The English Reformation* (*Schocken). Detailed study down to 1559, with useful bibliography.

T. M. Parker, *The English Reformation to 1558,* 2nd ed. (*Oxford). Excellent short account.

G. H. Williams, *The Radical Reformation* (Westminster, 1962). Encyclopedic and indispensable study of the Anabaptists and other left-wing reformers.

F. H. Littell, *The Anabaptist View of the Church,* 2nd ed. (Starr King, 1958). Perceptive, brief introduction.

The Catholic Reformation

H. Daniel-Rops, *The Catholic Reformation* (Dutton, 1962). Admirable study by a French Catholic scholar.

A. G. Dickens, *The Counter-Reformation* (*Holt). Comprehensive survey by an English Protestant scholar.

B. J. Kidd, *The Counter-Reformation* (S. P. C. K., 1933). Scholarly account by an Anglican.

P. Janelle, *The Catholic Reformation* (Bruce, 1951). Scholarly account by a Catholic.

R. Fülop-Miller, *Jesuits: History of the Society of Jesus* (*Capricorn), and H. Boehmer, *The Jesuits* (Castle, 1928). Respectively, by a Catholic and a Protestant.

Protestantism and Progress

M. Weber, *The Protestant Ethic and the Spirit of Capitalism* (*Scribner's). Advances the famous thesis on the interrelationship of religion and economics.

R. H. Tawney, *Religion and the Rise of Capitalism* (*Mentor). Turns the Weber thesis around to emphasize economic motivation.

L. W. Spitz, ed., *The Reformation: Basic Interpretations* (*Heath). Useful introduction to divergent scholarly views.

E. Troeltsch, *Protestantism and Progress* (*Beacon). By a leading modern religious philosopher.

P. Tillich, *The Protestant Era* (*Phoenix). Abridged from a longer study by a ranking modern theologian.

Sources

H. S. Bettenson, ed., *Documents of the Christian Church,* 2nd ed. (*Oxford). Admirable compilation, particularly valuable for the Reformation.

E. G. Rupp and B. Drewery, eds., *Martin Luther* (St. Martin's, 1970). An anthology of his significant writings, with helpful editorial comment.

H. J. Hillerbrand, *The Reformation in Its Own Words* (*Torchbooks). Another useful compilation of primary material.

Châteillon, *Concerning Heretics,* ed. R. H. Bainton (Columbia Univ., 1935). One of the earliest arguments for religious freedom, not merely toleration.

Dynastic Politics and Warfare

1494-1648

The Balance of Power

Historians have chosen a number of different dates to mark the watershed between medieval and modern. Protestants pick 1517 and the Ninety-Five Theses, while Americans often think of 1492 as the great year. For the kingdoms of western Europe, historians single out the appearance of strong, ambitious monarchs—1461, Louis XI in France; 1469, the marriage of Ferdinand of Aragon and Isabella of Castile; 1485, Henry VII and the advent of the Tudors in England. For international relations they are likely to choose a more obscure date—1494, when Charles VIII of France began what has been called the first modern war by leading his army over the Alps toward the conquest of Italy.

All such dates are arbitrary, for, as our discussion of the Renaissance has shown, the dividing line between medieval and modern culture cannot be placed in a single country or a single year. Moreover, it can be argued that what really makes the modern world "modern" is the combination of rationalism, natural science, technology, and economic organization that has given men a new power over natural resources. By this standard, the great change came in the eighteenth century, and the sixteenth and seventeenth were but preparation. Still, for the historian of international relations, a difference between the medieval and modern organization of the European state system is noticeable as early as the late 1400s.

The Competitive State System

Western society, in early modern times, was a group of states, big, middle-sized, and small, each striving to grow, usually by annexing other states or at least bringing them under some sort of control. At any given moment some states were on the offensive, trying to

sive, trying to preserve what they had. Even states we now think of as peaceful small democracies, like Sweden and Denmark, took the offensive in quest of territorial empire three centuries ago, and Sweden almost became a great power.

The constituent units in this competitive system are usually termed sovereign states, which means in practice that their rulers had armed forces to implement their policies. After the height of feudal disintegration, perhaps in the tenth century, a continuous though irregular process of reducing the number of sovereign states got under way and lasted down to World War I. If a feudal lord with armed retainers can be called sovereign because he could make war on his own initiative, then the tenth-century West had thousands of sovereign units. By the end of the Middle Ages, however, the little feudal units had been absorbed into much bigger states over much of the West, with the partial exception of much-fragmented Germany. When local wars occurred, they were seldom wars between states but rather civil wars, risings of dissident nobles against their sovereigns. The shadowy unity of Western Christendom was destroyed at the end of the Middle Ages, but so too was the real disunity of numerous local units capable of organizing war among themselves.

As the modern state system began to take shape in the fifteenth and sixteenth centuries, the three well-organized monarchies of Spain, France, and England dominated western Europe; the smaller states of Scotland, Portugal, and Scandinavia generally played a subordinate role. In central Europe, the Holy Roman Empire, with its many quasi-sovereign member states, did not have the kind of internal unity enjoyed by the Atlantic powers. Yet under the leadership of the Austrian Hapsburgs, the empire took a leading part in international competition. Between France and the em-

century dukes of Burgundy had tried to weld many small units into a revived middle kingdom. Out of this zone have come the states of Holland, Belgium, Luxembourg, Switzerland, and Italy. Renaissance Italy, as we have already seen, was divided into several sovereign states that comprised a junior state system with wars, diplomacy, and balance of power. As early as the fourteenth century, Italy anticipated on a small scale the international politics of Europe in later centuries. To the southeast was the new and expanding Ottoman Empire, with European lands reaching to the central Danube valley. To the east, Muscovite Russia was beginning to become a great state, and Poland-Lithuania was already great in size if not in power.

Over the last five hundred years certain states have attempted to disrupt this state system: sixteenth-century Spain; the France of Louis XIV in the seventeenth century and of the Revolution and Napoleon a century later; the Germany of the Kaiser and Hitler and, to a lesser degree, the Russia of Stalin in the twentieth century. They have tried to reduce or obliterate the sovereignty of other states. Each time this has happened, the threatened units sooner or later joined together in a coalition against the aggressive power to maintain the system and, in the time-honored phrase, to restore or redress the balance of power. The phrase is a descriptive one, not a moral principle, and it is a convenient thread through the intricacies of international politics in the modern West. We take up this thread in 1494.

Sixteenth-century woodcut: an army besieging a city.

Dynastic State and Nation State

First, however, we must examine briefly the nature of the political units that made up the competitive state system. It is the custom to call them dynastic states up to about the end of the eighteenth century and nation states thereafter. What this distinction implies may be found in the change of title imposed on Louis XVI by the Revolution in 1791—from king of France, which suggests that the kingdom was real estate belonging to the Bourbon dynasty, to king of the French, which suggests that he was the leader accepted by the French nation. In the early modern period some states were loose agglomerations of formerly independent units that might be separated from each other by foreign territory, that sometimes spoke different languages, and that were tied together almost solely by the ruling dynasty. The widely scattered Hapsburg realm is a good example. In war and diplomacy the dynastic ruler and his circle of nobles and bureaucrats acted as a team with a certain team spirit, but the various peoples in such a dynastic state had relatively little sense of patriotism, of common national effort and ambitions. Early modern wars were not total wars, and, except in their disastrous effects on government finances, and on taxes, they scarcely touched the lives of the common people who were not actually in the way of contending armies

trying to live off the land. In the peace settlements, no one talked about "national self-determination of peoples" or worried greatly about transferring areas and populations from one dynasty to another.

On the other hand, the distinction between dynastic states and nation states must not be overdrawn. Especially in the great Atlantic monarchies a degree of national patriotism existed in the sixteenth century and, in England and France, it had already been evident during the Hundred Years' War when the English referred scornfully to the French as frogs, and Frenchmen retaliated by calling the English *les godons,* the French mispronunciation of *goddams.* At the time of the great Spanish Armada (1588) Englishmen showed intense patriotic emotion, hating and fearing Spaniards both as foreigners and as militantly anti-Protestant Catholics. Even in divided Germany, Luther could count on Germans to dislike Italians. Hatred of the foreigner bound men together at least as effectively as love of one another.

The differences between the present-day state and the early modern state are generally exaggerated today. They are real, and they make the dynastic wars of the sixteenth, seventeenth, and even eighteenth centuries seem petty and bewildering, but they are not in the main differences in kind. They are differences in the degree of efficiency, of centralization, of the ability to command vast numbers of men and great resources, and of the rapidity of movement.

The Instruments of Foreign Policy

By 1500, almost all the European sovereign states possessed in at least rudimentary form most of the social and political organs of a modern state, lacking only a large literate population brought up in the ritual and faith of national patriotism. Notably they had two essential instruments: a professional diplomatic service and a professional army. The fifteenth and sixteenth centuries saw the steady development of modern diplomatic agencies and methods. Governments established central foreign offices or ministries, sent diplomats and regular missions to foreign courts, and organized espionage under the cover of open diplomacy. Formal peace conferences were held and formal treaties were signed, with all the ceremony and protocol we associate with such occasions. Finally, to govern these formal relations a set of rules began to take shape that is rather too grandly termed "international law," for it often proved impossible to enforce.

The apparatus of international politics developed most fully in Renaissance Italy and found its classic expression in the admirably organized diplomatic service of the Republic of Venice. The detailed reports Venetian ambassadors sent back to the Senate from abroad are among the first documents of intelligence work we have. They are careful political and social studies of the personalities and lands involved rather than mere gossipy cloak-and-dagger reports. In those days, the diplomat was a most important maker of policy in his own right. With rapid travel impossible, his government could not communicate with him in time to prescribe his acts minutely, and he often had to make important decisions on his own. Good or bad diplomacy, good or bad intelligence about foreign lands, made a vital difference in a state's success or failure in the struggle for power.

The armed forces made still more difference. The early modern centuries were the great days of the professional soldier, freed from the limitations of feudal warfare and not yet tied to the immense economic requirements and inhuman scale of modern warfare. The officer class in particular could plan, drill, and campaign on a fairly large but quite manageable scale; they could, in effect, handle warfare as a skill, even as an art or a pleasure. The common soldiers, too, for the most part were mercenaries; the word "soldier" in fact comes from *solidus,* the Latin for "piece of money." Some of these mercenaries were recruited at home, usually among the poor and dispossessed, sometimes by impressment. Others were foreigners who made a career of soldiering, particularly Swiss and Germans; thousands of them served in the armies of Francis I of France together with Englishmen, Scots, Poles, Italians, Albanians, and Greeks.

These professional forces were often trained to parade, to dress ranks, and to keep discipline, and they were whipped if they broke discipline, though threats of punishment did not always prevent desertions when pay was late or rations inadequate. Each regiment or unit commonly wore the same uniforms, but whole armies usually displayed such an extraordinary variety of garb that in battle recognition of friend and foe was not easy. Tactics and strategy in the field were under the control of an officer hierarchy that culminated in a commanding general, who in turn was subject to some control by the central government. In short, though these armies would look anarchic to a modern professional of the spit-and-polish school, they were far better organized and disciplined than feudal levies had been.

Yet the early modern armies also show many feudal survivals, many forms of entrenched privilege, many ways of twisting away from centralized control. The officer class continued to preserve many of its old habits of chivalry, such as the duel, which often seriously menaced internal discipline. If the feudal lord no longer brought his own knights for the forty days of allotted time, his descendant as regimental colonel often raised his own regiment and financed it himself. Weapons were of an extraordinary variety. Reminders of the old hand-to-hand fighting survived in the sword and in the pike, the long shaft used by foot soldiers against the armored knight and his mount. Hand firearms—arquebus, musket, pistol, and many others—were slow-loading and slow-firing, and usually not even capable of being aimed with any accuracy. The cannon, quite unstandardized as to parts and caliber, and heavy and hard to move, fired solid balls, rather than exploding shells.

Armies on the march lived mostly off the land, even when they were in home territory. But they were beginning to develop the elaborate modern organization of supply and the modern service of engineers. Both the growth of military technology and differences of national temperament were reflected in the shift of military predominance from Spain to France about 1600. Spain, the great fighting nation of the sixteenth century on land, excelled in infantry, where the pike was a major weapon. France, the great fighting nation of the seventeenth and early eighteenth centuries on land, excelled in artillery, engineering, and fortification, all services that were more plebeian, less suited to the former feudal nobility than infantry and cavalry.

Meanwhile, the first modern navies were also growing up. In the later Middle Ages, Venice, Genoa, and Pisa had all begun to assemble fleets of galleys disciplined both as individual ships and in fleet maneuvers. In the Renaissance, Venice took the lead with its arsenal and its detailed code of maritime regulations. Naval organization, naval supply, the dispatch and handling of ships, all required more orderly centralized methods than an army; they could not tolerate the survival of feudal individualism, indiscipline, and lack of planning. The officer class, as in the armies, was predominantly aristocratic, but it came usually from the more adventurous, the less custom-ridden part of that class. During the sixteenth century, naval supremacy passed out of the Mediterranean to the Atlantic, where it rested briefly with Spain, and thence passed in the seventeenth century to the northern maritime powers of England, Holland, and France.

II Hapsburg and Valois, Tudor, and Orange

The Italian Wars of Charles VIII and Louis XII

Charles VIII of France (1483–1498) inherited from his parsimonious father Louis XI a well-filled treasury and a good army. He continued Louis' policy of extending the royal domain by marrying the heiress of the duchy of Brittany, hitherto largely independent of the French crown. Apparently secure on the home front, Charles decided to expand abroad. As the remote heir of the Angevins who had seized the throne of Naples in the thirteenth century, Charles disputed the right of the Aragonese Ferrante to hold that throne. He chose to invade Italy, however, not only because he had this tenuous genealogical claim but also because Renaissance Italy was rich, and was divided into small rival political units—it looked, in short, to be easy picking. So it was at first, for in the winter of 1494–1495 Charles paraded his army through to Naples in triumph. But his acquisition of Brittany had already disturbed his neighbors, and his possession of Naples threatened the balance of power in Italy. The French intrusion provoked the first of the great modern coalitions, the so-called Holy League composed of the papacy (which, remember, was also an Italian territorial state), the empire, Spain, Venice, Milan, and soon England. This coalition forced the French armies out of Italy without much trouble in 1495.

Charles was followed on the French throne by his cousin of the Orléans branch of the Valois family, Louis XII (1498–1515). Louis married Charles' widow to make sure of Brittany, and then tried again in Italy, reinforced by still another genealogical claim, this time to Milan. Since his grandmother came from the Visconti family, Louis regarded the Sforza dukes as simple usurpers; he proceeded to drive Il Moro from Milan in 1499. In this second French invasion, the play of alliances was much subtler and more complicated, quite worthy of the age of Machiavelli. Louis tried to insure himself from the isolation that had ruined Charles by allying in 1500 with Ferdinand of Aragon, with whom he agreed to partition Naples. Then, in 1508, Louis helped form one of those cynical coalitions that look on paper as though they could break the balance-of-power principle, because they are the union of the strong against a much weaker victim. This was the League of Cambray, in which Louis, Ferdinand, Pope Julius II, and the emperor Maximilian joined to divide up the lands held in the lower Po Valley by the rich but—on land—militarily weak Republic of Venice.

The practical trouble with such combinations is that the combiners do not really trust one another, and usually fall to quarreling over the pickings. All went well for the despoilers until Ferdinand, having taken the Neapolitan towns he wanted, decided to desert Louis. The pope, frightened at the prospect that France and the empire might squeeze him out entirely, in 1511 formed another "Holy League" against France with Venice and Ferdinand, later joined by Henry VIII of England and the emperor Maximilian. Despite some early successes in the field, the French could not hold out against such a coalition, for they now had a war on two fronts. Henry VIII attacked the north of France and won at Guinegate (1513) the "battle of the spurs," so called from the speed with which the French cavalry spurred their flight from the battlefield. In Italy too the French were defeated, and Louis XII, like Charles VIII, was checkmated.

Charles V versus Francis I

These two French efforts were, however, merely preliminaries. The important phase of this first great modern test of the balance of power was to follow immediately, and to take a basically different form. For there were now really two aggressors: the French house of Valois, still bent on expansion, and the house of Hapsburg. When the Hapsburg Charles V succeeded his grandfather Maximilian as emperor in 1519, he was a disturber by the mere fact of his existence rather than by temperament or intent. He had inherited Spain, the Low Countries, the Hapsburg lands in central Europe as well as the headship of the Holy Roman Empire, and the preponderance in Italy. He apparently had France squeezed in a perfect vise.

The vise almost closed. Louis XII's successor, Francis I (1515–1547), was badly defeated by the largely Spanish Hapsburg forces at Pavia in 1525 and was himself taken prisoner and held in Madrid until he signed a treaty giving up all the Valois Italian claims and ceding the duchy of Burgundy. This treaty he repudiated the moment he was safely back in France. It is probable that Charles V would not have destroyed France entirely even had he been able to; in these early modern wars there were accepted limits to what might decently be done to the defeated. The belligerents convey the impression of engaging in a kind of professional athleticism that was often bloody and unscrupulous yet subject to certain rules of the game. The players sometimes changed sides; one of the imperial commanders at the battle of Pavia in which the French were so severely beaten was the Constable de Bourbon, a great French noble at odds with his king.

The same Bourbon commanded the Spanish and German mercenaries of the emperor at the time of the horrible sack of Rome in 1527. Pope Clement VII (1523–1534), a Medici and a good Italian at heart, had first supported Charles V but turned against him after his victory at Pavia. In the League of Cognac, 1526, he allied himself with the other main Italian powers

Francis I of France: portrait by Joos van Cleve.

and with Francis. In reply, Charles besieged Rome, but he did not plan the sack, which took place when his mercenaries became infuriated by delays in pay and supplies. By the end of the decade, Charles had made peace with the pope and with Francis, and in 1530 he was crowned by the pope as emperor and as king of Italy, the last ruler to receive this double crown, this inheritance of Charlemagne. But the world over which Charles symbolically ruled was very different from that of Charlemagne, and Charles was in fact no emperor but a new dynast in a new conflict of power.

France was still in the vise between the Spanish

and the German and Netherlandish holdings of Charles, and Francis I, a proud, consciously virile Renaissance prince, was not one to accept for long so precarious a position—above all, a position in which he lost face. He used the death of the Sforza ruler of Milan in 1535 to reopen the old claim to Milan and to begin the struggle once more. Neither Francis nor Charles lived to see the end of this particular phase of the Hapsburg-Valois rivalry. Neither side secured decisive military victory. In 1559 the important Treaty of Cateau-Cambrésis confirmed Hapsburg control of Milan and Naples. It marked the failure of France to acquire a real foothold in Italy, but it also marked the failure of the Hapsburgs to reduce the real strength of France, which retained the important bishoprics of Metz, Toul, and Verdun on her northeastern frontier, first occupied during the 1550s. The Hapsburg vise had not closed largely because France proved militarily, economically, and politically strong enough to resist the pressure. But the vise itself was a most imperfect instrument; Charles' German arm was paralyzed by the political consequences of the Reformation and the stubborn resistance of Protestant princes.

The last phase of the personal duel between the aging rivals, Charles and Francis, shows how many variables entered the play of the balance of power. To gain allies, Francis did not hesitate to turn to Charles' rebellious German subjects. Although head of a Catholic country, whose king had long been called "the eldest son of the Church," he allied himself with the Protestant duke of Cleves and even concluded an alliance with the Muslim Ottoman emperor, Suleiman the Magnificent, who attacked Charles from the rear in Hungary.

One other participant in the complex struggles of the first half of the sixteenth century was England, which, though not yet a great power, was already a major element in international politics. The men who set English policy were probably not guided by a consciously held theory of the balance of power, but they often behaved as though they had arrived intuitively at the conclusion that they should intervene on behalf of the group that was being defeated. In addition, England had on her northern border an independent Scotland, which tended to side with France, the great hereditary English enemy. Yet the English were quite capable of supporting the hereditary enemy if they thought Charles V was too strong. After Charles had won at Pavia and taken Rome, the English minister Wolsey worked out an alliance with France in 1527. The English were also capable of reversing themselves. In 1543, when Charles was beset by Protestants and Turks, Henry VIII came to his aid against France, but not too vigorously. In the campaign of 1544, when a German army was actually marching on Paris down the Marne valley, the English had landed on the Channel coast and, had they really pressed matters, Paris might have fallen. But the English rather deliberately besieged the Channel port of Boulogne, and Francis escaped with his capital city intact.

The Wars of Philip II

The first great Hapsburg effort to dominate Europe ended with the Peace of Augsburg and the Treaty of Cateau-Cambrésis four years later. The second effort at domination was less Hapsburg than Spanish. In 1556, Charles V abdicated both his Spanish and imperial crowns and retired to a monastery, where he died two years later. His brother, who became Emperor Ferdinand I (1556–1564), secured the Austrian Haps-

Marble bust of Philip II of Spain, from the workshop of Leone Leoni.

burg territories. His son, King Philip II of Spain (1556–1598), got also the Spanish lands overseas, the Burgundian inheritance of the Netherlands, and Milan and Naples in Italy. Even without Germany, Philip's realm was a supranational state, drawing much gold and silver from the New World and threatening France, England, and the whole balance of power. Like his father, Philip II found Protestantism intolerable, a divisive force that must be wiped out by force if necessary. His attempt to invade England and restore Catholicism has made him one of the villains of Anglo-Saxon and Protestant tradition, the cold-blooded "devil of the south." In fact, he was no lover of war for its own sake but a serious hard-working administrator and a devout and dutiful Catholic.

Philip had five major points of involvement. (1) So long as Italy remained divided into the five major units of Milan, Venice, Tuscany, Papal States, and Naples, it was to be a stake in the balance of power, a source of lands to be annexed by expansionist states. (2) In France Philip was bound to appear as the Catholic champion in the civil and religious strife that prevailed during the second half of the century. (3) In the Mediterranean, which Ottoman naval power was threatening to turn into a Muslim lake, the Spanish fleet, under Philip's illegitimate half-brother Don John of Austria, participated in a Christian victory over the Ottoman fleet off the west coast of Greece in 1571. This

Europe in 1555

Possessions of the House of Hapsburg
- Austrian
- Spanish

···· Boundary of the Empire
■ Battle sites

NORWAY

North Sea

SCOTLAND
Edinburgh

DENMARK
Copenhagen

Balti...

Stock...

IRELAND
Dublin

ENGLAND
Bosworth Field ■
London
Canterbury
Calais

Atlantic Ocean

Amsterdam
Leiden
NETHERLANDS
Antwerp
Cleves
Münster

Bremen
Elbe R.
BRANDENBURG
Berlin
Oder R.

Wittenberg
Torgau
HESSE
Leipzig
SAXONY
SILES...
Wartburg

LUXEMBOURG
Verdun
Metz
Speyer
THE EMPIRE
Prague
BOHEMIA

Vervins
Seine R.
Paris

Ivry ■

BRITTANY

Nantes

Loire R.

La Rochelle

FRANCE

AUVERGNE

Cognac

FRANCHE COMTÉ
Toul
WÜRTTEM-BERG
Danube R.
Augsburg
Constance
BAVARIA
Basel
Zurich
SWITZERLAND
BURGUNDY
Geneva
Rhône R.
SAVOY
TYROL

MORAVIA
AUSTRIA
Vienna
STYRIA

HU...

Trent
CARINTHIA
CARNIOLA

Avignon (to the Papacy)
PROVENCE

Milan
Pavia ■
Po R.
Padua
Bologna
Venice

VENETIAN REPUBLIC
Adriatic Sea

Genoa

PORTUGAL
Lisbon
Tagus R.

Valladolid
Tordesillas

SPAIN
NAVARRE
BASQUE PROV.

Madrid
Toledo

Ebro R.

ARAGON

CASTILE

Guadalquivir R.

Palos
Seville

Cadiz

CORSICA
(to Genoa)

BALEARIC IS.

TUSCANY
PAPAL STATES
Rome

NAPLES
Naples

SARDINIA

Mediterranean Sea

(Tributary to Ottoman Empire)

B A R B A R Y   S T A T E S

SICILY

MALTA

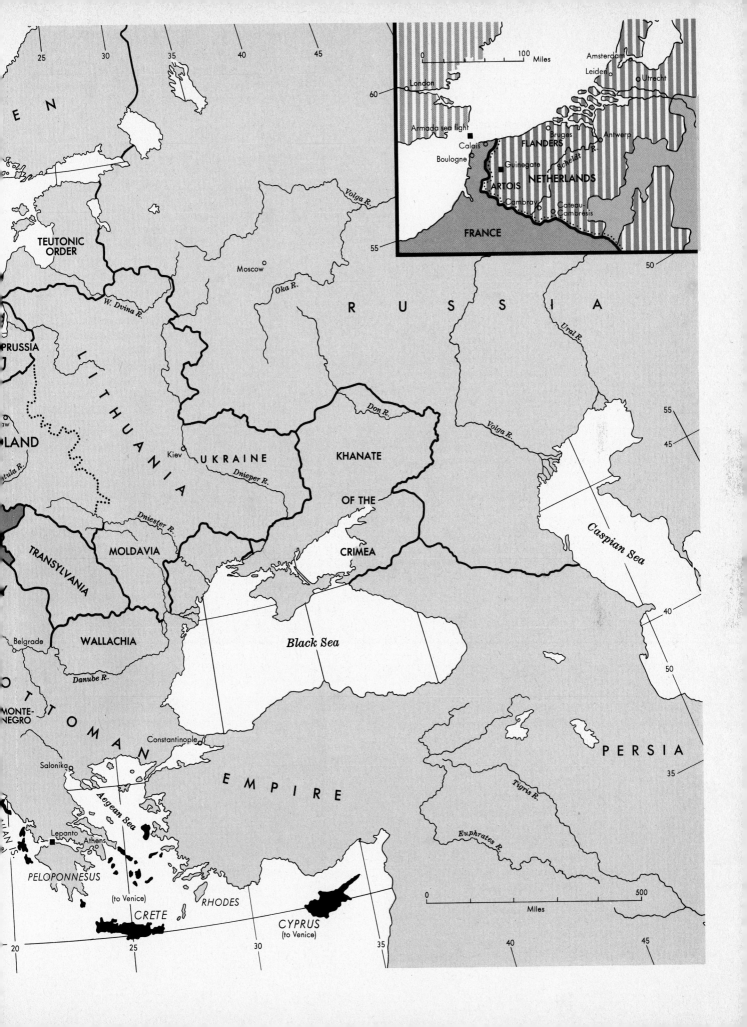

TEUTONIC
ORDER

PRUSSIA

L I T H U A N I A

POLAND

Vistula R.

W. Dvina R.

Moscow

Oka R.

R   U   S   S   I   A

Volga R.

Ural R.

Kiev

U K R A I N E

Dnieper R.

Don R.

KHANATE

OF THE

CRIMEA

Volga R.

55

45

Caspian Sea

Dniester R.

TRANSYLVANIA

MOLDAVIA

40

50

Belgrade

WALLACHIA

Black Sea

MONTE-
NEGRO

OTTOMAN

Danube R.

PERSIA

Constantinople

Salonika

EMPIRE

35

Lepanto

Athens

Aegean Sea

Tigris R.

PELOPONNESUS

(to Venice)

RHODES

CRETE

CYPRUS
(to Venice)

Euphrates R.

Amsterdam

Leiden

Utrecht

0   100 Miles

London

60

Armada sea fight

Calais

FLANDERS

Bruges

Antwerp

Boulogne

Guinegate

R.

Scheldt

ARTOIS

NETHERLANDS

Cambray

Cateau-
Cambresis

FRANCE

55

50

0   500

Miles

20   25   30   35   40   45

battle of Lepanto checked but did not immediately roll back Ottoman expansion. (4) In the New World and on the wide seas connecting it with the Old World, England and France were beginning to challenge the monopoly Spain and Portugal had tried to set up, as the next chapter will relate. (5) In the Netherlands, the revolt of Philip's Dutch Protestant subjects soon involved him also in a struggle with their champion, Tudor England.

The Dutch revolt was the dramatic focus of Philip's wars. Charles V had come to count heavily on the wealth of the Netherlands, estimated to be the highest per capita in Europe, to finance his constant wars. But he made no attempt to integrate into a unified superstate the seventeen provinces of the Netherlands, which were very jealous of their traditional autonomy. There were few effective institutions to bind the seventeen together; each province had its own medieval Estates or Assembly, dominated by the nobility and wealthy merchants, which raised taxes and armies. In the mid-sixteenth century the area was still overwhelmingly Catholic, with small minorities of Anabaptists and Lutherans; Calvinism was just starting to move northward across the French border.

Whereas Charles V had liked the Netherlands and made Brussels his favorite place of residence, Philip II was thoroughly Spanish in outlook and never visited the area after the early years of his reign. Not only Philip's temperament and nature antagonized his subjects in the Low Countries but also his up-to-date ideas about centralized efficient rule, which led him to curtail their political and economic liberties. The inhabitants cherished their traditional autonomy and, as a commercial and seafaring people, they were intent on conducting business without the restrictions imposed on trade and industry by Spanish regulations. Those who were Protestant resented and feared Philip's use of the Inquisition in the Netherlands.

This explosive mixture of religion, politics, and economic interests produced the revolt. Philip sent Spanish garrisons to the Netherlands and attempted to enforce edicts against heretics. Opposition, which centered at first in the privileged classes who had been most affected by Philip's political restrictions, soon spread to the common people. In 1566, when a group of two hundred nobles petitioned Philip's regent to adopt a more moderate policy, an official sneeringly referred to "these beggars." The name stuck, proudly adopted by the rebels. The political restlessness, combined with an economic slump and the growing success of the Calvinists in winning converts, touched off riots in August 1566, which resulted in heavy destruction of Catholic churches in such major centers as Ghent, Antwerp, and Amsterdam. Philip responded to this "Calvinist fury" in 1567 by dispatching to the Netherlands an army of twenty thousand Spaniards headed by the unyielding, politically stupid duke of Alba.

In those days the Spanish infantry was the best in Europe, and the rebels were ill armed and ill prepared. Their eventual success was a heroic achievement against great odds; it was, however, no extraordinary victory of weakness over strength, but rather a victory fully consonant with a fact of Western political life— that no thoroughly disaffected population can be long held down by force alone. Alba had the force, and he set up a Council of Troubles—later dubbed the Council of Blood—which resorted to executions, confiscations, and severe taxation on a large scale. The number of victims executed under the Council of Blood totaled about a thousand, yet all the repression accomplished was to heighten the opposition to Spanish policy. In 1573 Alba gave up in despair.

Meantime, the rebel "Beggars" turned to a kind of naval guerrilla warfare, gained control of the ports of the populous northern province of Holland, and then ended effective Spanish authority in Holland and adjacent areas. Large numbers of Protestant refugees, especially Calvinists, from other provinces resettled themselves in Holland as a result. The historical split was appearing between the largely Catholic southern Netherlands and the mainly Protestant north—to use popular terminology, between Belgium and Holland (the name of the province is often, though inaccurately, applied to all seven northern provinces). It was to be a religious, not a linguistic split, for Dutch was the language both of the north and of Flanders in the south; French was spoken only in the Walloon country of the southeast. North and south had much to unite them, and union of all seventeen provinces was the goal of the rebel leader, William of Orange, the Silent, prince in the 1570s. William, who got his nickname because his silences could be discreet or deceptive by turn, was a convivial nobleman with firm political convictions but few religious ones (he was, at different periods, a Lutheran, a Catholic, and a Calvinist).

William's goal of unity seemed almost assured in the wake of widespread revulsion at the "Spanish Fury" of 1576, when Spanish troops, desperate because their pay was two years in arrears, sacked the great Belgian port of Antwerp and massacred several thousand of its inhabitants. But in 1578, when the duke of Parma arrived to govern the Netherlands, Phillip's policies at last showed signs of a willingness to compromise in the face of facts. By political concessions to old privileges of self-rule, Parma won back the ten southern provinces, which remained largely Catholic after the exodus of many Calvinists to the north. It was too late to win back the northern provinces, except perhaps by radical religious concessions, which Philip could not make.

In 1581 the Dutch took the decisive step of declaring themselves independent of the Spanish Crown. They made good that declaration by their courageous use of their now much better-organized land forces and by the fact that Philip faced grave internal economic problems just when he had been drawn into fighting on other fronts. He had to cope with the Turks, the French Protestants, and the anti-Spanish moderate wing of French Catholics. In 1584 the Dutch were deprived of their first great national leader when William the Silent was assassinated. But his death did not profit the Spanish cause since it created a hero-martyr not only to the Dutch but to all Protestants.

In 1585 the English queen, Elizabeth I, after long hesitancy, finally came out on the side of the Dutch and sent an army to their aid. The English had been sympathetic with the Dutch all along, but Elizabeth had feared that, with France in the midst of civil war, a Franco-Spanish alliance against English and Dutch was quite possible. But here too Philip showed himself incapable of diplomacy: he permitted France to maneuver into neutrality, and he provoked England by fomenting Catholic plots against Elizabeth. The English in turn provoked Spain: for years they had been preying on Spanish commerce on the high seas, and Hawkins, Drake, and other sailors had been raiding Spanish possessions in the new world.

The great armada of unwieldy men-of-war that Philip sent out to invade England was defeated in the Channel, in July 1588, by a skillfully deployed lighter English fleet, and was utterly destroyed afterward by a great storm. The battle was the beginning of the end of Spanish preponderance, the beginning of English greatness in international politics, and the decisive step in the achievement of Dutch independence. These por-

tentous results were not so evident in 1588 as they are now; but even at the time the defeat of the Spanish Armada was viewed as a great event, and the storm that finished its destruction was christened the "Protestant wind."

In 1598 Philip II died in the great, severe palace of the Escorial he had built near Madrid. He had ordered an open coffin put beside his sick bed, and a skull with a crown of gold. Save for the seven northern provinces of the Netherlands—and even these had never officially given up—the great possessions that had been his when he began his reign were intact. In 1580 he had added Portugal by conquest and brought the whole Iberian peninsula under a single rule. Yet he left his kingdom worn out, drained of men and money. And whatever his goals in international politics had been, whether a Spanish hegemony, a revived Western empire, or merely the extinction of the Protestant heresy, he had realized none of them.

III The Catholic Monarchies: Spain and France

The states that took part in these dynastic and religious wars experienced an uneven working out of the new

The Escorial, the combined palace, monastery, and mausoleum built by Philip II near Madrid.

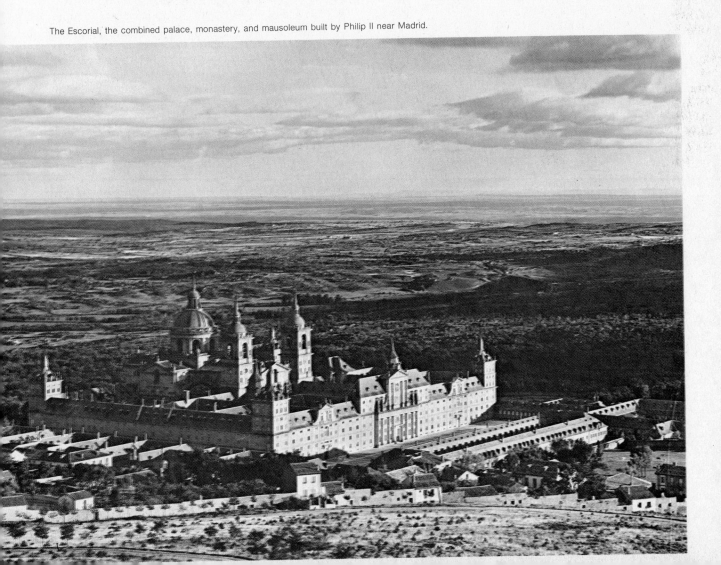

businesslike aims and methods characterizing the passage of domestic politics from the medieval to the modern world. They all had paid professional armies and paid professional civilian bureaucrats. They had a central financial system, a central legal system that made some attempt to apply the law uniformly to all subjects, and a central authority—king, king and council, king and parliament, estates, cortes, or other assembly—that could make new laws. Such labels as Age of Absolutism and Divine Right Monarchy are frequently pinned on the early modern centuries, and not without reason. Over most of Europe the ultimate control of administration usually rested with a hereditary monarch who claimed the God-given right to make final decisions. But, while the greater nobles were losing power and influence to the monarchy, the lesser nobles continued to dominate the countryside, where medieval local privileges survived vigorously almost everywhere, together with local ways of life quite different from those of the court and the capital.

Spanish Absolutism

Sixteenth-century Spain offers a case study of the clash between the ideal of absolutism and the recalcitrance of the varied groups on which the monarchy sought to impose its centralized, standardized rules. The reigns of two hard-working monarchs, the emperor Charles V (as king of Spain he was Charles I, 1516–1556) and Philip II, span almost the whole century. Charles, who was more a medieval survival than a modern king, did little to remodel the instruments of government he had inherited from his grandparents, Ferdinand and Isabella. Brought up in the Low Countries, he came to Spain a stranger, with a Flemish entourage that already had the modern northern European contempt for the "backward" south. Charles' election to the imperial throne in 1519 made him further suspect in Spain; the aristocrats were restless in the face of the new monarchical dignity, and the municipalities disliked the growth of central fiscal controls. In 1520 a league of Spanish cities, led by Toledo, rose up in the revolt of the *comuneros* (the name applied to the rebels). The comuneros were put down in 1521, but Charles had been frightened out of what reforming zeal he may have had and in the future did his best not to offend his Spanish subjects.

Philip II, unlike his father, grew up as a Spaniard first of all, and was much more willing and able to build a more professional centralized regime in Spain. He devised a system of councils, topped by a council of state, which were manned by great nobles but had only advisory powers. Final decisions rested with Philip, and the details were worked out by a series of private secretaries and local organs of government, not staffed by nobles. Philip also reduced the Cortes, the representative assemblies, to practical impotence. In Castile, nobles and priests, because they did not pay direct taxes, no longer attended the session of the Cortes, and the delegates of the cities were left as a powerless rump. The Cortes of Aragon, while retaining more power, was seldom convoked by Philip. Above all, Philip had assured sources of income—his tax of a fifth of the value of the precious cargoes from America, direct taxes from the constituent states of his realm, revenues from the royal estates and from the sale of offices and patents of nobility, revenues from the authorized sale, at royal profit, of dispensations allowed by the pope (permission to eat meat on Fridays and during Lent, and even something very close to the very indulgences that had raised Germany against the pope). Philip, like most continental monarchs of his time, had no need to worry over representative bodies with control of the purse. Yet he was always heavily in debt and on three occasions suspended payments on his obligations; his bankruptcies triggered that of the famous Fugger firm in Augsburg.

Even in this matter of revenue, where Philip's power at first sight looks so complete, the limitations of the absolute monarch of early modern times are clear. Except by borrowing and hand-to-mouth expedients like the sale of offices, he could not notably increase his income. He could not summon any representative group together and get them to vote new monies. In the first place, the constituent parts of his realm, Castile, Aragon, Navarre and the Basque provinces (both at the western end of the Pyrenees, adjoining France), the Italian lands, the Low Countries, the Americas, and the newest Spanish lands, named after the monarch himself, the Philippine Islands, had no common organs of consultation. Each had to be dealt with as a separate problem, and the slowness of communication with his far-flung domains further delayed the always deliberate process of decision making. For the most part the nobility and clergy were tax exempt, and could not be called upon for unusual financial sacrifices. Add to all this the difficulty of collection, the opportunities for graft, and the lack of a long-accumulated administrative and financial experience, and one can see why Philip could not have introduced a more systematic general taxation.

Outside the financial sphere, the obstacles to really effective centralization were even more serious. The union of the crowns of Aragon and Castile, achieved by the marriage of Ferdinand and Isabella, had by no means made a unified Spain. To this day regionalism—to give it a mild name—is probably more intense in Spain than in any other large European state. In those days, some of the provinces did not even accept extradition arrangements for the surrender of criminals within the peninsula. Many of them could and did levy customs dues on goods from the others. The northern regions, which had never been totally conquered by the Muslims, preserved all sorts of privileges known as *fueros*. Aragon still kept the office of *justicia mayor*, a judge nominated by the Crown but for life and entrusted with an authority somewhat remotely like that of the United States Supreme Court.

What the house of Austria, as the Hapsburg dynasty was termed in Spain, might have accomplished had they been able to expend their full energies on uniting and developing their Spanish lands can never be known. What they did do was exhaust the peninsula and weaken their lands overseas in the effort to secure hegemony over Europe and subdue the Protestant heresy. This was indeed the great age of Spain, when both on land and on sea the Spanish were admired as the best fighters, when Spain seemed to be the richest of states and destined to be the mistress of both the Americas. It was also the age of Loyola and Cervantes, the golden age of Spanish religion, literature, and art, but it was a brief flowering, and Spanish greatness largely vanished in the seventeenth century.

The Spanish Economy

Spain is a classical instance of a great state's failure to maintain a sound economic underpinning for its greatness. The Iberian peninsula is mountainous, and its central tableland is subject to droughts, but its agricultural potential is considerable, more than that of Italy for example; and it has mineral resources, notably iron. Spain was the first of the major European states to secure lands overseas and to develop the navy and merchant marine to integrate the vast resources of the New World with a base in the Old World. Yet all this wealth slipped through Spain's fingers in a few generations. An important factor here was the immense cost of the wars of Charles V and Philip II; in particular, the Low Countries, which had brought much revenue to Charles, became a pure drain on Philip's overburdened finances.

Governmental expenditure on armed forces, though in itself unproductive, is not fatal to a national economy if it stimulates greater productivity in the nation and its dependencies. But this was not true of sixteenth-century Spain. She drew from the New World immense amounts of silver and many commodities— sugar, indigo, tobacco, cocoa, hides—without which she could hardly have fought her European wars. But all this was not enough to pay for world dominion. The bullion passed through Spanish hands into those of bankers and merchants in other European countries, partly to pay for the Spanish armies and navies, and partly to pay for the manufactured goods sent to the New World. These goods, which the colonies were forbidden to make for themselves, Spain could not supply from her own meager industrial production. Although a royal decree gave Spanish merchants a monopoly on trade with the Indies, as the century wore on they were reduced to the role of middlemen, sending to the Indies items imported from the rest of Europe. In addition, the English, Dutch, and other competitors invaded their theoretical monopoly by large-scale smuggling of goods into Spain's colonies. Thus, while Spain's governmental expenditures did prime the economic pumps, the pumps were foreign, not Spanish, and by 1600 Spain's home industry was on the decline.

The free-trade economists of the nineteenth century attributed Spain's failure to exploit her economic opportunities to the prevalence of monopoly under governmental supervision. Sixteenth-century Spain was certainly moving toward the economic policy called mercantilism (the reference is not to individual merchants but to the mercantile or commercial system), which was to reach its fullest development in seventeenth-century France. Although Spain lacked the true mercantilist passion for building national wealth under government auspices, she used many mercantilist techniques, the endless regulation in general and the narrow channeling of colonial trade in particular. In Castile, a single institution, the Casa de Contratación (House of Trade) in Seville, controlled every transaction with the Indies and licensed every export and import. The amount of paperwork, in an age unblessed by typewriters and copiers, to say nothing of computers, was staggering.

Beyond all this, the whole direction of Spanish civilization diverted creative energies away from industrial channels. Warfare, politics, religion, art, farming, or simply living like a hidalgo (*hijo de algo,* "son of somebody," hence "nobleman," "gentleman") were all respectable activities. But what Americans call business was not an activity on which Spanish society put a premium. Not that Spaniards were lazy: the epitome of so much we think of as Spanish, Don Quixote, was hardly a lazy man, but his activity was not exactly productive of material wealth. If we take into consideration the numerous holidays, the habit of the siesta, the large numbers of beggars, soldiers, priests, monks, and hidalgos, as well as the lack of encouragement to new enterprises and techniques, and the heavy hand of an inefficient bureaucracy, then it becomes clear that the total Spanish effort was bound to be inadequate in competition with nations better organized for modern economic life. Spain, in short, presents almost the antithesis of the picture of what goes into the "capitalist spirit" drawn by Weber in his hypothesis on the Protestant ethic.

The Spanish Style

Yet the Spanish supremacy, though shortlived, was real enough, and it helped make our present-day world. Half the Americas speak Spanish (or a rather similar tongue, Portuguese) and carry, however altered, a cultural inheritance from the Iberian peninsula. French, Dutch, and English national unity and national spirit were hardened in resistance to Spanish aggression. The Spanish character, the Spanish "style," was set—some may say hardened—in this Golden Age, which has left to the West some magnificent paintings and one of the few really universal books, *Don Quixote* by Miguel de Cervantes (1547–1616). This Spanish style is not at all like those of France and Italy, so often tied with Spain as "Latin"—a term that is very misleading if the "Latin" peoples are grouped together as "sunny." For the Spanish spirit is among the most serious, most darkly passionate, most unsmiling in the West; it is a striving spirit, carrying to the extreme the chivalric point of honor.

In art this spirit stands out in the paintings of a master who was Spanish only by adoption, El Greco (1541–1614). "The Greek," born on Crete, was schooled in the late Byzantine manner of painting and later studied with Titian in Venice. In his thirties he settled at Toledo, the religious capital of Castile, which in medieval days had been the intellectual center of Muslim Spain. El Greco's Byzantine and High Renaissance training served as foundations for a highly personal way of dealing with religious themes best illustrated in his masterpiece, *The Burial of the Count of Orgaz,* in the church of Santo Tomé at Toledo. This fourteenth-century nobleman had made generous endowments in honor of Saint Augustine and Saint Stephen, both of whom, according to legend, miraculously appeared after his death to bury his body. The painting shows both the earthly and heavenly realms, as the saints gently lift the corpse in the presence of aristo-cratic mourners, who gaze upward toward the angel bearing the count's soul to heaven. There the Virgin and St. John are waiting to intercede for him with Christ and St. Peter.

The lower scene might almost have been painted by Titian or another great portraitist of the Renaissance, even though the mourners have the grave, prominent eyes of the Byzantine school. The upper scene could only have been the work of El Greco. The billowing clouds are pearly gray with a cold, luminous quality (one critic has called it "ectoplasmic"); the elongated, slender figures have tapering fingers, narrow heads, and unnaturally large Byzantine eyes; even the cherubs are slim, with none of the pink chubbiness usually associated with them. Stretching toward heaven like a Gothic pinnacle, *The Burial of the Count of Orgaz* is an extraordinary effort to record the mystic's unrecordable experience.

Two other paintings by El Greco provide additional insights into the Spanish spirit during the Catholic Reformation. One is his portrait of Cardinal Niño de Guevara, the Archbishop of Toledo and the Grand Inquisitor of Spain, which one historian has labeled "terrifying" because it conveys so vividly the sitter's combination of tension, asceticism and bigotry. The other is *A View of Toledo,* the first Spanish landscape painting, depicting the city's majestic hilltop site above the gorge of the Tagus River. To make the composition more dramatic El Greco rearranged the location of the city's landmarks and filled the nighttime sky with "ectoplasmic" clouds and reflected lightning, communicating a sense of eeriness and foreboding.

In religion, during the generations following Ignatius Loyola, the Spanish style was expressed most strikingly in the careers of Saint Teresa of Avila (1515–1582) and Saint John of the Cross (1542–1591), who brought back the tortured ecstasies of the early Christian ascetics and added a dark, rebellious note of their own. Theirs was no attempt to withdraw into monastic isolation but a heroic effort to combat this world of the senses and thus transcend it. They worked vigorously together to reform Spanish monasticism, and John, in particular, was harshly persecuted by established religious interests. They were both familiar figures to the Spanish common people, who in their own way identified themselves with these saints in their struggle. Here is part of an account of what followed the death of John of the Cross:

El Greco's portrait of Cardinal Don Fernando Niño de Guevara.

Hardly had breath ceased than . . . crowds assembled in the street and poured into the convent. Pressing into the room where he lay, they knelt to kiss his feet and hands. They cut off pieces from his clothes and bandages and even pulled out the swabs that had been placed on his sores. Others took snippings from his hair and tore off his nails, and would have cut pieces from his flesh had it not been forbidden. At his funeral these scenes were repeated. Forcing their way past the friars who guarded his body, the mob tore off his habit and even took parts of his ulcered flesh.*

The creations of Cervantes, in their very different way, likewise carry the mark of the Spanish style. Spain is Don Quixote tilting with the windmills, aflame for the Dulcinea he has invented, quite mad. But it is also the knight's servant, Sancho Panza, conventional, earthy, unheroic, and sane enough, though his sanity protects him not at all from sharing his master's misadventures. Cervantes almost certainly meant no more than an amusing satire of popular tales of chivalry. But his story has got caught up in the web of symbolism we live by, and the Don and his reluctant follower are for us Spain forever racked between fantasy and common sense. This tension runs all through *Don Quixote*. Chivalry is indeed silly, and worth satire—gentle satire:

> "I would inform you, Sancho, that it is a point of honor with knights-errant to go for a month at a time without eating, and when they do eat, it is whatever may be at hand. You would certainly know that if you had read the histories as I have. There are many of them, and in none have I found any mention of knights eating unless it was by chance or at some sumptuous banquet that was tendered them; on other days they fasted. And even though it is well understood that, being men like us, they could not go without food entirely, any more than they could fail to satisfy the other necessities of nature, nevertheless, since they spent the greater part of their lives in forests and desert places without any cook to prepare their meals. . ."
>
> "Pardon me, your Grace," said Sancho, "but seeing that, as I have told you, I do not know how to read or write, I am consequently not familiar with the rules of the knightly calling. Hereafter, I will stuff my saddlebags with all manner of dried fruit for your Grace, but inasmuch as I am not a knight, I shall lay in for myself a stock of fowls and other more substantial fare."†

The extreme of pride—pride of status, of faith, of nation—has seemed to the outside world the mark of Spain. Perhaps there is little to choose among the triumphant prides of nations in triumph. Yet as the "shot heard round the world" sounds very American, so the Cid, the legendary hero of the reconquest from the Muslims, is very Spanish in these verses as he goes off to his Crusade:

> *Por necesidad batallo*
> *Y una vez puesto en la silla*
> *Se va ensanchando Castilla*
> *Delante de mi caballo.*   [*I fight by necessity:*
> *But once I am in the saddle,*
> *Castile goes widening out*
> *Ahead of my horse.*]

*G. Brenan, "A Short Life of St. John of the Cross," in *The Golden Horizon*, ed. C. Connolly (London, 1953), pp. 475–476.

† *Don Quixote*, trans. Samuel Putnam (New York, 1949), 1:78–79.

France: The Last Valois Kings

North of the Pyrenees the long-established French monarchy began to move toward a more efficient absolutism after the Hundred Years' War, particularly under Louis XI. In this development France had certain advantages. None of its provinces—not even Brittany with its Celtic language and autonomous traditions, nor Provence with its language of the troubadours, its ties with Italy, its earlier history as a separate unit—shows quite the intense regionalism that may be found in Catalonia or the Spanish Basque provinces. Moreover, unlike the Iberian peninsula, Italy, or Greece, most of France is not cut up by mountain ranges into isolated compartments. Yet despite these assets France was still imperfectly tied together under Francis I (1515–1547). Many provinces, especially Brittany and others that had come under direct Valois rule fairly recently, retained their own local representative bodies (Estates), their own local courts (parlements), and many other privileges. The national bureaucracy was as yet only a patchwork, and the nobility, though it had lost most of its old governmental functions to royal appointees, held on to feudal memories and attitudes.

As we have seen, however, the kingdom of Francis I was strong enough to counter the threat of encirclement by Charles V. The king himself was not another Louis XI, however. Self-indulgence weakened his health and distracted him from the business of government; his extravagant court and, far more, his frequent wars drained the finances of the state. Yet in many respects Francis was a good Renaissance despot, thoroughly at home in the age of Machiavelli. At the beginning of his reign he extended the royal gains made at papal expense in the Pragmatic Sanction of Bourges (1438). In the Concordat of Bologna (1516), the pope allowed the king a very great increase in control over the Gallican church, including the important right to choose bishops and abbots. In the face of treason, Francis responded by confiscating the estates of the Constable de Bourbon when he defected to the Hapsburgs. In adversity he had courage: witness his successful recovery after the disaster at Pavia in 1525. In diplomacy he was unscrupulous and flexible: witness his alliances with the Turks and with the German Protestants. Good-looking (until his health broke down), amorous, lavish, courtly, Francis did things in the grand manner. It is reported that it took eighteen thousand horses and pack animals to move the king and his court on their frequent journeys. He built the famous châteaux of Chambord and Fontainebleau, and in Paris he remodeled the great palace of the Louvre and founded the Collège de France, second only to the old Sorbonne as an educational center. He patronized Leonardo, Cellini, and other artists and men of letters.

Francis was the last strong monarch of the house of Valois. After his death in 1547, his son Henry II and his grandsons were barely able to maintain the prestige of the Crown in the face of crippling disorders. The second half of the sixteenth century was the age of French civil and religious wars, a crisis that almost undid the centralizing work of Louis XI and his successors.

The religious map of France in the 1550s showed a division by class as well as by territory. While Protestantism scarcely touched the French peasantry, except in parts of the south, the Huguenots were strong among the nobility and among the rising classes of capitalists and artisans. The region of Paris, Brittany, most of Normandy, and the northern areas bordering on the Low Countries remained ardently Catholic. Protestantism was gaining in the southwest and in south-central France, especially in the lands of the old Albigensian heresy. Even in these regions, however, the employer class was more likely to be Protestant, the workers to be Catholic. The French nobility took up Protestantism partly in response to a missionary campaign directed toward them from Geneva and partly for political reasons. The old tradition of local feudal independence among the nobles encouraged resistance to the centralized Catholic monarchy and its agents. The German princes in revolt had everything to gain in a worldly way by confiscation of church property and establishment of an Erastian Lutheran church. But, after the Concordat of 1516, the French kings had everything to lose by a Protestant movement that strengthened their restive nobility and that in its Calvinist form was the very opposite of Erastian.

Sporadic warfare began soon after the death of Henry II in 1559 (ironically, he was fatally wounded in a tournament celebrating the Treaty of Cateau-Cambrésis). For the next generation the crown passed in succession to Henry's three sons—Francis II (1559–1560), Charles IX (1560–1574), and Henry III (1574–1589)—and France was torn by civil and religious strife. Since Charles IX was a boy of ten at his accession, authority was exercised by his mother, Catherine de' Medici, who shared the humanistic and artistic tastes of her famous Florentine family and, contrary to Protestant prejudice, had no particular religious convictions. But Catherine was determined to preserve intact the magnificent royal inheritance of her sons, which seemed to be threatened by the rapid growth of the Huguenots, by their increasing pressure for official recognition, and by Catholic counterpressure against concessions. What especially worried Catherine was the apparent polarization of the high nobility by the religious issue—the great family of Guise was zealously dedicated to the Catholic cause, and the powerful families of Bourbon and Montmorency to the Huguenot.

Success in scattered fighting during the 1560s netted the Huguenots some gains. Their ambitious leader, Coligny, who was linked to the Montmorencys, gained great influence over the unstable Charles IX and apparently seriously hoped to take over control of the government. Panicky at the danger to the prospects for her sons and to her own position, Catherine threw in her lot with the Guises and persuaded Charles to follow suit. The result was the massacre of Huguenots on Saint Bartholomew's Day (August 24, 1572). Three thousand victims fell in Paris, including Coligny, many of them dragged from their beds in the first hours of the morning according to a prearranged plan; thousands more perished in the provinces. In spite of Saint Bartholomew's Day and subsequent reverses in the field, the Huguenots remained strong. As the warfare continued, the Catholic nobles organized a threatening league headed by the Guises, and both sides negotiated with foreigners for help, the Catholics with Spain and the Protestants with England. Thus the French crown found itself pushed into opposition to both groups.

The French civil and religious strife culminated in the War of the Three Henrys (1585–1589)—named for Henry III, the Valois king and the last surviving grandson of Francis I; Henry, duke of Guise, head of the Catholic League; and the Bourbon Henry of Navarre, the Protestant cousin and heir-apparent of the childless king (his grandmother had been the sister of Francis I). The threat that a Protestant might succeed pushed the Catholic League to propose violating the rules of succession by making an uncle of Henry of Navarre king, the Catholic cardinal of Bourbon. But this attempt to alter the succession alienated moderate French opinion, already disturbed by the extremes of both Catholics and Protestants.

Paris, on the other hand, was fanatically Catholic, and a popular insurrection there (May 1588), frightened Henry III out of his capital, which triumphantly acclaimed Guise as king. Henry III responded by conniving at the assassination of the two great men of the Catholic League, Henry of Guise and his brother Louis. Infuriated, the league rose in full revolt, and Henry III took refuge in the camp of Henry of Navarre, where he in turn was assassinated by a monk.

The First Bourbon: Henry IV

Henry of Navarre was now by law Henry IV (1589–1610), the first king of the house of Bourbon. In the decisive battle of Ivry (March 1590) he defeated the Catholics, who had set up the aged cardinal of Bourbon as "King Charles X." But Henry's subsequent efforts to besiege Paris were repeatedly frustrated by Spanish troops sent down from Flanders by Philip II. Philip planned to have the French Estates General put Henry aside and bestow the crown on the Spanish infanta, Isabella, daughter of Philip II and his third wife, Elizabeth of Valois, who was the child of Henry II and Catherine de' Medici. In the face of this new threat, Henry was persuaded that if he would abjure his own Protestant faith he could rally the moderate Catholics and secure at least tolerated status for the Protestants. He turned Catholic in 1593 and Paris surrendered, giving rise to the perhaps apocryphal tale that he had remarked, "Paris is well worth a Mass." Henry now declared war against Spain and brought it to a successful conclusion with the Treaty of Vervins, 1598, which essentially confirmed the Cateau-Cambrésis settlement of 1559.

Within France the Edict of Nantes, also in 1598, endeavored to achieve a lasting religious settlement. While it did not bring complete religious freedom, it did provide for a large measure of toleration. The Huguenots were granted substantial civil liberties and were allowed the exercise of their religion in certain towns and in the households of great Huguenot nobles. Public worship by Huguenots was forbidden in episcopal and archiepiscopal cities, and most particularly in Paris. Of the two hundred towns where Huguenots could worship, they were to fortify and garrison one hundred at government expense as symbols of safeguard.

The intellectual preparation for the Edict of Nantes and for the revival of the French monarchy under Henry IV had been in large part the work of a group of men known as *politiques,* a term that comes closer to meaning "political moralist" than "politician." The greatest of them, Jean Bodin, who died in 1596, held that the sole possibility of peace and quiet in a divided France lay in obedience to a king above petty civil strife. Bodin and his colleagues stressed the need for political unity to maintain law and order, yet they were not absolutists but moderates who by no means preached that the king must be obeyed no matter what he did. The politiques were convinced that under the supremacy of the French state Frenchmen should be allowed to practice different forms of the Christian religion. They believed that the basic aim of the belligerents in the religious wars—to put down by force those who disagreed on matters of faith—was un-Christian. Here is how one of them, Michel de l'Hospital, who was also a practicing Catholic, stated their position:

Portrait of Henry IV (Henry of Navarre).

> If they are Christians, those who try to spread Christianity with arms, swords, and pistols do indeed go contrary to their professed faith, which is to suffer force, not to inflict it. . . . Nor is their argument, that they take arms in the cause of God, a valid one, for the cause of God is not one that can be so defended with such arms. . . . Our religion did not take its beginnings from force of arms, and is not to be kept and strengthened by force of arms. . . .
>
> Let us pray God for the heretics, and do all we can to reduce and convert them; gentleness will do more than harshness. Let us get rid of those devilish names of seditious factions, Lutherans, Huguenots, Papists: let us not change the name of Christian.*

Henry IV was particularly fortunate in arriving on the French scene when the passions of civil war were nearing exhaustion and the nation was ready for pacification. The high degree of success he achieved also depended greatly on his own personal qualities. A realist rather than a cynic, as the remark about Paris being

*P. J. S. Dufey, ed., *Oeuvres complètes de Michel de l'Hospital* (Paris, 1824), 1:395–402. Our translation.

worth a Mass might suggest, Henry balanced concessions to the Huguenots with generous subsidies to the Catholic League for disbanding its troops, and he declined to summon the Estates General because of its potential for proving troublesome. Other kings in other days, like Louis XI of France and Henry VII of England, had accomplished the restoration of law and order, but only Henry of Navarre became a genuinely popular hero. Witty, dashing, with a pronounced taste for pretty women and bawdy stories, he was the most human king the French had had for a long time, and the best-liked monarch in their whole history. His court casually included his wife, his mistresses, and his children, legitimate and otherwise. He made jokes about his financial difficulties. And, most of all, he convinced his subjects that he was truly concerned for their welfare; Henry IV is still remembered as the king who remarked that every peasant should have a chicken in his pot on Sunday.

Henry's economic experts reclaimed marshes for farm land, encouraged the luxury crafts in Paris, and planted thousands of mulberry trees to foster the culture and manufacture of silk. They extended canals and launched a program of building roads and bridges that eventually won France the reputation of maintaining the best highways in Europe. Faced with a heavy deficit when he took office, Henry's chief minister, the Huguenot Sully (1559–1641), systematically lowered it until he brought government income and expenditure into balance. His search for new revenues had some unhappy consequences, however. He not only continued the old custom of selling government offices but permitted the beneficiary to transmit the office to his heir on payment of an annual fee—a lucrative new source of royal income but an even greater source of future difficulty, since more and more officeholders were more concerned with enjoying and protecting their vested interests than with the faithful execution of their duties. For the rest, the incidence of taxation remained lopsided, with some provinces much more heavily burdened than others, and with the poor paying much more than their fair share. Collection remained in the hands of contractors called "farmers," and the treasury suffered loss of revenue from entrusting this public function to often unscrupulous private entrepreneurs. Fiscal weakness was to remain the Achilles' heel of the French monarchy for the next two centuries.

IV The Protestant States:
Tudor England and the Dutch Republic
Henry VIII, 1509–1547

In England Henry VII had already established the new Tudor monarchy on a firm footing. That Henry VIII did not run through his heritage and leave an exhausted treasury and discredited monarchy was not because he lacked the will to spend lavishly. As Martin Luther wrote of him, "Junker Heintz will be God and does whatever he lusts."* Henry loved display, elaborate palaces (Hampton Court, near London, is the best known), and all the trappings of Renaissance monarchy. His "summit conference" with Francis I, a kindred luxurious spirit, near Calais in 1520 has gone down in tradition as the Field of the Cloth of Gold. Democratic critics have often accused European royalty of ruinous expenditures on palaces, retinues, pensions, mistresses, and high living in general; yet such expenditures were usually a relatively small part of government outlays. War was the really major cause of disastrous financial difficulties for modern governments. Henry's six wives, his court, his frequent royal journeys did not beggar England; the wars of Charles V and Philip II did beggar Spain.

Henry VIII made war in a gingerly manner, never really risking big English armies on the Continent, and contenting himself with playing a rather cautious game of balance of power. He made full use of the opportu-

nities afforded him by the English Reformation to add to royal revenues by confiscation of monastic property, and, even more important, by rewarding his loyal followers with lands so confiscated. Henry thus followed in the footsteps of his father in helping create a new upper class, which soon became a titled or noble class. In contrast to France, the new class was on the whole loyal to the Crown and yet, in contrast to some of the German states, by no means subservient to the Crown, by no means a mere ennobled bureaucracy. Under Henry VIII and his successors the newly rich continued to thrive, and many other Englishmen prospered. But Tudor England also had a class of the newly poor as a result of the great enclosures of land for sheepfarming; small farmers, who lost their right to pasture animals on former common lands now enclosed in private estates, lost the margin that had permitted them to make ends meet.

Lacking the patience to attend to administrative details, Henry relied heavily on members of the new Tudor nobility as his chief assistants—Wolsey in the early part of his reign, then Cranmer who as archbishop of Canterbury enabled Henry to marry Anne Boleyn, and, above all, Thomas Cromwell, later made earl of Essex, who superintended the precarious ramifications of the break with Rome. Cromwell exploited the printing press to disseminate propaganda favoring the royal point of view. He was a master administrator, who endeavored to make the royal administration more loyal, professional, and efficient, less tied to the king's household and to special interests, in short, more modern in character. He achieved a great deal, but he antagonized other ambitious royal servants. Discredited with the king by the action of his enemies, Cromwell was executed in 1540. Wolsey, too, had been disgraced and died awaiting execution.

Henry could be ruthless, yet he could be tactful and diplomatic, as in his handling of Parliament to get everything he wanted, including statutes that separated the English church from Rome, and grants for his wars and conferences. Henry's Parliaments were very far from being elected legislatures based on wide suffrage. The House of Lords had a safe majority of men—titled nobles and, after 1534, bishops of the Anglican church—who were in fact of Tudor creation or allegiance. The House of Commons was composed of the knights of the shire, chosen by the freeholders of the shires, and of the burgesses, representatives of incorporated towns or boroughs (not by any means all towns). In most boroughs, a very narrow electorate chose these members of Parliament. Since the majority of the people of the shires were agricultural workers or tenants, rather than freeholders of land, the county franchise, too, was limited. The knights of the shire were chosen from among, and largely by, the squires and the lesser country gentlemen. Royal favor and royal patronage, as well as the patronage of the great lords, could pretty well mold the shape of a House of Commons.

Still, even the Tudor Parliaments were nearer a

*Quoted in J. J. Scarisbrick, *Henry VIII* (Berkeley, 1968), p. 526.

modern legislative assembly than the parallel assemblies of the Continent. The great point of difference lay in the composition of the House of Commons, which had emerged from the Middle Ages not as a body representing an urban bourgeoisie but as a composite of the rural landed gentry and the ruling groups in the towns. On the Continent, the assemblies corresponding to the English Parliament usually sat in three distinct houses—one representing the clergy, another all the nobles, great and small, and a third the lay commoners. Some countries, as for instance Sweden, had four estates—clergy, nobles, townsmen, and peasants.

Historians today emphasize the fact that the political differences between England and the Continent reflected differences in social structure. England certainly had a nobility or aristocracy ranging from barons through viscounts, earls, and marquesses to dukes at the top. These nobles, plus Anglican bishops, composed the House of Lords. In England, younger sons of nobles were not themselves titled nobles, as they were on the Continent, but were members, usually top members, of a complex group. In addition to the younger sons and descendants of nobles this group included the squires and rich bankers and merchants, who almost always acquired landed estates and became squires. It also included leading lawyers and civil servants, the Anglican clergy, dons at Oxford and Cambridge (who at first were usually in Anglican orders), officers in the army and navy, and a scattering of others in the liberal professions. This large and diverse group was never a closed caste and remained open to socially mobile men from the lower classes. The imprecise terms "gentry" and "gentlemen" are sometimes applied to this group, although the former is too exclusively rural in connotation and the latter is not always accurate in its implication that gentlemen invariably own enough property or capital so that they do not have to work for a living. Perhaps "ruling elite" or "establishment" would be as good names as any for this uniquely English class.

By the beginning of the Tudor era Parliament had already obtained much more than the purely advisory powers that were all that the French Estates General, for instance, really had. Parliament emerged from the Middle Ages with the power to make laws or statutes, which did, however, require royal consent. In terms of constitutional structure, the Tudor parliaments could have quarreled as violently with the Crown as the Stuart parliaments did in the next century. Yet, although the Tudor monarchs had their difficulties with Parliament, they usually got what they wanted without serious constitutional crises. This was particularly true of Henry VIII and Elizabeth I, who succeeded in part, as we have noted, because their parliaments, if not precisely packed, were generally recruited from men indebted to the Crown for their good fortune. But the Tudors also succeeded because they were skillful rulers, willing to use their prestige and gifts of persuasion to win the consent of Parliament, careful to observe the constitutional and human decencies. Both Henry and

Elizabeth were good, hearty persons, sure of themselves and their dignity, immensely popular with all classes of their subjects. Both were fortunate enough to be able to incorporate in their persons strong national feelings of patriotic resistance to the two most hated foreign foes, the Roman church and the Spanish monarchy.

Edward VI and Mary

The course of Tudor domestic history, however, did not run with perfect smoothness. Henry VII had faced two pretenders; Henry VIII met opposition to his religious policy. A Catholic minority, strong in the north, continued throughout the sixteenth century to oppose the Protestant majority, sometimes in arms, sometimes in intrigues. The death of Henry VIII in 1547 marked the beginning of a period of extraordinary religious oscillation.

Henry was succeeded by his only son, the ten-year-old Edward VI, borne by his third wife, Jane Seymour. Led by the young king's uncle, the Duke of Somerset, Edward's government pushed on into Protestant ways. The Six Articles, by which Henry had sought to preserve the essentials of Roman Catholic theology, worship, and even church organization, were repealed in 1547. The legal title of the statute commonly called the Six Articles had been "An Act for Abolishing Diversity in Opinion." The goal was still uniformity, and in the brief reign of Edward VI an effort was made to prescribe uniformity of religious worship through a prayerbook and articles of faith duly imposed by Parliament. Cranmer, archbishop of Canterbury, was much influenced by the ideas of Zwingli, and had committed himself by his marriage—as did Luther—to a clear, symbolic break with Roman Catholicism. Under his supervision, the patient majority of the English people was pushed into Protestant worship.

Then, in 1553, the young king, Edward VI, always a frail boy, died. Protestant intriguers vainly attempted to secure the crown for a Protestant, Lady Jane Grey, a great-granddaughter of Henry VII and a quiet, scholarly young woman with no ambitions. But Edward VI was followed by his older sister Mary, daughter of Catherine of Aragon, whom Henry VIII had put aside. Mary had been brought up a Catholic, and at once began to restore the old ways. Of course there was a rebellion, which flared into the open when Mary announced a marriage treaty by which she was to wed Philip II of Spain. Yet Mary prevailed against the rebels, and Lady Jane Grey was executed for a plot in which she had never really participated. A Catholic cardinal was made archbishop of Canterbury under Rome, and Cranmer was burned at the stake. Catholic forms of worship came back to the parishes, but significantly the church land settlement of Henry VIII remained undisturbed. The vigorous persecution of Protestants—most of the nearly three hundred people burnt were from the lower classes, and many were women—gave Mary her lasting epithet of Bloody and laid the foundations of the English Protestant hatred and suspicion of Catholicism, traces of which still survive today.

Elizabeth I

When Mary died after a short reign, in 1558, the last of Henry's children left was Elizabeth, daughter of Anne Boleyn. She had been declared illegitimate by Parliament in 1536 at her father's request. Henry's last will, however, rehabilitated her, and she now succeeded as Elizabeth I (1558–1603). She had been brought up a Protestant, and once more the English churchgoer was required to switch religion. This time the Anglican church was firmly established; the prayer book and Thirty-nine Articles of 1563 issued under Elizabeth (and noted in the preceding chapter) have remained

to this day the essential documents of the Anglican faith.

The Elizabethan settlement, moderate and permanent though it was, did not fully solve the religious problem. England still had a Catholic party, Catholic Spain was a serious enemy, and independent Scotland could always be counted on to take the anti-English side. The new queen of Scotland was Mary Stuart, granddaughter of Henry VIII's sister Margaret, and therefore the heiress to the English throne should Elizabeth die without issue. Mary, who was Catholic and whose mother was a member of the fanatically Catholic Guise family of France, did not wait for Elizabeth's death to press her claim. On the ground that Elizabeth was illegitimate, she assumed the title of queen of England and Scotland.

Meantime, numerous Protestant groups not satisfied with the Thirty-nine Articles were coming to the fore. Collectively, these people were called Puritans, since they wished to purify the Anglican church of what they considered papist survivals in belief, ritual, and church government. In practice, their proposals ranged from moderate to radical. The moderates would have settled for a simpler ritual and retained the office of bishop. The Presbyterians would have replaced bishops with councils (synods) of elders, or presbyters, and adopted the full Calvinist theology. The Brownists, named for their leader Robert Browne, would have gone still further and made each congregation an independent body.

Thus Elizabeth faced a decidedly grim prospect during the early years of her reign. The troubles of Edward and Mary had undone some of the work of the two Henrys; dissension seemed all around her; yet she was to reign for nearly fifty years. Her personality was hardly heartwarming. She was vain (or simply proud), not altogether immune to flattery, but too intelligent to be led astray by it in great matters. She was a good Renaissance realist (a better one than Machiavelli himself), somewhat too overpowering and impressive for a woman, but very effective in the pageantry and posing of public life. She was loved by her people if not by her intimates. She never married, but in the early years of her reign she played off foreign and domestic suitors one against another with excellent results for her foreign policy, in which she was always trying to avoid the expenses and dangers of war, trying to get something for nothing. One may believe that her spinsterhood settled on her at first as no more than a policy of state, and later as a convenient habit. She had male favorites, but probably not lovers.

Mistrusting the great aristocrats, Elizabeth picked her ministers from the ranks just below the nobility, talented men like Burleigh and Walsingham who put her government in splendid order. Thanks to skillful diplomacy, which made full use of the French and Dutch opposition to Spain, the showdown with Philip was postponed until 1588, when the kingdom was ready for it. Mary, Queen of Scots, proved no match at all

Portrait of Queen Elizabeth I by an unknown artist. The map of England is at her feet.

for her gifted cousin, not merely because she was not a good politician, but even more because she had no sure Scottish base to work from. Mary was Catholic, and Scotland under the leadership of John Knox was on its way to becoming one of the great centers of Calvinism. Mary managed everything wrong, including, and perhaps most important in a puritanical land, her love affairs. Her subjects revolted against her, and she was forced in 1568 to take refuge in England, where Elizabeth had her put in confinement. Mary alive was at the very least a constant temptation to all who wanted to overthrow Elizabeth. Letters, which Mary declared were forged, and over which historians still debate, involved her in what was certainly a real conspiracy against Elizabeth, and she was tried, convicted, and executed in 1587, to become a romantic legend.

The dramatic crisis of Elizabeth's reign was the war with Spain, resolved in the defeat of the great Spanish Armada in 1588. But her old age was not to be altogether serene. Forced to turn frequently to Parliament for approval of financial measures, she met mounting criticism of her religious policy from Puritan members of the House of Commons. She got her money not by making concessions to the Puritans but by grudgingly conceding more rights to the Commons. The Commons responded not with expressions of gratitude but with bolder criticism of the queen's policy, and at what proved to be the last meeting of Parliament Elizabeth attended, failed to salute her appearance with the usual salvo of applause. The stage was being set for the great seventeenth-century confrontation between the Crown and Parliament.

During Elizabeth's final years the stage was also being set for a drama that was to have an even longer run—the Irish question. The ruling Anglo-Irish landed class was out of touch with the native peasants. In 1542 the country had been made a kingdom, but hardly an independent one, since the crowns of England and Ireland were to be held by the same person. Earlier, in 1495, a statute had put the Irish Parliament firmly under English control and had made laws enacted by the English Parliament applicable to Ireland as well. Attempts to enforce Protestant legislation passed by the English Parliament outraged the native Irish, who had remained faithful Catholics. In 1597 the Irish rose in revolt; the rebellion was put down bloodily in 1601, but the basic Irish problem remained unsolved. The favorite of Elizabeth's old age, the Earl of Essex, lost influence by his failure to cope with the Irish rebels; he then became involved in a plot against the queen and was executed.

The English Renaissance

The Age of Elizabeth, then, was marked by intrigue, war, rebellion, and personal and party strife. Yet there were solid foundations under the state and society that produced the wealth and victories of the Elizabethan Age and its attainments in literature, music, architecture, and science. The economy prospered in an era of unbridled individual enterprise that was often unscrupulous and, in raids on the commerce of foreigners like the Spaniards, piratical. The solid administrative system was based on a substantial degree of national unity made possible by the absence of the extreme local differences and conflicts encountered on the Continent. A common sentiment kept Englishmen together and traced for most of them limits beyond which they would not carry disagreement. Elizabeth herself played a large part in holding her subjects together. Her religious policy, for example, was directed at stretching the already broad principles and practices of the Church of England so that they would cover near-Catholicism at one extreme and near-Congregationalism at the other. There was a limit to this stretching, and Elizabeth did not grant either Catholics or Brownists the right to practice their religion publicly. But, in contrast to Mary's severity, Elizabeth's persecution was largely a matter of fining offenders.

The Age of Elizabeth was marked by a great flowering of culture that extended beyond the chronological limits of her reign, 1558 to 1603, back to the reign of Henry VIII and forward to that of her successor, James I. This was the English Renaissance, when ladies and gentlemen cultivated all the muses, played the lute, sang madrigals, admired contemporary painting, and dressed as did their counterparts in the pacesetter of European style, Italy. The glory of the English Renaissance resided in its literature, for England was not a land of great original creations in music and the plastic arts. The greatness of Elizabethan England, when it is not in the deeds of Drake, Hawkins, Thomas Cromwell, Burleigh, and the Tudors themselves, lies in the words of Thomas More, William Shakespeare, Francis Bacon, Edmund Spenser, Ben Jonson, and many others who are part of the formal higher education of English-speaking people all over the world.

Their writings have suffered popular admiration and neglect as well as the thorough academic working-over that goes with the status of established classics. They belong to a culture now four hundred years past, and their authors wrote English before its structure and its word order were tamed, partly by the influence of French prose, into their present straightforward simplicity. For most of us, they are much easier to read about than to read. Yet on the whole they have survived intact as classics, and Shakespeare, notably, continues even outside the English-speaking world to be a kind of George Washington of letters, above reproach. He is the necessary great writer of a great people, as is Dante for the Italians, Goethe for the Germans, Pascal or Molière or Racine for the French, Cervantes for the Spanish, Tolstoy or Dostoevsky for the Russians.

These Elizabethans are overwhelmingly exuberant; they are exuberant even in refinement, full-blooded even in erudition. To a later generation, the polite, orderly admirers of measure and sense in the late seventeenth and eighteenth centuries, these Elizabethans were uncouth, undisciplined. To the nineteenth-century romantics, they were brothers in romance. The love of the excessive is obvious in much Elizabethan writing, in the interminable, allusion-packed, allegory-mad stanzas of Spenser's *Faerie Queene*, in the piling up of quotations from the ancient Greeks and Romans, in Shakespeare's fondness for puns and all kinds of rhetorical devices, in the extraordinarily bloody tragedies—remember, for example, the stage littered with corpses at the end of *Hamlet*.

The Elizabethans were also exuberant patriots, lovers of their country in the first flush of its worldly success. Here is one of the most famous speeches in Shakespeare, that of the dying John of Gaunt in *Richard II*, in itself an admirable sample of the English Renaissance, right down to the inevitable allusion to Greco-Roman mythology:

> *This royal throne of kings, this scepter'd isle,*
> *This earth of majesty, this seat of Mars,*
> *This other Eden, demi-paradise,*
> *This fortress built by Nature for herself*
> *Against infection and the hand of war,*
> *This happy breed of men, this little world,*
> *This precious stone set in the silver sea,*
> *Which serves it in the office of a wall*
> *Or as a moat defensive to a house,*
> *Against the envy of less happier lands,*
> *This blessed plot, this earth, this realm, this England.*

The Dutch Republic

Almost contemporaneous with the Elizabethan Age was the great age of the Dutch, which extended from the late sixteenth century through the first three quarters of the seventeenth. The United Provinces of the Northern Netherlands, as we have seen, gained effective independence from Spain before the death of Philip II, though formal international recognition of their status was delayed until 1648. The Dutch state was a republic in the midst of monarchies, but it was an aristocratic merchant society, far from being a popular democracy. Despite its small size (approximately that of the state of Maryland), it was a great power, colonizing in Asia, Africa, and the Americas, trading everywhere, supporting an active and efficient navy.

In economic life, the Dutch were the pacesetters of seventeenth-century Europe, and Amsterdam succeeded Antwerp (as Antwerp had earlier succeeded Bruges) as the major trading center of northwestern Europe. Dutch ships played a predominant role in the international carrying trade: in the mid-seventeenth century it is estimated that the Dutch operated between half and three-quarters of the world's merchant vessels. The Dutch also controlled the very lucrative North Sea herring fisheries. Their East India Company, founded in 1602, assembled and exploited a commercial empire. It paid large regular dividends and was a pioneer instance of the joint-stock company, sponsored by the state and pooling the resources of many businessmen who would scarcely have risked such a formidable undertaking on an individual basis. The Bank of Amsterdam, founded in 1609, was also a model, minting its own florins and so innovative in services to depositors that it made Amsterdam the financial capital of Europe. The Dutch invented life insurance and perfected the actuarial calculations on which it is based. Specialized industries flourished in particular cities and towns: diamond cutting, printing, and bookbinding at Amsterdam; shipbuilding at Zaandam; gin distilling at Schiedam; woolens at Leiden and linens at Haarlem. The Dutch, together with their Catholic cousins under Spanish rule in Flanders, were in the van of European agricultural progress; they created new farm plots called polders by diking and draining lands formerly under the sea, and they experimented with new techniques of scientific farming and with new crops. Among the latter were tulips, imported from the Ottoman Empire; the growing of tulip bulbs in the fields around Haarlem set off a wild financial speculation, the "Tulipomania" of the 1630s.

In government, the Dutch republic was no model of up-to-date efficiency, for the United Provinces were united in name only, fragmented by Dutch deference to traditional local home rule. The seven provinces sent delegates (*Hooge Moogende*, "high mightinesses") to the Estates General, which functioned like a diplomatic congress rather than a central legislature. Each province did have a chief executive, the stadholder, originally the local lieutenant of the Spanish king in the days of Hapsburg rule, and the fact that most of the provinces chose as stadholder the incumbent prince of the house of Orange made him a symbol of national unity. Twice in the seventeenth century, however, the preponderance of the Orange stadholder was challenged by the ranking local official of the most important province, the grand pensionary of Holland. In the first quarter of the century the grand pensionary, Jan van Olden Barneveldt, who was also the organizer of the East India Company, dominated Dutch politics until he was executed because of his support for Arminian doctrines of free will against Calvinist predestination. In the third quarter, the grand pensionary, Jan De Witt, an actuarial expert, ran the republic until he was lynched by a mob when the soldiers of Louis XIV overran an ill-prepared Holland in the 1670s.

In religion, Dutch practicality brought wide toleration. The beneficiaries were the substantial minority of Catholics, Protestant dissidents from Calvinist orthodoxy—Lutherans, Anabaptists, and eventually even Arminians—and Jewish refugees from Spain, Portugal, Poland, and Lithuania. The Jews made a considerable contribution to Dutch prosperity, and a still larger one was made by Calvinist refugees from the southern

Vermeer's "View of Delft," painted ca. 1658.

Netherlands. Dutch freedom made Holland a major publishing center of works in French and English and carried Dutch universities, especially that at Leiden, to the top of the European learned world. Individual Dutchmen made distinguished contributions to European culture, and the name of one of them—Rembrandt—has become a synonym for artistic genius. (Further particulars of Dutch artistic and intellectual achievements will be found in Chapter 15.)

The style of Dutch civilization in its great age was solid, reasonable, sober, but far from colorless, by no means puritanical in any ascetic sense. It is also a persuasive exhibit in support of Weber's thesis on the Protestant ethic. This little nation, through intelligence, hard work, hard trading, and adventurous exploration—and exploitation—overseas, won a high place in the world. But by 1700 the great days of the Dutch republic were coming to an end, as it was eclipsed by its larger and more powerful neighbors, Britain, France, and Prussia. Like the Swedes, who won a brief preponderance at about the same time, the Dutch did not have the resources at home to support the status of a great power.

V   Germany and the Thirty Years' War

Like the great wars of the sixteenth century, the Thirty Years' War, 1618–1648, was in part a conflict over religion, and like them it had a Hapsburg focus. This time, however, the focus was more on the Austrian than the Spanish Hapsburgs, and so the bulk of the fighting took place in Germany. While the Hapsburg emperor, Ferdinand II (1619–1637), did not aspire to universal rule, he did make the last serious political and military effort to unify Germany under Catholic rule. The Thirty Years' War began as a conflict between Catholics and Protestants; it ended as an almost purely political struggle to reduce the power of the Hapsburgs in favor of France and a newcomer to high international politics, Sweden.

The Peace of Augsburg in 1555 did not bring complete religious peace to Germany. It did not recognize Calvinism, to say nothing of the more radical Protestant sects, and it left unsettled the problem of ecclesiastical reservation. On this latter issue, an imperial decree provided that if a Catholic prelate were converted to Protestantism the property formerly under his control should remain in Catholic hands. But this

The hanging of thieves during the Thirty Years' War: a contemporary engraving.

was a one-sided proclamation; it had not been formally negotiated with the Protestants, who greatly resented it.

By the opening of the seventeenth century, the religious situation in Germany was becoming increasingly unsettled. In spite of the Augsburg peace, Calvinism had spread rapidly since 1555. Calvinist princes, ignoring the provision in the settlement against proselytizing, sponsored active missions in both Lutheran and Catholic regions. They also banded together in the Protestant Union (1608), which led Catholic German states to form the rival Catholic League (1609). It is important to note that more than religion was involved and that both the Union and the League had political ambitions as well. Both represented the interests of German particularism—that is, of the individual states—against those of the Holy Roman Empire, even though the Catholic League and its leader, Maximilian of Bavaria, were to ally with the emperor Ferdinand.

The German religious situation concerned the Spanish Hapsburgs as well as their Austrian cousins. After the Dutch revolt, the Spaniards wanted to stabilize a line of communications between their Belgian and Italian lands traversing the Rhine valley and the Alps. The Dutch and the French both wanted to thwart Spanish plans of securing this overland route, and the Bourbon monarchs of France did not relish the idea of being encircled by Hapsburg territory any more than their Valois predecessors had. A major physical obstacle blocking Spanish communications was the Palatinate, a rich vineyard area in the Rhineland ruled by a Calvinist elector.

The Struggle over Bohemia and the Palatinate, 1618–1625

In 1618 the Elector Palatine was Frederick, who also headed the Protestant Union and was married to the daughter of James I of England. Frederick hoped to break the Catholic hold on the office of emperor upon

the death of the emperor Matthias, who was old and childless and had already chosen as his heir the strongly Catholic Hapsburg prince, Ferdinand. The electors of Saxony, Brandenburg, and the Palatinate were Protestants; if there could be four Protestant electors instead of three when Matthias died, the majority could then install a Protestant emperor. Because three electors were Catholic archbishops the only way to elect an additional Protestant was to oust the one lay Catholic elector, the king of Bohemia, a position filled in name by the emperor Matthias and in practice by his heir, Ferdinand, who was styled "king-elect."

Bohemia, today a part of Czechoslovakia, was then a Hapsburg crown land; its Czech inhabitants wanted local independence from the rule of Germans and of Vienna. Some Czechs expressed their national defiance of the Germans by following the faith that John Hus had taught them two centuries before, and that was called Utraquism (from the Latin for "both") because it gave the laity communion in both wine and bread. While Utraquists, Lutherans, and Calvinists were all tolerated in Bohemia, the state religion was Catholic, and the prospect of Ferdinand's becoming king of Bohemia and then emperor alarmed Czech Protestants. When Protestant leaders opposing invasion of Czech religious liberties were arrested, a revolt broke out, beginning with the famous defenestration of Prague (May 23, 1618), in which two Catholic imperial governors were thrown out of a window into a courtyard seventy feet below. They landed on a pile of dung, and escaped with their lives.

The Czech rebels set up their own government and offered the crown of Bohemia to Frederick of the Palatinate. Frederick went off to Prague but without making adequate provision for defense of his home territories in the Rhineland, which the Spaniards occupied in 1620. Meantime, Catholics in Bohemia, Spain, and Flanders rallied against the Czech rebels with money and men. On the death of the emperor Matthias in 1619, the imperial electors chose the Hapsburg Ferdinand as his successor (Emperor Ferdinand II, 1619–1637). Maximilian of Bavaria, head of the Catholic League, supported Ferdinand's cause in Bohemia in return for a promise of receiving Frederick's electoral post; even the Lutheran elector of Saxony also supported Ferdinand. The Protestant Union remained neutral, as did England, although the Protestant Frederick was very popular in his father-in-law's kingdom. In Bohemia, Maximilian and the Catholic forces won the battle of the White Mountain (1620); derisively nicknamed the "winter king" because of his brief tenure, Frederick fled, and Ferdinand made the Bohemian throne hereditary in his own family. He also abolished toleration of Czech Utraquists and Calvinists, but granted it temporarily to Lutherans because of his obligations to the elector of Saxony. He executed the leaders of the rebellion, confiscated their lands, and sanctioned terrible destruction in Bohemia.

The continued presence of Spanish forces in the Palatinate upset the balance of power. The Lutheran king of Denmark, Christian IV (1588–1648), feared the Hapsburgs would move north toward the Baltic; the French faced a new Hapsburg encirclement; and the Dutch were threatened by an immediate Spanish attack. The Dutch made an alliance with Christian IV, and another with the fugitive Frederick, agreeing to subsidize his attempt to reconquer the Palatinate. When fighting resumed, Frederick was defeated again, whereupon the emperor Ferdinand transferred the Palatine electorate to Maximilian of Bavaria (1625).

In France, meantime, Cardinal Richelieu, chief minister of Louis XIII (1610–1643), recognized the Hapsburg danger and took steps to counter it. He was ready to arrange a dynastic marriage between the future Charles I of England and Louis XIII's sister, Henrietta Maria, and to make an alliance with other Protestants: Frederick, the Dutch, Christian IV, and Gustavus Adolphus, the Lutheran king of Sweden. By the summer of 1624 the new coalition was taking shape, but was shattered by Spanish victories in Holland (1625) and the unwillingness of Gustavus to serve under the Danes, traditional enemies of the Swedes. Christian IV had to defend the Protestants alone.

Intervention by Denmark and Sweden, 1625–1635

A vigorous and ambitious monarch, King Christian IV had taken full advantage of the increased authority that Lutheranism gave to royalty. When he intervened in the war, he sought not only to defend his coreligionists but also to extend Danish political and economic hegemony over northern Germany. To check the Danish invasion, the German Catholics enlisted the help of the private army of Wallenstein (1583–1634), a general who, though born of a German Protestant family in Bohemia, was reared a Catholic and fought on the imperial side. He recruited and paid an army that lived off the land by requisition and plunder,

sometimes at the expense of Catholic and imperial sympathizers. Wallenstein, who had bought huge tracts of Bohemian real estate confiscated from Czech rebels, was in fact a German condottiere, a private citizen seeking to becoming a ruling prince, perhaps even emperor of a rejuvenated Germany. He never came close to success, but his army was a major factor in the war at its most critical period. Together with the forces of the Catholic League under Count Tilly, Wallenstein's army defeated the Danes and moved northward into Danish territory.

Then, at the height of the imperial and Catholic success, the emperor Ferdinand and his advisers overreached themselves. In the Edict of Restitution (1629) they attempted a one-sided resolution of the long-vexing question of ecclesiastical reservation by demanding the restoration of all clerical estates that had passed from Catholic to Lutheran hands since 1551, three generations earlier. The edict also affirmed the Augsburg exclusion of the Calvinists and the radical Protestants from toleration. The Treaty of Lübeck, also in 1629, allowed Christian IV to recover his Danish lands but exacted from him a promise not to intervene again in Germany. This seemed to the outside world a sign that Hapsburg power was actually spreading to the Baltic, a region thoroughly Protestant and hitherto only on the margin of imperial control. The old pattern was then repeated: the Hapsburgs were trespassing beyond their customary spheres of influence; those upon whom they encroached resisted the trespass; and the trespasser was finally forced to withdraw.

More and more the emperor Ferdinand became indebted to the ambitious Wallenstein, and less and less could he control him. Wallenstein planned to found a new Baltic trading company with the remnants of the Hanseatic organization, and by opening the Baltic to the Spaniards make possible a complete victory over the Dutch. When Ferdinand asked him for troops to use in Italy against the French, Wallenstein, intent on his northern plans, refused. Soon Ferdinand dismissed Wallenstein, leaving the imperial forces under the command of Tilly and of Maximilian of Bavaria, who had been alarmed by Wallenstein's activities and was placated by his departure. If Ferdinand had also placated the Protestants by revoking the Edict of Restitution, peace might have been possible. But he failed to do so, and the war resumed with Gustavus Adolphus as the Protestant champion.

Called the Lion of the North, Gustavus Adolphus (reigned 1611–1632) was a much stronger champion than Christian had been. Like Christian, he had ambitions for political control over northern Germany, and he hoped that Sweden might assume the old Hanseatic economic leadership. He had tamed the unruly Swedish nobility, given his country an efficient government and a sound economy, taken lessons from the Dutch in military tactics, and proved himself and his armies against Russia and Poland by establishing a Swedish foothold on the eastern shores of the Baltic, notably

Europe in 1648

Brandenburg-Prussia
Austrian Hapsburg Lands
Spanish Hapsburg Lands
Swedish possessions
Venetian possessions
Ottoman Empire

- - - Boundary of the Holy Roman Empire

■ Battle sites

Approximate division line between Puritans and Cavaliers in England, May, 1643

North Sea

NORWAY

Oslo

Stock

SW

DENMARK

Copenhagen

Balti

SCOTLAND

Edinburgh
Dunbar • Berwick

ULSTER

Drogheda

IRELAND

Dublin

Wexford

Preston
Marston Moor

ENGLAND

Nottingham

Worcester
Naseby

London

Atlantic Ocean

Lübeck
POMERANIA

Texel
Bremen
Hamburg
BRANDENBURG

UNITED NETHERLANDS
Osnabrück
Berlin

THE

Elbe R.
Oder R.

Münster
Magdeburg

SPANISH NETHERLANDS
Rhône R.
WEST-PHALIA
Lützen

SILE

Rocroy
Paris

Seine R.
Verdun
PALATINATE
Heidelberg
SAXONY

Nantes

Orléans

Metz
Toul

EMPIRE

BOHEMIA

Prague

Loire R.

Strasbourg

ALSACE

MORAV

FRANCE

FRANCHE COMTÉ

Danube R.

AUSTRIA

Vienna

BAVARIA

STYRIA

Bordeaux

SWITZERLAND

VALTELLINE

Geneva

TYROL

CARINTHIA

CARNIOLA

H

SAVOY

Rhône R.

PIEDMONT

MILAN

Avignon (to the Papacy)

Genoa

Po R.

Venice

VENETIAN REPUBLIC

PORTUGAL

Burgos

Marseilles

Florence

PAPAL STATES

Lisbon

SPAIN

Madrid

Ebro R.

Tagus R.

Barcelona

CORSICA (to Genoa)

Rome

Ra

NAPLES

Guadalquivir R.

Valencia

BALEARIC IS.

Naples

Seville

Granada

SARDINIA

Mediterranean Sea

Palermo

SICILY

0   500
Miles

ALGIERS
(Tributary to Ottoman Empire)

TUNIS

MALTA

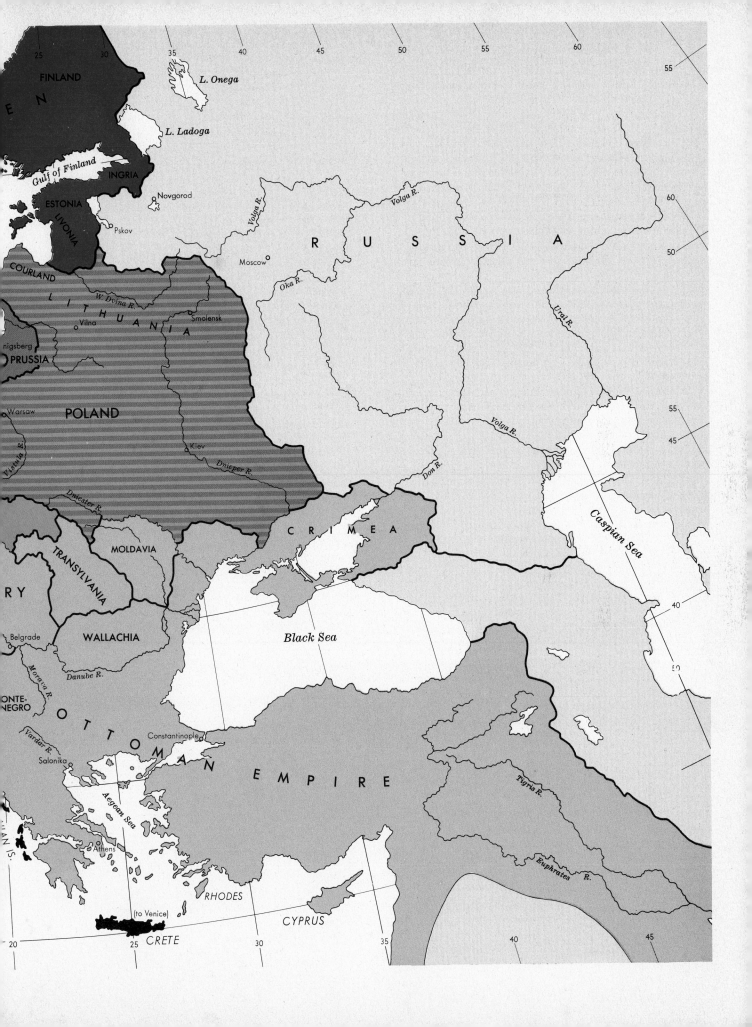

FINLAND

L. Onega

L. Ladoga

Gulf of Finland

INGRIA

ESTONIA

Novgorod

LIVONIA

Pskov

COURLAND

RUSSIA

Volga R.

Volga R.

LITHUANIA

W. Dvina R.

Vilna

Smolensk

Moscow

Oka R.

Ural R.

nigsberg

PRUSSIA

Warsaw

POLAND

Kiev

Dnieper R.

Volga R.

Vistula R.

Don R.

Dniester R.

Caspian Sea

MOLDAVIA

CRIMEA

TRANSYLVANIA

RY

Belgrade

WALLACHIA

Black Sea

40

Morava R.

Danube R.

ONTE-
NEGRO

O T T O M A N

Vardar R.

Constantinople

Salonika

Tigris R.

E M P I R E

Aegean Sea

N IS.

Athens

Euphrates R.

RHODES

CYPRUS

(to Venice)

CRETE

German states secured the right to conduct their own foreign affairs, making treaties among themselves and with foreign powers if these were not directed against the emperor. This last was a face-saving for the Hapsburgs, for the fact that the constituent states now had their own foreign services, their own armies, their own finances—three earmarks of independent sovereignty—showed that the Holy Roman Empire of the German nation was no longer a viable political entity. The Westphalian settlement also recognized formally the independence of the Dutch republic, already independent in fact for over half a century, and of the Swiss confederation, the nucleus of which had first broken away from Hapsburg control during the later Middle Ages.

For more than two centuries after 1648, the Thirty Years' War was blamed for everything that later went wrong in Germany. We know now that the economic decline of Germany had begun well before the war opened in 1618 and that the figures of deaths and destruction recorded in contemporary chronicles were inflated and are highly unreliable. Yet, even when allowance is made for exaggerations, scholars estimate that the overall diminution in the German population was from about twenty-one million in 1618 to less than thirteen and a half million in 1648. Some historians also trace to this destructive war aspects of modern Germany that have made her a disturbing influence in the modern world. They point to a national sense of inferiority heightened by her delayed achievement of national unity, a lack of the slow ripening in self-government that a more orderly growth in early modern times might have encouraged, a too strong need for authority and obedience brought out in response to the anarchic conditions of the seventeenth century. These are dangerously big generalizations that are at most suggestive; they can by no means be proved.

On the other hand, it is evident that the final outcome of the war raised almost as many problems as it solved. It did not end hostilities between two of the chief belligerents, France and Spain, who continued to fight for another eleven years. The Peace of Westphalia satisfied neither the pope, who denounced it, nor many Protestants, who felt betrayed by it. Politically, the fresh successes of German particularism limited the Hapsburgs' direct power in Germany to their family lands and enabled such states as Bavaria, Saxony and, above all, Brandenburg-Prussia to move to the fore in German affairs. In addition, non-Austrian Germans harbored bitter resentment against the Hapsburgs for having fought this most terrible of dynastic and religious wars to protect family interests. And it was a most terrible war, not just because of its length but because of its savage character and the large armies involved. The Swedish force alone numbered two hundred thousand at its peak and was the largest to be put in the field since Roman days. Despite the enormous loss of life, however, the war made little change in the social hierarchy of Germany; once the fighting was over, the nobility often succeeded in forcing the peasants back onto the lands by denying them the right to leave their village or engage in home industry. One can appreciate why some recent historians have pronounced the Thirty Years' War a crucial event in the development of a crisis in seventeenth-century Europe, which Chapter 15 examines in more detail.

Reading Suggestions on Dynastic Politics and Warfare

General Accounts

The New Cambridge Modern History (Cambridge Univ.). The first four volumes of this lengthy collaborative project contain much information on the topics covered in this chapter.

H. G. Koenigsberger and G. L. Mosse, *Europe in the Sixteenth Century* (*Holt). An excellent survey with useful bibliographical footnotes.

E. F. Rice, Jr., *The Foundations of Early Modern Europe, 1460–1559* and R. S. Dunn, *The Age of Religious Wars, 1559–1689* (*Norton). Enlightening brief surveys; part of a series published recently.

J. H. Elliott, *Europe Divided, 1559–1598* (*Torchbooks). Useful introduction to the Age of Philip II.

M. R. O'Connell, *The Counter Reformation, 1559–1610,* and C. J. Friedrich, *The Age of the Baroque, 1610–1660* (*Torchbooks). Comprehensive volumes, with full bibliographies, in the Rise of Modern Europe series. Friedrich's is particularly stimulating.

H. Trevor-Roper, ed., *The Age of Expansion* (McGraw-Hill, 1968). Sumptuously illustrated collaborative volume touching on many topics in European and world history from the mid-sixteenth to mid-seventeenth century.

The Cambridge Economic History of Europe, Vol. 4: *The Economy of Expanding Europe in the Sixteenth and Seventeenth Centuries* (Cambridge Univ., 1967). Scholarly chapters by experts on selected aspects of the economy rather than a general survey.

War and Diplomacy, 1494–1598

L. Dehio, *The Precarious Balance: Four Centuries of the European Power Struggle* (*Vintage). A German historian interprets the shifting balance of power, beginning with the sixteenth century.

G. Mattingly, *Renaissance Diplomacy* (*Sentry). A stimulating and indispensable introduction.

C. Petrie, *Earlier Diplomatic History, 1492–1713* (Macmillan, 1949). A useful manual.

C. H. Carter, *The Secret Diplomacy of the Habsburgs, 1598–1625* (Columbia Univ., 1964.) An instructive case study in diplomatic history.

C. W. C. Oman, *A History of the Art of War in the Sixteenth Century* (Dutton, 1973). Highly interesting study of a neglected aspect of history.

J. F. C. Fuller, *A Military History of the Western World,* 3 vols. (*Funk & Wagnalls). By an informative, somewhat unorthodox general; volumes I and II contain material relevant to this chapter.

Spain

J. Lynch, *Spain under the Habsburgs,* 2 vols. (Oxford Univ., 1964, 1969). A thorough and up-to-date scholarly study; the first volume treats the sixteenth century, and the second the seventeenth.

J. H. Elliott, *Imperial Spain, 1469–1716* (E. Arnold, 1963). Another good scholarly introduction. Elliott is the author of an important monograph: *The River of Catalans: A Study in the Decline of Spain, 1598–1640* (Cambridge Univ., 1963).

R. T. Davies, *The Golden Century of Spain* (*Torchbooks) and *Spain in Decline, 1621–1700* (St. Martin's, 1957). Popular accounts addressed to the general reader.

K. Brandi, *The Emperor Charles V* (*Humanities). Thorough study of the ruler of a troubled dynastic conglomerate.

C. Petrie, *Philip II of Spain* (Norton, 1963). An interesting and impartial biography.

F. Braudel, *The Mediterranean and the Mediterranean World in the Age of Philip II,* 2 vols. (Harper, 1972). An important geographical and socio-economic study of Spain's involvement with Italy and the Ottoman Empire.

France

A. Guérard, *France in the Classical Age: The Life and Death of an Ideal* (Braziller, 1956). Lively, provocative, and highly personal interpretation of French history from the Renaissance to Napoleon.

J. E. Neale, *The Age of Catherine de' Medici* (*Torchbooks). Excellent short introduction to the French civil and religious wars.

J. W. Thompson, *The Wars of Religion in France, 1559–1576* (Univ. of Chicago, 1909). A detailed narrative; still very useful.

J. Héritier, *Catherine de Medici* (St. Martin's, 1963). A sound biography.

A. J. Grant, *The Huguenots* (Butterworth, 1934). A brief and reasonably dispassionate study.

W. J. Stankiewicz, *Politics and Religion in Seventeenth Century France* (Univ. of California, 1960). Goes back to the politiques of the late sixteenth century.

Q. Hurst, *Henry of Navarre* (Appleton, 1938). Standard biography.

England

C. Read, *The Tudors* (*Norton). Excellent introduction to the interrelations of personalities and politics. Read also published *The Government of England under Elizabeth* (*Univ. of Virginia) and scholarly studies of her chief ministers.

J. D. Mackie, *The Earlier Tudors, 1485–1558,* and J. B. Black, *The Reign of Elizabeth, 1558–1603* (Clarendon, 1952, 1960). Comprehensive, scholarly volumes in the Oxford History of England.

S. T. Bindoff, *Tudor England* (*Penguin). Sound, scholarly introduction.

G. R. Elton, *The Tudor Revolution in Government* (*Cambridge Univ.). Important study of the shift to a bureaucratic state.

J. J. Scarisbrick, *Henry VIII* (*Univ. of California). The first new scholarly biography in more than half a century; may be supplemented by the still more recent psychological study by L. B. Smith, *Henry VIII: The Mask of Royalty* (*Sentry).

J. E. Neale, *Queen Elizabeth I: A Biography* (*Anchor). By a great scholar, author also of *The Elizabethan House of Commons* (*Penguin) and *Elizabeth I and Her Parliaments,* 2 vols. (Cape, 1953, 1957).

E. Jenkins, *Elizabeth the Great* (*Capricorn). Sound biography focused more on the person than the queen.

W. MacCaffrey, *The Shaping of the Elizabethan Regime* (*Princeton Univ.). Able study of her early years in power.

W. P. Haugaard, *Elizabeth and the English Reformation* (Cambridge Univ., 1968). Excellent scholarly assessment.

G. Mattingly, *The Armada* (*Sentry). A truly great work of history.

A. Fraser, *Mary, Queen of Scots* (*Dell). Recent biography of Elizabeth's impulsive antagonist.

The Dutch Republic

C. J. Cadoux, *Philip of Spain and the Netherlands* (Butterworth, 1947). Moderate restatement of the liberal Protestant view of the question.

P. Geyl, *The Revolt of the Netherlands, 1555–1609* (*Barnes & Noble) and *The Netherlands in the Seventeenth Century,* 2 vols. (Barnes & Noble, 1961, 1964). Detailed studies by a distinguished Dutch historian who regrets the disruption of the unity of the Low Countries. A briefer statement may be found in his *History of the Low Countries* (St. Martin's, 1964).

J. Huizinga, *Dutch Civilization in the Seventeenth Century and Other Essays* (*Torchbooks). The title essay is a thoughtful evaluation by another distinguished Dutch historian.

C. V. Wedgwood, *William the Silent* (*Norton). Sound biography of the Dutch national hero.

V. Barbour, *Capitalism in Amsterdam in the Seventeenth Century* (*Ann Arbor). Illuminating study of an important factor in Dutch success.

Germany and the Thirty Years' War

H. Holborn, *A History of Modern Germany.* Vol. 2: *The Reformation* (Knopf, 1959). This authoritative study goes down to 1648.

C. V. Wedgwood, *The Thirty Years' War* (*Anchor). Full and generally well-balanced narrative.

S. H. Steinberg, *The "Thirty Years' War" and the Conflict for European Hegemony, 1600–1660* (*Norton). Briefer, more recent account.

G. Pagès, *The Thirty Years' War* (*Torchbooks). Translation of an older French study, stressing the diplomatic side of the war.

T. K. Rabb, ed., *The Thirty Years' War: Problems of Motive, Extent, and Effect* (*Heath). Sampler of differing views of these controversial questions.

M. Roberts, *Gustavus Adolphus: A History of Sweden, 1611–1632,* 2 vols. (Longmans, 1953, 1958). Sympathetic detailed biography.

Sources and Fiction

N. Roelker, ed., *The Paris of Henry of Navarre* (Harvard Univ., 1958). Selections from the informative *Mémoires-journaux* of Pierre de l'Estoile, a rich source of social history.

H. Haydn, ed., *The Portable Elizabethan Reader* (*Viking). A good anthology.

S. Putnam, ed., *The Portable Cervantes* (*Viking). Selections from the editor's admirable translation of *Don Quixote.*

H. J. C. von Grimmelshausen, *Simplicius Simplicissimus* (*Bobbs-Merrill). Picaresque but realistic novel written in the seventeenth century and set against the background of war-ravaged Germany.

W. Scott, *Kenilworth* (*Airmont). By the famous Scottish novelist of the romantic era; the setting is Elizabethan England.

The Expansion of Europe in Early Modern Times

Exploration and Expansion, Old and New

During the early modern centuries, when Europeans were experiencing the Renaissance and the Reformation, with its long aftermath of traumatic conflict, some of them took part in a remarkable expansion that carried European sailors, merchants, missionaries, settlers, and adventurers to almost every quarter of the globe. What Westerners confidently call "the known world" moved outward at a breathtaking pace, although relatively few Westerners, then or now, realized that non-Western peoples—the Chinese or American Indians, for example—had their own different concept of the "known world." In the age of Homer, the known world of the West had encompassed little more than the eastern Mediterranean and its fringes. Under Alexander the Great and the Romans, it was still centered on the Mediterranean and the western fringes of Asia, with much of the interior of Europe and Africa hazy or blank, and with the Americas still unsuspected. Then the explorations of the late Middle Ages launched a continuous process that culminated in the full fruition of geographical knowledge.

Westerners were not the first people to move and migrate over vast reaches of water. Even earlier than the Viking voyages in the Atlantic, the Polynesians, for example, who came from southern China, had accomplished the daring feat of settling remote Pacific islands. But the Polynesians and other early migrants kept no written records and no significant ties with their places of origin. They were not societies in expansion, but groups of individuals on the move. The expansion of the West was very different. From the very start in ancient Greece and Rome, records were kept, maps were made, and the nucleus always remained in touch with its offshoots. Western society has expanded *as a society*, often as a group of states.

The modern Western expansion, which began in the mid-fifteenth century, differed also in important ways from the expansion that had carried the cultures of the ancient Near East as far as western and northern Europe. In the first place, this modern expansion was much faster and covered more ground. Although some secrets of the Arctic and the Antarctic, some details of the wilder interiors of the world, were not known to us until the twentieth century, it is broadly true that the whole world was revealed to Europeans within two and a half or three centuries after 1450—within four long lifetimes. In the second place, this modern expansion was the first time our Western society crossed great oceans. Ancient and medieval Western navigation had clung to the narrow seas and the shorelines. The ancients had even commonly drawn up their boats on land to spend the night. Now Westerners crossed the Atlantic and the Pacific, far from the protecting land. In the third place, this expansion carried Westerners well outside the orbit of relations with Byzantines and Muslims, who were also successors to the cultures of Socrates and Christ, into relations with a bewildering variety of races, creeds, and cultures, from naked savages to cultivated Chinese. Not since the Germanic peoples had been tamed and converted in the early Middle Ages had Westerners come into close contact with primitive peoples. Finally, and of very great importance, expanding Europe possessed a margin of superior material and technological strength that enabled Western society to do what no society had ever done before—extend its influence around the world.

An important element of that margin was the possession of firearms; yet firearms could be legally or illegally acquired by non-Europeans, and very soon were. The strength by which Europeans overcame the world was a compound of technological and economic superiority and of superior political and social organization, which in turn permitted superior military organization. This superiority was not applied from a

centuries since the invasion by the "Indo-Europeans" considerable human intermixture had undoubtedly occurred. Yet even today the upper classes in most of India are lighter in color than the lower.

The most striking thing about Indian culture was the high place occupied by the priestly caste, the Brahmins. The Brahmin faith has strains of a most otherworldly belief in the evils of the life of the flesh and the attainment of salvation by a mystic transcendence of the flesh in ascetic denial. With this is a doctrine of the transmigration of souls, in which sinful life leads to reincarnation in lower animal life, and virtuous life leads, at least in some forms of Hindu belief, to ultimate freedom from flesh of any sort and reunion with the perfect, the ineffable. But official Brahminism became a series of rigid and complicated rituals, and the religion of the common people retained from earlier times an elaborate polytheism lush with gods and goddesses who were by no means ethereal, but fleshly indeed. Against all this worldliness there rose in the sixth century B.C. a great religious leader, Gautama Buddha, himself of noble stock. Buddhism accepts the basic Brahminical concept of the evil of this world of the flesh, but it finds salvation, the nirvana of peaceful release from the chain of earthly birth and rebirth, in a life ascetic but not withdrawn, a life of charity and good works. Although Buddhism died out in the land of its birth, it spread to China, Japan, and southeastern Asia.

In these lands it took two forms, still existing. In the northern lands of Tibet, China, Japan, the Mahayana (Great Vehicle) continued in theology to emphasize Buddha's strong ethical desire to make nirvana available to all. In southeastern Asia and Ceylon, the Hinayana (Lesser Vehicle) prevailed. In theory, the Hinayana relies more on ritual, and its monks are wholly detached from the world. Buddhism remains one of the world's great higher religions. It has made some converts among Western intellectuals, especially in an altered form known as Zen Buddhism, originally a kind of Japanese stoicism.

The religious thought of India has left a residue of greater otherworldliness, of greater emphasis on a mystical subduing of the flesh, of a revulsion from the struggle for wealth, satisfaction of the common human appetites, worldly place and power, than has Christianity or Islam. In practice, Indian life, even before the Europeans came, displayed plenty of violence, plenty of greed, cruelty, and self-indulgence. Except as superstition and taboo and ritual, little of the higher religions had seeped down to the masses. To some Western minds, the educated classes of India have seemed to take refuge in otherworldly doctrines as a psychological defense against the worldly superiority of the West and the poverty and superstition of their own masses. But the fact remains that for three hundred years educated Indians have insisted that they feel differently about the universe and man's place in it than do we, that theirs is a higher spirituality.

China

China, too, resisted the West, and in many ways more successfully than did India. A very old civilization that goes back several thousand years before Christ was established in the valleys of the Yangtze and the Yellow rivers. Like the other civilizations bordering the great nomadic Eurasian heartland—the Mesopotamian, the Indian, the European—it was subject to periodic incursions of tribesmen. It was against such incursions that the famous Great Wall of China was built in the third century B.C. On the whole, the Chinese protected their basic institutions against the victorious nomads, whom they absorbed after a few generations. At just about the time when the first Europeans were setting up permanent trade relations with China, the last of these "barbarian" conquests occurred. Early in the seventeenth century, Mongolian tribes established a state of their own in eastern Manchuria, to the north of China proper. In 1644, they seized the Chinese capital of Peking and established a dynasty that lasted until 1911. But the Manchus, like other outsiders before them, left Chinese institutions almost untouched.

Chinese history is by no means the uneventful record of a "frozen" and unchanging society that some Westerners have thought. It is filled with the rise and fall of dynasties; with periods of effective governmental centralization and periods of "feudal" disintegration; with wars, plagues, and famines; and with the gradual spread of Chinese culture southward and eastward to the region of Canton, to Vietnam, to Korea, and to Japan. Under the flux many elements of continuity existed. At the base of Chinese social life was a communal village organization, held together by very strong family ties, a cult of ancestor worship, and a tradition of hard work on the farm. The Chinese village, basically unchanged until the Communist reform of our own day, was one of the oldest socio-economic organizations in the civilized world. At the top of this society was an emperor, the Son of Heaven, whose subjects were conditioned to at least formal imperial unity in somewhat the same manner as early medieval Westerners were conditioned to the unity of Roman Catholic Christendom.

The business of running this vast empire was entrusted to one of the most remarkable ruling classes history has recorded, the mandarins, a bureaucracy of intellectuals, or at least of men who could pass examinations in literary and philosophical classics requiring a rigorously trained memory. The mandarin class, though it was susceptible to graft and to nepotism and proved not very resilient in the face of new European ideas, had served the state for thousands of years, and its existence is one of the reasons for the extraordinary stability of Chinese society. Although in theory the class was one open to talents, the necessary education was too expensive and too difficult for any but a few gifted, lucky, and persistent poor boys. Just as in India, then, China had a small upper class that enjoyed a style of living hardly available to aristocracy in the medieval

A mandarin: engraving from John Ogilby's "Atlas Chinensis," 1671.

West, and an immense population at the very margin of existence.

It has often been remarked that China never had a religion, in the sense that Buddhism, Christianity, and Islam are religions with a firm doctrine of salvation. The Chinese millions had their superstitions, their demons, their otherworld. But the upper class took little interest in mysticism and otherworldliness; they demonstrated a realistic acceptance of the world as it is, and a concern with human relations, with politeness and decorum. Their conventional Confucianism was a code of manners and morals, not a sacramental religion. Confucius, a sage who flourished in the fifth century B.C., was no prophet but a moralist who taught an ethical system of temperance, decorum, obedience to those who were wise and good. This lack of commitment to an otherworldly religion, however, has by no means made the Chinese more receptive to Western ideas. Down to the establishment of the Communist regime at any rate, China resisted westernization more effectively than any other great culture.

The Portuguese Empire

The empire that the Portuguese founded in Asia and Africa was a trading empire, not an empire of settlement. They established along the coasts of Africa, India, and China a series of posts over which they hoisted the Portuguese flag as a sign that these bits of territory had been annexed to the Portuguese crown. Such posts were often called factories after the factors or commercial agents who were stationed there to trade with the natives. As all the European colonial powers were to do later on, the Portuguese offered guns, knives, cheap cloth, and gadgets of all sorts. In return they got gold and silver (when they could), pepper and other spices, still essential for making meat palatable in pre-refrigeration days, silks and other luxuries, and, finally, raw materials such as cotton and, in Brazil, tobacco and sugar.

Two guiding principles of this trade were accepted by almost all contemporaries, whether in the mother country or in the colonies, as simple facts of life. First, in this trade the mother country was the determining element, and would naturally provide manufactured goods and services while the colony produced raw materials. Second, foreigners, nationals of other European lands, were excluded from this trade; they could not deal directly with the colony or take part in the commerce between mother country and colony. The Portuguese, in sum, followed a policy of mercantilism, symbolized by the virtual monopoly Lisbon exercised over European imports of pepper and cinnamon during the sixteenth century.

Armed forces were essential to the establishment and maintenance of this colonial system. Relatively small land forces proved sufficient both to keep the natives under control and to ward off rival European powers from the trading posts. A large and efficient navy was also necessary, for the easiest way to raid a rival's trade was to wait until its fruits were neatly concentrated in the hold of a merchant vessel, and then take it at sea as a prize. Pirates were often openly an unofficial adjunct of a given navy, called privateers and operating only against enemies or neutrals, never against their own nationals. A navy was, then, essential to protect the sea routes of a colonial power. The Portu-

guese fleet was not only a merchant fleet; under the command of governors like Albuquerque, it was a great military fleet that brushed aside Arab opposition and for a few decades ruled the oceans of the Old World.

The Portuguese made no serious attempt to settle large numbers of their own people either in the hot coastlands of Africa or in the already densely populated lands of India and the Far East. Nor, with the one exception we are about to encounter, did they attempt to make over these natives into pseudo-Portuguese. Many natives were enlisted in the armed forces or used as domestic help and in subordinate posts such as clerks, and they inevitably picked up, however imperfectly, the language and culture of the colonial power. But neither among the primitive tribes of Africa nor among the Indian and Chinese masses did this process of europeanization go very fast or far. The Portuguese left the old ruling chiefs and old ruling classes pretty much as they had found them. The native upper classes monopolized most of the limited European wares, and Europe could not yet flood non-European markets with cheap manufactured goods made by power-driven machinery. Nothing Western touched the masses of natives in the

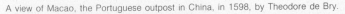

A view of Macao, the Portuguese outpost in China, in 1598, by Theodore de Bry.

AMACAO.

sixteenth century, nothing tempted them away from their millennial ways of life, in anything like the degree our twentieth-century West attracts and tempts the East.

There is one exception. The Portuguese and the Spanish, and even their relatively secular-minded rivals, the English, Dutch, and French, did attempt to Christianize the natives. Some of these attempts were coercive, as at Goa where the Portuguese pulled down all the native temples and made it impossible to practice traditional religion. From the first, however, much sincerity, devotion, and hard work also went into the missionary movement. The earliest missionaries underestimated the obstacles they were to encounter. Many of them were in a sense partly converted themselves; that is, they came to be very fond of their charges and convinced that these were in fact almost Christians already. Some of the Jesuits in China, the first European intellectuals to live in this very civilized country, seriously believed that with just a bit more effort the full reconciliation between Christianity and Confucianism could be achieved.

From the start, difficulties arose between the missionaries, anxious to protect their charges, and the traders and colonial officials, driven by their very place in the system to try to exploit the natives. Local chiefs and monarchs regarded converts as potential traitors, more loyal to their Western faith than to their Eastern rulers. Finances and manpower were always serious problems, with so many to convert and tend, and with so few men and so little money to do the work. Measured in statistical terms, the effort to convert India and the Far East to Christianity did not make a serious impression on the masses—something under a million converts by 1600. The greatest missionary successes tended to occur in areas of Buddhism; then in a state of decay comparable to that of Catholicism on the eve of the Reformation, and the greatest failures in areas of Islam, for Muslims have very seldom abandoned their faith for any other. Yet the influence of Christianity cannot be measured in terms of actual church memberships in the East; it has been far greater on the upper and intellectual classes than on the masses and is an important part of the whole Western impact on the East.

The Portuguese, though first in the field in the East, very soon had to yield to newer rivals. Like the Spaniards, they suffered from an inadequate home industry; their banking, their business methods, their initiative—if not their scruples—were not up to competition with the aggressive expanding powers of northwest Europe. Though monopolizing the import of pepper from the East, they sought the assistance of the more knowledgeable merchant community of Antwerp in distributing the pepper to European markets. The cloth and other wares they traded in the East they often had to import from countries with more developed industries. After the sixteenth century, they ceased to add to their empire and their wealth, and sank back

to a secondary place in international politics. A great epic poem, the *Lusiads* (1572) of Luis de Camoëns (Camões), is their monument.

The sixty years of union between the Spanish and Portuguese monarchies, 1580–1640, accelerated the decline of Portugal's imperial fortunes by involving her in prolonged worldwide warfare with Spain's great adversary, the Dutch republic. Better-equipped and better-disciplined Dutch forces drove the Portuguese from most of their posts in Indonesia and from Ceylon and parts of the Indian coast. Yet a Portuguese empire did survive along the old route around Africa to Goa, on the island of Timor in Indonesia, and in Macao in China. And it survived all the way down to 1974, when the overthrow of the right-wing dictatorship in Lisbon ended the stubborn Portuguese effort to resist the increasingly determined attempts by natives to expel the Portuguese from their major African colonies —Portuguese Guinea and Angola on the west coast, and Mozambique on the east. Thus the first colonial empire in Africa became the last. It endured so long because until 1974 the Portuguese never voluntarily relinquished any territories; the Republic of India had to seize Goa by force in 1961. Another reason for the longevity of the empire in the face of such active and hungry competitors as the French, Dutch, and British lay in the fact that, while Portugal's most successful rivals took away her leadership, they left her a partner in the competition. Finally, the survival of the Portuguese empire was greatly aided by the fact that the greatest of the European imperial powers, England, remained through modern times in alliance with Portugal. The complete victory of France or the Netherlands in the colonial scramble might possibly have brought an end to the Portuguese empire.

III West by Sea to the Indies
Columbus and Later Explorers

In the earliest days of concerted effort to explore the oceans, the rulers of Spain had been too busy disposing of the last Muslim state in the peninsula, Granada, and uniting the disparate parts of Spain to patronize scientific exploration as the Portuguese had done. But individual Spanish traders were active, and Spain was growing in prosperity. When Portuguese mariners found the three groups of Atlantic islands—Azores, Madeira, and Canaries—a papal decree assigned the Canaries to the crown of Castile and the others to Portugal. Once the marriage of Ferdinand and Isabella had united Aragon and Castile, Queen Isabella wanted to catch up with the Portuguese. So in 1491, when the fall of Granada seemed imminent, she commissioned Columbus to try out his plan to reach India by going west.

Columbus (1451–1506) was an Italian, born in Genoa. He was essentially self-educated and, at least in navigation and geography, had educated himself very well. His central conception, that it would be possible to reach the Far East—"the Indies"—by sailing westward from Spain, was not uniquely his. That the earth is a globe was a notion entertained by ancient Greek geographers and revived with the renaissance of the classics. Toscanelli at Florence in 1474, Behaim at Nuremberg in the very year of Columbus' voyage, published maps that showed the earth as a globe—but without the Americas, and with the combined Atlantic and Pacific much narrower than they are in fact. The growth of oceanic navigation had made it possible to act on this notion by deliberately sailing west on the Atlantic. But it was still a strikingly novel idea, and a persistent, innovating personality was needed to win support for such an expedition.

With the sole aim of reaching the Indies Columbus might not have been able to set out. But, as his commission from Queen Isabella shows, he was also charged to discover and secure for the Spanish crown new islands and territories, a mission that probably reflects the importance of ancient and medieval legends about Atlantis, Saint Brendan's isle, and other lands beyond the Azores. Even if he did not reach the Indies, there seemed a chance that he would reach something new.

He reached a New World. Setting out from Palos near Cadiz on August 3, 1492, in three very small ships, he made a landfall on an island of the Bahama group on October 12 of the same year, and eventually went on to discover the large islands we know as Cuba and Santo Domingo (Haiti). On a second voyage, in 1493, he went out with seventeen ships and some fifteen hundred colonists, explored further in the Caribbean, and laid the foundations of the Spanish Empire in America. On his third voyage in 1498–1500, he reached the mouth of the Orinoco in South America but encountered difficulties among his colonists and was sent home in irons by the royal governor Bobadilla, who took over the administration of the Indies for the Crown. He was released on his return to Spain, and in 1502–1504 made a fourth and final voyage, in which he reached the mainland at Honduras. He died in comparative obscurity in Spain (1506), totally unaware that he had reached, not Asia, but a new continent.

That continent was, by a caprice of history, not destined to bear his name, though it is now liberally sprinkled with other place names in his honor. News of Columbus' voyage soon spread by word of mouth in Europe, for printing was still in its infancy. There were no newspapers or geographical institutes; the international learned class—the humanists—were more interested in Greek manuscripts than in strange lands; and, from early Portuguese days on, governments had done their best to keep their discoveries as secret as possible. The most effective spreading of the word in print about the New World was done by another Italian in the Spanish service, Amerigo Vespucci, who wrote copiously about his alleged explorations in the immediate footsteps of Columbus. Scholars doubt that Vespucci really made all the discoveries, from the southeastern United States to the tip of South America, that he claimed to have made. But his letters came to the attention of a German theoretical geographer, Martin Waldseemüller, who in 1507 published a map blocking out a landmass in the southern part of the New World that he labeled, from the latinized form of Vespucci's first name, America.

After Columbus, the roster of discovery grew rapidly. Ponce de León reached Florida in 1512, and Balboa in 1513 crossed the Isthmus of Panama and saw a limitless ocean, on the other side of which the Indies did indeed lie, for it was the Pacific. Many other Spaniards and Portuguese in these first two decades of the sixteenth century explored in detail the coasts of what was to be Latin America. It was now quite clear that an immense landmass lay athwart the westward route from Europe to Asia, and that even the narrow Isthmus of Panama was an obstacle not readily to be overcome by a canal. Maritime exploration then turned to the problem of getting around the Americas by sea and into the Pacific. North America proved an obstacle indeed, for none of the great estuaries—Chesapeake, Delaware, Hudson—promising though they looked to the first explorers, did more than dent the great continent, the breadth of which was totally unknown. The St. Lawrence looked even better, for to its first French explorers it seemed like the sought-for strait. But even the St. Lawrence gave out, and the rapids near Montreal, which showed it was only another river after all, received the ironic name of Lachine (China), for this was not the way to China. Not until the mid-nineteenth century was the usually ice-choked "Northwest Passage" in the Arctic discovered by the Englishman Sir John Franklin.

The "Southwest Passage" was found only a generation after Columbus in the course of an expedition that is the most extraordinary of all the great voyages of discovery. Ferdinand Magellan, a Portuguese in the Spanish service, set out in 1519 with a royal commission bidding him to find a way westward to the Spice Islands of Asia. Skirting the coast of South America, he found and guided his ships through the difficult fog-bound passage that bears his name, the Straits of Magellan, reached the Pacific, and crossed it in a voyage of incredible hardship. Scurvy alone, a disease we now know to be caused by lack of vitamin C, meant that he and his men had to surmount torturing illness. After he had reached the islands now known as the Philippines, Magellan was killed in a skirmish with the natives. One of his captains, however, kept on along the known route by the Indian Ocean and the coast of Africa. On September 8, 1522, the *Victoria* and her crew of 18 men—out of 5 ships and 243 men that had sailed in 1519—landed at Cadiz. For the first time, men had circumnavigated the earth and had proved empirically that the world is round.

What these explorations cost in terms of human suffering, what courage and resolution were needed to carry them through, is very hard for our easy-traveling generation to imagine. Here, from the bare report the sailor Pigafetta gives of Magellan's expedition, is a firsthand account of one of the crises:

> Wednesday, the twenty-eighth of November, 1520, we came forth out of the said strait, and entered into the Pacific sea, where we remained three months and twenty days without taking in provisions or other refreshments, and we only ate old biscuit reduced to powder, and full of grubs, and stinking from the dirt which the rats had made on it when eating the good biscuit, and we drank water that was yellow and stinking. We also ate the ox hides which were under the mainyard. . . . Besides the above-named evils, this misfortune which I will mention was the worst, it was that the upper and lower gums of most of our men grew so much that they could not eat, and in this way so many suffered, that nineteen died.*

Foundation of the Spanish Empire

As a by-product of Magellan's voyage, the Spaniards who had sponsored him got a foothold in the Far East, which they had reached by sailing west. As we have seen, by the Treaty of Tordesillas in 1494 Spain and Portugal had divided the world—the world open to trade and empire—along a line that cut through the Atlantic in such a way that Brazil became Portuguese. This same line, extended round the world, cut the Pacific so that some of the islands Magellan discovered came into the Spanish half. Spain conveniently treated the Philippines as if they also came in the Spanish half of the globe, though they are just outside it, and colonized them from Mexico.

Up to now, we have concerned ourselves mostly with maritime explorations and the founding of coastal trading stations. The Spaniards in the New World, however, very soon explored by land, and acquired thousands of square miles of territory. To the explorer by sea there succeeded the conquistador, often of the impoverished, noble hidalgo class, half explorer, half soldier and administrator, and all adventurer. Of the conquistadores, two, Hernando Cortés and Francisco Pizarro, have come down in history with a special aura of tough romance. With a handful of men they conquered the only two civilized regions of the New World: the Aztec empire of Mexico, taken by Cortés with 600 soldiers in 1519, and the Inca empire of Peru, taken by Pizarro with 180 soldiers in 1531–1533. The narrative of these conquests, whether in the classic nineteenth-century histories of the American William Prescott or in the narratives of actual participants, remains among the most fascinating if not among the most edifying chapters of Western history. A book of this scope cannot do justice to the drama of the conquerors of Mexico and Peru, nor to the many other Spaniards who in search of glory, salvation, gold, and excitement toiled up and down these strange new lands—Quesada in New Granada (later Colombia); Coronado, de Soto,

*Lord Stanley of Alderly, *The First Voyage Round the World by Magellan, translated from the accounts of Pigafetta, and other contemporary writers* (London, 1874), pp. 64–65.

and Cabeza de Vaca in the southwest of what became the United States; Mendoza in La Plata (the lands around the river Plate—today Uruguay and Argentina); Valdivia in Chile; Alvarado in Guatemala; and many others, not least Ponce de León hunting for the fountain of eternal youth in Florida.

Unlike the great cultures of India and the Far East, the pre-Columbian cultures of the Americas crumbled under the impact of the Europeans. From Mexico to Bolivia, Paraguay, and Patagonia (in southern Argentina), millions of people survive who are of American Indian stock, and any understanding of Latin America requires some knowledge of their folkways and traditions. Mexican artists and intellectuals in our day proudly hold up their Indian heritage against the Yankees, and against their own europeanized nineteenth-century rulers. But the structure of the Aztec and the Inca empires has simply not survived. The sun god in whose name the Inca ruled, the bloody Aztec god of war, Huitzilopochtli, are no longer a part of the lives of men, as are Confucius and Buddha. Yet the fact that the civilizations of Peru and Central America once existed as large territorial states, and made high achievements in art and science, is further evidence against naive Western notions of white superiority.

Well before the end of the sixteenth century, the work of the conquistadores had been done, and in Latin America the first of the true European colonial empires—in contrast to the trading empires in Africa and Asia—had been founded. Nowhere, save in the region of La Plata and in central Chile, was the native Indian stock eliminated and replaced by a population almost entirely of Old World stock—something that has happened in the United States and Canada save for a tiny Indian minority. Over vast reaches of Mexico and Central and South America, a crust of Spanish or Portuguese formed at the top of society and made Spanish or Portuguese the language of culture; a class of mixed blood, the *mestizos,* was gradually formed from the union, formal or informal, of Europeans and natives; and in many regions the Indians continued to maintain their stock and their old ways of life almost untouched. Finally, wherever, as in the Caribbean, the Indians were exterminated under the pressure of civilization, or, as in Brazil, they proved inadequate as a labor force, the importation of slaves from Africa added another ingredient to the racial mixture.

Moreover, geography and the circumstances of settlement by separate groups of adventurers in each region combined to create a number of separate units of settlement tied together only by their dependence on the Crown and destined to become the independent nation-states of Latin America today. Geography alone was perhaps a fatal obstacle to any subsequent union of the colonies, such as was achieved by the English colonies that became the United States of America. Between such apparently close neighbors as the present Argentine and Chile, for instance, lay the great chain of the Andes, crossed only with great difficulty by high

Machu Picchu, ancient Inca city in the Andes of Peru. Corn and potatoes were grown on the terraces.

mountain passes. Also between the colonies of La Plata and the colonies of Peru and New Granada lay the Andes and the vast tropical rain forests of the Amazon basin, still almost unconquered today. The highlands of Mexico and Central America are as much invitations to local independence as were the mountains of Hellas to the ancient Greeks. Cuba and the other Caribbean islands have the natural independence of islands.

Latin American Empires Evaluated

The Spaniards transported to the New World the centralized administrative institutions of Castile. At the top of the hierarchy were two viceroyalties, that of Peru with its capital at Lima and that of New Spain with its capital at Mexico City. From Lima the viceroy ruled for the Crown over the Spanish part of South America, except Venezuela. From Mexico City the viceroy ruled over the mainland north of Panama, the West Indies, Venezuela, and the Philippines, Each capital had an *audiencia,* a powerful body staffed by professional law-

yers and operating both as a court of law and as an advisory council. During the sixteenth century additional audiencias were established in Santo Domingo, Guatemala, Panama, New Granada, Quito, Manila, and other major centers. In Madrid, a special Council of the Indies formulated colonial policy and supervised its execution.

This was certainly a centralized, paternalistic system of government, which has rightly enough been contrasted with the "salutary neglect" in which the North American colonies were generally left by the home government until the crisis that led to the American Revolution. But it was not—given the vast areas and the varied peoples under its control, it could not be—as rigid in practice as it was in theory. The rudiments of popular consultation of the Spanish colonists existed in the *cabildos abiertos* or assemblies of citizens in the towns. Moreover, as time went on the bureaucracy itself came to be filled largely with colonials, men who had never been in the home country, and who developed a sense of local patriotism and independence.

Early sixteenth-century stone carving of the Aztec god Zipe Totec.

Castrovirrena: a Peruvian mining town in 1613. Llamas are being led toward the town from the works.

Madrid and Seville were simply too far away to enforce all their decisions. Notably in the matter of trade, it proved impossible to maintain the rigid monopolies of mercantilistic theory, which sought to confine trade wholly to the mother country, and to prohibit, or severely limit, domestic industry in the colonies. Local officials connived at a smuggling trade with the English, Dutch, French, and North Americans, which in the eighteenth century reached large proportions.

The hand of Spain was heaviest in the initial period of exploitation, when the rich and easily mined deposits of the precious metals in Mexico and Peru were skimmed off for the benefit both of the Spanish crown, which always got its *quinto,* or fifth, and of the conquistadores and their successors, Spaniards all. This gold and silver did the natives no good, but in the long run it did no good to Spain, since it went to finance a vain bid for European supremacy and to pay for wares needed by the colonies that the mother country did not produce. By the early seventeenth century, when the output of precious metals began a long decline, the economy and society of Spanish America had stabilized. The economy was not progressive, but neither was it hopelessly backward. Colonial wares—sugar, tobacco, chocolate, cotton, hides, and much else— flowed out of Latin America in exchange for manufactured goods and for services. Creoles (American-born of pure European stock) and mestizos were the chief beneficiaries of this trade. Above the African slaves in the social pyramid, but well below the mestizos, were the native Indians. This, then, was a system of social caste based on color, one that never became so rigid as that in North America but that still damaged native pride and self-respect.

Especially in the Caribbean, but to a degree everywhere, the whites tried to use native labor on farms, in the mines, and in transport. The results were disastrous, for epidemics of smallpox and other new diseases introduced by the Europeans decimated the ranks of the native population. In the West Indies the Carib Indians were wiped out, and in central Mexico, scholars have estimated, the total population fell from about nineteen million when Cortés arrived to only some two and a half million eighty years later. Here, as with the gold and silver, some ironic spirit of history seems to have taken revenge on the whites: though the question of the origin of syphilis is still disputed, many historians of medicine believe that it was brought from the West Indies, where it was mild, to Western civilization, where it became virulent. The attempt to regiment native labor in a plantation system or to put it on a semimanorial system of forced labor, known as the *encomienda,* proved almost as disastrous. The encomiendas, which had been developed in Spain itself for lands reconquered from the Muslims, grouped farming villages whose inhabitants were "commended" to the protection of a conquistador or colonist. The "protector" thereby acquired both a source of income without engaging in demeaning labor and an economic base for a potential defiance of central authority. The shortage of native labor made recourse to black slaves inevitable. A final element in the social and racial situation was the character of the colonial whites, who tended to be aggressive and insensitive; by and large, except for some clerics, the gentler souls stayed home.

Yet against all these forces making for harshness and cruelty, there were counteracting forces. Spanish imperial policy toward the natives was in aim by no means ungenerous, and even in execution holds up well in the long and harsh record of intercourse between whites and nonwhites all over the globe. The New Laws of 1542 forbade the transmission of encomiendas by inheritance, thereby striking a blow against feudal decentralization. The New Laws also forbade the enslavement of native Indians, who were regarded as wards of the Crown. The central government in Spain passed many laws to protect the Indians, and though these were often flouted in the colonies—a phenomenon not unknown in the English colonies—they put a limit to wholesale exploitation of the natives. Their cause was championed by men of great distinction, and notably by Bartolomé de las Casas (1474–1566), "Father of the Indians," bishop of Chiapas in Mexico.

Unlike their counterparts in Africa and Asia, the Indian masses were converted to Christianity. More than Spanish pride was involved in the grandiose religious edifices constructed by the colonists and in their elaborate services. Many priests seemed to realize the need to fill the void left in the lives of the Indians by the destruction of old temples and the suppression of complex pagan rituals. Church and state in the Spanish and Portuguese colonies in the New World worked hand in hand, undisturbed for generations by the troubles roused in Europe by the Protestant Reformation and the rise of a secular anti-Christian movement. The Jesuits in Paraguay set up among the Guarani Indians a remarkable society, a benevolent despotism, a utopia of good order, good habits, and eternal childhood for the Guarani. On the northern fringes of the Spanish world, where it was to meet the Anglo-Saxons, a long line of missions in California and the Southwest held the frontier. Everywhere save in wildest Amazonia and other untamed areas, the Christianity of the Roman Catholic church brought to the natives a veneer of Western tradition, and made them in some sense part of this strange new society of the white men.

In their close union of church and state, in their very close ties with the home country, in their mercantilist economics, and in still other respects, the Portuguese settlements in Brazil resembled those of the Spaniards elsewhere in Latin America. Yet there were significant differences. The Portuguese settlements were almost entirely rural: Brazil had nothing to compare with the urban splendor of Mexico City or Lima. A large number of black slaves were imported into the tropical areas of Brazil, and, because the white males drew no sexual color line, the races became more thoroughly mixed in colonial times than they did in most

Spanish colonies except Cuba. Finally, perhaps because of the relative proximity of Brazil to European waters, the Portuguese had more troubles with rival nations than the Spaniards did. The existence on relatively recent maps of those fragments of imperial hopes—French Guiana, Surinam (Netherlands Guiana, partially autonomous in 1975 and scheduled for independence by the end of the year), and Guyana (independent since 1966, but a British colony before then)—bears witness to the fact that the northern maritime nations made a serious effort to settle on the northern fringes of Brazil.

IV   The North Atlantic Powers and Russia

Spain and Portugal enjoyed a generation's head start in exploration and one of nearly a century in founding empires of settlement. Without this head start, which they owed in part to their position as heirs of the Mediterranean trade, Spain and Portugal could scarcely have made the great mark in the world that they did. For the northern Atlantic states soon made up for their late start. As early as 1497 the Cabots, father and son, Italians in the English service, saw something of the North American coast, and gave the English territorial claims based on their explorations. In the first half of the sixteenth century the explorations of another Italian, Verrazzano, and the Frenchman Jacques Cartier gave France competing claims, which were reinforced in the early seventeenth century by the detailed explorations of Champlain. Dutch claims began with the voyages of Henry Hudson, an Englishman who entered their service in 1609.

English, Dutch, and Swedes in North America

The English did not immediately follow up the work of the Cabots. Instead, they put their energies into the profitable business of interloping, that is, of breaking into the Spanish trading monopoly. John Hawkins, in 1562, started the English slave trade, and his nephew, Francis Drake, penetrated to the Pacific, reached California, which he claimed for England under the name of New Albion, and returned to England by the Pacific and Indian oceans, completing the first English circumnavigation of the globe (1577–1580). Under Sir Humphrey Gilbert in 1583 the English staked out a claim to Newfoundland, which gave them a share in the great fishing grounds off northeastern North America.

In 1584, Sir Walter Raleigh unsuccessfully attempted to found a settlement on Roanoke Island (in present-day North Carolina) in a land the English named Virginia, after their Virgin Queen, Elizabeth. Early in the next century the English established two permanent footholds at Jamestown in Virginia (1607) and at Plymouth on Massachusetts Bay (1620). Both were to become colonies of settlement, in which the sparse Indian population was exterminated and replaced by men and women for the most part of British stock. But in their inception both were nearer the pattern of trading posts set by the Spanish and Portuguese. Both were established by chartered trading companies with headquarters in England; both, and especially the Virginian, cherished at first high hopes that they would find, as the Spaniards had, great stores of precious metals. Both were disappointed in these hopes and only just managed to survive the first terrible years of hardship. Tobacco, first cultivated in 1612, and the almost legendary Captain John Smith, explorer and man of resourcefulness, saved the Virginia colony; and furs (notably beaver), codfish, and Calvinist toughness saved Plymouth. Both colonies gradually built up an agricultural economy, supplemented by trade with the mother country and interloping trade with the West Indies. Neither received more than a few tens of thousands of immigrants from abroad. Yet both these and the later colonies expanded by natural increase in a country of abundant land for the taking. The thirteen colonies by 1776 were a substantial series of settlements with almost three million inhabitants.

Before these English colonies were completed one important and one very minor foreign group had to be pushed out. The Dutch, following up the explorations of Hudson, had founded the colony of New Amsterdam (1626) at the mouth of the river that bears his name and had begun to push into the fur trade. This made them rivals of the English and of the French, farther north in Canada. In a war with England in the 1660s, however, the Dutch lost New Amsterdam, which was annexed by the English in 1664 and renamed New York. The Dutch, though very few in number, left descendants prominent in the future United States, as such names as *Stuyvesant, Schuyler,* and *Roosevelt* suggest.

The minor competitors were the Swedes, who founded Fort Christiana (1638) on the Delaware near present-day Wilmington. But New Sweden was never a great enterprise, and in 1655 Fort Christiana was taken over by the Dutch, who in turn were ousted by the English. Pennsylvania, chartered to the wealthy English Quaker William Penn in 1681, filled the vacuum left by the expulsion of Swedes and Dutch from the Delaware. It was to become the keystone colony before it became the keystone state.

The arch of colonies, in which Pennsylvania formed the keystone, reached from Maine to Georgia and numbered thirteen, each founded separately and each with its own charter. American tradition perhaps exaggerates the differences between the southern and northern groups of colonies. Massachusetts was not wholly settled by democratic plain people, "Roundheads," nor was Virginia settled wholly by great English landowners, gentlemen or "Cavaliers," and their retainers. All the colonies were settled by a varied human lot, which ranged from the gentry at the top down to members of the poorest classes, who immigrated either as indentured servants or as impressed seamen who deserted ship.

Still, it is true that New England was for the most part settled by Calvinist Independents (Congregationalists), already committed to wide local self-government and to a distrust of a land-owning aristocracy; and it is true that the southern colonies, especially tidewater Virginia, were settled for the most part by Anglicans used to the existence of social distinctions and to large landholdings. In Virginia, the Church of England became the established church; in Massachusetts, the Puritan Congregationalists, nonconformists in the homeland, almost automatically became conformists in their new home, and set up their own variety of state church. Geography, climate, and a complex of social and economic factors drove the South to plantation monoculture of tobacco, rice, indigo, or cotton even in colonial days and drove New England and the Middle Colonies to small farming by independent farmer-owners and to small-scale industry and commerce. Yet the small farmers in the Piedmont sections of Virginia and the Carolinas represented a very northern mixture of Presbyterians, Scotch-Irish, and Germans from Pennsylvania. Some historians hold that the natural environment, and not any original difference of social structure and religious belief, accounts for the diverging cultures of North and South and their eventual armed conflict.

To us who are their heirs, it has seemed that these English colonists brought with them the religious freedom, the government by discussion, and the democratic society of which we are so proud. So they did, though they brought the seeds, the potentialities, rather than the fully developed institutions. These colonists came from an England where the concept of freedom of religion was only beginning to emerge; it was quite natural for the Virginians and the New Englanders to set up state churches. Yet these immigrants represented too many conflicting religious groups to enforce anything like the religious uniformity that prevailed in the Spanish colonies or in Canada. Even in Calvinist New England "heresy" appeared from the start, with the presence of Baptists, Quakers, and even Anglicans. Moreover, some of the colonies were founded by groups that from the first practiced religious freedom and separated church and state. In Pennsylvania, founded by Quakers who believed firmly in such separation; in Maryland, founded in part to give refuge to the most distrusted of groups at home, the Catholics; in Rhode Island, founded by Roger Williams and others unwilling to conform to the orthodoxy of Massachusetts Bay—in all these colonies there was something like the complete religious freedom that was later embodied in the Constitution of the United States.

The seeds of democracy, too, existed, although the early settlers, not only in Virginia but even in the North, readily accepted class distinctions. No formal colonial nobility ever arose, however, and the early tendency to develop a privileged gentry or squirearchy in the coastal regions was balanced by the equalitarianism of the frontier and by careers open to talent in the towns. Government by discussion was firmly planted in the colonies from the start. All of them, even the proprietary colonies, which were granted to a single proprietor (Pennsylvania) or to a group of proprietors (the Carolinas and Georgia), had some kind of colonial legislative body.

Here we come to the critical difference between the English colonies in the New World and the Spanish and French colonies. In Spain and France the governments were already centralized bureaucratic monarchies; their representative assemblies were no more than consultative and had no power over taxation. Royal governors in Latin America and in New France could really run their provinces, leaning on men they appointed and recalled, and raising funds by their own authority. England, while also a monarchy, was a parliamentary monarchy, torn by two revolutions in the seventeenth century. Though the Crown was represented in most colonies by a royal governor, the English government had no such bureaucracy as the Spanish and French had. Royal governors in the English colonies had hardly even a clerical staff and met with great difficulty in raising money from their legislative assemblies. The history of the colonies is full of bickerings in which the governor, with little local support and only sporadic backing from the home government, was often stalemated. Furthermore, in all the colonies the established landowners, merchants and professional men, though not necessarily all adult males, participated not only in colonial assemblies but also in local units of government—towns in New England, counties elsewhere. Finally, the settlers brought with them the common law of England, with its trial by jury and its absence of bureaucratic administrative law.

New France
To the north of the thirteen colonies, in the region of the Bay of Fundy and in the St. Lawrence basin, the French built on the work of Cartier and Champlain. New France was to be for a century and a half a serious threat to its southern neighbors. The St. Lawrence and the Great Lakes gave the French easy access to the heart of the continent, in contrast to the Appalachian ranges that stood between the English and the Mississippi. The French were also impelled westward by their search for furs, which are goods of great value and comparatively little bulk, easily carried in canoes and small boats. Moreover, led by the Jesuits, the Catholic French gave proof of a far greater missionary zeal than did the Protestant English. The priest, as well as the *coureur des bois* (trapper), led the push westward. Finally, the French in North America were guided by a conscious imperial policy directed from the France of the Bourbon monarchs, *la grande nation* at the height of its prestige and power.

Accordingly, it was the French, not the English, who explored the interior of the continent. By 1712 they had built up a line of isolated trading posts, with miles of empty space between, thinly populated by Indians, which completely encircled the English colonies on the Atlantic coast. The story of these French explorers, missionaries, and traders, admirably told by the American historian Francis Parkman, is one of the most fascinating pages of history. The names of many of them—La Salle, Père Marquette, Joliet, Frontenac, Cadillac, Iberville—are a part of our American heritage. Lines of outposts led westward from Quebec to the Great Lakes, and other lines moved northward up the Mississippi to meet them from Mobile and New Orleans, where a colony named Louisiana, after Louis XIV, had been founded at the beginning of the eighteenth century.

Yet, impressive though this French imperial thrust looks on the map, it was far too lightly held to be equal to the task of pushing the English into the sea. It was a trading empire with military ambitions, and except in Quebec it never became a true colony of settlement. And even there it never grew in the critical eighteenth century beyond a few thousand inhabitants. Frenchmen simply did not come over in sufficient numbers, and those who did come spread themselves out over vast distances as traders and simple adventurers. Frenchmen who might have come, the Huguenots who might have settled down as did the Yankee Puritans, were excluded by a royal policy bent on maintaining the Catholic faith in New France.

The Indies, West and East
The northwestern European maritime powers intruded upon the pioneer Spanish and Portuguese both in the New World and in the Old. The French, Dutch, and English all sought to gain footholds in South America, but had to settle for the unimportant Guianas. They broke up thoroughly the Spanish hold on the Caribbean, however, and ultimately made that sea of many islands a kaleidoscope of colonial jurisdictions and a center of constant naval wars and piracy. Today, these West Indian islands are a depressed area, with the tourist industry their main hope; in early modern times, however, they were one of the great prizes of imperialism. The cheap slave labor that had replaced the exterminated Carib Indians raised for their masters on the plantations the great staple crops: tobacco, fruits, coffee, and, most basic of all, cane sugar (there was then no threat of competition from the beet sugar that northern countries began to produce around 1800).

By 1715 the French, Dutch, and English had also laid the bases of trading and colonial empires in Asia and Africa. India proved to be the richest prize, and the most ardently fought for. The Mogul Empire was not strong enough in southern India to keep the Europeans out, but it did prove strong enough to confine them on the whole to the coastal fringes. Gradually, in the course of the seventeenth century both the French and the English established themselves in India on the heels of decaying Portuguese power and wealth. The English defeated a Portuguese fleet in 1612 and immediately thereafter got trading rights at Surat on the western coast. Although the able and active Mogul emperor Aurangzeb tried to revoke their rights in 1685, he soon found their naval and mercantile power too much to withstand. In 1690, the English founded in Bengal in eastern India the city they were to make famous, Calcutta. Meanwhile, the French had got a foothold on the south coast near Madras, at Pondichéry, and soon had established other stations. By the beginning of the eighteenth century, the stage was set in India as in North America for the decisive struggle for overseas empire between France and Britain.

Both countries operated in India, as they had initially in North America, by means of chartered trading companies, the English East India Company and the French Compagnie des Indes Orientales. In their trading activities the companies were backed up by their governments when it was evident that the whole relation with India could not be purely commercial and that some territories around the trading posts had to be held. Although both countries became involved in Indian politics and warfare to support their trading companies, neither attempted to found a New England or New France in the East.

The Dutch entered even more vigorously into the competition, founding their own East India (1602) and West India (1621) companies. In sharp contrast to the close government supervision exerted by Spain and Portugal over colonial activities every step of the way, the Dutch granted these private business ventures full sovereign powers. They had the right to maintain their own fighting fleets and armies, declare war and wage it, negotiate peace, and govern dependent territories. The Netherlands East India Company succeeded in pushing the Portuguese out of Ceylon and then, bypassing India proper, concentrated on southeastern Asia, especially the East Indies. Here again they pushed the Portuguese out, save for part of the island of Timor, and they also discouraged English interlopers. And through it all the company paid an annual dividend averaging 18 percent. In spite of their rapid decline as a great power in the eighteenth century, the Dutch got so firm a hold in Java and Sumatra that their empire in Indonesia was to last until the mid-twentieth century.

Africa and the Far East

To reach the East all three of the northern maritime powers used the ocean route around Africa that the Portuguese had pioneered in the fifteenth century. All three got African posts, with the Dutch occupying the strategic Cape of Good Hope at the southern tip of the continent in 1652. While the cape was at first a fitting station for Dutch ships on the long voyage to Indonesia and the Far East, it was empty except for primitive tribes and had a temperate climate. Though immigration was never heavy, a colony of settlement grew up peopled by Dutch and by French Huguenots, the ancestors of the Afrikaners of South Africa today. In West Africa the Dutch took from the Portuguese posts on the Gold and Guinea coasts and won a share of the increasingly lucrative slave trade.

The French also worked down the Atlantic coast, taking Senegal (1626) at the westernmost point of the African bulge, and later acquiring in the Indian Ocean the large island of Madagascar and the smaller one of Mauritius, taken from the Dutch. The British secured a foothold at the mouth of the Gambia River near Senegal (1662) and later made acquisitions at the expense of the French and the Dutch. Thus by the eighteenth century a map of Africa and adjacent waters shows a series of coastal stations controlled by various European powers. But the interior remained for the most part unexplored, untouched except by slavers and native traders. Only in the nineteenth century was "the Dark Continent" opened to European expansion.

The Far East, too, was not truly opened to Western imperialism until the nineteenth century. In China, the Portuguese did cling to Macao, and the Dutch, on their heels as always, obtained a station on Taiwan (1624), an island that the Portuguese had christened Formosa ("beautiful"). The Jesuits, bringing with them European instruments and learning that interested the Chinese, were tolerated in the seventeenth century, but they made little headway in missionary activity. At bottom the Chinese, convinced that their empire was the Middle Kingdom, central in a spiritual and cultural sense, regarded most Europeans as barbarians who should be paying them tribute.

In Japan, the reaction against European penetration was even stronger than in China. The Portuguese won trading privileges in the sixteenth century, followed by the Dutch in 1609; meantime, the great Jesuit missionary, Francis Xavier, began work in 1549. Though Christianity did not make wholesale conversions, it did make considerable headway. The Tokugawa family, the feudal military rulers of Japan from 1600 to 1868, feared Christianity not only as a threat to national traditions but also as a threat to their own rule, because of the opportunities it might give European powers to intervene in Japanese politics and intrigue with their enemies. They therefore decided to close their land entirely to foreign dangers. In the early seventeenth century, they suppressed Christianity by force and sealed off Japan. Foreigners were refused entry, and Japanese were refused exit; even the building of large ships capable of sailing the ocean was forbidden. The Dutch, who had persuaded the Japanese that Protestants were less subversive than the Catholic Portuguese, were allowed, under strict supervision, to retain an island in Nagasaki harbor, where after 1715 they were limited to two ships a year. Not until the American Commodore Perry came to Japan in 1853 was this amazing self-blockade really broken.

East by Land to the Pacific

The expansion of Europe in the early modern centuries was not restricted to the Atlantic maritime powers. The

The Great Wall of China, built in the third century B.C. to guarantee an isolation that proved elusive.

Russian exploration and conquest of Siberia offer all sorts of parallels with European expansion in the New World, from the chronological (the Russians crossed the Urals from Europe into Asia in 1483) to the political, for the expanding Muscovite state of Russia was a "new" monarchy, newer in some ways than the Spain of Charles V and Philip II or the England of Elizabeth I. This Russian movement has also been likened to the American expansion from the Atlantic seaboard to the Pacific. Compared with the Russian advance to the Pacific, the American westward movement was relatively slow: the Russians covered some five thousand miles in about forty years; we took longer to go a shorter distance. But the Russian advance left vast areas "behind the lines" unsettled and unabsorbed, whereas our own more gradual movement was more thorough. In contrast to the American, who faced formidable mountains and deserts, the Russian had easier going on the enormous flatlands of the Siberian river basins. For the Americans too, the Indians often posed serious military and political problems, whereas the Siberian tribesmen, widely scattered across the area, seem on the whole to have helped the Russians. Though enormous

in extent, Siberia continued to be very sparsely inhabited.

The victories of Ivan the Terrible over the Volga Tatars led to the first major advances, with private enterprise in the van. By the end of the sixteenth century the Stroganov family had obtained huge concessions in the Ural area, where they made a great fortune in the fur trade and discovered and exploited Russia's first iron mines. The Stroganovs hired bands of Cossack explorers, who led the eastward movement; their Daniel Boone was the famous Yermak, whose exploits took on legendary proportions. At a suitable point on a river basin, the spearhead of the advance party would build a wooden palisade and begin to collect furs from the surrounding area. Almost before the defense of each new position had been consolidated, the restless advance guard would have moved hundreds of miles farther eastward to repeat the process until Okhotsk on the Pacific was reached in the 1640s.

The government followed at some distance behind with administrators and tax collectors, soldiers and priests, as each new district was opened up. A Siberian bureau in Moscow had nominal responsibility for the

The Dutch outpost in Nagasaki harbor, 1689.

government of the huge area, but decisions had to be made on the spot because of the communications problem, although the Russians had an efficient postal service working quite early. Thus the Siberians always tended to have the independence traditionally associated with men of the wide open spaces, and reinforced by the Cossack and outlaw traditions from which many of them sprang. Because Ohkotsk and its neighborhood along the Pacific were intensely cold, and the ocean frozen for many months in the year, the Russians were soon looking enviously southward toward the valley of the Amur River, which flowed into the Pacific at a point where the harbors were open all the year round.

Explorations in this area brought the Russians into contact with the Chinese, whose lands they were now casually invading. But the Chinese government of the period did not care very much about these regions, which, from its own point of view, were far-northerly outposts. In 1689 the Chinese signed with Moscow the Treaty of Nerchinsk, the first they had concluded with any European state. The treaty stabilized the frontier, demilitarized the Amur valley, and kept the Russians out of Manchuria, the home territory of the ruling Chinese dynasty, though it recognized the Russian ad-

vances farther north. It also provided the two powers with a buffer zone of Mongolian territory, which acknowledged Chinese overlordship. Thus, with almost incredible speed the Russians had acquired an empire whose riches are still incompletely exploited today and had staked out a future as an Asian power with interests in the Pacific at just about the time the English took New Amsterdam from the Dutch.

North by Sea to the Arctic

By 1715, the expansion of Europe was beginning to affect almost every part of the globe. European explorers, missionaries, traders, proconsuls of empire, had spread out in all directions. Even Arctic exploration, stimulated by the hope of finding a Northwest or a Northeast Passage that would shorten the route to the Far East, had already gone a long way by the beginning of the eighteenth century. Henry Hudson had found not only the Hudson River but also Hudson's Bay in the far north of Canada. In the late seventeenth century, English adventurers and investors formed an enterprise that still flourishes in Canada today—the Hudson's Bay Company, originally set up for fur trading along the great bay to the northwest of the French settlement in Quebec. In the late sixteenth century, the Dutch had penetrated far into the European Arctic, had discovered the island of Spitsbergen to the north of Norway, and had ranged eastward across the Barents Sea named after their leader. Early in the eighteenth century the Russians also explored most of the long Arctic coasts of their empire, and the Dane Bering, in Russian service, discovered the Aleutian Islands and the sea and strait bearing his name separating northeastern Siberia from Alaska.

V The Impact of Expansion
The Human and Economic Record

The record of European expansion contains pages as grim as any in history. The African slave trade, begun by the Portuguese and entered by other peoples for its financial gains, is a series of horrors, from the rounding up of the slaves by native chieftains in Africa through their transportation across the Atlantic to their sale in the Indies. What strikes a modern most of all is the matter-of-fact acceptance of this trade, as if the blacks were so much livestock. The Dutch slave ship *St. Jan* (note the irony of the saint's name) started off for Curaçao in the West Indies in 1659. Her log recorded every day or so deaths of slaves aboard, until between June 30 and October 29 a total of 59 men, 47 women, and 4 children had died. There were still 95 slaves aboard when disaster struck, thus matter-of-factly recorded:

> *Nov. 1.* Lost our ship on the Reef of Rocus, and all hands immediately took to the boat, as there was no prospect of saving the slaves, for we must abandon the ship in consequence of the heavy surf.

> *Nov. 4.* Arrived with the boat at the island of Curaçao; the Hon'ble Governor Beck ordered two sloops to take the slaves off the wreck, one of which sloops with eighty four slaves on board was captured by a privateer.*

And here is the Hon'ble Governor Beck's report to his Board of Directors in Holland:

> What causes us most grief here is, that your honors have thereby lost such a fine lot of negroes and such a fast sailing bark which has been our right arm here.

> Although I have strained every nerve to overtake the robbers of the negroes and bark, as stated in my last, yet have I not been as successful as I wished. . . .

> We regret exceedingly that such rovers should have been the cause of the ill success of the zeal we feel to attract the Spanish traders hither for your honors' benefit, . . . for the augmentation of commerce and the sale of the negroes which are to come here more and more in your honors' ships and for your account. . . .

> I have witnessed with pleasure your honors' diligence in providing us here from time to time with negroes. That will

*E. Donnan, ed., *Documents Illustrative of the History of the Slave Trade to America*, (Washington, D.C., 1930), 1:143.

be the only bait to allure hither the Spanish nation, as well from the Main as from other parts, to carry on trade of any importance. But the more subtly and quietly the trade to and on this island can be carried on, the better will it be for this place and yours.*

Americans need hardly be reminded of the fact that we virtually exterminated the native Indian population east of the Mississippi and that, if they massacred us when they could, we replied in kind often enough, and with superior means. There were, of course, exceptions to this bloody rule. In New England, missionaries like John Eliot did set up little bands of "praying Indians," and in Pennsylvania, the record of the relations between the Quakers and the Indians was excellent. The white man's diseases, which in those days could hardly have been controlled, and the white man's alcoholic drinks, which were quite as hard to control, did more to exterminate the red men than did fire and sword.

Seen in terms of economics, however, the expansion of Europe in early modern times was by no means the pure "exploitation" and "plundering" it sometimes appears to be in the rhetoric of antiimperialists. There was robbery, just as there was murder or enslavement. There was, in dealing with the natives, even more giving of slight or nominal value in exchange for land and goods of great value. Just as all Americans are familiar with the slogan "The only good Indian is a dead Indian," so they know for how little the Indians sold the island of Manhattan. Finally, the almost universally applied mercantilist policy kept money and manufacturing in the hands of the home country. It relegated the colonies to the production of raw materials, a role that tended to keep even colonies of settlement in a relatively primitive and economically dependent condition.

While Europeans took the lion's share of colonial wealth in the early modern centuries, some of the silver from America financed European imports of spices and luxuries from Asia. Not many European mercantilist monopolies were watertight in practice so that enterprising natives shared in the new trade and its profits. Although few Europeans settled in India or in Africa, their wares, and especially their weapons, began gradually the modernizing process that would ultimately produce the worldwide "revolution of rising expectations" of our own day. By the eighteenth century this process was only beginning, and in particular few of the improvements in public health and sanitation that Europeans would bring to the East later on had yet come about; nor had greater public order come to India or Africa as it eventually would.

Effects of Expansion on the West

The West has in its turn been greatly affected by its relations with other peoples. The list of items that have

*Ibid., 1:150–151.

come into Western life since Marco Polo and Columbus is long. It includes foodstuffs above all; utensils and gadgets, pipes for smoking, hammocks and pajamas; styles of architecture and painting, bungalows and Japanese prints; and much else. Some of the novelties caught on more quickly than others. Tobacco, brought into Spain in the mid-sixteenth century as a soothing drug, had established itself by the seventeenth century as essential to the peace of mind of many European males. Maize or Indian corn (in Europe, "corn" refers to cereal grains in general) was imported from the New World and widely cultivated in well-watered areas of Spain and Italy. Potatoes, on the other hand, though their calorie content is high and though they are cheaper to grow in most climates than the staple bread-stuffs, did not immediately catch on in Europe. In France, they had to be popularized in a regular campaign that took generations to be effective. Tomatoes, the "love-apples" of our great-grandfathers, were long believed to be poisonous and were cultivated only for their looks. Tea and coffee, which Europeans and North Americans now take for granted as imports everyone uses, were just beginning to become available in large quantities by 1700.

Among Westerners, knowledge of non-European beliefs and institutions eventually penetrated to the level of popular culture, where it is marked by a host of words—"powwow," "kowtow," "taboo," "totem," for instance. At the highest level of cultural interchange, that of religion and ethical ideas, however, the West took little from the new worlds opened after Columbus. The first impression of Westerners, not only when they met the relatively primitive cultures of the New World, but even when they met the old cultures of the East, was that they had nothing to learn from them. Once the process of interchange had gone far enough, some individuals were impressed with the mysticism and otherworldliness of Hindu philosophy and religion, and with the high but quite this-worldly ethics of Chinese Confucianism. Others came to admire the dignity and simplicity of the lives of many primitive peoples. But for the most part what struck the Europeans—when they bothered at all to think about anything more than money making and empire building—was the poverty, dirt, and superstition they found among the masses in India and China, the low material standards of primitive peoples everywhere, the heathenness of the heathens.

Yet exposure to these very different cultures also stimulated Western minds and broadened intellectual horizons. The first effect was perhaps no more than to increase the fund of the marvelous and incredible. Early accounts of the New World are full of giants and pygmies, El Dorados where the streets are paved with gold, fountains of eternal youth, wonderful plants and animals. Soon, however, serious science was encouraged. A dip into any of the early accounts of voyages, say the famous collection edited in English by Richard Hakluyt in 1582, gives an impression more of the realis-

tic sense and careful observation of these travelers than of their credulity and exaggerations. Here is modern geography already well on its way to maturity, and here too are the foundations of the modern social sciences of anthropology, comparative government, even of economics. A good example is the report by an early seventeenth-century Italian traveler on the puzzling Hindu institution of caste:

> The whole Gentile-people of *India* is divided into many sects or parties of men, known and distinguisht by descent or pedigree, as the Tribes of the Jews sometimes were; yet they inhabit the Country promiscuously mingled together, in every City and Land several Races one with another. 'Tis reckon'd that they are in all eighty four; some say more, making a more exact and subtle division. Every one of these hath a particular name, and also a special office and Employment in the Commonwealth, from which none of the descendants of that Race ever swerve; they never rise nor fall, nor change condition: whence some are Husbandmen, others Mechanicks, as Taylers, Shoemakers and the like; others Factors or Merchants, such as they whom we call *Banians*, but they in their Language more correctly *Vania*; others, Souldiers, as the *Ragiaputi*; . . . so many Races which they reckon are reduc'd to four principal, which, if I mistake not, are the Brachmans, the Souldiers, the Merchants and the Artificers; from whom by more minute subdivision all the rest are deriv'd, in such number as in the whole people there are various professions of men.*

It may well be that the intellectual effects of the great discoveries were on the whole unsettling, disturbing. They helped, along with the new astronomy, the new mechanics, the Protestant Reformation, and much else, to break the medieval "cake of custom." They helped, literally, to make a New World of ideas and ideals. Such changes are always hard on ordinary human beings, for they demand that men change their minds, something that most of us find very hard to do.

The great discoveries also helped to revolutionize the economy and society of Europe; we already have seen some instances of how this came about. By the middle of the seventeenth century, Spain is estimated to have imported eighteen thousand tons of bullion from the Americas—enough to increase the gold supply of Europe by 20 percent and the silver supply by 300 percent. Everywhere new coins were circulated, and everywhere prices rose—by some 400 percent in Spain during the sixteenth century, by less dramatic but substantial amounts elsewhere. This rise in prices accompanied and helped to cause a general economic expansion that ultimately produced the Industrial Revolution.

In the long process of inflation and expansion, which has continued with ups and downs to the present, some groups gained and others lost. In general, merchants, financiers, and businessmen in general enjoyed a rising standard of living. Those on relatively fixed incomes suffered, including landed proprietors, unless

*E. Grey, ed., *The Travels of Pietro della Valle in India* (London, 1892), 1:78–79.

they turned to large-scale capitalist farming, and also governments, unless they were able to find new sources of income. Wage earners, artisans, peasants, and the general majority of people usually did not find their incomes keeping pace with the rise in prices. In short, here as elsewhere, the effects of expansion were unsettling, even harsh, as well as stimulating.

The American historian Walter P. Webb, in *The Great Frontier*, made a still more sweeping generalization about the effects of expansion. The vast lands of the "frontier" in the New World, he maintained, were a bonanza or windfall, and supplied the real force behind the great increase in man's power to get more out of his natural environment with less sacrifice—and this unprecedented wealth and power, in turn, constitute the great innovation of modern Western civilization. As a sympathetic British historian recently observed, Webb's frontier thesis "deserves two cheers for gallantry, although not—regrettably—three cheers for success." * Once again we find that the attempt to make a single explanation of the great movements of history is dangerous. The opportunities for expansion that the discoveries gave to Europeans were obviously one factor in the rapid growth of productivity, population, and technical skills. By the late sixteenth century the easily acquired supplies of silver from the New World were priming the pumps of developing capitalism in northwest Europe.

But, by the mid-seventeenth century, the effects of this particular pump-priming were fading, as silver became scarcer and more costly, and as the colonial manufactures began to increase, and the colonial market for European goods to diminish, in defiance of the strictures of mercantilism. The frontier theory of modern Western capitalist society is no more convincing as a sole explanation than, say, the Marxist theory of economic determinism or the Weber thesis about the Protestant ethic. The roots of the great discoveries themselves, like the roots of capitalism, Protestantism and modern science, lie deep in the Middle Ages. Before

*J. H. Elliott, *The Old World and the New* (Cambridge, 1970), p. 59.

new worlds could be accessible to European enterprise trade, navigation and government organization all had to arrive at the point where Henry the Navigator, Columbus, da Gama, and the others could proceed methodically to the explorations and the conquests that had been there, after all, for the Greeks, the Phoenicians, the Romans, or the Vikings to make, had they been able and willing.

Toward One World

"There is only one world, and although we speak of the Old World and the New, this is because the latter was lately discovered by us, and not because there are two." * These words were written by a Spaniard in sixteenth-century Peru. By the beginning of the eighteenth century—although there were still blank spots on the map, especially in the African interior and the Pacific northwest of America, and although Japan and China still tried to exclude European influence—it was already clear that only one system of international politics existed in the world. All general European wars now tended to be world wars, fought, if only by privateers, on the seven seas and, if only by savages and frontiersmen, on distant continents. Sooner or later, any considerable transfer of territory overseas and any great accession of strength or wealth in any quarter of the globe affected the international balance of power.

The One World of the eighteenth century was not one world of the spirit; the great mass of Europeans were ignorant of what really went on in the hearts and minds of men elsewhere. But already Western goods penetrated almost everywhere, led by firearms and liquor, but followed by a great many other commodities, not all of them "cheap and nasty," as later critics of imperialism would complain. Already an educated minority was appearing, from professional geographers to journalists, diplomats, and businessmen, who dealt with what were now quite literally the affairs of the world.

*Ibid., p. 102.

Reading Suggestions on the Expansion of Europe
Background and General Accounts

J. H. Parry, *The Age of Reconnaissance* (*Mentor) and *The Establishment of the European Hegemony, 1415–1715: Trade and Exploration in the Age of the Renaissance* (*Torchbooks). Excellent introductions by a ranking expert in the field.

C. E. Nowell, *The Great Discoveries and the First Colonial Empires* (*Cornell Univ.). Handy brief introduction.

B. Penrose, *Travel and Discovery in the Renaissance, 1420–1620* (*Atheneum). Very informative survey with accounts of voyages not easily available elsewhere.

J. N. L. Baker, *A History of Geographical Discovery and Exploration*, rev. ed. (Barnes & Noble, 1963). A standard work.

P. Sykes, *A History of Exploration from the Earliest Times to the Present* (Routledge, 1934). A comprehensive treatment of the subject.

C. R. Beazley, *The Dawn of Modern Geography*, 3 vols. (John Murray, 1897–1906). An authoritative account; stops in 1420 but useful for the background of this chapter.

G. Jones, *The Norse Atlantic Saga* (Oxford Univ., 1964). A reliable summary of Viking exploration.

H. Trevor-Roper, ed., *The Age of Expansion: Europe and the World, 1559–1660* (McGraw-Hill, 1968). Less comprehensive in treatment than the title suggests, but with enlightening chapters on the Spaniards, the Dutch, and the Far East.

The Portuguese

C. R. Boxer, *The Portuguese Seaborne Empire, 1415–1825* (Knopf, 1969). Admirable study in the History of Human Society series. Boxer has also written a succinct survey covering the same period: *Four Centuries of Portuguese Expansion* (*Univ. of California).

E. Sanceau, *Henry the Navigator* (Norton, 1947). A good biography of the Portuguese sponsor of exploration.

H. H. Hart, *Sea Road to the Indies* (Macmillan, 1950). Deals with da Gama and other Portuguese explorers.

C. McK. Parr, *So Noble a Captain* (Crowell, 1953). A very scholarly treatment of Magellan and his circumnavigation.

The Spaniards

J. H. Parry, *The Spanish Seaborne Empire* (Knopf, 1966). Excellent account in the useful History of Human Society series.

S. E. Morison, *Admiral of the Ocean Sea,* 2 vols. (Little, Brown, 1942). The best book on Columbus; by a historian who retraced Columbus' route in a small ship. He has also published the briefer *Christopher Columbus, Mariner* (*Mentor).

C. H. Haring, *The Spanish Empire in America* (*Harcourt). A standard treatment of the subject.

W. H. Prescott, *The Conquest of Mexico* and *The Conquest of Peru* (many editions). Celebrated narratives written more than a century ago; may be sampled in various abridgments, among them *The Portable Prescott* (*Viking).

L. B. Hanke, *The Spanish Struggle for Justice in the Conquest of America* (*Little, Brown). Study of an important and often neglected side of the Spanish record.

The Dutch

C. R. Boxer, *The Dutch Seaborne Empire, 1600–1800* (Hutchinson, 1965). Full, up-to-date survey by a capable scholar: another volume in the History of Human Society series.

A. Hyma, *The Dutch in the Far East* (Wahr, 1942). Stressing social and economic developments.

B. H. M. Vlekke, *Nusantara: A History of Indonesia,* rev. ed. (Lorenz, 1959). Introduction to the most important region of Dutch imperial activity.

The French and the British

J. B. Brebner, *The Explorers of North America, 1492–1806* (*Meridian). Good brief survey.

G. Lanctot, *History of Canada,* 2 vols. (Harvard Univ., 1963–1964). Detailed study to 1713; by a French-Canadian scholar.

G. M. Wrong, *The Rise and Fall of New France,* 2 vols. (Macmillan, 1928). Sound study by an English-Canadian scholar.

S. E. Morison, ed., *The Parkman Reader* (Little, Brown, 1955). Selections from the celebrated multivolumed *France and England in North America* by the nineteenth-century historian Francis Parkman.

J. H. Rose, ed., *The Cambridge History of the British Empire,* Vol. 1 (Cambridge Univ., 1929). Detailed survey to 1783.

Africa, Asia, and the Pacific

H. Labouret, *Africa before the White Man* (Walker, 1963); B. David-son, *Africa in History* (Macmillan, 1969); R. Oliver and J. D. Fage, *A Short History of Africa* (*Penguin). Three helpful introductions. Fage has also written *A History of West Africa* (*Cambridge Univ.) and other useful books on the continent.

B. Davidson, *The African Slave Trade* (*Atlantic Monthly). By a prolific writer on African history.

A. L. Basham, *The Wonder That Was India* (*Evergreen). A more careful survey of Indian history up to the Muslim invasions than the title might suggest.

E. O. Reischauer and J. K. Fairbank, *East Asia: The Great Tradition* (Houghton, 1960). An expert survey of China, Japan, and Korea from the beginnings. Reischauer has also written *Japan: The Story of a Nation* (*Knopf).

R. Grousset, *The Rise and Splendor of the Chinese Empire* (*Univ. of California). An enlightening study of Chinese culture.

K. S. Latourette, *China* (*Spectrum). Excellent introduction.

G. B. Sansom, *A History of Japan, 1334–1615* and *A History of Japan, 1615–1867* (*Knopf). Perceptive accounts by a leading British expert.

C. Lloyd, *Pacific Horizons* (Allen & Unwin, 1946), and *Captain Cook* (Faber & Faber, 1952). Readable modern reviews of early Pacific exploration.

The Americas

J. Soustelle, *Daily Life of the Aztecs on the Eve of the Spanish Conquest* (*Stanford Univ.). Instructive study by an anthropologist.

S. J. and B. Stein, *Colonial Heritage of Latin America* (*Oxford Univ.). Essays stressing its economic dependence on the mother countries.

A. P. Newton, *The European Nations in the West Indies, 1493–1688* (Black, 1933). Excellent study of a great arena of colonial rivalry.

C. M. Andrews, *The Colonial Period of American History,* Vols. 1, 2, 3 (*Yale Univ.). Detailed study of the European settlements.

D. J. Boorstin, *Americans: The Colonial Experience* (*Vintage). A provocative briefer treatment.

L. B. Wright, *Cultural Life of the American Colonies, 1607–1763* (*Torchbooks). An especially good volume in the New American Nation series.

The Impact of Expansion

J. H. Elliott, *The Old World and the New, 1492–1650* (*Cambridge Univ.). Stimulating lectures on the impact of the New World upon the Old.

The Cambridge Economic History, Vol. 4 (Cambridge Univ., 1967). Scholarly essays on expanding Europe in the sixteenth and seventeenth centuries.

W. P. Webb, *The Great Frontier: An Interpretation of World History* (Houghton, 1952). Assigns the New World a crucial role in the developing wealth and power of the Old.

E. J. Hamilton, *American Treasure and the Price Revolution in Spain, 1501–1650* (Harvard Univ., 1934). Long a standard study, but its stress on the central role of bullion has been challenged by more recent scholarship.

Sources and Historical Fiction

I. R. Blacker, ed., *The Portable Hakluyt's Voyages* (*Viking). Excerpts from the famous late sixteenth-century collection.

J. R. Levenson, *European Expansion and the Counter-Example of

Asia (*Prentice-Hall). Materials on technology, religion, social structure, and "spirit."

E. D. Genovese and R. Foner, *Slavery in the New World* (*Prentice-Hall). Materials on the comparative slave policies of the imperial powers.

L. Wallace, *The Fair God* (*Popular Library). A real thriller, a century old, on the Aztecs of Mexico; by the author of *Ben Hur*.

C. S. Forester, *To the Indies* (Little, Brown, 1940). Fine novel on Columbus.

R. Sabatini, *The Sea Hawk* (Houghton, 1923). A good melodramatic novel of adventures on the sea in the late sixteenth century.

W. Cather, *Shadows on the Rock* (*Random House). Sensitive re-creation of life in New France by a twentieth-century American novelist.

Divine-Right Monarchy— and Revolution

Introduction

The Peace of Westphalia in 1648 brought to a close not only the Thirty Years' War but also a whole epoch in European history. It ended the age of the Reformation and Counter-Reformation, when wars were both religious and dynastic in motivation and the chief threats to a stable international balance came from the Catholic Hapsburgs and from the militant Protestants of Germany, the Netherlands, and Scandinavia. After 1648 religion, though continuing to be a major source of friction in France and the British Isles, ceased to be a significant international issue. The main force jeopardizing the European balance was the entirely secular ambition of Bourbon France, for seventy-two years— 1643 to 1715—under a single monarch, Louis XIV, who inherited the throne at the age of four and a half. Louis was the embodiment of the characteristic early modern form of royal absolutism, monarchy by divine right, and he was the very personification of royal pride, elegance, and luxury. To the French, Louis XIV was *le grand monarque,* and his long, long reign marked the culmination of their *grand siècle,* the great century that had begun under Cardinal Richelieu in the twenty years before Louis' accession and that was marked by the international triumph of French arms and French diplomacy and, still more, of French ways of writing, building, dressing, and eating, the whole style of life of the upper classes in *la grande nation.*

While the culture of *la grande nation* went from one triumph to another, Louis XIV's bid for political hegemony was ultimately checked. His most resolute opponent was England, still in the throes of the greatest political upheaval in her history. The upheaval resulted from the collision between the forces of the Stuart monarchy and High Church Anglicanism, on the one hand, and those of Parliament and the Puritans, on the other. The final settlement was a compromise weighted in favor of the parliamentary side, but still a compromise

and therefore compatible with the modern image of England as the country of gradual, orderly change. This was not the image prevailing in the seventeenth century, after decades of violence and flux, with one English king executed and another obliged to go into exile. In those days England was synonymous with revolution.

The English political turmoil was not the only seventeenth-century revolution. Alfred North Whitehead, the eminent English mathematician and philosopher of the early twentieth century, called the 1600s "the century of genius." It was the century of Galileo and Francis Bacon, of Descartes and Pascal, of Newton and Locke, and of many others who helped to lay the foundations of modern science, to provide it with indispensable tools, and to establish the patterns of thought and procedure that we call rational, empirical, and inductive. This intellectual and scientific revolution had repercussions more far-reaching than those emanating from the court or the culture of Louis XIV's France or even from the England of revolution and civil war. The "century of genius" was the prelude to what has been termed "the great modern revolution," the practical applications of the new science and technology to the production of raw materials and finished goods—the agricultural and industrial revolutions.

Some historians of the mid-twentieth century have found the mid-seventeenth century an age of crisis comparable in its disturbing effects to the famines and Black Death of the fourteenth century. Demographers note the decline in population not only in war-ravaged Germany but in Spain and some other countries as well. Economic historians point to the severely depressing effects of the Thirty Years' War and also to the social upheavals accompanying the struggle between the capitalism of the rising middle class and the agrarianism of the traditional landed classes. Political historians stress the multiplicity of revolutions, successful and abortive, against extravagant, corrupt, and inefficient monarchies not just in England but in Portugal, Spain, France, and elsewhere. Still other historians, however, while admitting that the seventeenth century experienced more than its share of troubles, reject these attempts to find a single dominant pattern, whether demographic, economic, or political. To them it was an age of crises (in the plural, not the singular) whose interrelations have not yet been convincingly demonstrated.

II Bourbon France
Louis XIII and Richelieu

France's *grand siècle* was almost blighted in the bud when, in 1610, in the prime of his career, the capable and popular Henry IV was assassinated by a madman. The new king, Louis XIII (1610–1643), was only nine years old; the queen mother, Marie de' Medici, served as regent but showed little of her famous family's political skill. Her Italian favorites and French nobles, Cath-

olic and Huguenot alike, carried on a hectic competition that threatened to undo all that Henry IV had accomplished. During these troubles the French representative body, the Estates General, met in 1614 for what was destined to be its last session until 1789 on the eve of the great French Revolution. Significantly, the meeting was paralyzed by tensions between the noble deputies of the second estate and the bourgeois of the third. Meanwhile, Louis XIII, though barely in his teens, attempted to assert his personal authority and reduce the role of his mother. Poorly educated, sickly, nervous, and subject to spells of depression, Louis needed expert help.

He was fortunate in securing the assistance of the remarkably talented Richelieu (1585–1642), who proved to be an efficient administrator and a sincere but not an ardent Catholic as bishop of a remote diocese in western France. Tiring of provincial life, Richelieu moved to Paris and showed great skill and considerable unscrupulousness in political maneuvering during the confused days of Marie de' Medici's regency. He emerged as the conciliator between the king and

An illustration from Abraham Bosse's "Le Palais Royal" (1640) gives a good picture of French fashions and tastes.

his mother, and was rewarded with election to the College of Cardinals and then, in 1624, with selection by Louis as his chief minister. While the king maintained a lively interest in affairs of state, Richelieu was the virtual ruler of France for the next eighteen years. He proved to be a good Machiavellian and a good politique, subordinating religion and every nonpolitical consideration to *raison d'état* (reason of state), a phrase that he probably coined himself.

When Richelieu entered the king's service, he claimed to have promised Louis that he would "ruin the Huguenot party, humble the pride of the great nobles, recall all his subjects to their duty, and raise his name among foreign nations to the level where it ought to be." * The promise proved to be a largely accurate forecast of Richelieu's program and accomplishments. *Raison d'état* made the "ruin" of the Huguenots his first priority, for the political privileges they had received by the Edict of Nantes made them a major obstacle to the creation of a centralized state. The hundred fortified towns they governed, chiefly in southwestern France, constituted a state within the state, a hundred centers of potential rebellion that Richelieu was determined to bring under control. Alarmed, the Huguenots did in fact rebel. It took the royal forces fourteen months to besiege and take their chief stronghold, the Atlantic port of La Rochelle, which finally fell in 1628 after the besiegers constructed a great jetty to seal off the access of its harbor to the sea. (Louis XIII, incidentally, was so excited by the project that he wanted to lend the masons a hand in the work.) Thereupon Richelieu canceled the political and military clauses of the Edict of Nantes but left intact its grant of partial religious toleration to the Huguenots.

The siege of La Rochelle lasted so long because France had no navy worthy of the name. In the next ten years Richelieu created a fleet of thirty-eight warships for the Atlantic and, for the Mediterranean, a dozen galleys manned by slaves (an exception to the rule that whites were never enslaved in the modern West). Meanwhile, he guided France expertly through the Thirty Years' War, committing French resources only when concrete gains seemed possible, and ensuring favorable publicity by supplying exaggerated accounts of French victories to the *Gazette de France*. In every way Richelieu was a great practitioner of realistic power politics.

Raison d'état, indeed, motivated all his policies. He lived in elaborate style, accompanied on his travels by his private choir and corps of musicians, not just because he was fond of music but because he believed such a retinue befitted the chief minister of a splendid kingdom. In 1635, he founded the famous French Academy, to compile a dictionary of the French language and to set the standards and style of the national culture. He tried to humble the factious nobles, though

with only partial success, by ordering the destruction of some of their châteaux and forbidding the favorite aristocratic indulgence of private duels. More effective was his transfer of supervision over the local administration from nobles and from officeholders of dubious loyalty who had purchased their posts to the more reliable *intendants*. These royal officials had existed earlier but performed only minor functions; now they were given greatly increased powers over justice and the police and especially over apportioning and collecting taxes.

Richelieu made possible *la grande nation* of Louis XIV by building an efficient, centralized state. But in a sense he built too well, making the French governments so centralized, so professionally bureaucratic, that it had no place for the give-and-take of politics. Except for attempting to equalize the incidence of taxes among the provinces of France, Richelieu did little to remedy the chronic fiscal weakness of the government, particularly corruption in tax collection and the piling up of deficits. His concentration on *raison d'état* led him to take an extraordinarily callous view of the subjects on whose loyal performance of their duties the welfare of the state depended. He once wrote: "All politicians agree that when the people are too comfortable it is impossible to keep them within the bounds of their duty . . . they must be compared to mules which, being used to burdens, are spoiled more by rest than by labour." *

Mazarin and the Fronde

The deaths of Richelieu and Louis XIII in successive years (1642, 1643), the accession of a child king, and the regency of the hated Hapsburg queen mother, Anne of Austria (she was a Hapsburg from Spain, where the dynasty was called the house of Austria)—all seemed to threaten a repetition of the crisis following the death of Henry IV. The crisis was averted, or at any rate delayed, by the new chief minister, Mazarin (1602–1661). Picked and schooled by Richelieu himself, Mazarin, too, was a cardinal (though not a priest as his predecessor had been) and a past master of *raison d'état*. He, too, was careless about the finances of the French state, but, unlike Richelieu, he amassed an immense personal fortune during his public career, bestowing lavish gifts on his five Italian nieces, who married into the high French nobility, and collecting a magnificent library, which he willed to the French state. He antagonized both branches of the French aristocracy—the nobles of the sword, descendants of feudal magnates, and the nobles of the robe (the reference is to the gowns worn by judges and other officials), descendants of commoners who had bought their way into government office. The former resented being excluded from the regency by a foreigner; the latter, who had invested heavily in government securities, particu-

*Quoted in C. J. Friedrich, *The Age of the Baroque, 1610–1660* (New York, 1952), p. 198 n. Our translation.

*Quoted in C. V. Wedgwood, *Richelieu and the French Monarchy* (New York, 1950), p. 137.

Triple portrait of Richelieu, by Champaigne.

larly disliked Mazarin's casual way of borrowing money to meet war expenses and then letting the interest payments on government loans fall into arrears.

The discontent boiled over in the Fronde, 1648–1653, named for the slingshot used by Parisian children to hurl pellets at passersby, and one of the several midcentury uprisings in Europe. Some of the rioting involved participation by the peasantry and the common people of Paris, both impoverished by the economic depression accompanying the final campaigns of the Thirty Years' War. But the Fronde was essentially a noble revolt, led first by the judges of the Parlement of Paris, a high court and a stronghold of the nobles of the robe, and then, after the Peace of Westphalia, by aristocratic officers returned from the Thirty Years' War. Various "princes of the blood," relatives of the royal family, intervened with their private armies. Though Mazarin twice had to flee France and go into exile, the upshot of the Fronde was to confirm him in power and to pave the way for the personal rule of Louis XIV. The youthful king got a bad fright when

the frondeurs actually broke into his bedroom, and he resolved to hold firmly to the reins of state. The Fronde failed essentially because it had no real roots in the country, not even in the rising middle classes. It was a struggle for power between Mazarin and his new bureaucracy and two privileged groups of nobles. Each noble group distrusted the other, and the nobles of the sword were also split by personal feuds; all Mazarin had to do was apply the old Roman maxim "Divide and rule."

Le Grand Monarque

When Mazarin died in 1661, Louis XIV began to rule as well as to reign. At the age of twenty-two the king already displayed an impressive royal presence, as reported by Madame de Motteville, a seasoned observer of the French court:

> As the single desire for glory and to fulfill all the duties of a great king occupied his whole heart, by applying himself

to toil he began to like it; and the eagerness he had to learn all the things that were necessary to him soon made him full of that knowledge. His great good sense and his good intentions now made visible in him the rudiments of general knowledge which had been hidden from all who did not see him in private. . . .

He was agreeable personally, civil and easy of access to every one; but with a lofty and serious air which impressed the public with respect and awe . . . , though he was familiar and gay with ladies.*

Louis continued to be "familiar and gay with ladies" until finally, after the death of his Spanish queen, he settled down in the 1680s to a proper middle-aged marriage with Madame de Maintenon, a Huguenot turned devout Catholic who had been the governess of his illegitimate children.

Louis XIV, the "Sun King," succeeded so well as *le grand monarque* because by education, temperament, and physique he was ideally suited to the role. It has been remarked that he had received from Mazarin just enough education to be guided always by *raison d'état,* though not by reason itself. Endowed with excellent manners—"civil and easy of access to everyone," as Mme de Motteville observed—he also had admirable

self-discipline, patience, and staying power. He never lost his temper in public and went through long daily hours in council meetings and elaborate ceremonials with unwearied attention and even enjoyment, to which his conspicuous lack of a sense of humor may have contributed. He had an iron physical constitution, which enabled him to withstand a rigorous schedule, made him indifferent to heat and to cold, and allowed him to survive both a lifetime of gross overeating (an autopsy revealed his stomach was twice normal size) and the crude medical treatment of the day.

He was five feet five inches tall—a fairly impressive height for the day—and added to his stature by shoes with high red heels. To provide a suitable setting for the Sun King, to neutralize the high nobility politically by isolating it in the ceaseless ceremonies and petty intrigues of court life, and also to prevent a repetition of the frondeurs' intrusion into his bedroom in Paris, he moved the capital from Paris to Versailles, a dozen miles away. There on sandy wasteland he built his celebrated palace more than a third of a mile long, flanked by elaborate stables and other outbuildings, approached from Paris by a majestic avenue, and set in an immense formal garden with fourteen hundred fountains, the water for which had to be pumped up from the River Seine at staggering expense. Versailles housed, mainly in cramped uncomfortable quarters, a

*_Memoirs of Madame de Motteville,_ trans. K. P. Wormeley (Boston, 1902), 3:243.

The Palace of Versailles: an engraving by P. Menant.

court of ten thousand, including dependents and servants of all sorts.

Divine-Right Monarchy

The admired and imitated French state, of which Versailles was the symbol and Louis XIV the embodiment, can also stand as the best historical example of divine-right monarchy. Perhaps Louis never actually said, "L'état c'est moi" (I am the state), but the phrase has stuck, and it certainly summarizes his convictions about his role. In theory, Louis was for his subjects no mere man but the representative of God on earth—or at least in France. He was not elected by his subjects, nor did he acquire his throne by force of arms; rather, he was born to a position God had planned for the legitimate male heir of the tenth-century Hugh Capet. As God's agent, his word was final, for to challenge it would be to challenge the whole structure of God's universe. Disobedience was a religious as well as a political offense.

Though Louis has been dead less than three centuries, the ideas and sentiments centered on this divine-right monarchy seem so utterly alien today that it takes an effort of the historical imagination not to dismiss them as nonsense. Two clues may help us to understand why they were once held so widely and so firmly. The first is the survival of the characteristic medieval view that right decisions in government are not arrived at by experiment and discussion, but by "finding" the authoritative answer provided for in God's scheme of things. In the days of Louis XIV many people still believed that God through his chosen agents directly managed the state. The second clue lies in the deliberate efforts of Henry IV and Richelieu as well as Louis XIV to fuse the sixteen million inhabitants of France into a single national unit. The problem was to make these millions who were used to thinking and behaving as Normans, Bretons, Flemings, Alsatians, Burgundians, Gascons, Basques, and Provençaux to think and behave as Frenchmen. The makers of the Bourbon monarchy could not rely on a common language, for only a minority as yet spoke standard French; and they could not rely on a common educational system, a common national press, or a common participation in political life, for all of these lay in the future. They could, and did, attempt to set up the king as a symbol of common Frenchness. The king collected taxes, raised armies, touched in a hundred ways the lives of his subjects who had to feel that the king had a right to do all this and that he was doing it *for* them rather than *to* them. A king who was the agent of God was the kind of ruler they could accept.

Divine-right monarchy, with its corollary of obedience on the part of subjects, is thus one phase in the growth of the modern centralized nation-state. It was an institution that appealed to old theological ideas, such as the biblical admonition to obey the powers that be, for "the powers that be are ordained of God," but it was also inspired by the newer ideas of binding men together in a productive, efficient state. In practice, naturally, the institution did not wholly correspond to theories about it. Louis XIV was not the French state, and his rule was not absolute in any full sense of that word. He simply did not have the physical means for controlling in detail what his subjects did, a control much more extensive under modern techniques of communication, propaganda, and administration than it ever was in the days of "absolute" monarchy. Medieval survivals made for diversities in laws, customs, weights and measures, as well as language, that all stood in the way of uniformity. Important groups still clung to medieval rights and immunities, which they felt did not depend on the king's will. Many of these groups were corporations—municipal councils, courts like the parlements in Paris and in some provincial capitals, economic groups such as guilds—which usually possessed written charters and traditional privileges difficult for the government to override. Particularly troublesome were the aristocratic and religious forces, both Catholic and Huguenot, that had been involved in the civil strife of the late sixteenth century.

Nobles, Catholics, and Huguenots

In all the important countries of Europe the feudal nobles maintained themselves into early modern times; the degree to which they were integrated into the new machinery of state was of crucial importance in the development of modern Europe. In Hapsburg Spain, as indeed in the Hapsburg lands of central Europe, the old nobility generally accepted the new strength of the Crown, but maintained much of their privilege and all their old pride of status. In Prussia, as a later chapter will show, they were successfully integrated into the new order, becoming on the whole faithful servants or soldiers of the Crown, but with a social status that set them well above mere bourgeois bureaucrats. In England, as we shall shortly see, the nobility achieved a unique compromise with the Crown. In France, the nobles of the sword were in effect shoved aside by the Crown and deprived for the most part of major political functions, but they were allowed to retain social and economic privileges and important roles as officers in the king's army.

This process of reducing the old French nobility to relative powerlessness at least in national political life had begun during the fifteenth century and had been hastened by the religious and civil wars of the next century. An important part of the nobility, perhaps nearly half, had espoused the Protestant cause, in large part from sheer opposition to the Crown. The victory of Henry IV, purchased by his conversion to Catholicism, was a defeat for the nobility. Under Richelieu and Louis XIV the process was completed by the increasing use of commoners in the task of running the government, from the great ministers of state, through the intendants, down to local administrators and judges. These commoners were usually elevated to the nobility of the robe, which did not have at first the social prestige of the nobility of the sword. The Fronde demonstrated that these new nobles could not be counted upon as loyal supporters of the Crown. Among the old nobles they aroused a contemptuous envy, summed up in the famous complaint of the ultra-aristocratic duc de Saint-Simon that only "vile bourgeois" had the confidence of the king; the nobles of the sword knew they were shelved. By the end of Louis' reign, however, the two kinds of nobility had become better amalgamated, giving the whole order a new lease on life.

In medieval times, the clergy had been a separate order, backed by the supranational power and prestige of the papacy and possessing privileges not wholly in the control of the Crown. Even under Louis XIV the French clergy continued to possess important corporate privileges. They were not subject to royal taxation; they contributed of their own free will a gift of money that they voted in their own assembly. In the centralized France that emerged from the Hundred Years' War the Crown had fostered the evolution of a national Gallican church, firmly Catholic but also controlled by the monarchy, and friendly to new political, social, and economic ideas. Under Louis XIV the Gallican union of throne and altar reached a high point in 1682 when a great assembly of French clerics drew up the Declaration of Gallican Liberties, asserting in effect that the "rules and customs admitted by France and the Gallican church" were just as important as the traditional authority of the papacy. "Ocean itself, immense though it is, has its limits," pronounced Bishop Bossuet, a great defender of Louis's monarchy by divine right. In practice, however, the flamboyant new Gallican claims for French royal authority did not prove to be very important.

Louis XIV took as the goal of his religious policy the application of a traditional French motto—*un roi, une loi, une foi* (one king, one law, one faith). Whereas Richelieu had attacked only the political privileges of the Huguenots, Louis attacked their fundamental right of toleration and finally abolished it. He began by pulling down Huguenot churches not specifically authorized by the Edict of Nantes, then put restrictions on Huguenots' education, their admission to the professions, and their right to marry outside their faith. A campaign for converting Protestants to the Roman faith assumed a coercive aspect through the notorious *dragonnades,* the billeting of dragoons in Huguenot households as a persuasive measure. Misled by exaggerated reports of the success achieved, and pressed by the fanatically anti-Huguenot lower Catholic clergy, Louis revoked the Edict of Nantes in 1685. After the revocation, fifty thousand Huguenot families fled abroad, notably to Prussia, Belgium, Holland and the Dutch colony in South Africa, England (where they were given a chapel in Canterbury cathedral itself), and the colonies of British North America, as the name of New Rochelle, New York, reminds us. The practical skills and the intellectual gifts of the refugees strengthened the lands that received them, and the departure of industrious workmen and of thousands of veteran sailors, soldiers, and officers weakened the mother country. Some Huguenots remained in France, worshiping underground in spite of persecution.

Within the Catholic church itself, Louis had to contend with two important elements that refused to accept his Gallicanism. The Quietists, a group of religious enthusiasts led by Madame Guyon, sought for a more mystical and emotional faith. Their tendency to exhibitionism and self-righteousness combined with their zeal for publicity belied their name of Quietist and offended the king's sense of propriety. The Jansenists, sometimes called the Puritans of the Catholic church, were a high-minded group whose most distinguished spokesman was the scientist and philosopher Pascal. Named for Cornelius Jansen, bishop of Ypres in the early seventeenth century, the Jansenists took an almost Calvinistic stand on the issue of predestination. They stressed the need to obey the authority of God rather than that of man, no matter how exalted the position of the particular man might be. They therefore questioned both the authority of the pope (and of his agents, the Jesuits) and that of the king. On the surface, Louis was successful in repressing both Quietists and Jansenists, but the latter in particular survived to trouble his successors in the eighteenth century.

The Royal Administration

Just as Louis XIV was never wholly master of the religious beliefs and practices of his subjects, he never quite succeeded in building up an administrative machine wholly under royal control. At Versailles he had three long conferences weekly with his ministers, who headed departments essentially like those of any modern state—War, Finance, Foreign Affairs, Interior. The king kept this top administrative level on an intimate scale; he usually had only four ministers at one time, and gave them virtually permanent tenure. Colbert served as controller general for eighteen years, and Le Tellier for thirty-four as secretary of state for the Army, a portfolio later entrusted to his son, who had been ennobled as the marquis de Louvois. All told, only sixteen ministers held office during the fifty-four years of his personal reign.

From Louis XIV and his ministers, who were directly responsible to him, a chain of command proceeded down through the intendants, whose number was fixed at thirty, with each at the head of a *généralité,* a big administrative unit roughly corresponding to the older province. Below the intendants were their subordinates, the *subdélégués,* and at the bottom were the towns and villages of France, which sometimes defied or ignored the royal command. Even the indefatigable Louis could do no more than exercise general supervision over the affairs of his large and complex kingdom. And he probably could not have achieved even partial success without the invention of printing. For the familiar government printed forms to be filled out were already in existence. And they are still there, duly filled out and filed in their hundreds of thousands in the local archives of France.

In practice, the royal administration was full of difficulties and contradictions. There were many conflicting jurisdictions, survivals of feudalism and the medieval struggle to control feudalism. The officials of Louis XIV, by the very fact of being nobles of the robes, possessed a privileged status they could hand down to their heirs. They, too, tended to form a "corporation" and to be more their own masters in their own bailiwicks than the theory of royal absolutism would allow. The key provincial administrators, the intendants, may seem to have been no more than agents of the Crown. Yet anyone who pursues in local history the detailed records of what they actually did finds that many of them exercised considerable initiative on their own. Nor was the old administrative device of moving the intendants about from one généralité to another sufficient to overcome this centrifugal tendency.

A particularly important potential for trouble existed in the parlements, the supreme courts of appeal in the various provinces, of which one, the Parlement of Paris, enjoyed special prestige and power from its place at the capital and from the size of its territorial jurisdiction, almost half of the kingdom. The judges who staffed the courts headed the nobility of the robe, owned their offices, and were not removable at the will of the king. In addition to the usual work of a court of appeals, the parlements claimed through their function of registering royal edicts before they went into force something approaching the right of judicial review. That is, they claimed to be able to refuse registration of an edict if they thought it unconstitutional, not in accord with higher law of the land. Although the claim negated theoretical royal absolutism, Louis got around it in his own lifetime. The Parlement of Paris had already lost a round in its struggle with the royal power by entering the lists against Mazarin in the Fronde. Now Louis successfully utilized another old institution, the *lit de justice* (literally, "bed of justice"), in which he summoned the Parlement of Paris before him in a formal session and ordered the justices to register a royal edict. In this way, for instance, he enforced measures against Jansenism, which was strong among the judges. But the parlements, too, were to plague his eighteenth-century successors.

Mercantilism and Colbert

Just as divine-right monarchy was not peculiarly French, so the mercantilism identified with the France of Louis XIV was common to many other Western states; but, like divine-right rule, it flourished most characteristically under the Sun King. Mercantilism was part and parcel of the early modern effort to construct strong, efficient political units. The mercantilists quite frankly aimed to make their nation as self-sustaining as possible, as independent as possible of the need to import goods from other nations, which were its rivals and its potential enemies. The mercantilists held that production within a nation should provide the necessities of life for a hard-working population, and the necessities of power for the nation to fight and win wars. They believed that these goals required planning and control from above. They were all for sweeping away the remnants of such medieval institutions as the manor and the guild, which, they felt, reduced the energies and abilities needed in an expanding economy. But they did not believe, as the free-trade economists would later believe, that all that was necessary was to leave individuals free to do whatever they thought would enrich themselves. Instead, the mercantilists would channel the national economic effort by protective tariffs, by government subsidies, by grants of monopolies, by industries directly run by the government, and by encouraging scientific and technological research.

The mercantilists viewed overseas possessions as a special part of France that should be run from the homeland by a strong government. Already in the seventeenth century many foodstuffs and raw materials were more easily available overseas than in Europe. Colonies, therefore, should be encouraged to provide necessities so that the mother country need not import them from her competitors. In return, the mother country would supply industrial goods to the colonies and have a monopoly over colonial trade. This mercantilistic attitude toward colonies was held not only by France and Spain but by the less absolutist governments of England and Holland.

The great French practitioner of mercantilism was Colbert (1619–1683), who had served his apprenticeship under Mazarin and advanced rapidly to become controller general early in the personal reign of Louis. He never quite attained the supremacy reached by Richelieu and Mazarin; he was the collaborator, never the master, of Louis XIV. Other great ministers, Louvois for military affairs especially, stood in the way of his supremacy. Yet Colbert was influential in all matters affecting the French economy, most interested in foreign trade and in the colonies, and therefore in the merchant marine and in the navy. His hand was in everything, in invention, in technological education, in designing and building ships, in attracting foreign experts to settle in France.

Among the industries he fostered were the processing of sugar, chocolate, and tobacco from the colonies; the production of military goods by iron foundries and textile mills; and the luxuries for which the French have been famous ever since. The Gobelins tapestry enterprise in Paris was taken over by the state and its output expanded to include elegant furniture, for which the king was a major customer. Glassblowers and lacemakers were lured away from Venice, despite strenuous efforts by the Venetian republic, including the use of poison, to keep their valuable techniques secret. In a blow against French competitors Colbert imposed heavy tariffs on some Dutch and English products. To promote trade with the colonies and also with the Baltic and the Mediterranean he financed a battery of trading companies, of which only the French East India Company eventually succeeded.

At home, Colbert encouraged reforestation, so that iron foundries could have abundant supplies of charcoal (then essential for smelting); he also promoted the planting of mulberry trees to nourish the silkworms vital to textile output. He even attempted—vainly, as it turned out—to impose what we could call quality control by ordering that defective goods should be prominently exhibited in public, along with the name of the offending producer, and that for a third offense the culprit himself was to be exhibited. He also endeavored, again for the most part in vain, to break down the barriers to internal free trade, like provincial and municipal tariffs or local restrictions on the shipment of grain to other parts of France. He did, however, sponsor the construction of important roads and canals; the Canal du Midi (of the south) linking the Atlantic port of Bordeaux and the Mediterranean port of Narbonne reduced transport charges between the two seas by three-fourths and was described as the greatest engineering feat since Roman days.

Whether the great prosperity France achieved in the first thirty years of Louis's reign came about because of, or in spite of, the mercantilist policies of Colbert is a question difficult to answer. Under the mercantilist regime at any rate, France did attain an undoubted leadership in European industry and commerce. That lead she lost, in part because the last two wars of Louis XIV were ruinously expensive, in part because in the eighteenth century France's rival, England, took to the new methods of power machinery and concentrated on large-scale production of inexpensive goods. France remained largely true to the policies set by Colbert—relatively small-scale production of a variety of luxuries and other consumer goods. But the difference between French and English industry was also a difference in

the focus of national energies. France, like Spain before her, spent an undue proportion of her national product in an unfruitful effort to achieve the political domination of both Europe and the overseas world through the force of arms.

The Goals and Instruments of French Expansion

France was the real victor in the Thirty Years' War, acquiring lands on her northeastern frontier. In a postscript to the main conflict, she continued fighting with Spain until at the Peace of the Pyrenees, 1659, Mazarin secured additional territories: Artois, in the north adjoining Flanders, and Roussillon, at the Catalan-speaking Mediterranean end of the Pyrenees. Well recovered from the wounds of her own religious wars and prospering economically, France was ready for further expansion when the young and ambitious monarch began his personal rule in 1661.

What were the goals of that expansion? To complete the gains of 1648 and 1659 and secure the kingdom's "natural frontiers" along the Rhine and the Alps? To wage a mercantilist war against France's major economic competitors, Holland and England? Or to revive the multinational empire that Charlemagne had ruled nine hundred years earlier? Historians today tend to believe that Louis pursued each of these goals in sequence, as he became more and more powerful and more and more convinced that the proper occupation of a king was the aggrandizement of his kingdom. In addition, Louis was keenly aware of the potentials of cultural imperialism, and he wanted the French language, French taste in the arts, and French social ways to spread their influence over Europe.

While French cultural imperialism went from triumph to triumph, Louis' political and military designs won some successes but met ultimate failure. In North America, in India, in Holland, and on the Rhine, and in dozens of other places, the agents of Louis were working to increase their master's power and prestige. Other peoples became convinced that France was threatening things that they held dear—life, property, independence, self-respect. Under this threat, most of the European states allied themselves against the French aggressor and beat him.

Louis XIV and his talented experts fashioned splendid instruments to support an aggressive foreign policy. In 1661 half a dozen men made up the whole Ministry of Foreign Affairs; half a century later, it had a huge staff of clerks, archivists, coders (and decoders) of secret messages, renegade priests and ladies of easy virtue who operated as clandestine agents, great lords and prelates who lent their dignity to important missions, and professional assistants who did most of their work. The growth of the French army was still more impressive, from a peacetime force of twenty thousand

Nicholas Largillière's "Louis XIV and His Heirs."

to a wartime one almost twenty times larger. In size, the armies of Louis XIV were beginning to assume a truly modern look.

In quality, however, French forces were rather less modern. The ranks were filled not with citizen soldiers raised by some kind of universal conscription but with mercenaries and the victims of impressment. Leadership may be described as semiprofessional. Both the basic larger unit, the regiment, and the basic smaller one, the company, were not only led but also recruited and paid by their commanders—colonel and captain, respectively. These men were usually nobles, who purchased their commissions and behaved as though they were a combination of condottieri and of feudal lords bringing their private forces to do battle for their overlord.

Nevertheless, Louis and his lieutenants almost revolutionized the character of France's fighting forces. At the Ministry of War the father-and-son team of Le Tellier and Louvois arranged the grouping of regiments in a brigade under a general to bring them under closer control. They also introduced two new ranks of officer, major and lieutenant colonel, to give more opportunity to talented commoners; these new commissions were awarded only for merit and were not available for purchase, like a colonelcy or captaincy. Supplies were more abundant, pay was more regular, and an effort was made to weed out the "deadbeats" who appeared only on regimental paydays. The inspector general, Martinet, made his name a byword for the enforcement of rigorous drilling and discipline.

In the field, during Louis' early wars, the king had the invaluable help of two senior commanders, Condé and Turenne, both veterans of the Thirty Years' War. French armies showed particular strength in artillery, engineering and siege techniques, all particularly important in those days before wars of rapid movement, when armies moved ponderously and did much fighting in the waterlogged Low Countries. The French boasted an engineer of genius, Vauban, of whom it was said that a town he besieged was indefensible and one he defended was impregnable (two centuries later, the little city of Belfort in Alsace, which he had fortified, withstood a long Prussian siege). While military medical

Hotel des Invalides from the south.

services remained crude and sketchy, a large veteran's hospital was built in Paris, the Hôtel des Invalides, one of the most impressive monuments of *le grande siècle*.

The First Two Wars of Louis XIV

The main thrust of Louis XIV, unlike that of the Valois, which had been toward Italy, was northeast, toward the Low Countries and Germany. He sought also to secure Spain, if not quite as a direct annexation, at least as a French satellite with a French ruler. Finally, French commitments overseas in North America and in India drove him to attempt, against English and Dutch rivals, the establishment of a great French empire outside Europe.

The first actual war of Louis XIV was a minor affair, but it showed how he was going to move. When he married the daughter of Philip IV of Spain, his bride had renounced her rights of inheritance; now Louis claimed that, since her dowry had never been paid, the renunciation was invalid. His lawyers dug up an old family rule, the right of "devolution," on which he based his claim that lands in Belgium (then the Spanish Netherlands) should have devolved upon his wife. In the ensuing War of Devolution with Spain, 1667–1668, Turenne won victories, but Louis did not press his advantage. The Dutch, just north of Belgium, felt alarmed for their independence and also for their prosperity because of the discriminatory tariff against their goods introduced by Colbert in 1667. They entered into a Triple Alliance with England and Sweden to prevent Louis's upsetting the balance of power. A compromise peace at Aix-la-Chapelle, 1668, awarded Louis only Lille and other towns on the Franco-Belgian border.

Furious at the Dutch because of their economic ascendancy, their Calvinism, and, most of all, their republicanism, Louis resolved to teach them a lesson. He isolated them diplomatically by buying off Sweden and England, their former partners in the Triple Alliance. In 1672 French forces invaded Holland. The terrified Dutch lynched their bourgeois leader, Jan de Witt, whom they blamed for their military unpreparedness, and turned to the youthful stadholder of Holland (and of several other provinces), William III of Orange, the great-grandson of the martyred hero of Dutch independence, William the Silent. The French advance was halted by the desperate expedient of opening the dikes and flooding polders with the sea water from which they had been reclaimed. Even without the strong leadership of William of Orange, Europe would probably have responded to the threat of French domination by forming an anti-French alliance. As it was, Spain, the Holy Roman Empire, and the German state of Brandenburg-Prussia joined against France and her allies. The coalition was not very effective, and French diplomacy separated the allies at the treaties of Nijmegen (Nimwegen) in 1678–1679 (there were six separate peace arrangements, all told). Holland was left intact at the cost of promising neutrality, and the French gave up their tariff on Dutch goods; Spain ceded to France the Franche Comté (county of Burgundy), part of the Hapsburgs' Burgundian inheritance, plus some towns in Belgium; Prussia, which had defeated Louis' ally, Sweden, at Fehrbellin (1675), was obliged by French pressure to return the Swedes' lands in Germany. The power and prestige of France were now at their peak, as rulers all over Europe, and in particular the host of princelets in Germany, copied the standards of Versailles.

The Last Two Wars

Yet in the last three decades of Louis' reign most of his assets were dissipated, especially the concrete ones of wealth and efficient organization. Not content with the prestige he had won in his first two wars, Louis embroiled himself with most of the Western world in what looked like an effort to destroy the independence of Holland and most of western Germany, and to bring the Iberian peninsula under a French ruler. The prelude to new military aggression was the juridical aggression of the "chambers of reunion," special courts set up by the French, in the early 1680s, to tidy up the loose ends of the peace settlements of the past generation. There were loose ends aplenty on the northern and eastern frontiers of France, a zone of political fragmentation and confused feudal remnants, many of which were under the suzerainty of the Holy Roman emperor. After examining the documents in disputed cases the chambers of reunion "reunited" many strategic bits of land to territories acquainted earlier by France. The French did not hesitate to threaten force to back up these awards, as they did in the case of the former free city of Strasbourg, the chief town of Alsace.

Continued French nibbling at lands in western Germany and Louis' assertion of a dynastic claim to most of the lands of the German elector Palatine set off the third of his wars, the War of the League of Augsburg, 1688–1697. The league against him was put together by his old foe, William of Orange, who after 1688 shared the throne of England with his wife Mary,

daughter of James II. From then on England was thoroughly committed to take sides against Louis. The League of Augsburg also included Spain, the Holy Roman Empire, and the Alpine state of Savoy, which was threatened by Louis' tactics of "reunion." The great naval victory of the English over the French at Cape La Hogue in 1692 showed that England, not France, was to be mistress of the seas. But on land the honors were more nearly even. William was beaten in battle in the Low Countries time and again, but he was never decisively crushed. In Ireland, French attempts to intervene on behalf of the deposed English king, James II, were foiled at the battle of the Boyne (July 1690), the anniversary of which is still celebrated by Protestant "Orangemen" in northern Ireland. France and England also exchanged blows in India and in the West Indies and North America, where the colonists called the conflict King William's War.

The Peace of Ryswick (1697) ending the War of the League of Augsburg was a peace without victory,

Mignard's equestrian portrait of Louis XIV.

The peace congress at Utrecht, 1713.

a general agreement to keep things as they were. It lasted barely four years, for in 1701 Louis XIV took a step that led to his last and greatest conflict, the War of the Spanish Succession (1701–1714). Charles II, the Hapsburg king of Spain and Louis' brother-in-law, died in 1700 without a direct heir. For several years the diplomats of Europe had been striving to arrange a succession that would avoid putting on the throne either a French Bourbon or an Austrian Hapsburg. Although they agreed on a Bavarian prince, he died in 1699, and plans were made to partition the Spanish inheritance between Hapsburgs and Bourbons. Then Charles II died after making a new will that bequeathed his lands intact to Philip of Anjou, grandson of Louis XIV. Louis, after much soul searching, accepted on behalf of Philip, even though he had signed the treaty of partition. The threat to the balance of power was neatly summarized in the remark a gloating Frenchman is supposed to have made, "There are no longer any Pyrenees." England, Holland, Savoy, the Holy Roman Empire, and many German states formed the Grand Alliance to preserve the Pyrenees.

In the bloody war that followed, the French were gradually worn down in defeat. In North America they lost Acadia (Nova Scotia) to the English, and in Europe they were beaten by the allies in four major battles, beginning with Blenheim (1704) and concluding with Malplaquet (1709). The allied armies were commanded by two great generals, Prince Eugene of Savoy and the English John Churchill, Duke of Marlborough. But the French were not annihilated, and Malplaquet cost the Allies twenty thousand casualties, at least as many as the French suffered. By scraping the bottom of the barrel for men and money, the French managed even after Malplaquet to keep armies in the field.

Moreover, the Grand Alliance was weakening. The English, now following their famous policy of keeping any single continental power from attaining too strong a position, were almost as anxious to prevent the union of the Austrian and Spanish inheritances under a Hapsburg as to prevent the union of France and Spain under a Bourbon. At home, they faced a possible disputed succession to the throne, and the mercantile classes were sick of a war that was injuring trade and seemed unlikely to bring any compensating gains. In 1710, the Tory party, inclined toward peace, won a parliamentary majority and began negotiations that culminated in a series of treaties at Utrecht in 1713.

Utrecht was a typical balance-of-power peace, which contained France without humiliating her. She lost to England Newfoundland, Nova Scotia, and the Hudson's Bay territories, but she preserved Quebec and Louisiana, as well as her Caribbean islands. Louis gained in a sense what he had gone to war over, for Philip of Anjou was formally recognized as King Philip V of Spain and secured the Spanish lands overseas. The

French and Spanish crowns were however, by specific provision, never to be held by the same person, so the allies, too, had won a point. Furthermore, England took from Spain the Mediterranean island of Minorca, which she handed back later in the century, and the great Rock of Gibraltar guarding the Atlantic entrance to the Mediterranean, which (as of the mid-1970s) the Spanish are still seeking to recover. The English also gained, by an agreement called the Asiento, the right to supply slaves to the Spanish colonies, a right that gave them also opportunities for smuggling.

The Austrian Hapsburgs, denied the main Spanish succession, were compensated with Belgium and the former Spanish possessions in Italy, Milan and Naples. In Belgium, now the Austrian Netherlands, the Dutch were granted the right to garrison certain fortified towns, the "barrier fortresses," for better defense against possible French aggression. For faithfulness to the Grand Alliance Savoy was rewarded with Sicily; although forced to exchange this prize in 1720 for the lesser island of Sardinia, the Duke of Savoy could call himself king of Sardinia and thus began the long process that united Italy under the crown of Savoy in the nineteenth century. The elector of Brandenburg, too, was rewarded with a royal title, king *in* (not *of*) Prussia, which lay outside the Holy Roman Empire at the southeastern corner of the Baltic.

In all the general European settlements of modern times—Westphalia, Utrecht, Vienna, Versailles—historians discern imperfections that would lead to subsequent unsettlement and another general war. Utrecht is no exception, though of all the settlements it is the one in which victors and vanquished seem closest. First of all, the rivalry between France and England for empire overseas was undiminished. In India, as in North America, each nation was to continue after Utrecht as before, the effort to oust the other from land and trade. In Europe, the Dutch were not really protected against the French by the barrier fortresses in the Austrian Netherlands, and the Austrian Hapsburg emperor, Charles VI, never forgot that he wanted to be "Charles III" of Spain and never gave up hope that he might be able to upset the Utrecht decision. The distribution of Italian lands satisfied nobody, Italian or outsider, and the next two decades were filled with acrimonious negotiations over Italy. In short, no one seemed to have quite what he wanted—which is one of the difficulties of arriving at compromise solutions.

French Aggression in Review

Proponents of the view that Europe underwent a severe crisis during the seventeenth century can find much evidence in the horrors resulting from Louis XIV's aggressions. The total cost of his wars in human lives and economic resources was very great, especially in the deliberate French devastation of the German Palatinate during the War of the League of Augsburg. The battle of Malplaquet, which left forty thousand men wounded, dying, or dead in an area of ten square miles, was not surpassed in bloodshed until Borodino in Napoleon's Russian campaign, a century later. Behind the lines there was much suffering, too, notably in the great famine that struck France in 1693–1694. And the year of Malplaquet, 1709, was one of the grimmest in modern French history, when bitter cold, crop failures, famine, and relentless government efforts to stave off bankruptcy by collecting more taxes caused almost universal misery. The Parisians complained bitterly in this parody of the Lord's Prayer: "Our Father which art at Versailles, thy name is hallowed no more, thy Kingdom is great no more, thy will is no longer done on earth or on the waters. Give us this day thy bread which on all sides we lack. . . ." * These wars were not simply struggles among professional armies directed by professional politicians; they were wars among peoples, wars that brought out feelings of patriotism and hatred for the foreigner and the aggressor, though these feelings lacked as yet the intensity of modern nationalism.

Thus, in comparison with the wars of nationalism and revolution that were to follow and the wars of religion that had gone before, the wars of Louis XIV lacked the all-out drives of "total" wars. Louis set himself up as a champion of Catholicism, especially after the revocation of the Edict of Nantes in 1685, and William of Orange was hailed as a Protestant champion. Yet Louis, unlike his predecessor in aggression, Philip II of Spain, did not entertain any real hope of stamping out Protestantism among the Dutch. William's Protestant victory at the Boyne brought new indignities to Irish Catholics, while in England and New England the French were dreaded as Catholics. In the end, however, the Grand Alliance against Louis was a complete mixture of Catholic and Protestant in which religion played a comparatively minor role.

No lay substitute for the crusading religious spirit had emerged. Unlike Napoleon, Louis XIV was not the product of a revolution; unlike Hitler, he was not the product of a humiliating national defeat. He was indeed the Sun King, presiding over a dazzling court, but he was also the legitimate, even conventional, ruler of a land long used to prominence in Europe. The aggression of Louis XIV was, like the culture of his France, a relatively moderate "classical" aggression, lacking the heaven-storming fervor of aggressions born of revolution.

III Stuart England

English-speaking people throughout the world tend to believe that England has always had a representative

---

*G. R. R. Treasure, *Seventeenth Century France* (London, 1966), p. 413.

and constitutional government and never went through the stage of divine-right monarchy that France and other continental states experienced. This belief is largely correct, but it would be better stated as follows: To the extent that English government utilized the new methods of professional administration developed in the fifteenth and sixteenth centuries, it may be considered potentially just as absolute as any divine-right monarchy. But representative government provided a check on this potential through the concept of a constitution, a set of rules not to be altered by the ordinary processes of government. These rules might be written down, but they might also be unwritten, a consensus about certain traditions. They came to be regarded as limiting the authority not only of the king but even of a government elected by a majority of the people, a guarantee to individuals that they had "civil rights" and might do certain things even though men in posts of authority disapproved. Without these rules and habits of constitutionalism, and without powerful and widespread human convictions backing them up, the machinery of parliamentary government could be as ruthlessly absolute as any totalitarian government.

In seventeenth-century England the development of potentially absolute institutions was checked and modified by the continued growth of representative institutions. In France kings and ministers were able to govern without the Estates General. In England Parliament met in 1629 and quarreled violently with King Charles I, who then governed for eleven years without calling Parliament. But in 1640 he felt obliged to call Parliament and, though he dismissed it at once when it proved recalcitrant, he had to call another in that same year. This was the famous Long Parliament, which sat—with changes of personnel and with interruptions—for twenty years, and which made the revolution that ended the threat of absolute divine-right monarchy in England. If we understand why Charles, unlike his French counterpart, was obliged to call Parliament, we have gone a long way toward understanding why England had a head start in modern representative government.

Two very basic reasons go back to medieval history. First, as we have already seen, in the English Parliament the House of Commons represented two different social groups not brought together in one house on the Continent, the aristocratic "knights of the shire" and the "burgesses" of the towns and cities. The strength of the Commons lay in the practical working together of both groups, which intermarried quite freely and, in spite of some economic and social tensions, tended to form a single ruling class with membership open to talented and energetic men from the lower classes.

Second, local government continued to be run by magistrates who were not directly dependent on the Crown. We must not exaggerate: England, too, had its bureaucrats, its clerks and officials in the royal pay. But whereas in France and in other continental countries the new bureaucracy tended to take over almost all governmental business, especially financial and judicial affairs, in England the gentry and the higher nobility continued to do important local work. The Elizabethan Poor Law of 1601 put the care of the needy not under any national ministry but squarely on the smallest local units, the parishes, where decisions lay ultimately with the amateur, unpaid justices of the peace, recruited from the gentry. In short, the privileged classes were not, as in France, shelved, thrust aside by paid agents of the central government; nor did they, as in Prussia, become themselves mere agents of the Crown. Instead, they preserved a secure base in local government and an equally firm base in the House of Commons. When Charles I tried to govern without the consent of these privileged classes, when he tried to raise from them and their dependents money to run a bureaucratic government without these privileged amateurs, they had a solid institutional basis from which to resist.

But they had to struggle. They had to fight a civil war. No matter how much emphasis the historian may put on the social and institutional side, he cannot ignore what looks like the sheer accident of human personality. The Tudors from Henry VII to Elizabeth I, with some faltering under Edward VI and Mary, had been strong personalities and had been firmly—quite as firmly as any Valois or Hapsburg—convinced that they were called to absolute monarchy. They had slowly built up a very strong personal rule, handling their parliaments skillfully, giving in occasionally in detail, but holding the reins firmly. Henry VIII and his daughter Elizabeth both commanded the kind of devotion from their subjects that can be built in time into formidable personal rule; their successors could not command such emotional loyalty.

Elizabeth I was childless, and in 1603 she was succeeded by the son of her old rival and cousin, Mary, Queen of Scots. James Stuart, already king of Scotland as James VI, became James I of England (1603–1625), thus bringing the two countries, still legally separate, under the same personal rule. James was a pedant by temperament, very sure of himself, and above all sure that he was as much a divine-right monarch as his French cousins. He was a Scot, and as a foreigner an object of distrust to his English subjects. He lacked entirely the Tudor heartiness and tact, the gift of winning people to him. His son Charles I (1625–1649), under whom the divine-right experiment came to an end, had many more of the graces of a monarch than his father, but he was still no man to continue the work of the Tudors. He was quite as sure as his father had been that God had called him to rule England, but he could neither make the happy compromises the Tudors made nor revive their broad popular appeals.

The fundamental fact about the actual break between the first two Stuarts and their parliamentary opponents is that both were in a sense revolutionaries. Both were seeking to bend the line of English constitutional growth away from the Tudor compromise of a strong crown working with and through a late medieval parliament based on the alliance of nobility, gentry, and commercial classes. James and Charles were seeking to bend the line toward divine-right monarchy of the continental type; the parliamentarians were seeking to bend it toward something even newer, the establishment of a legislative body possessing the final authority in both the making and the carrying out of law and policy.

Behind this struggle lay the fact that the business of state was gradually growing in scope and therefore in cost. The money required by Stuarts—and indeed by Bourbons, Hapsburgs, and the rest of the continental monarchs—did not go just for high living by royalty and the support of parasitic nobles; it went to run a government that was beginning to assume many new functions. Foreign relations, for example, were beginning to take on modern forms, with a central foreign office, ambassadors, clerks, travel allowances, and the like, all requiring more money and personnel. James I and Charles I failed to get the money they needed because those from whom they sought it, the ruling classes, succeeded in placing the raising and spending of it in their own hands through parliamentary supremacy. The Parliament that won that supremacy was a kind of committee of the ruling classes; it was not a democratic legislature, since only a small fraction of the population could vote for members of the Commons.

In this struggle between Crown and Parliament religion played a major part in welding both sides into cohesive fighting groups. The struggle for power in England was in part a struggle to impose a uniform worship on Englishmen. The royalist cause was identified with High Church Anglicanism, that is, with an episcopalian church government and a liturgy and theology that made it a sacramental religion relatively free from left-wing Protestant austerities. The parliamentary cause, at first supported by many moderate Low Church Anglicans, also attracted a strong Puritan or Calvinist element. Later, it came under the control of the Presbyterians and then of the extreme Puritans, who were known as Independents of Congregationalists. The term "Puritanism" in seventeenth-century England is a confusing one, for it was used as a blanket to cover a wide range of religious groups, from moderate evangelical Anglicans all the way to the radical splinter sects of the 1640s and 1650s. The core of Puritanism went back to Zwingli and Calvin, to the repudiation of Catholic sacramental religion and the rejection of music and the adornment of churches. It placed a positive emphasis on sermons, on simplicity in church and out, and on "purifying" the tie between the worshiper and

Portrait of James I by Daniel Mytens, 1621.

his God of what the Puritans considered Catholic "superstitions" and "corruptions."

The Reign of James I, 1603–1625

In the troubled reign of James I, three major issues emerged that intensified the struggle in which his son was to go under—money, foreign policy, and religion. In all three issues, the Crown and its opposition each tried to bend the line of constitutional development in its own direction. In raising money, James sought to make the most of revenues that did not require a parliamentary grant. Parliament sought to make the most of its own control over the purse strings by insisting on the principle that any new revenue raising had to be approved by parliament. When James levied an import duty without a parliamentary grant, an importer of dried currants named Bate refused to pay.

Van Dyck's portrait of Charles I hunting, ca. 1635.

in fact a new claim for parliamentary control of foreign affairs. James responded by dissolving Parliament and imprisoning four of its leaders. The Spanish marriage fell through, but the betrothal of Charles in 1624 to the French princess Henrietta Maria, sister of Louis XIII, who was also Catholic, was hardly more popular with the English people.

In religion, Elizabeth, though refusing to permit public services by Catholics and Puritans, had allowed much variety of practice within the Anglican church. James summed up his policy in the phrase "no bishop, no king"—by which he meant that the enforcement of the bishops' monarchical authority in religion was essential to the maintenance of his own monarchical power. James at once took steps against what he held to be Puritan nonconformity. He called a conference of Anglican bishops and leading Puritans at Hampton Court in 1604, at which he presided in person and used the full force of his pedantic scholarship against the Puritans. After the conference dissolved with no real meeting of minds, royal policy continued to favor the High Church, anti-Puritan party. In spite of James' failure to achieve anything like religious agreement among his subjects, his reign is a landmark in the history of Christianity among English-speaking peoples. In 1611, after seven years' labor, a committee of forty-seven ministers authorized by him achieved the English translation of the Bible that is still widely used. The King James Version remains a masterpiece of Elizabethan prose, perhaps the most remarkable literary achievement a committee has ever made.

Bate's case was decided in favor of the Crown by the Court of Exchequer, and the decision attracted much attention because the judges held the king's powers in general to be absolute. Then a royal "benevolence"—a euphemism for a contribution exacted from an individual—was resisted by a certain St. John, and his appeal was sustained by the chief justice, Sir Edward Coke. James summarily dismissed Coke from office and thereby drew attention once again to his broad use of the royal prerogative.

The Tudors had regarded foreign affairs as entirely a matter of royal prerogative. The delicate problem of marriage for Elizabeth I, for instance, had concerned her Parliaments and the public; but Parliament made no attempt to dictate a marriage, and Elizabeth was careful not to offend her subjects in her own tentative negotiations. On the other hand, when James I openly sought a princess of hated Spain as a wife for his son Charles, the Commons in 1621 made public petition against the Spanish marriage. When James rebuked them for meddling, the House drew up the Great Protestation, the first of the great documents of the English Revolution, in which they used what they claimed were the historic privileges of Parliament to assert what was

The Difficulties of Charles I, 1625–1642

Under Charles I, all his father's difficulties came to a head very quickly. England was involved in a minor war against Spain, and though the members of Parliament hated Spain, they were most reluctant to grant Charles funds to support the English forces. Meanwhile, in spite of his French queen, Charles also became involved in a war against France. This he financed in part by a forced loan from his wealthier subjects and by quartering troops in private houses at the householders' expense. Consequently, Parliament in 1628 passed the Petition of Right—"the Stuart Magna Carta"—which first explicitly stated some of the most basic rules of modern constitutional government: No taxation without the consent of Parliament; no billeting of soldiers in private houses; no martial law in time of peace; no one to be imprisoned except on a specific charge and subject to the protection of regular legal procedure. All these principles were limitations on the Crown.

Charles consented to the Petition of Right in order to secure new grants of money from Parliament. But he also collected duties not sanctioned by Parliament, which thereupon protested by resolutions not only against his unauthorized taxes but also against his High Church policy. The king now veered from conciliation to firmness; in 1629 he had Sir John Eliot, mover of the resolutions, arrested together with eight other members, and then dissolved Parliament. Eliot died a prisoner in the Tower of London, the first martyr on the parliamentary side.

For the next eleven years, 1629–1640, Charles governed without a Parliament. He squeezed every penny he could get out of royal revenues that did not require parliamentary authorization, never quite breaking with precedent by imposing a wholly new tax, but stretching precedent beyond what his opponents thought reasonable. Ship money illustrates Charles' methods. It had been levied by the Crown before, but only on coastal towns for naval expenditures in wartime; Charles now imposed ship money on inland areas and in peacetime. When John Hampden, a very rich gentleman from inland Buckinghamshire refused to pay it, he lost his case in court (1637) but gained wide public support for challenging the king's fiscal expedients.

In religious matters, Charles was under the guidance of a very High Church Archbishop of Canterbury, William Laud, who systematically enforced Anglican conformity and deprived even moderate Puritans of their pulpits. Puritans were sometimes brought before the Star Chamber, long a highly respected administrative court but now gaining a reputation for high-handedness because it denied the accused the safeguards of the common law. In civil matters, Charles made use of an opportunist conservative, Thomas Wentworth, earl of Strafford, who had deserted the parliamentary side and went on to become lord lieutenant of Ireland.

England was seething with repressed political and religious passions underneath the outward calm of these years of personal rule. Yet, to judge from the imperfect statistics available, the relative weight of the taxation that offended so many Englishmen was less than on the Continent and far less than taxation in any modern Western state. The Englishmen who resisted the Crown by taking arms against it were not downtrodden, poverty-stricken people revolting from despair, but self-assertive, hopeful people defending their civil rights and their own forms of worship as well as seeking power and wealth.

The attempts of twentieth-century historians to isolate the economic motives of seventeenth-century English revolutionaries have stirred up a great scholarly controversy, which is linked with efforts to find a Europe-wide crisis in the middle 1600s. The debate has centered on the role of the gentry, that large group of landed aristocrats just under the high nobility, who did much of the fighting in the civil wars. R. H. Tawney, a Labor party intellectual, claimed that the more enterprising, more capitalistic gentleman farmers, rather like rural bourgeois, supported the Puritans. His antagonist,

Hugh Trevor-Roper of Oxford, asserted that on the contrary the gentry backing the Puritans were those who were barely holding their own or sinking down the economic scale in the face of inflation, the enclosure of lands for sheep farming, and the competition of the secular owners of former monastic lands. Neutral historians tend to conclude that these are suggestive though overabstract attempts to define the undefinable, the role of an amorphous social class whose economic status varied and whose political decisions were by no means necessarily made on economic grounds.

Charles I could perhaps have weathered his financial difficulties for a long time if he had not had to contend with the Scots. Laud's attempt to enforce the English High Church ritual and organization came up against the three-generations-old Scottish Presbyterian "Kirk." In 1638, a "Solemn League and Covenant" bound the members of the Kirk to resist Charles by force if need be. Charles marched north against the Scots and worked out a compromise with them in 1639. But even this mild campaign was too much for the treasury, and in 1640 Charles had to call Parliament back into session for the first time in eleven years. This Short Parliament denied him any money until the piled-up grievances against Charles and his father were settled; it was dissolved almost at once. Then the Scots went to war again, and Charles, defeated in a skirmish, bought them off by promising the Scottish army £850 a day until peace was made. Since he could not raise £850 a day, he had to call another Parliament, which became the famous Long Parliament of the Revolution.

Since the Scottish army would not be disbanded until it was paid off, the Long Parliament held it as a club over Charles' head and put through a great series of reforms striking at the heart of the royal power. It abolished ship money and other disputed taxes. It disbanded the unpopular royal administrative courts, such as the Star Chamber, which had become symbols of Stuart absolutism. Up to now, Parliament had been called and dismissed at the pleasure of the Crown; the Triennial Act of 1640 made obligatory the summoning of future Parliaments every three years, even if the Crown did not wish to do so. Parliament also attacked the royal favorites, whom Charles reluctantly abandoned. Archbishop Laud was removed, and Strafford, declared guilty of treason, was executed in May 1641.

Meanwhile, Strafford's harsh policy toward the Irish had borne fruit in a rebellion that amounted to an abortive war for national independence by Irish Catholics and that caused the massacre of thirty thousand Protestants in the northern Irish region of Ulster. Parliament, unwilling to trust Charles with an army to put down this rebellion, drew up in 1641 the Grand Remonstrance summarizing all its complaints. Charles now made a final attempt to repeat the tactics that had worked in 1629. Early in 1642, he ordered the arrest of five of his leading opponents in the House of Commons, including Hampden of the ship-money case. The five took refuge in the privileged political sanctuary of the City of London, where the king could not reach them. Charles I left for the north and in the summer of 1642 rallied an army at Nottingham; Parliament simply took over the central government. The Civil War had begun.

During these first years of political jockeying signs were already evident that strong groups in England and in Parliament wanted something more than a return to the Tudor balance between Crown and Parliament, and between religious conservatives and religious radicals. In politics, the Nineteen Propositions that Parliament submitted to the king in June 1642 would have established parliamentary supremacy over the army, the royal administration, the church, and even the rearing of the royal children. Charles turned down the propositions. In religion, the Root and Branch Bill, introduced in 1641 but not enacted into law, would have radically reformed the Church of England, destroying "root and branch," the bishops and much of what had already become traditional in Anglican religious practices. The moderates in politics and religion were plainly going to have trouble defending their middle-of-the-road policies among the extremists of a nation split by civil war.

The Civil War, 1642–1649

England split along lines partly territorial, partly social and economic, and partly religious. The royalist strength lay largely in the north and west, relatively less urban and less prosperous than other parts and largely controlled by country gentlemen loyal to throne

The House of Commons as shown on the Great Seal of England used by the Commonwealth, 1651.

and altar. Parliamentary strength lay largely in the south and east, especially in the great city of London and in East Anglia, where Puritanism commanded wide support among the gentry. The Scots were always in the offing, distrustful of an English Parliament but quite as distrustful of a king who had sought to foist episcopacy on their kirk.

In the field, the struggle was at first indecisive. The royalists, or Cavaliers, recruited from gentlemen used to riding, had the initial advantage of superior cavalry. What swung the balance to the side of Parliament was the development of a special force, recruited from ardent Puritans in the eastern counties, and gradually forged under strict discipline into the famous "Ironsides." Their leader was a Puritan gentleman named Oliver Cromwell (1599–1658), who won a crucial battle at Marston Moor in 1644. The parliamentary army, now reorganized into the New Model Army, staffed by radicals in religion and politics, stood as Roundheads (from their short-cropped hair, something like a crewcut) against the Cavaliers. At the battle of Naseby in 1645, the New Model was completely victorious over the king, and Charles in desperation took refuge with the Scottish army, who turned him over to the English Parliament in return for £400,000 back pay.

Now a situation arose that was to be repeated, with variations for time and place, in the French Revolution in 1792 and the Russian Revolution in 1917. The group of moderates who had begun the revolution and who still controlled the Long Parliament were confronted by the much more radical group who controlled the New Model Army. In religion, the moderates, seeking to retain some ecclesiastical discipline and formality, were Presbyterians or Low Church Anglicans; in politics, they were constitutional monarchists. The radicals, who were opposed to churches disciplined from a central organization, were Independents or Congregationalists, and they already so distrusted Charles that they were able at least to contemplate that extraordinary possibility, an England under a republican form of government. The situation was complicated by the Presbyterian Scots, who regarded the radical Roundheads as religious anarchists.

The years after 1645 were filled with difficult negotiations, during which Charles stalled for time to gain Scottish help. In 1648, Cromwell beat the invading Scots at Preston, and his army seized the king. Parliament, with the moderates still in control, now refused to do what the army wanted, to dethrone Charles. The Roundhead leaders then ordered Colonel Pride to exclude by force from the Commons ninety-six Presbyterian members. This the Colonel did in December 1648, in true military fashion, with no pretense of legality. After "Pride's Purge" only some sixty radicals remained of the more than five hundred members originally composing the Long Parliament; they were known henceforth as the Rump Parliament. The Rump brought Charles to trial before a special high court of trustworthy radicals, who condemned him to death. On January 30, 1649, Charles I was beheaded.

Cromwell and the Interregnum, 1649–1660

The subsequent eleven years are known to historians as the Interregnum, the interval between two monarchical reigns. This bit of English understatement should not disguise the fact that England was now a republic, under the government known as the Commonwealth. Since the radicals did not dare to call a free election, which would almost certainly have gone against them, the Rump Parliament continued to sit. Thus, from the start, the Commonwealth was the dictatorship of a radical minority come to power through the tight organization of the New Model Army. From the start, too, Cromwell was the dominating personality of the new government. In religion an earnest and sincere Independent, but no fanatic, a patriotic Englishman, strong-minded, stubborn, but not power-mad, by no means unwilling to compromise, Cromwell was nevertheless a prisoner of his position.

He faced a divided England, where the majority was no doubt royalist at heart and certainly sick of the fighting, the confiscations, the endless changes of the last decade. He faced a hostile Scotland and an even more hostile Ireland, where the disorders in England had encouraged the Catholic Irish to rebel once more in 1649. In 1650, Charles II, eldest son of the martyred Charles I, landed in Scotland, accepted the Covenant (thereby guaranteeing the Presbyterian faith as the established Scottish kirk), and led a Scottish army once more against the English. Once more, the English army proved unbeatable at the battle of Worcester (1651), and the hope of the Stuarts took refuge on the Continent, after a romantic escape in disguise. Finally, Cromwell faced a war with Holland (1652–1654) brought on by the Navigation Act of 1651, which deliberately struck at the Dutch carrying trade. It was a typically mercantilistic measure, which forbade the importation of goods into England and the colonies except in English ships or in ships of the country producing the imported goods.

By 1654, Cromwell had mastered all his foes. He himself went to Ireland and suppressed the rebellion with bloodshed that is still not forgotten. In the so-called Cromwellian Settlement, he dispossessed native Irish landholders in favor of Protestants; he achieved order in Ireland, but not peace. He brought the naval war with the Dutch to a victorious close in 1654. Later, Cromwell also waged an aggressive war against Spain (1656–1658), from whom the English acquired the rich Caribbean sugar island of Jamaica. Even in this time of troubles, the British Empire kept growing.

Cromwell, however, could not master the Rump Parliament, which brushed aside his suggestions for an increase in its membership and a reform of its procedures. In April 1653 he forced its dissolution by appearing in Parliament with a body of soldiers. In December 1653 he took the decisive step of inaugurating the regime called the Protectorate, with himself as "lord protector" of England, Scotland, and Ireland, and with a written constitution—the only one Britain has ever had—the Instrument of Government. It provided for an elected Parliament with a single house of 460 members, who were in fact chosen by Puritan sympathizers, since no royalist dared vote. Even so, the lord protector had constant troubles with his parliaments and in 1657 yielded to pressure and modified the Instrument of Government to provide for a second parliamentary house and to put limits on the lord protector's power. Meanwhile, to maintain order, Cromwell had divided the country into twelve military districts, each with a major general commanding a military force.

Oliver Cromwell died in 1658 and was succeeded as lord protector by his son Richard, who was a nonentity. The army soon seized control, and some of its leaders regarded the restoration of the Stuarts as the best way to end the chronic political turbulence. To ensure the legality of the move, General Monk, commander of the Protectorate's forces in Scotland, summoned back the Rump and readmitted the surviving members excluded by Pride's Purge. This partially reconstituted Long Parliament enacted the formalities of restoration, and in 1660 Charles Stuart returned from exile to reign as Charles II.

The Revolution in Review

Was there a Reign of Terror in the English Revolution? Perhaps not, since much of the bloodshed occurred in formal battles between organized armies and was not the revolutionary bloodshed of guillotine, lynching, and judicial murder. Nevertheless, Charles I was beheaded; Strafford, Laud, and others suffered the death penalty; royalists had their properties confiscated. Above all, the Puritans at the height of their rule in the early 1650s attempted to enforce on the whole population the difficult, austere life of the Puritan ideal. This enforcement took the familiar form of "blue laws," of prohibitions on horse racing, gambling, cock fighting, bear baiting, dancing on the green, fancy dress, the theater, on a host of ordinary phases of daily living. This English Reign of Terror and Virtue, coming too early for modern techniques of propaganda and regimentation, was not entirely effective. Many an Anglican clergyman, though officially "plundered"—that is, deprived of his living—continued worship in private houses; many a cock fight went on in secluded spots. Nevertheless, the strict code was there, with earnest persons to try to enforce it, and with implacable enemies to oppose it. The remark of the Victorian historian Macaulay—that the Puritans prohibited bear baiting not because it gave pain to the bear but because it gave pleasure to the spectators—is a sample of the deep hostility that still survives in England toward the reign of the Puritan "saints."

Many Englishmen have seemed rather ashamed of their great revolution, preferring to call it the Civil War or the Great Rebellion, and recalling instead as their Glorious Revolution the decorous movement of 1688–1689, to which we shall come in a moment. Yet the events of 1640–1660 are of major importance, not only in the history of England, but in the history of the West. Here for the first time the monarchy was challenged in a major revolt by politically active private citizens; though the Stuarts were ultimately restored, no English king could ever hope to rule again without a Parliament, or revive the Court of Star Chamber, or take ship money, benevolences, and other controversial taxes. Parliament thenceforward retained that critical weapon of the legislative body in a limited monarchy, control of the public purse by periodic grants of taxes.

Another basic freedom owes much to this English experience. Freedom of speech was a fundamental tenet of the Puritans, even though at the height of their power they did not live up to it. It received a classic expression from the poet John Milton, who was the secretary of the Commonwealth, in his *Areopagitica* (the reference is to the Council of the Areopagus in ancient Athens). While Milton defended free speech principally for an intellectual and moral elite, one of his arguments was characteristically English: attempts to curb free expression just won't work. In practice, the voluminous pamphlet literature of the early years of the great turmoil is a lively manifestation of free speech in action. The extraordinary fermentations of radical minorities foreshadowed modern political and social thought. One such group, the Levelers, found many sympathizers in the revolutionary army and advanced a program later carried by emigrants to the American colonies. They called for political democracy, universal suffrage, regularly summoned parliaments, progressive taxation, separation of church and state, and protection of the individual against arbitrary arrest. There were even hints of the collectivist drive toward economic equality, a goal closely tied to biblical ideas in those days. The Diggers, for example, were a small sect that preached the sharing of earthly goods in a kind of communism. They actually dug up public lands in Surrey near London and began planting vegetables; they were driven off, but not before they had got their ideas into circulation. The Fifth Monarchy men, the Millenarians, and a dozen other radical sects preached the Second Coming of Christ and the achievement of some kind of utopia on earth.

Still more important, there emerged from the English Revolution even more clearly than from the religious wars on the Continent, the conception of religious toleration. The Independents, while they were in opposition, stood firmly on the right of religious groups to

worship God as they wished. Though in their brief tenure of power they showed a willingness to persecute, they were never firmly enough in the saddle to make England into a seventeenth-century Geneva. At least one sect held to the idea and practice of religious toleration as a positive good. The Quakers, led by George Fox (1624–1691), were Puritans of the Puritans. They themselves eschewed all worldly show, finding even buttons ostentatious. They found the names of days and months indecently pagan, the polite form "you" in the singular a piece of social hypocrisy, and legal oaths or oathtaking most impious. Hence they met for worship on what they called First Day rather than the day of the sun god; they addressed another person as "thee" or "thou"; and they took so seriously the Protestant doctrine of the priesthood of the believer that they did entirely without a formal ordained ministry. In the Religious Society of Friends, as they are properly known, any worshiper who felt the spirit move might testify in what other sects would call a sermon. Friends felt too deeply the impossibility of forcing anyone to see the "inner light" for them to coerce people to accept their faith. They would abstain entirely from force, particularly from war, and would go their own way in Christian peace.

The Restoration, 1660–1688

The Restoration of 1660 kept Parliament essentially supreme but attempted to undo some of the work of the Revolution. Anglicanism was restored in England and Ireland, though not as a state church in Scotland. Against the "dissenters," as Protestants who would not accept the Church of England were then termed, the so-called Clarendon Code set up all sorts of restrictions. For instance, by the Five Mile Act all Protestant ministers who refused to subscribe to Anglican orthodoxy were forbidden to come within five miles of any town where they had previously preached. Yet the dissenters continued to dissent without heroic sufferings. In characteristically English fashion, the Test Act of 1672, which prescribed communion according to the Church of England on all officeholders, local as well as national, was simply got around in various ways, though it was not actually repealed until 1828. One way was "occasional conformity," by which a dissenter of not too strict conscience might worship as a Congregationalist, say, all year, but might once or twice take Anglican communion. Another, developed in the eighteenth century, was to permit dissenters to hold office, and then pass annually a bill of indemnity legalizing their illegal acts. Dissenters remained numerous, especially among the artisans and middle-class merchants, and as time went on they grew powerful, so that the "nonconformist conscience" was a major factor in English public life. Indeed, the three-century progression of names by which these non-Anglican Protestants were called is a neat summary of their rise in status—the hostile term "dissenter" became "nonconformist" in the nineteenth century and "Free Churchman" in the twentieth.

The Restoration was also a revulsion against Puritan ways. The reign of Charles II (1660–1685) was a period of moral looseness, of gay court life, of the Restoration drama with its ribald wit (the Puritans in power had closed the theaters), of the public pursuit of pleasure, at least among the upper classes. But the new Stuarts had not acquired political wisdom. Charles II dissipated some of the fund of good will with which he started by following a foreign policy that seemed to patriotic Englishmen too subservient to the wicked French king Louis XIV. The cynic is tempted to point out that, if Charles's alliance with Louis in 1670 was most un-English, it did result in the final extinction of any Dutch threat to English seapower. And it sealed a very important English acquisition, that of New Amsterdam, now New York, first taken in the Anglo-Dutch War of 1664–1667.

What really undid the later Stuarts and revealed their political ineptitude was the Catholic problem. Charles II had come under Catholic influence through his French mother and very possibly embraced the Roman religion before he died in 1685. Since he left no legitimate children, the crown passed to his brother, James II (1685–1688), who was already a declared Catholic. In the hope of enlisting the support of the dissenters for the toleration of Catholics, James II issued in 1687 a Declaration of Indulgence, granting freedom of worship to *all* denominations, Protestant dissenters as well as Catholics, in England and Scotland. This was in the abstract an admirable step toward full religious liberty; but to the great majority of Englishmen Catholicism still seemed the great menace to the English nation, and it was always possible to stir them to an

Seventeenth-century Dutch engraving: fireworks in London celebrating the coronation of King William III and Queen Mary II.

irrational pitch by an appeal to their fear of "popery." Actually, by the end of the seventeenth century the few remaining Catholics in England were glad to be left in something like the status of the dissenters and were no real danger to a country overwhelmingly Protestant. In Ireland, however, the Catholics remained an unappeasable majority.

The political situation was much like that under Charles I; the Crown wanted one thing, Parliament wanted another. Although James II made no attempt to dissolve Parliament or to arrest members, he simply went over Parliament's head by issuing decrees, like the Declaration of Indulgence granting full religious toleration, in accordance with what he called the "power of dispensation." Early in his reign, he had made a piddling rebellion by the duke of Monmouth, a bastard son of Charles II, the excuse for two ominous policies. First, his judges organized the "bloody assizes," which punished suspected rebel sympathizers with a severity that seemed out of all proportion to the extent of the rebellion. Second, he created a standing army of thirty thousand men, part of whom he stationed near London in what appeared an attempt to intimidate the capital. To contemporaries it looked as though James were plotting to force both Catholicism and divine-right monarchy on an unwilling England. The result was the Glorious Revolution.

The Glorious Revolution and its Aftermath, 1688–1714

The actual revolution was a coup d'etat engineered at first by a group of James' parliamentary opponents who were called Whigs, in contrast to the Tories who tended to support at least some of the policies of the later Stuart monarchs. The Whigs were the direct heirs of the moderates of the Long Parliament, and they represented an alliance of the great lords and the prosperous London merchants.

James II married twice. By his first marriage he had two daughters, both Protestant—Mary, who had married William of Orange, the Dutch opponent of Louis XIV, and Anne. Then in 1688 a son was born to James and his Catholic second wife, thus apparently making the passage of the crown to a Catholic heir inevitable. The Whig leaders responded with a barrage of propaganda, including a whispering campaign to the effect that the queen had not even been pregnant and a new-born babe had been smuggled into her chamber in a warming pan, so that there might be a Catholic heir. Then the Whigs and some Tories negotiated with William of Orange, who could hardly turn down a proposition that would give him the solid assets of English power in his struggle with Louis XIV. He accepted the offer of the English crown, which he was to share with his wife, the couple reigning as William III (1689–1702) and Mary II (1689–1694). On November 5, 1688, William landed at Tor Bay on the Devon coast with some fourteen thousand soldiers. When James heard the news, he tried to rally support, but everywhere the great lords and even the normally conservative country gentlemen were on the side of the Protestant hero. James fled from London to France in December 1688, giving William an almost bloodless victory.

Early in 1689 Parliament formally offered the crown to William on terms that were soon enacted into law as the Bill of Rights. This famous document, summing up the constitutional practices that Parliament had been working for since the Petition of Right in 1628, is in fact almost a succinct form of written constitution. It lays down the essential principles of parliamentary supremacy—control of the purse, prohibition of the royal power of dispensation, and frequent meetings of Parliament. Three major steps were necessary after 1689 to convert Britain into a parliamentary democracy in which the Crown has purely symbolic functions as the focus of patriotic loyalty. These were, first, the concentration of executive direction in a committee of the majority party in the Parliament—that is, the Cabinet headed by a prime minister, the work of the eighteenth and early nineteenth centuries; second, the establishment of universal suffrage and payment of members of the Commons, the work of the nineteenth century, completed in the twentieth; and third, the abolition of the power of the House of Lords to veto legislation passed by the Commons, the work of the early twentieth century. Thus we can see that full democracy was still a long way off in 1689. William III and Mary II were real rulers, who did not think of themselves as purely ornamental monarchs, without power over policy.

Childless, they were succeeded by Mary's younger sister, Anne (1702–1714). Anne and her nonentity of a husband strove hard to leave an heir to the throne, but all their many children were stillborn or died in childhood. The exiled Catholic Stuarts, however, did better. The little boy born to James II in 1688 and brought up at the court of St. Germain near Paris, grew up to be known as the "Old Pretender." But in 1701 Parliament passed the Act of Settlement, which settled the crown, in default of heirs to Anne, the heir apparent to the sick William III, not on the Catholic pretender but on the Protestant Sophia of Hanover or her issue. Sophia was a granddaughter of James I, and the daughter of Frederick of the Palatinate, the "Winter King" of Bohemia in the Thirty Years' War. On Anne's death in 1714, the crown therefore passed to Sophia's son, George, first king of the house of Hanover. This settlement clearly established the fact that Parliament, and not the divinely ordained succession of the eldest male in direct descent, made the king of England.

In order to ensure the Hanoverian succession in both the Stuart kingdoms, Scotland as well as England, the formal union of the two was completed in 1707 as the United Kingdom of Great Britain. Scotland gave up its own parliament and sent sixteen peers to the Lords and forty-five members to Commons of the Parliament of the United Kingdom at Westminster. The Union Jack, with the superimposed crosses of Saint George (for England) and Saint Andrew (for Scotland), became the national flag of Great Britain. Although the union met with some opposition from both English and Scots, on the whole it went through with surprising ease, so great was Protestant fear of a possible return of the Catholic Stuarts. And, in spite of occasional sentimental outbreaks of Scottish nationalism even in our own day, the union has worked very well. With the whole of England and the colonies open to Scottish politicians and businessmen, the nation famed for its thrifty and canny citizens achieved a prosperity it had never known before.

The Glorious Revolution did not, however, settle one other perennial problem—Ireland. The Catholic Irish rose in support of the exiled James II and were put down at the Boyne in 1690. William then attempted to apply moderation in his dealings with Ireland, but the Protestant "garrison" there soon forced him to return to the Cromwellian policy. Although Catholic worship was not actually forbidden, all sorts of galling restrictions were imposed on the Catholic Irish, including the prohibition of Catholic schools. Moreover, economic persecution was added to the religious, as Irish trade came under stringent mercantilist regulation. This was the Ireland whose misery inspired Jonathan Swift in 1729 to make his "modest proposal" that the impoverished Irish sell their babies as articles of food.

IV The Century of Genius

In the seventeenth century the cultural, as well as the political, hegemony of Europe passed from Italy and Spain to France, England, and Holland. Especially in literature, the France of *le grand siècle* set the imprint of its classical style on the West through the writings of Corneille, Racine, Molière, Boileau, Bossuet, and a host of others. Yet the men who exerted the greatest influence on our culture were not exclusively French and were rather philosophers and scientists than men of letters. The Italian Galileo and the Englishman Newton, together with the Frenchmen Descartes and Pascal, launched the modern scientific revolution and prompted Whitehead to claim that ever since their day we "have been living upon the accumulated capital of ideas provided . . . by the genius of the seventeenth century." *

*A. N. Whitehead, *Science and the Modern World* (New York, 1948), p. 58.

Portrait of Descartes by Frans Hals.

The Scientific Revolution

A major role in the cultivation of a new scientific attitude was taken by the English intellectual and politician Francis Bacon (1561–1626). Though not himself a successful practitioner of science, Bacon was the tireless proponent of the need for the observation of phenomena and the patient accumulation of data. In *The Great Instauration* (the word means "restoration") he wrote:

> For all those who before me have applied themselves to the invention of arts have but cast a glance or two upon facts and examples and experience, and straightway proceeded, as if invention were nothing more than an exercise of thought, to invoke their own spirits to give them oracles. I, on the contrary, dwelling purely and constantly among the facts of nature, withdraw my intellect from them no further than may suffice to let the images and rays of natural objects meet in a point, as they do in the sense of vision. . . . And by these means I suppose that I have established for ever a true and lawful marriage between the empirical and the rational faculty, the unkind and ill-starred divorce and separation of which has thrown into confusion all the affairs of the human family.*

*M. T. McClure, ed., *Bacon: Selections* (New York, 1928), pp. 14–15.

By relying on the empirical faculty, which learns from experience, Bacon was promoting what he called induction, which proceeds from the particular to the general. Deduction, the medieval mode of reasoning still in fashion in Bacon's day, by contrast, proceeds from the general to the particular. Deduction is not necessarily antiscientific, for it sometimes produces the hunches advancing theoretical science. What Bacon particularly attacked was the inclination of deductive reason to accept general axioms as "settled and immovable." Ranking high among such established axioms were the views of the universe associated with two authorities of antiquity, Aristotle and Ptolemy. Bacon's contemporary, Galileo (1564–1642), ridiculed blind acceptance of ancient authorities and thereby became embroiled with the Church.

Galileo was also one of the scores of individuals—some famous, some unknown or now forgotten—who contributed to the new instruments that permitted the more exact measurements and more detailed observations of inductive science. It is probable, for example, that Dutch glassmakers first put two lenses together and discovered that they could obtain a greater magnification. By 1610 Galileo was using the new device in the form of a telescope to study the heavens, and later in the century two Dutchmen employed it in the form of a microscope—Swammerdam to analyze blood (he probably discovered the red corpuscles), and Van Leeuwenhoek to view and describe protozoa and bacteria. Working from the experiments of Galileo, other technicians developed such instruments of measurement as the thermometer and the barometer. Using the barometer, the Frenchman Pascal (1623–1662) proved that what we term air pressure diminished with altitude. From this he went on to counter the old adage "Nature abhors a vacuum" by showing that a vacuum is possible.

Charles II of England roared with laughter on being told that members of his Royal Society were weighing the air. Yet the Royal Society for Improving Natural Knowledge, founded in 1662, and its French counterpart, the Académie des Sciences (1666), were important promoters of scientific investigation. The one, in characteristic English fashion, was a private undertaking, though with a royal charter; the other, sponsored by Colbert for the greater glory of Louis XIV and *la grande nation*, was a government institution, whose fellows received salaries and also instructions to avoid discussion of religion and politics. Both societies financed experiments and both published scientific articles in their house organs, the *Philosophical Transactions* and *Journal des savants*.

An international scientific community arose through the formal exchanges of the corresponding secretaries of such academies, and also through the private correspondence among members and their acquaintances. Both professional men and aristocrats joined learned societies, and many a gentleman and an occasional lady dabbled in a private laboratory or observatory. Some did more than dabble, among them Robert Boyle (1627–1691), son of an Irish earl, who discovered the law of physics named after him: that under compression the volume of a gas is inversely proportional to the amount of pressure. While many scientists still published in Latin, their discoveries were popularized in books and articles in the vernacular.

Meantime, the basic language of science—mathematics—was taking a great leap forward. In 1585 Stevin, a Fleming, published *The Decimal, Teaching with Unheard-of Ease How to Perform All Calculations Necessary among Men by Whole Numbers without Fractions*. Another great time-saver was devised by the Scot Napier, with his *Marvelous Rule of Logarithms* (1616), which shortened the laborious processes of multiplying, dividing, and finding square roots. Descartes (1596–1650) worked out analytical geometry, which brought geometry and algebra together through the "Cartesian coordinates," as in the plotting of an equation on a graph. The mathematical achievements of the century culminated in a method for dealing with variables and probabilities. Pascal made a beginning with studies of games of chance, and Dutch insurance actuaries devised tables to estimate the life expectancy of their clients. The English Newton and the German Leibniz (1646–1716), apparently quite independently of each other, invented the calculus. The practical value of these innovations is indicated by the fact that without the calculus, and without Cartesian geometry, Newton could never have made the calculations supporting his revolutionary hypotheses in astronomy and physics.

In astronomy the heliocentric theory advanced by Copernicus in the sixteenth century proved to be only a beginning. It raised many difficulties, notably when observation of planetary orbits did not confirm Copernicus' belief that the planets revolved about the sun in circular paths. The German Kepler (1571–1630) opened the way to a resolution by proving mathematically that the orbits were in fact elliptical. Then Galileo's telescope revealed the existence of spots on the sun, rings around Saturn, and moonlike satellites around Jupiter. All this evidence of corruption in high places led Galileo to publish a book in 1632 defending the heliocentric concept and ridiculing supporters of the traditional geocentric theory. But the Church, headed by traditionalists, brought Galileo before the Inquisition, which placed his book on the *Index* of prohibited works and sentenced him to what amounted to perpetual house arrest. Despite the public recantation Galileo was obliged to make, he is reported to have had the last word, "and yet it does move"—the Earth is not stationary, as the Church insists, but a planet behaving like other planets.

An even more celebrated story recounts Galileo's experiment of dropping balls of different weights from the Leaning Tower of Pisa to test Aristotle's theory that objects fall with velocities proportional to their weight.

While the story itself may be apocryphal, Galileo did in fact disprove Aristotle. Galileo's studies of projectiles, pendulums, and falling and rolling bodies helped establish modern ideas of acceleration and inertia, which Newton later formulated mathematically.

In 1687 Newton published the laws of motion, together with other great discoveries, in *Philosophiae Naturalis Principia Mathematica* (Mathematical Principles of Natural Philosophy). Since he had made many of these findings two decades earlier, when he was still an undergraduate at Cambridge, Newton fits the popular concept of physics as the young man's science par excellence. He went on to secure abundant recognition in his later years, gaining a professorship at Cambridge, a knighthood, the presidency of the Royal Society, and the well-paid post of master of the Mint. Even Newton, however, was not fully modern, for he often devoted himself to experiments in alchemy and unsuccessful efforts to determine the accurate dates of biblical events.

Newton's greatest contribution was the law of gravitation. It followed from his laws of motion, which picture bodies moving not in straightforward fashion of themselves but only in response to forces impressed upon them. These forces are at work in the mutual attraction of the sun, the planets, and their satellites, which are thereby held in their orbits. Newton stated the formula that the force of gravitation is proportional to the product of the masses of two bodies attracted one to the other, and inversely proportional to the square of the distance between them. Newton also promoted the development of optics by using a prism to separate sunlight into the colors of the spectrum. He demonstrated that objects only appear to be colored: their color is not intrinsic but the result of reflection and absorption of light.

Meanwhile, the mechanistic views of the physicists were invading geology and physiology. In 1600, the Englishman Gilbert, in a study of magnetism, suggested that the earth itself was a giant magnet. In 1628, Harvey, the physician of Charles I, published his demonstration that the human heart is a pump driving the blood around a single circulatory system. Harvey's theory, confirmed a generation later by the discovery through microscopic observation of the capillary connections between arteries and veins, discredited the hypothesis, handed down from Galen in classical antiquity, that the blood in the arteries moved quite separately from that in the veins. Finally, in 1679, the Italian Borelli showed that the human arm is a lever, and that muscles do mechanical work.

World-Machine and Rationalism

All these investigations in the various sciences tended to undermine the older Aristotelian concept of something "perfect." Instead of perfect circles, post-Copernican astronomy posited ellipses; instead of bodies moving in straightforward fashion of themselves Newton pictured bodies responding only to forces impressed upon them. All these investigations, in short, suggested a new major scientific generalization, a law of uniformity that simplified and explained and that coordinated many separate laws into one general law. Galileo almost made this achievement, but got into trouble with the Church for suggesting that the earth was not stationary, as had always been thought. It was Newton who finally drew everything together in the grand mechanical conception that has been called the Newtonian world-machine.

The Newtonian world-machine, and the new science of which it was the product, had very important theological and philosophical implications. Natural science of itself does not deal with the great problems of theology and philosophy. It does not give men ends or purposes but rather means, and its theories are explanations, not moral justifications. Yet, historically, the rise of modern science was associated with a definite world-view and system of values, for which the best name is probably *rationalism.* This is a broad term. It is possible to be at the same time a rationalist and a believer in a supernatural God, like Thomas Aquinas and other medieval Schoolmen. In the early modern West, however, rationalism tended to banish God entirely from the universe or at least to reduce him to a First Cause that started the world-machine going but then did not interfere with its operation. The new mechanistic interpretation of the universe regarded God not as the incomprehensible Creator and Judge but simply as the architect of a world-machine whose operations man could grasp if only he would apply his reason properly.

The rationalism and materialism engendered by the scientific revolution found a most articulate spokesman in René Descartes. When he was a young man, as his *Discourse on Method* (1637) relates, he resolved to mistrust all authorities, theological or intellectual. His skepticism swept everything aside until he concluded that there was one thing only he could not doubt: his own existence. There must be reality in the self engaged in the processes of thinking and doubting—in the famous formulation, "Cogito ergo sum" (I think, therefore I am). From this one indubitable fact Descartes reconstructed the world until he arrived at God, a deity poles apart from older patriarchal concepts, a supreme geometer whose mathematical orderliness foreshadowed the great engineer of the Newtonian world-machine. But where Newton would proceed inductively, at least in part, by relying on the data of scientific observations and experiments, Descartes proceeded deductively, deriving the universe and God ultimately from "Cogito ergo sum."

The world that Descartes reconstructed proved to be two separate worlds—that of mind and soul, on the one hand, and that of body and matter, on the other. We confront the famous Cartesian dualism, which the twentieth-century philosopher-mathematician White-head claimed so hypnotized succeeding generations of philosophers that modern philosophy was ruined by their futile endeavors to put matter into mind or mind into matter and thus resolve the dualism. Descartes himself claimed competence to deal in detail only with the material world, yet the way in which he dealt with it intimated that it was the only world that counted. Witness his boast that if given matter and space, he could construct the universe himself.

Progress—and Pessimism

Scientist and rationalist helped greatly to establish in the minds of educated men throughout the West two complementary concepts that were to give the Enlightenment of the eighteenth century a pattern of action toward social change, a pattern still of driving force in our world. These were, first, the concept of a regular "natural" order underlying the irregularity and confusion of the universe as it appears to unreflecting man in his daily experience; and, second, the concept of a human faculty, best called reason, obscured in most men by their faulty traditional upbringing, but capable of being brought into effective play by good—that is, rational—upbringing. Both these concepts can be found in some form in our Western tradition at least as far back as the Greeks. What gives them novelty and force at the end of the seventeenth century is their being welded into the doctrine of progress—the belief that all human beings can attain here on earth a state of happiness, of perfection, hitherto in the West thought to be possible only for Christians in a state of grace, and for them only in a heaven after death.

By no means all the great minds of the seventeenth century shared this optimistic belief in progress and the infallibility of reason. The many-sided legacy of this century of genius is evident, for example, in the contrast between the two most important political writings issuing from the English Revolution—Thomas Hobbes' *Leviathan* and John Locke's *Second Treatise of Government*. Published in 1651 and much influenced by the disorders of the English Civil War, *Leviathan* is steeped in Machiavellian pessimism about the inherent sinfulness of man. The state of nature, when men live without government, is a state of war, Hobbes argues, where men prey upon their fellows and human life is "solitary, poor, nasty, brutish, short." Men's only recourse is to agree among themselves to submit absolutely to the Leviathan, an all-powerful state that will force men into peace.

In a sense, Hobbes turned the contract theory of government upside down by having men consent to yield all their liberties. With Locke it is right side up again. Locke, who knew Robert Boyle and was closely linked with the Royal Society, was also a close associate of the Whig leaders who engineered the Glorious Revo-

lution. His *Second Treatise of Government*, published in 1690 as a defense of their actions, accepted neither the divine-right theory of absolutism nor the Hobbesian justification of absolutism out of desperation. Locke paints a generally cheerful picture of the state of nature, which suffers only from the "inconvenience" (note the mild terminology) of lacking an impartial judicial authority. To secure such an authority men contract among themselves to accept a government, not the omnipotent Leviathan, but a government that respects a man's life, liberty, and property. Should the king seize property by imposing unauthorized taxes or should he follow policies like those of James II, then his subjects are justified in overthrowing their monarch. Locke's relative optimism and his enthusiasm for constitutional government nourished the major current of political thought in the next century, culminating in the American and French revolutions. But events after 1789 brought Hobbesian despair and authoritarianism to the surface once more.

Meantime, exponents of the older Christian tradition continued to flourish on the Continent. One example is the energetic Frenchman Vincent de Paul (1581–1660), who served seven years as a slave in a Turkish galley. While insisting on the observance of strict orthodoxy, Vincent also instituted the systematic care of foundlings, sponsored missions to rural areas neglected by the Church, and launched the Daughters of Charity, an organization that would enable well-to-do women to undertake the good works Vincent believed their wealth and status obligated them to perform.

Another example is Blaise Pascal, who also believed in charity, but in the sense of God's incomprehensible love rather than of philanthropy. Pascal, indeed, was a one-man summation of the complexities of the century of genius. He won an important place in the history of mathematics and physics by his work with air pressure and vacuums and, at the practical level, by his invention of a calculating machine and his establishment of the first horse-drawn bus line in Paris. Yet he was profoundly otherworldly as well and became a spokesman for the high-minded puritanical Jansenists, whose doctrines he defended in lively epigrammatic French, with the skill, fervor, and onesidedness of the born pamphleteer. He dismissed as unworthy the concepts of God as mere master geometer or engineer and sought instead for the Lord of Abraham and the Old Testament prophets. He underwent a great mystical experience one night in November 1654 when he felt with absolute certainty the presence of God and of Christ. He spent his final years in religious meditation and left unfinished at his death one of the most remarkable works of Christian apologetics in existence, the *Pensées* (Thoughts). Here he wrote:

Man is but a being filled with error. This error is natural, and, without grace, ineffaceable. Nothing shows him the truth: everything deceives him. These two principles of truth, reason and the senses, besides lacking sincerity, reciprocally deceive each other. The senses deceive reason by false appearances: and just as they cheat reason they are cheated by her in turn: she has her revenge. Passions of the soul trouble the senses, and give them false impressions. They emulously lie and deceive each other.*

A final example is Baruch Spinoza (1632–1677), who tried to reconcile the God of Science and the God of Scripture. Spinoza constructed a system of ethical axioms as rigorously Cartesian and logical as a series of mathematical propositions. He also tried to reunite the Cartesian opposites, matter with mind, body with soul, by asserting that God was present everywhere and in everything. His pantheism caused his ostracism in Holland by his fellow Jews and also by the Christians, who considered him an atheist; his rejection of rationalism and materialism offended intellectuals. Spinoza found few admirers until the romantic revolt against the abstractions and oversimplifications of the Enlightenment.

Literature

Just as Henry IV, Richelieu, and Louis XIV brought greater order to French politics after the civil and religious upheavals of the sixteenth century, so the writers of the seventeenth century disciplined French writing after the Renaissance extravagance of a genius like Rabelais. It was the Age of Classicism, which insisted on the observance of elaborate rules, on the authority of models from classical antiquity, and on the employment of a more polite vocabulary. In the early 1600s the example of greater refinement in manners and speech was set by the circle who met in the Paris *salon* (reception room) of an aristocratic hostess, the marquise de Rambouillet. Later, proper behavior was standardized by the court ceremonial at Versailles and proper vocabulary by the famous dictionary of the French language that the experts of the academy founded by Richelieu finished compiling in the 1690s after more than a half century of labor. Boileau (1636–1711), the chief literary critic of the day, set the rules for writing poetry with his pronouncement "Que toujours le bon sens s'accorde avec le rhyme" (Always have good sense agree with the rhyme). Exaggerated notions of propriety outlawed from polite usage the French counterparts of such terms as *spit* and *vomit* and obliged writers to seek euphemisms for dozens of commonplace activities. Already there are indications of the social cleavage that produced the revolution of 1789 in the enormous gap between the classical French of the court and the plainer, coarser language of the average French person.

On the other hand, the linguistic purification of the seventeenth century also brought substantial benefits. Without its discipline, French could never have won its unique reputation for clarity and elegance. The leading tragic dramatists of *le grand siècle* made observance of all the classical do's and don'ts not an end in itself but a means to probe deeply into the endless variety of human personalities. Corneille (1606–1684) and Racine (1639–1699) usually chose plots from Greek mythology and wrote in the rhymed couplets called alexandrines (the iambic hexameter used for a poem about Alexander the Great). They also respected the unities decreed by Aristotle's *Poetics,* which restricted the action of play to a single place, to one twenty-four-hour span of time, and to a single topic. Within this rigid form the genius of Corneille and Racine created moving portraits of people upholding exalted ideals of honor or crushed by overwhelming emotion. The French tragedies of the seventeenth century are worthy successors to the Greek dramas of the fifth century B.C. not merely because of their classical form but also because of their psychological insight and emotional power.

As a writer of comedies Molière (1622–1673), the other great dramatist of the age, was less constrained to employ a dignified vocabulary and to heed the other canons of classicism. The main characters of his satirical comedies were not only sharply etched individuals but social types as well—the overrefined pedantic ladies of the salons in *Les Précieuses Ridicules,* the hypocrite in *Tartuffe,* the miser in *L'Avare,* the ignorant and self-important newly rich in *Le Bourgeois Gentilhomme.* In Molière, as in all good satire, there is more than a touch of moralizing, and didactic overtones are also present in two other characteristic works of the Great Century. The *Fables* of La Fontaine (1621–1695) which reworked in lively fashion tales borrowed from antiquity, vindicated the author's contention that while he imitated the classics he was by no means enslaved to them. The *Maxims* of La Rochefoucauld (1613–1680), cast in epigrammatic prose of classic purity, were less down to earth in language but even more disenchanted in their estimates of human nature: "We all have enough strength to bear the misfortunes of others." "We generally give praise only to gain it for ourselves." "We always find something not altogether displeasing in the misfortunes of our friends." *

Seventeenth-century English literature also had its cynics, notably Wycherley, Congreve, and the other playwrights who wrote the witty, bawdy, and disillusioned Restoration comedies. Under Charles II and his successors the pendulum of public taste and morality

*B. Pascal, *Thoughts, Letters, and Opuscules,* trans. O. W. Wright (Boston, 1882), p. 192.

*The Maxims of La Rochefoucauld, trans. F. G. Stevens (London, 1939), pp. 9, 49, 173.

Diego Velásquez "The Maids of Honor," 1656.

made a particularly violent swing in reaction to the midcentury Puritans who had closed down the theaters as dens of sinfulness. One of those Puritans, John Milton (1608–1674), the secretary of Oliver Cromwell, produced a truly major work of literature, *Paradise Lost,* the only English epic in the grand manner that still attracts many readers. Though Milton was a classical scholar of staggering erudition, his often complex style and his profound belief in Christian humanism really made him a belated representative of an earlier literary age, the last great man of the English Renaissance.

What was needed to prepare for the classical age of English letters was the modernization of the English language by pruning the elaborate flourishes, standardizing the chaotic spelling, and eliminating the long flights of rhetoric characteristic of Elizabethan and early seventeenth century prose. Under the influence of John Dryden (1631–1700), English began to model itself on French, adopting its straightforward word order, its comparatively brief sentences, and its polish,

neatness, and clarity. English letters were ready for the Augustan age, which lasted through the first half of the eighteenth century.

V The Baroque Era

Baroque, the label usually applied to the arts of the seventeenth century, probably comes from the Portuguese *barroco,* an irregular or mishapen pearl. Some critics have seized upon the suggestion of deformity to deprecate the impurity of seventeenth-century art in contrast to the purity of the Renaissance. Especially among Protestants, the reputation of baroque has suffered because it was identified with the Counter-Reformation and many of its leading artists appeared to be propagandists for Rome. In addition, many viewers may be repelled by the flamboyance of such baroque works as the enormous baldachin, the sculptured canopy over the main altar of Saint Peter's in Rome, or the acres of canvases by Rubens in the Louvre that seem to be populated mainly by hefty pink female flesh.

It is true that baroque art was closely associated with the Jesuits, with the successors of Philip II in Spain, and above all with Rome during the century following the Council of Trent. Papal patronage reached a pinnacle in the pontificate of Urban VIII (1623–1644), the head of the free-spending Barberini family. It is also true that Catholic reformers enlisted the arts in propagating the faith and endowing it with greater emotional intensity. Yet it is equally true that not all the baroque masters were Catholic—Rembrandt, for instance, was a Mennonite, and Sir Christopher Wren an Anglican—nor were all their patrons Catholic prelates or grandees. Portraits of the Protestant Charles I of England brought Van Dyck fame and wealth, and in the Dutch Republic, where the Calvinist churches frowned on all ornamentation, painters won support from the business community and sometimes became prosperous businessmen themselves.

The unprecedented financial success of some artists is one of the distinguishing characteristics of baroque: Rubens, Van Dyck, Wren, and Bernini were able to live like lords, in contrast to the relatively austere existence of such Renaissance masters as Leonardo and Michelangelo. A second characteristic is the baroque stress on sheer size exemplified by the vast canvases of Rubens, the immense palace of Versailles, and Bernini's baldachin in Saint Peter's and his grandiose colonnade outside. A third characteristic is the preoccupation with theatricality, as painters intensified the use of *chiaroscuro* to create the illusion of brilliant lighting and placed figures in the immediate foreground of a canvas to draw the spectator into the scene as a participant. A final characteristic is the realistic depiction of a wide range of humanity, clowns, beggars, gypsies, cardsharps, cripples and dwarfs as well as ordinary people praying, laughing, or eating. In France, for example, Georges de La Tour (1593–1653) took everyday subjects—a woman retrieving a flea as she undresses is a famous instance—and executed them in a nighttime setting that permitted dramatic contrasts of light and shadow.

Painting

The most restrained baroque painter was probably Velásquez (1599–1660), who spent thirty-four years at the court of Philip IV of Spain, interrupted only by two trips to Italy where he purchased for his patron masterpieces by Titian and other Renaissance masters now housed in Madrid's Prado. Velásquez was fascinated by the solution of difficult technical problems. He needed all his skill to soften the receding chins and thick lips of the Hapsburgs and yet make his portraits of Philip IV and the royal family instantly recognizable. His greatest feat of technical wizardry is *The*

Maids of Honor, which has a room to itself in the Prado. A little princess, having her portrait painted, is surrounded by a pet dog, dwarfs, and other attendants; it is the moment when the royal parents are looking in on the scene, but only their reflections are seen, in a mirror at the rear of the room. As Velásquez turns to greet them and looks at the viewer, the latter realizes he is standing where the royal couple must have stood. Painted with the adroit use of mirrors, *The Maids of Honor* is a splendid example of baroque attempts to make the spectator an active participant.

Unlike the aristocratic Velásquez, the Flemish Rubens (1577–1640) was the baroque counterpart of the Renaissance universal man. A diplomat and linguist, an ardent student of antiquity and archaeology, he amassed a fortune from his painting and collected impressive honors (knighting by Charles I of England, elevation to the nobility by the King of Spain). Rubens made his studio, with its two hundred students, a veritable factory of art, and he himself is estimated to have contributed at least in part to over two thousand pictures, whose subjects ranged from simple portraits to

Rubens' "Marie de' Medici Landing in Marseilles."

A Rembrandt self-portrait (1640).

ambitious political themes. He painted the ceiling of the Whitehall Banqueting Hall in London saluting James I as the uniter of Scotland and England; he did an allegory of the city of Antwerp as Andromeda, a mythological princess who was chained to a rock until she was liberated, in this instance by a Spanish governor; and he was commissioned by Marie de' Medici, the widow of Henry IV of France, to execute a series of canvases glorifying Henry and herself. As monarchs by divine right, Henry and Marie are portrayed more as mythological figures than as mere mortals; artistically, the pictures are significant for the generous employment of the mother-of-pearl flesh tones, which are Rubens' hallmark.

One of Rubens' pupils was his fellow Fleming, Van Dyck (1599–1641), whose portraits of Charles I captured the casual elegance and confident authority of the Stuart monarch, making him appear the embodiment of Castiglione's ideal courtier. Although courtly values had few followers among the Flemings' northern neighbors in the Netherlands, the officers of Dutch civic guards and the governing boards of guilds and other important organizations of Dutch merchants liked to be portrayed for posterity. Middle-class families favored small cheerful pictures, preferably showing the leisure activities cherished by these hard-working people. The consequence was a veritable explosion of artistic enterprise that coincided with the heyday of Dutch prosperity during the first two-thirds of the century. With the French invasion of the 1670s, both the economic and artistic hegemony of the Dutch began to fade.

Seventeenth-century Dutch painters were admired both for their subtle depiction of light and color in landscapes and for their talented exploitation of the artistic possibilities of the interiors of Dutch houses, with their highly polished or well-scrubbed floors and their strong contrasts of light and shade. The best-known baroque painters in the Netherlands are Frans Hals (1580–1666) and Rembrandt (1609–1669). Hals used bold strokes to paint cheerful contingents of civic guards, laughing musicians, and tavern topers. As he aged, he himself became a chronic toper; yet in his eighties, a penniless inmate in a poorhouse, he painted the most remarkable group portrait of baroque art— *The Women Regents of the Haarlem Hospital,* dour, formidable, and ageing matrons in all their Calvinist severity.

Rembrandt, too, attained fame early, then slipped into obscurity and poverty; he documented his troubles in a series of moving self-portraits. He, too, executed famous group portraits—*The Night Watch* and *The Syndics of the Drapers' Guild* (this last arranged by a friend in the textile business, but all the proceeds went to his creditors). Rembrandt painted an exceptional scientific subject, *The Anatomy Lesson of Dr. Tulp,* with a physician explaining the structure of blood vessels and tendons in the arm of an executed criminal, about the only kind

of cadaver available to anatomists in those days. Rembrandt's paintings often show the fascination with *chiaroscuro* and with the gold evening light that is so typical of baroque, and he often strives for direct involvement of the viewer as well. In successive sketches for *Ecce Homo,* when Pilate allows the crowd to choose between Christ and Barabbas, Rembrandt progressively eliminated the crowd, and the beholder of the final version realizes that he is one of an unseen multitude choosing Barabbas over Christ. In his difficult later years, when he lived in the most squalid quarter of Amsterdam, Rembrandt seemed particularly drawn to biblical figures and their tribulations—Saul and David, the prodigal son and his father—and used residents of the Jewish ghetto as models. Consequently, Rembrandt has been called the greatest Protestant religious painter, a rare exception to the rule that Protestant tradition has not welcomed the visual arts.

Architecture and the Art of Living

To obtain a fair sample of baroque painting one should visit the Louvre, the Prado, the National Gallery in London, the Rijksmuseum in Amsterdam, the Metropolitan in New York and perhaps half a dozen other institutions. To sample baroque architecture and urban planning one need visit only Rome, where Urban VIII and other popes sponsored churches, palaces, gardens, fountains, avenues, and piazzas in a determination to make their capital the most spectacular city in Europe. A tour should begin at Saint Peter's, which, apart from Michelangelo's dome, is a legacy of baroque rather than the Renaissance. The proportions of Michelangelo's Greek-cross design were destroyed when a greatly lengthened nave was constructed in the early 1600s. With the vast space of the nave leading into the vast space beneath the dome, it was imperative to find a way of filling the latter.

Urban VIII entrusted the commission to the young architect, Bernini (1598–1680), who hit on the ingenious solution of the baldachin or tabernacle, an enormously magnified and strengthened version of the flimsy little canopy used to cover the sacrament. Four enormous spiral bronze columns, modeled after those supposedly used in Solomon's temple, support an elaborate bronze canopy, topped by an orb and a cross, the papal emblems. The decoration made generous use of the Barberini family symbols, the bees and the laurel. This 85-foot-high structure filled the void without blocking the view from the nave through the apse. To secure the bronze for the columns and canopy the bronze roof of the Pantheon, the best preserved monument of ancient Rome, was melted down—whence the epigram of Urban VIII's physician, *Quod non fecerunt Barbari, fecerunt Barberini* (What the Barbarians didn't do, the Barberini did).

Under a successor of Urban, Alexander VII

Bernini's baldacchino above the main altar at St. Peter's, Rome.

(1655–1667), Bernini undertook to fill the void between the baldachin and the wall of the apse, producing what is known, with astonishing understatement, as Saint Peter's chair. It is an elaborately carved throne borne on the shoulders of four great bronze figures, the front pair representing two Latin fathers (Saint Ambrose and Saint Augustine) and the rear pair two Greek fathers (Saint Athanasius and Saint Chrysostom). Their positions were intended to symbolize the ideal of unity between Latin and Greek churches as well as the preponderance of the Latin. Around and above the throne are clouds leading up to a sunburst of golden rays and heavenly creatures, in the midst of which is a dove, symbol of the Holy Spirit. This fantastic creation of marble, glass, stucco, and bronze is perhaps the ultimate statement of the baroque obsession with drama and illusion.

Also under Alexander VII Bernini tackled the problem of framing the open space facing the facade of Saint Peter's, where crowds receive the papal blessing on special occasions. Employing a trick of stage design, he extended two wings from the façade to mitigate the disproportion of the façade, which was too wide for its height. Beyond the trapezoidal area he built a great oval piazza flanked by curving colonnades, each with row upon row of simple Doric columns, which have been likened to formations of papal soldiers, and the whole compared to "the arms of Mother Church gathering in her children."

Architect, painter, sculptor, engineer, and improvisor, rewarded by his patrons with handsome fees and flattering honors, Bernini stood in the great tradition of the universal man of the Renaissance. Yet, as the leading sculptor of the seventeenth century, he contributed to the precipitous decline of that medium from its Renaissance pinnacle, in the judgment of some critics. Their major evidence is his *Ecstasy of Saint Teresa*, which not only expressed her mystical experience of divine love in physical terms (as she herself had expressed it) but also prompted another of Bernini's theatrical productions. He converted a chapel in the Roman church of Santa Maria della Vittoria into a miniature theater, with sculptured boxes on the sides containing portraits of the family that had commissioned the work. On a little stage in the center he placed Teresa, voluminously gowned and swooning back onto a cloud, with a smiling angel standing by and holding the fire-tipped dart of divine love; the white marble figures are spotlighted by bright rays appearing to come from heaven but actually entering through a hidden window.

Purely as an architect, Bernini was a conservative and made only cautious departures from the classical norms of the Renaissance. His chief rival, Borromini (1599–1667), was a daring experimenter who abandoned the straight lines and right angles of classicism. In the little Roman church of San Carlo alle Quattro Fontane he ingeniously combined concave and convex surfaces to make a compact curving structure that utilized with full efficiency a small plot of land.

Although Borromini's innovations influenced fanciful late baroque buildings in Austria, Germany, and Latin America, conservatism prevailed elsewhere, most significantly in the France of Louis XIV, which replaced Rome as the trend-setter of Europe in the last third of the century. Advanced Baroque design received one setback when a major addition to the Louvre was executed in classical style, and another when the same style was chosen for the exterior of the palace at Versailles. Still, there are Baroque qualities at Versailles— the superhuman dimensions the conscious effort to be overwhelming, and the opulent interior with its allegorical paintings and the famous Hall of Mirrors, a long narrow gallery where the installation of a large mirror opposite each window creates the illusion of spaciousness. Altogether, the palace was a splendid setting for the endless ceremonies surrounding the sun king, even if it was not a comfortable residence for the thousands who inhabited it.

Beyond the palace stretches an enormous park, with statues, fountains, pavilions, and a mile-long canal that became a backdrop for fireworks displays on state occasions. Landscape architects raised their craft to a fine art in keeping the plantings close to the palace carefully manicured and leaving those more distant in their natural state. After Louis moved to Versailles, he did not neglect Paris but added to it some fine squares surrounded by the townhouses of the aristocracy with his own statue in the center (the Place Vendôme is a good surviving example). He also provided the Louvre with a majestic western approach, the broad tree-lined avenue of the Champs Elysées.

In England, baroque building was much diluted by Palladio's classicism. Under Charles II the Surveyor-General (chief architect) was Christopher Wren (1632–1723), a talented engineer and astronomer, who was deluged with commissions after the great fire destroyed much of London in 1666. He directed the rebuilding of fifty-one parish churches in addition to designing a new Saint Paul's Cathedral. Saint Paul's, in particular, strained his capacity to fuse varying styles into a harmonious whole: the walls are supported by concealed Gothic flying buttresses; the main facade and the dome are classical; and the twin towers have curving lines in the manner of Borromini. Perhaps Saint Paul's is most baroque in being so self-consciously grand, as if it were quite aware that it was and would remain *the* landmark of London and that its dome would be copied for the Pantheon in eighteenth-century Paris and the Capitol in nineteenth-century Washington.

England's purest baroque monument is Blenheim Palace in Oxfordshire, named in honor of the Duke of Marlborough's victory over the French in 1704, pre-

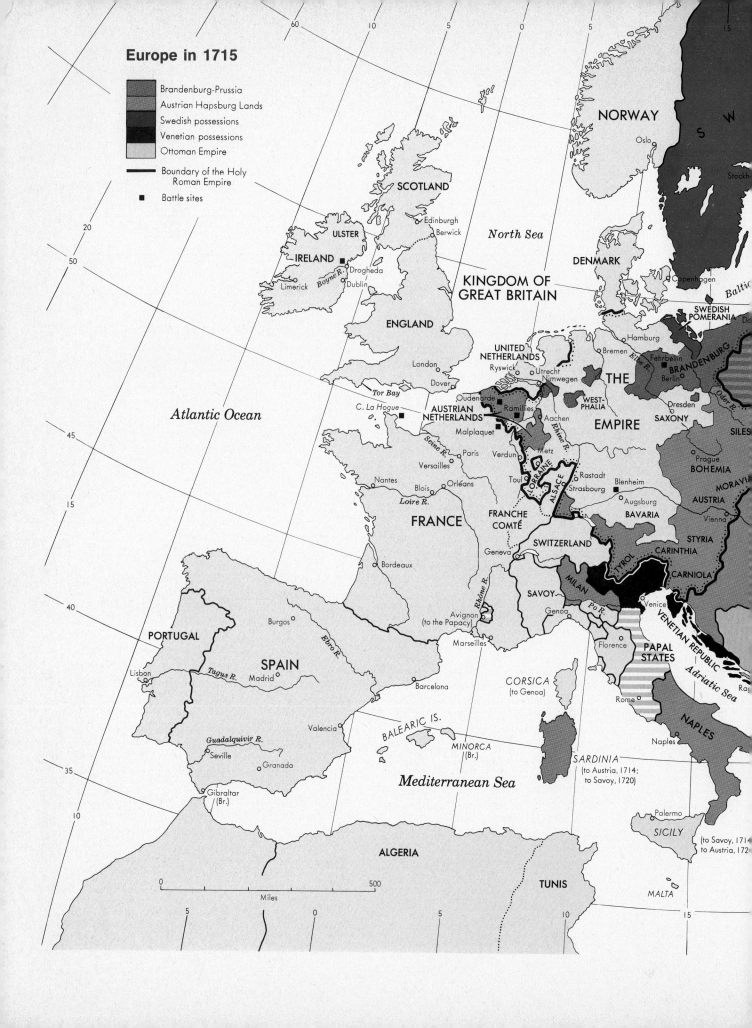

Europe in 1715

Legend:
- Brandenburg-Prussia
- Austrian Hapsburg Lands
- Swedish possessions
- Venetian possessions
- Ottoman Empire
- ▬▬ Boundary of the Holy Roman Empire
- ■ Battle sites

NORWAY
Oslo
S W

SCOTLAND
Edinburgh
Berwick

North Sea

DENMARK
Copenhagen
Baltic
Stockholm

ULSTER
IRELAND
Drogheda
Dublin
Limerick
Boyne R.

KINGDOM OF GREAT BRITAIN

ENGLAND
London
Dover

SWEDISH POMERANIA
Hamburg
Bremen
Fehrbellin
Berlin
BRANDENBURG
Elbe R.
Oder R.
Dresden
SAXONY
SILES

UNITED NETHERLANDS
Ryswick
Utrecht
Nimwegen
WEST-PHALIA
Aachen
THE EMPIRE

Tor Bay
C. La Hogue
AUSTRIAN NETHERLANDS
Oudenarde
Ramillies
Malplaquet

Atlantic Ocean

Paris
Versailles
Verdun
Metz
Toul
LORRAINE
ALSACE
Rastadt
Strasbourg
Blenheim
Augsburg
Rhine R.
BOHEMIA
Prague
MORAVIA
AUSTRIA
Vienna
STYRIA

Nantes
Blois
Orléans
Loire R.

FRANCE

FRANCHE COMTÉ

SWITZERLAND
Geneva

Bordeaux

Rhône R.

SAVOY
Genoa
MILAN
Po R.
Venice
VENETIAN REPUBLIC
Adriatic Sea
Rag

Avignon (to the Papacy)
Marseilles

Florence
PAPAL STATES
Rome

NAPLES
Naples

PORTUGAL
Lisbon
Tagus R.
Burgos
Madrid
SPAIN
Ebro R.

Barcelona

CORSICA (to Genoa)

Valencia

Guadalquivir R.
Seville
Granada
Gibraltar (Br.)

BALEARIC IS.

MINORCA (Br.)

SARDINIA (to Austria, 1714; to Savoy, 1720)

Mediterranean Sea

SICILY
(to Savoy, 1714;
to Austria, 172)
Palermo

ALGERIA

TUNIS

MALTA

0   500
Miles

FINLAND

L. Onega

L. Ladoga

Nystadt

Gulf of Finland

St. Petersburg

INGRIA

Narva

Novgorod

ESTONIA

LIVONIA

Pskov

COURLAND

W. Dvina R.

Vilna

nigsberg

LITHUANIA

PRUSSIA

Warsaw

POLAND

Vistula R.

Kiev

Smolensk

Moscow

Oka R.

Volga R.

R   U   S   S   I   A

Dnieper R.

Poltava

Dniester R.

TRANSYLVANIA

MOLDAVIA

NGARY

arlovitz

Passarovitz

de

WALLACHIA

Danube R.

CRIMEA

Black Sea

Volga R.

Don R.

Caspian Sea

55

45

40

50

35

PERSIA

ONTE-
EGRO

O   T   T   O   M   A   Ñ

Vardar R.

Salonika

Constantinople

E   M   P   I   R   E

Tigris R.

Aegean Sea

Athens

Euphrates R.

RHODES

CYPRUS

CRETE

20

25

30

35

40

45

Inset map

ENGLAND

Calais

ARTOIS
1659

ALSACE
1648–1681

Paris

LORRAINE
1766

THE EMPIRE

FRANCHE COMTÉ
1678

FRANCE

1601

Rhône R.

Avignon

ROUSSILLON
1659

CORSICA
1768

Growth of France
1559-1769
— Boundary of the Empire, 1559

60

55

50

St. Paul's Cathedral, London, begun in 1675.

sented to him by a grateful government, and financed in part by subscriptions from a grateful public. The architect Vanbrugh (1664–1726), who was also a leading Restoration playwright, designed Blenheim less as a residence than as a vast theatrical setting. The immense courtyard was overwhelmingly impressive, but the kitchens were a quarter of a mile from the main dining-room! Voltaire observed that if the rooms had been as wide as the walls were thick Blenheim would have been more livable.

The arts of good living made substantial progress in the seventeenth century, despite the ravages of disease and famine, which are estimated to have reduced the European population by at least 15 percent between 1648 and 1713. The expansion of Europe overseas made available the new beverages of coffee, tea, and cocoa, new cotton materials, and luxuries like Chinese porcelain and lacquered ware. Exotic tropical woods made possible the technique of marquetry, that is, inlaying and veneering furniture with different kinds of wood. On the whole, furniture was becoming more specialized: dining chairs replaced dining benches; chairs were made both with arms and, to accommodate hoopskirts, without; Louis XIV had his *chaise percée* (pierced chair) to accomplish his morning duties in his bedchamber.

Chests were made more convenient for storage by the installation of drawers; and when the chest became baroque and acquired a curved front and greater space, it was termed a commode. Kneehole writing desks appeared, and, especially in England, drop-leaf gateleg tables, which could stand in a narrow space by a wall or be opened up as a dining or gaming table. For dining, table napkins came into use along with individual plates and glasses in place of communal bowls and vessels. Families of moderate means could afford these innovations as well as a teapot, a pitcher, and a few items of plain silver and thus participated in what amounted to a revolution in domestic arrangements.

Music

Baroque composers, especially in Italy, moved further along the paths laid out by their Renaissance predecessors. In Rome, Frescobaldi (1583–1644) exploited the dramatic potentialities of the pipe organ, attracting thousands to his recitals at St. Peter's. In Venice, Monteverdi (1567–1643) wrote the first important operas to back up his contention that "speech should be the master of music, not its servant." The opera, a characteristically baroque compound of music and drama proved so popular that Venice soon had sixteen opera houses, which were already focusing on the celebrity of the chief singers rather than on the overall quality of the supporting cast and the orchestra. The star system reached its height at Naples, where conservatories (originally institutions for "conserving" orphans) specialized in voice training. Many Neapolitan operas were loose collections of arias designed to show off the talents of the stars, and the effect of unreality was heightened by the custom of having the male roles sung by women and some of the female by *castrati,* male sopranos.

At its best seventeenth-century opera rose above the level of stilted artificiality. In England, Purcell (1658–1695), the organist of Westminster Abbey, produced a masterpiece for the graduation exercises of a girls' school, the beautiful and moving *Dido and Aeneas.* Louis XIV, appreciating the obvious value of opera in enhancing the resplendence of his court, imported from Italy the talented Lully (1632–1687), who was not only a musician and a dancer but also a speculator and politician who vied with Molière as "cultural director" of court life. Lully's operas on mythological themes are now for the most part forgotten, but the overtures and dances that he wrote for them were the prelude to the eighteenth-century achievements in instrumental music.

Reading Suggestions on Divine-Right Monarchy— and Revolution

Europe in General

R. S. Dunn, *The Age of Religious Wars, 1559–1689* (*Norton). Crisp, comprehensive, and up-to-date survey.

M. Ashley, *The Golden Century* (Praeger, 1969). Another valuable recent introduction to seventeenth-century Europe.

C. J. Friedrich, *The Age of the Baroque, 1610–1660;* F. L. Nussbaum, *The Triumph of Science and Reason, 1660–1685;* J. B. Wolf, *The Emergence of the Great Powers, 1685–1715* (*Torchbooks). Detailed, scholarly volumes, with very full bibliographies; in the Rise of Modern Europe series.

A. Vagts, *A History of Militarism* (*Free Press), and E. M. Earle, ed., *Makers of Modern Strategy* (*Princeton Univ.). Both are helpful on seventeenth-century warfare.

E. F. Heckscher, *Mercantilism,* rev. ed., 2 vols. (Macmillan, 1955). A famous and controversial work.

F. L. Nussbaum, *A History of Economic Institutions in Modern Europe* (Crofts, 1933). An abridgement of Sombart's *Modern Capitalism,* arguing that war is economically creative; the arguments are attacked by J. U. Nef, *War and Human Progress* (*Norton).

R. B. Merriman, *Six Contemporaneous Revolutions* (Clarendon, 1938). Lectures focused on the midcentury upheavals. The implications of this crisis are examined by the essays in T. Aston, ed., *Crisis in Europe, 1560–1660* (*Anchor).

France

G. R. R. Treasure, *Seventeenth Century France* (Rivingtons, 1966). Full and lucid survey.

J. D. Lough, *An Introduction to Seventeenth Century France* (*McKay). Designed for the student of literature and useful for anyone interested in the subject.

A. Guérard, *France in the Classical Age: The Life and Death of an Ideal,* rev. ed. (Braziller, 1956). Stimulating interpretation of early modern France.

C. J. Burckhardt, *Richelieu: His Rise to Power* and *Assertion of Power and Cold War* (Allen & Unwin, 1964 and 1970). Scholarly two-volume study of the great cardinal.

O. Ranum, *Richelieu and the Councillors of Louis XIII* (Oxford Univ., 1963). An important monograph on administration.

C. V. Wedgwood, *Richelieu and the French Monarchy* (*Collier). Sound brief evaluation.

D. Bitton, *The French Nobility in Crisis, 1560–1640* (Stanford Univ., 1969). Sound study of their declining role.

A. Lublinskaya, *French Absolutism: The Crucial Phase 1620–1629* (Cambridge Univ., 1968). From the standpoint of a Russian Communist scholar.

J. B. Wolf, *Louis XIV* (*Norton). Detailed, scholarly biography, stressing politics.

P. Goubert, *Louis XIV and Twenty Million Frenchmen* (*Vintage). The relations between the Sun King and his subjects.

W. H. Lewis *The Splendid Century* (*Morrow). Stresses the nature of society in France under Louis XIV.

W. J. Stankiewicz, *Politics and Religion in Seventeenth Century France* (Univ. of California, 1960). Illuminating study of their interrelations.

W. C. Scoville, *The Persecution of the Huguenots and French Economic Development, 1680–1720* (Univ. of California, 1960). Enlightening evaluation.

C. W. Cole, *Colbert and a Century of French Mercantilism,* 2 vols. (Columbia Univ., 1939). A solid, detailed study.

J. E. King, *Science and Rationalism in the Administration of Louis XIV* (Johns Hopkins Univ., 1949). Monograph showing the relations between intellectual and political history.

W. F. Church, ed., *The Impact of Absolutism in France* (*Wiley). Useful selections from source materials and commentaries on the era of Richelieu and Louis XIV.

England

M. Ashley, *England in the Seventeenth Century* (*Penguin), and C. Hill, *The Century of Revolution, 1603–1714* (*Norton). Two sound surveys by experts.

G. Davies, *The Early Stuarts 1603–1660,* and G. N. Clark, *The Later Stuarts, 1660–1714,* rev. eds. (Clarendon, 1949). More detailed scholarly treatments, in the Oxford History of England.

W. Notestein, *The English People on the Eve of Colonization, 1603–1630* (*Torchbooks). Admirable social history.

C. W. Bridenbaugh, *Vexed and Troubled Englishmen, 1590–1642* (Oxford Univ., 1968). A more recent study covering much of the same ground as Notestein's book.

C. V. Wedgwood, *The King's Peace, 1637–1641; The King's War, 1641–1647;* and *A Coffin for King Charles* (Macmillan, 1955–1964). Detailed study of the Great Rebellion by a ranking expert.

S. R. Gardiner, *History of England, 1603–1642,* 10 vols.; *History of the Great Civil War, 1642–1649,* 4 vols.; and *History of the Commonwealth and Protectorate, 1649–1656* (Longmans, 1904–1913). An older major work of detailed history. Gardiner's views may be sampled in his brief textbook, *The First Two Stuarts and the Puritan Revolution, 1603–1660,* first published in 1876 and recently reprinted (*Apollo).

D. H. Willson, *King James VI and I* (Holt, 1956). Sound appraisal of the first Stuart.

C. Hibbert, *Charles I* (Harper, 1968). Useful biography.

P. Zagorin, *The Court and the Country* (Routledge, 1969). Appraisal of the origins of the English Revolution.

L. Stone, *The Crisis of the Aristocracy, 1558–1641* (*Oxford Univ.) and *Social Change and Revolution in England, 1540–1640* (*Barnes and Noble). Important studies by a scholar who is an expert on the controversy over the role of the gentry. That controversy is neatly summarized in J. H. Hexter, *Reappraisals in History* (*Torchbooks).

C. V. Wedgwood, *Oliver Cromwell,* rev. ed. (Duckworth, 1973) and C. Hill, *God's Englishman* (*Torchbooks). Perhaps the soundest of recent works on Cromwell.

G. Davies, *The Restoration of Charles II, 1658–1660* (Huntington Library, 1955). An authoritative monograph.

A. Bryant, *King Charles II* (Longmans, 1931). Unusually sympathetic in tone.

F. C. Turner, *James II* (Macmillan, 1948). Balanced treatment of a ruler generally subject to partisan interpretation.

S. B. Baxter, *William III and the Defense of European Liberty* (Harcourt, 1966). Recent and sympathetic.

J. R. Tanner, *English Constitutional Conflicts of the Seventeenth Century* (*Cambridge Univ.). Full and scholarly.

C. Hill, *The World Turned Upside Down* (*Compass). Sketch of the radical ideas advanced during the English Revolution. May be supplemented by the older study of G. P. Gooch, *English Democratic Ideas in the Seventeenth Century* (*Torchbooks).

O. F. Morshead, ed., *Everybody's Pepys* (Harcourt, 1926). A useful abridgment of the famous diary kept during the 1660s; a fascinating document of social history.

The Century of Genius

P. Smith, *A History of Modern Culture,* Vol. 1 (Holt, 1930). An older work, and a mine of information on aspects of culture often neglected in intellectual histories.

C. Brinton, *The Shaping of Modern Thought* (*Spectrum). A survey of intellectual history from the Renaissance on.

H. F. Kearney, *Origins of the Scientific Revolution* (*Barnes & Noble). A many-sided introduction to this controversial topic.

H. Butterfield, *The Origins of Modern Science, 1300–1800* (*Free Press). A lively and controversial survey, minimizing the contribution of scientists before Galileo.

A. N. Whitehead, *Science and the Modern World* (*Free Press). An incisive and influential critique of what modern science really means and implies; rather difficult but well worth the effort.

A. R. Hall, *The Scientific Revolution, 1500–1800* (*Beacon). A solid account, written from the standpoint of the historian.

L. S. Feuer, *The Scientific Intellectual: The Psychological and Sociological Origins of Modern Science* (Basic Books, 1963). A stimulating interpretation from a more controversial point of view.

E. J. Dijksterhuis, *The Mechanization of the World Picture* (Clarendon, 1961). Informative study of the intellectual impact of science.

F. H. Anderson, *Francis Bacon: His Career and His Thought* (Univ. of Southern California, 1962). A good appraisal of an important pioneer.

B. Willey, *The Seventeenth Century Background* (*Anchor). Essays on Descartes, Hobbes, Milton, and other figures in the intellectual life of the century.

E. Mortimer, *Blaise Pascal* (Harper, 1959). A sympathetic and well-written study.

F. Baumer, *Religion and the Rise of Skepticism* (Harcourt, 1960). Assesses the spiritual impact of science.

S. E. Bethell, *The Cultural Revolution of the Seventeenth Century* (Roy, 1951). A literary study with fruitful suggestions for the historian of ideas.

The Baroque

J. S. Held and D. Posner, *17th and 18th Century Art* (Prentice-Hall; Harry N. Abrams, 1972). A recent systematic survey of painting, sculpture and architecture, handsomely illustrated.

G. Bazin, *The Baroque* (New York Graphic Society, 1968). Less systematic but more suggestive assessment. Bazin is also the author of a brief introduction, *Baroque and Rococo Art* (*Praeger).

A. C. Sewter, *Baroque and Rococo* (*Harcourt). Compact introduction.

V. L. Tapié, *The Age of Grandeur* (Weidenfeld & Nicolson, 1960). A review of baroque and classical art throughout Europe.

R. N. Hatton, *Europe in the Age of Louis XIV* (*Harcourt). Instructive study of the links among economic, social, and cultural developments.

F. Haskell, *Patrons and Painters* (*Harper & Row). Enlightening examination of the relationship between Italian society and art in the baroque era.

M. R. Bukofzer, *Music in the Baroque Era* (Norton, 1947). A standard introduction.

R. Wittkower, *Art and Architecture in Italy, 1600–1700,* 3rd ed. (1973) and A. Blunt, *Art and Architecture in France, 1500–1700* (1953). Two scholarly volumes in "The Pelican History of Art" (Penguin).

Historical Fiction

A. Dumas, *The Three Musketeers* (*Washington Square); *The Man in the Iron Mask* (*Airmont). Swashbuckling yarns of seventeenth-century France, based on careful research.

T. Gautier, *Captain Fracasse* (Bigelow Smith, 1910). A good picaresque tale, based on conscientious research; set in the France of Louis XIII.

A. Manzoni, *The Betrothed,* trans. A. Colquhoun (*Dutton). Milan about 1630; a famous Italian novel.

N. Hawthorne, *The Scarlet Letter* (*many editions). The best introduction to the Puritan spirit through fiction.

R. Graves, *Wife to Mr. Milton* (Creative Age, 1944). A good novel; not kind to Milton.

W. M. Thackeray, *Henry Esmond* (*several editions). Set in England about 1700.

Illustrations

ℐndex